PREHISTORIC GUIANA

PREHISTORIC GUIANA

Denis Williams

Ian Randle Publishers
Kingston • Miami

First published in Jamaica, 2003 by
Ian Randle Publishers
11 Cunningham Avenue, Kingston 6

A catalogue record of this book is available
from the National Library of Jamaica.

National Library of Jamaica Cataloguing In Publication Data

Williams, Denis
    Prehistoric Guiana/ Denis Williams

p.:ill., maps; cm

Bibliography : p. .-Includes index

ISBN 976-637-156-3 Hardback
ISBN 976-637-080-X Paperback

1. Guyana - History   2.   Guyana - Civilization
I. Title

988   dc 21

and in the United States by
Ian Randle Publishers Inc
www.ianrandlepublishers.com

© 2003 Government of Guyana

ISBN 0-9729358-7-8 Paperback
ISBN 0-9729358-8-6 Hardback

All rights reserved. No part of this publication may be
reproduced, stored in a retrieval system, or transmitted
in any form or by any means electronic, mechanical,
photocopying, recording, or otherwise, without
the prior permission of the publishers.

Printed and bound in the United States

Guyane française	41
Summary	44
Brazilian Guiana	44
The Coast	44
The Hinterland	45
Venezuelan Guyana	48
Archaeology and language	48
Summary	53
THE PALEO-INDIGENOUS PEOPLES	55
Introduction	55
The paleo-environments	56
The Coast	56
The Hinterland	57
The Andean Heritage	62
Introduction	62
Settlement pattern	67
Subsistence	69
PEOPLES OF THE TROPICAL FOREST ARCHAIC	76
Demography	76
Warao pioneers on the Western Guiana Littoral	76
The Southeastern Subzone	76
The Northwestern Subzone	81
Settlement pattern	86
The Coast	86
The Hinterland	90
Economy	100
Niche variation on the Western Guiana Littoral	100
Changing local environments of the swamps	104
The adaptive value of niche variation	111
Traditional bases of intensification	130
Development of the canoe manufacturing industry	136
The tools	136
The industry	141
The aftermath	145
The Archaic on *terra firme*	149
Parameters of the study	149
The parietal artifacts	151
The mobiliary artifacts	161
Modified rock in Archaic culture history	162
Petroglyphs	162
Controlled resource exploitation	185
The mediating agent	188

CONTENTS

Text Figures	ix
Text Tables	xv
List of Maps	xvi
Message from the Government of Guyana	xvii
Denis Williams – A Biographical Note	xix
Foreword	xxiii
EDITOR'S PREFACE	xxvi
PREFACE	xvii
INTRODUCTION	1
The setting	1
The Western Guiana Littoral	2
The Eastern Guiana Littoral	2
The Western Guiana Hinterland	4
The Eastern Guiana Hinterland	5
Political and cultural divisions	5
Sources for the study of prehistory	6
Introduction	6
Artificial depressions	7
Shell mounds	8
Petroglyphs and pictographs	10
Earthworks	11
Pottery	11
Rock alignments	12
Human skeletal remains	14
Summary	14
History of research	16
Guyana	16
The Europeans 1866 - 1899	17
The North Americans 1900s - 1960	22
The early stage 1900s - 1939	22
The late stage 1939 - 1960	26
Introduction	26
The professionals	26
The local amateurs	32
Summary	34
Suriname	35
The local amateurs	35
The professionals	38
Summary	40

Imposition of the petroglyphic *grapheme*	190
Sharpening grooves	191
Bedrock mortars	200
Chipping station	202
Regional demographic dispersals	203

THE FIRST FARMERS — 207
Introduction — 207
- The environment of the swamp edge — 207
- The preagricultural ceramists of Hosororo Creek — 215
- First farmers on the Western Guiana Littoral — 225
- Antecedents of the pioneer horticulturists — 233

The Formative — 236
- Adaptive responses to environmental freshening — 236
- The Arawak dispersals — 237
- The Carib dispersals — 240

The transition to horticulture on the Western Guiana Littoral — 242
- The Aruka Basin — 242
- The Mabaruma chronologies — 245
- The Warao legacy — 248
- The relations of production in manioc horticulture — 257
- The horticulturist radiation — 260

Mabaruma: origin, characterization, chronology — 267
- The conventional Mabaruma phase — 267
- Apostaderan motifs — 268
- Guarguapan motifs — 270
- Macapaiman motifs — 270

Domestication of the land on the Aruka River — 272
Recharacterization of the Mabaruma phase — 277
- Horticulturist alliances — 279

Periodification of the Mabaruma phase — 280
Iconography — 282
The Formative interaction sphere — 290
The Protohistoric Mabaruma interaction sphere — 297
The Proto-Eastern Maipuran Arawak migrations — 301
- Introduction — 301
- Proto-Easterners on the upper Essequibo — 304

Mound dwellers on the Eastern Guiana Littoral — 317
- Introduction — 317
- Hertenrits and its aftermath — 326
- The reef dwellers — 326

The Proto-Northern/Proto-Eastern Arawo convergence — 339
The demise of the Orinoco-Amazon interaction corridor — 343

The Carib migrations	346
Introduction	346
Western Karinya	350
Eastern Karinya	359
The Akawaio dispersal	367
Period I	380
Period 11	383
Belief, magic, death and the forms of art	394
The woman potter in sacred and secular art	397
Inter-ethnic frontiers	400
The North Rupununi Savannas	402
The North Pakaraimas	403
ORIGIN AND DISSEMINATION OF TROPICAL FOREST CULTURE IN THE GUIANAS	406
Introduction	406
The principal migrations	408
The Coast and Coastal Hinterland	408
The Hinterland	410
The circum-Guiana migrations	410
Contrasting horticulturist adaptations	412
The Intermediate Area and the Guianas	414
LITERATURE CITED	429
INDEX	465

TEXT FIGURES

Chapter 1: Introduction

1. Map. The "Island" of Guiana — 1
2. Waropoko, Upper Waini — 8
3. Makatau: the cave system — 10
4. Daub fragments in archaeological contexts — 13
5. Barabina. Differentially preserved human bones — 14
6. The Waramuri excavations 1866 — 17
7. N.O. Poonai *(1923 - 1996)* — 33
8. C.J. Hering and Suriname archaeology — 35
9. Sipaliwini Savanna. Some stone artifacts — 38
10. Guyane française. Raised fields at Kourou — 41
11. Guyane française. Human-footed bird — 43
12. Marajó Island. Pottery of the Marajoara phase — 46
13. Some Guiana sites of the Polychrome Tradition — 47
14. Upper Orinoco. The Barraricoid Tradition — 51
15. Major Carib language groups — 52
16. Carib languages of the Guianas — 53

Chapter 2:

1. Northern Guyana during the Riss-Würn interglacial — 56
2. Proposed forest refuges — 59
3. Rainfall northern South America — 60
4. Pleniglacial rainfall/rainforest relationships — 61
5. Paleo-indigenous projectile point, Guyana — 63
6. Wenamu River. Paleo-Indigenous scraper — 64
7. Projectile point, Puruni River, Guyana — 65
8. Projectile points: Puruni and Ireng Rivers — 66
9. Projectile point, La Culebra, upper Orinoco — 70
10. a. Archaeological beeswax; b. Fish spear, Rio Amazon — 73
11. Fish trident: lower Amazon — 73

Chapter 3:

1. Piraka shell mound — 76
2. Shrimping, climate and river discharge — 78
3. Mounds on the basement edge: Piraka, Kabakaburi — 79
4. Piraka. Cremation efficiencies — 81

5.	Barabina shell mound: bone bundle, storage pit	82
6.	Barabina: correlation of burial orientations, solstitial points and mean monthly rainfall	85
7.	Subzones of the Western Guiana Littoral	87
8.	Archaic occupations in the Guianas	91
9.	Job's Tears *(Coix Lachrynta Jobi)*	94
10.	*Pedra Pintado,* Rio Brinco	95
11.	Upper Rio Branco	96
12.	Petroglyph distributions, Makatau Cave	97
13.	Barkbeater, Pomeroon River	99
14.	Waini River. Section	102
14a.	Chronology of Midden Types	105
15.	Archaic mining products: a. iron ore, b. steatite	108
16.	Honeycomb tubeworm in shellfish refuse, Barabina	110
17.	Steatite deposits in the Kauiramembu Range	112
18.	Peat deposits on the basement edge, Kabakaburi	114
19.	a. Peat, Pomeroon River, b. Conch, Waiwaru Creek	115
20.	Waramuri shell mound: the stratigraphic profile	116
21.	Upper Waini River. Test pit on Wahana Island	118
22.	Excavations at Piraka Pomeroon River	119
23.	The Zebra Nerite (Puperita pupa)	122
23.	Haimarakabra shell mound: the stone tool inventory	123
25.	Alaka phase: early shellfishing toolkit	127
26.	Moruka River. Seasonally inundated grass savannas	128
27.	Upper Waini River. Wahana Island: the site plan	134
28.	Pomeroon River: the boatbuilding tradition	137
29.	The stone ax in canoe manufacture	138
30.	Evolution of stone working technology	139
31.	Evolution of the stone adze Southeastern Subzone	139
32.	Stone adze fracture patterns	140
33.	A late Archaic stone adze	141
34.	Moruka River. Tools on imported quartz	142
35.	Pomeroon River. The mature stone tool industry	145
36.	Environments of the Warapana and Siriki mounds	146
37.	The monkey in a. Archaic, b. Horticulturist art	148
38.	Petroglyphic, pictographic sample area	150
39.	Game animals and fish in Archaic petroglyphs	151
40.	Geological basis of petroglyph distributions	155
41.	Enumerative petroglyph elements	157
42.	Enumerative petroglyph dispersion	157
43.	Upper Waini Fish trap petroglyphs	160

44. Rio Branco. Bedrock mortar	161
45. Burro Burro River, Guyana. Archaic quartz tools	162
46. The Enumerative petroglyph type	164
47. The petroglyphic grapheme	166
48. New Mexico. The petroglyphic tally	167
49. Petroglyph directional/notational elements	168
50. The Cuneiform petroglyph subtype	170
51. Fish Trap petroglyphs	171
52. Upper Essequibo River. The food web	172
53. Fish Trap petroglyphs. a. Amazon, b. Waini Rivers	174
54. Geological sketch map of the Guiana Shield	175
54. Upper Mazaruni River. The Tramen pictograph	178
56. Comparative phosphene patterns	182
57. Comparative phosphene patterns Brazil, Guyana	183
58. Regional Enumerative petroglyph elements	184
59. The petroglyph technique of pecking and abrasion	186
60. The petroglyph toolkit	187
61. Massed punctuation, Makatau Mountain, Rupununi Savannas	189
62. Upper Essequibo. Comparative water levels 1994, 1996	191
63. Archaic water levels from sonar data	192
64. Size grades of stone tools from sharpening grooves	194
65. Orenoque River. Bedrock mortar	201
66. Rio Branco - Kassikaityu	205
67. Rio Branco. Some sharpening grooves	205

Chapter 4:

1. The Seba profile	208
2. Comparative pollen diagrams: a. Colombia, b. Guyana	209
2a. Seba Creek; the pollen diagram	210
3. Barabina foothills. Transect thru rain forest	213
4. Seba Creek	218
5. The AWB manuscript [1905]	219
6. The Hosororo Creek excavations	220
7. Hosororo Creek. North-south section	223
8. Hosororo Creek. Characteristics of *Wanaina Plain* pottery	226
9a. Hosororo Creek. Stages in the loss of feldspar temper	229
9b. Hosororo Creek. Clay tempered pottery	231
10. Wahana Island shell mound. Intrusive oyster refuse	233
11. Hosororo Creek. Percussion-made stone adze	234
12. Wahana Island. The cave site	235

13.	*The Timehri* petroglyph in the Orinoco Basin	238
14.	Traditional costume in a fertility dance, Colombia	239
15.	The *Timehri* petroglyph in the Amazon Basin	240
16.	*Mauritia flexuosa* in swamp forest	243
17.	Freshening diagram	243
18.	Irrigation horticulture	243
18a.	Slash-and-burn horticulture	243
19.	Hosororo Creek, a. low tide, b, high tide	249
20.	Flour of the Moriche palm	250
20a.	Distribution of Moriche palms	253
21.	Age estimates on the Moriche palm	254
22.	Arawak household utensils used in manioc processing	259
23.	Early Formative vessel shapes	261
24.	Aruka River. King Vulture	267
25.	Corentyne River: King Vulture	267
26.	Apostadero pottery. Vessel shapes and decoration	269
27.	Mabaruma phase: Apostaderan decorative motifs	271
28.	The lower Aruka River	273
29.	The upper Aruka-Kaituma watershed	274
30.	Hosororo Creek. Freshwater for the upper Aruka, Formative vessel shapes. a. Hobediah. b. Hotaquai	275
31.	Hosororo-Baffancas, Hosororo Waini interaction	278
32.	Classic Mabaruma vessel shapes	281
33.	Ritualizing of the manioc root	283
34.	The Classic Mabaruma biomorphic adorno (armature)	284
35.	Classic Mabaruma. Conventionalized elements	285
36.	Classic Mabaruma. The stereotype	286
37.	Akawaio tattoo patterns	287
38.	Karinya red-on-white painted pottery	288
39.	Some Archaic and modern mortuary symbols	289
40.	The Amazon-Orinoco corridor (Coastal)	291
41.	The Amazon-Orinoco corridor (Southeast)	292
41a.	Amazon-Orinoco corridor (Coastal Hinterland)	293
42.	Pottery of the Recht-door-Zee trade entrepôt	294
43.	Koriabo Point. A Mabaruma trade entrepôt	296
44.	Regional dispersion of Postclassic traits	299-300
45.	Wonotobo Falls. The Proto-Eastern migration	302
46.	Kurupukari Falls Essequibo River	304
47.	Kurupukari Falls. Saladoid vessel shapes	305
48.	Saladoid white-on-red painted decoration, Kurupukari Falls	306
49.	Kurupukari Falls. Apoteri Incised decorative motifs	307

50.	Kurupukari Falls. Incised/Modeled decorative elements	309
51.	Kurupukari Falls. Incised urn lids/bowls	310
52.	Kurupukari Falls. Hypothetical function of the basin urn lid	311
53.	Some funerary ceramic vessels	312
54.	Distributions of some mortuary symbols	313
55.	Kurupukari Falls. Polychrome techniques	315
56.	*Apoteri Incised* motifs in the Guarita Subtradition	315
57.	*Apoteri Incised* in Saladoid and Polychrome inventories	316
58.	Pioneering settlements on the Eastern Guiana Littoral	319
59.	Seasonally inundated grass savannas	320
60.	Prins Bernard Polder. Excavated wooden shovel	326
61.	Eastern Guiana Littoral. The Barbakoeba reef site	327
62.	Eastern Guiana Littoral. Raised horticultural plots	328
63.	The coastal interfleuves	329
64.	Eastern Guiana Littoral. Arawak and Carib camp sites	332
65.	Head/foot symbols among horticulturists	335
66.	Arawak stilt house, Orealla (contemporary)	336
67.	Corentyne River. Excavations at Marjorie Landing, Orealla	340
68.	Orealla complex. Vessel shapes, decoration, stone tools	341
69.	Dutch pioneers on the Berbice and Canje Rivers	344
70.	Arawak vessels dredged from the Berbice River	345
71.	Pomeroon River. Zoned Incised Crosshatch on urn lid	347
72.	Some Carib tribes of Colombia and northern Venezuela	349
73.	Waiwaru Creek. Canoe landing	350
74.	Jacobus Farm, Pomeroon River. Irrigation horticulture	351
75.	Waiwaru Market. Karinya pottery decoration	352
76.	Waiwaru Market. Diagnostic vessel shapes	353
77.	Progradation on the Pomeroon right bank	354
78.	Pomeroon River	355
79.	Comparative ceramic traits Aruka and Cauca Rivers	356
80.	Comparative mortuary symbols of horticulturists	357
81.	Pottery of the Moruki and Pomeroon Rivers	358
82.	Comparative traits. Eastern, Western Karinya ceramics	360
83.	Shaft tombs. a. upper Rio Cauca, b. northern Amapá	361
83.	Artifacts of western Venezuela and Colombia in Guyana	362
85.	Eastern Karinya settlement pattern	364
86.	The Territory of Amapá, Brazil	366
87.	Ceramics of the Koriabo phase	369
88.	Mazaruni River. Quartz Island	371
89.	Braided channel on the Mazaruni River	372

90. Quartz Island. Sketch plan	374
91. Quartz Island. Intrusive decorative traits	377
91a. Contemporary red-on-white painted turtle, Waiwaru Creek	379
92. Quartz Island. The stratified sample	381
93. Rare carved wooden staff, Mazaruni River	382
94. Essequibo River. Late prehistoric Akawaio migration	384
95. Potaro River. Late prehistoric Akawaio migration	386
96. Comparaive ceramic traits: Waiwaru, Koriabo, Mazagio	391
97. Koriabo phase Essequibo River. *Tangas*	398
98. Evolution of an Arawak magical sign in Akawaio ceramics	399
99. Convergence of disparate mortuary symbols Demerara River	402
100. Impedimenta of the *kenainta* in a contemporary cave	404

Chapter 5:

1.	The principal migrations	411
2.	Essequibo River. Fort Zeelandia: a still rising water table?	414
3.	Kurupukari Falls. Early motifs of the Guarita Subtradition	420
4.	Ceramics of the Poc6 phase, Nhamunda/Trombetas Rivers	421
5.	Apoteri Incised elements in the Marajoara phase	423
6.	Distributions of the scroll-and-step-fret motif	425

TEXT TABLES

A.	Contrasting subzones of the Western Guiana Littoral	3
B.	Contrasting traits in Coastal and Hinterland cultures	15
C.	Piraka shell mound. Skeletal sample by age-group	77
D.	Comparative frequencies of *Rhizophora species* at culmination of the Holocene sea level rise Eastern Guiana Littoral	82
E.	Barabina shell mound. Burial frequencies, upper limb flexure/level, orientation.	84
F.	Barabina shell mound. Diatoms/level	90
G	Barabina shell mound. Fishbone frequencies/level	109
H.	Percentage ratios of waste chips in stone tool manufacture	190
I.	a. length/depth relationships of sharpening grooves h. Size grades of tools derived from Table I.a.	193
J.	Comparative means sharpening grooves Siparuni, Essequibo	196
K.	Comparative means sharpening grooves Siparuni, Essequibo	197
L.	Hosororo Creek. Number/size C. rhizophorael level	216
M.	Hosororo Creek. Ceramic frequencies/level Units 3,4	221
N.	Hosororo Creek. a. ceramics, b. stone	224
O.	Internal relationships of Carib languages	241
P.	Initial dates of some preagricultural shell mounds	251
Q.	The Buckleburg-1 site. Temper types/level	322
R.	Kamarang River. Regrowth farms over the past 100 years	388
S.	Diversity at several stages of succession	389
T.	Early sites of the Koriabo phase in Coastal Suriname	393

MAPS

Major Carib language groups, Figure 1.15	52
Carib languages of the Guianas, Figure 1.16	53
Northern Guyana in the Riss-Würm interglacial, Figure 2.1	56
Proposed forest refuges of the Guianas, Figure 2.2	59
Hypothetical reconstruction of late Pleniglacial rainfall, Amazonia, Figure 2.3	60
Hypothetical reconstruction of late Plenigacial forest refuges, Figure 2.4	61
Piraka shell mound, Figure 3.3	79
The Western Guiana Littoral, Figure 3.7	87
Archaic occupations in the Guianas, Figure 3.8	91
The Upper Rio Branco, Figure 3.11	96
The Waini-Barima watershed, Figure 3.14	102
Steatite deposits, upper Barama River, Figure 3.17	112
Wahana Island, Waini River, Figure 3.27	134
The petroglyph sample area, Figure 3.38	150
Petroglyph distributions, the geological base, Figure 3.40	155
The Guiana Shield, Figure 3.54	175
The Rio Branco-Kassikaityu corridor, Figure 3.66	205
The lower Aruka River, Figure 4.28	273
The Aruka-Kaituma watershed, Figure 4.29	274
Hosororo-Barrancas, Hosororo-Waini routes, Figure 4.31	278
Orinoco-Amazon corridor (Coastal), Figure 4.40	291
Orinoco-Amazon corridor (Southeast), Figure 4.41	292
Orinoco-Amazon corridor (Coastal Hinterland) Figure 4.41a	293
Wonotobo Falls, Corentyne River, Figure 4.45	302
Kurupukari Falls, Essequibo River, Figure 4.46	304
The Eastern Guiana Littoral, Figure 4.58	319
Proto-Eastern Arawak expansion, Figure 4.64	332
The Dutch on the Berbice and Canje Rivers, Figure 4.69	344
Possible Carib migrations, Figure 4.72	349
Progradation on the Mouth of the Moruka, Figure 4.77	354
Early Karinya settlement pattern, Figure 4.85	364
Territory of Amapá, Brazil, Figure 4.86	366
Principal migrations of horticulturists, Figure 5.1	411
Patamona dance festival, North Pakaraimas, Figure 5.7	426

MESSAGE FROM THE GOVERNMENT OF GUYANA

It has been said that in order to know where we are going, we should have an understanding of from whence we came.

This work *Prehistoric Guiana* by Denis Williams, provides for us Guyanese, and in fact Caribbean people, a platform to do just that. As Mark Plew states, 'This work represents the first major synthesis of the prehistory of Guyana'. It, however, does more. By providing a unique insight into the prehistory of Guyana through serious dedicated archaeological research over an extended period of time, a rich treasure trove is revealed to us from which we can chart the path to our progressive development.

The study of human history and prehistory, through the excavation of sites and the analysis of physical remains, was a pre-eminent part of the life of Denis Williams. This is evident from the record of his travels and his works. He was therefore able to compare the progress of human existence over time and, as a result, had an insight into the direction in which man is headed.

The compass of Williams' interest was not, however, restricted to prehistory. He was a consummate artist, novelist and archaeologist, a remarkable man and one of the most accomplished and versatile scholars of Guyana. His blend of artist and archaeologist allowed him to look with a 'different eye' at his research and the treatment of our cultural heritage. This unusual combination in one individual created a holistic approach which has now formed a tapestry enabling us to experience arousals of our own interest in the past, an appreciation of that past and a profound respect for the indigenous peoples' relationship with the environment. Certainly there are lessons to learn here concerning our relationship with the present and the foundations we lay for the future.

Denis Williams developed an interest in archaeology while working as an artist on an archaeological project in the Sudan. This was further stimulated after his return to Guyana in 1967 in the Mazaruni District. The artist in him guided his initial research which focused on the petroglyphic inscriptions or rock art of the ancient Amerindians as reflected in his Master's thesis to the University of Guyana in 1979 entitled, 'The Aishalton petroglyph complex in the prehistory of the Rupununi savannas'.

His appointment in 1977 as Director of the newly created Walter Roth Museum of Anthropology (founded at his initiative and in recognition of another pioneer in anthropology and archaeology, Dr Walter Roth) enabled him to fervently pursue his interest in researching the prehistory and archaeology of Guyana which had not been carried out by a Guyanese scholar up to that time.

In this book, Denis Williams, provides a unique insight into the archaeological research conducted in Guyana. His was the work of a pioneer whose great effort contributed to the recognition of the need through serious and unstinting research to reconstruct the prehistoric cultures and, thus, helped to give impetus to the continuing development of archaeological research in Guyana and the quest for knowledge about our earliest inhabitants.

Prehistoric Guiana focuses on the prehistory of the ancient Amerindian culture in what is now known as Guyana, the land of many waters, but it is a major work for this region, especially northern South America. It is a great source of information for scholars and gives other archaeologists and anthropologists the encouragement to continue further intensive research. It is hoped that the publication of this work will stimulate and encourage young Guyanese and Caribbean researchers to follow in the author's path of endeavour. His life work began the development of a Guyanese archaeological tradition that is in no way complete. It is for others to take up where he was forced to leave off.

Whether in his work as an artist, teacher, writer or archaeologist, Denis Williams provides an outstanding example of a Guyanese thinker. One who was willing to explore his own country with humility and wonder. It is in the very publication of *Prehistoric Guiana* that his heart's desire to share his knowledge of the prehistory of his country is achieved.

The publication of this major archaeological work is a result not only of the author's work but also the hundreds of Amerindian people from the various villages of the hinterland who, for over two decades, shared their knowledge; the staff of the Walter Roth Museum, especially Ms Jennifer Wishart, Denis Williams' colleague; Dr Mark Plew, Chair and Professor of Anthropology of Boise State University, as editor, and his staff and students who were critical in preparing the manuscript for publication; Dr Betty Meggers, Research Associate of the Smithsonian Institution, a friend and associate of Denis who also contributed to the Foreword; the support and encouragement of Mrs Toni Williams and all of the author's children, especially Ms Evelyn Williams, one of his daughters, who designed this extraordinary cover for the publication; and, Ian Randle who responded to my request for assistance in having this work published.

The Ministry of Culture, Youth and Sport wishes to extend its deepest gratitude and thanks to all those who helped – Guyanese and non-Guyanese, government officials and civil society, researchers, and just interested persons – in making the publication of this work a reality. Here is an example of people who came from various continents, diverse institutions, and different backgrounds overcoming barriers of all kinds, who collaborated on publishing this first major archeological work by a Guyanese. This 'coming together' was in itself of special significance.

May all who read it be enlightened about our rich prehistoric cultural heritage and learn from this remarkable work by Denis Williams, a true son of Guyana and the Caribbean.

Gail Teixeira
The Minister of Culture, Youth and Sport,
Guyana

DENIS WILLIAMS – A BIOGRAPHICAL NOTE

Denis Williams worked as an artist, art historian, novelist, anthropologist and archaeologist on three continents. He put his intellectual powers, creative genius and energy into a wide range of interrelated work in Britain, Nigeria and Guyana. He was a true polymath.

He was born on February 1, 1923 in Georgetown, Guyana to Joseph Alexander (a merchant) and Isabel (nee Adonis) Williams. In 1949, he married Catherine Hughes with whom he had five children – Janice, Evelyn, Isabel, Charlotte and Beatrice. The marriage ended in divorce in 1974. His second marriage to Toni Marian Dixon (poultry farmer and horticulturist) in 1975 produced another five children – Miles, Morag, Everard, Rachael and Denis. His last child, Kibilerie, was born to Jennifer Wishart, his companion for many years.

Educated in Georgetown, earning his Senior Cambridge School Certificate in 1941, Denis Williams was awarded the British Council's first scholarship in the colony to study art in Britain. He was a fine arts student at Camberwell School of Art from 1946-48 where William Coldstream, Lawrence Gowing and Claude Rogers were among his lecturers. The paintings Denis Williams produced in this period had been favourably noted by Wyndham Lewis.

On his return home in mid-1949, he worked intensively on a series of paintings in oils on sacking – *Plantation Studies*, *Origins*, *Burden and Release* – which were shown at private exhibitions. The paintings aroused considerable comment and some hostility. Unfulfilled in the Georgetown environment and not finding the teaching position he had hoped for, he returned to England in 1950.

Back in London with a body of new work, he asked Wyndham Lewis for his critical response. The result was a one-man show at Gimpel Fils in December 1950. Its centrepiece was the painting *Human World,* which was reproduced in *Time* magazine and bought by public subscription in British Guiana. This painting became the first piece of artwork in the now extensive National Collection. This exhibition resulted in Denis Williams becoming a visiting tutor at the prestigious Slade and a lecturer at the Central School of Fine ARTS. Subsequently, he had several successful one-man exhibitions at Gimpel Fils. He also exhibited widely in group exhibitions, including the Daily Express Young Artists' Exhibition in 1955, in which Lucien Freud won the first prize and Williams, with *Painting in Six Related Rhythms,* was a runner up.

Of his London experience, Williams had ambivalent feelings and was full of inner conflict. He admitted that it was:

> not only formative, but to a degree even determinative, however, given the circumstances of the day, acceptance at this level was in fact the most inacceptable, indeed, probably the most humiliating of choices open to the Colonial Artist.

1956 proved a turning point with an exhibition entitled *This is Tomorrow* at the Whitechapel Gallery, as Williams felt he had reached the end of the road with 'pseudo-European' painting. The resulting reaction was to get back to his roots and become the person he now knew he really was.

The ten years in Britain were followed by ten years in Africa. The first five (1957-62) were spent in the Sudan, lecturing in fine arts and art history at the Technical Institute of African Studies in Khartoum. The Sudan experience stimulated his interest in archaeology. He travelled the deserts of Northern Sudan studying the remains of antique Napatan and Meroitic cultures (the latter, perhaps, the very earliest of Iron Age societies on the continent), sketching newly-excavated artifacts. The Sudan became the setting of his first work of fiction, *Other Leopards,* now a classic of Caribbean literature. Autobiographical in content, it explores the sense of alienation which Denis experienced as a colonial black Englishman in an African Muslim culture.

It was in 1962 that Denis Williams moved to Nigeria and lectured in African Studies at the University of Ife and at the University of Lagos in 1966. Extensive research among the iron and bronze-working societies of West Africa led to his writing of a magisterial survey of African classical sculpture and metallurgy, the monumental and pioneering *Icon and Image: A Study of Sacred and Secular Forms of African Classical Art* (1974). At both universities he founded museum collections of African artifacts and edited journals of African studies. Denis Williams was possibly the first art historian of African descent to write about sub-Saharan Africa, thereby preparing for the establishment of art-historical teaching at the University of Ife. He documented Yoruba Masquerade Festivals which no other research scholar has seen, and his published papers on Yoruba brass casting are still among the best available sources.

It was while in Nigeria that he wrote his second novel, *The Third Temptation,* set in Wales (the home of his first wife), which employed the complex narrative technique of the then new *nouveau roman,* and which had nothing to do with his African experience.

Uncomfortable in Europe and Africa, Williams felt he was at the stage where he should return home to his own 'primordial world', the interior of Guyana, and contribute to the development of his country. He lived from 1968 to 1974 in Issano, the middle Mazaruni area of the Guyana hinterland, where he established a farm with his wife Toni. It was Toni who found the first ancient Amerindian artifact which formed the beginning of Denis' extensive collection and the beginning of his research into *Prehistoric Guiana.* In Issano he continued writing, painting and, subsequently, researching Amerindian tribal art, particularly the petroglyphs. He described this as a '*tremendous*' period of his life, one free of '*twentieth-century anxieties*'. Building his own house and acting as mid-wife when his wife gave birth to their daughter Morag created a new dimension to his way of life. He started work on a novel set in the Guyana rain forest, *The Sperm of God,* in which he examined the 'mongrel, polyglot society' of the New World where, unlike the Old, there is no 'purity of sperm' – themes which later emerged in his book *Image and Idea in the Arts of Guyana* (1970). He started work, painting the immense central panel, 'Majestas', of a triptych for a new church at nearby Kamarang. During his period in Issano he visited Georgetown several times to deliver a series of lectures.

Aubrey Williams said of Denis Williams:

> You have to know the man. He lives his life totally . . . You can't divide it up: the agricultural from the scientific, from the archaeological, from the creative in the sense of his sculpture and painting.

Eventually, for the sake of the children, Denis Williams left his primordial haven for Georgetown where he settled in 1974, becoming the new Republic's Director of Art. Two years later he founded and became the first Principal of the Burrowes School of Art, encouraging fellow Guyanese artists, especially the young, the East Indian Guyanese and the Indigenous Indian, in a field previously dominated by Guyanese of African descent. During this period he painted a vast mural, Memorabilia II, in the newly opened Cultural Centre in Georgetown. He was appointed Director of Art for the Ministry of Education, Social Development and Culture in Guyana (1977). In I 978, Williams served as Chairman of the National Trust of Guyana. His last position as Director of the Walter Roth Museum of Anthropology, which he founded, indicated his great interest in archaeology (in which he obtained an MA in Prehistory in 1979 from the University of Guyana). In 1980, he was a Visiting Research Scholar in the Department of Anthropology at the Smithsonian Institution. His publication 'Petroglyphs in the Prehistory of Northern Amazonia and the Antilles'(*Advances in World Archaeology,* Vol. 4,1985)was one of the highlights of his research. He obtained a DLitt (Honoris causa) from the University of the West Indies in 1989.

Wilson Harris wrote:

> Denis Williams' migration from a realm of brilliant painting to literature and archaeology was natural and right for him within his pursuit of symbol and actuality. His final sanctuary lay in exhaustive analyses of the skeleton of history of South America, Guyana, to which he returned in the late 1960's.

In the weeks leading up to his death, Denis worked hard on the manuscript for *Prehistoric Guiana* which he was able to complete.

A few of Denis Williams publications include: *Giglioli in Guyana 1922-1972* (biography); *Images and Idea in the Arts of the Caribbean* (1970); *Habitat and Culture in Ancient Guyana* (1984); *Petroglyphs in the Northern Amazonia and the Antilles*; (1985) *Ancient Guyana* (1985); *Amazonia Petroglyphs* (1985); *Prehistoric Culture of the Iwokrama Rain Forest Reserve* (1996); and numerous articles in *Archaeology and Anthropology: Journal of the Walter Roth Museum of Archaeology and Anthropology.*

At his funeral on July 4, 1998, Ian McDonald paid tribute by describing Denis Williams as a West Indian Leonardo da Vinci, filled with that fervent eagerness to understand all the world's mysteries, which the scientist Louis Pasteur called 'the inner god, which leads to every thing'. McDonald quoted from a passage about da Vinci, that greatest of all Renaissance men, which he felt could also have been used to describe Denis Williams:

> It seemed that nothing was impossible for him, that he could attempt anything – and understand anything. He composed treatise after treatise; with supreme self-confidence, he sought to penetrate the secrets of art, water, air, mankind, the world. He was interested in geology, in fossils, in ancient architectures and in the formation of mountains. He investigated the origins of milk, colic, tears, drunkenness, madness and dreams. He talked of writing what the soul is. He dreamed of flying like an eagle or a kite and began to draw plans of flying machines. Alongside a drawing of a bird in a cage he [da Vinci] wrote: 'my thoughts turn to hope'.

Denis Williams has been the recipient of several national and international awards. The government of Guyana honoured him with the Golden Arrow of Achievement in 1973 and the Cacique Crown of Honour in 1989. He was also presented with a Certification of Recognition, the Gabriel Mistral award for culture by the Organisation of American States in 1994 and, shortly before his death, with the 'Cowrie Circle' by the Commonwealth Association of Museums in 1998.

Toni Williams
Georgetown, 2002

FOREWORD

No part of the New World has fascinated Europeans more than Amazonia, and within Amazonia, the Guianas. Reporting on the first descent of the Amazon in 1542, Carvajal described villages ruled by women who lived in stone houses, worshiped the sun, ate from gold and silver utensils, and wore woolen clothing. When efforts to find El Dorado in the northern Andes failed, the search moved east, stimulated by tales of a huge lake lined with settlements containing "great riches of gold" (Hemming 1978:152-3). During subsequent decades, numerous large and well equipped expeditions sought in vain for the lake and the "great and golden city of Manoa," characterized by Ralegh as the capital of the "large rich and bewtiful empyre of Guiana." Despite illness, starvation, physical hardship, and loss of life, and despite first-hand reports by returning captives denying its existence, the search continued until the end of the 16th century, when it was abandoned only for lack of financial support (Hemming 1978). Nevertheless, Lake Parima continued to appear on maps for another hundred years, constituting "by far the biggest and most persistent hoax ever perpetrated by geographers (Gheerbrant 1992:43; Alés and Pouyllau 1992; Nicholl 1995).

After a long hiatus, the myth of El Dorado has been revived by anthropologists. Whitehead (1991:256), who considers Ralegh's account to be accurate, contends that Lokono chieftains "constituted a powerful polity that straddled the Amazon and Orinoco drainage basins in the area of the Sierra Acarai/Tumuc Humuc, linking the Corentyn and Berbice with the Paru and Trombetas rivers"; that these "upland polities...controlled both the trade in precious metals and other trans-Guyana commerce," and that ""we are dealing with civilizations of considerable complexity, possibly even protostates" (1994:38,44,48). He attributes the failure to find archaeological evidence of gold working to the fact that the locations of gold deposits were a secret ritually guarded by the Guyana chieftains (1991:257) and considers a Tairona-style gold pendant dredged from the Mazaruni River to be "dramatic, direct confirmation of the credibility of many sixteenth and seventeenth century sources that have until now been regarded as deeply suspect" (1990:19). Bray (1997:51), by contrast, attributes it to either prehispanic trade or postcolumbian importation from northern Colombia.

Four kinds of evidence have bearing on the credibility of the chronicles: (1) historical, (2) environmental, (3) ethnographical, and (4) archaeological. Historians deplore "archaeological naiveté in the face of historical documents" (Galloway 1992:182; Lightfoot 1995:206) and warn us that the early explorers saw "with a distorted vision, the result of preconceived ideas, unfailing credulity, and an abundant superstition" (Rothery 1995: 10; Flint 1992); that "it is important to remember that the testimonies were presented with the aim of gaining Crown support for further expeditions and therefore may have been exaggerated" (Newson 1996:223; Carlson 1996:25), and that the Europeans "wrote stories for self-justification and glory; it was not necessary that they portray the places they went and the people they saw accurately—just that they do it convincingly" (Galloway 1992:193).

Ecologists, biologists, climatologists, limnologists, geologists, sedimentologists, agronomists, and other natural scientists have compiled a vast amount of environmental evidence for the predominance of delicately balanced ecosystems in the neotropical lowlands and their inherent limitations for sustainable intensive exploitation by large sedentary human populations (e.g. Eden 1990; Jordan 1985; Sioli 1984; Richards 1996). The inherent deficiencies of infertile soil and warm humid climate are periodically augmented by long and short-term droughts that alter the composition, distribution, and density of plants and animals (Meggers 1994). The effectiveness of the biotic adaptations is reflected in the degradation that follows their disruption, whether by abandonment of traditional behavior by indigenous groups (Henley 1982:50-53; Eden 1974:32, Clark and Uhl 1984) or by commercial efforts at "development," such as the ill-fated Jarí Project (Fearnside 1988). In spite of such evidence, the impression persists among anthropologists that no serious impediments exist to sustainable intensive exploitation of Amazonia.

Ethnographers have compiled an extensive literature documenting the sustainability of the indigenous adaptation to the tropical forest. Detailed knowledge of the flora and fauna, small and frequently moved villages, extensive exchange networks, taboos, and other cultural behavior are comprehensible as risk-minimizing measures in the context of fluctuating and uncertain resources (Meggers 1996). Although some ethnologists consider that surviving Amazonians maintain population densities well below carrying capacity (Gregson 1992:436; Wagley 1977:24; Descola 1994:310), others have documented subsistence stress among such communities as a result of exceptionally dry weather, catastrophic flooding, and other unpredictable hazards (Lizot 1974:7; Baksh and Johnson 1990:212).

Archaeological evidence, which can resolve the debate, is disputed. Are extensive habitation sites the product of multiple reoccupations by relatively small communities during hundreds of years or do they represent large permanent settlements? Thus far, the first pattern has been identified by archaeological fieldwork on the coast and interior of Guyana (Evans and Meggers 1960), on the Ventuari and Manipiare rivers in Venezuela (Meggers, Evans, and Cruxent 1960), on the Rio Negro (Simões and Kalkmann 1987) and on the coast of Amapá in Brazil (Meggers and Evans 1957), as well as in other parts of Brazilian Amazonia. The second pattern has been inferred from investigations on the margins of the Guianas, specifically on the lower middle Orinoco (Roosevelt 1980), on the lower Rio Negro (Heckenberger et al 1999), and on Marijó Island (Roosevelt 1991). In this volume, Denis Williams provides the first comprehensive approach to reconstructing the history and characteristics of human settlement of the Guianas. In contrast to his predecessors, most of whom limit themselves to one category of phenomena, he takes a holistic approach and, not having been formally trained in any of the disciplines involved, he has escaped indoctrination by establishment positions. He integrates a wide variety of evidence from original research with previously published archaeological, geological, ecological, ethnographic, climatic, botanical, and even nutritional data. He interprets changes in faunal remains and tool types in the context of alterations in the coastal habitats, which in turn are correlated with changes in climate. He infers the existence of kinship networks from the presence of exotic raw materials implying long-distance exchange. He relates the locations and content of petroglyphs and sharpening grooves to tool size and to climatic fluctuation. He draws on first-hand acquaintance with indigenous groups to attribute changes in settlement pattern to subsistence stress. He correlates the occurrences of distinctive petroglyphs and the changes in mortuary practices with episodes of immigration, which are also reflected in the distributions of the major language families. Finally, he associates the speakers of Warau, Arawak, and Carib languages with the three major ceramic traditions—Mabaruma, Koriabo, and Atisté—and traces their movements through time and space using the temporal and spatial distributions of these ceramic traditions.

This summary does not communicate the complexity of the synthesis Williams provides, but it gives an idea of the wide range of evidence he has drawn together. His perspective benefits from an unusual combination of scientific judgment and artistic insight, which leads him to see relationships between phenomena that others have missed. It deserves careful consideration by all those concerned with understanding the past, assessing the present, and directing the future exploitation of the Guianas.

Betty J. Meggers

EDITOR'S PREFACE

With the passing of Denis Williams, Guyana lost one of its most accomplished and remarkable scholars. In the area of archaeology, he had no peers. For some twenty-five years and with little financial assistance, he pioneered the archaeology of Guyana. Traveling from one end of the country to the other, he conducted surveys and excavations and routinely published his findings. The prolific nature of his life's work is reflected in *Prehistoric Guiana*. This most important work represents the first major synthesis of the prehistory of Guyana. Sadly, however, Denis Williams passed away before completing the final version of his important work. At the urging of Jennifer Wishart, Dr. Williams' long-time colleague, and Minister Gail Teixeira, Ministry of Culture, Youth and Sport, I agreed to assist in editing and preparing the manuscript for publication.

At the time of his passing, only a hard copy of the manuscript remained. The manuscript contained handwritten notes of edits in the hand of Dr. Williams and Ms. Wishart. With these notations in mind, I completed an edit of the manuscript which was then scanned and reformatted to reflect the original document as much as possible. At the suggestion of Dr. Betty Meggers, Smithsonian Institution, who reviewed portions of the manuscript, I changed numerical notations from Spanish to English style and standardized measurements. A number of illustrations were drafted based on Dr. Williams sketches, while others, which had been drawn in pencil by Dr. Williams, were inked for publication. Overall, the book remains almost exactly as Dr. Williams left it.

It has taken almost a year to complete the preparation of *Prehistoric Guiana*. Without the assistance of many individuals the task would not have been completed. A number of my staff have worked diligently to bring the manuscript to press. Faith Brigham spent many weeks scanning and reformatting the text. Brian Glassic scanned and prepared a number of photographs, while Richard Benedict drafted and inked a number of artifact drawings. Jennifer Wishart helped me decipher a number of Dr. Williams' notes, provided insight regarding the intent of specific sections of the book, and assisted with the location of missing illustrations. Dr. Betty Meggers read and commented on sections of the manuscript and offered valuable advice throughout the process. Finally, the publication of this book has been insured by the commitment and efforts of Toni Williams, Jennifer Wishart, and the Honourable Gail Teixeira, Minister of Culture, Youth and Sport, who recognized the significance of *Prehistoric Guiana* and have worked to insure that the book will be available to the scholarly community and the people of Guyana.

Mark G. Plew
December 2000

PREFACE

This book has been on its way ever since I first took up residence 'Among the Indians of Guiana,' in particular among the great Akawaio of the Mazaruni Basin, three decades ago. The perspective gained from direct daily contact with a people who have occupied the same territory continuously for the past two thousand years is sobering. The psychic autonomy engendered by this level of adaptation to the tropical forest, bolstered by their century-old Hallelujah faith, has proven an effective shield against the multi-faceted and often unwelcome intrusions of the state. As the missionaries may take a long time realizing, the Akawaio need no one.

Their sense of pride and self-sufficiency is equaled by that of their linguistic ancestors, the Karinya, whose acquaintance I have enjoyed for just a decade, and intermittently at that, in the course of excavating their ancestral territory on the upper Pomeroon. There they maintain an impenetrable isolation in the midst of a predominantly Arawak culture, relatively recently arrived. Notwithstanding my only recent acquaintance with it, knowledge of the archaeology of the Karinya provided the keystone in reconstructing the prehistoric cultures of the entire Guiana Coast down to the Mouth of the Amazon. They are now a very diminished people, whose antiquity in the area is attested, nonetheless, by the religious behaviors they have shared with, first, the very ancient Warao, and secondly with groups on the western Venezuela Coast and in Colombia. Over time, Karinya culture appears to have enjoyed an interaction sphere, albeit disjunct, along the north coast of South America from Caribbean Colombia to the Mouth of the Amazon.

As it comes into better focus, this may explain similarities between the cosmology of the Karinya and the Warao, whose languages likewise appear to suggest a distribution area stretching from the Mouth of the Orinoco River to the west of Lake Maracaibo.

The relationship between the Warao and the Orinocan Arawaks is more clearly in evidence archaeologically. It was initiated on the Aruka River around 1600 B.C. and survives to the present day.

I have enjoyed more intermittent acquaintances with the Patamona of the North Pakaraimas, the Makusi of the North Rupununi Savannas, the Wapisiana of the South Rupununi Savannas (who contributed years of labor to the study of the remarkable petroglyph corpus there), and the Waiwai of the rain forest to the far South.

Working among these very different and historically distinct peoples over the past thirty years not only has provided a most important base for archaeological interpretation (they remain 'tethered' to specific niches) but also has revealed the vacuity of appellations such as 'Amerindian', 'aborigines', 'natives', 'Boks', etc.

In the name "Guiana" is enshrined the several mutually distinctive histories of all these peoples, our spiritual ancestors. There simply is no alternative route to a national self image. For their patient and loving collaboration over the years, they head the list of my acknowledgments.

At the same time, the search for the past of these ancestors of ours has involved access to the resources of museum institutions of various colleagues abroad. Also, it has involved discussions and correspondence across the continents. Outstanding has been the relationship with the Smithsonian Institution initiated by Walter Roth and F.W. Hodge in 1913 and continued under successive Chiefs of the Bureau of American Ethnology. I have benefitted in manifold ways from this relationship, in particular as a Visiting Research Scholar in the internship program during the fall of 1980. As a meeting ground for Latin American scholars, the Smithsonian has no equal in the southern continent. I am grateful also to the U.S. Government for participation in their International Visitor Program in 1985. This Program permitted first-hand acquaintance with museum institutions across the length and breadth of the United States, a package otherwise wholly beyond my means. Lacking the library and laboratory facilities of the great European and North American institutions, relationships of this kind, shared also in lesser degree with colleagues at other American institutions, and in Europe particularly with the Albert Egges van Giffen Instituut voor prae- en proto-historie, University of Leiden, and with the University of Amsterdam, represent a most useful form of collaboration, especially valuable in not being institutionalized. Nearer home, I have benefitted in various ways from collaboration with colleagues at the National Museum in Caracas, the Museu de los Indios in Rio de Janeiro, the Goeldi Museum in Belem and, in Suriname, the Surinaams Museet. Without the friendship and support of these colleagues, and especially the library and laboratory resources they invariably were able to negotiate on my behalf, *Prehistoric Guiana* definitely could not have been written in Guyana. Written elsewhere, it would have lacked many of the hands-on relationships in anthropological space and time which above all I have sought to perceive and present. For this latter privilege, unquestionably my greatest debt is to the Government of Guyana for financing the programs of the Walter Roth Museum that have provided the research materials presented here.

This book could never have been conceived, either, without the hard work and loyalty of my Jennifer, whose opinions were the acid bath of all data, from whatever source, coming my way.

28 October 1996

REFERENCES CITED

Alés, Catherine and Michel Pouyllau
  1992   La conquete de l'inutile: les géographies imaginaires de l'El Dorado. *L'Homme* 32 (122-124): 271-308.

Baksh, Michael and Allen Johnson
  1990   Insurance policies among the Machiguenga: an ethnographic analysis of risk management in a non-westem society. In *Risk and Uncertainty in Tribal and Peasant Economies,* edited by E. Cashdan, pp. 287-295. London: Academic Press.

Bray, Warwick
  1997   Metallurgy and anthropology: two studies from prehispanic America. *Museo del Oro Bul* 42:36-55. Bogotá: Banco de la República.

Carlson, Catherine C.
  1996   The (in)significance of atlantic salmon. *FederalArchaeology 8* (3-4):22-30.

Clark, Kathleen E. and Christopher Uhl
  1984   Deterioro de la vida de subsistencia tradicional en San Carlos de Rio Negro. *Interciencia 9:358-365.*

Descola, Philippe
  1994   *In the society of nature: a native ecology of Amazonia.* New York: Cambridge University Press.

Eden, Michael J.
  1974   Ecological aspects of development among the Piaroa and Guahibo Indians of the Upper Orinoco Basin. *Antropológica 39:25-56.*
  1990   *Ecology and land management in Amazonia.* London: Bellhaven Press.

Evans, Clifford and Betty J. Meggers
  1960   Archeological investigations in British Guiana. *Bureau of American Ethnology Bul.* 177. Washington DC, Smithsonian Institution.

Evans, Clifford, Betty J. Meggers, and José M. Cruxent
  1960   Preliminary results of archeological investigations along the Orinoco and Ventuari Rivers, Venezuela. *Actas del 33° Congreso Internacional de Americanistas,* pp. 359-369, San José, Costa Rica.

Fearnside, Philip M.
  1988   Jarí at age 19: lessons for Brazil's silvicultural plans at Carajás. *Interciencia* 13:12-24.

Flint, Valerie I.J.
1992 *The imaginative landscape of Christopher Columbus.* Princeton: Princeton University Press.

Galloway, Patricia
1992 The unexamined habitus: direct historical analogy and the archaeology of the text. In *Representations in Archaeology,* edited by J. C. Gardin and C.S. Peebles, pp. 178-195. Bloomington: University of Indiana Press.

Gheerbrant, Alain
1992 *The Amazon; past, present, and future.* New York: Harry N. Abrams.

Gregson, Ted L.
1992 Fishing in the waters of Amazonia: native subsistence economies in a tropical rain forest. *American Anthropologist* 94:428-440.

Heaton, H.D., editor
1934 The discovery of the Amazon according to the account of Friar Gaspar de Carvajal and other documents. *American Geographical Society Special Publ.* 17. New York.

Heckenberger, Michael J., James B. Peterson, and Eduardo Gcés Neves
1999 Village size and permanence in Amazonia: two archaeological examples from Brazil. *Latin American Antiquity* 10:353-376.

Hemming, John
1978 *The search for El Dorado.* London: Michael Joseph Ltd.

Henley, Paul
1982 *The Panare: tradition and change on the Amazonian frontier.* New Haven: Yale University Press.

Jordan, Carl F.
1985 *Nutrient cycling in tropical forest ecosystems.* New York: John Wiley and Sons.

Lightfoot, Kent G.
1995 Culture contact studies: redefining the relationship between prehistoric and historic archaeology. *American Antiquity* 60:199-217.

Lizot, Jacques
1974 El Río de los Periquitos: breve ralato de un viaje entre los Yanomami del alto Siapa. *Antropológica* 37:3-23.

Meggers, Betty J.
  1994 Archeological evidence for the impact of mega-Niño events on Amazonia during the past two millennia. *Climatic Change* 28: 321-338.
  1996 *Amazonia: man and culture in a counterfeit paradise.* Second Edition. Washington DC, Smithsonian Institution Press.

Meggers, Betty J. and Clifford Evans
  1957 Archeological investigations at the mouth of the Amazon. *Bureau of American Ethnology Bul.* 167. Washington DC, Smithsonian Institution.

Newson, Linda A.
  1996 Between Orellana and Acuña: a lost century in the history of the north-west Amazon. *Bull. Inst.Fr. d'etudes Anines* 25:203-231.

Nicholl, Charles
  1995 *The creature in the map: a journey to El Dorado.* New York: William Morrow and Co.

Richards, Paul W.
  1996 *The tropical rain forest.* Second Edition. New York: Cambridge University Press.

Roosevelt, Anna C.
  1980 *Prehistoric maize and manoic subsistence along the Amazon and Orinoco.* New York: Academic Press.
  1991 *Moundbuilders of the Amazon.* SanDiego: AcademicPress.

Rothery, Guy Cadogan
  1995 *The Amazons.* London, Senate.

Simoes, Mario F. and Ana Lúcia Kalkmann
  1987 Pesquisas arqueológicas no médio Rio Negro (Amazonas). *Revista de Arqueologia* 4:83-116.

Sioli, Harald, editor
  1984 *The Amazon: limnology and landscape ecology of a mighty river and its basin.* Dordrecht: Dr.W. Junk Publishers.

Wagley, Charles
  1977 *Welcome of tears: the Tapirapé Indians of central Brazil.* New York: Oxford University Press.

Whitehead, Neil L.
1990 The Mazaruni pectoral: a golden artefact discovered in Guyana and the historical sources concerning native metallurgy in the Caribbean, Orinoco and northern Amazonia. *Archaeology and Anthropology* 7:19-38. Georgetown.
1991 Los señores de los epuremei: un examen de la transformación del comercio y la política indígenas en el Amazonas y Orinoco 1492-1800. In *Etnohistoria del Amazonas,* P. Jorna et al, coordinadores, pp. 255-263. Quito: AbyaYala.
1994 The ancient amerindian polities of the Amazon, the Orinoco, and the Atlantic coast: a preliminary analysis of their passage from antiquity to extinction. In *Amazonian Indians,* A.C. Roosevelt, editor, pp. 33-53. Tucson, University of Arizona Press.

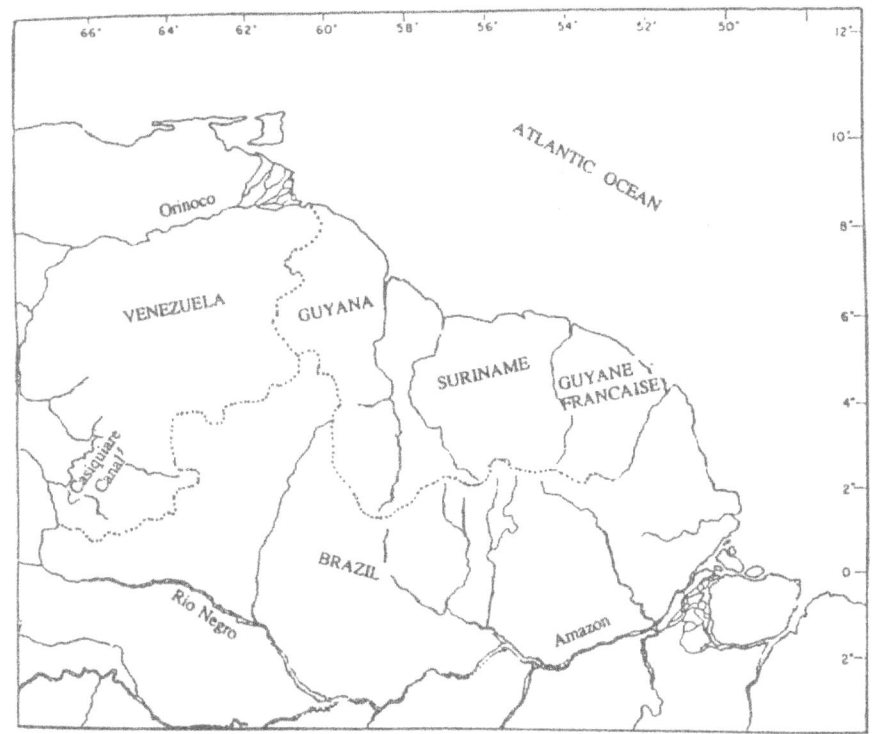

Figure 1.1. Map. The "Island" of Guiana.

1. INTRODUCTION

The setting

The Precambrian Guiana Shield, which forms the nucleus of the Island of Guiana (i.e. bounded by the courses of the Amazon and Orinoco Rivers and their bridging stream the Casiquiare Canal) is divided into roughly equal but contrasting sectors by the valleys of the Rio Branco, Rupununi and Essequibo Rivers. These sectors define an Eastern and a Western Guiana, each fringed by a littoral of variable inland extension and independent morphology. Western Guiana comprises the southern portion of the Venezuelan Territory of Amacuro, as well as the State of Bolivar and the Territory of Amazonas. It includes, also, portions of Amazonas and Roraima States in Brazil and, in Guyana, the portion of Essequibo County that lies to the north of the east-west trending stretch of the upper Rupununi River. Eastern Guiana comprises the Brazilian State of Amapá, the northern portion of the State of Pari and the eastern portion of the State of Roraima, as well as the national territories of Guyane française, Suriname and the southern portion of the County of Essequibo, in Guyana. Toward the middle of the Shield are the Pakaraima Mountains, covering some 73,000 square kilometers. These are large mesa and high plateau mountains reaching 2810 m on Mt. Roraima in Guyana and 3014 m on Mt. Neblina in Brazil, Figure 1.1.

The Western Guiana Littoral

Co-terminous with the Western Guiana Coast of Krook (1970) is an expanse of peat swamps and tidal clay flats under swamp and marsh forest of Recent date. With the culmination of the eustatic rise in the sea level along the Guiana Coast around 6000 years ago, these tidal clay flats and marshes occupied the sediment basin formed to seaward of an interglacial shoreline which extended in a great arc between the mouths of the Orinoco and Essequibo Rivers some distance inland from the present day sea coast. This fossil shoreline represents the initial stage of a shoreline of submergence (Strahler 1975:554), highly embayed and irregular, with ragged peninsulas formed by the valleys of the northeast-trending Barima and Waini Rivers. These bays, peninsulas and elongated islands extend the upland-wetland interface many times the length of its defining arc, in this way affording maximum intergrading of the two great biotic systems of the Western Guiana Littoral: rainforest on the uplands and fresh- or brackish-water forest on the lowlands. Areal relationships between fresh- and brackish-water forest have changed substantially in the past in phase with variable magnitudes of marine influence through time.

The Western Guiana Littoral is believed subject to continuing tectonic subsidence, increasing in magnitude toward the Orinoco Delta (Brinkman and Pons 1968: 5, 9, 21). With the Holocene rise in the sea level, eustatic peat of varying depth was deposited in the swamps on top of the subsiding clay sediments. The east-west gradient produced by this subsidence has resulted in the peat deposits of the west being more substantial than those around the Essequibo estuary in the east. Marked edaphic differences lead to the recognition of northwestern and southeastern subzones in the Western Guiana Littoral. Contrasts in elevation, rainfall, drainage, water quality, vegetation, etcetera, between these subzones are shown in Table A. These contrasting subzones correspond approximately with Zones 2 and 5 in the classification of the Guyana forests (see De Milde and de Groot 1970). They are also of contrasting subsistence potential.

On the Western Guiana Littoral, the combination of extensive peat swamps bounded on the one hand by rain forest and on the other by a wide, shallow inshore shelf, produces a distinctive coastal type (Ray et al 1984) that is characterized by extremely high productivities (Perlman 1980).

The Eastern Guiana Littoral

East of the Mouth of the Essequibo River, the drainage area of which covers some 45.8×10^3 km^2, the coastal peat swamps of the North West, deposited in Recent time, give way to the complex of geological units, comprising the Guiana Coastal Plain, which stretches with variable inland extension to the Mouth of the Oyapoc. These units comprise an Old Coastal Plain of Pleistocene age, a Young Coastal Plain of Recent date and a complex of *chenier* ridges running at distances varying between 5 - 10 km inland more or less parallel to the shoreline. The Old

Table A. Contrasting subzones of the Western Guiana Littoral

		SE subzone	NW subzone
Vegetation[1]			
Forest type (ha):			
1	Mixed forest	435,800	551,950
1b	Mora forest	54,450	3,150
1d	Liane forest	250	--
1l	Mixed upland forest	27,100	--
1m	Mixed undulating forest	1,100	--
2c	Wallaba forest	31,450	--
3	Mora forest	69,350	8,000
3b	Mora forest	34,300	29,800
3e	Swamp forest	3,800	530,400
4	Mangrove forest	4,600	32,150
4a	Mangrove woodland	6,050	48,300
	Open swamp	20,550	1,350
Soil type		Tertiary white sands; Latosols	Peat on marine clay; Latosols
Rainfall[2]		1780 - 2410 mm	2410 - 2790 mm
Water quality		Blackwater pH 4.0	Whitewater pH 7.0
Tectonic subsidence[3]		slight to absent	Pronounced

[1] De Milde and de Groot (1970)
[2] Persaud (1983)
[3] Brinkman and Pons (1968)

Coastal Plain is evident as disjunct erosional remnants of marine sediments ranging in elevation between 3 - 5 meters. The Young Coastal Plain comprises marine clays that were deposited in erosion gullies of the Old Coastal Plain during the Holocene rise in the sea level. The narrow, elongated subparallel bundles of sand or shell constituting the *chenier* ridges were deposited on top of the sediments of the Young Coastal Plain at highest wave level during periods of progradation of the coastline. Beyond the Oyapoc, the coast trends sharply southward to the Mouth of the Amazon, immediately entering the Intertropical Realm which lies seasonally within the trade winds of both hemispheres in contrast to the Tropical Realm of the remainder of the coast, which lies permanently within the trade winds of the northern hemisphere.

The Guiana Coast, one of only a few true *chenier* plain coasts anywhere, represents one of the world's most dynamic environments because of the speed with which morphological changes occur there. The fine-grained sediments comprising it are supplied by the Amazon, which annually delivers something on the order of 1000 tons of clay to the ocean, some 22-30% of which are deposited by the North Equatorial Current along low-lying portions of the coastline of Guyana, Suriname and Guyane trancaise (Wells and Coleman 1981a). The type of clay minerals providing the main component of these young marine clays derive from weathering at high altitudes in the Andes where conditions are comparable to those obtaining in moderate climatic zones (Janssen 1976). This accounts for the high fertility of the Eastern Guiana Littoral and its outstanding biotic richness, in which respect it is comparable to the *varzea* of the Amazon floodplain, which derives from the same source.

Extensive mudflats and associated intertidal mudbanks migrate alongshore from southeast to northwest at an average 1.5 km/yr. Mechanisms controlling this unique coastal feature are treated in Augustinus, (1978) and Wells and Coleman (1981a). As these colossal subtidal mudbanks proceed northwestward in a well defined 30-year cycle, the coast is continually modified by alternate largescale depositional and erosional events. Intertidal mudflats, the subaerial extensions of these subtidal mudbanks or mudshoals, occur every 30 - 60 km along the coast. A typical mudflat/mudbank system is 10 - 20 km wide, extends offshore and slopes 0.050. Intertidal exposures range between 2 - 5 km (Allersma 1968; Brown 1943; Clapperton 1993; Wells and Coleman 1981a).

Offshore, the North Equatorial Current flows northwestward with a maximum surface velocity of about 1 m/sec around April. This figure drops to 0.7 - 0.3 m/sec during the second half of the year (Allersma 1968). Sediments brought down from the Guyana rivers are deposited by this current off the south coast of Trinidad (Bleackley 1956; see also Olsen 1973). The volume of these sediments is small when compared with the flow of marine sediments along the coast. The North Equatorial Current may have aided prehistoric communication with the Eastern Caribbean (e.g. see Boomert 1979a:111).

The Western Guiana Hinterland

Beyond the Coastal Plain lie two other geological units which constitute the Western Guiana Hinterland. The first of these comprises the folded Precambrian metasediments, metavolcanics, gneisses and granites of the Guiana Shield. Superimposed upon this crystalline basement, a once extensive sandstone plateau, the Roraima Formation, has weathered and eroded into the giant table mountains *(tepui)* of southern Venezuela, northern Brazil and western Guyana. In this *Pantepui* of the biogeographers, land rising above 1000 meters may exceed 80,000 km^2, while the area above 1500 meters may exceed 10,000 km² and the surfaces of the highest table mountains may approximate 5000 km² (Steyermark 1982:200). These elevations sharply distinguish the area to the west of the Essequibo-Rio Branco watershed from that to the east of it. Its radial drainage pattern has provided distributaries for prehistoric cultural traits moving northward to the Atlantic *via* the Wenamu and Barama Rivers, southward to the Amazon *via* the Ireng and Rio Branco, eastward to the Essequibo *via* the Mazaruni, Cuyuni, Potaro and Siparuni Rivers and westward to the upper Orinoco *via* the Rio Ventuari. From the remotest antiquity, the Caroni has facilitated the bridging of the Orinoco-Amazon watershed *via* the Guiana Highlands.

During the rains, May-July, when the Rio Branco cannot discharge into the swollen Amazon mainstream, its waters back up in its tributary, the Takutu, flooding the Rupununi Savannas in places to depths in excess of two meters. During the dry season, the savannas dry out completely.

The Eastern Guiana Hinterland

The Eastern Guiana Hinterland is dominated by a low-lying, polygonally dissected landscape whose small, rounded laterite-covered hills rise from seasonally flooded lowlands that severely limit the scope of human occupancy (Hurault 1989; Kroonenberg and Mellitz 1983; Meggers and Evans 1957; Simões and Araujo-Costa 1978). The emergent rocks of the Guiana Shield narrow progressively west to east to disappear altogether in the Brazilian Territory of Amapá. Correspondingly, the three Guianas diminish areally west to east. The coast range of Guyane française attains a maximum elevation of 800 in and projects in a few small pffshore islands. Due to the east-west direction of the Amazon-Atlantic watershed, the streams of the Eastern Guiana Hinterland flow either northward to the Atlantic or southward to the Amazon, facilitating north-south communication *via* the Essequibo and Corentyne Rivers. Main tributaries of the Essequibo lead westward to the Pakaraimas.

Political and cultural divisions

The national histories of the Guiana territories are as diverse as their edmic divisions. They are contained in five major European languages spoken by around five million people across the region. This diversity has been a major factor in political and cultural development. The process of rapid indigenization of archaeological scholarship in Brazil that followed on the pioneering work of Smithsonian archaeologists Meggers and Evans at the Mouth of the Amazon in the forties was paralleled in Venezuela following on the pioneering works of the North Americans Bennett, Kidder and Osgood conuriencing in the early thirties. Compared to the rest of the Guianas, Brazil and Venezuela are relatively old independent nation states with European-type cultural infrastructures. A vastly different situation obtained in what may be called the Colonial Guianas (British, Dutch and French) by virtue of their dependent political status, their chronically strapped economies, their perfunctory educational and cultural institutions and their racially mixed populations of overwhelmingly ex-slaves and indentured laborers. While in Brazilian and Venezuelan Guiana it was relatively easy to graft archaeological inquiry on to pre-existing European-type cultural infrastructures characterized by museums, universities, specialized libraries, etc., in the Colonial Guianas this was definitely a pioneering undertaking at the time of the take-off of Amazonian archaeology in the, immediate post-World War II years. Suriname became a self-governing part of the Kingdom of the Netherlands in 1954, while Guyana achieved political independence from Great Britain only in 1966. To the present, French Guiana remains a *département* of metropolitan France and prospects for its political and economic advancement are thought at present to be not encouraging. In terms of regional integration, Suriname was accepted into the Caribbean Community - an economic and cultural bloc of English-speaking ex-colonial states - only in 1995.

Among the relatively recent immigrant populations of these "Three Guianas" the concept of history appertains to specific ancestral concerns of each that spell identity and survival, and hardly at all to the notion of cultural evolution in the Island of Guiana as a whole. There is, in contrast, the "problem" of the Native American whose historical concerns embrace the entire territory and who implacably views all non-Native Americans as intruders and despoilers there. With an area of some 1.6×10^6 km^2, Guiana occupies somewhat more than a quarter of the area of the rain forests of the Amazon Basin and boasts an antiquity directly associated with the Early Man migrations into the southern continent 12,000 or more years ago. The development of archaeology in the Guianas must therefore be seen as apposite to global concerns regarding the recoverable history of the rain forest and its sustainable exploitation, as well as to problems centering on the past and future of its non-immigrant populations. With the increasing articulateness and national organization of the indigenes these two concerns bid fair to proving a single inseparable problem in the anthropology of the future: overpopulation (Williams 1996a).

Sources for the study of prehistory
Introduction

Sources for the study of the ancient cultures of the Guianas are many and diverse. Shell mound complexes, petroglyphs, pictographs, stone tools and weapons, earthworks, pottery, artificial depressions, rock alignments, rock circles and related structures, and human burials, taken together, have stimulated a sizeable though uneven literature during the past hundred or so years. To the present, emphasis has been placed mainly on study of the horticultural period, as evidenced in its diagnostic ceramic complexes. Undue emphasis on ceramic classification and analysis has led to an unfortunate neglect of the earlier periods, concerning which the shell mounds, petroglyphs and pictographs are eloquently representative of the incomparably vaster time span covered by the Archaic cultures. Whereas, on the Coast, shell mounds constitute the only pathway to knowledge of Archaic cultures and environments, in the Hinterland this pathway is provided by the numerous specimens of modified bedrock that constitute the principal surviving archaeological evidences of the period. At the same time, both on the Coast and in the Hinterland, aspects of the antecedent paleo-Indigenous cultures are evidenced in odd finds of stone tools, implements and chipping stations that permit comparisons with various equally ancient cultures elsewhere in South America. The cultural uniformity of the Guianas on all time levels suggests that the potentials for integration of Coastal and Hinterland data sets are promising.

Artificial depressions

Inexplicably neglected in the study of the ancient past are myriads of artificial depressions that have been reported in the Guiana rivers for well over the past two hundred years, assuming them to have been the subject of Horstman's intriguing reference on the Rupununi River in 1740 to "a stone covered with various letters and some figures, also the seat of the fundament, also the calves of the legs and the heels of him who wrote it" (in Harris and de Villiers 1911:173). Well over a thousand of these artificial depressions may occur at a given site, evidently indicating sustained exploitation of a rain forest environment that otherwise characteristically conceals every other trace of human occupancy. Carefully measured and plotted with respect to elevation above prevailing water level in the river (pwl), these data may be related to a given cross section of riverbed plotted by sonar equipment. Such data are of the utmost importance in the matter of reconstructing water level movements in the remote past. These may be identified with one or other of the Holocene arid intervals that have been indicated in Amazonia by palynology. Moreover, since certain of these depressions may be diagnostic of the kinds of stone tool that were manufactured or maintained in them, numerical analysis may aid their classification and therefore identification of specific tool types which otherwise may be no longer in evidence. Such reconstructions may be indicative, in turn, of the associated kinds of cultural activities.

These kinds of data are statistically revealing where samples are very large ($n = >850$ specimens) and derive from both banks of a river, artificial depressions being mostly encountered on only one riverbank or on isolated boulders in the stream. Because of this, water level observations recorded on one bank of a river usually lack corroboration by evidences deriving from the immediately opposite bank. Such paired data sets, though unusual, provide a useful control for evaluating the significance of water level inferences deriving from sites elsewhere in a particular river basin. Combined, these kinds of data from major drainages of the

Guianas evidently carry potentials for reconstructing movements of the water table, and hence the picture of probable past vegetations, regionally.

Variable flood stages of a river in the remote past may also be evidenced by deposits of varnish on riverbed or riverbank outcrops. Such deposits may have formed at different times and in discrete layers of mutually contrasting color. Imposition of artificial depressions may be associated with one or other of such deposits, permitting inferences to be drawn concerning the local sequence.

Shell mounds. Thirty-odd shell mounds have been reported or recorded on the edge of the immense peat swamps of the Western Guiana Littoral (Anon [J.L.Smith] 1866; Bennett 1866; Brett 1868; Bullbrook 1953; Meggers and Evans 1955; Osgood 1946; Verrill 1918). Around one-half of these have been excavated during the past 135 years. Shell mounds occur with variable frequencies in both the Northwestern and Southeastern Subzones of the Western Guiana Littoral. An interim report on a project for their survey and excavation is given in Williams (1981). In the Southeastern Subzone, Brett (1868:433) reported a shell mound "near the Akawini" River. This has now been identified with the Warapana shell mound, not hitherto reported. A number of ground, or ground and polished stone artifacts, labelled "Waramuri Mound" or "Waramuri", are in the Im Thurn Collection, Walter Roth Museum. Artifacts from Brett's Waramuri excavations of 1866, reported to have been deposited in the Christy Collection by Sir John Lubbock (Im Thurn 1883:413) are not listed in a recent inventory of Guyanese artifacts held in London's Museum of Mankind. Information volunteered by local residents on the existence of shell mounds on the Aruquiaha and Yaramai Creeks, upper Pomeroon River, was not substantiated in the field. Very possibly, as indeed remains the belief of certain local residents, the shell mounds of the Southeastern Subzone number more than the four already excavated there. However, their paucity relative to complexes reported or recorded in the biotically richer Northwestern Subzone is evidently a function of the respective subsistence potentials of these contrasting areas of the Western Guiana Littoral.

Figure 1.2. Waropoko,Upper Waini

In the Northwestern Subzone, the mound at Querow (Quiaro), recorded in the 1981 report, has now been identified with Kuiaru (Gazeteer of Guyana), Kwiaru on some maps. A few stone artifacts from this site are in the Everard Im Thurn Collection, Walter Roth Museum. Shell mounds reported on Bamboo (Kamuata) Creek and on the Waiwa River (Evans and Meggers 1960:35) have never been investigated. Poonai (1978) reported shell mounds in the swamps near Waropoko on the upper Waini River, Figure 1.2. Of these, the mounds at Alaka Creek, Alaka Island and Sand Creek have been excavated (Evans and Meggers 1960). A mound locally reported on Aiyekowa Creek, left bank Waini River, is probably the *Pawaieykemoo* mentioned from hearsay by Im Thurn (1883:412). Also locally reported is a shell mound at Assakata, on Assakata Creek, a tributary of the Biara,which empties into the Baramani River.

More to the northwest, another shell mound complex centered on the lower Aruka River appears to have included a number of still unexcavated sites along the Barima River which, together with the Waini, drains the swamps of the Northwestern Subzone. In this Lower Aruka Complex, the shell mound at Hobo was destroyed without trace for the installation of the Mabaruma airstrip. A small overgrown mound was discovered, and excavated, on the edge of the swamps at Kokerital, nearby (Williams MS). Verrill's report of shell mounds on small hills between Kumaka and Barabina were not confirmed in recent survey. The Barabina mound has been excavated repeatedly (Osgood 1946; Verrill 1918; Williams 1981; see Roosevelt 1995, Williams 1997). Local folk report investigations there by "Old Roth" as well as by a North American, Elizabeth Tull, who removed a few "head bones" (Cyril Emmanuel pers. comm. 1979). A fair degree of credibility must attach to an unsolicited report of a shell mound "behind the pig pens" at Camp Papaya, near Matthews Ridge, made by a National Serviceman in 1981. Peter Fredericks, the present (1988) Warao occupant of the shell mound at Akawabi, claimed that his parents occupy a shell mound at Surprise Hill on the Kaituma River, "just before Port Kaituma."

The shell mounds of the Western Guiana Littoral thus comprise three spatially discrete complexes on the basement edge between the Orinoco and Essequibo estuaries: the upper Pomeroon, upper Waini and lower Aruka complexes. No other shell mounds are known along the Guiana Coast. Barring the deposit at Hosororo Creek, shell mounds reported on both banks of the Amazon near its mouth (Hilbert 1959; Roosevelt et al 1991) were not affiliated to these complexes. The mounds of the Western Guiana Littoral appear to have been affiliated, with progressively decreasing antiquity, to shell mound complexes on Trinidad and in northeastern South America.

The potentials of shell mound complexes on the Western Guiana Littoral for restructuring long vanished environments remain to be fully exploited. The Guyana mounds comprise species of shellfish that no longer survive anywhere along the coast. They are therefore excellent indicators of environmental change during archaeological time. Since the formation of these mound complexes coincided with peat deposition in the sediment basin of the North West during the eustatic rise in the sea level, episodes of peat deposition that were coincident with deposition of the remains of now vanished shellfish species should be diagnostic of stages in the evolution of the coastal swamps. In this process, changes in the prevailing fauna indicate shifts in the critical balance between marine influence and the influence of run-off in these low-lying swamps.

Intercalated in the peat of this sediment basin, deposits of shell sand indicate a marine incursion during the Amazonian arid interval of +/- 4000 b.p. (Williams 1982, 1992). Palynological analysis of peat associated with these shell sand deposits may contribute data on water table fluctuations during the Archaic. Such data may potentially correlate with water table fluctuations in hinterland rivers as evidenced by zonation in complexes of artificial depressions. Alternatively, they may correlate with arid intervals evidenced by island building increments of sand in hinterland rivers resulting from periodic watershed erosion in phase with episodes of torrential rainfall.

Petroglyphs and pictographs

Petroglyph distributions in the Guianas and in northern South America as a whole have been discussed by Schomburgk (1841:108). Various distribution maps are available (Dubelaar 1986, Dubelaar MS; de Valencia et al 1987; Sujo Volsky 1975; Williams 1985). New specimens are being continually discovered (Williams 1994, 1996). Homogeneity in petroglyph content across the various territories of northern Amazonia has been noted by Dubelaar (1986), Humboldt (1852-1853) and Schomburgk (1841; cf. Mallery 1893). This homogeneity has permitted classification of the petroglyphs of northern Amazonia into three great Traditions, or Series, representing hunter-gatherers in, respectively, the savannas and rain forest, as well as those peripatetic horticulturists who migrated out of the lower Rio Negro, in due course encircling the Guiana land mass and colonizing the Antilles. The iconographic homogeneity of each petroglyph Tradition permits diagnosis of inter-relationships between disparate groups occupying a particular niche, such as a river drainage, or even a fortuitously located cave or rock shelter, on different time levels. Plans and dimensions of petroglyphic

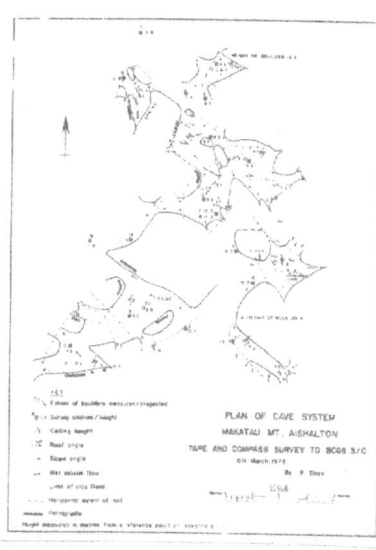

Figure 1.3. Makatau cave.

chambers in a particular cave system may be indicative of the probable size of the occupying band, and even of the distribution of its constituent families, Figure 1.3. Excavation of a cave floor may furnish evidences of a prehistoric dietary and the associated toolkit (e.g. Mentz Ribeiro et al 1987, 1989), and thus suggest prevailing levels of nutrition. Petroglyphs and pictographs may depict tools and weapons such as fish spears, projectile points, stone axes, etc., or implements in impermanent materials such as a wide range of basketry fish traps which enjoy poor survival potential in the Tropical Forest environment (Hurault et al 1963; Williams 1985). Tools recovered in a datable context at the foot of a petroglyph boulder may provide a time slot for the associated petroglyph Tradition. Petroglyphs permanently located below critical low water in various rivers of the Guianas (Brown 1873; Dubelaar 1986; Toutouri 1983; Williams 1978; Winter 1881) permit identification of the now submerged horizon on which they were imposed during one or other of the arid intervals of the Holocene. Certain petroglyphs and pictographs in the hinterland are diagnostic of belief systems that are independently evidenced in the archaeology of the Archaic shell mound cultures of the Western Guiana Littoral, thereby suggesting the unity and antiquity of Tropical Forest Culture.

Earthworks

Horticulturists on the Eastern Guiana Littoral constructed remarkable mound platforms surrounded by moats and elevated farm plots that are unique in the Guianas. An extensive raised-field complex straddling the low-lying Canje-Berbice-Abary watersheds, unusual so far inland, suggests wetter conditions at the time they were constructed. Whitehead (pers. comm. 1994) reported a date at around A.D. 1,000 on uncontexted charcoal extracted from the base of one of these mounds. Surface collecting on the fringes of the area yielded sherds of the Abary phase of around this date, originally identified and defined on the Eastern Guiana Littoral (Evans and Meggers 1960). These earthworks carry potentials for suggesting key elements in the social structure of groups occupying the coastal alluvium when contrasted with groups occupying *terra firme*.

A curious trench surrounds a small hill in the Commewijne District of Suriname. Though roughly contemporary with the coastal and coastal-hinterland mound structures and raised fields, this hill trench is thought not to have functioned as a moat (Versteeg 1981). Similar features are reported in Guyane française (Abonnenc 1952; Toutouri 1983; Maziére 1995:51) and possibly in the Territory of Amapá in Brazil (Meggers and Evans 1957:76).

Pottery

The most ubiquitous of prehistoric remains, pottery, was in fact the latest to have been recognized as such (Im Thurn 1884; Quelch 1894). This was a direct result of colonial agricultural and industrial expansion towards the end of the nineteenth century, when forests were being mechanically felled and the coastal shell and sand reefs put to the plough. The restricted scope of such operations means that, in the Guianas, knowledge of archaeological ceramics remained largely coastal and riverain on to the advent of local air travel. Various ceramic styles have been identified and defined on the coast (Boomert 1979, 1980, 1981; Evans and Meggers 1960; Geijskes 1960-1961; Goodland 1964; Im Thurn 1884; Meggers and Evans 1955; Poonai 1962; Quelch 1894; Sanoja O. 1979) as well as in the hinterland (Barse pers. comm. 1988; Barse 1989, 1990; Boomert 1983; Boomert and Kroonenberg 1977; Cruxent and Rouse 1959, 1961; Evans and Meggers 1960; Evans et al 1960; Groene 1976; Hilbert and Hilbert 1980; Meggers and Evans 1957; Mentz Ribeiro et al 1986, 1987, 1989; Miller 1992; Roget et Roy 1975; Roosevelt 1995; Rostain 1994, 1994a; Roy 1978; Tarble 1985; Tarble and Zucchi 1984; Vargas and Sanoja 1970; Versteeg 1978, 1980; Weber 1990; Zucchi 1985; Zucchi et al 1984; Zucchi and Tarble 1984).

The earliest mention of archaeological pottery was made by Im Thurn (1884) shortly after his quoting (1883:3 89) Waterton's premature claim that the Guiana Indian had left no record behind him, either on parchment or on stone or in earthenware, to say what he had done. As it now transpires, archaeological ceramics are extremely well distributed along almost every watercourse of this Land of Many Waters. Along with potsherds, excavation may yield fragments of tempered potters' clay which, besides contributing to reconstruction of local industries may also be indicative of very long distance trade networks.

Long distance trade networks may also be indicated by distributions of certain ceramic tempering materials, such as nodules of decayed steatite or of chlorite schist, the specialized quarries of which are known. Trade networks indicated by distributions of such ceramic raw materials may have originated in Archaic polities, again indicating the antiquity of Tropical Forest adaptations in the Guianas.

Ceramic decoration may suggest the world of myth, ritual or the supernatural. Representations include anthropomorphic, zoomorphic and geometric elements in specific contexts, e.g., burials (Meggers and Evans 1957: Pls. 17 - 19). In the case of certain anthropomorphs, physiographic characteristics shared with Archaic models in contrasting media (e.g. de Valencia et al 1987: Figure 155/0/1) suggest extreme longevity for the associated than atological beliefs. Certain gender-specific roles seem suggested by the longevity of these elements.

Daub fragments surviving in archaeological refuse may be indicative of a particular house type (Wishart 1982). Leaf impressions on such daub fragments may be sufficiently specific to indicate the plant species utilized at a given site, e.g., dhalebana *(Geonoma sp.)* and thus suggest an aspect of the prevailing vegetational environment, Figure 1.4a - e.

Rock alignments. Cobbles or boulders of granite or other igneous rocks (Brown 1873) occur as alignments, rock circles or rock piles over large areas in the Eastern

Guiana Hinterland. To the present, most have remained undisturbed, or only minimally disturbed, protected *in situ* by sacred memory (Baldwin 1946; Henderson 1952; Hurault et al 1963; Meggers and Evans 1957; Schomburgk 1848). Free-standing rock features have been thought (Boomert 1981) to comprise six categories:

Figure 1.4 a-e
a. Daub fragment showing wattle
    impression. Recht-door-Zee.
b. Daub fragment showing palm leaf
    impression. Recht-door-Zee.
c. Daub fragment showing impression
    of withes. Recht-door-Zee.
d. Daub fragment showing impression of
    dhalebana palm leaf *(Geonoma sp)*.
    Corentyne River.
e. *Dhalebana palm*, Mahaica River.

(*i*) alignments, (*ii*) rock circles, (*iii*) single, standing stones, (*iv*) stone piles, (*v*) figures and (*vi*) walls of stone. Boomert provides a useful bibliography. Though frequently reported, their significance remains unknown.

Human skeletal remains

In the prevailing acid soils of most of Guyana, human skeletal remains disintegrate completely within a period of around 250 years. Human bones preserved in exceptional conditions in the artificial mounds and shell ridges of coastal Suriname date appreciably earlier, the latter as far back as the opening centuries of the Christian Era. Earliest of all, surviving the passage of millennia, are numerous skeletons in various stages of preservation in the shell mounds of the Guyana swamps, Figure 1.5.

Figure 1.5.

Barabina.
Human skeletal remains in various stages of pretervation. On a single level, the sample may range from intact specimens to bone dust.

In the Hinterland, bones encountered in ceramic burial jars, as in the rock shelters of the Rupununi Savannas, survive no longer than bones interred directly in the soil. Granted their inevitably poor state of preservation in the acid soils of most of Amazonia, these materials have attracted only limited attention from physical anthropologists. Nonetheless, burials continue to be excavated and to pose bioarchaeological questions that remain a long way from being addressed. Such questions concern, for example, the relative nutritional status of shellfishers in the northwestern swamps who consumed, on the one hand, exclusively arthropods (crab) or, on the other, exclusively gastropods (snails), over immense time periods and within specific kinds of microhabitats. Again, in a situation in which the shift from food collecting to food production is poorly understood diachronically, the apparently enormous time span involved in the transition may be more unequivocally indicated by isotopic analysis of amino acids in bone collagen than can at present be suggested by purely archaeological methods. Analyses such as these are not readily available to the Amazonian archaeologist. This notwithstanding, the available materials exhibit very good potentials for the interpretation of mortuary behaviors within the context of prevailing religious beliefs and cosmology.

Summary

The above review of the range of sources for the study of the ancient cultures of the Guianas lends scant support to the notion of the inherent poverty of the Tropical Forest Lowlands as regards the availability of archaeological materials. According to this view, most of what was made and used by Tropical Forest peoples was perishable and soon destroyed by the humid climate, the only significant exception having been pottery (Lathrap 1970:63; Meggers 1984; Meggers et al 1988). Thus, although Amazonia comprises more than half the area of Brazil, data on hunter-gatherers there are thought too sparse and imprecise to warrant discussion (Schmitz 1987). The perceived difficulties are compounded by the scale of the territory and the complexity of the biotic and abiotic environments to which human groups have been adapting continuously over the millennia. In exploiting the various source materials reviewed above, the challenge is one of identifying unknown cultural systems with particular biotic and abiotic environments some of which may have passed into oblivion with the human groups they supported. The canvas is immense and its time depth embraces the many foci provided by the contrasting categories of sources outlined above. Granted the areal magnitude of the territory and the multitude of microenvironments involved, some lasting centuries in the archaeological record while others spanned millennia, its contrasting resources are best seen as representing basically two complementary data sets, Coastal and Hinterland, each comprising a range of traits specific to a particular niche, and, in many cases, associated with subsistence potentials which, over time, contributed to regional integration, Table B.

Table B. Contrasting traits in Coastal and Hinterland cultures

	Coast	Hinterland
Formative 3500 b.p.	pottery earthworks bounded cemeteries	rock alignments stone tools/weapons modified bedrock caves/rock shelters
Archaic 7200 b.p.	shell mounds bounded cemeteries	stone tools/weapons caves/rock shelters modified bedrock
Paleo-Indigenous 11,000 b.p.		stone tools/weapons caves/rock shelters modified bedrock

History of research
Guyana

Though lacking somewhat in constancy, the history of archaeological investigations in Guyana is of an antiquity that is comparable to any elsewhere in the Americas. The quest of the Dutch governor, Gravesande, spade and pickaxe in hand, for the remains of Phoenicians and Carthaginians on the Essequibo-Demerara watershed in 1767 (Harris and de Villiers 1911:534) anticipated by a good two decades Thomas Jefferson's stratigraphic excavations in Virginia, while the seminal trenching of the Waramuri shell mound on the Moruka River by the local missionary of the Society for the Propagation of the Gospel, W. H. Brett, in 1865 (Anon [J.L.Smith] 1866; Bennett 1866; Brett 1868) anticipated by two years publication of Wyman's initial investigations on the St John's River, Florida.

Brett's work at Waramuri led to the discovery and subsequent excavation of several shell mounds on the neighboring Pomeroon River. Two problems providing research foci at this pioneering stage were to persist in the archaeology of the Western Guiana Littoral for most of the following century. The first concerned the relative antiquity of the mounds and the levels of cultural development represented by their makers, while the second referred to sea levels thought to have prevailed at the time at which these once coastal mounds, now sequestered under dense rain forest, had accumulated. These two problems survived in Guyanese archaeology despite the shifts in theoretical orientation that accompanied the replacing of its pioneering European colonial amateurs by North American professional practitioners around the turn of the century.

The period of these European amateurs lasted from around 1860 to around 1899. Following upon it, the development of archaeology in Guyana was guided by the theoretical concepts of trained North Americans working in the country and/or in adjacent territories and attaching to one or other of the great American museums of Natural History. The period culminated with the investigations of Smithsonian archaeologists, Clifford Evans and Betty J. Meggers, fresh from their doctoral investigations at the Mouth of the Amazon.

The North American period lasted between 1900 - 1960. It was itself subdivided into early and late stages. The early stage, 1900 - 1939, was defined by the investigations of A. Hyatt Verrill, W.C. Farabee, Walter Edmund Roth and others, while the late stage, 1940 - 1960, was defined by the investigations of J.E.L. Carter, J.A. Bullbrook, Cornelius Osgood, Clifford Evans and Betty J. Meggers, the latter two publishing either independently or as a team. Whereas the broad-based surveys of the early workers usefully identified a number of archaeological sites on the coast and in the hinterland, the work of the later investigators was marked for the first time by stratigraphic control, description, measurement, classification and interpretation. The respective contributions of the two periods are characterized in

what follows.
The Europeans 1866 - 1899
Excavation of the Waramuri shell mound, Moruka River, in 1866, Figure 1.6, was a direct consequence of the publication, during the previous year, of Lubbock's *Prehistoric Times*. Pioneered by a British missionary, the Waramuri

Figure 1.6. Waramuri shell Mound, Moruka River, 1866: the earliest known excavation in the Guianas. For the entertainment of the Governor's party, "Some wild-looking Waraus brought forward their decorated shields and engaged in friendly contest with each other" (Brett 1866:430).

excavation was immediately taken up by the British colonial administration in Guyana, with the result that certain of its artifacts were dispatched to Sir Joseph Hooker, at the time Britain's most eminent scientist. A colleague of Darwin and Lyell, Hooker had been an adjudicator in 1859 of the priority claims concerning natural selection as the mechanism for evolution, which had been advanced simultaneously by Charles Darwin and Alfred Russell Wallace. Thus, in the hands of Church and State, the prevailing Classical Evolutionism came to provide a handy paradigm for explaining the human remains unexpectedly encountered in excavation of the various shell mounds now being opened on the Western Guiana Littoral.

Samples of the human skeletal remains from these excavations were forwarded by Sir Joseph Hooker to Sir John Lubbock. Although the latter's opinions seem not to have been recorded, these skeletal materials appeared to an eye-witness at the Waramuri excavations to have been similar to those reported from Lubbock's Danish shell mounds. The skulls were thought "small but of extraordinary thickness," the most perfect specimen having been found remarkable for the absence of forehead and for what appeared to be projecting rims round the eye sockets. Brett, their excavator, likewise noted of these skulls that they were of "great thickness," about a quarter of an inch. As elsewhere, the implied evidence of biological evolution was translated into social and cultural terms, and the Warainuri skeletal materials were interpreted as the remains of a "stunted squalid horde of savages." As among the Danes, cannibalism was automatically inferred from the numbers of human bones that apparently had been split open for extracting the marrow. Evidently, such practices represented the earliest stage in Lewis Henry Morgan's evolutionary model of human, social and cultural development: savagery - barbarism - civilization - though, in light of obvious differences in the respective cultural levels of Dane and Indian, and in keeping with Morgan's precepts, it was found necessary to allocate to the Indian an evolutionary slot appropriate to his perceived social and cultural status. Thus, Im Thurn (1883:410):

> The earlier stages of civilisation through which A people passes are much the same in all parts of the world and at all periods of the world's history; and so, just as the primitive European made kitchen-middens in the far-off so-called 'prehistoric ages', certain Indians made them a very few centuries ago in South America and possibly -- in very remote parts of the continent --, still make them even now.

Therefore, relative to the ages of those in Denmark, the shell mounds of the Western Guiana Littoral were thought just to have preceded the voyages of Columbus. The comparison thus set in time and place an earlier population which pre-Evolutionist writers had been content to characterize simply as "an anterior race of men" (Humboldt 1853,ii:472), "a former race of men" (Brown 1873:256) or "a race long past away" (Winter 1881:21). These antique peoples may have been affiliated to Egyptians, Etruscans or even Africans (Blair 1980/1857).

Everard (later Sir Everard) Im Thurn (1852 - 1932), a monumental figure in Guyanese anthropology, was a protegé of Sir Joseph Hooker, who had in fact been instrumental in securing his appointment to the curatorship of the British Guiana Museum, a position he took up in 1877 with an interest in natural history that had preceded his admission to Oxford in 1871. Combined with a zest for exploration, intimate contact with a variety of unacculturated peoples, his connections with leading British research institutions such as Kew Gardens, the Royal Anthropological Institute and the Royal Geographic Society, not to mention a personal acquaintance with E. B. Tylor, Im Thurn was soon set on the anthropological career that culminated in his presidency of the Royal Anthropological Institute in 1919 - 1920.

As a British colonial administrator at the height of empire, anthropology to Im Thurn was candidly an instrument of imperialism:

> "I think that better understanding of native ways of thought is needed by us, whether at home or abroad, who take part in the further development of the already great and splendid lands of our tropical Empire, and of the fundamentally loyal Native subjects of the British Crown".

Thus, having experienced the aboriginal population of British Guiana in its long established equilibrium with its habitat, the naturalist, in the words of his biographer (Marett 1934), proved just the man to prepare the way for the introduction of a perceived higher civilization, being best placed in time to judge how a new balance could be struck between immemorial custom and the ways of the wider world.

The year before his arrival in British Guiana, Harper's (1876) article, *The Tribes of British Guiana*, had been published in the Journal of the Royal Anthropological Institute. In it, Harper turned to what was then known of Mexican culture as the probable source of developments to the south and southeast. In a series of migrations from the north and northwest, the stronger and fiercer tribes had subdued or displaced the weaker and less warlike ones. In the struggle, the stronger tribes had occupied the more favored niches, the weaker having been compelled to move into less desirable environments. As Harper's ingenious hypothesis was to have a lasting effect on Im Thurn's outlook on the origins of the indigenes of Guiana, it is cited more fully below:

> Each movement in the north caused a general commotion, which shook, displaced, or broke in fragments various tribes on the American continent. The offshoots and fragments of such tribes, not being able to maintain an independent position in more favored localities, were sometimes driven into lowlands and swamps like Guiana.

Suggested routes of such migrations were *via* the Isthmus of Panama, by sea along the coast or through the Caribbean island chain *via* Trinidad and Tobago.

In the year of his arrival, Im Thurn re-excavated Brett's shell mound at Kabakaburi and was present at the opening of the newly discovered shell mound at Piraka, not far off. Int Thurn was thus under immediate pressure to explain the origin and contents of these mounds. A place in the history of mankind needed to be found for the subject peoples whom he had been mandated to lead to "higher civilization." The new Carter/Harper migration/displacement model proved fully adequate to explaining the contents of the shell mound, i.e., its types of shellfish species, types of stone tools and the discrete strata that could be observed at certain sites. Im Thurn (1883:416) concluded that the shell mounds had been made by strangers to the Guiana Coast, that the intrusion had been from the sea rather than over land and that the intruders had been fierce Caribs. In accordance with the Harper model, certain of the rock engravings of British Guiana were found readily comparable with Mexican picture writing *(ibid* 406).

The implications of this for the cultural sequence on the Western Guiana Littoral was that the material remains there had resulted from the occupations of two distinct groups, Carib cannibals from the islands occupying sites on lowlying terrain near the sea coast and their less warlike victims, the aboriginals of Guiana. The shell mounds represented the refuse of these recent intruders, but Im Thurn did not specify the hearthlands of the aborigines.

Subsequent writers (e.g. Quelch 1894), while associating the remains at certain coastal sites with Carib occupancy, remained content to regard the patently more ancient artifacts, such as petroglyphs, concerning which the contemporary native could offer no explanation, as works of some other considerably more ancient and advanced race. Thus, the dichotomy perceived by Im Thurn in the peopling of the Western Guiana Littoral remained unchallenged.

The second problem in the pioneering period in Guyana archaeology concerned the sea level prevailing at the time the shell mounds had accumulated. Granted the faunal variety that is represented in these mounds, few species of which had survived at the time of the earliest investigations, the sea level problem was evidently directly associated with environmental change of some significant magnitude on that lowlying coast. However, notwithstanding his impeccable scientific connections in Great Britain, this problem had been ignored by Im Thurn. Committed to the migration/displacement model, Im Thurn (1883:419) was obliged to regard the shells comprising these mounds as manuports even though, in one of his earliest comments on the Waramuri excavations, Brett (to Archdeacon Jones 1866) had long attributed the disappearance of these shellfish species to drastic changes in the sea level:

> "In former days, when these shellfish (many kinds of which are scarcely known on our muddy shores) must have abounded, and Waramuri ridge, now separated by 10 or 12 miles of alluvial deposit from the sea was probably a promontory or an island" ...

The contemporary historian, Bennett (1866:253), likewise adverted to a time when the prevailing coastal forests had been submerged under Atlantic billows which had rolled to the base of Waramuri Hill, then an island. On the other hand, Im Thurn (1879, 1883), who never entered the sea level debate, was content to speak only of "islands of firm ground in the midst of the swamps," possibly referring to certain sandy, forested hummocks in the Pomeroon swamps rather than to the more elevated rock outcrops of the North West, which he knew well.

Concerns regarding possible changes in the mound environment at Waramuri since its formation were taken up by Richard (later Sir Richard) Owen, Superintendent of the British Museum Department of Natural History, who advised that specimens of its constituent shells should be sent to the British Museum for determination (Brett to Archeacon Jones 1866):

> "The knowledge so acquired might throw light on the kind and degree of change of coast line, or other evidence of geological action to which the locality of the mound may have been subject".

There is no evidence that this most important line of inquiry was ever followed up. More in keeping with his own interests and the spirit of the times, Owen insisted on re-internment of the excavated human skeletal remains "in deference to the feelings of the Indians with respect to the religious veneration they evinced for the resting places of their ancestors and the sanctity of sepulture." Formal re-internment in the presence of the natives was recommended, though, granted the prevailing world interest in human craniology, a qualification relating to the treatment of independent skulls was prudently appended: "The foregoing observations do not apply to human crania that may be discovered by the mission under other circumstances in tumuli or mounds" (loc. cit.).

There is no record that either shell samples or human crania were ever dispatched to the British Museum. The projected studies in environmental change on the Western Guiana Littoral were accordingly never undertaken, while the opportunity for pioneering osteological research on the aborigines was also lost. Towards the end of the century, the British curator of the Guiana Museum (Quelch 1894) laid confident claim to an improving outlook "adown the vista of knowledge" of the Guyana past, but fifty years later his successor, Peberdy (1945) yet found cause to lament:

> For too long South American archaeology has appeared to be the special prerogative and hunting ground for students and specialists of research from the United States of America. Splendid work

has been accomplished by American archaeologists in Venezuela, Colombia and Brazil and it is surely not too much to ask that our own people take a lively interest in the rich archaeological material from British South America.

The North Americans 1900s - 1960
The Early Stage 1900s - 1939

The redirection of Guyanese anthropology from the European to the North American sphere was the work of one man, himself European and a British colonial administrator at that. Of a Hungarian family that had emigrated to Australia, Walter Edmund Roth (1861 - 1933) spent the early part of his career as Protector of the Aboriginees in Queensland, an ideal preparation for a post which he took up in British Guiana in 1907 as Stipendiary Magistrate, first at Makasima on the Pomeroon River, and later at Christianburgh, on the Demerara River. Roth's earliest fullscale work in Guyana, *Animism and Folklore of the Guiana Indians*, was published in 1915 as the Thirtieth Annual Report of the Bureau of American Ethnology. It was followed in 1924 by the now classic *An Introductory Study of the Arts, Crafts and Customs of the Guiana Indians*, published as the Thirty-eighth Annual Report of the Bureau of American Ethnology. In 1929, his *Additional Studies of the Arts, Crafts and Customs of the Guiana Indians* was published as Bulletin 91 of the Bureau of American Ethnology. In that year, Roth was appointed Curator of the British Guiana Museum. In this capacity he conducted an archaeological reconnaissance on the Aruka River which yielded by far the most representative collection ever made of the ceramics which later inquiry (Meggers and Evans 1955) would designate the Mabaruma phase. Roth's profusely illustrated classification of these materials, *A Preliminary Survey of Certain Prehistoric Potteryware from the North Western District of British Guiana* [1930] remains unpublished. On his death in 1933 the flag of the United States Embassy in Trinidad was flown at half mast.

Thus, to all intents and purposes and very apposite to the future development of anthropology in Guyana, Roth was perceived throughout his career as an American scholar. Although he counted among his colleagues some of the leading practitioners of the day on both sides of the Atlantic, his anthropological career was never officially recognized by any British institution. His long association with the Bureau of American Ethnology spanned the stewardships of Jesse Walter Fewkes, F.W. Hodge and Matthew Stirling. Roth's great value to North American anthropology, as Im Thurn's had been to British, lay in his permanent residence among as yet unacculturated indigenous groups at a time when practically nothing was known of the southern continent. For this reason, the expenses of his researches were generously met by the Bureau, which, in addition, proved a willing publisher. His lifelong postings in hinterland areas of Guyana, added to his great zest for travel and exploration, as well as his ready intimacy with the indigenes, proved an ideal experience for adopting the new Boasian concepts in American anthropology, which sought "evidences of man's behavior among men in their natural environs" rather than in the idealized constructs and sweeping generalizations of the Classical Evolutionists. This quite unique experience of hinterland Guyana proved a powerful stimulus for his ready adoption of the new direction in American anthropology. Accordingly, Roth's theoretical orientation was rapidly revolutionized. Whereas as late as 1903 Roth had been dispatching to Tylor at Oxford frequent Aboriginal Reports from Queensland on topics such as probes into the lowest strata of the human mind, the relation of a man to his clan-animal name, the rebirth of ancestral souls, etc. *(Letters received 1902 - 1931,* University of Guyana), there is no hint whatsoever of any such concerns in his publications for the Bureau after arriving in Guyana a few years later.

Boasian thought explicitly denied the existence of a distinctive mental equipment in primitive man. The new theorists found no trace of a lower mental organization in any of the extant races of man. Further, the thesis of a single unilineal development of cultural traits the world over that had provided the theoretical basis of the investigations of im. Thum and others was now unequivocally rejected. If it was claimed that human culture had run such a course, then the assertion remained to be proven on the basis of detailed studies of the historical process involved through study of particular cultures and by demonstration of analogies in their development. Boasian analysis now definitely disproved the existence of far-reaching homologies of the kind which hitherto had permitted arranging all the manifold cultural lines of human groups in an ascending scale in which each can be assigned its proper place. Roth's break with the imperialist anthropology of Im Thurn, and indeed of Tylor, was therefore absolute. Consequently, unfortunately for the discipline, communication between these contemporaries in Guyanese anthropology remained apparently non-existent throughout.

Living among the indigenes of Guyana before the final stages of their acculturation, Roth immediately began publishing from direct observations of their material and spiritual culture. His first paper appeared within a year of his arrival, initiating a record of systematic investigations that spanned the next quarter of a century. Together, these investigations produced that varied harvest of facts and artifacts as empirical evidence of cultural processes of the living about which, at the time, virtually nothing was known. As Fewkes remarked in anticipation of the publication of his Additional Studies (Letters received September 19, 1925):

> "You certainly have a fund of information about the tribes of which we have little knowledge, and your adventures and studies should, I think, make a volume as interesting as any we have published

> ...I was very much pleased with your last volume and think it one of the best we have published --so much in it is new to ethnologists ... "

Roth's final contribution was the archaeological survey of the Aruka River which yielded the most comprehensive collection of potsherds yet assembled at any site on the Western Guiana Littoral. Though as yet unpublished, it remains a critical source for the study of the earliest horticulturists so far known in the Guianas, all the more valuable for the light it throws on early relationships between first farmers on the lower Aruka and lower Orinoco Rivers.

Early North American initiatives in Guyana were contributed to by William Curtis Farabee of the University Museum, University of Pennsylvania, who made anthropometric investigations and other observations among the Makusi and Wapisiana of southern Guyana and northern Brazil during 1913 - 1914. Farabee's direct contribution to the archaeology of the Guianas was his *Some South American Petroglyphs* published in the Holmes Anniversary volume (1916). Many of the petroglyphs of this remote area of the Atlantic-Amazon watershed, here documented by drawings, photographs or measurements, have never been relocated, in addition to which Farabee provided technical and classificatory information (e.g. contrasting types of gravure, differences between typical savanna and riverine glyphs) which contributed significantly to subsequent petroglyph analysis.

At around this time, Joyce (1916:254) was reverting at second hand to Brett's notion of ancient higher sea levels on the Guiana Coast. The idea was elaborated upon by Lovén (1935:115) who saw the Aruka hills as continental relics that had survived erosion in some remote geological period which also had seen transformation of former sea bottom into mangrove swamps.

Farabee was followed into Guyana by the wealthy amateur, A. Hyatt Verrill (1918, 1918a), whose quest for the element of time depth in the cultures he studied was severely limited for want of an adequate methodological base. Systematic ceramic analysis and the classification of stone tools yet lay very much in the future, in addition to which Verrill evinced scant interest in natural or cultural stratigraphy. For these reasons, the unilineal thinking of his predecessors constituted the only available pathway to the interpretation of his materials, so that, while omitting to mention any of the nineteenth century writers, these writers, notably Im Thurn, Quelch and, to a lesser extent, Brett, nevertheless provided the Evolutionist framework by means of which his excavated materials were evaluated. Thus, having opened the Barabina mound a good half century after Brett's pioneering investigations on the Pomeroon and Monika Rivers, Verrill still found his skeletal materials representing a "type of man with heavy, thick skull devoid of visible sutures, projecting heavy orbital ridges, extremely low forehead, strong-pointed jaws and eyes close together." The dentition was of interest, the molars having been "all out of proportion to the premolars, which were abnormally small."

In keeping with the migration/displacement model of Im Thurn, Verrill identified two distinct types of shell mound on the Western Guiana Littoral. The first was located in the Northwestern Subzone, on the emergent rocks of the Guiana Shield that defined the limits of the sediment basin, its specimens frequently located many miles from the present day sea coast or estuaries, while the second comprised immense concentrations of shells in the lowlands of the Southeastern Subzone, nearer the sea. While these latter may have been post Columbian in origin, the former were evidently very much older, having been formed at a time when, in Verrill's opinion, "the entire district was covered by the sea and the present-day hills rose as islands from the waves." Here, Verrill found the erstwhile action of the sea evidenced in numerous undercut and wave-worn ledges and boulders, as well as in small areas of sea beaches and shell sand beneath the thin layers of vegetable mould and alluvium at the base of the hills. Unfortunately, these observations could not be confirmed in subsequent surveys by the present author, and nor have the alleged erosional evidences on the emergent rocks ever been recorded in later archaeological or geological literature (e.g. Bleackley 1956; Osgood - 1946; Pollard 1956). This notwithstanding, mortuary data deriving from Verrill's investigations on the Eastern Guiana Littoral provided useful support for earlier observations on burial ritual there provided by Quelch (1894) and Im Thurn (1884). Resulting from the rapid expansion of the sugar industry, Verrill's mortuary data proved the last to be collected on the coastal alluvium.

Like his predecessors Brett and Im Thurn, Verrill concluded that two distinct races had inhabited the Western Guiana Littoral in prehistoric times, one a primitive fish-eating group which had not yet developed the art of ceramic decoration or of well made stone implements. The other group was more highly developed, skilled in the manufacture of beautifully finished stone implements, with pottery-making developed to an art. These latter appear to have inhabited the country and driven off or destroyed its more peaceful shellfishing occupants whose land and villages they seized. Thus, while declining to claim it, Verrill had located the putative cannibals' victims of Im Thurn.

The next contribution to the archaeology of the Western Guiana Littoral was made by the British geologist, J. A. Bullbrook, stationed in Trinidad since 1913. Prior association with archaeological methodology through his acquaintance with the Egyptologist Oric Bates in the Sudan, combined with his geological training, resulted in the outstanding report *On the Excavation of a Shell Mound at Palo Seco, Trinidad, BWI* edited with admiration many years later (1953) by Irving Rouse for Yale University. Bullbrook had already completed these excavations at the time he made acquaintance in the early twenties with the archaeology of the Western Guiana Littoral through occasional visits to Guyana which took him to the shell mound at

Koriabo on the Barima River as well as to an unspecified site on the Aruka. River. Although any notes that may have resulted from these visits have unfortunately not survived, Bullbrook's experience of the swamp basin stimulated a brief comment on the sea level debate.

Thus, by the time that the early phase of the North American period was brought to an end with the commencement of World War II, the two main problems that had provided the foci of inquiry for the nineteenth century pioneers had attained a respectable antiquity. It was now thought that at least some of the shell mounds of the Western Guiana Littoral had accumulated in a now vanished environment, and that the area had been inhabited by at least two distinct races representing contrasting levels of development.

The Late Stage 1939 - 1960

Introduction. The post-World War period differed from the period of the pioneers by virtue of a new theoretical orientation which involved the introduction of ceramic classification and a concern with structuring local chronologies. Although as yet still strictly confined to the coast, certain archaeological cultures were defined and a few area syntheses were constructed. The culture-area concept in North American ethnology now introduced the additional problem of the definition, origin and locus of dissemination of Tropical Forest Culture.

The professionals. Commencing in the early forties, the archaeology of horticulturists on the Western Guiana Littoral came to be linked by one worker or another to events at the Mouth of the Orinoco River. The notion had originated with the one-off excavation of an associate, of Bullbrook's, a British Army officer also posted in Trinidad, at the time on a brief visit to Guyana. Having unearthed a *cache* of near intact plain pottery vessels and a few ground stone tools at Seba, 145 km up the Demerara River, Major (then Lieut.) J.E.L Carter (1943) was led to speculate that in their lack of decoration these vessels probably represented the southern limit of Arawak penetration from the lower Orinoco. According to Carter, the main current of Arawak culture coming down that river had turned sharply north and passed through Trinidad to the Caribbean islands, while "a small southerly eddy" had accounted for the simple undecorated pottery of this Seba assemblage, whose geographical setting suggested to Carter a trading center and place of cultural exchange. The supposed factors in such cultural exchange were not identified, though various distances were cited (some unreliably) indicating potential relationships with the Mouth of the Waini River, with Koriabo on the Barima River, with Los Barrancos on the lower Orinoco River and even with Bullbrook's site at Erin on the south coast of Trinidad. The indicated collaboration with Bullbrook, as well as with Cornelius Osgood, a member of the Yale Caribbean Anthropology Program whom Carter had met in Trinidad in 1941, played a part in furthering Carter's ideas, for, impressed with certain similarities between pottery he saw in

Trinidad and pottery he had recently excavated on the lower Orinoco, Osgood lost no time in planning a visit to Guyana.

Within months of Carter's publication, Osgood (1946) was in the North West attempting to reconstruct the cultural sequence there. Resuming Verrill's investigations, which he considered the most significant contribution to the archaeology of Guyana since the pioneering days of Brett, Osgood, while rejecting many of Verrill's views on ancient sea levels, nonetheless found Verrill's evidence "indisputable." However, Osgood dismissed Verrill's correlation between deposition of shellfish refuse and erosion of the coastal rocks by a still rising sea. "What we need to know and do not," he objected, "is the age of the beach lines and the source of the shells." Unfortunately, Osgood did not bother to verify the existence of the erosion data that had been so critical to Verrill's reconstruction. Even more unfortunate was the loss in the Georgetown fire of 1945 of the results of Osgood's investigations at the critical Barabina shell mound and elsewhere in coastal Guyana. However, from his field notebooks and certain of his salvaged materials, Osgood was able in the following year to publish his valuable *British Guiana Archaeology to 1945*, which summarized investigations to that date and included a brief report on his own excavations in the North West and on the Demerara Coast. Employing twelve shovelmen, Osgood had trenched the Barabina mound in a single day, describing the digging as "the lightest possible work." However cavalier the approach may now seem, that undertaking represented the very first stratigraphically controlled excavation ever undertaken in Guyana, in which respect it marked an important advance in local shell mound archaeology. But for the loss of his excavated materials and granted the near advent of the radiocarbon era, Osgood may well have answered questions -- posed by Verrill's excavations and thus concluded the sea level debate after a good 80 years of speculation. That was not to be, however, and there the matter rested for another 40 and more years. As his trenching of the Barabina shell mound merely confirmed the main findings of Verrill, and as his attempts at ceramic classification (1946:53) were in fact overtaken by later scholarship, the outstanding outcome of Osgood's investigations was the support he was early able to offer to the Carter hypothesis of an Orinocan origin of the pottery of northwestern Guyana. Through this support, and well before the definitive investigations of Evans and Meggers in Guyana, Carter's exploratory formulation of Arawak migrations on the lower Orinoco River was now firmly ensconced in the realm of archaeological fact (Osgood 1946:48).

The highwater mark of archaeological investigations during the period was reached in the work of Smithsonian archaeologists Clifford Evans and Betty J. Meggers following six months of fieldwork in 1952-1953. Returning to the North West, the authors defined the Archaic Alaka phase and horticulturist Mabaruma and Koriabo phases on the basis of excavations at 23 sites during a period of just over a month. Of these, six were sites of the Alaka phase. Among other things, these investigations (1960:25) supported Verrill's observations that two types of shell mounds occur in northwestern Guyana. As had been postulated by Verrill, the authors also suspected the existence of an independent shellfishing culture on the Pomeroon River, in the Southeastern Subzone, though they were unable to investigate this possibility. As regards the Alaka sequence, the authors (1960:59) were careful to emphasize the preliminary nature of their findings, and chose to present these findings only as a basis for future investigations, their evidences having been found not sufficiently strong or clear cut for the interpretations proffered to be considered final. Also, the provisional nature of their interpretations of the Alaka phase must be understood in light of the smallness of the sample (20%) in an inventory totaling thirty-odd known shell mounds scattered across some 3500 km^2 of intertidal swamps, Appendix A. Moreover, the sample was derived only in the Northwestern Subzone of the Western Guiana Littoral, the Southeastern Subzone having remained uninvestigated since the days of Im Thurn.

The permanent and outstanding outcome of the investigations of Evans and Meggers was the identification, definition and characterization of the major archaeological cultures of Guyana chronologically interpreted. Publication of the now classic *Archaeological Investigations in British Guiana* (1960), together with the earlier *Archaeological Investigations at the Mouth of the Amazon* (1957) laid the foundation for all subsequent inquiry into the prehistory of the Guianas. Combined, the scope and timing of these two reports were to prove seminal to South American archaeologists from many territories. The standardized ordering of the mountainous new data which the authors had made available at the very dawn of scientific archaeology in the Lowlands provided a firm foundation for further inquiry, notably in ceramic description, classification and, seriation, now taken for granted by scholars of the Libby era. Already by 1956 these achievements had earned them the Certificate Award of the Washington Academy of Sciences, conferred each year on outstanding scientists under 40. With this man-and-wife team, the Certificate was awarded for the first time ever in anthropology, which had to be accommodated in the biological sciences.

As elsewhere in the southern continent, the publication of Steward's *Handbook of South American Indians* constituted a landmark in the development of anthropology. Originally simply classificatory in intention, Steward's (1948:674) review later took on certain developmental overtones with consequent theoretical implications for Tropical Forest archaeology (see for example Evans 1971). Steward (1949:759) suggested that Tropical Forest culture represented a derivation from the culture of the Intermediate Area, the route followed having been southeastward along the north coast of South America into the Amazon Basin. In this view, there was relatively little cultural diffusion inland, either from the Orinoco Basin or from the

Andes, though a few traits may have spread from Colombia *via* the upper Orinoco River. On the evidences of the probable direction of flow within the Tropical Forest, and of the rich material remains in evidence there, the Guianas and the lower Amazon were postulated as the center of dispersal of Tropical Forest Culture.

These were the hypotheses that provided the research focus for the pioneering investigations of Evans and Meggers in the Guianas. British Guiana (now Guyana) was selected for its size and topographic characteristics. If, in confirmation of the Steward hypothesis, evidence of prehistoric communication between the Coast and the Hinterland was to be found, this seemed the best place to look for it. An itinerary was therefore planned to include parts of the country where evidences of migration or diffusion might have been expected to show up had such evidences existed. Thus, for the first time ever, archaeological investigations were designed to encompass not only the coastal and riverine areas of the Guianas but also the savannas of *terra firme* that span part of the Orinoco-Amazon watershed, as well as the upper Essequibo to the southeast, which spans the Amazon-Atlantic watershed. Left out of account was the territory to the east of the Essequibo River, i.e., the Berbice and Corentyne Basins which, as a result, remain largely unknown to the present.

The strategy was designed to test the hypothesis of Tropical Forest origins in the Intermediate Area by investigating the major postulated migration/diffusion routes, i.e., along the Atlantic coast to the Mouth of the Amazon, or, alternatively, up the Orinoco and into the Amazon Basin *via*, the Rio Negro. In demonstrating that neither of these routes had ever been used, Evans and Meggers (1960:340) concluded that rather than representing the fountainhead of Tropical Forest cultural development the Guianas had acted merely as a recipient of culture traits and complexes. The antiquity of settlement by Tropical Forest groups there appeared to the authors to have been greatest at both margins of the area, i.e., the Mouth of the Orinoco and the Mouth of the Amazon, implying primary migrations and/or diffusion down these two rivers *from the west*. Spread along the coast was apparently extremely slow, and toward the Interior practically nil. Infiltration had undoubtedly been farther inland than the immediate fringes, though the authors could find no evidence in archaeology or ethnography to suggest that penetration had been deep or significant.

The earliest ceramists on the Western Guiana Littoral were considered by Evans and Meggers to have arrived there at around the time that the authors' Alaka phase had completed its transition to horticulture, i.e., around A.D. 500 (Evans and Meggers 1960:145, 335, Figure 126). The authors were the first to raise the question of a relationship between the shellfishing and the pottery-making cultures of the Western Guiana Littoral. With this question, the issue of cultural chronology on the Western Guiana Littoral came to be subsumed within the larger one of the place of origin and diffusion of Tropical Forest culture.

The antiquity of settlement at the Mouth of the Amazon was subsequently established by a series of radiocarbon dates commencing in the fourth millennium B.C. for the shell mounds of the Mina phase (Simões 1981). Meggers and Evans (1978:554) immediately recognized the significance of this antiquity for the cultural sequence on the Western Guiana Littoral, where the Alaka phase, near the Mouth of the Orinoco River, exhibited sufficient similarities in ceramic traits with those of the Mina phase at the Mouth of the Amazon to have been considered a plausible stepping stone to northeastern Brazil from a supposed origin in the more or less contemporary Puerto Hormigo, a shellfishing culture with ceramics on the Caribbean coast of Colombia. Retrodiction of the antiquity of the Alaka phase now reintroduced the question of its unequivocal terminal date, an issue on which debate has since been searching and prolonged, though inconclusive (Evans and Meggers 1964; Lathrap 1964, 1966,1970; Willey 1971:374, fn 49). As Willey saw it:

> The question obviously bears on the terminal date for the Alaka phase of Guyana, for if Mabaruma can be dated back to the early part of Period II, then the Alaka culture must have been assimilating to agriculture and ceramics at about this time rather than a thousand years or so later.

Accordingly, Willey (ibid Figure 6.2) placed inception of the Alaka phase in his Period I, (?)5000 B.C, permitting it in due course to have been modified by the Barrancoid Series sometime during the first millennium B.C. This modification is recognized as the Mabaruma phase (or Mabaruma Subseries) during Period III, with inception dating between A.D. 300 - 700. Implicit in this accommodation is the notion of the derivation of the Mabaruma phase from the Barrancoid Tradition, first hypothesized by Carter in the early forties, confirmed soon thereafter by Osgood and never since questioned. Without challenging that proposition, which constituted the linch pin of the conventional Mabaruma chronology, Willey merely questioned the timing of the event.

Though not an archaeologist of the Guianas, Lathrap (1964, 1966, 1970, 1973, 1975) had meanwhile taken inquiry in an altogether different direction. Lathrap proposed a specifically Amazonian origin of great antiquity for Tropical Forest Culture, suggesting that, as early as 4000 - 5000 B.C., *Manihot esculenta* had been developed as a highly productive staple in the lowlands of northern South America. In this view, Tropical Forest Culture had reached a high state of efficiency by around 3000 B.C., and already had extended over great areas of northern South America, where, by around 1000 B.C., it had replaced the shellfishing Alaka culture on the Western Guiana Littoral. Lathrap (1970:63) explicitly rejected the notion that Tropical Forest Culture had evolved out of any earlier shellfishing culture. According to this author, "There is no doubt that the Tropical Forest intruders moved onto the Guiana Coast from the floodplain of the Lower Orinoco." As regards these early horticulturists, Lathrap (1970:64) cited unspecified "detailed documentation" of the displacement there of the Archaic Alaka phase of the Western Guiana Littoral by a fully developed Tropical Forest Barrancoid culture. With the Alaka phase thus summarily replaced by an intruding Barrancoid group, there was obviously no point in seeking the ceramic ancestors of these Barrancoids locally. Accordingly, along with the Venezuelan Coast, Lathrap eliminated the Guiana Coast from further consideration. Incredibly, that decision followed by just a few years Lathrap's (1966:565) own archaeologically derived evidence of early interaction between Barrancoids on the lower Orinoco and ceramists at Mabaruma, in Guyana. On that basis, and perhaps having misread the ambiguities in the Alaka-Mabaruma sequence perceived by Evans and Meggers (1960:64) he had urged a backward revision of Mabaruma inception to around 700 or 800 B.C." As with Osgood regarding the establishment of an unequivocally causal relationship between peaking of the eustatic sea level rise and the emergence of Archaic culture on the Western Guiana Littoral, so also with Lathrap. In each case the data to hand had been simply insufficient to support quite original perceptions. The picture of Mabaruma origins and affiliations surviving in the literature might have been very different today had Lathrap, and not Osgood, chosen to exploit his early hunches by direct investigations on the lower Aruka River. One would have thought that the anomaly of a steatite-tempered Mabaruma Incised (or Barrancas Incised) sherd occurring in a Saladero deposit most certainly merited further investigation. This would have been a simple undertaking had not prior convictions and a possible misreading of ambiguities in the Alaka-Mabaruma sequence stood in the way of Lathrap's correctly evaluating the striking ceramic evidence that he had himself unearthed. In the event, Lathrap was content to abandon this bit of hard evidence in favor of a naked conjecture which, unfortunately, was to leave a permanent mark in Mabaruma research.

Thus, at the end of the North American investigations, the Guianas had entered the mainstream of archaeological debate, though problems relating to the cultural sequence on the Western Guiana Littoral and the history of sea level fluctuations there, first enunciated by Brett a good hundred years earlier, yet remained unresolved. As has been seen, the notion of successive occupations of the Western Guiana Littoral by at least two groups, one very primitive and the other somewhat less so, which had first been proposed by Brett and his contemporaries, survived among all subsequent workers on to the final decades of the North American period, at around which time the relatively new question of the place of origin and dissemination of Tropical Forest Culture was raised by Julian Steward (1948:886):

> The Guianas were not culturally homogeneous, but it is impossible at present to establish their subdivisions with certainty. It would be profitable to examine further the distinctions between the coastal area, the inland mountain-savanna area, and the Amazonian area which Gillin has sketched.

> Systematic comparisons of *Arawakan* and *Cariban* Culture would also be helpful. From the point of view of dispersal of these cultures, more knowledge of the coastal and Amazonian tribes is essential. As these disappeared before their culture was recorded, the problem is thrown squarely to archaeology.

By the end of the North American period, the definition of the horticultural Mabaruma phase had come to provide a measure of contrast with the earlier shellfishing Alaka phase on the Western Guiana Littoral, though, at the hands of its various excavators (e.g. Verrill 1918, Osgood 1946, Evans and Meggers 1960) chronological relationships between the two cultures yet remained unclear. It has been shown that the notion of the derivation of the horticulturist Mabaruma phase from the lower Orinoco, first advanced as a vague supposition by a thoroughly inexperienced young British soldier on a brief visit to the colony, found ready acceptance and rapid confirmation by the eminent Yale archaeologist, Osgood, and has survived to the present, directly subscribed to by Evans and Meggers (1960, 1964), Lathrap (1964, 1966, 1970) and indirectly by Willey (1971), and others. To date, this critically important cultural sequence remains undemonstrated. Unfortunately, the sea level debate did not survive the loss of Osgood's materials in the Georgetown fire of 1945.

A late sequel to the North American period was a joint expedition, in 1985, of the Centro de Investigaciones Indigenas de Puerto Rico to the Waiwai of southern Guyana in collaboration with the Walter Roth Museum. The team comprised Peter Roe of the University of Maryland, George Mentore, a Guyanese, of the University of Virginia and Peter Siegel, then a doctoral candidate of SUNY (Goldstein 1987; Siegel 1987).

The local amateurs

Commencing during the decade of the forties, and possibly resulting from the well publicized activities of visiting professionals such as Carter, Osgood and Evans and Meggers, certain local individuals began to evince a new interest in the antiquities of the country and recorded in print such archaeological artifacts as they encountered during the course of their other activities. Typically, such persons were well educated and prominent in other fields, such as surveying, law, business or government, but they differed from the expatriate amateurs of the previous century in an apparently total absence of curiosity concerning the origin of the indigenes or the nature of past environments. They reported in a responsible manner, but generally eschewed the commitment of interpretation. Moreover, despite the existence of a national museum since the mid-nineteenth century, the objects they described have rarely survived, though the writings are invariably of locational interest with respect to sites that today are mostly destroyed.

In this category are Vincent Roth's (1944) carefully mapped and illustrated description of a horticulturist bead factory on the Mahaica River, Peberdy's (1948) equally well illustrated report on the rock paintings on Tramen Mountain, upper Mazaruni River; Henderson's (1952) report on stone circles in the North Pakaraimas; Poonai's (1962) description, among the earliest, of raised horticultural fields ("humped hills") and urn cemeteries on the Canje-Corentyne watershed; Goodland's (1964) intriguing description of the discovery of the moated Joanna mound with the airborne help of the British Army in the environs of Blackbush Polder and Haniff's (1967) report on petroglyphs in the North Rupununi Savannas. These were all one-off reports, with no commitment of their authors to sustained inquiry on the related topic, or any other. Nonetheless, although they generally affected the hearty/ironic tone of the British expatriate of yesteryear (the voice of the clubman), their place in the literature is assured, if only on account of the apparent demise of the anthropological amateur in post-Independence Guyana. In deriving his Amerindians from Egypt *via* Atlantis, Poonai, a young Guyanese solicitor, Figure 1.7, struck precisely the note of earnestness eschewed by the pre-Independence British clubman in the context of a disintegrating empire. For his part, Poonai represented a remarkable survival of the Speculative Period in North American archaeology, which had come to an end around 1840. His intellectual antecedent was the early nineteenth century British naturalist, Charles Waterton, "the first mover of his discoveries," rather than the scientifically restless North Americans of the mid-twentieth century.

Figure 1.7. N.O. Ponnai (1923-1996)

Summary. Guyana took into national independence exactly 100 years of archaeological investigations dating back to the pioneering work of Brett in 1866. Despite its status as a British colony throughout this period, the interest of the British in the archaeology of the country did not survive the turn of the century. From that time, the development of the science came increasingly under the influence of North American professionals representing a variety of institutions, notably the Caribbean Anthropology Program of Yale University of the 1930s (Bullbrook, Carter, Rouse) and the Smithsonian Latin American Program of the 1960s (Evans, Meggers).

In the context of the developmental sequence proposed for North American archaeology (Willey and Sabloff 1974), a Classificatory-Descriptive Period commenced with Brett's investigations in the 1860s and lasted on to Roth's survey on the Aruka River in 1930. Although, in North America, the Classificatory-Descriptive Period had come to an end by around 1914, the succeeding Classificatory-Historical Period (Chronology) was not initiated in Guyana until the investigations of Osgood (1946). Thus, as in the Caribbean, archaeological development in Guyana tended to lag behind events in North America by a good three to four decades (see Watters 1976).

Osgood's pioneering work in stratification and ceramic classification was unfortunately aborted with the loss of his excavated materials. This added to the just mentioned time lag by a few years, since the integration of seriation with metrical stratigraphy (the 'sistema Ford' of Latin American archaeologists), the identification of independent ceramic phases and traditions in the structuring of cultural sequences, and the framing of area syntheses, all constituting the new theoretical orientation in North American archaeology, had to await the investigations of Evans and Meggers in the early fifties and publication of their results in the following decade.

By this time, the succeeding Classificatory-Historical Period (Context and Function) in North American archaeology (1940 - 1960) was being already replaced by the Explanatory Period. This second half of the Classificatory-Descriptive Period, with its emphasis on the potentials of artifacts for revealing aspects of group behaviors and relationships, particularly as expressed in settlement pattern, was represented by Meggers and Evans' (1979) experimental formulation of Taruma village succession based on the seriated sequence of 24 sites on the upper Essequibo, as well as by Siegel's (1987) site structure analyses among the modern Walwai.

Thus, resulting from the contributions of prominent North American professionals, the archaeology of Guyana was early drawn into the discourse on the origin and dissemination of Tropical Forest Culture. For this reason, and possibly also on account of its English language background in a region whose primary research is conducted in five major European languages, its scholarship has maintained a central place in the archaeology of the Guianas since the problem was first enunciated by Steward half a century ago. To the present, this critical problem remains unresolved, but the archaeological chronology structured by Clifford Evans and Betty J Meggers, its most distinguished investigators, has in the meantime provided the indispensable base for the interpretation of ceramic materials which, following upon their seminal publication, *Archaeological Investigations in British Guiana*, began coming to light in neighboring Suriname.

Suriname
The local amateurs

It is obvious that Suriname is in need of archaeological research to serve as a basis for the history of that country

At the time that the above comment was made by the then Director of the Suriname Museum, D.C. Geijskes (1960-1961), odd educated expatriate amateurs had in fact been assembling small collections of curiosities over at least the previous 100 years. However, since excavation had rarely been attempted, the demographic and environmental issues that had provided key research foci and a developing literature in Guyana during the same period were notably lacking in Suriname.

Inception of this type of investigation dates to around 1860, at which time an enthusiastic Dutch plantation owner in Suriname, C.J. Hering, Figure 1.8a, began shipping artifacts, mainly stone axes, back to the National Museum of Antiquities in Leiden. In 1879, Hering's diligence was recognized by the award of a silver medal of that institution. A few years later the Netherlands Government commissioned him to undertake a petroglyph survey on the Marowijne and Coppename Rivers and to investigate further any other remains of the early peoples. Fortified by this

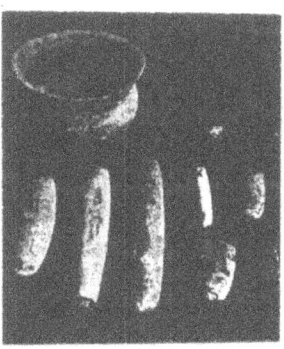
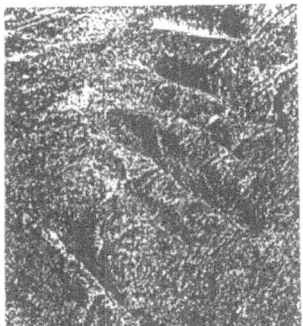

Figure 1. 8 a-c. **a**. C.J. Hering, pioneer of Suriname archaeology *(after Versteeg 1983)*. **b**. Stone axes, Suriname. **c**. Grinding grooves, Coppename River, Suriname *(b,c, after Bubberman 1972)*.

assignment, Hering undertook investigations at an old settlement in Coronie District from which he was able to dispatch to Leiden some stone axes, fragments of a ceramic jar, a wooden club, human skeletal remains, shells and bones (Versteeg 1983).

Hering's collection of Suriname stone axes, Figure 1.8b, soon began to stimulate a European scholarship. Among the earliest reports were those presented to the Congress of Americanists in 1877 and 1878 (Leemans 1878,1879). The collection of Suriname artifacts was officially mentioned in the 1882 - 1883 Report of the Leiden Museum (Leemans 1884). Other writers on the Hering collection were Spitzly (1890) and Schmeltz (1904). Hering himself (1899:54-58) listed certain items in the catalog of the Netherlands Nyest Indies Exhibition in Haarlem in 1899. *On West Indian Stone Implements and other Indian Relics* by the physical anthropologist ten Kate had been published in 1889. It reflected strongly the thinking of Im Thurn's previously published (1883, 1884) inquiries on the subject. This latter is chiefly noteworthy as an early attempt at stone ax classfication. It stimulated efforts at stone ax classification in Suriname during the following century (e.g. Boomert 1979a; Bubberman 1972; Penard and Penard 4917).

Among items dispatched by Hering to Leiden were a few watercolor drawings of petroglyphs at Bigiston on the Marowijne *(Fr:* Marouini) River now in the Rijksmuseum voor Volkerkunde, Leiden (Dubelaar 1986:286; Versteeg 1983:6; see also Penard and Penard 1917; Geijskes 1960 - 1961). The Marowijne River petroglyphs were again taken up by the Penard brothers, whose rather fanciful interpretations of their significance are no longer remembered. A member of the Corentyne expedition of 1910 - 1911, Lieut. C. C. Käyser of the Royal Dutch Navy (1912) reported two petroglyphs on its tributary, the Lucie River, so named for his wife! The Corentyne petroglyphs were more fully reported by Gonggryp (1920). Specimens at individual sites there were reported by Stahel (1927), IJzerman (1931) and Hellinga (1954). According to Dubelaar, (1986:16) the year 1968 represents the watershed between the incidental recording of petroglyphs in Suriname and their systematic exploration and inventorying, principally at his own hands. As against a mere 37 specimens known to that date, systematic survey now reported 168 new items, his assiduous co-worker having been the forester, F.C. Bubberman (1972,1973,1974,1977). Thus, as with the stone implements, the line of study initiated by Hering in the late nineteenth century was to bear ample fruit during the twentieth.

Frequently accompanying the petroglyphs are various kinds of grinding and milling surfaces, early observed by de Goeje (1906) on the Tapanahoni. These were first formally reported by the Penard brothers (1917) who correctly interpreted the most numerous type, the *slijpgroeven,* Figure 1.8c, as specialized sharpening sites in prehistoric stone tool industries. Others were recorded by ten Kate (1914 - 1917),

Stahel (1927), and D'Audretsch (1957). The earliest classification was made by Ahlbrinck as a result of his explorations in the upper Corentyne in 1927. Albrinck's types were: (1) long, narrow and deep, with sharp upper edges, (2) long, wide and shallow, with dull upper edges, (3) egg-shaped and shallow, with sharp upper edges, and (4) round, shallow and flat. Stahel associated these artifacts with rapids in the rivers, while D'Audretsch correlated their density at a given site with population size. During the Hevea-Coppename Expedition of 1943 - 1944, Geijskes reportedly mapped, photographed and measured 30 specimens at two sites on the Rechter Coppename River, employing the Ahlbrinck classification.

The Penard brothers, permanently confined by illness to a room in Paramaribo, appear to have pioneered the study of Amazon stones, the local name of which -- Maroni stones -- suggests an associated trade with Brazil *via* that river. De Goeje reported the recovery of an olive green specimen and mentioned other occurrences in Suriname, but in his view the trade with the lower Amazon was carried in canoes *via* the Atlantic coast. An exhaustive study of these artifacts was made by Boomert (1987), an expatriate archaeologist at the time attached to the Suriname Museum.

Following on Hering's early ceramic collecting, prehistoric potteryware was casually reported by odd individuals (e.g. Feriz 1956; Geijskes 1960-1961; Goethals MS; Stahel 1927). Peter Goethals, a student of Osgood at Yale University, conducted fieldwork in coastal Suriname during six months in 1961. His collections and unpublished manuscript contributed to the definition of the Koriabo phase of Evans and Meggers (1960:150). At the 32nd International Conference of Americanists, Feriz (1956) presented a report on certain potsherds from Suriname which "embodied degenerate elements of the highly remarkable ceramic art of Marajó Island in the Amazon Delta." Archaeological salvage during bauxite mining operations in the Suriname hinterland in 1958 triggered Geijskes' illustrated report on the pottery, stone artifacts, etc., the first ever report of this kind in Suriname. With the publication the following year of his *History of Archaeological Investigations in Surinam*, Geijskes not surprisingly remained profoundly disappointed with what had been achieved during the immediately preceding one hundred years:

> It is strongly urged that the archaeological investigation of Surinam which, so far, had been sketchily undertaken in Europe and America, be conducted in Surinam itself.

Assuming his vision was of a native Suriname archaeology, this was a problematic dream, for Geijskes, like all of his predecessors, was himself an expatriate and trained in a discipline other than anthropology. During the period represented, archaeological activity in Suriname had been contributed to by members of professions such as the Church, geology, linguistics, forestry, agriculture, government and the navy, the experts having invariably been Dutch and usually transient. Thus, the opportunity for training in Suriname did not exist. The solitary anthropologist, ten Kate, had visited Suriname only briefly in 1885 - 1886. Appointed to the curatorship of the Suriname Museum in 1956, shortly after the country had become a self-governing territory of the Kingdom of the Netherlands (1954), Geijskes was himself a biologist. His curatorship is marked in the literature for his donation of the Kwatta and Hertenrits skeletal collections to the Royal Tropical Institute in Amsterdam, where they provided materials for the doctoral thesis of another Dutch national, Tacoma (1963). Geijskes' advocacy of the nationalization of archaeology in Suriname thus appears to reflect other than the purely academic aspirations of the Suriname people themselves. In 1965, Geijskes retired after 27 years as a government official in Suriname and returned to Holland. The local situation remained unaltered. The period of local amateur activity reviewed in his 1960 - 1961 publication differed from the European period in Guyana by virtue of the transitoriness of its main protagonists, in the one-off nature of their contributions, in its lack of research objectives and in a virtually complete absence of excavation. Suriname therefore remained outside of the mainstream discourse of American archaeology throughout.

The professionals

Suriname's first professional archaeologist, a Dutch doctoral candidate of the State University of Leiden, was attached to the Suriname Museum between 1973 - 1975. His successor, also Dutch, left Suriname in 1981 and presented his doctoral thesis in 1985. A Dutch trained Suriname native archaeologist was appointed in 1984. An outstanding contribution of the period was the report of the southern Suriname Sipaliwini Complex, Figure 1.9.

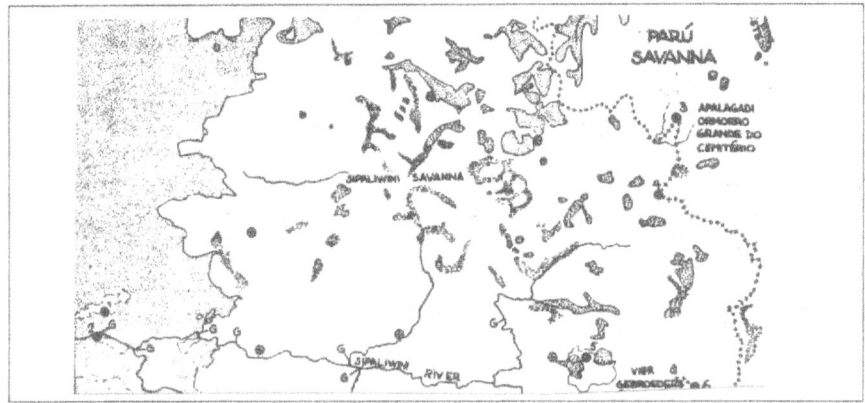

Figure 1.9 **a,b**. Sipaliwini Savannas, southern Suriname

The discovery was made by Bubberman in 1962 but not published until much later (e.g. Boomert 1977, 1980; Bubberman 1974). According to Boomert, the complex comprised some 29 sites with an inventory mainly consisting of waste cores and flakes, hammerstones, choppers, scrapers, knives and projectile points on quartz and rhyolite, Figure 1.9. On the basis of projectile point typology, an affiliation has been suggested with the Canaima and Las Casitas complexes of Venezuela. However, the Sipaliwini Complex remains undated. In the absence of any similarly extensive site in the Guianas, the display of its artifacts in the Suriname Museum continues to attract very considerable interest in the country's newly found sense of prehistoric time depth.

The expansion of the petroglyph inventory was accompanied by an advance in classification. Technologically, Dubelaar (1977, 1979, 1986) identified four impositional modes in Suriname petroglyphs: (*a*) planed line, (*b*), groove, (*c*) modeling, (*d*) leveling. Typologically, three classes were recognized: (1) a simple anthropomorph often associated with geometrical elements such as spirals, circles, etc., (2) a composite figure of the type identified by Kock-Grünberg with a dance costume on the upper Vaupés and, (3) a more naturalistic, three-dimensional figure exemplified by certain specimens at King Willem Falls on the Corentyne and Tapanahoni Rivers. The notion that petroglyphs functioned as a script of any description - pictographic, syllabic or alphabetic (cf. Hellinga 1954) -- was rejected by Dubelaar (1982), the basic requirements for such a function being order and some level of repetition of signs.

As has been seen, the initial notice of Suriname pottery dates back to Hering's investigation of a site "... in District Coronie, behind the abandoned plantation *The Hope* situated beside the plantation *Burnside*... a large mound of shell and sand mixed with bones and broken Amerindian pottery." As a Dutch planter, Hering personified the process of Europeanization of the Eastern Guiana Littoral that had been set in train by the first settlers during the seventeenth century (Goethals MS; Hurault 1972; van Berkel 1948; see also de Forrest's map of 1625), but not recorded until the closing years of the nineteenth century, e.g. Im Thurn (18 84), Quelch (1894), both on the newly disturbed sand and shell reefs of the Guyana coastlands. Hering's note therefore constitutes the earliest mention of one of the most remarkable features of the horticultural period in Suriname, the artificial mounds and raised field complexes of the coastal plain. In the event, these mounds and artificially raised fields were to remain unexcavated on to the middle of the twentieth century. Although the formal study of Suriname pottery dates back to Goethal's (1951) excavations, that event was rapidly overtaken by escalating interest in these raised field complexes and habitation mounds, culminating with Geijskes' excavation of the most famous of them all, the Hertenrits, in 1957 (Geijskes 1960/1961).

Subsequent work showed use of this farming technique to have extended eastward to Guyane française (Rostain 1991, 1994, 1994a, 1995; Rostain and Frenay 1991) and westward to both coastal and hinterland Guyana (Goodland 1964; Poonai 1962; Simon pers. comm. 1990). It has been suggested (Michael Eden pers. comm. 1994) that occurrences of the hinterland specimens on the low-lying Berbice-Canje watershed may indicate wetter soils locally at the time that the mounds were constructed. If so, a version of the watertable horticulture reported in certain Peruvian coastal valleys (West 1979) may seem implied.

To date, most of what is known of the horticultural period in Suriname derives from investigations on the Coastal Plain (Boomert 1977, 1980, 1983, 1993; Boomert and Kroonenberg 1977; Versteeg 1978, 1980, 1983, 1985, 1991; Versteeg and Bubberman 1992). Horticultural sites recorded or reported in the hinterland are few (Boomert 1981,1983; Boomert and Kroonenberg 1977; Versteeg 1978, 1980, 1981). Archaeological chronologies for Suriname, and Suriname and adjacent territories, place inception of horticultural subsistence on the coast at around A.D. 250 (Boomert 1993; Versteeg and Bubberman 1992) and in hinterland Suriname at around 2000 B.C. (Versteeg and Bubberman 1992). This latter date is not acknowledged in Boomert (1993). With his earliest coastal site located at Buckleburg-1, Versteeg recognized a broad continuum, Buckleburg-Hertenrits-Kwatta-Barbakoeba, which is claimed to have "spread over the Suriname plains from the Orinoco area." This opinion was somewhat modified in Boomert's (1993) view that the peopling of the Guiana coast resulted from the incursion of bearers of three major ceramic traditions -- Saladoid and Arauquinoid from the middle and lower Orinoco valley, and Marajoaroid from the lower Amazon.

Summary

In the context of the intellectual history of North American archaeology, the Classificatory-Descriptive Period survived in Suriname on to the time of arrival of the first professional in 1973 or a good sixty years following on its demise in the United States. Even so, the nature of the materials investigated offered only limited scope for description and classification. In the absence of excavation, the one-off nature of the reports and lack of commitment to sustained inquiry by workers principally trained in other disciplines, the period is comparable to that of the local amateurs which, in Guyana, terminated the North American Period and may in fact have derived from it. In the succeeding Classificatory-Historical Period (Chronology), stratigraphic excavations at sites of the artificial mounds and associated raised horticultural fields represented a significant advance in the archaeology of the Guiana Coast.

Guyane française

> Par manque de credits, de specialistes et de bonnes volontes, de nombreux sites archéologiques restent encore idexploites en Guyane.

The above opinion of a local columnist *(vide* Dubelaar 1984:206) was published as late as 1975. The situation remained unaltered during most of the following two decades. Although raised field complexes had been discovered in the coastal swamps at Kourou as early as 1964 during the initial surveys of the *Centre National d'Etudes Spatiales*, Figure 1.10., no one had paid them the slightest attention, attributing their authorship to convicts from the penal settlement on Devil's Island. Systematic investigations were undertaken there only during 1989 - 1991 in the *Projet Savanes* of ORSTOM, *l'Institut française de recherche scientifique pour le developpement en cooperation*. The survey was undertaken by Stephen Rostain in collaboration with Pierre Frenay of *l'Institut Geographique National*. After further pioneering work in coastal archaeology, Rostain's doctoral thesis was submitted to the University of Paris in 1994. Rostain's interests subsequently led to Colombia.

Figure 1.10. Guyane française. Raised fields in the swamps at Kourou *(Courtesy Stephen Rostain)*.

Guyane française differs from the ex-British and ex-Dutch territories of the northeastern South American coast in being not an ex-colony but an integral part of the French Republic, represented in the French Parliament by a senator and a deputy and with close economic and cultural ties to the metropole. On to 1945, its history was dominated by the location of the notorious penal settlement on Devil's Island, the period having been characterized by a general indifference to intellectual concerns. Nonetheless, a beginning in cuno collecting appears to have been made as early as 1872 with the dispatch of a stone ax from the Approuague to the Cayenne National Archives (Abonnenc 1952). In the ensuing hundred or so years, sporadic observations on modified rock were made by Crevaux (1883), Geay (1903), Reichlen and, Reichlen (19431946) and Abonnenc (1952), the latter compiling a useful inventory based on his own researches as well as those of Reichlen and Reichlen and others. Of the 120 sites listed, 94 were of assemblages of grinding and milling surfaces, a comment perhaps on the low level of interest in excavation during the period. Resultingly, the literature is scanty and refers mainly to the recording of petroglyph sites. The discovery in 1948 by a geodesic engineer (Hurault et al 1963) of a petroglyph complex in the forests of the Marouini headwaters is of interest today in its representation of typically savanna elements, suggesting significant environmental change since modification of the respective boulders.

One useful result of the overwhelming early concern with grinding surfaces was an attempt at standardizing the local terminology. A distinction originally made by Geay between *polissoirs à gouttière* and *polissoirs à cupule* was elaborated upon by Deman et Lefebvre (1974):

> "Le trait en fuseau est défini en ces terms: trait poli dont
> la section est un angle et qui présente en plan la forme d'un
> fuseau effilé et peu profond aux extrémites; it s'elargit et
> s'approfondit progressivement vers le milieu".

Accordingly, *traits en fuseau* were now definitively distinguished from cupules, a distinction that permits independent analysis of these strangely neglected artifacts.

A rare ground and polished stone carving from the upper Oyapoc reported in a private collection by Abonnenc (1952) represents the figure of a bird resting on a human foot, Figure 1.11. Thought by its owner to have been of considerable age, it was claimed by its finder, a local miner, to have been recovered at a depth of around two meters in a gold working on Sikini Creek. While the provenience may be reliable, experience counsels that miners notoriously exaggerate the depths at which such artifacts were recovered, often simply from bravado but more frequently in an attempt to enhance their value in the eyes of a prospective purchaser. In the case of stone carvings, the situation is worsened by their universal rarity in the Guianas. This obviates any possibility of their typological or technological classification and the recognition of styles and periods. In its opposition of the symbol of flight and the symbol of human rootedness on the earth, which may occasionally be found repeated

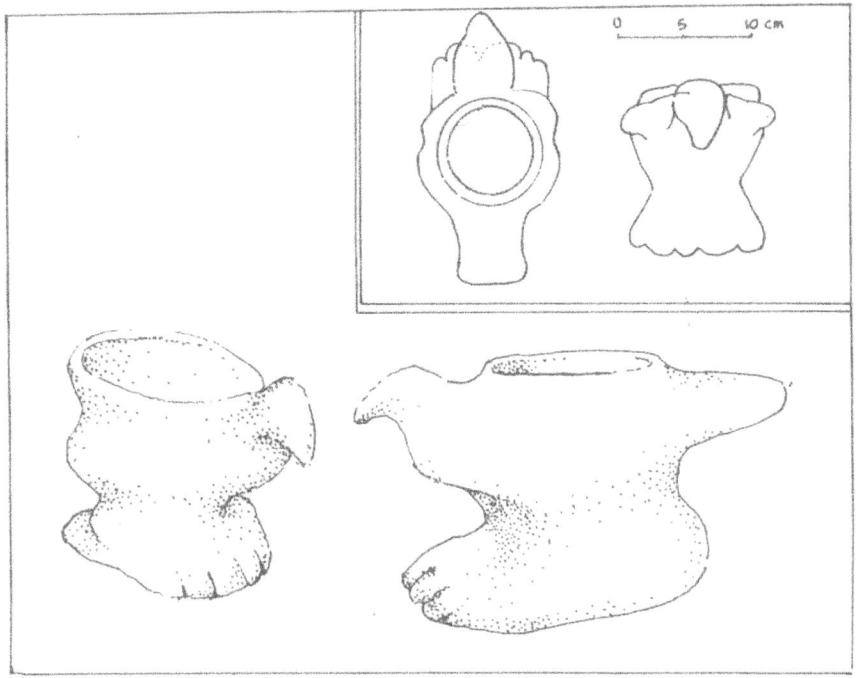

Figure 1.11. Guyana française. Human-footed bird. Stone *(after Abonnenc 1952)*.

in other contexts and in other forms, the object is nonetheless of extreme iconographic importance for the light it now sheds on certain cosmological beliefs.

Because of the poverty of the literature, on the very rare occasions that ceramics were encountered in this Classificatory-Descriptive Period (e.g. Boyé 1974; Groene 1976; Roget et Roy 1975) they could be interpreted only in light of typological resemblances perceived to exist between selected decorated motifs in a given sample and decorative motifs of, invariably, the Koriabo phase which had been identified and defined in Guyana some two decades earlier (Meggers and Evans 1955; Evans and Meggers 1960). Obviously, the value of such comparisons was always limited.

L'Association Guyanaise d'Archèologie et d'Ethnographie (L'AGAE) was founded in 1979. Publication of the cultural sequence for coastal Guyane française (Rostain 1994, 1994a, 1995), while initiating the Classificatory-Historical Period (Chronology) after a time lag of some 80 years, at the same time provided data that have been found useful in structuring an area synthesis of the Guiana Littoral.

Summary

Based mainly on the reporting and/or curating of modified stone, especially grinding surfaces and petroglyphs, the archaeological record in Guyane française goes back at least 100 years; but while displaying a time depth more or less equal to the Guyana and Suriname records, the characteristically Classificatory-Descriptive literature remained relatively meagre throughout. The first, and so far only, professional reporting of the Classificatory-Historical Period (Chronology) was made in 1994 by an expatriate scientist who moved on shortly afterwards.

Brazilian Guiana
The Coast

> The pottery from Caviana, Maracá, and Brazilian Guiana shows a number of affinities to that of Marajó in abstracted traits, such as the presence of funerary urns, painted geometric designs, and the joining of eyebrows to the nose in anthropomorphic faces, but the actual designs and vessel shapes are usually quite different.

Although Guyana boasts indisputable priority in the history of archaeological investigations in the Region as a whole, the research problem that continues to dominate inquiry -- the place of origin and dissemination of Tropical Forest Culture -- was first put to the archaeological test not there but along the northeastern Brazilian coast, in the Territory of Amapá. At the time the above observation was made in 1945 (Meggers 1947:209) the problem had not yet been formulated by Steward, though already Meggers was drawing attention to striking typological similarities between certain ceramic specimens from the upper Amazon and specimens from sites on Marajó Island at the Mouth of the Amazon. Not yet having visited the area, Meggers' observations were based on study collections in various North American museum institutions as well as on the available published materials:

> Illustrations of isolated vessels from the Upper Amazon are scattered through the literature. An anthropomorphic urn reproduced by Nordenskiold... from the Rio Napo [eastern Ecuador] and a vessel from the Rio Aguarico [eastern Ecuador] described by Gillin show remarkable similarities to those from Marajó. Another anthropomorphic urn from the Rio Napo, corresponds closely to the tubular Maracá type. Urns from the Rio Japurá, Itacoatiara and Miracanguera [central Amazon] are reminiscent of the styles at the mouth of the Amazon.

Thus, by the time that Steward (1948:885) had come to proposing the Guianas as the center of dispersal of Tropical Forest Culture, deriving from an ultimate source in the Circum-Caribbean area, Meggers was already formulating the preliminary outlines of an alternative hypothesis. The fieldwork now undertaken with Clifford Evans at the Mouth of the Amazon, and particularly in the Territory of Amapá, was designed to test that hypothesis.

Although the area had been visited repeatedly by explorers, treasure seekers and scientists since 1870, there had as yet been no systematic archaeological work at this strategically "classic spot" (cf. Hartt 1871; Penna 1877; Steere 1927), so that neither the extent nor the chronology of the sites was then known. That situation was changed profoundly and for all time after their year of investigations at the Mouth of the Amazon and on the northeast coast of Brazil, July 1948 - July 1949.

Their investigations in the Territory of Amapá combined 22 excavated sites with museum collections deriving from the earlier excavations of Nimuendaju, Lima Guedes and Coudreau. Of the three prehistoric cultures identified in the Territory of Amapá, the Arua was uniquely represented on both sides of the eastward flowing Rio Araguari, which divides the area into northern and southern sectors. Cultural refuse of the Aristé phase was resticted to the northern portion of the Territory, while refuse of the Mazagão phase was restricted to the south. A local tradition on the Rio Maracá represented a late offshoot of the Mazagão phase. Although these investigations were taken as far to the north as the mouth of the Oyapoc, the authors could detect no evidence whatsoever in support of the Steward hypothesis of a coastwise migration of groups originating in a Circum-Caribbean hearth. As Evans (1971/1955) put it, "There is not one bit of related material." Obviously, Tropical Forest Culture had entered the Guianas by some other route.

The Hinterland

The technically sophisticated and decoratively elaborate pottery of the Marajoara culture on Marajó Island presented a seeming anomaly of monumental proportions in the context of the typically Tropical Forest complexes that preceded and followed it there. The difficulty of reconciling this evidently complex culture with the egalitarian cultures represented not only at the Mouth of the Amazon but also in the Territoy of Amapá, both to the north and to the south, constituted a powerful stimulus for seeking Marajoara origins elsewhere than in the immediate Tropical Forest environment.

The authors' six-month field season in British Guiana (= Guyana) had been undertaken during 1952-1953 with their earlier joint manuscript *Archeological Investigations at the Mouth of the Amazon (1957)* still in press. Following on the Guyana fieldwork, and with the resulting *Archeological Investigations in British Guiana* still in preparation, a new period of fieldwork was undertaken on the Rio Napo, eastern Ecuador, in 1956. The experience provided, at long last, confirmation of Meggers' (1947) preliminary hypothesis, conceived more than a decade earlier while examining the Beal-Steere Marajoara collection in the University of Michigan Museum of Anthropology, of a direct link between Marajoara and certain ceramic cultures on the upper Amazon:

> We found exactly what we were looking for. The links with the Marajoara culture of the lower

Amazon are very, very strong, and our theory of movement downriver is definitely proven.
- *(Letters to Vincent Roth, July 11, 1957)*

Resulting from their work in eastern Ecuador, the authors (1968:94, Figure 68) now found that most of the diagnostic traits of their Napo phase also occur along the middle Amazon between the Rio Japurá and the Rio Tapajós as well as on Marajó Island. This distribution led to their formulation of the Polychrome Horizon Style (Meggers and Evans 1961), Figure 1.12.

> The Polychrome Tradition is defined by the presence of polychrome painting, excising and double-line incising. Subtraditions are defined by the presence of these plus subtradition diagnostics: dentate, drag-and-jab, push-and-jab punctation for the Saracá Subtradition; grooving and waist flanges for the Guarita Subtradition, etc. *(Meggers pers. comm. 1991).*

On the basis of their having detected certain Napo-like ceramic traits in the Colombian Highlands, notably anthropomorphic urns featuring "swollen" lower limbs, the authors considered the associated Polychrome Tradition to have originated somewhere in the northwest of South America around 2000 years ago (Evans and Meggers 1968:94; Meggers pers. comm. 1991). In the Guianas, the Tradition

Figure 1.12. Marajoara phase. The Polychrome Tradition *(after Meggers and Evans 1957).*

is represented by a number of sites on the Amazon left bank below the Mouth of the Rio Negro, Figure 1.13. At least three subtraditions have been recognized -- the Guarita, Miracanguera and Saracá (Lathrap 1970:155; Miller 1992) -- which may indicate a respectable antiquity for the Tradition in the area. In due course, Lathrap (1970:120) claimed to have detected "blatantly" Barrancoid characteristics in the early levels of certain Central Amazon sites, on which basis the Guarita and Miracanguera Subtraditions were postulated by him to have evolved out of this earlier Barrancoid style.

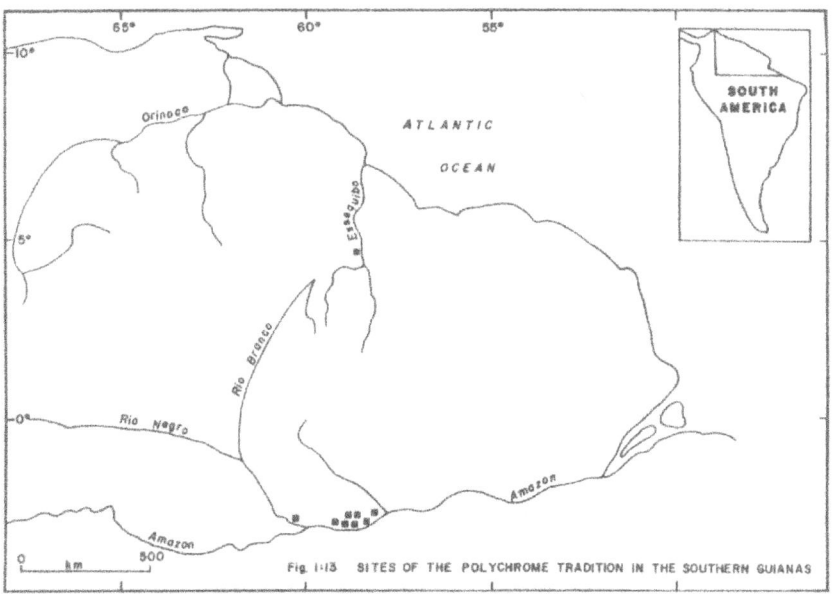

Figure 1. 13. Sites of the Polychrome Tradition in the southern Guianas

Although archaeological inquiry in the hinterland has been slight and sporadic (Schmitz 1987), the cultural sequence there has been pushed back to the Archaic on the upper Rio Branco (Mentz Ribeiro et al 1987). In the Caverna da Pedra Pintada, on the lower Amazon, Roosevelt et al (1996) report a deposit spanning the paleo-Indigenous to late prehistoric periods, about 11,200 b.p. to A.D. 1450. Formative pottery there returned dates between 3600 - 3200 b.p., which are contemporaneous with dates representing the horticulturist Boa Vista phase on the Rio Trombetas, 3280 +/- 45 b.p., and 2950 +/- 130 b.p. (Weber 1990) and with initial dates for horticulture at Hosororo Creek on the Western Guiana Littoral (Williams 1992).

Venezuelan Guayana

Covering nearly half the national territory of Venezuela, the *Macizo de Guayana* is extremely difficult terrain. This is reflected in the relative paucity of archaeological investigations conducted there. The Classificatory-Historical Period has provided evidence of occupation on the upper Orinoco dating back to 7000 B.C. (Barse 1989, 1990, MS., pers. comm. 1988) with implications of a regional trade network already based on the jasper outcrops of the Roraima Supergroup in the Pakaraima Mountains. A series of red, and sometimes green, vitric tuffs occurs on Mt. Roraima over a limited vertical interval near the middle of this succession. Although similar intercalations are found as far east as the Tafelberg in Suriname, and as far south as the Urupi Formation in Brazil, jasper appears to be absent in the west, beyond 63 - 64° W (Gibbs and Barron 1994:119). Jasper employed in the small, barbed, contracting-stem projectile points reported by Barse around Puerto Ayacucho may have derived from outcrops in the Canaima Savannas, now well known for its industry of flake and core tools (Cruxent 1971:37). Indeed, this rock material has dominated toolmaking throughout the Western Guiana Hinterland from the time of the very earliest migrations into the lowlands. The small, stemmed or unstemmed Canaima points are thought (Rouse and Cruxent 1963:42) to indicate the survival of the paleo-Indigenous lifeway as evidenced in the Rio Pedregal sequence in western Venezuela. Small, contracting-stem points similar to Barse's specimens have been recovered in various Archaic contexts across the continent (Barse 1997). They may represent a modification of the large points of paleo-Indigenous subsistence in a drastically altered environment.

The Classificatory-Historical Period is also represented in ceramic complexes on the middle Orinoco (Cruxent and Rouse 1961; Evans, Meggers and Cruxent 1960; Tarble 1985 and Zuechi 1991). Tarble (1985) and Zucchi (1985) present models of Carib migrations and dispersals down the Orinoco. Results of excavations at Parmana on the middle Orinoco has contributed to knowledge of early horticulture in the lowlands. Initial occupation there was represented by two radiocarbon series: 810 - 940 B.C., and 2030 - 3475 B.C. (Roosevelt 1980; Rouse and Allaire 1978). A choice between them was based on independent thermoluminescence assays (Zucchi et al 1984). Although the results favored the younger series, C^{14} dates subsequently obtained for ceramics in the third or even fourth millennium B.C. on the lower Amazon suggest that in future the long Parmana chronology may need to be revisited. The suggestion of an early extended ceramic horizon in the lowlands that was unrelated to either the Orinocan Saladoid or Barrancoid Traditions presents an implicit challenge to the Steward model of the origin and dissemination of Tropical Forest Culture.

Archaeology and language

A few archaeologists (Uthrap 1970; Rouse 1985; Tarble 1985; Zucchi 1985,

1991) have had recourse to the phylogeny of language in order to explain certain ceramic distributions and thus reconstruct routes of past migrations in the Guianas. The Region is dominated by two of the three great language groups of Amazonia -- Arawak and Carib. Warao, long considered an independent language (Mason 1950) has now been classified with the Chibcha and Shiriana groups in a macro-Chibchan phylum (Greenberg 1960; Greenberg et al 1986). Granberry (1971, 1993) points to a possible affiliation between Warao and the Timucua language of Florida, with separation estimated at around 3000 - 2000 B.C., or around the time of the Colonial Formative dispersal which witnessed the diffusion of certain ceramic traits from Colombia into the southeastern United States (Ford 1969:187; Meggers and Evans 1978:554). Granberry (1993:41) cites structural and lexical evidences suggesting that Timucua probably originated as a native language in northwestern Amazonia, its grammar being quite clearly Waroid-based. In this reconstruction, Warao proper, as well as Warao-related languages, were spoken from an indeterminate time in the past until at least the time of Spanish intervention along the Caribbean littoral of northern South America from somewhere to the west of Lake Maracaibo east to and including the Orinoco Delta. More than this, a few resemblances to non-Maipuran Arawak may point toward possible contact with pre-Maipuran Arawak speakers perhaps as early as 3500 B.C., presumably somewhere along the upper reaches of the Rio Negro near its confluence with the Amazon, the area identified by Lathrap (1970) as the possible hearth of Proto-Maipuran Arawak. Warao may therefore be a relic of an extremely ancient language in Amazonia, today confined to the Orinoco Delta and northwestern Guyana. Archaeologists have not so far had recourse to linguistic data to explain the distributions of Warao culture, though Wilbert (1979:134) cites Warao oral tradition of a time when their ancestral territory encompassed the island of Trinidad, then still connected to the South American mainland.

Arawak is today the largest and most important language group in South America though, in the Guianas, it is represented by only one of its seven branches -- Maipuran. It is thought that around 4500 - 5000 years ago the seven branches of Arawak diverged from a Proto-Arawakan language located somewhere between the headwaters of the Ucayali and the Madre de Dois Rivers on the upper Amazon (Noble 1965). On the other hand, Migliazza (1982) sees the upper Amazon (between the Ucayali and upper Purus Rivers in the west and the upper Madeira River in the east) as only one of two centers of dispersal for these languages, the other having been located somewhere on the northern coast of South America, outside of Amazonia. In this view, the present dispersion of Arawak results from dispersals from these northern and southern homelands.

Speakers of Proto-Arawakan in the northern homeland are thought to have separated from Taino and Guamo between 5000 - 4500 b.p. moving to north of the

Orinoco near the coast of Venezuela. While Taino spread northward into the Caribbean, Black Carib and its daughter languages, Igneri and Lokono, are thought to have spread eastward reaching the coastal Guianas around 1500 b.p.

In the southern homeland, northern Maipuran Arawak was meanwhile separating from pre-Andine, arriving in the central Amazon around 2600 b.p., subsequently spreading west and north along the Amazon and up the Rio Negro. From the Rio Negro, it expanded *via* the Casiquiare Canal into the upper Orinoco Basin, penetrating eastern areas of the Guiana land mass by around 1500 b.p. and giving rise to Wapisiana, Patikur, Baniwa, et cetera.

Lowland archaeologists have paid close attention to these reconstructions of Arawak dispersals and have sought the appropriate correlates in the material culture (Lathrap 1970; Rouse 1985; Zucchi 1991). In Lathrap's view (1970:74), horticulturist speakers of Proto-Arawakan located on the central Amazon flood plain around 3000 B.C. began to disperse north and south in quest of suitable areas of alluvial bottomlands. The northern migrants moved up the Rio Negro, thence *via* the Casiquiare Canal into the Orinoco, which they occupied for a prolonged period until pressure from newer groups forced them onto the Venezuelan Coast and, ultimately, out into the Antilles where they were the Tainos encountered by Columbus. Proto-Maipuran successors and conquerors of these pioneers likewise followed the Orinocan route between 1000 and 500 B.C. Besides displacing their ancestors there, these later migrants are thought to have fanned out along the Venezuelan and Guyana coasts.

Unfortunately, due to a lack of direct archaeological experience in the lowlands, Lathrap's highly idealized reconstruction of Arawakan origins and dispersals was based on various secondary sources as well as on unevaluated previously published reports. Moreover, to some extent his model may have resulted from prior commitment to the hypothesis of the displacement of the Alaka culture at the Mouth of the Orinoco River by a fully developed Barrancoid culture. It has been seen that in advancing this hypothesis Lathrap was obliged to disregard evidence which he had himself unearthed indicating the existence of Mabaruma Barrancoids at around the time of his own retrodicted date for the initiation of Barrancoid culture. The presence of these Mabaruma folk on the lower Aruka River at this time evidently ran counter to Lathrap's original model of the displacement of the Alaka culture by a fully fledged Barrancoid culture on the lower Orinoco. Therefore the proposition was never repeated by Lathrap. It has since been ignored in the literature. In a series of tests conducted on the upper Orinoco, Zucchi (1991) was unable to identify on the ground the archaeological correlates of this arm of Lathrap's postulated Arawak dispersal. On the other hand, undoubted Barrancoid materials of apparently early date have since been reported or recorded on the upper Orinoco River (Barse 1989, 1990; Meggers pers. comm.), Figure 1.14.

Figure 1.14. Barrancoid sherds, upper Rio Siapa, upper Orinoco.
(Courtesy Betty J. Meggers)

Other ceramic distributions suggested to Lathrap (1970:120) that by a contrasting route certain proto-Maipuran Arawaks, also originating on the Rio Negro, descended the Amazon into Brazilian Guiana. The then available C^{14} dates located early Barrancoids on the central Amazon during the closing years of the first millennium B.C. or the opening years of the Christian Era.

In the related model of Rouse (1985), proto-Maipuran Arawaks centered on the Rio Negro began to disperse in a "pincer movement" around the Island of Guiana during the second millennium B.C. One group descended the Amazon to the Atlantic Coast, in the process developing a new, proto-Eastern language which it carried to the Guiana Coast. Other proto-Maipuran speakers, advancing down the Orinoco *via* the Casiquiare Canal, eventually developed a new, proto-Northern language. In due course, they penetrated the Guiana Coastal Plain and moved south to, or close to, proto-Easterners coming up from the south. This model remains to be put to the archaeological test.

The great mass of Carib languages occurs to the north of the Amazon, where they have been classified into northern and southern groups. The areal extensions of these groups differ somewhat according to the reconstructions of different linguists, Figures 1.15, 1.16.

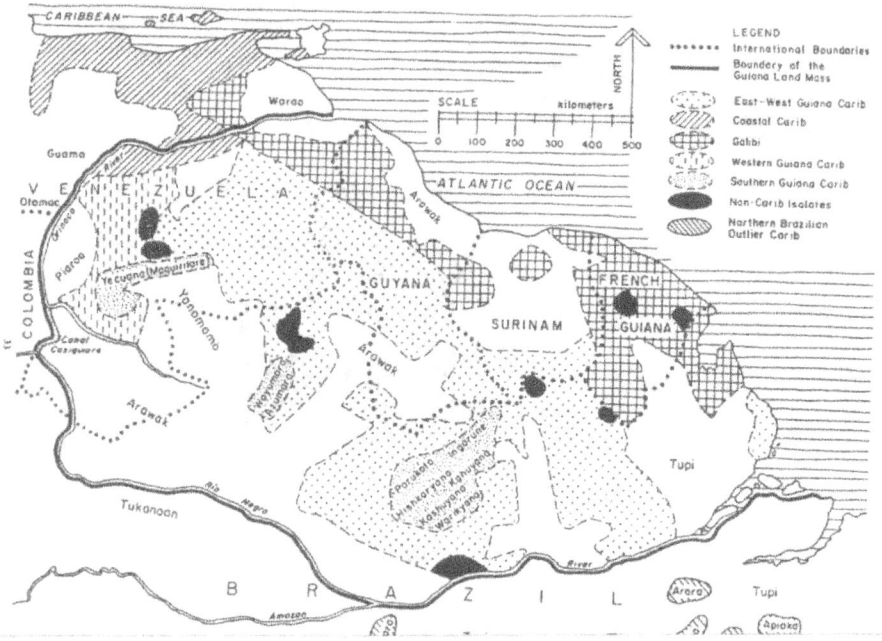

Figure 1.15. Major Carib language groups ca. A.D. 1700 *(after Migliazza 1982)*.

According to Migliazza (1982), these languages began to diverge around 4500 or 4000 b.p., the greater diversity being exhibited, by Northern Carib, which suggests that its distribution area includes proto-Carib's homeland and center of dispersal. Around 3500 b.p., western Guiana Carib separated from proto northern-Carib. On the Eastern Guiana Littoral, Galibi differentiated during the next millennium. Shortly after this, around 2000 b.p., languages of the central Guiana subfamily (Trio, Pemon, Kapon, Pauxiana, Wayana, et cetera) crystallized. Around 1000 b.p., most of the present day languages comprising the southern family, as well as certain subgroups of the northern family, originated.

Durbin's (1977) reconstruction is particularly attractive to archaeology on account of its being more areally specific. Here, the major blocs of Carib speakers follow disjunct distributions that potentially are more readily reconcilable with

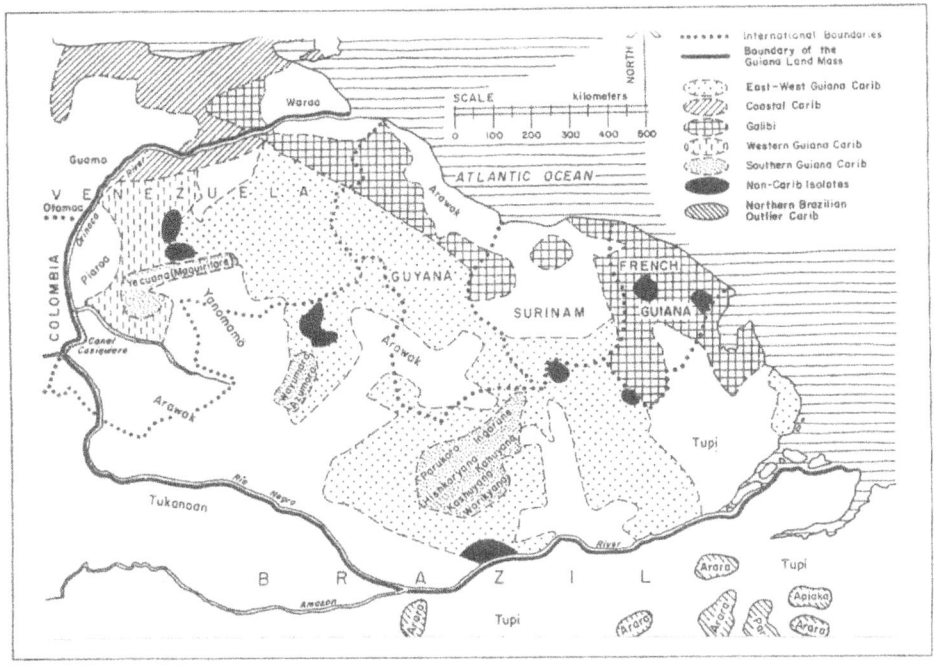

Figure 1.16. Carib languages of the Guiana land mass *(after Durbin 1977)*.

ceramic distributions. On the Eastern Guiana Littoral, for example, the island occupied by Galibi in Suriname should correlate with a specific ceramic complex, while, even more significantly, the restriction of Galibi to the northern portion of the Territory of Amapá and of East-West Guiana Carib to the southern portion of that Territory may be found to correlate with differences to which attention has long been drawn between ceramic complexes to the north and south, respectively, of the Rio Araguari (Meggers and Evans 1957:158).

Summary

The centrality of Guyana in the archaeological history of the Region resulted from two unrelated causes: (*a*) temporal priority of archaeological excavations at the unique shell mound complexes of the Western Guiana Littoral, and (*b*) the geographic importance of the country with respect to the problem of the origins of Tropical Forest Culture originally posed by Steward (1948:886) and first addressed by Evans and Meggers (1960). Excavation of certain Archaic shell mounds during the sixties of the nineteenth century generated two research foci that survived in archaeological inquiry over the ensuing hundred years and more. These two foci related to the nature of the cultural sequence on the Western Guiana Littoral and to determination of sea level movements thought to have been responsible for certain archaeologically detected environmental changes there. Geographically, Guyana is ideally located for detecting early Tropical Forest traits that may have been present on its principal margins, defined by the courses of the Orinoco and Amazon Rivers.

As regards the cultural sequence on the Western Guiana Littoral, the Classical Evolutionist model was inadequate for interpreting the available data, while Boasian Particularism was only poorly applied in Roth's pioneer survey on the Aruka Basin. The problem was addressed in the Classificatory-Historical Period (Chronology) by Osgood (1946) and Evans and Meggers (1960). The value of Osgood's investigations was compromised by the loss of his excavated materials before they could have been adequately studied. Reconstruction of the cultural sequence by Evans and Meggers was based on admittedly inadequate sampling of the shell mounds (1960:59). Accordingly, the critical issue of Mabaruma origins, and thus of the origins of first farming in Guyana, remained unresolved. At that stage in the inquiry, also, the issue of the cultural sequence on the Guyana Coast came to be subsumed in the wider issue of the place of origin and dissemination of Tropical Forest Culture and to some extent was obscured by it (Meggers and Evans 1978:552). Resultingly, key problems posed by the earliest investigators (i.e., the identity of the coastal pioneers, main features of their now vanished environment and the changing nature of its subsistence resources, unique anywhere in the Guianas) remained unaddressed.

The sea level debate, which had engaged the attention of certain of the foremost British scientists of the day, maintained its momentum into the present century in the observations of Verrill, Bullbrook and Osgood, when finally it became bogged down for want of adequate data, all of these investigations having been ludicrously brief and limited in scope. Yet the antiquity that has been claimed for horticultural origins in northwestern Guyana (e.g. Lathrap 1964, 1966) cannot be understood in the absence of a clear picture of sea level fluctuations on those low-lying swamplands. Unfortunately, that debate had lost currency entirely by the time Steward's model was presented.

While being basically a reinterpretation of that model, which saw Tropical Forest Culture deriving, and degenerating, from the Circum-Caribbean Area, the model of Clifford Evans and Betty J. Meggers, though challenged by Lathrap (1970), survives to the present day (e.g. Sanoja 1979, 1983, and others). The Lathrap model, meanwhile, found a measure of support in the linguistically derived model of Rouse (1985). However, the Rouse model yet remains to be put to the archaeological test.

2. THE PALEO-INDIGENOUS PEOPLES

Introduction

Certain structural transformations in this dynamic coastal environment modified its productivities over time. The environmental stages outlined below have been recognized as a basis for restructuring the cultural sequence.

i. 13,000-10,000 b.p. Following on the dry late Pleni-glacial, the climate of northern South America became wetter (Van der Hammen 1974; Van der Hammen and Absy 1994). Rivers now carried increasing amounts of water (cf. Roeleveld 1969). Riverbed fish ponds were submerged.

ii. 10,000-7200 b.p. In the early centuries, Trinidad still formed part of the South American mainland. The littoral line lay farther out to sea, with rivers cutting through coastal grass savannas (Van der Hammen 1963: Figure 22;1974: Figure 18). Bones of a late Pleistocene megafauna recovered in South Trinidad (Boomert 1982, and Natural History Museum Port of Spain) suggest that such animals may once have grazed these savannas (cf. Harris 1976; Hoffman and Lynch 1990).

iii. 7200-6000 b.p. The sea reached the line of emergence of the rocks of the Guiana Shield, representing an absolute sea level rise and a marine-to-brackish coastal zone. Human exploitation of the mangrove epi-fauna and the intertidal mudflats is evidenced in the Southeastern Subzone. In the Northwestern Subzone, an abundance of marine shellfish evidences the hypersaline environment immediately preceding the sea level peak (Roeleveld 1969).

iv. 6000-4000 b.p. A relative sea level rise followed on cessation of the absolute sea level rise (Brinkman and Pons 1968). A brackish water epifauna is associated with the mangroves at this time.

v. 4000-3550 b.p. Around 4000 b.p., an arid interval supervened (Absy 1982, 1985; Van der Hammen 1974). Two marine incursions are evidenced in coastal streams. Marine shellfish now dominate in the mangroves.

vi. 3550-2030 b.p. Around 3550, tectonic subsidence ceased locally. Environmental freshening dropped below the critical level for survival of economic shellfish species. There was a shift in the means of production.

vii. 2030 b.p. The arid interval ended. In the gradually ameliorating environment, coastal horticulturists colonized the rain forest.

The paleo-environments
The Coast

The late Pleniglacial coastline of the Western Guiana Littoral (26,000-21,000 to 14,000-13,000 b.p.) stood much further out to sea than at present. At that time, swamp and marsh forest stood directly behind a belt of shoreline mangroves, and behind the mangroves dry grass savannas extended all the way back to the emergent rocks of the Guiana Shield Complex. When the post-glacial sea began to rise, it rapidly entered the river valleys that traversed these grass savannas and later covered their higher parts. The Demerara River valley was already flooded as far upstream as Linden when the sea stood around 36 m below its present level, probably between 11,500 and 8600 b.p. (Van der Hammen 1963), Figure 2.1.

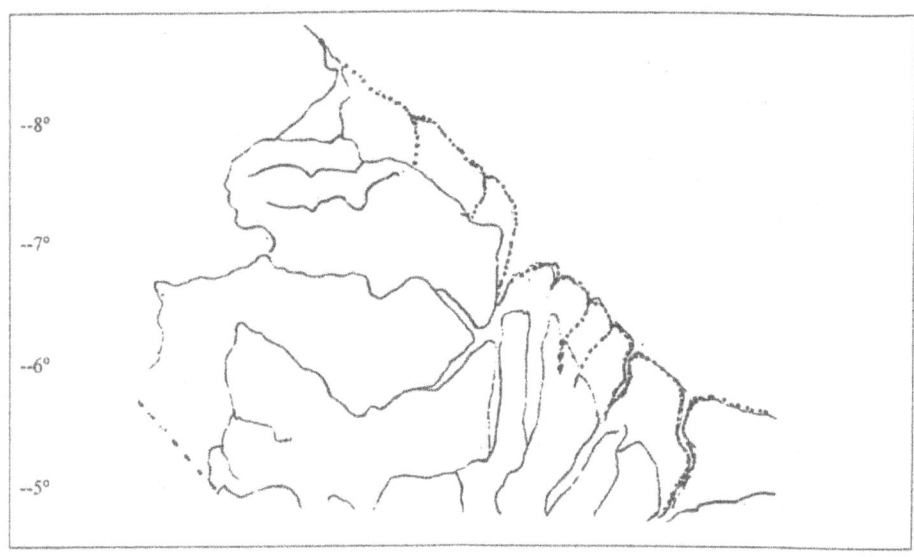

Figure 2.1. Extension of the sea during the Riss-Würm interglacial, the situation during the highest Holocene sea level having been almost the same (*after Van der Hammen 1963*).

As the sea level rose, its sediments attracted vegetation which was successively submerged to give rise to new growths at higher elevations. A hundred and fifty years ago hydraulic engineers drilling in Georgetown's Cummingsburg Ward on the Eastern Guiana Littoral encountered two layers of decaying *Avicennia nitida* at depths of 3.6 and 15.0 m, respectively (Martin 1967:120). Correlation of the depth of the lower of these deposits with similarly deep but undated remains at Ogle Bridge just outside Georgetown suggests that by 8000 years ago the coastline there had reached almost its maximum seaward extension. Around 7200 years ago, mangrove was growing 5.4 m below present ground level a bit to the south of Paramaribo, in Suriname (Roeleveld 1969). Around 7000 years ago, *Avicennia* had gained a foothold again 3.60 m below Georgetown's present day Cummingsburg, and for another thousand years the sea continued to deposit marine clays along this highly unstable shoreline.

At around this time, the earliest known pioneers, apparently a small group of Warao, were in occupation at Piraka on the Southeastern Subzone of the Western Guiana Littoral. On the low-lying basement edge which constitutes part of the upper Pomeroon Basin, the warm, shallow waters had attracted a brackish-water fauna associated with stands of *Rhizophora mangle*. Though unknown in the area at the present time, mangrove growth in former times remains in evidence there as substantial subsurface peat deposits. The date of this early human occupation, 7230 +/- 90 b.p. (Beta 27055), is regarded as marking the end of the paleo-Indigenous period on the Guiana Coast.

There is no evidence of human occupancy at this time in the Northwestern Subzone of the Western Guiana Littoral, nearer the Orinoco Delta; the earliest known human occupation there dates a few centuries later. The shallow sea continued to advance toward the crescent of emergent rocks of the crystalline basement. As yet, the peat swamps that characterize the area had not begun to form; such peat growth awaited establishment of the mangrove forests that accompanied the advance of brackish conditions up the deeply incised river valleys. A local informant on the Barima River (Captain Roberts) reports fallen trees *(tacoubas)*, representing a lower land surface, sticking out from the riverbank at Koriabo Point well below the present minimum low water of the dry season. The environmental stages outlined below have been recognized as a basis for restructuring the cultural sequence on the Western Guiana Littoral.

The Hinterland

Although the problem of accounting for the existence of savannas in the wet tropics has not been resolved to the satisfaction of all concerned (Huber 1982; Sarmiento 1984; see Hills 1965), savannas are of undoubted age in the Guianas and have fluctuated areally with the oscillating climates of the Pleistocene and the Holocene. Commencing during the late Pleistocene, around 26,000 b.p., cold, dry conditions prevailed in the Guiana savannas lasting on to around 14,000 years ago. A warmer period, characterized by increased rainfall, followed between 14,000 - 10,000 years b.p. Other shorter and less intense dry episodes have marked the Holocene, especially between 11,000 and 9500 b. p., and around 4000 b.p., but these are thought (e.g. Brown 1977) to have caused no important fragmentation of the flora. However, available archaeological evidences (e.g. Mentz Ribeiro et al 1989) show that a dry period around 4000 b.p. coincided with human occupancy of the Rupununi Savannas. Around this time, a pattern of alternating extensions of savanna woodland and open grass savannas that had characterized the Rupununi vegetation during the Holocene gave way to the open savannas of the present day (Wijmstra and Van der Hammen 1966). Thus, climatic fluctuations resulting in the alternation of humid and more and periods continued into Recent times.

Haffer's (1969) theory of forest fragmentation in Amazonia during periods of sustained reduced precipitation has been widely supported by other workers in biogeography, as well as in geomorphology, palynology and archaeology (e.g. Absy 1982, 1985; Brown 1977; Meggers 1975, 1977, 1979; Prance 1973, 1982; Vanzolini 1970). Refuge theory holds that forest and non-forest biomes changed continuously in distribution during the geological past, breaking the forest up into isolated blocks, or *refugia*, which subsequently expanded and coalesced under the varying humid to and climatic conditions of certain geological time intervals, especially during the Quaternary (Haffer 1982:9). The forest refuge has been defined (Brown and Ab'Saber 1979) as a region in which there exists sufficient continuity of favorable climate, soils, topography and vegetation to maintain the integration of formerly more widespread landscapes and biotas. This makes the preservation of organisms associated with these conditions more probable than their extinction, populations there being permitted to evolve under diverse environmental pressures and in accordance with their respective plasticities. In the evolution of the forests, *refugia* have therefore functioned as centers of endemism, evidenced at the present time by disjunct distributions of certain species of birds, reptiles and plants.

While displaying a high level of concordance with regard to their locations, the sizes of these *refugia* vary significantly. Thus, whereas most workers identify a Guiana Refuge in southern areas of the British, Dutch and French ex-colonial territories, the largest of these refuges (Prance 1973) stretches west to east from the Pakaraima Mountains to the Oyapoc, while the smallest (Vanzolini 1970) straddles the southern borders of Suriname and Guyana française and extends minimally into the Brazalian State of Pará and the Territory of Amapá. Brown's (1977) Guiana Refuge is connected by a narrow corridor to an Oyapock Refuge. Prance (1982) later restructured his Guiana Refuge into separate Western and Eastern Guiana refuges, the Western still occupying most of central Guyana as well as most of southwest

Suriname. The distributions of Haffer, Prance and Vanzolini have been summarized by de Granville (1982), Figure 2.2a. Brown's distribution is given in Figure 2.2b.

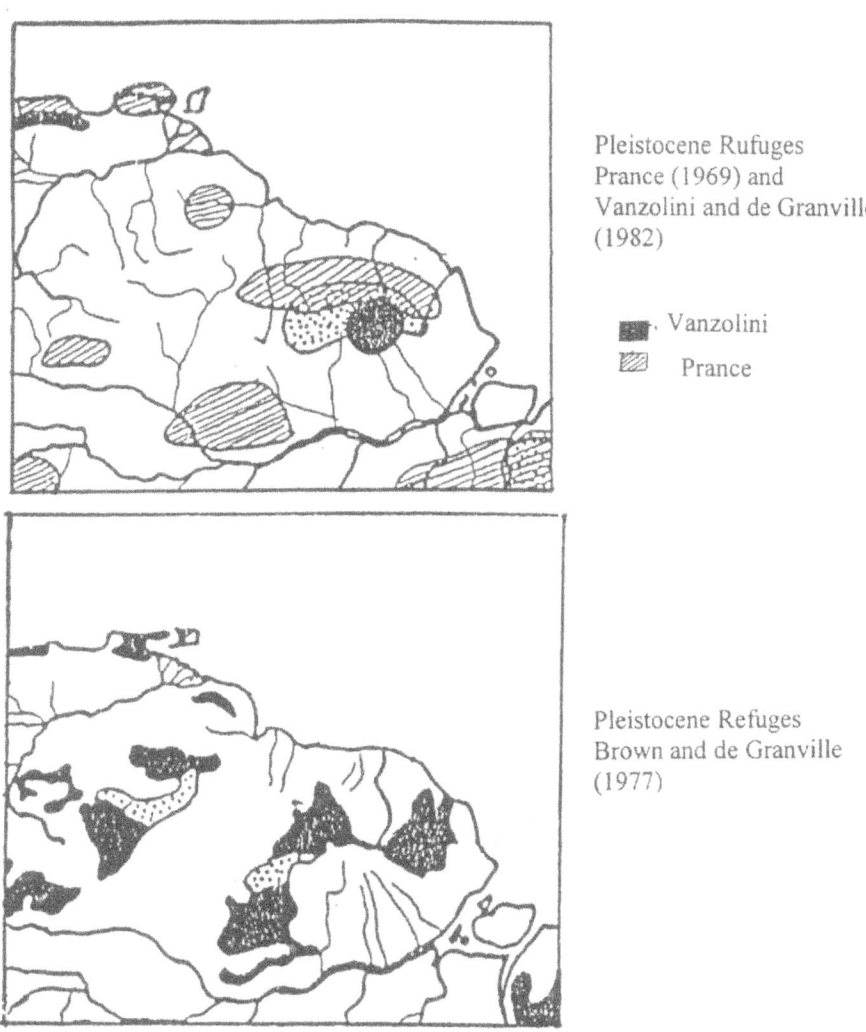

Pleistocene Rufuges
Prance (1969) and
Vanzolini and de Granville
(1982)

▰ Vanzolini
▨ Prance

Pleistocene Refuges
Brown and de Granville
(1977)

Figure 2.2a,b. a. Summary of forest refuges, after de Granville 1982.
 b. Forest refuges according to Brown (1977).

In a more recent inquiry, Van der Hammen and Absy (1994) show that in certain areas, savanna type vegetation and savanna forest had replaced the rain forest during the late Pleniglacial (ca. 22,000-13,000 b.p.), at which time the Amazonian forest may have been split up into one major west Amazonian and several other medium-sized forest refuges distributed across eastern areas. To the authors, these conditions suggested a rainfall decline on the order of 500 to 1000 mm (25% - 40%). Applying these data to a modern rainfall map, Figure 2.3, permitted reconstruction of late Pleniglacial rainfall, Figures 2.4a,b.

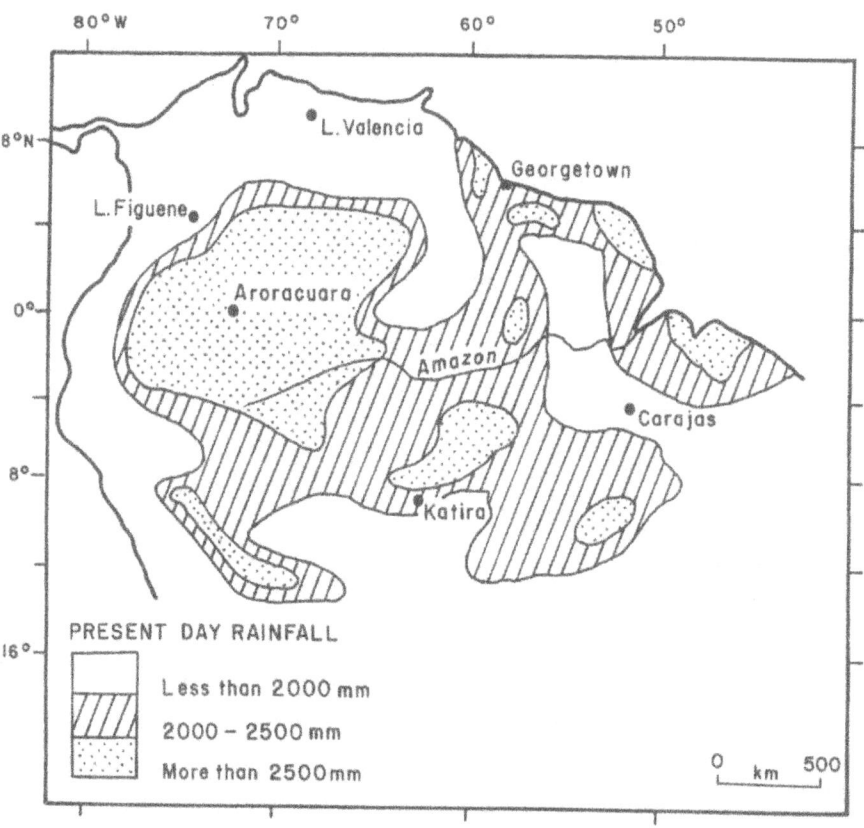

Figure 2.3. Rainfall map of northern South America, not including Andean and Pacific areas (*after Van der Hammen and Absy 1994*).

At a 40% rainfall reduction, the authors' *refugia* distributions in the Guianas display a remarkable congruence with *refugia* proposed by the biogeographers and others to explain existing centers of species diversity or endemism.

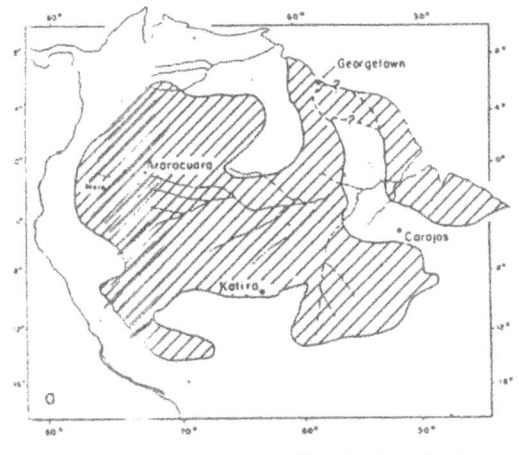

2.4a. Area of >1500 mm rainfall and approximate (rain) forest area at a general rainfall reduction of 25%.

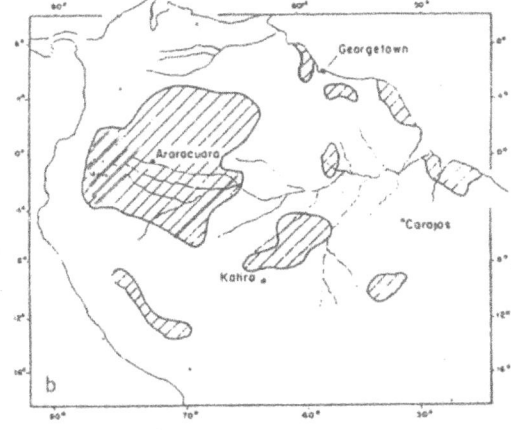

2.4b. Area of >1500 mm rainfall and approximate (rain) forest area at a general rainfall reduction of 40%. (after Van der Hammen and Absy 1994).

However, attention has been drawn to the fact that oscillations in the vegetational cover of the rain forest do not necessarily require an explanation in refuge theory; species composition in forest communities in eastern Ecuador, regarded as representing a permanently wet *refugium*, had in fact apparently changed markedly during the Last Glacial Maximum (summarized in Clapperton

1993:146). It was concluded that the tropical rain forest constantly undergoes change, during interglaciations as well as during glaciations. The two viewpoints are probably both reasonable and not mutually exclusive. As will be seen, the archaeology of the Guianas yields dated evidences of forest fragmentation during the Holocene, both on the Coast and in the Hinterland.

The Andean Heritage
Introduction

It is generally accepted that man first entered South America over land from North America at a time when favorable conditions prevailed in the Isthmus of Panama. This is suggested by the distribution of certain fluted projectile points whose general characteristics indicate affiliation to the specialized big game Clovis point of New Mexico. Points of this description are known from Mexico (Di Peso 1955; Lorenzo 1953, 1964), Costa Rica (Snarkis 1979; Swauger and Mayer-Oakes 1952), Guatemala (Coe 1960), and Belize (Hester 1985; Kelly 1993). Their conventional time range, 11,500 - 11,000 b.p., has been narrowed recently to 11,200-10,900 b.p. (Hoffecker et al 1993). Claims for pre-Clovis occupations in the Americas have mostly been greeted with skepticism (Meltzer et al 1994; Lynch 1990; Morlan 1988; Grayson 1988 and others), though recent data from southern Chile seem to indicate a generalized hunting and food gathering economy there in excess of 12,000 years ago (eg. Dillehay 1984; see also *Guardian Weekly* Feb. 23, 1997). The associated stone-working technology included bifacial flaking, and pecking-and-grinding. The pre-Clovis debate therefore continues.

Points of Clovis affiliation are thought to have spread rapidly through South America, reaching the southern tip of Argentina by around 9000 B.C. (Bird 1969, 1988, 1993). A certain stemmed, fluted, round-shouldered type known from the earliest levels at Palli Aike Cave and Fells Cave in Argentina has been designated Magellan-1. Similar points have since been recovered in stratified deposits at Los Toldos, also in Argentina, and at El Inga in highland Ecuador (Bell 1960; Cardich 1987; Mayer-Oakes 1963). Scattered finds have been reported also from the Central and Western Cordilleras in Colombia, as well as from the Ecuadorian coast (Willey 1971:46). Bird (1969) reported a doubtful specimen from Uruguay.

Taken with the available dates from Fell's Cave (Bird 1988:Table 17), this distribution has suggested a direct and more or less rapid transit of the Andean Chain (Haynes 1964; Hester 1973; Lynch 1978; Lothrop 1961; Mayer-Oakes 1963; Sauer 1944; Willey 1971) by specifically highland-adapted groups (Mayer-Oakes 1963) who eschewed exploitation of the Lowland environment (Lothrop 1961; Lynch 1978:473). However, the implications of certain large, stemmed, unstemmed and, in one case, fluted, points from the Guiana area, early reviewed in the literature (Evans and Meggers 1960:21; Willey 1971:60) remain to be considered. Granted the narrow time range represented by the technology of the Clovis point, the occurrence of affiliated specimens in Guyana indicates that the earliest migrants into the southern continent did in fact readily and rapidly adapt to the lowland environment and indeed appear to have penetrated as far as the Western Guiana Littoral by about the time that their fellows had completed the transit of the Andean Chain. At around this time, the late Pleniglacial forest refuges, comprising a major west Amazonian refuge and several other medium-sized *refugia* in eastern areas, may have been recoalescing, Figure 2.3b. As the climate became wetter, water levels in the rivers began to rise. In this environment of relatively shallow streams and vast areas of open savanna, conditions for the long distance migration of small human groups living off the land would appear to have been optimal.

The earliest mention of what have since come, to be recognized as paleo-indigenous artifacts in the Guianas are two projectile points on quartz and jasper, respectively, which, according to Roth (1924:170., Pl.36A), were recovered in the northwest coastal area of Guyana, Figure 2.5a,b.

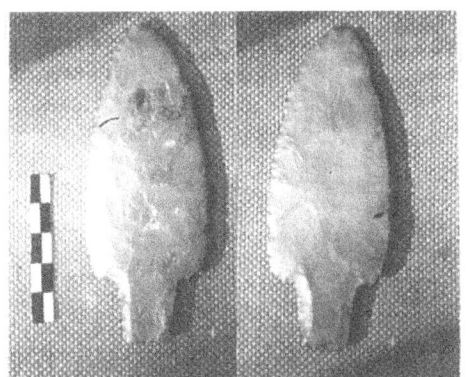 

Figure 2.5a,b. a. Northwestern Guyana. Magellan-1 type projectile point on crystal quartz. b. Northwestern Guyana. Projectile point on jasper, with channel scar on one face of the stem.

The outstanding attribute of the Magellan-1 type point is its size. It measures 110 x 44 x 6 mm, the tip having broken off approximately 6 mm below the point. The contracting stem is 20 mm long. The blade is ovoid-triangulate in outline with rounded shoulders. Flutes are 42 and 30 mm long, respectively, 11 - 13 mm wide, imparting a biconcave cross section to the stem, which displays the Clovis-Folsom trait of lateral grinding. The remarkable thinness achieved by percussion flaking on such a large specimen is evidently attributable to the flaking properties of crystal quartz when contrasted with other kinds of rock materials employed in flint knapping. In Clovis technology, a point manufactured from obsidian was not flaked as thin as points of equal length manufactured from chalcedony or crystal quartz (Tankersley 1994; see also Bird 1969).

The other point from the Western Guiana Littoral, Figure 2.5b, is even larger. At 160 mm, its surviving length falls short of its original length by a centimeter or so. Its width at the waist is 47 mm, and thickness varies between 10 - 11 mm. The contracting stem is 22 mm long. Pendant tangs flare outwards, producing a distinctive blade contour. A shallow channel scar along one face of the stem is 26 mm long, 7 mm wide. The rock material is red jasper.

Probably referring to the time level represented by these large points of the Western Guiana Littoral is the blade-like scraper or knife from the Western Guiana Hinterland shown in Figure 2.6. The specimen, which is on red jasper, was dredged up in the Wenatnu River, which rises in the North Pakaraimas and empties into the Cuyuni River. It evidently represents the industry of large, plano-convex scrapers on red or green jasper reported by Cruxent (1971) in the Guiana Highlands. This tool constitutes something of an early postglacial horizon marker across northeast and east Brazil, with occurances

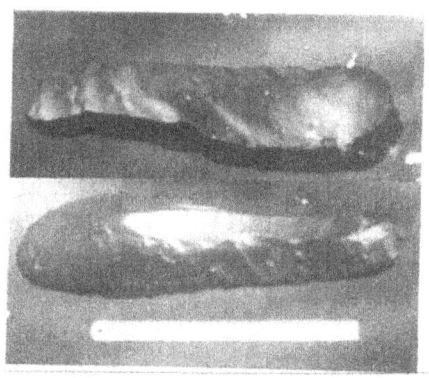

Figure 2.6. Scraper, Wenamu River, Guyana

in Pernambuco, Piaui, Minas Gerais, Goia, Mato Grosso and Sao Paulo, where it served a multitude of purposes, e.g., as scraper, knife, chopper, ax, polisher, nutting stone, anvil, etc. (Barbosa 1992:145). The type is known from the earliest level at El Inga, in Ecuador (Willey 1971:46, Figure 2.16g,h).

Also from the Western Guiana Hinterland is the lanceolate point with rounded base shown in Figure 2.7. Its surviving length is 85 mm, the original having probably exceeded 120 mm. It is 45 mm wide, 13 mm thick. Crudely chipped on a curved flake of green jasper, it remains asymmetrical in both profile and contour, which may account for its having fractured across the waist. It derives from the Puruni River, a tributary of the lower Mazaruni, where it was recovered in dredging operations. This provenience attests to the deep penetration of the river valleys of the Western Guiana Hinterland by paleo-indigenous groups exploiting the radial drainage of the Pakaraimas as water levels in these rivers began to rise toward the ending of the Pleistocene and the rain forest commenced to re-coalesce in phase with the prevailing moister conditions.

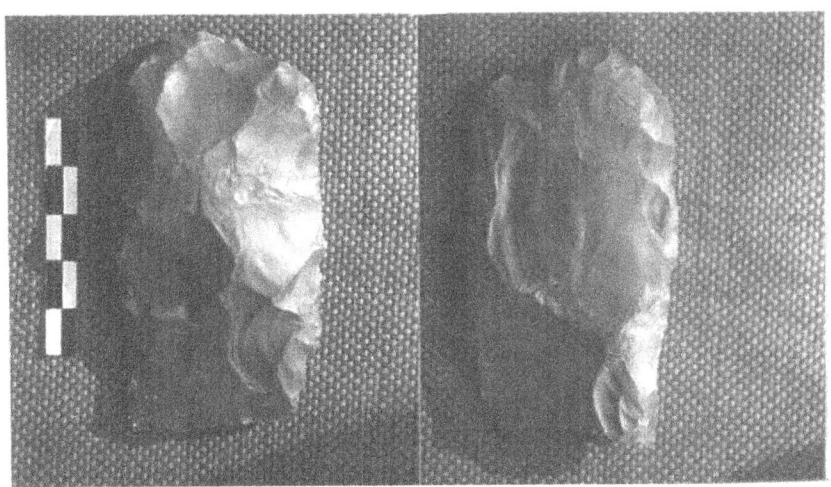

Figure 2.7. Puruni River, Guyana.

The reduction process of this type of point is distinctive. Comprehensive chipping on the obverse surface contrasts with a markedly cursory treatment of the reverse surface, which was only minimally modified by the removal of a few coarse flakes and some trimming of the edges. This treatment is reminiscent of certain lanceolate points of the Andean Ayampitín Complex. A long sequence on the punas of the Peruvian Central Sierra, commencing at between 9000 - 8000 B.C., includes two lanceolate types. One was bifacially chipped on chert, while the other, typically on chalcedony, exhibited chipping characteristics exactly similar to the Mazaruni specimen. This latter occurred at the very beginning of the sequence and disappeared during its final stages, while the former commenced near the middle of the sequence and survived to the end. As with the other points, the Mazaruni specimen differs from its Andean prototype only by virtue of its exceptional size. The Andean specimen was regarded by its excavator (Hurtado de Mendoza 1987:198) as apparently representing the survival of an ancient unifacial chipping technique. Together, these specimens represent a lanceolate projectile point horizon in South American prehistory whose sites have been encountered from the northern Andes to the southern tip of the continent and span contrasting elevational zones with the type site located at Ayampitín, in Argentina (Lumbreras 1974:32).

Also made on a curved flake, the specimen shown in Figure 2.8a measures 120 mm maximum diameter. The rock material is chalcedony, a concretionary quartzite deriving from the greenstone belt in northwestern Guyana and occurring also as far to the south as the Akawainna Mountains on the Essequibo River. Eroded nodules, the probable source of these points, occur also in streams in the Pakaraimas (Barron pers. comm. 1990). The specimen was dredged up in the Puruni River. Its pentagonal form is regarded as possibly a modification of the true leaf shape (Willey 1971:48, Figure 2-19 left). It is an undoubted early type in the Central Andes, dating at various sites there between 9500 and 5500 B.C. (Hurtado de Mendoza 1987:219, Pl. 2a; Lothrop 1961:118; McNeish 1971:164; see Evans and Meggers 1960: Pl. 8b). It occurs abruptly and in relative abundance around the middle of the Pedras Gordas sequence on the punas of the Peruvian Central Sierra and maintained its popularity into the most recent levels, i.e., more or less contemporaneously with the bifacial Ayampitín points (Hurtado de Mendoza 1987:219, Figure 10.1).

The point shown in Figure 2.8b was dredged up in the Ireng River in the North Rupununi Savannas near the Good Hope ranch (Evans and Meggers 1960:22, Pl. 8a). It is on red jasper, and is of composite contour. The surviving length, 144 mm, represents an original in excess of 165 mm. Maximum width at the waist is modified by four notches on each edge. Above the notches, the recurved blade tapers to a needle-like point. The edges end in pendent tangs. The 27 mm long stem is constricted at the neck, bulges gently and tapers to a round base. A specimen from the South Savannas, 80 mm long, 35 mm wide and 9 mm thick, on crystal quartz, is also bilaterally notched. Here the tangs are less well developed than in the larger specimen and only one edge of the stem bulges below the constricted neck. Other small specimens on jasper are known from the North Savannas and the Kopenang River.

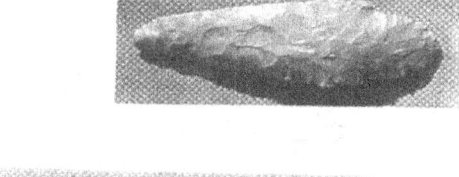

Figure 2.8a, b. Projectile points a, Puruni River, b, Ireng River, Guyana.

Evans and Meggers (1960:22) early pointed to the similarity of the large specimen from the Ireng River to certain points reported from early sites in coastal Peru, such as Pampa de los Fosiles and Pampa de Paijan. Recent work by Pelegrin and Chauchat (1993) provides a wealth of detail supporting the comparison, e.g., the elongated stem with convex contours, pendant tangs, the recurved blade edges chipped to a needle-like point, the characteristically large sizes (110 - 150 mm with variants as much as 220 mm) and odd specimens exhibiting notched edges. In replication experiment, the authors reconstructed the percussion flaking reduction process from a Chivateros-type biface through a leaf-shape preform to the characteristic Paijan point (1993: Figure 2). A single radiocarbon date at +/- 9000 b.p. was considered minimal. Willey (1971:57) regards the Pakian point complexes of the Peruvian north coast as dating at around 6000 - 5000 B.C., and as representing the low-elevation component in the pattern of seasonal transhumance that characterized one of his early Andean Hunting-Collecting tradition cultures.

If there is any substance in these comparisons between the Guiana and Andean points, then the time span represented ranges between 9500 - 4200 B.C., covering the Old South American Hunting tradition and the Andean Hunting-Collecting tradition in the chronological sequence for the Peruvian Highlands, or Preceramic Periods I - IV (Willey 1971:Figures 2-2, 3-8.). Granted the unequivocal affiliation of at least one of these points to the Clovis technological tradition, initial penetration of the Lowlands was evidently early. Large (+/-200 mm) triangular, elongated points on chalcedony with broad, fluted stems reported on the Rio Negro (Roosevelt et al 1996) suggest an affiliation with these otherwise unique points from Guyana. They, too, suggest that initiation of the regional sequence for the Guianas did not lag far behind the Peruvian.

Settlement pattern

The close typological relationship between these points from the Central Andes and the Western Guiana Hinterland appears to reflect the dispersion of the late Pleistocene forest refuges that have been postulated in explanation of the disjunct distributions of certain animal and plant species in northern South America.

Comparison of the Guianese and Andean points is aided by the fact that the rock materials universally employed in manufacture of the Guiana specimens -- red or green jasper or crystal quartz -- derive from specific occurrences in the Pakaraima Mountains, a relict block of Roraima Supergroup rocks spanning parts of the national territories of Guyana, Venezuela and Brazil and culminating in a tripartite border on Mount Roraima (2810 m). The Roraima Supergroup rocks comprise a thick sequence of sedimentary units overlying the crystalline rocks of the Guiana Shield. The underlying red or green jasper occurs no further west than 64°. Obviously, the very restricted occurrences of this jasper in the Guiana land mass was of extreme economic importance to the earliest migrants and indeed may have provided the *raison d'etre* for the initial peopling of the territory. The various types of projectile points made on this jasper in Guiana therefore are of uncommon diagnostic interest.

The economic alternative to this jasper, crystal quartz, is of even more restricted occurrence in the Roraima Highlands, being confined to the right bank of the upper Mazaruni River, off the eastern edge of the escarpment of the Roraima Formation in the area of the projection of that Formation to the southeast. One explanation of this very localized occurrence is that the highly siliceous, non-porous nature of the Formation rocks effectively blocked the passage of hydrothermal fluids originating in the underlying basement, at the same time contributing to their cooling and crystalization.

Quartz crystals primarily occur in veins or pegmatites, less frequently in eltivial, colluvial or alluvial deposits. Quartz dykes may be detected by the vigilant eye in ravines, streams or gravel beds, or encountered under varying depths of overburden. Thus, exploitation of this resource implies intimate knowledge of the terrain, at least semi-sedentary habitation and involves no specialized equipment (Weihrauch et al 1977:29). Projectile points made on crystal quartz and reported from sites as far apart as the Western Guiana Littoral and the South Rupununi Savannas doubtless derived from this source. Significantly, tools deriving directly from an Andean complex, characterized by rock materials such as obsidian (Ecuador) or basalt, chert and quartzite (Argentina) are so far unknown in Guianese assemblages.

The dispersion of the paleo-Indigenous tools cited above suggests that the routes of the earliest migrations followed the radial drainage of the Pakaraima Mountains from a core area centered on these strategic outcrops of jasper and quartz. Cruxent (1971:32) reports a workshop in the Guayana Highlands yielding large retouched flakes on red and green jasper with plano-convex scrapers similar to the specimen from the Wenamu River shown in Figure 2.6. Evidently, these all represent the same industry. To the north, however, Cruxent (1972, 1972a) reports an industry at Tupuken, near the confluence of the Yuruari and Cuyuni Rivers in which large, coarse flakes were produced by battering quartz and basalt cobbles against stone anvils.

From this core area, main routes led northward *via* the Wenamu River to the Cuyuni (on both of which streams tools of the paleo-Indigenes have been recovered) thence overland to the headwaters of the Barama River, which drains from the Imataka Mountains and leads *via* the Waini to the coast. Eastward, the Mazaruni, Cuyuni and Potaro Rivers have all yielded specimens of Early Preceramic tools. Another route led southward *via* the Ireng River and its tributary the Takutu, which empties into the Rio Branco.

Subsistence

The settlement pattern indicated by the dispersion of these workshops and the distinctive large projectile points that were produced in them suggests that the earliest migrations followed gallery forest, into major refuge areas in the ameliorating climatic conditions and rising water levels of the late Pleistocene. Unfortunately, the surviving materials mostly represent casual finds, though the recently excavated *Caverna da Pedra Pintada* in the vicinity of Mont Alegre on the lower Amazon left bank contained strata with material reported as spanning the paleo-Indigenous to late prehistoric periods, about 11,200 b.p. to A.D. 1450 (Roosevelt et al 1996). Interestingly, the large projectile points of the Western Guiana Hinterland were not represented in this inventory, suggesting the absence of fish ponds on dried out stream beds there. Elsewhere in the Guianas, as also in the Andes (e.g. see Lynch 1978:487) the available evidences permit setting the upper limit of the paleo-Indigenous period at around 7000 B.C., by which time the late Pleistocene big game had all become extinct. Due to the virtual absence of habitable caves which may have provided camp sites for the earliest Guyanese, the representative tools and implements invariably lack the spatial and temporal contexts that are indispensible for cultural reconstruction and intersite comparisons. Thus, notwithstanding the various typological similarities of the large Guyana points to the Andean points cited, in the absence of stratigraphic reference, few inferences can be drawn with respect to the subsistence system represented. The mere survival of Clovis/Magellan-1 projectile point technology on the Western Guiana Littoral does not in itself provide a sufficient reason for inferring big game hunting in lowland subsistence. It has been observed (Hester 1973) that since most of South America beyond the Andean Chain lies below 500 meters, its equatorial position ensured that much of the area occupied by the Guianas, Venezuela and Brazil would not have been particularly favorable for human occupation during the glacial maximum. On the other hand, early migrants entering South America by way of the Andes were able to follow the same environmental zone for several thousands of miles to the absolute southern tip of the continent, hunting big game that were adapted to specific environmental zones. In this scenario, movement of only 100 miles or so to the east or to the west would have been sufficient to force such hunters to enter quite different environmental zones and to have changed their economy. The large Guiana points certainly suggest a shift from big game to some other form of hunting.

Nonetheless, bones of a late Pleistocene megafauna are now known from lowland sites such as Taima-Taima and Muaco in western Venezuela and even from the Pitch Lake on the Island of Trinidad, this latter having then still been connected to the South American mainland (e.g. see Harris 1976). Thus, their presence in appropriate lowland habitats may be inferred elsewhere in northern South America, at least onto the end of the paleo-Indigenous period. This notwithstanding, the size, shape and weight of the Guiana points suggest that they are unlikely ever to have been employed in hunting a late Pleistocene megafauna. Thus, morphologically, they lend a measure of support to Hester's hypothesis. The sizes of these points suggest that in the ameliorating climate of the late glacial (p.58.i) in which was initiated the cultural sequence in the Guianas, the overwhelming subsistence emphasis involved other forms of protein capture. By around 6000 - 5000 years ago, the climate was apparently already comparable to that prevailing in modern conditions, for at around this time torrential rainfall is indicated by massive sediment transport at various locations in the Pakaraima Mountains (Schubert 1986). In the meantime the sea had attained its present level along the Guiana Coast. Extrapolating from present day dry-season conditions, the attenuated watercourses of hinterland areas at the end of the Pleistocene had been characterized by stretches of exposed riverbed alternating with permanent riverbed ponds and shallow cataracts, both extremely rich in fish fauna. These streams now were seasonally bank-full, necessitating an altered pattern of exploitation, as seems indicated by the modified sizes of the associated projectile points. On the upper Orinoco right bank, the Provincial-1 site, around 20 km downstream from Puerto Ayacucho, yielded a radiocarbon date on a hearth sample at 9020 +/- 100 b.p., or 7070 B.C. (Barse 1989:254). Associated was a fragment of ground stone interpreted as possibly representing the butt end of a stone ax. Upriver, at La Culebra, near its confluence with the Cataniapo, stratified excavations recovered flake scrapers on locally occurring crystal quartz as well as two small, contracting-stem projectile points on, respectively, pink jasper and a grayish-black grainy chert, both rock materials being reported as non-local. La Culebra is estimated to date between 5000 - 4000 B.C. (Barse 1989:357), Figure 2.9.

Figure 2.9. L. Culebra, Upper Orioco
(after Barse 1989: Figure 19).

On comparative grounds, their excavator very plausibly estimate these points to date at between 6500 and 4000 B.C. In due course, these small points would be universally distributed in the Guianas, for example on the Canaima, Rupununi and Sipaliwini Savannas. The location of the La Culebra site on the upper Orinoco, far to the west of the only geologically attested occurrences of jasper in Western Guiana, already suggests the system of interdependence between *terra firme* and the surrounding alluvium which would characterize cultural evolution throughout the Archaic and into the horticultural period.

The Archaic period is negatively defined in North American archaeology on the absence of either a specialized big-game hunting adaptation or a sedentary horticultural adaptation. In the tropical forest lowlands, by contrast, where a big game hunting adaptation has never been demonstrated, the Archaic is not so readily distinguished from the preceding paleo-Indigenous stage. Purely on the grounds of stone tool technology, the [Andean] chronology of the large points discussed above suggests that, with the higher water levels that characterized the now drastically changing coastal and hinterland environments (p. 59: ii, iii above), these large points ceased to be manufactured around 4200 B.C. in favor of the various small stemmed or unstemmed points on red or green jasper that characterize the Archaic in the Guianas. Should this prove to have been in fact the case, it would accord quite nicely with the available environmental data, which indicate that, by this time, both on the Coast and in the Hinterland, the late glacial landscape had changed beyond recognition, necessitating certain critical shifts in subsistence technology. Where the find spots of their characteristic tools suggest that the camp sites of the paleo-Indigenes were located along the attenuated streams of the late Pleistocene and the early Holocene, these sites now were submerged by the rising water levels of the mid-Holocene. Such now submerged riverain camp sites are known in the Archaic.

Adaptation to the late Pleistocene environment thus seems to have involved a basic shift in protein capture from big game hunting in the Andes to generalized hunting and collecting in the lowlands. Migrating groups carried Andean mental templates in stone working eastwards. The prevailing low sea levels and attenuated watercourses would have permitted fish to be taken with hand-held spears in shallow pools and cataracts dotting the dried out riverbeds. But though attested in Archaic rock art (e.g. Hurault et al 1963), there is as yet no evidence of paleo-Indigenous spear fishing in the Guianas. Peaking of the sea level rise around 4000 B.C., combined with now wetter climates and increased runoff, resulted in enhanced depths in the rivers and submergence of the riverbed pools, enforcing a modified fishing technology. The timing of this shift appears to have varied greatly, perhaps depending on prevailing water levels. Thus, whereas the new small points are already in evidence on the upper Orinoco River during the eighth to seventh millennium B.C., (Barse 1990) the large, Andean type points survived in the streams of western Guiana well into the fifth millennium B.C. The small, stemmed points from the Mouth of the Amazon show the diet there to have derived mainly from plants, fish, reptiles, mollusks, birds and large mammals. This represents much the same diet as in the Itaparica Tradition, which, characterized by the large, unifacial bladelike scrapers shown at Figure 2.6, was spreading over the eastern tropical parklands of Brazil after around 11,000 b.p. (Barbosa 1992; Schmitz 1987). By contrast, when compared with their Andean counterparts, the large sizes of the bifacial points from the Western Guiana Hinterland are difficult to reconcile with the notion of hunting the small and characteristically cryptic terrestrial mammals of the tropical forest. At lengths ranging between 11 - 17 cm, they would have been excessively vulnerable to impact fracture with no compensating advantage in efficiency. Very likely, they served some more specialized purpose, as seems hinted at in their very shape.

The incompatability between these large points with terrestrial hunting in the tropical forest environment is best illustrated by two comparisons. The first is with the Magellan-1 point, the prototype of one of the earliest of the Guiana specimens. The formal conservatism and wide dispersion of this point type suggests optimum efficiency for taking big game at its known size range of 6 - 8 cm. At sizes approaching double this range, as in the Guiana specimens, efficiency in hunting the late Pleistocene terrestrial megafauna can be expected to have declined correspondingly.

The second comparison is based on Flenniken's (1985:273) replication experiments on post-impact fracture patterns in a number of points of Magellan-1 size range. Eleven specimens measuring between 5.5 - 7.0 cm were mounted on hand-held spears and employed to dispatch two 75 kg adult male goats. The results showed that 72.7 % of the damage sustained by these points occurred in or very close to the shaft area, and that *all fractures resulted from artifact bending*. Notwithstanding the very much smaller sizes of the goats in Flenniken's experiment when contrasted with a large late Pleistocene mammal, the results are comparable with fracture patterns on typical Magellan-1 points from Fell's Cave and El Inga (Bird 1969:57), in both of which cases the nature and position of the fractures related to the overall form, relative thinness and manner of hafting of the points. By contrast, in spite of their unusual length, not one of the surviving Andean type points from the Guianas exhibits damage to the basal area. They all sustained damage, if at all, only to the tip. Since game animals of the tropical forest rarely exceed the weight of the goats in the Flenniken experiment, the question of the purpose for which these large points of the Guianas were conceived remains to be addressed.

This question would appear a good deal less problematic were the points interpreted as having once been hafted to fish spears. A wealth of fish spears, fish traps, and stone projectile points are represented in the Archaic petroglyph inventory of the Guianas (Brown 1873; Dubelaar 1982, 1986; Evans and Meggers 1960: Figure 86b; Farabee 1916; Im Thurn 1883:Pl.ix; de Valencia et al 1987:Pls. 162, 292, 295; Wallace 1889; Williams 1979a, 1985, 1994). Line sinkers recovered in Archaic contexts indicate use of the cadell in the shallow inshore waters of the Western Guiana Littoral commencing well before the sea had attained its present level (6885 + /- 85 b.p. SI 5075) (Williams 1981). Fish protein thus appears to have underpinned Archaic subsisence from the earliest period and may represent the survival of paleo-Indigenous spear fishing on the dried out riverbeds of the end of the Pleistocene.

An Archaic petroglyph in Guyane française depicts a fish spear associated with an identifiable and popular fish species, the haimara (*Hoplias malabaricus*) (Hurault et al 1963:Figure 12). Spear fishing by lamplight is widely described during the nineteenth century. On the Amazon, Bates (cited in Smith 1981:51) described the activity as illuminated by flaming torches of green bark stripped from palm fronds (i.e., palm bast primed with beeswax). Lumps of molten beeswax, the archaeological correlates of such torches, occur in an Archaic context on the Western Guiana Littoral (Williams 1981:27), Figure 2.10. Elsewhere, spear fishing has been described by Roth (1924:192), Gillin (1948:828) and Smith (1981:51). Smith described a metal-tipped trident, the gig, 2.5 m long and used with modern torches to take the same fish species as is described in the petroglyph from Guyane française, Figure 2.11. In the past, such points were made of wood. What preceded this form is not known and, according to Smith, the archaeological record is unlikely to provide an answer.

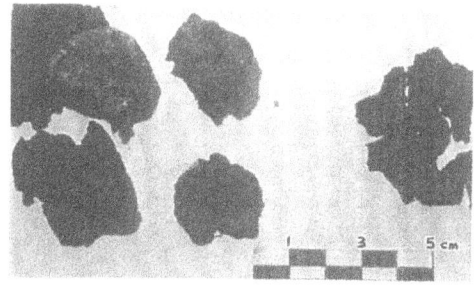

Figure 2.10. Barabina shell mound. Beeswax residues from a palm-bast flambeau.
Figure 2.11. Itacoatiara, lower Amazon. The gig (*after Smith 1981: Figure 4.5*).

In fact, it seems that, as described by Smith, the characteristics of the gig might themselves provide a credible answer to the question of the unusual sizes of the paleo-Indigenous projectile points from Western Guiana. The gig is weighted distally not only by its three metal points, each 10 cm long, but also by a pronounced bulge emphasized by a compensating tapering of the proximal end of the shaft. The weight distribution of this implement is thus overwhelmingly concentrated at its fore-end, which seems more compatible with vertical rather than with horizontal use. Grasped around mid-point of the shaft, the fisherman with upraised arm, representing a total height of approximately 2.0 m, man and implement, allowed the point a vertical range of 1.0 - 1.5 m before it entered the water surface.

The Guiana specimens exhibit weights ranging between 29.5 - 102.4 g (mean 57.6 g). In its present damaged condition, the lightest specimen, the Paijan point (39.5 g), is roughly the maximum size of the standard Paijan point of the Peruvian north coast (11 - 15 cm), usually made on rhyolite. Its excavators (Pelegrin and Chauchat 1993) themselves interpret the classic Paijan point as a specialized fishing implement, having never encountered it in archaeological association with bones of a late Pleistocene megafauna. Since the Guiana and Rio Negro points are all considerably heavier than the Paijan specimen, a spear fitted with one or other of them would probably have been weighted as effectively as a modern gig and been just as efficient on the vertical or near vertical trajectory that was required for fishing the shallow hinterland pools and cataracts of the late Pleistocene and early Holocene.

Thus, when comparison is made with modern spear fishing, a better "fit" would seem to result concerning the probable function of these outsize points of the paleo-Indigenes than when comparison is made with conventional points employed in terrestrial hunting in a tropical forest environment. The evidence is only presumptive, but combined with the independently attested paramountcy of fish as a protein resource on both the Archaic and horticultural time levels, it does seem to suggest that the prototype of the modern fish spear may have been a paleo-Indigenous weapon fitted with a point designed by both weight and shape for vertical travel over a distance of just a few centimeters. The invariably minimally damaged condition of these points upon recovery and the total absence of the basal fractures that would have resulted from bending upon impact with terrestrial game animals of even moderate sizes, seem to support our hypothesis of their use on fish spears.

Thus, use of the term paleo-Indian in the sense of the big game hunting economies of North America and the Andes is unwarranted at present in the tropical forest lowlands, where early post-glacial adaptation was to a radically different environment. At this time of forest fragmentation and attenuated river discharge, human groups appear to have established their camp sites adjacent to the riverbed ponds and cataracts of *terra firme*, where, as in the present-day dry season, the shallow, teaming waters are readily exploited by the fish spear. Therefore, much of the material remains of these pioneers was deposited on a horizon of sandbanks, riverine islands or low, riverbank outcrops which, in due course, were permanently submerged by the higher water levels of the middle and late Holocene. This is mainly where they are recovered at the present time, during the dredging operations of miners and rarely, so far as is known, in caves such as were occupied by their fellows at higher latitudes. These important adaptive differences are recognized in the term *paleo-Indigene*, which seems to us to carry specific connotations of ancestry and continuity.

Sustained paleo-Indigenous exploitation of the unique jasper exposures in the Pakaraimas yields a readily identified settlement pattern deriving from the biotic poverty of the area. This poverty enforced long-distance expeditions down to the biotically rich river valleys and gallery forests of the Pakaraima drainage. As has been seen, occasional fishing forays are in evidence even as far afield as the fossil coastline and its estuaries. These kinds of evidences carry implications of a demographic nature for groups pioneering the settlement of the Guianas. As presently known, their tool distributions indicate that, residentially, these pioneers were tethered to some of the edaphically poorest territory in the region. The present Patamona population has been described as typical of developing countries. It is characterized by a population pyramid with a broad base and narrow apex indicating high fertility and mortality rates and low life expectancy (Dangour and Ismail 1995). It seems highly unlikely that the paleo-Indigenous ancestors of the Patamona could have enjoyed a significantly different status as regards diet and nutrition in the biotically poor North Pakaraimas where their remains are well distributed. It will be seen that the techno-economic infrastructure of these apparently small but mobile paleo-Indigenous peoples was inherited and vastly expanded by their Archaic successors, whose enhanced mobility in a changing landscape in due course triggered the occupation of more or less the entire Guiana land mass, Figure 3.8. The indicated evolutionary continuum in this economically strategic area survives in the cultural memory of its present occupants, who provide a unique account (Whitehead 1996) of the meeting of first farmers and hunter-gatherers, with a reconstruction of subsequent relationships of, first, collaboration and, finally, integration.

3. PEOPLES OF THE TROPICAL FOREST ARCHAIC

Demography

Warao Pioneers on the Western Guiana Littoral

The Southeastern Subzone. As the sea level continued to rise along the Western Guiana Littoral, populations occupying favorable niches were necessarily small, comprising bands of perhaps no more than two or three extended families. The earliest known shell mound, Piraka, on the edge of the low, broken coastline of the Southeastern Subzone, measured only 11.4 x 11.0 x 1.8 m. Figures 3.1, 3.3.

Figure 3.1. Piraka shell mound. First excavated in 1877 and again in 1987, this mound has now fallen victim to indiscriminate logging.

The Piraka site was occupied initially around 7230 +/- 100 b.p. (Beta 27055). Settlement was initiated at the successor Kabakaburi mound 5340 +/- 100 b. p. (Beta 32188) suggesting the optimum lifespan of the Piraka mound was just under 2000 years. This compares well with the securely dated lifespan of the Barabina mound on the Northwestern Subzone, which, though areally larger, exhibits a similar depth of refuse representing 3000 years of accumulation.

Minimum growth rate of the Piraka mound, 0.85 mm/yr, indicates that accumulation of each 20 cm stratigraphic level represents around 170 years, or 8.8 human generations at an average 19.8 years per generation (Pianka 1974: Table 4.2). Estimated mortality thus ranged between 0.5 - 2.3 individuals per generation. At an estimated average band size of 15 individuals throughout the period, this gives a mortality rate of around 79 per thousand.

The skeletal sample comprised four adult males, two adult females, one of advanced and the other of undetermined age, six sub-adult or young adult (15 -21 yr) females, five infants and an adult of undetermined sex. Age of the oldest individual was > 50 yr. Age and sex determinations derived from standard non-metrical indicators (Brothwell 1981; Ubelaker 1989). Numbers in each age group are given in Table C.

Table C. Piraka shell mound. Skeletal sample by age groups

18 mos +/- 6 mos	2
6 yr +/- 21 mos	3
13 - 17 yr	1
15 - 21 yr	5
> 21 yr	6
> 50 yr	1

These data do not permit an estimate of life expectancy at birth, though the figure was evidently below 30 years. A sample of 51 individuals from the horticulturist Tingi Holo Ridge site on the Eastern Guiana Littoral, occupied between 1150 and 970 +/- 50 b. p., yielded a life expectancy figure at birth of 28 years, which Khudabux (1991:56) compared with a Late Woodland figure of 22 years. Most deaths there occurred very young (0 - 5 yr) or during the middle years (15 - 40 yr). In light of contrasts in the respective modes of production and differences in carrying capacity, the high mortality rate among horticulturists on the Eastern Guiana Littoral is of interest when compared with the Archaic Piraka population on the Western Guiana Littoral, both swampland communities subject to the changing environments of a fluctuating coastline.

In the sample from the Eastern Guiana Littoral, a high incidence of Harris lines indicating episodes of growth arrest that were associated with starvation or disease crises probably reflects seasonal fluctuations in the protein supply (Khudabux 1991). Cyclic fluctuation in the protein supply may be indicated on the Western Guiana Littoral as well. It is thought that a progressive decrease in annual bright sunshine for many consecutive years may be associated with decreased productivity at all levels of the food chain. Observed cyclic fluctuations in the shrimp catch there over an 11-year period are believed attributable to cyclic variations in annual mean sunshine (Persaud 1983), Figure 3.2a,b. A more short term cycle of periodicity in the shrimp catch appears to correlate with annual fluctuations in the discharge of the Essequibo River which negatively affected the sea bottom environment, Figure 3.2c. If this situation is extrapolated to the Archaic, the cyclic effect on primary productivity would have been compounded by archaeologically derived evidences of occasional prolonged drying out of the mudflats and consequent destruction of the mangrove epifauna which constituted the basic protein resource.

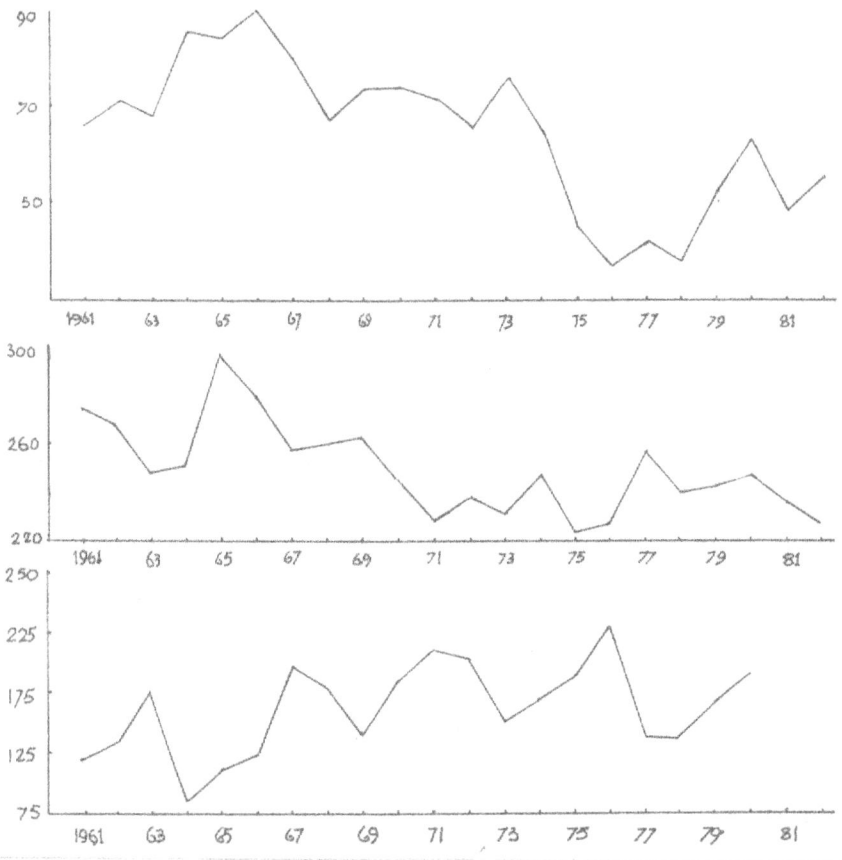

Figure 3.2a-c. Western Guiana Littoral. Annual or seasonal variations in shrimp catch, climate and river discharge (after Persaud 1983).

Chronic protein deficiency is indicated at the Piraka mound by virtue of the almost total reliance of its population on the small brackish-water snail, the Zebra Nerite (Puperita pupa). The impoverished diet that is implied by the accumulation of this almost pure deposit of a high-bulk, low-protein resource reflects the limited carrying capacity of this particular niche. Apart from sessile shellfish and crabs, the non-snail refuse included only beaks of wading birds. While the crab refuse implies the near proximity of exposed mudflats, the remains of wading birds suggest the diurnal penetration of the tides on the low, broken coastline of the southeastern swamp basin late in the sixth millennium B.C., Figure 3.3. Evidently, the bulk of dietary protein was provided more by collecting this minute snail off the mangrove roots than by inshore fishing, or, for want of adequate weapons, by hunting in the adjacent forest.

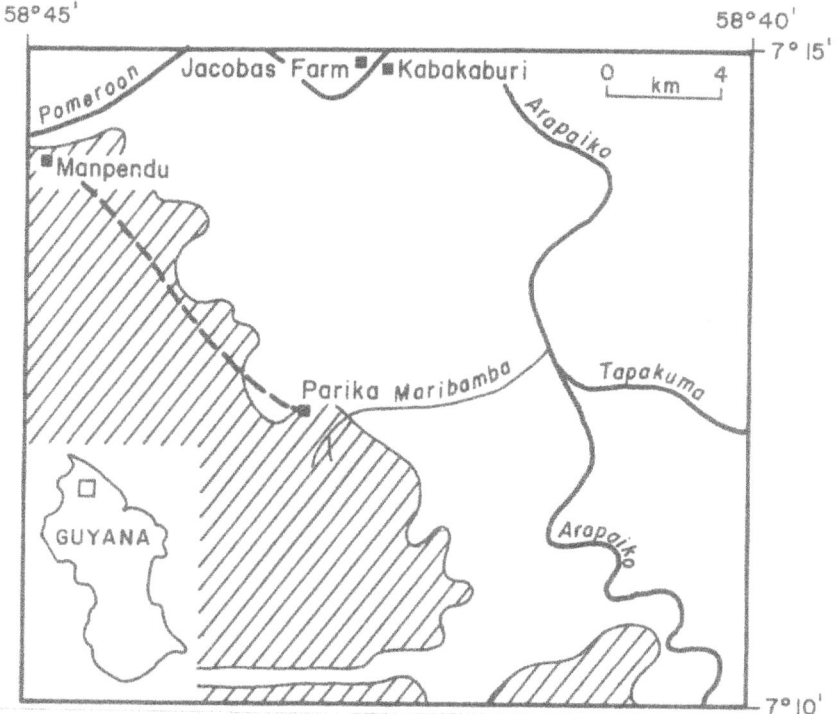

Figure 3.3. Piraka shell mound. Located directly on the Archaic shoreline, the site now is sequestered under rain forest ca. 65 km from the sea coast.

These factors appear to have been chronically limiting on population growth among this pioneering group, besides which the negative effects on its health status of virtually total reliance on a diet of nerites can be expected to have been severe. Notwithstanding sedentary occupation of the biotically rich swamp edge, their subsistence technology restricted the diet to sessile shellfish, crabs, and occasionally a ground-dwelling bird taken with a missile. On such a diet, it is unlikely that the recognized minimum five children at time of completed fertility (Howell 1976: Table 1) could ever have been realistically achieved or maintained. Further, in a population characterized by high recurrent mortality among young adult females (Table C), both the fertility rate and the crude birth rate can be expected to have remained permanently depressed.

The inherent inability of these shellfishers in any way to increase the productivity of the biota appears to have had the expected result of enforcing measures directed toward population regulation. Correlation between the numbers of infant deaths (5) and deaths of young adult females (5) in Table C seems to suggest attempts at population regulation. If this was achieved by means of prolonged lactation, then in such an impoverished group the strategem could have been life threatening to both mother and infant.

A correlation is suggested, through time, between periodically increased efficiency in cremation and intensity of consumption of unusual shellfish species such as the brackish-water Jamaica Lucine *(Lucina pectinatus)* and the freshwater snail *Ampullaria*, Figure 3.4. Accordingly, these are interpreted as famine options. Cremation efficiency was derived from the weight (g) of surviving parts or all of the cranium, femora and tibiae (representing the greatest volume of cortical bone in any given case) as a percentage of total bone residues per individual (Brothwell 1981:15). Sharp increases in cremation efficiency around the middle and ending of the occupation coincided with episodes of radical environmental change. The first appears to have been congruent with the freshwater climax of around 3300 B.C. which followed on culmination of the eustatic sea level rise as freshwater backup overcame the marine influence in the swamps. There is a corresponding critical decline in frequencies of the basic protein resource, the brackish-water Zebra Nerite. Simultaneously, the respective curves peak for consumption per level of Jamaica Lucine and Ampullaria. The second increase immediately preceded abandonment of the mound in conditions of an advancing shoreline and the irreversible disappearance of the mangroves (and the Zebra Nerite) locally. With the seaward advance of the shoreline, new mounds of nerites, e.g. at Kabakaburi, Warapana and Siriki, accumulated downstream. The relatively immense dimensions of these mounds implies consistent population expansion among later groups enjoying apparently more benign health conditions with the seaward advance of the mudflats.

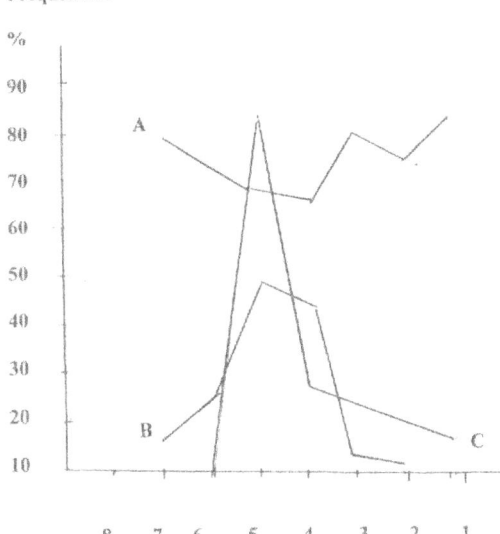

A. Mean combined weights of cremated cranium, femora and tibiae/level as a percentage of total bone residues/individual/level.

B. *Lucina pectinatus* frequencies/level.

C. *Ampullaria sp* frequencies/level

Figure 3.4. Piraka. Cremation efficiencies.

The Northwestern Subzone. A small deposit of shellfish measuring 12 x 20 x 0.3 m underlies the Archaic shell mound at Barabina, in the Northwestern Subzone. Designated Zone iv, it is overlain by a thin (0.5 cm) sterile layer (Zone iii) representing brief abandonment of the site not long after its initial occupation, around 6885 +/- 85 b.p. (SI 5075). This sterile layer is covered by refuse appertaining to the period of culmination of the sea level rise (Zone ii). The surface of Zone ii was subject to extreme weathering following on the abandonment of the mound. This surface is overlain by refuse of the horticulturist period, Zone i.

Refuse of the pioneering occupants rests directly on lateriticclay overlying the amphibole schist of the basement. It comprises mainly shells of *Strombus pugilis*,

Lucina pectinatus, Modiolus americanus and *Puperita pupa*, the deposit being overwhelmingly dominated by the first two. At this time, the Zebra Nerite was of relatively rare occurrence in the swamps. This being a brackish-water creature, the dominance of conch and clam at maximum sizes at inception of the deposit would seem to suggest the hypersaline environment that is thought to have preceded culmination of the eustatic rise in the sea level along the Guiana Coast. A pollen section at Matwaribo, in Suriname, indicates a progressive upward increase in local populations of *R mangle*, the most salt tolerant of mangrove species, as the sea rose to its present level, Table D.

Table D. Comparative frequencies of *Rhizophora* species at the culmination of the Holocene sea level rise on the Eastern Guiana Littoral.

Depth (cm)	R racemosa	R harrisonii	R mangle	R type (%)
105	10.1%	49.5%	32.5%	8.1%
315	9.4%	58.1%	24.3%	8.1%
585	8.3%	65.5%	18.6%	7.6%

Source: Roeleveld (1969)

The skeletal sample from Zone iv included three primary and five secondary burials. The primary burials, all tightly flexed, showed no consistency in deposition or orientation. All were recovered in the clay substratum (pH 7.5) in the area of greatest concentration of postmolds, suggesting interment in the earth floor of the associated dwelling. The secondary burials included a bone bundle comprising the long bones of a gracile individual. Once, apparently, these bones had been lashed together, Figure 3.5.

Figure 3.5. Bone bundle with storage pit, Barabina shell mound.

Bone bundles have been recovered in coastal contexts in preceramic Panama (McGimpsey 1956, 1958) and Ecuador (Stothert 1985). The Panama site, a shell mound at Cerro Mangote, returned a date at 6810 +/- 100 b.p., which just overlaps the youngest date in the sequence from Las Vegas, a local variant of early Tropical Forest Culture on the Santa Elena peninsula of south coastal Ecuador. The roughly contemporaneous date of the Barabina bone bundle appears to confirm Stothert's interpretation of the dispersion of this burial type as representing a broad affiliation between cultures along the coasts of Western Panama, Colombia and northern Peru, evident in northwestern South America perhaps as far back as 8000 b.p. Thus, affiliations already indicated by stone tool typology between the Andes and the lowlands on the Archaic time level may explain the occurrence of this distinctive trait on the Western Guiana Littoral. It may be worth recalling, on a somewhat later time level, the linguistic parallels cited by Granberry (1993:41) between the Timucua language of Florida and Warao-related languages of northwestern Amazonia, as well as certain resemblances thought to exist between Waroan and the pre-Maipuran Arawak languages of the upper Rio Negro. As has been seen, it is thought that Warao may very well be an extremely ancient language in Amazonia. Further, Wilbert (1972:113) cites various similarities between Waroan shamanic cults and those of central and southwestern North America. The Warao themselves claim a traditional history dating to a time, seven or eight thousand years ago, when the island of Trinidad still formed part of South America (Wilbert 1985). Our evidences of sedentary occupation at the Piraka and Barabina shell mounds a good thousand years in advance of culmination of the sea level rise lend strong support to Warao cultural memory.

The mixture of primary and secondary burials provides a further point of comparison between Barabina, Las Vegas and Cerro Mangote. At Barabina, heterogeneous burials did not survive into later levels. This distinguishes the mortuary behaviors of the pioneer occupants of the hill from all subsequent occupants. Secondary burial in Zone iv was represented by the disarticulated and co-mingled bones of four adults and an infant whose articulated cervical vertebrae suggest incomplete decomposition of the corpse before its redeposition. The secondary head burial of these pioneers represented an individual with complete sutural closure whose dental arcades exhibited wear consistent with artisanal use of the median incisors, caries on the second upper premolar, peridontal disease and third molar deficiency. High carbohydrate diets, such as were available to these swamp dwellers in the Moriche palm (*Mauritia flexuosa*) promote the formation of plaque, which is associated with both caries and peridontal disease (Wing and Brown 1979:89). Dental caries and peridontal disease have been attributed to nutritional stress and Vitamin C deficiency. A high incidence of carious teeth has been associated with Harris lines among horticulturists on the Eastern Guiana Littoral

(Khudabux 1989). Three cases of third molar deficiency were reported there in a sample of 20 individuals (Tacoma 1963). Zone ii yielded 18 burials; 14 coincided with the time of the culmination of the eustatic sea level rise, Table E.

Table E. Barabina shell mound. Burial frequencies, upper limb flexure/level; orientation

Level (cm)	Burial no.	Degree of upper limb flexure						Orientation
		Flexed		Tightly flexed		Semi-flexed		
		l	r	l	r	l	r	
40 - 60	B-22					150°	150°	280°
60 - 80	B - 07							disturbed
	B - 13					90°	180°	270°
	B - 23					60°	170°	270°
	B - 27					140°	140°	287°
	B - 34	30°				140°	140°	40°
	B - 37							
	B - 38					125°	90°	55°
	B - 42							280°
	B - 43	85°	90°					269°
	B - 55						180°	270°
	B - 56					120°	80°	265°
	B - 57					130°	70°	270°
	B - 65					170°	--	245°
	B - 69					120°	120°	270°
80-100	B - 01			10°	10°			210°
	B - 36	20°	30°					270°
						90°	180°	360°
100-150	B - 02	50°	30°					270°
	B - 03	60°	--			130°		225°
	B - 04							300°
	B - 16	10°	90°					130°
	B - 26							bone bundle
	B - 30							360°
	B - 39							268°
	B - 80							head burial

A shift in degree of flexure of the upper limbs corresponds with the time of culmination of the sea level rise. Simultaneously, there is a change in orientation, with the head of the deceased now pointing toward the west.

Cremation is introduced. This shift in burial practice indicates re-occupation of the hill, after a relatively brief period of abandonment, by newcomers whose tenure proved in the event long-lived. Progressive increases in burial frequencies per level among this later group may have been a function of unregulated population increase within the limited confines of the hill top. The successors of the pioneer occupants of the shell midden thus exhibited marked differences in deposition and orientation of the dead from their predecessors. At the same time, the burial mode sequence of these later arrivals itself displays a succession in which an earlier indifference to orientation is replaced by the practice of orienting the head of the deceased toward the precise direction of the setting sun (2700). Invariably now upper limbs are semi-flexed. The sequence seems to indicate a close relationship between conditions of environmental stress associated with the culmination of the sea level rise, high mortality, and the apparent influx of new migrants. However, despite the shift in the depositional pattern and the orientation of the head, continuity in the burial mode, notably the practice of cremation, suggests a consanguineal relationship between the more recent migrants and their hosts. Orientations of the majority of burials now oscillate between the solstices, interments having corresponded with the dry-season months, January to April, and August to December. No interments correspond to the rainiest months, May to July, Figure 3.6.

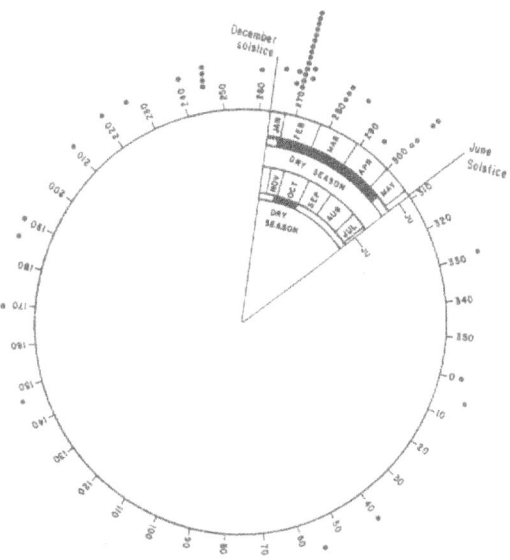

Figure 3.6. Barabina shell mound. Correlation of burial orientations, solstitial points and mean monthly rainfall. Burials concentrate in the annual dry seasons, January-May; October-November.

As the rivers begin flooding with the commencement of the first rains in May, fish migrate to shallow water up the creeks, beyond the tidal reach. Fishing activity in the mainstream is suspended. A consistent lack of burials during these months, over a period of millennia, suggests that these specialist fishers migrated inland with the fish during the rains.

Settlement pattern
The Coast

As has been seen, sedentary occupation of the Western Guiana Littoral preceded by over a thousand years the culmination of the eustatic sea level rise. By around 7,200 b.p., a small group was already in occupation at Piraka, on the low, broken coastline of the Southeastern Subzone. Around 200 years later another small group was in occupation at Barabina Hill, in the Northwestern Subzone. The coastline there was somewhat different from that of the present. The open grass savannas of the late Pleistocene, now being slowly covered by the encroaching sea, were cut by rivers up which the advance of the sea was introducing a new marine to brackish flora and fauna (p.59,iii). Shellfish species represented in the refuse of the pioneers there were the Caribbean Oyster (*Crassostrea rhizophorae* Guild.), the Fighting Conch (*Strombus pugilis*), the Jamaica Lucine (*Lucina pectinatus*), the Tulip Mussel (*Modiolus americanus*), the Zebra Nerite (*Puperita pupa*) and the Mangrove Land Crab (*Ucides cordatus*). These shellfish occurred at the optimum sizes that would be expected in the hypersaline environment that immediately preceded the culmination of the sea level rise. Large oyster shells were fused into glasslike concretions that are absent in later deposits, which had accumulated in a less saline environment. Their individual valves attained maximum diameters of up to 110 mm. Their dominance in the deposit evidences the ease with which these mollusks were procured relative to other available protein resources. Compared with fish, for example, which require apparatus of some kind for their capture, these shellfish were simply collected off the roots of the expanding stands of mangroves. Crab refuse likewise occurred in maximum densities, indicating the near proximity of exposed mudflats. This new and abundant supply of high quality protein undoubtedly explains the unprecedented attractiveness of coastal settlement in the centuries immediately preceding the culmination of the sea level rise.

At the contemporary Piraka shell mound in the Southeastern Subzone, the environment was brackish rather than saline, with the brackish-water Zebra Nerite therefore constituting the principal protein resource. The marked differences in local salinity levels along this stretch of coast probably were attributable to the close proximity of the estuary of the Essequibo River, then much wider than at present and apparently still encompassing the area occupied by the Piraka mound. The Essequibo is the *Rio Dulce* of early navigations along the "Wild Coast," famed for its freshwater discharge into the Atlantic well beyond its estuary (Benjamin 1982:30).

The periodic effect of this discharge on the marine food chain has been noted (p.80).

With the gradual rise of the post-glacial sea across the gently sloping (0.05 %) shelf, the steadily receding coastline created a shallow lagoon bounded to the south by the crescent of emergent rocks of the Guiana Shield. To the northwest of the Moruka River (the Northwestern Subzone) this crescent was fringed by scattered outcrops that formed those forested islands in the sediment basin which certain early observers perceptively considered to be erosional remnants of an ancient continental coastline. To the southeast of the Moruka River, towards the Essequibo estuary (the Southeastern Subzone) the rocks of the Guiana Shield were fringed by remnants of coarse Tertiary White Sands that formed low, forested islands on the edge of the swamps. As noted above, the Northwestern and Southeastern Subzones of the Western Guiana Littoral exhibit contrasting potentials for human subsistence. They cover, respectively, 3500 km^2 and 600 km^2, Figure 3.7a,b. Table A.

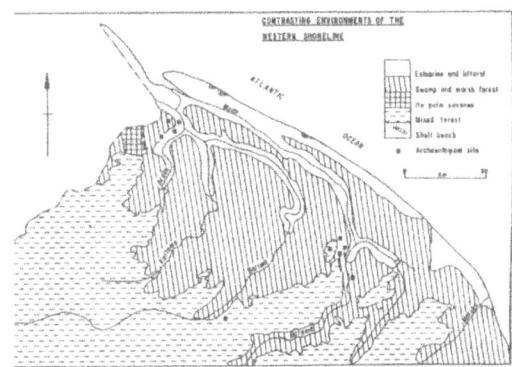
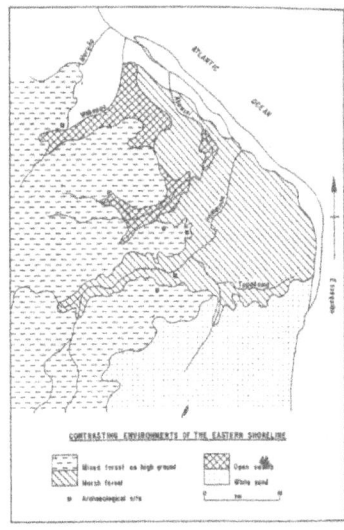

Figure 3.7a,b. The Western Guiana Littoral. **a.** Northwestern Subzone, **b.** Southeastern Subzone

Before the sea had attained its present level, it was theoretically possible to journey continuously within sight of land in this shallow lagoon from southern Trinidad to the Mouth of the Essequibo River and thus, by extension, to the Rupununi Savannas in the far south. This possibility seems endorsed by intrusive occurrences in the Trinidad Banwari Trace shell mound of artifacts thought to have been manufactured on Guiana greenstone. Appropriately, the initial date for Banwari Trace is 7180 +/- 80 b.p. (Harris 1976:37, 39, 40, 49). Interestingly, a large, stemmed, trianguloid point from eastern Trinidad, on local brown chert but regarded as comparable to the Guyana specimens, has been assigned in Trinidad archaeology to a time before the separation of that island from the South American mainland, though its similarity to specimens made after 6000 B.C. has been recognized (Hoffman and Lynch 1990).

With the formation of the Orinoco Delta at probably around 8000 b.p. (Van Andel 1967), backup commenced along its great tributary, the Barima River which, with its tributaries the Kaituma and Aruka, today drains the greater portion of the Northwestern Subzone. The gradual process of backup slowly transformed the shallow lagoons of the Western Guiana Littoral into mangrove-fringed freshwater swamps. Tectonic subsidence, increasing in magnitude westward between the Essequibo and Orinoco estuaries (Brinkman and Pons 1968) resulted in continual subsidence of these mangroves and consequent formation of the immense peat deposits that now characterize the Northwestern Subzone of the swamp basin. To the east of the Moruka River, a deposit of peaty clay stretching to the Essequibo Coast was formed in the Southeastern Subzone of the swamp basin.

As the rising sea initially penetrated the streams of the sediment basin, potable water became limiting. Human exploitation of the abundant brackish-water epifauna of the mangrove rhizophorae was possible only in proximity to natural springs or to the headwaters of creeks draining the emergent rocks of the crystalline basement. Differential deposition of shellfish species in the food refuse and intersite variations in their respective sizes and volumes indicate that the marine influence in the sediment basin lasted in places as much as seven hundred years, after which, as the influence of runoff supervened, the environment freshened and the intertidal mudflats were converted into the seasonally inundated grass savannas of the present day. Thus, the Western Guiana Littoral is by no means a homogeneous stretch of swamplands, but constitutes instead a mosaic of micro-environments that were created by the delicate balance maintained over the centuries between, on the one hand, marine influence on a coastline of, in parts, minimal elevation above mean sea level and, on the other, the influence of runoff from the major rivers draining the Imataka Range and other elevations of the coastal zone. The delicate nature of this balance rests to a large extent on the low gradient of the Barima River, 1.5 cm/km (Hydrometeorological Department, Georgetown) as well as on its rates of discharge into the *Boca Grande* of the Orinoco Delta.

As well as a physical base, these micro-environments have a biological base, notably in the estuarine ecosystem, which comprises rivermouths, tidal marshes, creeks and other marine-to-brackish water bodies in direct and constant interaction with the sea. The high biological productivity of this zone rests in the ability of estuarine sediments to absorb nutrient salts delivered from inland sources, which are there processed into a number of useful products and thus are not lost to the ocean floor (Hinrichsen 1996; Ogden 1987-1988; Schultz 1976).

In the Caribbean and in neighboring Venezuela, most island and mainland coastlines drop precipitously more than 2000 m within a few kilometers of shore, so that the area of shallow water that man most depends on for food is small. Since typically in tropical seas the warm surface waters rarely mix with the cold, nutrient-rich waters below, these areas of shallow water are extremely important in human subsistence. Therefore, on the Western Guiana Littoral, the low gradient of a warm, shallow shelf extending some 100 km offshore is a valued natural resource. As well as comprising a key element in the food chain, its mangrove canopy harbors hundreds of species of birds, notably great flocks of the scarlet ibis, while its estuaries shelter marine mammals such as manatees, otters, caiman, etc. It has been estimated that properly managed one hectare of mangroves in the Philippines can produce annually 100 kg fish, 25 kg shrimp, 15 kg crabmeat, 200 kg molluscs, and 40 kg sea cucumber (Hinrichsen 1996). Hence the unique attractiveness of this part of the mainland over the millennia.

Fish and shellfish of coastal and estuarine waters fall into two general groups: permanent residents and visitors. Typically, the permanent residents are smaller, feed on smaller items, and in fact may function as prey for the visitors, which include species that penetrate shallow waters and estuaries mainly on feeding forays but which also visit estuaries for a portion of their life cycles, e.g., appropriate sectors of the salinity gradients of coastal rivers are exploited at different stages in the development of these species. As a result of salinity gradient selection, the juveniles of many species are zoned preferentially over distances as great as 100 km or more in the coastal rivers. This pattern is reflected in occurrences of large numbers of very small fishes at the low salinity end of the gradient and smaller numbers of older, larger juveniles at higher salinity levels (Odum 1984). The pattern explains the differential contents of shell mounds along the same stretch of coastline but occupying contrasting areas of a given river drainage. At the same time salinity expressed in diatom frequencies may vary appreciably through time in the various levels of a given mound, Table F. A combination of extensive shallow water, estuaries and dense mangrove vegetation along its coasts and rivers renders the Western Guiana Littoral by far the most biologically productive area on the entire

Guiana Coast. This readily explains the unique occurrences there of all of the shell mounds known anywhere between the mouths of the Orinoco and Amazon Rivers.

Table F. Barabina shell mound. Diatom count/level.

Sample no:	Depth (cm)	Marine		Brackish			Fresh	
		M	MB	BM	B	BF	FB	F
P 17	20	-	-	-	-	5	3	-
P 15	40	-	-	2	27	1	8	-
P 13	60	2	-	-	1	1	-	-
P 11	80	-	-	-	1	-	-	-
P 9	100	-	-	-	-	-	1	-
P 7	120	-	-	-	-	-	-	1
P 5	140	-	-	-	1	-	1	-
P 3	160	-	1	-	-	-	1	-
P 1	180	-	-	-	-	-	2	-

Source: Jansma 1981. **Key: MB**, marine-brackish; **BM**, brackish-marine; **BF**, brackish-fresh; **FB**, fresh-brackish.

The Hinterland

Recent paleoecological research on alluvial deposits in the table mountains of the Gran Sabana indicates the onset of moist conditions there around 8000 to 10,000 b.p. (Schubert 1995; see also Schubert 1986; Rull 1991). This evidently continued the warming trend and increasing rainfall of the late glacial. It has been seen that the Holocene vegetation of the Rupununi Savannas was characterized by a pattern of alternating extensions of closed savanna woodland and open grass savannas on to around 5000 b.p., after which, and especially after 3000 b.p., open savanna supervened there. The dispersion of the large, Andean-type points of the paleo-Indigenous period, a few specimens of which were recovered in the Rupununi and Ireng River drainages, suggests the savanna-type environments favored as campsites by the earliest migrants.

After their imposition on the walls of Makatau Cave, in the South Rupununi Savannas, certain Archaic (Pit-and-Groove) petroglyph elements were sequestered beyond arm's reach of later occupants of the cave by the removal of 1.5 m of its floor in an episode of torrential rainfall (Williams 1979) which evidently had followed on sustained dry conditions there. The event may correlate with a period of torrential

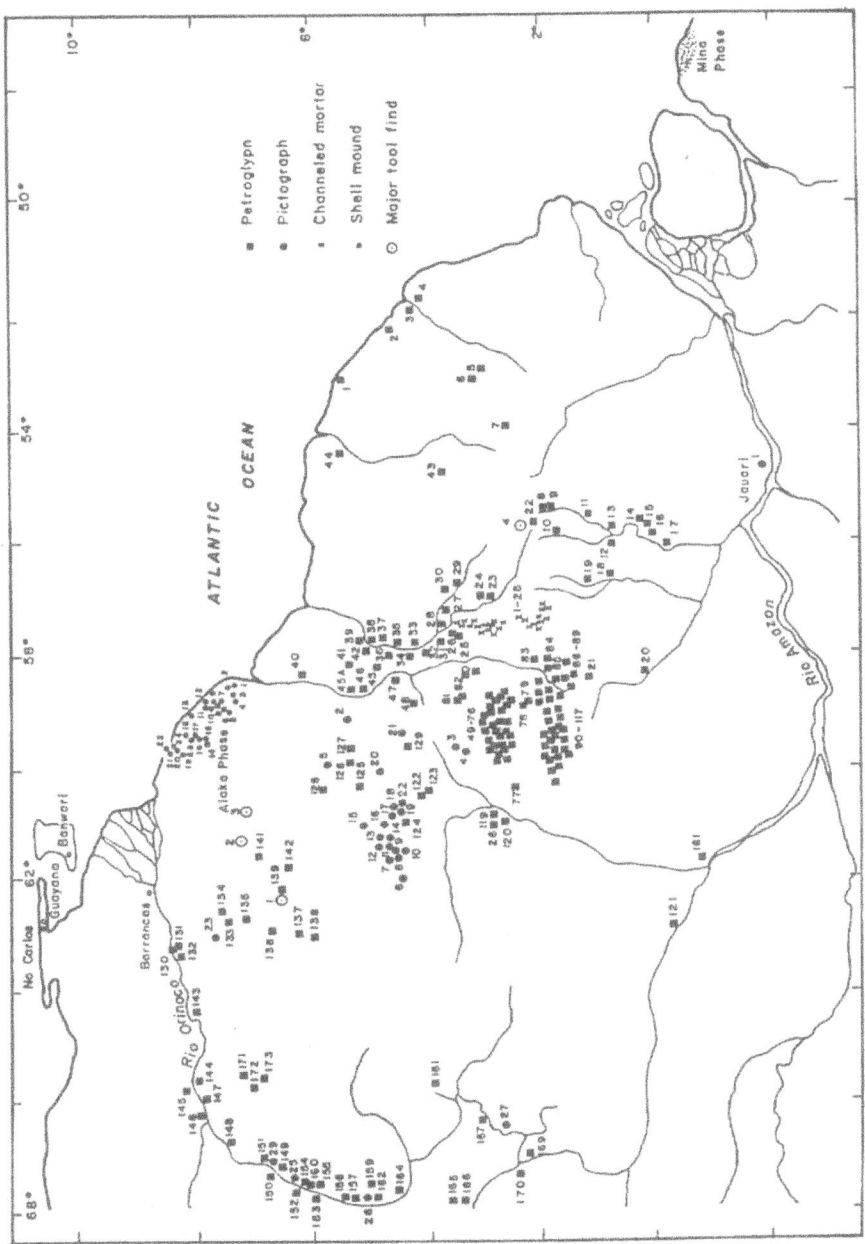

Figure 3.8. Archaic occupation of the Guianas.

rainfall reported in the Chimanta and Guaiquinima table mountains of the Roraima Formation and dated at between 6000 - 5100 b. p. These dates are congruent with the upper end of the estimated time range (5000 - 3000 B.C.) for the occurrence of the Pit-and-Groove petroglyph type in Eastern California and Nevada archaeology (Heizer and Baumhoff 1962:234).

C^{14} dates at 3950+/-180 b.p. and 3000+/-160 b.p. were obtained from Archaic food refuse in the Pedra Pintada Cave in the Rio Branco Savannas. Traces of pictograph paint from an even lower level in this food refuse suggest that inception of occupation there may have been significantly earlier (Mentz Ribeiro et al 1989). The date is important in lowland chronology since it associates imposition of a highly distinctive petroglyph, the Cuneiform Subtype, with conditions prevailing during the Amazonian arid interval of around 4000 b.p.

Though few and far between, caves were of undoubted importance to Archaic peoples in various areas of the Western Guiana Hinterland. Unfortunately, besides containing an occasional petroglyph or pictograph, caves have yielded few artifacts. However, the associated petroglyph typology, unquestionably diagnostic of the Archaic, has an important bearing on the settlement pattern. This is because the immobility of petroglyphs and pictographs implies a long-term association with a particular community whose cumulative investment in man-hours directed at specialist modification of the rock at least suggests a degree of sedentary occupation in any given case. Petroglyph distributions may therefore be diagnostic of important features of the settlement pattern.

Association of a particular petroglyph type with a given prehistoric culture derives from their classification into three great Traditions, or Series -- the Enmerative (with a Cuneiform Subtype), Fish Trap and Timehri Series, the first two representing aspects of Archaic subsistence, while the last is of the horticulturist period (Williams 1985). In the Guianas, they occur along rivers and creeks, on the savannas and in mountain areas, Figure 3.8.

By far the most direct means of reconstructing the Archaic settlement pattern in the Guiana hinterland is by survey and mapping of the various modified rocks in its many rivers and creeks, an activity which, as has been seen, provided the initial impetus for archaeological research in the British, Dutch and French Guianas, as well as in Brazilian Guiana, during the eighteenth and nineteenth centuries. Besides petroglyphs, these modified rocks comprise myriads of grinding surfaces diagnostic of tool manufacture and maintenance. These may be highly concentrated in a given stream or, alternatively, they may be widely dispersed. In some localities, also, modification of certain riverain boulders resulted from food preparation in bedrock mortars of a distinctive type, distributions of which relate to particular groups and a specific time level.

During the dry season of 1739 - 1740, the German traveler, Horstman (Harris and de Villiers 1911:173), managed to measure the height of Kurupukari (Traquari) Falls on the upper Essequibo River without once mentioning the striking petroglyphs prominently imposed on the rocks there, an omission which, compounded with his earlier failure to mention the equally spectacular petroglyphs at the "dangerous and diabolical" waterfall at Waraputa (Arapata), downstream, implies his total lack of interest in the subject. Today, two and a half centuries later, the modified rocks of these waterfalls, like many others across the Guianas, are recognized as evidence of the sedentary occupation of the rain forest by Archaic groups dispersing from the Rupununi Savannas to the south and the Pakaraima Mountains to the west during the rigors of the Amazonian arid interval of around 4000 years ago (Williams 1996a). The period was characterized by a low water table and low water levels in the rivers, so that, as with their paleo-Indigenous ancestors, the material remains of Archaic groups venturing into the rain forest at this time lie on a horizon which now is submerged most of the year.

Somewhat surprisingly, Horstman recorded with apparent interest on the Rupununi River "a stone with various letters and some figures, also the seat of the fundament, also the calves of the legs and the heels of him who wrote it." Judging from a copy from Horstman's manuscript made by the eighteenth century French cartographer D'Anville (Dubelaar 1986:173), the 'letters' and 'figures' were graffiti appertaining to the period of European exploration in the Guianas, while, apparently, the remainder of the report referred to the grinding surfaces encountered everywhere in the rivers, representing millennia of the manufacture of ground stone tools. Evidently, Horstman's attention had been arrested more by his encounter with the Roman alphabet in so unlikely an environment than by the depressions that he supposed had been imposed in the rock by the author of the inscriptions. Nonetheless, his record constitutes the earliest description of petroglyphs so far known anywhere in the Guianas, since which time they have been reported or recorded across the length and breadth of the region as mute evidence of long vanished stone working industries.

Because the overwhelming number of these artifacts refer to the period of Archaic expansion across the Guianas, and particularly to the period of the Amazonian arid interval, very many of them are located on the just mentioned submerged horizon and remain partly beyond reach of inquiry even during the lowest water levels of the dry season.

Also located on this submerged horizon, and on this account appertaining to either the paleo-Indigenous or Archaic time levels, is the chipping station encountered on the upper Burro Burro River, right bank Siparuni, left bank Essequibo. This workshop, comprising a pile of waterworn cobbles of vein quartz, discards and stoneworking debris, was located directly on the riverbank during a period of sustained low water but now lies submerged beneath around three meters of water during most of the year (Williams 1996).

Thus, Archaic groups occupying the rain forest lived mainly along its economic streams, attracted there principally by the abundant fish fauna concentrated around waterfalls and in deep pools in the riverbed as well as by shallow rapids suitable for fencing as fish pens. By virtue of differences in water quality, these streams differed in their potentials for supporting human populations, whitewater streams (= neutral reaction) being by far more biotically productive than blackwater streams (= acid reaction). But whereas on account of the purity of their waters the latter were favored for habitation, the former, though teeming with life, were avoided for residential use on account of the prevalence of disease vectors. Thus, notwithstanding its rich biological diversity, and a corresponding richness in Fish Trap petroglyphs and grinding surfaces, the Kassikaityu is known to the present day as The River of Death.

Also contributing to the Archaic settlement pattern were certain vegetal resources of specific distributions, e.g., the Moriche palm *(Mauritia flexuosa)*, the Brazilnut tree *(Bertholletia excelsa)* and the riparian grass Job's Tears (*Coix lachryma jobi*), all being outstanding starch producers. On the coast, moriche flour continued in use into living memory and may have been similarly important in the Archaic dietary in the Hinterland. Ethnographic parallels and the distributions of a distinctive type of bedrock mortar suggest the erstwhile importance of the Brazilnut to groups in southern Guyana, the upper Rio Branco and the coast of Guyane française, Figure 3.44. Used for "bead" aprons in Guyana into recent times, Job's Tears, Figure 3.9. is a traditional starch resource throughout the tropics (Andrew Gillison pers. comm. 1996).

Figure 3.9.
Job's Tears

The submerged horizon of the Archaic thus comprised campsites located along the attenuated rivers and creeks of an arid interval, as is indicated, for example, by the now submerged bedrock mortars of the Orenoque and New Rivers in southern Guyana, and of the upper Rio Branco in Brazil; fishing grounds that were centered on waterfalls, cataracts and deep ponds in the riverbeds; lithic workshops at selected rock exposures, such as the quartz vein at Inscription Rock on the Burro Burro River, or the concentrations of grinding surfaces at Big "S" Falls on the upper Siparuni River associated over the centuries with manufacture of the dugout canoe. The distinction frequently made between 'parietal' and 'mobiliary' specimens in the study of paleolithic art usefully distinguishes between these submerged petroglyphs, bedrock mortars, chipping stations and canoe manufacturing centers of the Archaic in the rain forest, on the one hand, and, on the other, the tools and implements of daily use which, from time to time, are recovered from now submerged sandbanks or forested islands in the rivers and creeks.

Of even greater antiquity than these submerged artifacts of the rain forest are various items of modified rock on the savannas. These mainly comprise petroglyphs, pictographs and grinding surfaces on suitable rock exposures or in caves, Figure 3. 10.

Figure 3. 10. Pedra Pintada, Rio Branco, Brazil (*after Mentz Ribeiro et al 1987*).

A number of caves or rock shelters on the upper Rio Branco are noted for their numerous pictographs associated with habitation refuse and dating to the arid interval of +/- 4000 b.p. Caves in the complex are Pedra Pintada, Pedra do Pereira, Pedra do Pingo, Pedra do Perdiz, Pedra do Sapo, Pedra do Machado, and Pedra do Sabao, Figure 3.11. Also known for their pictographs are the Cueva del Elefante,

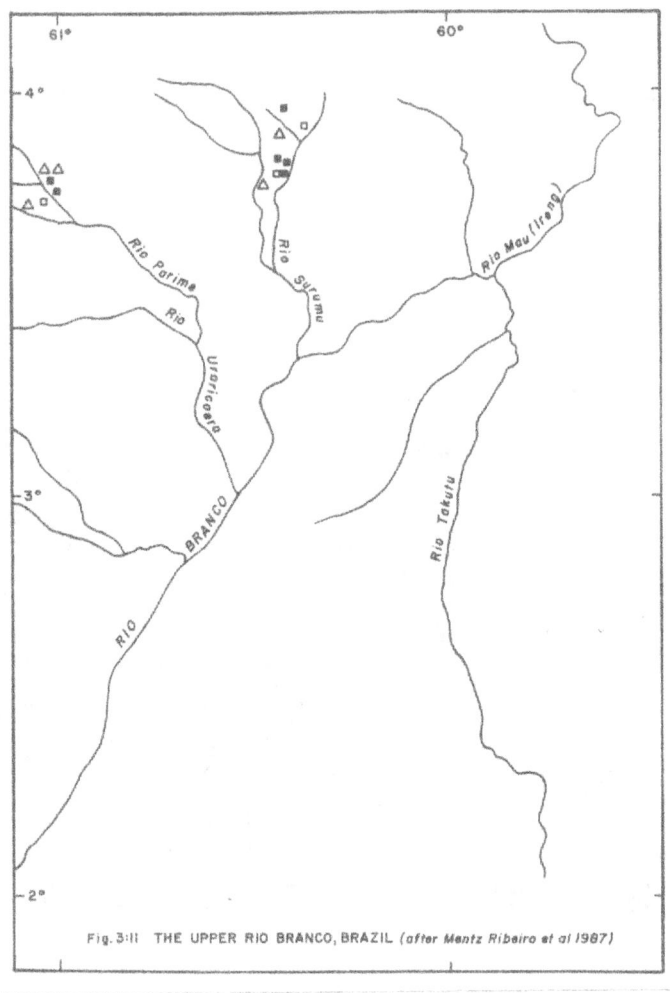

Figure 3.11. The upper Rio Branco, Brazil (*after Mentz Ribeiro et al 1987*).

a large rock shelter around 70 km to the southwest of Puerto Ordaz (Vargas and Sanoja 1970), and the Casa da Piedra at El Carmen on the Rio Parguaza (Cruxent 1946-1947), both in Bolivar State, Venezuela. The Tramen pictograph occupies a large rock shelter in the Merume Mountains on the headwaters of the Mazaruni River (Peberdy 1945, 1948) and small, painted rock shelters have been reported, in the North Pakaraimas (Henderson 1952). Petroglyphs occur in Makatau Cave, Rupununi Savannas (Williams 1979), Figure 3.12, as well as in Wahana Cave, upper Waini River.

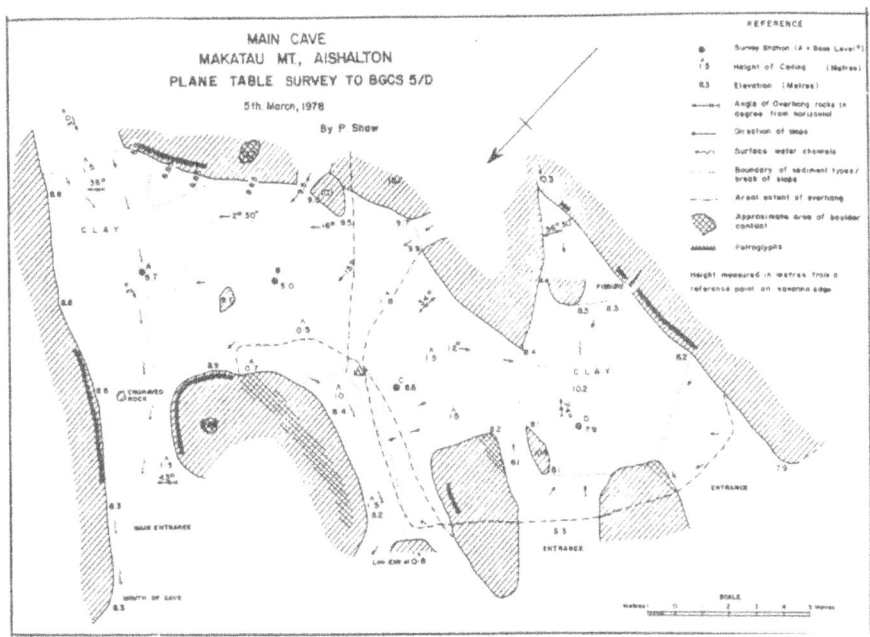

Figure 3.12. Makatau Cave, South Rupununi Savannas (after Shaw 1979).

The areas of individual chambers in Makatau Cave (< 100 m^2) suggest that band sizes were typically small. Judging from petroglyph typology there, the earliest band appears to have occupied three separate chambers, either simultaneously or at different times. If simultaneously, then the total band size could hardly have exceeded a score or so. The single chamber of the cave on Wahana Island was likewise small, with a maximum capacity of perhaps half a dozen. On the other hand, with an area of around 1000 m², El Elefante in Venezuelan Guayana could have slept well over 100, though, in view of its scattered resources, bands of this size were unlikely in the savannas.

Residential and ritual use of cave complexes and rock shelters indicate that particular bands were 'tethered' to specific resources while enjoying greater mobility than their fellows in the coastal zone. Game animals and fish represented in their petroglyphs and pictographs indicate that the hunters of *terra firme* were technically better equipped to exploit the available natural resources than were the coastal shellfishers. Typically portrayed were the range of characteristically small and cryptic game animals of the Tropical Forest, agouti, bush hog, caiman, monkey, sloth, etc. Bones of these animals sometimes are preserved in excavated food refuse in caves, unquestionably signifying habitation. However, numerous occurrences of freshwater snails in certain assemblages suggest famine episodes, which may have occurred with the annual flooding of the savannas. Being subject to extreme seasonal drought, savannas provide a lower arboreal mammalian biomass than mature forest that is subject to a less seasonal schedule of plant productivity (Eisenberg et al 1979:187) and since, in Guyana, 62% of all animals are arboreals (Simmons 1979:95), it was both expedient and profitable to locate these savanna settlements near to the forest. Petroglyph depictions of arboreals such as monkey and sloth indicate that the savanna hunter-gatherers turned to the forest consistently in order to supplement a seasonally fluctuating supply of animal protein. Following on the annual floods, residual pools in the dried out stream beds provided foci for the local food chain.

In the strategy of controlling basic production, the manufacture of the thousands of petroglyphs and pictographs that are scattered across the length and breadth of the Guianas (Schomburgk 1841) represented an energy input in subsistence technology on *terra firme* that was wholly absent in coastal infrastructures, where of course suitable rock exposures are few. To this degree, the subsistence regime on *terra firme* was energetically more 'expensive' (Price 1982) than on the coast. Contingent upon human appropriation of a given food item from the biota, whether animal or plant, was the obligation to the gods to render account of that trespass by imposition of a particular type of petroglyph element on a particular boulder, cave wall or cliff. As the mechanism which monitored the flow of energy through the sociocultural system in the interest of man's indefinite survival in the marginal environment of the savannas, the mediating structure erected between human and natural productivity in the form of petroglyph or pictograph manufacture itself involved considerable energy inputs in the mining and manuporting of selected rock materials to a given site, tool manufacture at that site, and expenditure of an indefinite number of man hours, days or perhaps even weeks in imposition of the appropriate glyphs by pecking and abrasion of the weathered surface of the prevailing Aminge granite. On the other hand, imposition of pictographs involved the appropriation of mainly organic raw materials for the manufacture of paints, notably the fruit of the Annato (*Bixa orellana*) and Crabnut (*Carapa guianensis*) plants. Production of this early synthetic, implying proximity to rain forest resources, again suggests a measure of sedentary occupation.

As evidenced in petroglyph distributions, Archaic habitations extended across the Guiana land mass as far to the east as the Oyapoc River and to the south as far as the Amazon. However, Archaic peoples did not exploit only the rivers, forests and savannas; their petroglyphs have been recorded in remote mountain fastnesses as well, which ethnographic parallels suggest were regarded as the "houses" of the game animals of the forest, accessible only through the mediation of the gods (Reichel-Dolmatoff 1971:99).

Thus, commencing around 7000 years ago, Archaic peoples began expanding across the Guianas, chiefly by way of its major streams. Very soon, some of their number occupied favorable niches in both subzones of the Western Guiana Littoral. In due course, and also *via* the hinterland rivers, others reached the Eastern Guiana Littoral in Guyane française. Distributions of their diagnostic artifacts indicate that communication between hinterland and coastal groups was continuous. For example, a bark beater on slate deriving from a coastal shell mound was inscribed with petroglyph elements diagnostic of the hunting economy of the savannas, Figure 3.13.

Figure 3.13. Barkbeater from a coastal shell mound, Guyana, with inscriptions of savanna hunter-gatherers. *University Museum of Archaeology, Cambridge No. Z1013*

Coastal/Hinterland interaction is evidenced again by occurrences of Fish Trap petroglyphs, a southern trait, on Wabana Island on the fossil shoreline of the Western Guiana Littoral. Another southern trait, the channeled mortar of the upper Orenoque River and the upper Rio Branco, is represented in the Archaic inventory of the Ile de Cayenne on the Eastern Guiana Littoral. In due course, and in conditions associated with the Amazonian arid interval of around 4000 b.p., the Archaic interaction sphere stretched from the Mouth of the Amazon River virtually to the Mouth of the Orinoco River. At around this time, the distinctive shell-tempered ceramics of the Mina phase from the Mouth of the Amazon made an abrupt appearance on the lower Aruka River, the last great tributary of the Barima River before it debouches into the *Boca Grande* of the Orinoco Delta.

Economy
Niche variation on the Western Guiana Littoral

From the time of the first settlements there, towards the end of the sixth millennium B.C., human subsistence on the Western Guiana Littoral had been conditioned by differentials in local hydraulic and tectonic conditions. These resulted in a mosaic of habitable niches, each of variable extension and duration, and separated by immense stretches of fresh water swamps bordered by mangroves. Middens comprising mainly shells of crabs harvested on now vanished intertidal mudflats cluster around rare granite exposures on marginally higher ground. Middens on the upper Waini River and the midden on Akawabi Creek on the Koriabo River are representative. Middens comprising mainly shells of the small, black-and-white-striped snail, the Zebra Nerite (*Puperita pupa*), are located in mangrove swamp. They occur in both subzones. The Piraka, Barabina and Koriabo Point middens are representative. The sole oyster-shell midden so far known is located on Hosororo hillfoot.

Snail-shell middens exhibit contrasts in structure, texture, color and permeability from crab-shell or oyster-shell middens. Permeability is a function of the substrate. From the amphibole schist of the basement edge, the 4 km-long Barabina Hill, 8° 13'N, 59° 49'W, in the Northwestern Subzone rises in eastern and western elevations to a maximum 21 m. The habitable area of the western elevation is confined to its level crown, measuring just 10 x 8 m. This constituted the growth point of the midden which, over time, accumulated irregularly downslope covering some 55 x 35 m. The broad, concave base of this refuse, resting on an impermeable substrate, contributed to the structural stability of the midden and formation of a soil profile that exhibits well defined A and B horizons. An A_o horizon (7.5R 2/2), 5 cm thick, overlies the shell surface. The A_1 horizon (2.5YR 5/6) gives way on 32 cm depth below the surface of the ground to an A_2 horizon (10R 5/8) extending to 130 cm depth below the surface. A B_1 horizon (7.5R N6) gives way on 138 cm below the surface to redeposited humus (5YR 2/2) overlying residual clay (2.5YR 5/6). An alternative specimen, the snail-shell Koriabo Point midden, 7° 33'N, 59° 40'W, on the Barima River, lacks the soil horizons of the Barabina midden. Instead, its upper 3.0 m comprise four equally spaced, bi-colored zones, each +/- 70 cm deep. The upper half of each zone is ocher-colored (10R 6/6); the lower half is gray-black (10R 3/2). There is no B horizon. The lower half of the midden comprises well washed, mobile, shiny nerite shells. Resting on kaolinitic clay, this free-draining zone inhibited formation of a B horizon. Similar color-banding is present in snail-shell middens on Kabakaburi Hill, 7° 14'N, 58° 43'W, and on Piraka Hill, 7 +/- 15'N, 58° 45'W, both on the Pomeroon River, Southeastern Subzone. The Kabakaburi deposit rests on residual clay, the Piraka on sand.

Crab-shell middens comprise an even-textured shell sand in their upper halves (10YR 6/6). In the lower halves, this shell sand is embedded in redeposited ash with the water retentive attributes of clay (7.5R N6). Horizontal cupping of the valves in oyster-shell middens favors homogenization of the deposit and inhibits soil formation.

Ash and charcoal are redeposited vertically or horizontally depending on the volume and intensity of local rainfall episodes and the permeability of the substrate. Where drainage is impeded in snail-shell middens, charcoal particles are consolidated in layers 2-3 cm thick which seal the interstices of shell fragments and inhibit further leaching. Soil particles accumulating above these consolidated layers increase the compaction of the shell refuse, constituting a floor for redeposition of further increments of ash and charcoal. Zoned banding results.

Snail-shell and crab-shell middens both exhibit massive horizontal conglomerates of shell, bones, etc., caused by rain water percolating through the overlying humus and combining with detrital carbon dioxide to form carbonic acid. This in turn dissolves calcium carbonate shell in upper levels to form a calcium bicarbonate solution which, percolating through the soil, precipitates the calcium carbonate that causes these concretions (Palmer and Williams 1977:25).

The founding nuclei at Piraka in the low-lying Southeastern Subzone and at Barabina Hill in the more elevated Northwestern Subzone occupied habitable niches a good thousand years before culmination of the eustatic rise in the sea level. These nuclei, deriving from peoples already adapted to the hinterland environment, provided propagules for the further colonization of the respective Southeastern and Northwestern Subzones. The results were the great shell mound complexes of the Western Guiana Littoral. Through time, and as a consequence of continued coastal evolution, these environments underwent drastic change, particularly resulting from culmination of the sea level rise and its aftermath. With environmental change, the subsistence pursuits of the settlers diverged.

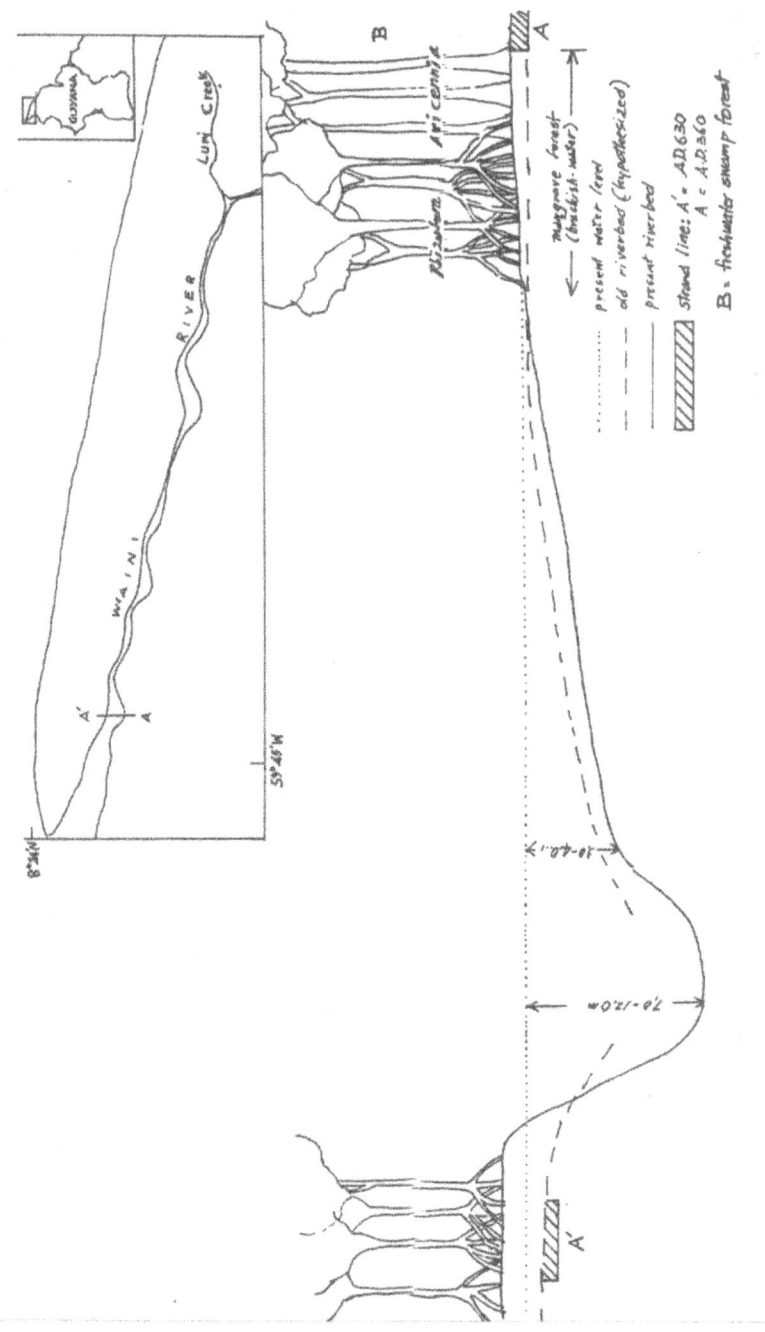

Figure 3.14. Section of the Waini at First Laguna. Left bank shell deposits absent above Luri Creek.

As the sea attained its present level on the Guiana Coast after around 6000 b.p., the marine influence was carried by the rivers to the limits of the swamp basin, in some cases as much as 220 km inland. In due course, however, the influence of run-off from the emergent basement rocks came to be felt along the swamp edge. Over time, run-off increased with increasing distance from the sea. Thus, in its coastal sector the Barima River now ebbed and flowed simultaneously under opposed hinterland and marine influences. In due course, and under the escalating influence of run-off, the marine influence retreated until it ceased to be felt on the swamp edge, now enjoying a permanently fresh environment. As equilibrium between the marine influence and the influence of run-off was achieved in the swamp basin, the intertidal mudflats of the Western Guiana Littoral were converted into the seasonally inundated grass savannas of the present day.

Rising water levels in the swamp basin associated with the freshening environment produced drastic changes in the riverain flora and fauna. With the seaward advance of fresh conditions, riverain stands of mangroves (=brackish-water) also advanced seaward. As higher levels of freshwater supervened, marsh (seasonally inundated) forest, characterized by economic stands of Mora *(Mora excelsa)* was replaced by swamp (permanently inundated) forest along the lower stretches of certain coastal streams, Figure 3.26. Concurrently, the submergence of the intertidal mudflats eliminated the traditional crab diet in certain communities, while with the seaward advance of the mangroves, the colonies of Zebra Nerite, the traditional brackish-water protein resource in other communities, also disappeared. Specialized gatherers of the Mangrove Oyster now saw the rapid demise of their traditional protein resource.

With the seaward advance of the mangroves, the site exploration territories of particular riverain communities were affected variably by differentials in the rates of freshening and in distances from the basement edge. Whereas on the Moruka River the distance of 19 km from the basement edge to the present day seashore lies well within the tidal range, on the neighboring Pomeroon River this distance is 65 km, and lies within the tidal counter currents. Therefore, faced with the identical problem of environmental freshening in the aftermath of the culmination of the sea level rise, the resettlement options of communities on these neighboring streams differed profoundly.

Over time, these once coastal mounds were sequestered under rain forest by the continued seaward advance of the intertidal zone and progressive growth of new belts of soil-forming mangroves (Stephens 1963; Wells and Coleman 1981a). The Mouth of the Waini, once located near the basement edge, now advanced seaward. Today, its former estuaries are identifiable as successive lagoons along its tidal reach. Progradation is evidenced at its present mouth by differences in the time each riverbank there was colonized by mangroves. Whereas peat on the left bank of the river mouth, representing former mangroves, returned a C^{14} date at 1590 +/- 90 b.p., or A.D. 360 (Beta 32186), peat from the right bank returned a date at 1320 +/- 70 b.p., or A.D. 630 (Beta 32185), Figure 3.14. Progradation continues, but due to the low gradient of the Waini, the shell mound cluster presently located some 90 km upstream on "The Beach" of Warao cultural memory still lies well within the tidal reach.

Due to a similarly low gradient, mangrove vegetation presently extends up the Barima River as far as Mt. Everard, ca. 170 km from the Orinoco Delta. The late survival of the Archaic group at Barabina, on its most seaward tributary the Aruka River, suggests that the intervening shell mounds may be of related ages, apparently having resulted from the slow downstream migration of the mangroves and their associated brackish-water fauna, following freshening on the basement edge after around 3700 B.C. The immense mudflat constituting the Waini-Barima watershed remained impassable until water levels rose sufficiently in the swamps to have permitted its having been bridged finally by small *itabos* (channels) through the forest. The contrasting midden types of the Western Guiana littoral are arranged chronologically in Figure 3.14a.

Changing local environments of the swamp basin

The bridging of the Waini-Barima watershed resulted in the breaching of the demographic barrier which, hitherto, had separated the founding nuclei in Southeastern and Northwestern Subzones. To the present day this barrier remains evidenced in the distribution of the respective place names, the Warao prefix *Wara* (kin) being specific to the W-aini (Our Place) side of the watershed and the Arawak prefix *Bara* (sea) to the *Bar*-ima side of the watershed.

Isolated on either side of this watershed and separated by hundreds of kilometers of mudflats, the founding nuclei at the snail-shell Barabina and Piraka middens represented the simplest level of adaptation to contrasting niches in the swamp basin. The limits of their respective economic catchment areas were determined by the proximity of abundant shellfish harvests in the nearby mangroves. The absence of bones of terrestrial mammals in their refuse indicates that exploitation of the nearby rain forest on elevated land was negligible. Stone working was irrelevant and remained rudimentary. At both nuclei, stone boiling is attested by numerous occurrences of fire-cracked pebbles of laterite and quartz (mean max. dia. 6.5 cm). A large, burnt cobble of laterite in the Piraka refuse (max. dia. 16.5 cm) was interpreted spontaneously by a Karinya laborer as a sweat stone (cf. Schomburgk 1841:157; also Thompson 1963:37). Two ground stone adzes from the earliest level of the Barabina mound attest the continued long-range interaction with *terra firme* which had secured the viability of paleo-Indigenous culture in northwestern areas of the Guianas from its beginnings.

Granted the mutual isolation of the founding nuclei on either side of this demographic divide, occurrences of ground stone tools in the Archaic Barabina mound in the Northwestern Subzone and their absence in the contemporary Piraka mound in the Southeastern Subzone, if not representing sampling error, suggests the possibility of divergent ancestries. The peopling of the Northwestern Subzone may have resulted from a migration, *via* the Wenamu and Barama Rivers, that differed from that which, perhaps *via* the Essequibo River, had resulted in the peopling of the Southeastern Subzone. Be that as it may, their subsequent evolution followed

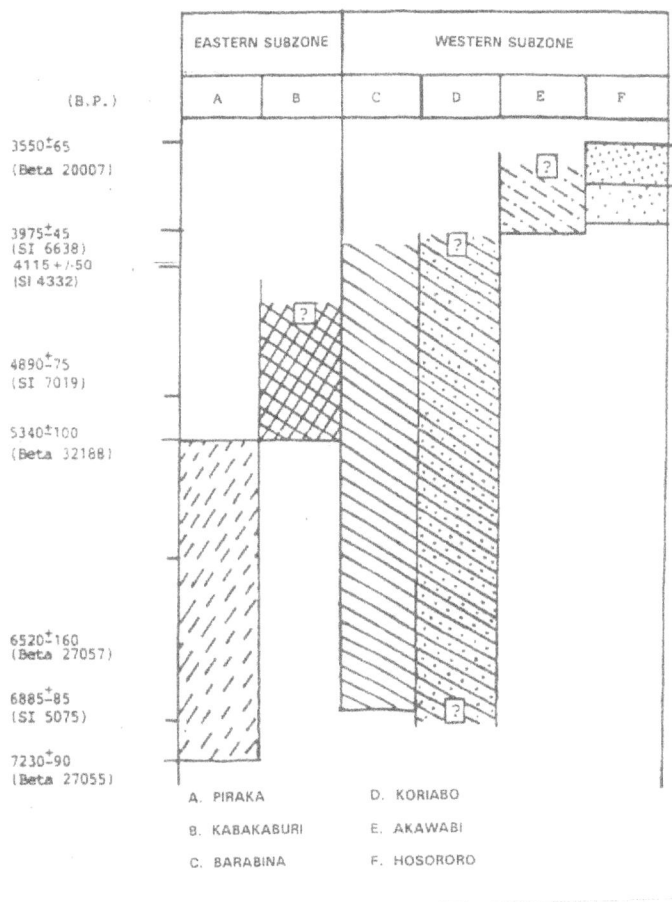

Figure 3.14 a. Chronology of midden types.

range of strategic rock materials deriving from various localities on *terra firme*, the Southeastern Subzone was characterized by an almost total absence of rock materials diametrically opposed pathways. The divergence was dictated by contrasts in the respective niches. Whereas the Northwestern Subzone was characterized by a wide of any description. There, the crescent of emergent rocks of the crystalline basement dwindle in elevation towards the Essequibo Delta and peter out as low, forested hummocks of poor economic potential to the swamps. These differences between niches assumed critical importance when, in the changing landscapes of the freshwater climax of 3300 B.C., the need for stone tools in the Southeastern Subzone became a factor in survival. The breaching of the Waini-Barima watershed then became imperative in the political economy of the Southeastern Subzone. (Bridging of the Waini-Barima watershed occurred once again, in British colonial political economy, with the opening of the Mora Passage during the present century, before which access to the Barima from the Atlantic had been *via* the Boca Grande of the Orinoco).

Freshening of the swamp basin followed on the culmination of the eustatic rise in the sea level around 4000 B.C. After that time, runoff began to counter the marine influence prevailing in the Barima and Waini Rivers as far inland as the crescent of emergent rocks of the swamp edge. The situation farthest from the sea is evidenced at the Koriabo Point shell mound on the Barima River in 7° 37' N, 59° 38' W. The earliest available C^{14} date for this midden, 6520 +/-160 b.p. or 4570 B.C. (Beta 27057) derived from charcoal on 3.0 m depth, representing some considerable time after initial occupation of the site. As the sea rose to its present level, the salt limit, and hence also the riverain brackish-water mangrove vegetation, penetrated much further upstream than at present. This is evidenced by rare occurrences of conch and 'clam in the refuse below 4.0 m depth. However, since the basic protein resource of the pioneer settlers remained the Zebra Nerite, the prevailing environment was Marine-Brackish (MB) in the diatom sequence shown in Table F. At around 5710 +/- 80 b. p., or 3760 B.C. (Beta 27056) fully brackish conditions (B) were indicated on 2.0 m depth by sporadic occurrences of the freshwater snail *Ampullaria* growing at modest sizes in the nerite deposit. Henceforth, *Ampullaria* sizes increased with decreasing mound depth in a Brackish-Fresh (BF) environment until, on the surface, specimens attained the V dimensions (100 - 110 mm max. dia.) typical of a freshwater habitat.

The location of this shell midden of the sediment basin in the Northwestern Subzone indicates the immense reach of the marine influence many centuries before the culmination of the sea level rise, evidently resulting from the extremely low gradient of the Barima River. As elsewhere on the basement edge, human settlement in the Marine-Brackish environment of the day was based on a nearby freshwater creek and survived the changes in ambient salinity that are indicated by the stratification of the various shellfish species. The date of the Marine-Brackish (MB) to Brackish (B) interface on this most remote area of the swamp edge, 3760 B.C., marks inception of the freshening conditions which, with the seaward movement of the freshwater front, had affected the lower coastal streams of the southeastern swamp basin by around 3300 B.C.

Koriabo Point was visited by the Venezuelan anthropologist, Elias Toro in 1905 (Osgood 1946), by the British archaeologist Bullbrook in 1920 (Osgood 1946), and by North American archaeologists Hyatt Verrill in 1918 (Verrill 1918a) and Evans and Meggers in 1953 (1960:67). Only Evans and Meggers recorded a shell mound there. They tested it briefly, correctly estimating its depth at around five meters. Koriabo Point is a snail-shell midden. This indicates a local environment of riverain mangroves (=brackish water) during the considerable period of its formation. Today, the environment is fresh (Mora forest, corkwood swamps). The mangrove zone is located some 40 km downstream, at Red Hill. In the low water levels of today's dry seasons, salt water penetrates inland as far as Anabisi Creek, around 20 km downstream from Koriabo Point, but during the rains run-off from the Imataka Hills forces the salt water back into the Orinoco Delta some 200 km distant.

This seasonal pattern presents a model of changing environments in the swamp basin as the hypersaline waters of a still rising sea were overcome by the escalating influence of run-off during the centuries after the sea level crest, cf. Figure 2.1. Changing local environments on the lower Barima River are evidenced by the faunal contents of the Koriabo mound.

The Barabina freshwater climax was not felt simultaneously across the swamp basin. Due to the severity of tectonic subsidence in the Northwestern Subzone when contrasted with the situation in the Southeastern Subzone, freshening in the Northwest was delayed by several centuries. As has been seen, the greater part of Period iii in the palcoenvironmental sequence on the Western Guiana Littoral (p. 59.iii) represented the tenure of the snail-shell Barabina midden by a reoccupying group following on its abandonment by the pioneer occupants. Since the arrival of the newcomers still significantly preceded the culmination of the sea level rise, surviving areas of intertidal mudflats provided bountiful seasonal supplies of the Mangrove Land Crab (*Ucides cordatus*), the carapaces and claws of which dominated the lower levels of their food refuse and accumulated also in discrete hillocks on the mound peripheries. Survival of these mudflats in the Northwestern Subzone long after they had been submerged in the Southeastern Subzone is attributable to the effects of tectonic subsidence locally and the associated relative rise in the sea level. The continuing rise in the sea level provided an effective brake on the advancing freshwater front, and consequently retarded the freshening process in the Northwest by several centuries.

The newcomers enjoyed a more complex culture than their predecessors. Their economic catchment area extended from the seacoast, now some 35 km distant, where they fished by cadell in the shallow inshore waters, into the Arukumai Hills on the Koriabo River around 50 km inland, where they mined ingots of specular iron ore, as well as up the Barima River to Koriabo Point on the basement edge, where they appear to have bartered for strategic rock materials such as andesite, quartzite, amphibolite, greywacke sandstone and chlorite schist, all of which survive in their refuse. These rock materials derived from various locations on the upper Barama River and appear to have been exploited and controlled exclusively by middlemen comprising the group at the Koriabo Point shell mound, who thus benefitted from their strategic location on the trail across the Barima-Barama watershed, a distance of around 30 km.

The enormous size of the Koriabo Point shell mound and its relatively great depth attest its strategic importance in the economy of the Western Guiana Littoral as the sole outpost of the mines on the upper Barima River. Its age and location suggest that it was probably founded by the group that reoccupied Barabina Hill precisely in response to the need to develop the stone tool industry which now underpinned their multifarious cultural pursuits, of which the exploration of iron ore in the Arukumai Hills was symptomatic. Unfortunately, for want of a knowledge of metals, the samples to hand profited them little notwithstanding evidences of purposeful battering, presumably with a view to tool manufacture of some sort. Figure 3.15a.

The newcomers occupied precisely the area on the crown of the hill that had been used by the pioneers, and suffered an increasingly high mortality rate in phase with a growing population (=density-dependent growth), Table C. As specialist fishers located in ready proximity to the sea (*Bara bina*), their most numerous stone tool was the line-sinker, identifiable by having been provided with a short tongue for lashing. Represented in a variety of sizes, numbers per level of line sinkers correlated with fish-bone frequencies through-

Figure 3.15,a,b. a. Barabina shell mound. Worked specular iron ore. Arukurnai Hills, Aruka River.

out the sequence. There was a marked decline in both at around the time of the culmination of the sea level rise, around 6000 years ago. Fishbone frequencies in independent excavation units (level 60 - 80 cm) display a similar decline at this time, doubtless due to the now brimful state of the rivers, Tables G.a,b.

Table G.a. Barabina shell mound. Unit 4: Fish and shellfish remains/level (g)

Level	Fish	Crab	Oyster	Clam	Rock shell	Mussel	Conch
16 - 40	81	6	144	25	13	-	-
40 - 60	695	-	96	17	-	-	-
60 - 80	462	12	252	50	12	5	126
80 - 100	546	-	184	34	-	-	-
100 - 110	933	16	784	29	4	16	12
110 - 120	sterile						
120 - 140	966	44	326	98	42	4	-

Table G.b. Barabina shell mound. Unit 14: Fish and shellfish remains/level (g)

Level (cm)	Fish	Shellfish					
		Crab	Oyster	Clam	Rock shell	Mussel	Conch
16 - 40	2611	-	-	-	-	-	-
40 - 60	4508	-	-	-	-	-	-
60 - 80	1512	-	98	47	12	14	95
80 - 100	1834	-	-	-	-	-	-
100 - 110	308	-	-	-	-	-	-
110 - 120	sterile						
120 - 140	1134	112	-	-	-	-	-

In both units, the decline in fish bone frequencies at the peak of the sea level rise was accompanied by simultaneous sharp increases/level of the saltwater mollusks, oysters, clam and conch, implying steeply rising salinity levels locally. The stratigraphic level dates at 5965 +/- 50 b.p. (SI 4333). The refuse therefore represents the faunal environment at the time of the culmination of the absolute sea level rise along the Western Guiana Littoral. As has been seen, the contemporaneous marked increase in the mortality rate was accompanied by a decisive shift in burial orientation, the head of the deceased being now unequivocally directed toward the setting sun (2700). Hunks of Honeycomb Tubeworm (*Phragmotopoma lapidosa*) in the refuse, Figure 3.16, suggest surviving areas of exposed mudflats.

Figure 3.16. Barabina shell mound.
Honeycomb Tubeworm in the food refuse.

In a column sample representing the Barabina profile, diatom counts were generally poor. Species ranged from marine to brackish in a sequence numbered 1-17. As indicators of the salinity of the water they characteristically inhabit, diatoms are divided into three major groups, marine (M), brackish (B) and freshwater (F). Marine diatoms may be subdivided into marine (M) and marine brackish (MB) groups, the latter preferring coastal waters. Brackish diatoms likewise can be subdivided into brackish-marine (BM), brackish (B) and brackish-fresh (BF) groups. However, the boundaries between species are not very sharp, since several species are eurylialine (tolerant of a wide range of conditions), while others are stenohaline (specific to a narrow range of conditions). As shown in Table F, only the uppermost samples in the column permitted conclusions to be drawn with any confidence concerning the environment of the mound. During accumulation of the lower part (P5 - P13), the environment was apparently brackish. On account of the small numbers involved, this cannot be stated with absolute certainty, though it is of interest to note that the only marine specimens occur simultaneously with the culmination of the sea level rise, supporting the evidence of the food refuse. Better preserved and more numerous specimens in the period following on this event, the uppermost two levels, indicate a decisively brackish environment nearing the time of abandonment of the site, 4115 +/- 50 b.p. (SI 4332). Thus, brackish conditions are independently evidenced in the Northwestern Subzone more than a thousand years after the transition to a fresh environment in the Southeastern Subzone. It will be recalled that a similar situation obtained in the days of the founding nuclei on the Western Guiana Littoral. Then, the Barabina environment had been hypersaline and the Piraka environment already brackish. This suggests that progradation of the mudflats which caused the once-coastal shell mounds to be sequestered under a mantle of rain forest on the basement edge was initiated much earlier in the geologically more stable Southeastern Subzone than it was in the still subsiding Northwestern Subzone. On the Western Guiana Littoral, the effects of tectonic subsidence were felt progressively more severe the nearer one approached the Orinoco Delta (Brinkman and Pons 1968). Increasing depths of peat deposits with travel northwestwards from the Essequibo River resulted from the differential effects of the relative rise in the sea level. Due to the variable influence of tectonic subsidence in the North West, this relative sea level rise survived appreciably the culmination of the absolute sea level rise. With travel in the opposite direction, the relatively deep peat deposits of the Northwestern Subzone peter out towards the Essequibo Coast in the Southeastern Subzone. There, a heavy peaty clay is the principal economic resource of an extensive modern rice industry. Thus, whereas, in the Southeastern Subzone, geological stability was a source of environmental stress and socio-cultural strain, these conditions were deferred for upwards of a thousand years in the geologically less stable Northwestern Subzone. Accordingly, the people of the Northwestern Subzone were spared the environmental 'time of troubles' which was initiated in the Southeastern Subzone around 3300 B.C. by local freshening, encroaching rain forest and seaward advance of the shoreline. Thus, as a defining factor in niche variation, its geology exercised a profoundly determining influence on socio-cultural evolution on the Western Guiana Littoral.

The adaptive value of niche variation

The contrasting niches of the Western Guiana Littoral, occupied by Archaic shellfishers a thousand or more years before the sea had attained its present level, provided a unique infrastructural base for the socio-cultural developments which resulted in the emergence of Tropical Forest Culture in this portion of the Guiana land mass. The burial orientations of the migrants who succeeded to the pioneer occupants at the Barabina shell mound suggest semi-permanent habitation, perhaps with seasonal camps located around the headwaters of various freshwater creeks. Thither, with the commencement of the rains in early May each year, fish migrate to spawn. The earliest toolkit of these migrants evidences a long-distance trade network which carried strategic rock materials from the upper Barama River into the lower Barima Basin *via* the portage at Koriabo Point. In this network, rock materials mined in the Kauramembu Mountains on the upper Barama River, Figure 3.17, were traded across the Barama-Barima watershed *via* Chinee Landing to Koriabo Point whence they were redistributed across the swamp basin as far as Barabina on the lower Aruka River. Notable among these was steatite. Because this rock material is unknown anywhere else in the geology of Guyana, its occurrences in archaeological deposits beyond the Barama River are uniquely diagnostic of certain aspects of

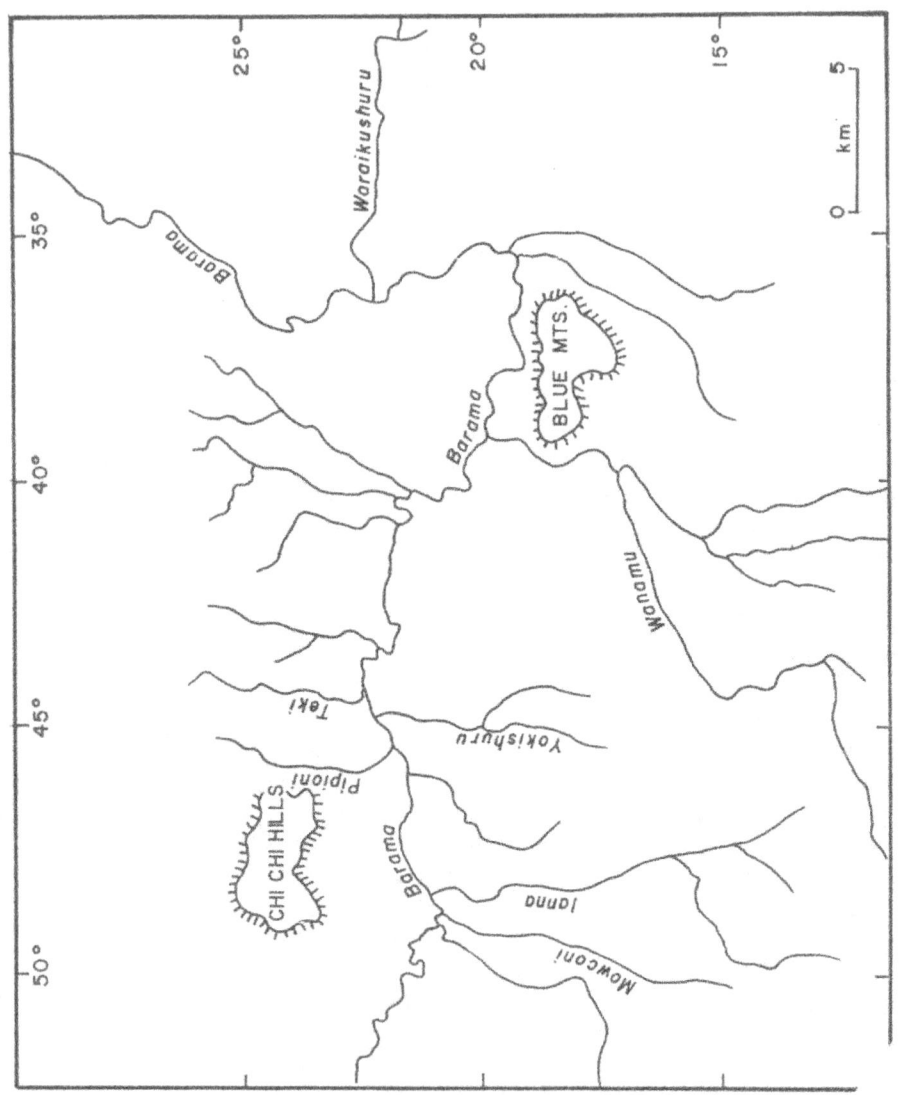

Figure 3.17 Map of the Kauramembu Hill area.

prehistoric interaction. It will be recalled that Lathrap (1966) supposed a steatite-tempered sherd occurring in an early ceramic deposit from Saladero at the Mouth of the Orinoco to have derived from Guyana. The indicated trade network, centered in the Kauramembu Hills, was of impressive antiquity. A nodule of decayed steatite, Figure 3.15b, was recovered 2.0 m deep in the Koriabo Point shell mound in refuse dating at 5710 +/- 80 b.p., suggesting the early interest in exotic raw materials that is exemplified by the occurrence of the ingot of specular iron ore in the Barabina mound around 200 km to the northwest, Figure 3.15a. A date at 6520 +/- 160 b.p. (Beta 25057) was returned on charcoal recovered 3.0 m deep in the Koriabo shell mound, the earliest deposits which lie, as yet unexcavated, on 5.0 m. Other rock materials prominently featured in this early trade network were andesite, quartzite, amphibolite and chlorite. Two anvil stones of quartz surrounded in the refuse by numerous waste chips, combined with the abundant quartz debris reported by Elias Toro in 1905 (Osgood 1946:32) and presently eroding out of the residual clay of the river terrace, also suggest the importance of the site as a chipping station. Nonetheless, as at Barabina, the toolkit remained rudimentary, representing mainly the technology of crude, amorphous chipping of cores and flakes characteristic of various early industries in northern South America (Evans and Meggers 1960:23; Sanoja 1969; Willey 1971:364; Williams 1978b:Figure 4). A pebble of amphibole schist displaying grinding facets consistent with use as a mano or whetstone and recovered in one of the early levels of the Koriabo Point shell mound indicates a reciprocal relationship with the lower Aruka River sites, amphibole schist being the prevailing rock material of the Aruka Hills. The complete characterization of this trade network awaits comprehensive excavation of the intervening shell mounds of the Barima Basin - Anabisi, Honobo, Mt. Everard and Drum Hill. For the moment, the importance of this trade network is merely as an indicator of the antiquity and scale of regional integration in the Northwestern Subzone during the three millennia and more that had elapsed since the arrival of the earliest permanent residents there.

As has been seen, shellfishers were in occupation of the Piraka site in the Southeastern Subzone ever since the effects of the rising sea first began to be felt there, around 7200 years ago. The mangrove vegetation which supported the brackish-water fauna that constituted their main protein resource remains in evidence there today as subsurface peat deposits directly on the basement edge. These deposits were overlain by the residual clay of the hilltop, Figure 3.18.

The hypersaline conditions prevailing at the inception of the Barabina shell mound in the Northwestern Subzone a thousand years before the cresting of the sea level rise never were in evidence at Piraka in the Southeastern Subzone. Like all other shell mounds in the Pomeroon Basin, the dense nerite deposit at Piraka indicates that the initial brackish environment had remained the same throughout. Such sustained brackish conditions may have resulted from proximity to the Mouth

Figure 3.18. Kabakaburi Hill, Pomeroon River. Peat underlying residual clay on the basement edge.

of the Essequibo River (the *Rio Dulce*), which once may have been much wider. In this scenario, the brackish environment of the pioneer settlers antedated formation of the present day freshwater swamp forest and extended to the basement edge. With the seaward advance of the shoreline, the now sequestered brackish-water vegetation on the basement edge was replaced by the freshwater swamps of the present day and the shellfishing lifeway ended.

Human exploitation of the mangrove epifauna may have ceased well before these mangroves disappeared. A peat deposit at Jacobus Farm on the basement edge near the Mouth of the Arapiako River shows mangroves still growing locally at 3170 +/- 70 b. p., (1170 B.C.), (Beta 44743), Figure 3.19a. Brackish conditions continue to be evidenced locally in the food refuse at nearby Waiwaru Market as late as 2150 +/- 70 b.p., (200 B.C.), (Beta 27649), Figure 3.19b.

 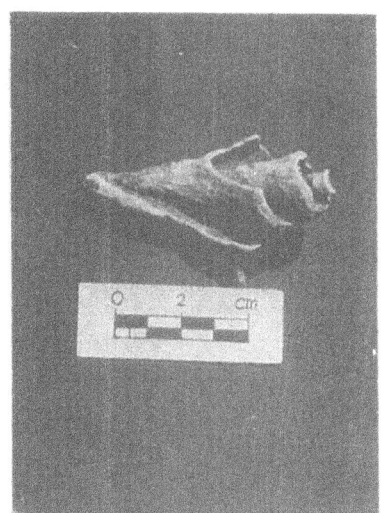

Figure 3.19 a,b. a. Jacobus Farm, Pomeroon River. Mangrove *rhizophorae* in peat deposit.
b. Waiwiaru Market, Pomeroon River. *Strombus pugilis* in the food refuse.

The propagule group responsible for sedentary occupation of the lower Moruka Basin at Waramuri Hill nearby appears to have derived from Piraka where, as noted above, stress conditions associated with the culmination of the sea level rise around 4000 B.C. are implied in increased cremation efficiency and a simultaneous recourse to famine options in the shellfish species utilized. It will be recalled that increased mortality and population movement were associated with the advent of the sea level peak at Barabina, far to the North West, Table E. On Waramuri Hill, salinization of the environment with the peaking of the sea level rise was offset by the presence of a perennial spring which supports a sizeable population there to the present day. Located on the absolute edge of the emergent rocks of the Guiana Shield with an illimitable expanse of productive mudflats stretching to the Atlantic, occupation of this forested hummock constituted, in the long run, a dynamic center of socio-cultural evolution after a thousand years of isolation and stasis among the propagule group that had initiated settlement in the Southeastern Subzone.

The changing local environments to which, over time, these Archaic shell-fishers adapted on Waramuri Hill are evidenced in the differing species of shellfish refuse accumulating in their food remains on the northern edge of the island. This mound comprises two well defined zones. The upper comprises a mantle of *terra preta* 20 - 40 cm thick, while the lower, 3.0 m deep, comprises shell sand containing variable quantities of Mangrove Oyster, Jamaica Lucine, Tulip Mussel, conch and, in the uppermost levels, increasing numbers of the Zebra Nerite. Differing frequencies of individual species permits division of this zone into three subzones, Figure 3.20.

Figure 3.20. Waramuri shell mound, Moruka River. The stratigraphic profile.

On to 1992, the Waramuri shell mound had not been investigated since its first opening by Brett in 1866. The predominantly crabshell matrix of this mound differed so remarkably from that of all others hitherto reported, which latter uniformly comprised the marble-sized, black-and-white striped Zebra Nerite, that it seemed some substance might exist for the claim, initiated by Brett, of contrasting prehistoric groups in occupation of the Western Guiana Littoral. As it transpires, no basis whatsoever exists for that claim, persistent though it proved among subsequent investigators. According to Evans and Meggers (1960:25), mounds of the Alaka phase which they identified and described are densely compacted refuse composed of shells (oyster, clam, mussel, snail, etc.), crab carapaces, and fish and animal bones and containing very crude percussion-made stone tools, with potsherds occasionally occurring on the surface and human skeletal remains scattered haphazardly throughout the refuse. On the other hand, mounds consisting mainly of nerite shells mixed with no dirt and little ash appeared to the authors to have been associated with one or other of their pottery-making cultures.

In point of fact, the only difference between these two types of shell mounds lies in the presence or absence, not of dirt, as reported above, but of variable quantities of shell sand deriving from the decomposition of innumerable crab parts. As is indicated at the Barabina and Kabakaburi mounds, dirt accumulates on shell mounds, and then in well defined layers, only during periods of abandonment, and such layers, sealed by further shell deposits after reoccupation of the mound, are readily recognizable in their respective profiles by texture, color, occasional root casts and of course the total absence of cultural refuse. The components mentioned above as constituting the contents of the typical Alaka phase shell mound occur in all of the shell mounds of the Western Guiana Littoral. Their densities depend on the attributes of a particular niche.

The most common component of these mounds, the tiny, round Zebra Nerite, stacks poorly when lacking a matrix of some kind, usually shell sand. Stability is maintained in this kind of mound only through its own internal pressures, and is lost with disturbance of these pressures during excavation, resulting in high mobility among its constituent shells. However, in certain conditions, this potentially mobile mass acquires structural support over time through the formation of massive horizontal conglomerates of shells, bones, etc. These conglomerates are caused by rain water percolating through humus comprising the upper layer of the mound. Rain water combines with detrital carbon dioxide to form carbonic acid, which in turn dissolves calcium carbonate shell in the upper layers to form a calcium bicarbonate solution. Percolating downward, this in due course precipitates the calcium carbonate that causes these massive concretions (Palmer and Williams 1977:25; see also Evans and Meggers 1960:29). As observed at the Koriabo Point shell mound, these concretions do not appear to form below a depth of around 3.0 m. Below this depth, excavation releases a continuous cascade of fresh, shiny nerite shells which, by undermining the mound structure, creates conditions conducive to its eventual collapse.

Mounds that are almost completely composed of shell sand are incomparably more stable, yielding sections that are subject to exact stratigraphic control to the greatest depths. The Waramuri and Wahana Island shell mounds are of this kind, Figure 3.21. They comprise overwhelmingly the residues of myriads of Mangrove Land Crabs that had attracted the very first settlers to the mudflats. Their difference

Figure 3.21. Test pit on Wahana Island, upper Waini River.

from other, nerite-based, shell mounds of the swamp basin is merely one of content, deriving from the type of niche inhabited by the occupying group. Whereas the Piraka group in the Southeastern Subzone harvested for upwards of a millennium the rich colonies of Zebra Nerites inhabiting the mangrove prop roots in their brackish environment, Figure 3.22, their descendants at Waramuri, on the adjacent Moruka River, harvested over just half that time the abundant colonies of crabs readily available in their mudflat environment.

Figure 3.22. Excavations at Piraka, Pomeroon River.

The zonation of the refuse in the Waramuri mound represents seven centuries of environmental change immediately following on the culmination of the eustatic sea level rise. The diagnostic shellfish species indicate (a) rapid salinization of rivers and creeks as a function of the cresting of the eustatic sea level rise, (b) alternate dessication and inundation of the intertidal mudflats and (c) eventual freshening of the environmnt. In this last stage, as the accumulated discharge of rivers draining the basement rocks gradually prevailed over the marine influence, the intertidal mudflats were converted into the seasonally inundated grass savannas of the present day. Since these changes were of pivotal importance in the sociocultural evolution of the entire Western Guiana Littoral, they each merit careful characterization.

(a) Salinization of rivers and creeks. While the massive accumulation of crab refuse that signals inception of mound growth implies the existence of extensive mudflats locally, the saline conditions that accompanied rapid retreat of the shoreline inland are indicated by various other specimens of an intertidal fauna mixed with this crab refuse. Occurrences of oyster, clam and conch at optimum sizes in the lowest levels of the mound are diagnostic of the high salinity levels obtaining at this initial stage of mound growth. Local stands of their substrate, the Red Mangrove, are implied along the Moruka River.

Diminishing sizes of certain shellfish species in the stratigraphic profile, e.g., *Strombus pugilis* and *Crassostrea rhizophorae,* are useful indicators of falling salinity levels prevailing locally during the development of the mound. All else being equal (e.g. temperature, water quality, etc.), optimum sizes of these shellfish will correlate with optimum salinity. However, these species were not equally well represented in the sample, besides which the Mangrove Oyster exhibits a wide range of tolerance of salinity (5 - 30%) and has been known to survive immersion in freshwater for limited periods (Bacon 1970; see also Loosanoff 1950). Also, its growth may be hampered by crowding on the substrate. This notwithstanding, its mean maximum diameters ranged between 100 - 54.6 mm from bottom to top of the stratigraphic profile. Mean maximum diameters of *Strombus pugilis* ranged between 90 - 35 mm. Because of its better numerical representation, and assuming a more or less steady rate of refuse accumulation, *Strombus* was favored as a more reliable indicator of diminishing salinity levels in the mound environment through time.

The period of high initial salinities represented by optimum mean maximum diameters of *Strombus pugilis (+/-* 90 mm) lasted well on two hundred years. In the 3.0 meter deep profile, a charcoal sample on 260 - 280 cm depth returned a C^{14} date at 5960 +/- 50 b.p., 4010 B.C. (Beta 57588), indicating initiation of mound development in the hypersaline conditions prevailing around the peak of the eustatic sea level rise. A charcoal sample on 180 - 200 cm depth returned a C^{14} date at 5740 +/- 50 b.p., 3790 B.C. (Beta 57586). This period of high ambient salinities was followed by an abrupt salinity decline which continued progressively through the upper two subzones. The gradual appearance of the brackish-water Zebra Nerite in the uppermost levels signaled slow freshening of the environment, during which time fissioning of the Waramuri community is indicated by inception of settlement on Haimarakabra shell mound. The top of the Haimarakabra mound dates at 5250 +/- 130 b.p. 3 300 B.C. (Beta 57590), representing the time of its abandonment and the shift to the Pomeroon River.

(b) Dessication/Inundation of the intertidal mudflats. Rapid incursion of the sea across a virtually flat shelf deposited marine sediments over the residual clays of the crystalline basement and initiated mangrove growth. On this "evolutionary coast," built up by deposition of mudflats which subsequently were colonized by permanent

vegetation (Wells and Coleman 1981a), the mangrove prop root provided the only substrate for the intertidal epifauna that constituted the subsistence base of these Archaic shellfishers. Zoning of this epifauna on each prop root provides a rough and ready diagnostic of water levels prevailing at the time particular shellfish species were harvested. *Crassostrea* occupies the middle, or oyster zone, which is around 30 cm in depth, with barnacles above and sponges and tunicates below it (Bacon 1970). Thus, oyster frequencies in the refuse are diagnostic of water levels prevailing in the economic catchment area of the mound during the relevant period of its growth.

This middle zone represents the difference between the levels of mean high and mean low water of neap tides. Oyster spat settling on the upper part of the prop roots die as a result of dessication. Below the level of mean low water of neap tides, dense growths of the Tulip Mussel *(Modiolus americanus)* occur among other organisms during periods of high salinites. *Modiolus* also may burrow in the mud beneath mangrove roots. Therefore, intercalations of mussel shells in the refuse indicate periods of lower than normal water levels locally. Relative thicknesses of these mussel layers constitute direct evidence of the durations of individual episodes of low water, Figure 3.20. The two lower zones of the profile exhibit three regularly spaced lenses of mussel shell of variable thickness, suggesting that these mollusks were harvested when water levels locally lay below the level of mean low water of neap tides. Durations of the respective low-water intervals varied from brief to prolonged. Similarly spaced mussel layers occur in the Barabina and Kabakaburi profiles as well as in the Brazilian *sambaqui* (Fairbridge 1976). At Waramuri, the major mussel deposit, varying between 40 - 50 cm in thickness, dates at +/- 3790 B.C., i.e., roughly contemporaneous with the furthest marine penetration in the swamp basin. In the subsequent freshwater rebound, a single and insubstantial mussel layer in the still accumulating crab refuse suggests the now increasing influence of run-off and the irreversible submergence of the intertidal mudflats.

During times of unusual and prolonged low elevations in the highwater maxima of neap tides, the shoreline stands far out to sea, beyond the intertidal zone, which now is permanently dessicated. At such times, the intertidal and sometimes even the subtidal fauna on mangrove prop roots are exposed to dessication. On the dried out mudflats, the bacteria, molds, tiny mollusks and crustaceans that represent the bottom of the food web perish (Rutzler and Feller 1987/88). This situation seems indicated periodically in the Waramuri mound by the recovery there of hunks of Honeycomb Tubeworm, Figure 3.16. Absence of crab refuse during such periods indicates the severity of the subsistence crises generated by these episodes of mudflat drying. The effect of dessication on the vegetation of the coastal environment is modeled in Figure 3.23.

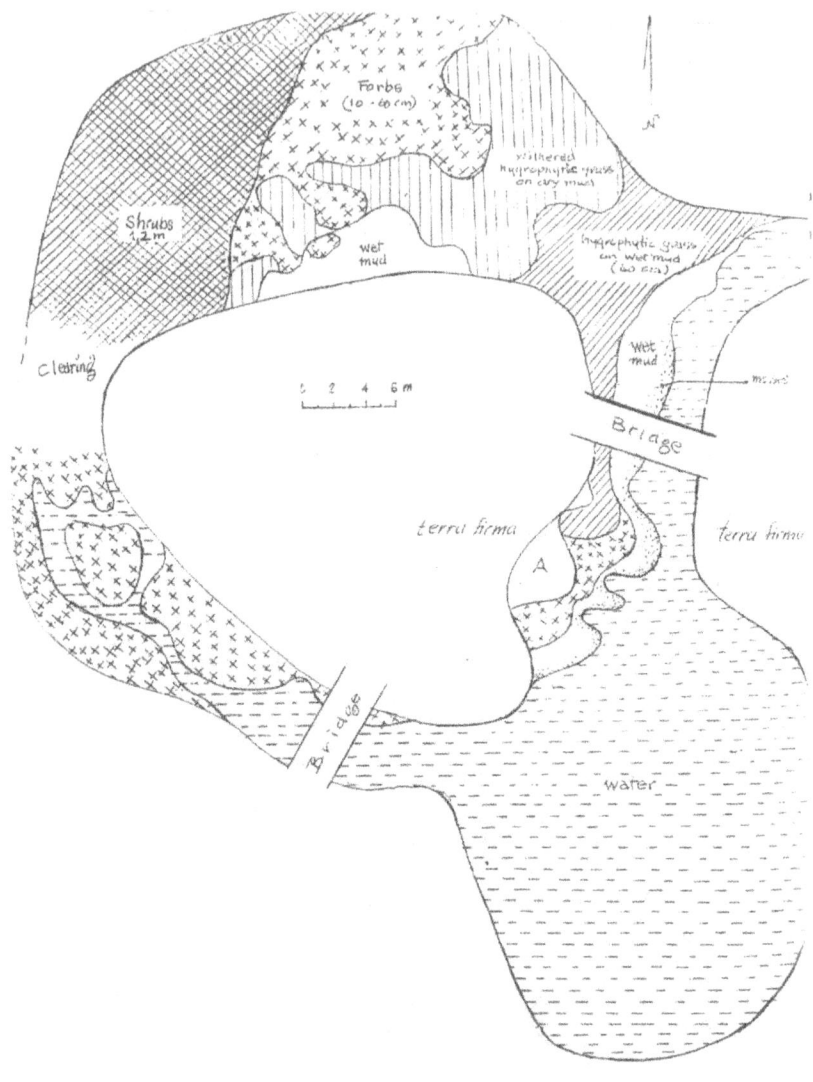

Figure 3.23. Manatee pond, Botanic Gardens Georgetown, Jan-March 1988. A moisture gradient trends SE-NW. Shallow water (< 30 cm) passes to wet mud, and dry mud (fissures 2-10 cm), supporting, successively, mosses, herbs and shrubs. As soil dries out, the (helophyte) grass withers and dies. Dried out mud is invaded by, first, forbs, then shrubs. Higher ground on the immediate pond edge, A., attracts (bahama) grass growing on *terra firme* ca. 85 cm above water level.

(c) Freshening of the environment. The Waramuri folk were ill-equipped for survival in an environment undergoing drastic and irreversible change after +/- 3300 B.C. The need for generating a versatile toolkit had never been felt by these pioneers on the highly productive mudflats. During the periodic stress episodes, their quest for the daily protein ration had led, not to the nearby rain forest, but to mussel beds in the mud below the mangroves.

In the approximately five hundred years represented by the upper two subzones, progressive freshening of the environment is indicated by regularly diminishing sizes of saltwater shellfish species. Towards the end of the period, the brackish-water Zebra Nerite began to appear in increasing frequencies. To specialist crab collectors, consumption of this marble-sized snail represented a shift to a famine option hitherto provided by standing resources of the now submerged Tulip Mussel. The uppermost zone of the mangrove prop root is host to no edible shellfish except the Zebra Nerite. Increasing reliance on this small and nutritionally poor snail at the expense of the traditional high-protein crab diet indicates the onset of sociocultural strain. Fissioning was a consequence of population pressure as decreasing food density on the mudflats coincided with declining productivity in the riverain mangroves after 3300 B.C. Reduction of the habitat of the land crab now increased the search time needed for providing the daily protein ration. Accordingly, a foraging strategy was adopted in which the low-return Zebra Nerite of the mangroves became more optimal than the high-return land crab of the vanishing mudflats. An accompanying increase in subsistence related tools signals subsistence-lack stress (Gibbon 1984:190), Figure 3.24.

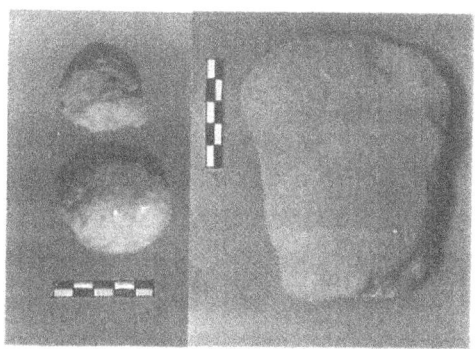

Figure 3.24. Haimorakabra shell mound, Moruka River. The stone tool inventory.

After virtually a total absence of ground stone tools, these now made an abrupt appearance in the workshops of the new Haimorakabra shell mound. The stone tool inventory there comprises implements never employed before anywhere on the

Western Guiana Littoral -- crude projectile points, choppers, hammerstones, anvil stones, chisels, scrapers and, most significantly, the specialized range of tools employed in the manufacture of the dugout canoe, i.e., adzes in many sizes and varieties, axes and whetstones.

The development of the dugout canoe on Haimarakabra Creek was the outstanding symptom of sociocultural strain in the radically altered environment. Factors inducing strain and thereby stimulating this remarkable development were (*i*) differences in the respective protein values of crustacean and molluscan shellfish ineats, (*ii*) differences in their respective harvesting costs and (*iii*) differences in their respective ease of procurement. These factors are examined below.

(i) Differences in protein value of crustacean and molluscan shellfish meats.

The meat of crustaceans yields between 17 - 22% protein, while that of mollusks yields between 15.3 - 18% protein (Borgstrom 1962:116; Waselkov 1987:Table 3.4). The Recomended Dietary Allowance (RDA) of protein per reference individual female is 55 g and per reference individual male 65g (Wing and Brown 1979: Figure 3.2). Therefore a harvest of around 60 crabs, representing the complement of a traditional collecting basket *(Warao: Kwa* = crab, *kwake* = crab basket. Creole *quake)*, each crab yielding 58.5 g meat in replication experiment, would have supplied 600 - 700 g protein or the RDA of an adult couple for just under a week.

The protein content of an Archaic meal is directly available archaeologically for comparison. Refuse from two meals dumped at different times against tree trunks on the edge of the camp site at Barabina and preserved as small hemispheres that were differentially weathered in relation to the remainder of the deposit provide an unusual insight into the protein content of an actual meal and the kinds and quantities of animals consumed toward the end of the third millennium B.C. One meal consisted of 1137 nerites (0.15 kg edible meat at a replicated 0.133 g per individual nerite); the remains of 35 crabs (= 2 kg edible meat at a replicated 58.5 g per individual crab); and bones of an estimated eight small fishes (vertebra diameters < 5mm) yielding an estimated 0.5 kg edible meat.

On a contrasting time level, refuse of another meal similarly dumped against a tree trunk on the edge of the camp site comprised 170 nerite shells (23 g edible meat), and the remains of 26 crabs (1.5 kg edible meat). Converted to values for shellfish protein and assuming an RDA of 65 g/day (male) and 55 g/day (female), the first meal would have been adequate in protein content for around 8 adult males and females (about the band size estimated from housepost distributions), while the second would have been adequate for around 6 adult males and females.

Acquiring the protein equivalent of 60 crabs would have necessitated harvesting between 25,000 - 35,000 nerites. This estimate seems supported by the volumes of storage pits for nerites excavated in the Barabina shell mound, each of which accommodated 24,000 - 54,000 individuals (Williams 1981:30).

(ii) Differences in harvesting costs. Selective exploitation of contrasting biotopes (mudflats, mangroves, rivers and creeks), represented by the refuse of these two meals, suggests optimization of the cost-benefits of protein capture against a background of seasonal abundances and scarcities. In the environment of the lower Moruka River at the time of the freshwater climax, the available options may not have been many. Nonetheless, the food refuse reveals consumption of crabs, snails and fish virtually to the end of occupancy.

The cost to an individual of harvesting a week's crab supply was around 1 hr, or just under 10 minutes per day. This labor input produced an RDA adequate for an adult couple. By contrast, in replication experiment, an hour's harvesting by an individual produced around 2000 Zebra Nerites, representing only 40 g protein. At this rate, the time required to produce an RDA adequate for an adult couple for one day would have been around three hours.

A high adult/juvenile ratio among shells of the Zebra Nerite in the deposit (3:1) suggests that efforts were made to counter this uneconomical harvesting rate by chopping and stripping the mangrove root *in situ*, as has been observed in recent practice on Trinidad (Bacon 1970). In this way, an average nine prop roots could be chopped and stripped per man per minute. But even at this rate, harvesting a complement of 6000 nerites, representing the daily protein ration of an adult couple, would have been at a cost of 2.6 hr. Evidently, therefore, a meal comprising protein deriving from only nerites was less cost effective than a meal combining protein deriving from the indicated combination of nerites, crab and fish.

(iii) Differences in relative ease of procurement. Whereas the RDA of crab meat for an adult couple could be harvested more or less on the doorstep, harvesting an equivalent complement of protein from the Zebra Nerite involved extended search of the mangroves. Search time related directly to the stocking of the mangrove plant, which, on the intertidal mudflats of the Western Guiana Littoral, occurs at a density of 25 plants/ha (de Milde and de Groot 1970). The inexorable seaward advance of the shoreline under the influence of run-off implies a corresponding advance of the mangrove belt and hence continually increasing search time per individual. Abandonment of the Waramuri site around 3300 B.C. suggests that the continued extension of its economic catchment area made necessary by the continuing advance of the mangrove belt had rendered protein capture from this source finally uneconomic.

Thus, the circumstances under which the dugout canoe first made its appearance on the Western Guiana Littoral are attributable directly to subsistence lack stress on the lower Moruka River. The continuing residential stability of the small Waramuri community there in face of the dire environmental reverses which the food refuse shows to have compromised carrying capacity during several preceding generations indicates the level of success achieved in attempting to devise an alternative system of protein capture notwithstanding the radical technoeconomic changes involved. From a traditional diet of pure, high-protein crab meat harvested virtually on the doorstep, the environmentally conditioned shift to a diet of low-protein nerites now involved simultaneous exploitation of the intertidal mudflats, the mangroves and the rivers and creeks in order to maintain cost effectiveness in protein capture.

Intensification was inevitable. Ironically, the accompanying technoeconomic change involved a choice among options which always had been available within the sociocultural system of the Western Guiana Littoral. For example, when hunting terrestrial quadrupeds became critical to survival among these traditionally mudflat-oriented crab collectors, the large, unifacially flaked projectile point *daborabaka* already existed somewhere in the system. A specimen was recovered in early refuse at Wahana Island, Figure 3.25g. Thus, it did not need to be reinvented when required among kinsmen on Waramuri Island, some 80 km to the southwest. This applied also to the specialized tootkit needed in the development of the dug-out canoe. In light of the ever-advancing shoreline and concurrent diminishing crab densities locally, economic survival now required more efficient watercraft than the woodskins of the paleo-Indigenous period. Their high level of specificity with regard to design and rock material notwithstanding, the knowledge required for the manufacture and use of the range of tools employed in canoe manufacture, as well as the sources of the necessary rock materials, long had been a resource of the sociocultural system which, however, yet remained to be exploited locally. Until stress conditions supervened, these available options had meant little to the Waramuri community in light of the efficiency of their traditional systems of resource utilization. With its freshwater spring and biotically rich mudflats, the community had been located ideally during the previous six hundred and more years to maximize exploitation of the available resources and at little infrastructural cost in the form of tools and implements. Accordingly, social organization had remained rudimentary.

The toolkit of their earliest shellfishing kinsmen had comprised organic materials such as bone for awls used in the manufacture of basketware and bushhog teeth for modifying wood. String for hammock manufacture was made from leaves of the ubiquitous Moriche palm. Dental arcades of certain excavated crania indicate artisanal use of the median incisors. Stone implements in daily use were unmodified pebbles and cobbles employed as hammerstones, manos or bark beaters, the latter used in the manufacture of bark cloth and woodskins. In this very rudimentary toolkit, the deliberate modification of stone involved merely striking flakes from rocks that already were characterized by sharp angles. These flakes were suitable for use as woodworking wedges. Fortuitously shaped cores were employed as line sinkers on cadels in inshore fishing (map: Inshore Waters). These latter were of only local distribution and remained unrepresented in cultural deposits distant from the seashore.

Figure 3.25. Early shellfishing toolkit. **a**. bone awl, **b**. spokeshave, **c**. scraper, **d**. hammerstone, **e**. boiling stone, **f**. bark beater, **g**. *daborabaka*, **h**. woodworking wedge, **i**. line sinker.

Occasional ground, or ground and polished ax or adze fragments recovered in early levels of the Barabina and Waramuri shell mounds represented the as yet unexploited availability of these advanced stoneworking technologies among the pioneering groups. The economic potentials of the ground stone technology represented by these odd artifacts remained as irrelevant on the mudflats of the lower Monika River as had been the technology of iron smelting among shellfishers on the lower Aruka River. Nonetheless, these artifacts had existed within the system, available for incorporation into the pre-existing toolkit of a given niche whenever the need arose. The sociocultural revolution represented by the emergence of the dugout canoe industry on an insignificant island in Haimorakabra Creek was therefore the product not only of environmental stress but also of capitalization, for the first time, of certain intellectual and material resources of the swamp basin.

The defining factor was the critical freshening of the environment and irreversible reduction of the local group to the unrelieved diet of low-protein nerites that is indicated in the uppermost level of their food refuse. The rising water level that contributed to the radical transformation of these ancient intertidal mudflats into the seasonally inundated grass savannas of the present day, Figure 3.26, remain in evidence on Haimorakabra Creek.

Figure 3.26. Moruka River. Seasonally inundated grass savannas, Haimorakabra Creek.

From its confluence with the Moruka River, and as far upstream as Bakassa Island, the riverain forest is dominated by an almost pure stand of Corkwood (*Pterocarpus officinalis*) overarching the stream. Immediately beyond Bakassa Island, the riverain vegetation comprises low, tangled bush under an open sky. This abrupt transition corresponds with contrasts in elevation of the riverbank. Whereas the stunted, upstream bush grows in around 60 cm of swamp with no visible riverbank, the Corkwood forest below Bakassa Island grows on a partly visible levee in around 30 cm of water. Thus, below Bakassa Island, a permanent drop in water level of around 30 cm would be sufficient to transform the present day swamp forest (permanently inundated) to marsh forest (seasonally inundated), thereby reintroducing the Mora forest (*Moa excelsa*), which is claimed in Warao cultural memory to have been burned by an infamous ancestor, one Pluto. The tradition survives in the name of Mora Island, farther upstream. This suggests that the demise of the Mora forests which, apparently, once occupied the floodplain on the tidal stretch of Haimorakabra Creek and which provided the valued raw material for the pioneering canoe manufacturing industry was a consequence of freshwater backing up in excess of the critical elevation for survival of the climax vegetation. The new water level eventually transformed erstwhile marsh forest (Mora forest) into the present day swamp forest (*Pterocarpus*). The evidently rapid transformation resulted in the demise of the canoe manufacturing industry on Haimorakabra Creek and the subsequent migration of its craftsmen to their ancestral territory on the neighboring Pomeroon River.

The date marking this critical transformation of the environment is indicated by a charcoal sample from the uppermost level of the successor mound on Haimorakabra Creek, 5250 +/- 130 b.p., 3300 B.C. (Beta 57590). This date also marks the transformation of a number of small, disparate economies on either side of the Barima/Waim "demographic divide" into an integrated socio-economic system that now resulted from the inflexible requirements of the canoe manufacturing industry. It was facilitated by the unique network of inland waterways brought into existence during the freshwater climax in the southeastern swamp basin, culminating a process that had commenced around 400 years earlier, Figure 3.14 a.

With the submergence of the intertidal mudflats, this divide was bridged between mudflat, or freshwater, adaptations in southeastern areas of the swamp basin, on the one hand, and *terra firme*, or brackish-water, adaptations in northwestern areas of the swamp basin on the other. On the Waini (freshwater) side of the divide, kinship ties between the Moruka Basin and the upper Waini River remain strong to the present day, while on the Barima (brackish-water) side of the divide, similarly strong kinship ties unite the Kaituma and Aruka Rivers, tributaries of the lower Barima. Between these, the Archaic shell mound site at Koriabo Point, long an outpost of the steatite mines on the upper Barama River, now was transformed into a redistributive center of interregional importance. In the new socioeconomic system, the raw materials and finished products of the canoe manufacturing industry were moved hundreds of kilometers across the Western Guiana Littoral as a result of intensification among the traditional crab collectors of the lower Moruka Basin.

Traditional bases of intensification

The most telling diagnostic of intensification in the lower Moruka Basin was the abrupt utilization of the ground stone tool. But even in this low-lying mudflat, bereft of suitable rock exposures, the occurrence of ground stone at the height of the freshwater climax five thousand years ago had not been unheralded. The recovery of a fragment of a ground stone ax out of context in the lower levels of the Waramuri shell mound indicates a traditional acquaintance with this stone working technique, which nonetheless had been of limited utility in the prevailing mudflat economy. It will be recalled that, elsewhere in the Northwestern Subzone, ground and polished stone adzes had occurred in the lowest level of the Barabina shell mound. Evidently intrusive and of doubtful utility there, these artifacts bear witness to the age-old relationship between *terra firme* and the Guiana Coast upon which the viability of swamp living had depended from the outset. But just as the advanced flint knapping of the paleo-Indigenous period had proven irrelevant to adaptation in the coastal swamplands and had fallen into desuetude there, so also did these later intrusions of ground stone technology among the early shellfishers of the Western Guiana Littoral. Evidently, these coastal shellfishers had preserved intact the age-old lines of communication with their ancestors of the Western Guiana Hinterland (e.g. Siparuni complex). At the same time, these early intrusions of ground stone in the refuse of communities as widely spaced across the swamps as those at Waramuri in the southeast and Barabina in the northwest indicate the importance these communities had attached to local communication links from very remote times.

Due to the uneven rates of submergence of the littoral mudflats and the immobility of most campsites in light of their all having been "tethered" to sources of potable water on the creek heads or at perennial springs, the crisis engendered by changing ambient salinities was experienced differentially in the various niches of the swamp basin. Thus, whereas the mudflats of the lower Moruka Basin were submerged more or less rapidly under the unbroken sheet of freshwater that today stretches back to the upper Waini drainage, mudflat submergence was a good deal less pressing elsewhere in the swamp basin as a result of contrasts in elevation, relative distance from the shoreline and, most importantly, the differential effects of tectonic subsidence. It has been seen that, due to this latter factor, a marine influence continued to be felt in the rest of the Northwestern Subzone a good thousand years and more after the environment in the Monika Basin had been transformed by the effects of the freshwater climax of 3300 B.C. Thus, areas of exposed mudflats and a brackish environment survived in other sectors of the Northwestern Subzone long after the intertidal mudflats of the lower Monika Basin had been transformed into the seasonally inundated freshwater grass savannas of the present day. Consequently, at the time of the subsistence crisis which on the lower Moruka River was occasioning the relocation of the canoe manufacturing industry to an ancestral site in the Southeastern Subzone, shellfishers in the remainder of the Northwestern Subzone continued to enjoy unmodified access to a variety of species of brackish-water and marine shellfish. These simultaneous differences in the salinity regime of the swamp basin were of extreme adaptive importance at the time of the subsistence crisis among crab collectors on the lower Moruka Basin. This is because the associated economic imbalance promoted conditions which now permitted relatively impoverished groups in the South East to fall back on the resources and skills of comparatively better off groups in the North West.

An example of such economic imbalance is evidenced in the profile of the Wahana Island shell mound on the upper Waini River. While the respective C^{14} dates indicate its approximate contemporaneity with the Waramuri mound, and this is confirmed by the accumulation of crab refuse comprising the respective deposits, the Waramuri environment was subject to a pattern of evolutionary change that was absent in the Wahana Island environment 80 km across the swamps to the northwest. The various lenses of Tulip Mussel which, in the Waramuri profile, indicate periodic sustained drying out of the mudflats and accompanying occurrences of local famine episodes are absent in the Wahana Island profile. Similar lenses of Tulip Mussel in the Barabina and Kabakaburi profiles indicate that the local mudflats there were subject to similar dessicating episodes. Perhaps due to its extensive granite ridge, such episodes of mudflat dessication are not in evidence at Wahana Island. Its Warao name (= *Black Sand by the Seashore*) implies that a sandy foreshore, now vanished, had remained a significant feature of the environment into the time of the freshwater climax.

Such economic imbalances created the complementaries by means of which, through time, the various socio-economic units of the swamp basin were integrated on a systemic basis. When the need arose, these units came to underpin the socio-cultural evolution of the entire Western Guiana Littoral.

Adoption of the specialized toolkit now required for manufacture of the dugout canoe in the lower Moruka Basin became possible because the required skills and material resources had been in existence earlier in scattered kin-based communities on both sides of the Barima/Waini divide. This is to say that the knowledge required for adapting to socio-cultural strain in a particular niche had been generated in various traditional infrastructures scattered across the Western Guiana Littoral during the several centuries following on the arrival of the founding nuclei at Piraka in the Southeastern and at Barabina in the Northwestern Subzones.

The requirements of the canoe manufacturing industry, which had emerged in the wake of the seaward advance of the shoreline and a freshening environment in the lower Moruka Basin, now involved tapping the intellectual and material resources of communities on the far side of the Barima-Waini divide. It has been shown that exploitation of their mineral resources had been a feature of the economies of communities on the Barima Basin ever since at least the sixth millennium. At around this time, steatite nodules mined on the upper Barama River were in evidence in the refuse of middlemen occupying the Koriabo Point shell mound. Simultaneously, the community on Barabina Hill in the Barima Basin was mining iron ore in the Arukumai Hills apparently for experiments in tool manufacture, Figure 3.15a,b. The early refuse at Barabina Hill exhibits chipping debris and tool discards indicating the importation of a range of rock materials from the Barama River mines. While the picture of this early trade in rock materials remains to be filled out by investigations at the as yet unexcavated intervening shell mounds at Anabisi, Honobo, Mt. Everard and Drum Hill, already the available data point to the strategic importance of the sites in the Barima Basin with respect to the exploitation of the mineral resources of *terra firme*.

In the higher water levels of the freshwater climax, the Waini-Barima watershed was bridged for the first time by means of a complex of shallow streams connected by man-made channels (*itabos*) which entered the Barima River below Koriabo Point. These had come into being with rising local water levels resulting from the gradual advance of the freshwater front. Now this network of small streams provided uninterrupted access to the Aruka Basin and thence to the Orinoco, Figure 3.14. This triumph of Archaic geography is attributable to the observation that, in the daily meeting of ebb and flow in creeks lying within the tidal counter-currents of major coastal streams, an absolute lack of current in the otherwise ever-flowing waters of the swamps is an unequivocal indicator of a submerged watershed. Where, from time immemorial, kilometers of impassable mudflats had separated these two major streams, with access possible only along the *terra firme* bush path to Chinee Landing on the distant Barama River, now an incomparably shorter route had been found across the mudflats of the Barima-Waini watershed. This resulted from careful plotting of the area of motionless water under which this watershed was submerged. Henceforth, it would be possible to journey continuously through these inland waterways from the Essequibo estuary to the Orinoco Delta. With the advent of the canoe manufacturing industry, a group of shell mounds clustered around a uniquely outcropping granite ridge on the upper Waini River now came into entrepreneurial prominence in the movements of men and materials along this highway.

Paramount in this complex was the shell mound on Wahana Island (N-9 in the terminology of Evans and Meggers 1960) at the mouth of Warapoco Creek and located on the Waini mainstream a few kilometers below the Morebo River, Figure

3.27. Down the Morebo flowed all traffic from the Barima River. Other small shell mounds in the complex are Alaka Creek, Assakata Creek, Aiyekowa Creek (probably the Pawaeiykemoo of Im Thurn 1883:412), Little Kaniaballi, Sand Creek and Quiaro. This compact settlement pattern resulted from the economically important north-south trending granite ridge commencing at Aiyekowa Creek on the left bank of the Waini River and ending at Alaka Creek on the Morebo River. Weathering and erosion of this granite had deposited areas of coarse sand on the very edge of the swamps, one of which may have survived in the Warao name Wahana. Another deposit survives on Alaka Creek, a left tributary of the Morebo. Some of these rare sand deposits appear to have contributed to the trade in rock materials moving into faraway swamp sites.

The primary importance of the Wahana Island granite exposure was as a tool grinding depot in the vast trade network that sprang up in the swamp basin in the wake of the canoe manufacturing industry on the lower Moruka River. In the dynamics of this trade, Wahana Island served as the meeting point of already well established local trade networks of the Barima and Waini Rivers, attracting lengthy stopovers by craftsmen from both sides of the watershed. Resultingly, the granite outcrops around Wahana Island, and especially those on Waropoko Creek, are covered with myriads of grinding surfaces attesting to the continuing viability of the industry across the centuries.

The present inhabitants of Wahana Island (1993), a Warao extended family numbering 14 individuals, claim that their village, Waropoko, was founded by one Waropoko, a native of Waramuri, 80 km to the southeast. The name evidently derives from *awarau* = kin and *-noko* = place. The suffix *-noko is* affixed to both verbs and nouns, e.g. *duhu* (sit) : *duhunoko* (seat); *ha* (hammock) : *hanoko* (house) (Edwards 1980). Hence, possibly also, *ohinoko* (Orinoco) = place of the Moriche palm. In any case *awarau* (kin) explains the similarity between place names such as Waropoko, Waramuri, Warapana (all Archaic sites) and Waraputa (an Archaic fishing ground at Waraputa Falls on the Essequibo River. Similarly, *awaranoka* (a place of learning) and *W-aini* (Our Place).

The Warao kinship network supported the system of exchange which distinguishes Early from Late Archaic shellfishing communities on the Western Guiana Littoral. Whereas the changing features of coastal geomorphology had contributed initially to the socio-economic isolation of the earlier inhabited niches, increasing exploration of the swamp basin and exploitation of its key geological resources later constituted a major contributory factor in the integration of the political economy. As knowledge of local mineral resources grew over time, a trade developed in nodules of decayed steatite and slivers of chlorite schist mined in the creek beds of the Kauramembu Hills. From Koriabo Point, the steatite nodules were transported down the Barima River to Hosororo Creek on the Aruku River. A sliver

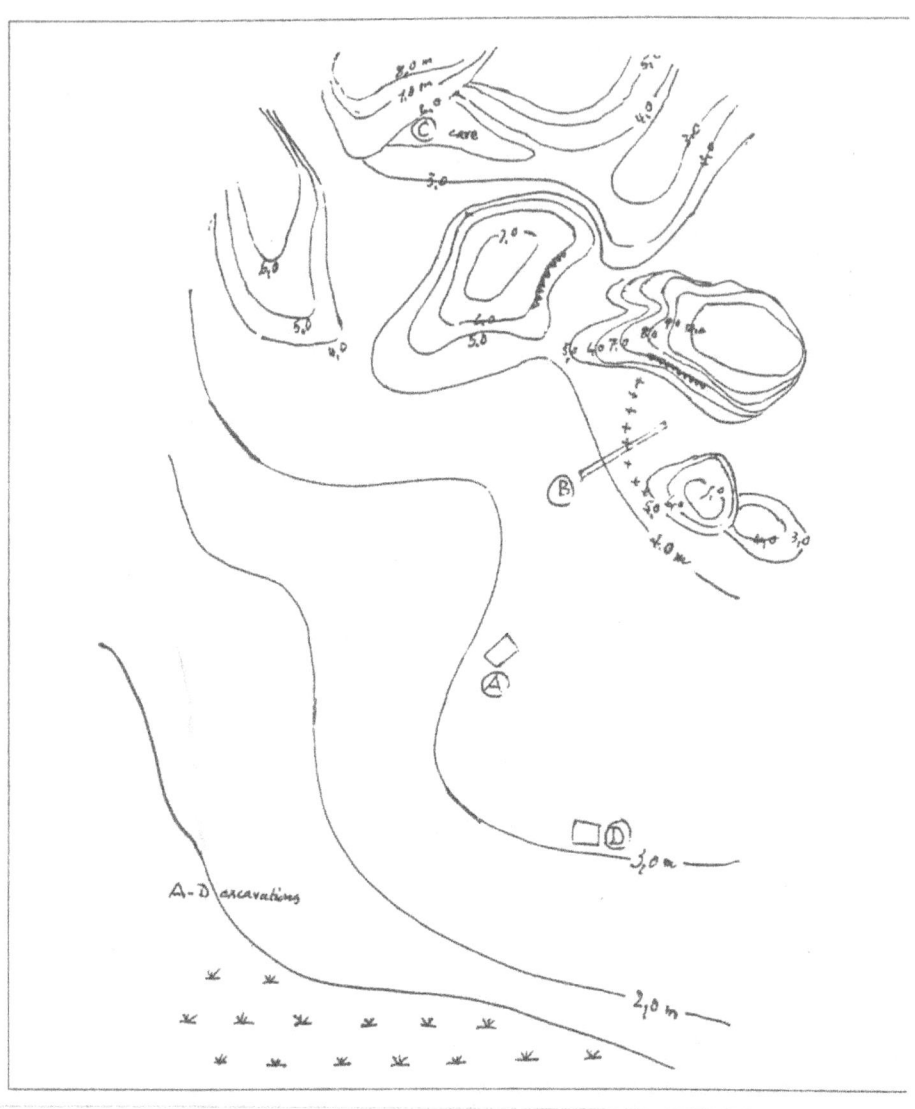

Figure 3.27. Waini River. Wahana Island: The Site Plan.

of chlorite schist recovered in the middle levels of the Piraka shell mound on the Pomeroon River indicates the southeastward extension of the trade before the ending of the fourth millennium B.C. The initial date for the successor mound at Kabakaburi nearby is 5340 +/- 100 b.p. (Beta 3218 8). Soon, pebbles and cobbles of andesite were being traded directly to Kabakaburi, in the stoneless swamps of the Southeastern Subzone, for use in the canoe industry there. Simultaneously, in the Northwestern Subzone, pebbles and cobbles of andesite, greywacke sandstone and amphibolite from the upper Barama River were being transported down the Barima River to Barabina on the lower Aruka River. In a complementary trade, following on the bridging of the Barima-Waini watershed, pebbles and cobbles of amphibole schist, the prevailing rock material of the Aruka Hills, were being transported in massive quantities to Wahana Island on the upper Waini River. These in turn were re-exported to the canoe workshops on the lower Moruka River in the southeast, where they were custom-made into blanks by specialist canoe craftsmen. Thereafter, they were re-exported to the granite ridge on Wahana Island for grinding into the specialized tools of the canoe industry.

Thus, the nature and scope of this trade network were determined by the geology of the swamp basin. Essential rock materials for the specialized tools of the industry were located on the upper Barama and lower Aruka Rivers. Granite outcrops for grinding these rock materials into finished products were located on the upper Waini River. Economic stands of the Mora tree, used for fashioning into canoes, were located on the basement edge on Haimarakabra Creek, lower Moruka River. The socio-economic integration of the region that is indicated by this basin-wide interlocking of local trade networks had its central stimulus in the advent of the freshwater climax toward the ending of the fourth millennium B.C. This was experienced first, and with the most profound socio-cultural consequences, in the South East.

At the time it was occupied by Waropoko, the ancestor of the present Warao community, the seashore constituted part of the economic catchment area of Wahana Island. This was not long before the sea had attained its present level. At that time, the island was 3.55 m lower than at present and was covered by a layer of black humus overlying bedrock. Discounting the effects of tectonic subsidence subsequently, the granite outcrop constituting its backbone rose a sheer 12 m. Instead of the present day freshwater swamps, the immediate surroundings constituted open mudflats. A lower Waini River drained these open mudflats, source of the Mangrove Land Crab whose refuse comprises the bulk of the shell mound. Marine mollusks occurring in significant numbers in the early food refuse denote the prevailing saline environment. Their sizes and densities declined in later levels. The gradually freshening conditions that are indicated by diminishing sizes per level of the various shellfish species in the Waramuri mound in the aftermath of the peaking of the sea level rise are in evidence also on Wahana Island. Progressively diminishing sizes and numbers per level of oysters in the Wahana Island profile similarly gave way to increasing numbers of the brackish-water Zebra Nerite in the uppermost 80 cm. Inception of this terminal stage of freshening has been dated at 4570 +/- 80 b.p., Cal B.C. 3370 - 3290 (Beta 69257). This is the period of the freshwater climax in the South East, among the socio-cultural consequences of which was the development of the dugout canoe by the Waramuri community. In its closing centuries the subsistence round at Waramuri similarly had been determined by the seaward advance of the mangroves.

The "time of troubles" that was initiated on the Waini side of the watershed by the freshwater climax of 3300 B.C. was not experienced on the Barima side for well over another thousand years. The economic imbalance that was created by these contrasting geological environments in the changing swamp regimes of the Western Guiana Littoral provided the basis of the balanced reciprocity that was essential to the sustained viability of the canoe manufacturing industry. With the disappearance of the intertidal mudflats in the southeast of the swamp basin, the subsistence of erstwhile crab collectors there now came to be based on the low-protein Zebra Nerite. This subsistence shift had been made possible only by the relocation of the industry to Kabakaburi on the upper Pomeroon River. Henceforth, Kabakaburi became the center of canoe manufacture. Thence, the continuing seaward advance of the mangroves was met by progressive relocation of habitation sites downriver. Over time, the Pomeroon would become renowned for the excellence of its canoes. The reputation survives in the boat building industry of the present day, Figure 3.28.

Development of the canoe manufacturing industry
The tools

The transformation of the trunk of a mature Mora tree into a dugout canoe some distance from the point of felling engaged communal energy coupled with a wide array of skills over a significant period of time. Now, these skills were incorporated into the traditional labor force of the crab collectors. The resulting, much more complex, relations of production involved occupation of a specialized manufacturing site independent of the old extended family compound on Waramuri Hill. Sand Hill on Haimarakabra Creek downstream was located ideally on permanently dry land in the midst of Mora forest. The dense refuse there is represented by a sample of 275 stone items, of which 220 were collected by Everard Im Thurn (Walter Roth Museum Im Thurn Collection). The remaining 55 items derived from stratigraphic excavation of two 2 x 2 m test pits. All of these latter were tools, in addition to which numerous stone chips indicated sustained *in situ* percussion flaking. Rock materials included pebbles and cobbles of amphibole schist, amphibolite, quartzite and fine-grained andesite, all deriving from the Barima side of the watershed to the far North West. The amphibole schist had derived from certain stream beds of the

Figure 3.28. Pomeroon River. The boat building tradition.

lower Aruka and the quartz from outcrops at Koriabo Point. Modification was by chipping, chipping and abrasion, grinding, and grinding and polishing. Unmodified waterworn pebbles of amphibole schist displayed one or more grinding facets, some stained with red coloring matter consistent with their having been employed as manos in the preparation of body paint. Hammerstones were on modified quartz pebbles that exhibit depressions on one or more surface. Crystal quartz was employed in the manufacture of knives, while the opaque vein quartz of Koriabo Point was modified by pecking for use as scrapers and choppers. Pecking was employed also in modifying large, bifacially flaked, stemless projectile points on quartz. Modification of quartz pebbles by pecking was known at sites on both the Northwestern and Southeastern Subzones. Large chisels with rectangular-sectioned butts were ground to sharp, wedge-shaped working edges. Sub-conical to rounded, rarely rhomboidal, waterworn pebbles exhibit grinding facets compatible with their having been used as whetstones. This item was numerically the best represented in both the im Thurn and the excavated collections. Certain waterworn cobbles of amphibole schist exhibited central depressions resulting from use as anvil stones. Damaged or discarded ground stone adzes/axes were represented by various bit, butt and shaft fragments on quartzite, amphibole schist and andesite.

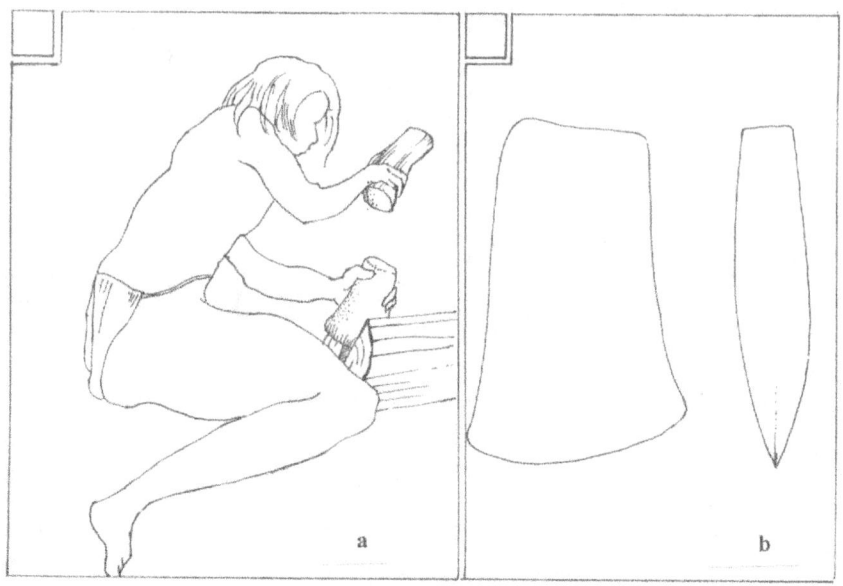

Figure 3.29a,b. Sand Hill, Haimarakabra Creek. The stone ax in canoe manufacture

Three types of ax were represented, petaloid, trapezoidal and bell-shaped, this latter displaying an unusual profile with outsloping shaft and wide, flaring bit, Figure 3.29b. Their shapes indicate a common absence of hafting, though asymmetric wear on the surviving bits is identical to wear occurring on hafted axes. In a sample of 18 specimens, all exhibited abrasion and/or spalling on the butts consistent with battering with a mallet and all had fractured horizontally across the shaft, apparently under percussion. Unhafted use in splitting wood in conjunction with the large stone chisels is suggested, Figure 29a.

The stone tool inventory at Sand Hill on Haimarakabra Creek as well as at the successor site on Kabakaburi Hill on the neighboring Pomeroon River, displays a gradual development in stone working technology from crude percussion flaking, to chipping and abrasion, to grinding, and grinding and polishing, Figure 3.30. These technological developments are paralleled by a concurrent typological evolution in the ground stone adze, the premiere tool in canoe manufacture, Figure 3.31. This resulted from problems faced in its efficient hafting, as is indicated in the range of fracture patterns represented by the surviving fragments. Because of their diagnostic potentials, these fracture patterns have been classified as follows, Figure 3.32.

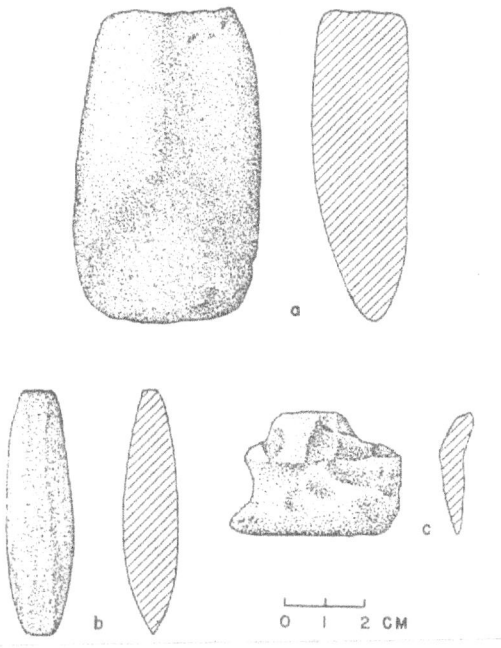

Figure 3.30. Evolution of stone working technology in the southeastern swamp basin.

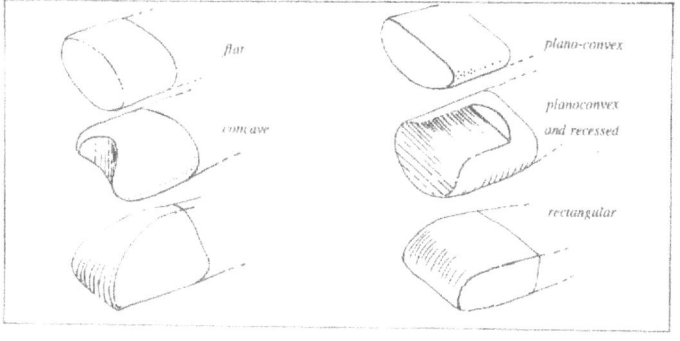

Figure 3.31. Evolution of the ground stone adze in the southeastern swamp basin.

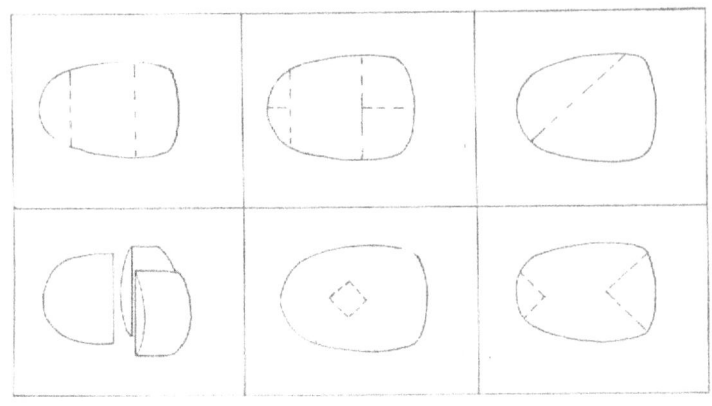

Figure 3.32. Fracture patterns of ground stone adzes employed in canoe manufacture.

i. *Simple vertical fracture.* A vertical fracture connects dorsal and ventral surfaces of butt or bit along a straight or curved line.

ii. *Compound fracture.* Two simultaneously occurring simple fractures meet at a right angle in butt or bit.

iii. *Oblique fracture.* Butt, bit and/or shaft are connected by a simple fracture.

iv. *Vertical/horizontal fracture.* Butt, bit and/or shaft fracture simultaneously vertically and horizontally.

v. *Core fracture.* Shaft fractures around a polyhedral core.

vi. *Wedge fracture.* A wedge comprising part or all of the edge of butt or bit is removed.

The most successful design, which anchored the helve simultaneously in both the butt and the shaft, survived into horticultural times, Figure 3.33. Typically it is associated with type *v* fracture.

Three weight grades characterize these Archaic adzes: 0.1 to 0.3 kg., 0.6 kg and 1.8 kg. This suggests a specialized function for each weight grade, and this is confirmed by ethnographic analogy. Contemporary Warao recognize two adze sizes in canoe manufacture: *nehara* (small) and *neharaija* (large) (Edwards 1980).

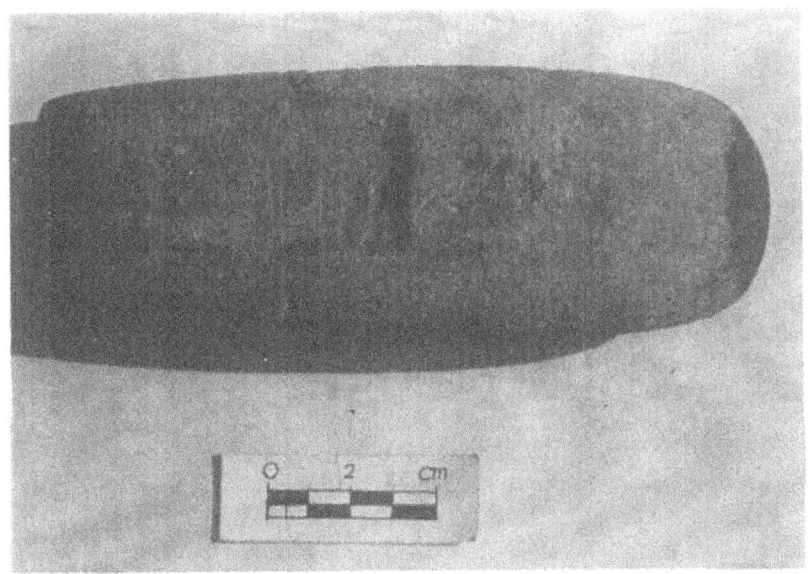

Figure 3.33. Archaic adze used in canoe manufacture.

The industry

The evidently *in situ* technological and typological development of the stone adze at Sand Hill implies resident specialist craftsmen there, while the density of the accompanying stone working refuse implies generations of locally transmitted skills. These skills may have been distinct from those of the actual manufacturers of the dugout canoes, whose knowledge successfully reduced the felled Mora log to a seaworthy vessel. Even with modern steel tools, this process is discussed in terms of months rather than of weeks or days, depending on the status of the craftsman, part-time or full-time. Some of the Sand Hill remains (food refuse, projectile points, cosmetic manos) suggest its occupation by part-time specialists supported by their womenfolk.

As has been seen, rock materials for the local industry derived from very distant locations across the Barima-Waini watershed. The obligatory ready supply of raw materials for manufacture of the stone tools of the industry implies trade relationships with communities in political control of these distant quarries. By virtue of their strategic locations, communities at Koriabo Point on the Barima River, Wahana Island on the Waini River and Barabina on the Aruka River functioned as independent factors in the indicated trade network. Their respective roles in the political integration of already existing local networks are examined below.

Koriabo Point. The shell mound rises from an old river terrace which stands 4.5 m above the dry season water level (May). Myriads of quartz chips embedded in the residual white clay at the foot of the mound cover an estimated 25 x 36 m. Although the depth of the mound at its apex is in excess of 5.0 m, excavation to 4.2

m depth yielded quartz chips only in the uppermost 1.50 m. Two quartz cobbles associated with chipping waste in the deposit had been employed as anvils. No stone tools were recovered. This stratigraphically late accumulation of quartz debris in the food remains suggests that at this time the export of quartz cobbles had been added to the local trade in rock materials from the Barama River. Now the industry was incorporated into the trade network that had followed on the bridging of the Barima-Waini watershed after around 3300 B.C. Bioindicators of local freshening around 3700 B.C. had begun to appear at Koriabo Point at a depth of 2.0 m from the surface (p. 107). This freshening was felt in southeastern parts of the coast some 400 years later.

Absence of stone tools in the Koriabo Point refuse suggests an extra-local focus in the industry. That focus was the canoe workshops of the lower Moruka and upper Pomeroon Rivers to the far southeast. There, the mound at Sand Hill on Haimarakabra Creek is covered also with myriads of quartz chips weathering out of the surface. Quartz cobbles mined at Koriabo Point had been manuported to Sand Hill to be chipped and pecked into the knives, scrapers, hammerstones, choppers and projectile points of the local inventory, Figure 3.34.

Figure 3.34. Sand Hill, Haimarakabra Creek. Tools manufactured on imported quartz.

The surface of the small, as yet unexcavated shell mound at Sand Creek on the lower left bank of Warapoco Creek above its confluence with the Waini River is littered also with modified and unmodified quartz chips. On the other side of the watershed, the site may have served as a waystation under the control of Wahana Island, which, though located within hailing distance across the swamps, is devoid of quartz refuse.

Besides quartz, the Koriabo Point refuse included the amphibolite, steatite, quartzite and greywacke sandstone of an older industry. Slate employed in the manufacture of the remarkable bark-beater from the Pomeroon River, Figure 3.13, may have passed through this entrepôt, since slate also derives from the Barama Group of the Barama-Mazartmi Assemblage and is characteristic of the Matthews Ridge Formation, upper Kaituma River (Williams et al 1967:12).

Wahana Island. The pebbles of andesite and quartzite recovered in fair quantities at Wahana Island undoubtedly derived from the Koriabo Point entrepôt. From this source, they were re-exported to the canoe workshops on the lower Moruka River. There, the Sand Hill refuse indicates local chipping of stone into the particular kinds of preforms required by the individual craftsmen. Hence the explicit typological evolution of the stone adze that is evidenced in the surviving debris there. But due to the absolute absence of suitable rock exposures on this low-lying southeastern edge of the basement, Figure 3.3, it was imperative to re-export these preforms to the granite ridge on the upper Waini River for grinding into the appropriate tools. Accordingly, the earliest occurrences of ground stone axes and adzes in the profile at Wahana Island date at 5290 +/- 90 b.p., or 3340 B.C. This is the time of the freshwater climax and the bridging of the Barima-Waini watershed. Tools recovered in excavation at Wahana Island exhibit the full technological range of the contemporary Sand Hill industry -- chipping, chipping and abrasion, grinding, and grinding and polishing. The Wahana Island refuse revealed no evidence of local stoneworking. The rock materials there were those of the trade with the Barima and Aruka Rivers.

Barabina Hill. In the canoe industry on Sand Hill, the most commonly sought after of these rock materials was the amphibole schist of the lower Aruka River, some 300 km to the northwest. This is the prevailing rock material of the Aruka Hills, the crusts of which are weathered to laterite and covered with residual clay. The pebbles of the trade were collected in local stream beds for stone boiling and reduction to simple tools and implements by crude percussion flaking. Though more than 100 km distant from Koriabo Point, pebbles from Barabina were delivered there more cheaply than rock materials deriving from the upper Barama River, across the watershed on *terra firme*. The amphibole schist of the lower Aruka River is represented in the refuse on Wahana Island and dominates the refuse on Haimarakabra Creek as well.

At the time that the first large, trapezoidal stone axes on amphibole schist appeared in the refuse on Wahana Island, the Mangrove Land Crab still constituted the principal protein resource there. A similar situation obtained on Barabina Hill, exemplifying the economic imbalance that had been created between niches by differential rates of freshening locally. The stone chipping on Barabina Hill was diagnostic of participation in the regional trade network by shellfishers whose own need of sophisticated stone tools still did not exist. The continued absence of such tools in their refuse suggests that the trade in this highly characteristic rock material was conducted against some otherwise unattainable good no longer in evidence, possibly the dugout canoe.

In the implied system of balanced reciprocity, the individual around whom labor was organized and through whom alliances were secured and maintained performed the functions of a headman. In these widely spaced communities, an absence of site stratification indicates that expansion of the industry resulting from positive feedback (more and better canoes -- more rapid access to strategic resources -- accelerating population growth -- more complex relations of production -- more and better canoes) was an adaptive response of basin-wide proportions. Hence the dispersion of the three great shell mound complexes of the Western Guiana Littoral on the lower Aruka River, the upper Waini River and the upper Pomeroon River, each community representing a point of critical economic importance in the regional industry. In this adaptive process, surpluses were not removed from the system in order to generate hierarchies in the more productive communities (Price 1982). Instead, a kin-based distribution of canoes, the corollary of the kin-based labor inputs in the relations of production, guaranteed the reinvestment of surpluses in the system, imparting to it continuing resilience. Thus, when, around 3300 B.C., the Sand Hill community finally dispersed and Kabakaburi Hill, yet within the advancing mangrove belt was occupied by the migrants, the tool inventory there evidenced the continued development of the dugout canoe on the basis of age-old alliances still linking the upper Waini, the lower Barima and the lower Aruka Rivers, Figure 3.35.

The enormous sizes of the successor mounds at Warapana and Siriki further downriver attest the successful adaptation of these already ancient Warao in an environment still being transformed by freshening consequent on the gradual seaward migration of the mangroves. As the community fissured over the centuries, elevated land was occupied nearer and nearer the advancing shoreline, Figures 3.36 a,b. In due course, Warao were in occupation as far as present day Charity, at that time probably located on an old mouth of the Pomeroon River. Since the proximity of the prevailing shoreline set a limit to any further advance, these shell mounds are both of unusual size, the Warapana community having expanded on a circular plan, perhaps originally around a central plaza, while, at Siriki, the community spread

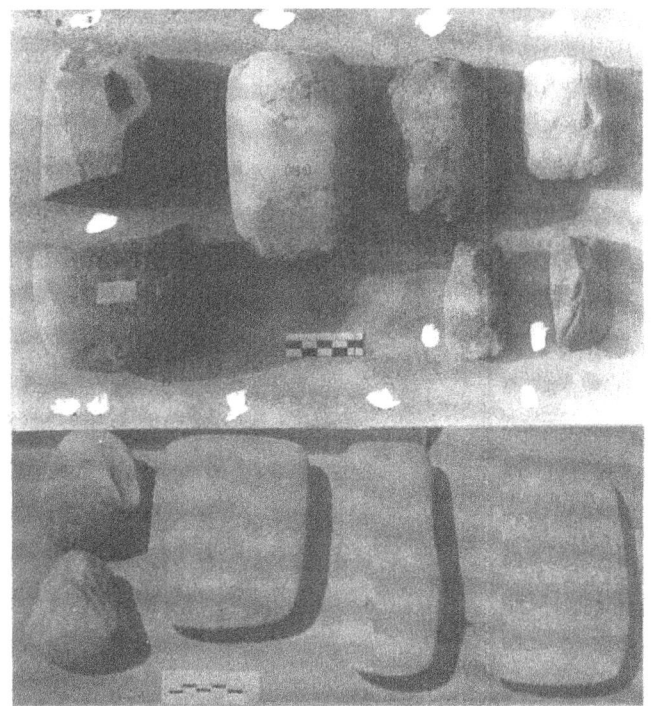

Figure 3.35. Piraka Pomeroon River. Stone tools of the mature canoe industry. Recovered on Maribamba (Marabunta) Creek in mora forest, Figure 3.3., they suggest *in situ* manufacture.

laterally. In each case a relatively large population and an extended time span seem indicated. Thus, by the end of the fourth millennium B.C., the swamp basin comprised a politically integrated system extending virtually from the Mouth of the Essequibo River to the Mouth of the Orinoco.

The aftermath

The lengthy evolution of the stone adze had resulted from problems posed by its efficient hafting for the task of reducing tropical hardwoods, *viz.*, Mora. So far, this evolution has been noted only on the Monika and Pomeroon Rivers, the core area of the canoe manufacturing industry. Although the problem was recognized elsewhere, it appears never to have been investigated so thoroughly and so consistently in other parts of the Western Guiana Littoral. This seems to suggest temporal priority for the Monika industry in a situation in which nothing is known with regard to the history of canoe manufacture in the Guianas. For this reason, the apparently unique development of the industry in the Southeastern Subzone of the Western Guiana Littoral needs to be understood in the context of known earlier stone working industries and their outcomes.

Notwithstanding the lengthy evolution of the stone adze in the local industry, Figure 3.31, the massive, semi-polished adzes, axes and whetstones of the Pomeroon River, Figure 3.35, were not unique to the Western Guiana Littoral at the time they

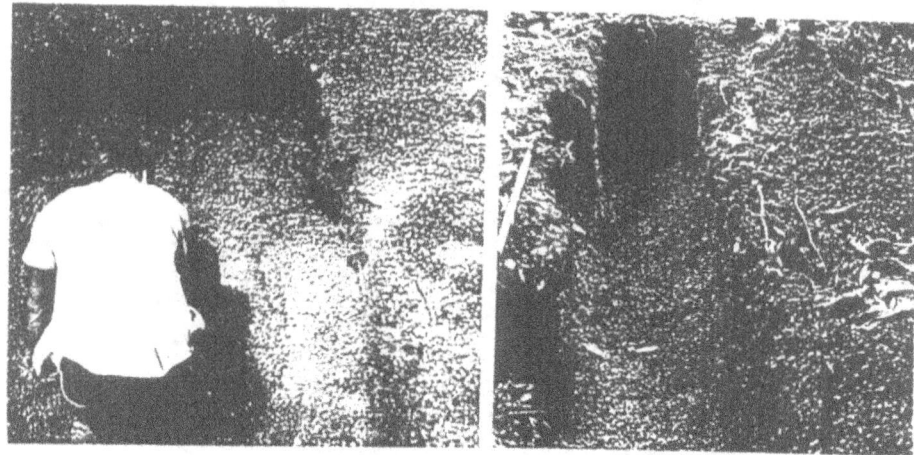

Figure 3.36a,b. **a.** Dry forest near Warapana shell mound, **b.** Shell mound at Siriki, near Charity.

were first employed there. An exactly similar toolkit was in use at contemporary sites of the Mina Tradition at the Mouth of the Amazon (Simões 1981: Figure 4ac). Radiocarbon dates for the Mina Tradition range between 3200 - 1600 B.C. (Simões 1981; see also Willey 1985), which suggests a technological horizon that was transforming socio-cultural systems in northeastern South America at around this time. It has been seen that a ground stone ax, dating at around 7000 B.C., has been recovered on the upper Orinoco River. The earliest ground stone adzes on the Western Guiana Littoral occur intrusively in early levels of the Barabina shell mound at around 5000 B.C. Thus, the adoption of this stoneworking technology in the Southeastern Subzone at around 3000 B.C. had resulted from an already old tradition of grinding and polishing stone. That tradition had been available to be exploited whenever the need arose. Associated with this tradition were various rock exposures in the streams of *terra firme* that were exploited in the grinding and polishing of stone implements. Similar rock exposures are unknown on the coast.

Certain tools from the as yet undated Castalia shell mound around the Mouth of the Cunia River, on the lower Amazon left bank, are identical to the Mina specimens. On the basis of similarities in subsistence, settlement pattern and ceramic technology, Castalia has been recognized as a culture of the Mina Tradition (Hilbert 1959). Distributions of certain Archaic petroglyphs indicate that this shell mound is located directly on a route which once crossed the Akarai watershed *via* the Mapuera, a tributary of the Trombetas, into the upper Essequibo River. The age of this route would seem to explain the appearance of the characteristic Mina toolkit on the Western Guiana Littoral when, abruptly, the need for intensification was felt there. In restructuring the prehistory of the Guianas, the vast scale of the various trade networks upon which rested the continuing viability of early communities needs constantly to be borne in mind, commencing with those early hunter-gatherers whose descent of the eastern Andes had initiated the exploitation of jasper in the Pakaraimas. As shown by finds of Archaic stone tools in the Sipaliwini Savannas of southern Suriname, the bridging of the Orinoco-Amazon watershed constitutes an essential part of this picture, main outlines of which were determined by the complimentarity between the resources of *terra firme* and those of the surrounding alluvial deposits, and by the adaptive "tethering" of a given community to its niche.

In due course, the seminal advance in regional integration that was initiated with the development of the dugout canoe affected Archaic communities far beyond the Western Guiana Littoral. As the shellfishing lifeway expanded northwestward along the old littoral line of northern South America, the diagnostic ground and polished trapezoidal axes of the Mina and Alaka Traditions appeared at Las Varas on the Gulf of Cariaco. Here, an abundance of large, trapezoidal adzes and axes dating between 2600 and 2000 B.C. were associated with conical "pestles" (Sanoja O. 1989:4., Figure 5). In the context of an expanding canoe industry, these "pestles" more plausibly suggest whetstones as used on the Pomeroon River and at Mina (cf. Simões 1981: Figure 4d,e). At Manicuare, further west and later in the sequence, the introduction of shell gouges is thought to have made possible the manufacture of the dugout canoe between 1730 and 1190 B.C. (Rouse and Cruxent 1963:46) or nearly a millennium later than at Las Varas. Diffusion of this trait along the South American coast is understood best against the background of the early Warao dispersion posited by the linguists.

The aftermath of the development of the dugout canoe on the Moruka River around 3300 B.C. was felt very soon in the Antilles. Levisa, the earliest Archaic site on Cuba, has been dated at 5140 +/- 170 b.p., or 3190 B.C. (GD 356). Virtually the entire Archaic inventory of Amazonian petroglyph elements (Williams 1978b, 1985) has been recorded in Greater Antillean pictographs (Delmonte y Rodriguez 1980; Veloz Maggiolo et al 1977). Granted the prior evolution of this inventory in specifically Amazonian environments, to be discussed later, a migration of significant magnitude would appear to have been involved on the late Archaic time level. The depiction of an "Enumerated" monkey on Cuba, Figure 3.37a, a highly distinctive Archaic petroglyph element in Amazonia, is of interest as indicating the survival there of an ancient system of controlled resource exploitation which in Amazonian environments had maintained an effective balance between carrying capacity and man's extractive behaviors in the biota (Williams 1979b, 1985). The stratagem proved not viable in the context of Archaic ecosystems in the Caribbean Islands, with the result that the monkey was exterminated in Cuba, the Dominican Republic and Jamaica, on all of which islands archaeology shows it to have been autochthonous (Veloz Maggiolo et al 1977:37). Certain petroglyph and pictograph distributions of an Amazonian iconography in the Lesser Antilles (Dubelaar 1995: Figure 104 - 106; Williams 1985: Table 7.1) seem also to indicate one or more Archaic migration from the mainland. The monkey appears to have survived on St. Kitts into the time of the Saladoid migrations, Figure 3.37b. So far, Archaic petroglyphs remain unknown there (see Dubelaar 1995; Laurie and Matheson 1973).

The long range human dispersals that are implied by the dispersion of Archaic artifacts of the Guianas during the fourth millennium B.C. indicate an interaction sphere that was delimited on the north by the Greater Antilles, on the south by the Brazilian northeast coast and on the west by the islands of the South Caribbean Chain (Aruba, Curacao and Bonaire) where the petroglyph/pictograph inventory is specifically Amazonian in iconography (see Hummelinck 1953, 1957, 1961-1962). This immense areal expansion of Archaic culture suggests more or less sustained population growth following upon the subsistence crisis that was engendered in the Southeastern Subzone of the swamp basin by the advent of the freshwater climax there around 3300 B.C. The indicated widely dispersed and interacting populations again hint at linguistic evidences of an earlier, much more extended Warao culture on the northwestern coast of South America and stand in sharp contrast to the situation of isolation and stasis which, for the thousand

Figure 3.37. a. Cuba, b. St. Kitts

and more years that preceded the culmination of the eustatic sea level rise had characterized the settlement pattern of the pioneering groups at Piraka in the Southeastern Subzone and Barabina in the Northwestern Subzone. The socio-cultural integration of the Western Guiana Littoral that resulted from the development there of the dugout canoe was a feature of the expanding knowledge of the rocks of the Guiana Shield which had been pioneered by its earliest Archaic occupants.

Sustained down the generations on to the coming of food production, this knowledge was a function of subsistence in the marginal environments of the Tropical Forest dating back to Archaic times. It was bound up with the exploitation of the biota by groups in no way equipped to enhance its productivity. Consequently, it involved an awareness of the contradiction between the imperatives of human subsistence and the potential for self-renewal in the biota in marginal environments. In the interests of man's indefinite survival, a resolution needed to be found to this critical contradiction. Since the biota would cease to exist if the energies extracted from it to maintain human life were not restored, human mortality (the reciprocal of human fertility) came to be apprehended as a function and condition of the continuing fertility of the biota itself, which, however, was apprehended as extra-human, supernatural, eternal. The image of the eternal and the supernatural was embodied in the permanence and implacable nature of rock -- the rocks of the streams, the savannas and mountains. Here was maintained the essential link between human mortality and divine immortality. In the continuing concourse of man and the supernaturals, certain of the emergent rocks of the Guiana Shield, imbued with the sacred, were modified in distinctive ways. These modifications are the petroglyphs and pictographs of our inquiry.

The Archaic on terra firme
Parameters of the study

Unlike the situation in the stoneless coastal swamps, where shellfishers had remained virtually without tools over nearly two millennia preceding the development of the dugout canoe, habitable niches for hinterland hunter-gatherers needed always to have included rock exposures suitable for tool manufacture and maintenance, food processing and the imposition of petroglyphs and pictographs. In the pursuit of these ends, the rocks of the Guiana Shield were modified in distinctive ways. These modified rocks, whether parietal or mobiliary, represent all that survives of the material culture of the Archaic on *terra firma*. As noted earlier, they are potentially of interest in the matter of restructuring aspects of the settlement pattern, subsistence system, group migrations and religious behaviors. Certain parietal specimens, e.g., grinding grooves, provide data for the reconstruction of Archaic water levels, and therefore of past climates.

Reflecting the above functions, petroglyphs/pictographs are distributed in every physiographic zone on *terra firme*, particularly in the west. Physiographic contrasts tend to correlate with contrasts in the elements represented. Since petroglyph imposition implies periodic or sustained human activity over variable time periods, selection of a representative sample was a potentially useful approach to interpreting spatial aspects of these activities.

The representative sample includes the Western Guiana Littoral and a hinterland comprising the Essequibo rain forests, the savannas and the Guiana Highlands. This is an area of some 28×10^4 km^2, or more than 20% of the 1.6×10^6 km^2 of the Guiana land mass, Figure 3.38.

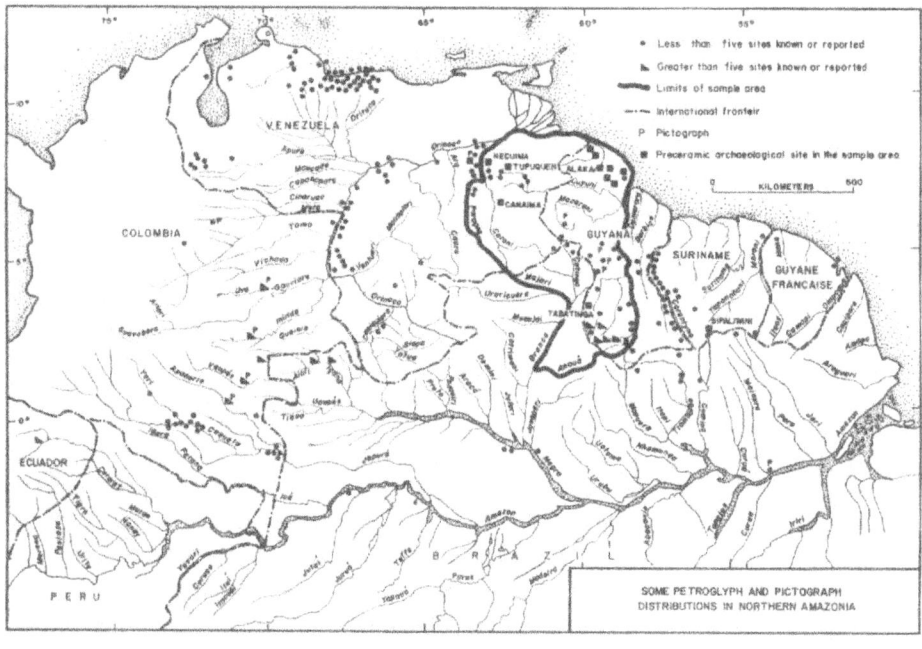

Figure 3.38. Location of the Sample Area and Distribution of Representative Petroglyph and Pictograph Sites in Northern Amazonia.

The parietal artifacts

Petroglyphs. Evidences of the varieties of protein capture that succeeded to the pond fishing of the paleo-Indigenes have survived, not only in conventional subsurface deposits of the sample area, such as at Pedra Pintada in the Rio Branco Savannas, but also in innumerable petroglyph representations of game animals encountered in the apparently once much more extensive savannas that link the Venezuelan llanos with the lower Amazon, Figure 3.39.

Figure 3.39. Game animals and fish in Archaic subsistence.

These petroglyph representations constitute a unique inventory of fauna taken by the Archaic hunter *in the prevailing environment*. When combined with the more traditional source for deriving the hunter-gatherer menu, e.g. excavation, the resulting picture is likely to be more detailed than may have derived from either source considered independently. While excavated food remains may be richer than petroglyphs in small items such as bird beaks, snail shells, palm seeds, etc., petroglyphs, made by the folk directly involved, survive both environmental change and the decay of their organic remains.

Unfortunately, considered as source material for reconstructing local or regional prehistory, the numerous petroglyphs of northern Amazonia so far have not attracted the attention that similar prehistoric manifestations have received in North America. Thousands occur in Venezuela alone (de Valencia et al 1987; Pollak Eltz 1976; Sujo Volksy 1975), notably on the Orinoco mainstream, on both flanks of the Coastal Cordillera and in the Andean foothills on the Colombian border. Surveys on the Quijos and Misagualli Rivers, upper Napo, in Ecuador, yielded 183 petroglyph elements (Porras G. 1961). An undetermined number has been reported or recorded on other tributaries of the upper Amazon, notably the Vaupés, Inirida, Guaviare, Apaporis and Caquetá (Dubelaar MS; Goodland 1979; Kock-Grünberg 1907, 1917; Reichel-Dolmatoff 1967, 1971; Schomburgk 1841; Silva Celis 1961; von Hildebrand 1975; Wallace 1889). Specimens have been reported on the Rio Branco savannas, in Brazil (Koch-Grünberg 1917; Mentz Ribeiro et al 1986, 1987, 1989; Schomburgk 1841). Around 1000 petroglyph and 150 pictograph elements have been recorded in Guyana (Brown 1873; Dubelaar 1986; Dubelaar and Berrangé 1979; Haniff 1967; Henderson 1952; Im Thurn 1879, 1883; Peberdy 1945, 1948; Poonai 1970; Williams 1978, 1979, 1979a,b, 1985, 1985a, 1994, 1996; Winter 1881). Dubelaar (1981a, 1986) has recorded 196 petroglyph elements in Suriname, where pictographs are unknown (Roth 1925). Thirty-three petroglyph elements have been recorded in Guyane française, where, again, pictographs are unknown (Abonnenc 1952; Boye 1974; Hurault et al 1963; Lefebre 1975; Rostain et Le Roux 1990; Toutouri 1983). Both petroglyphs and pictographs have been reported in the State of Para (Roosevelt et al 1996; Wallace 1889). Off western Venezuela, the Netherlands Antilles islands of Curacao, Aruba and Bonaire display some 200 pictograph and two petroglyph elements (Hummelinck 1953, 1957, 1961-1962, 1972). One of two petroglyph sites reported on Trinidad (Rouse 1953) was relocated by Boomert (pers. comm. 1982) and published by Dubelaar (1995). Bullen (1974) summarized various reports on petroglyphs in other parts of the Antilles (see also Dubelaar 1983). Dubelaar (1995) has presented the definitive survey. Numerous pictographs have been recorded in the Greater Antilles (Delmonte y Rodriguez 1980), but none in the Lesser.

This intimate and distinctive record of human adaptation to contrasting environments in northern Amazonia and the Antilles remains to be treated as an integrated whole. Notwithstanding the fact that particular assemblages have attracted notice over the past 250 years, there remain large gaps in our knowledge concerning the locations and contents of several sites. Some have been reported once with no record having been made (Brown 1873, 1876; Coudreau 1887; Humboldt 1852 - 1853; Schomburgk 1841). Others have been recorded once and never relocated (Blair 1980/1857; Dubelaar 1981; Farabee 1916; Goodland 1979; McTurk 1911). One site on the upper Marouini was discovered accidentally during forest felling for the erection of an observatory (Hurault et al 1963). In several countries, riverain glyphs lie below present day water levels (Brown 1873; Coudreau 1887; Dubelaar 1981; Evans and Meggers 1960; Farabee 1916; Lefebvre 1975; Porras G. 1961; Schomburgk 1848; von Hildebrand 1975; Williams 1978, 1979a,b, 1985). In the present pioneering state of the study, definitive inventories (e.g. Dubelaar 1986) are overtaken rapidly by later surveys (e.g. Williams 1994, 1996).

Discrepancies in recording petroglyph or pictograph elements are frequent enough to raise doubts concerning the reliability of the most meticulously compiled inventories. Doubt may attach also to the accuracy of detail in many an inventory (see Sujo Volksy 1975). This may result either from ambivalence in the surviving evidences (Dubelaar and Beffangé 1979; Hummelinck 1957) or from differing methods of recording the most unambiguous evidence (Mallery 1893:771). Site designations may be incorrect (Dubelaar 1981; Dubelaar and Berrangé 1979). Sites may have been partially or wholly destroyed through human (Hummelinck 1957; Pollak-Eltz 1976; Sanoja O. 1969; von Hildebrand 1975) or natural (Im Thurn 1883; Laurie and Matheson 1973; Schomburgk 1841) agencies. Of numerous specimens covering a rock barrier across the Berbice River a hundred years ago (Winter 1881), only 19 were detected in recent survey (Williams 1978). At certain terrestrial sites, glyphs are eroded terminally and vestigial traces of them may be revealed only through some transient conjunction in the angle and intensity of light and the chance location of a lucky observer. As a result of vegetal action between the mineral particles, glyphs approaching terminal erosion on granite disappear rapidly relative to their total life span. Specimens recorded by Goodland (n.d.) on the Aminge granite of the South Rupununi Savannas in 1971 could be detected only tactually in 1979. Exfoliation flakes on granite (Blair 1857) and diorite (Hummelinck 1961-1962) sometimes were employed to rough-in specific geometric elements preliminary to petroglyph imposition. The high level of accuracy attained in the imposition of concentric circles suggests attachment of these flakes to the end of a stick or string during execution. Pictographs fade to obliteration or are obscured by superimpositions (Hummelinck 1961-1962; Reichel-Dolmatoff 1967, 1971).

With available techniques of detection and recording, often in the context of the rain forest, compilation of a national or regional inventory of elements remains a formidable task. Nonetheless, progress beyond mere recording and description demands classification on a regional scale. An attempt has been made to classify Antillean materials (Bullen 1974), but this has not yet been achieved in northern Amazonia (see Sujo Volsky 1975). However, when the paucity of other kinds of preceramic remains in Amazonia is taken into account (Meggers 1982, 1994; Meggers and Evans 1978) special importance attaches to the study and interpretation of its petroglyph/pictograph materials.

Schomburgk's observation (1841) regarding their wide dispersion in northern Amazonia emphasizes the economic importance of the rocks of the Guiana Shield to the makers of these petroglyphs. The Shield offers a wide range of contrasts in elevation, soil types, mean annual precipitation, vegetational cover and water quality. These differentials are expressed as contrasting net primary productivities with concommitant variations in protein resources available to man. Dispersal of human populations across the various niches is facilitated by an extensive network of rivers and creeks, and evidences in the form of petroglyphs, pictographs, artificial depressions, bedrock mortars and dredged-up stone tools attest to differential exploitation of these contrasting niches. Accordingly, modified rocks exhibit a degree of functional zonation. The lowest zone, on riverbeds and riverbanks, is occupied by utilitarian artifacts such as polissoirs, bedrock mortars, and Fish Trap petroglyphs. On a middle zone, representing subsistence ritual, are the Enumerative petroglyphs of the savannas and forests. The uppermost zone, restricted to the mountain fastnesses, the abode of the supernaturals, is occupied by rare specimens of amorphous figuration and apparently sacred function.

It has been observed (Dubelaar 1974 - 1976) that with regard to South American petroglyphs as a whole it cannot at present be shown with certainty when or to what purpose they were made, what, if anything, they represent, or who made them and by what means. Contrasts with the state of petroglyph/pictograph inquiry in North America become sadly evident in statements such as this. Indeed, Dubelaar found the literature "a tiring if not discouraging affair," which may seem to be taking things a bit far, for when this immense distribution area is narrowed to encompass only northern Amazonia and its neighbors, research prospects become a good deal more encouraging on account of certain peculiarities in the data. These are: (*i*) the homogeneity of petroglyph and pictograph content across the various national territories, (*ii*) radiations of certain Amazonian petroglyph/pictograph elements into the Antilles on both Archaic and horticultural time levels, and (*iii*) influences of the arid interval of around 4000 years ago on petroglyph distributions in Amazonia.

Petroglyphs of the sample area constitute a reliable guide to the range of elements employed by Archaic hunter-gatherers across the Guianas. These elements provide the basis of the present classification. Classification, in turn, permits examining the implications of the above-mentioned peculiarities in the petroglyph/pictograph data for the Guianas as a whole. Some of these implications

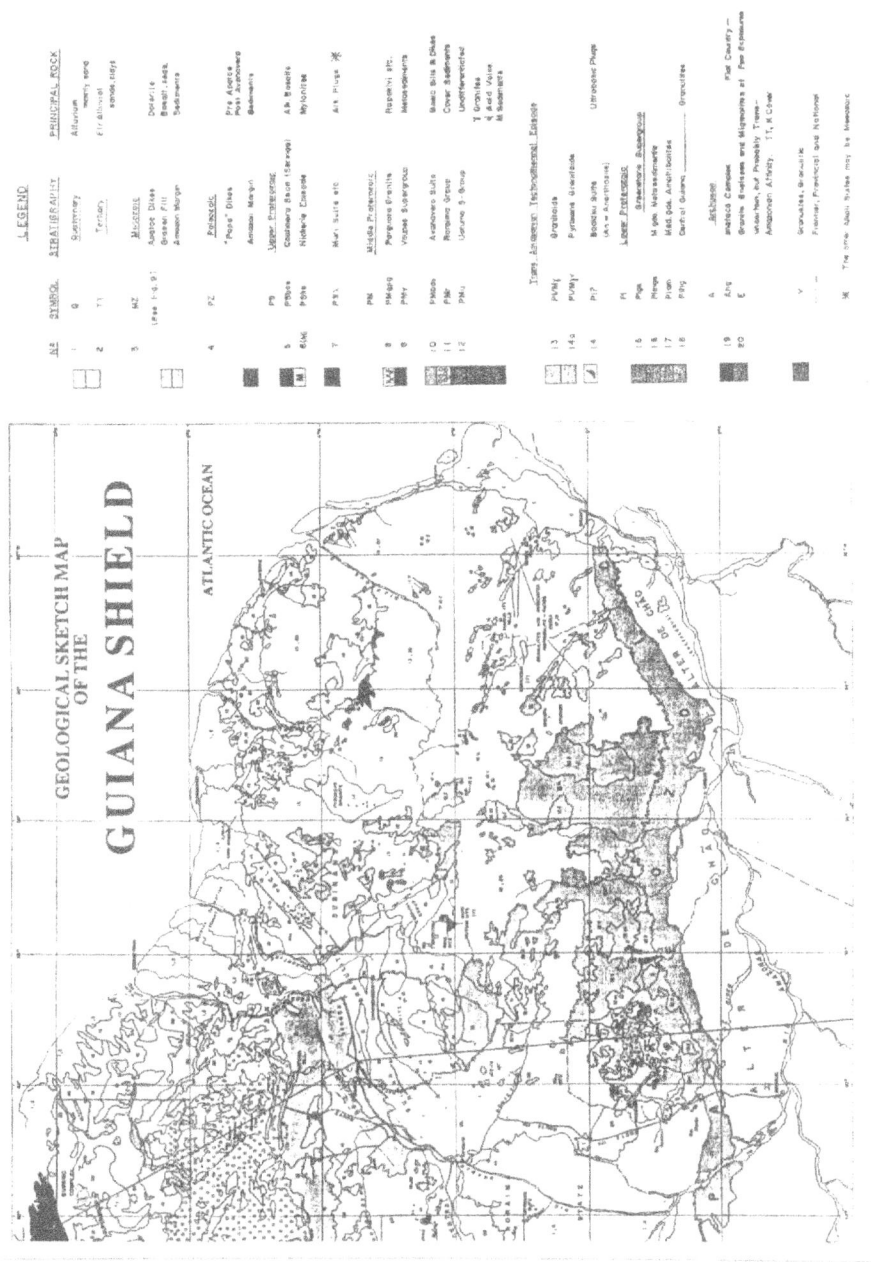

Figure 3.40. The Geological Basis of Petroglyph Distributions in the Orinoco and Amazon Basins.

are as follows:

(i) Homogeneity of petroglyph/pictograph content across the national territories.
Schomburgk's (1841) observation on petroglyph distributions in the Guianas is still the most explicit and the best remembered:

> I have followed these figures in Guiana, as in general over the northern portion of South America, more than a stretch of 700 miles in length and 500 in breadth, and found them here and there distributed over a superficial area of 350,000 square miles.

Restated in terms of the geology, Dubelaar (unpubl.) has observed:

> The younger geological formations, indicated by the notions 'Tertiary' and 'Quaternary,' are not likely to contain suitable rock surfaces. We studied the boundary between the Tertiary-Quaternary area and the area which is geologically older, for the Amazon and Oronoco Basin areas. This borderline between the Tertiary-Quaternary (abbreviated T.Q.) area and the older geological formations is shown on the map by a fat, broken line. It is striking how precisely petroglyph sites are in- or excluded by this boundary.

Dubelaar, Figure 3.40, acknowledged minor exceptions in his inventory, including a specimen on Trinidad. Nonetheless, the compactness of his distributions permits testing our classification, which recognizes three great petroglyph Traditions, or Series (Williams 1985). These are the Enumerative (or Aishalton), the Fish Trap and the Timehri. Only the first two are Archaic, the third is horticultural. The Enumerative Series includes a Cuneiform Subtype, so-called for its gravure characteristics. The elements comprising these three Series constitute the petroglyph inventory of northern Amazonia and the Antilles.

Elements of the Enumerative petroglyph fall into two classes: biomorphic and geometric, the latter being usually more numerous in a given assemblage. Occurrences include both petroglyphs and pictographs.

Biomorphic elements include anthropomorphs of specific characteristics, symmetric or asymmetric. Zoomorphs include deer, sloth, monkey, caiman, snake, peccary, agouti, turtle, bird, and fish, Figure 3.39. Phytomorphs are usually not specific with regard to the plant represented, though palms may be recognizable.

Seven kinds of geometric elements have been recognized, Figure 3.41. They are almost invariably associated with biomorphs. As shown in Figure 3.42, petroglyphs and pictographs of the Enumerative Series are of very wide dispersion in northern Amazonia and the Antilles.

The Enumerative Series dominates the rocks of the Guiana Shield. Its frequencies diminish west to east across northern Amazonia. Whereas thousands of glyphs have been reported in Venezuela, fewer than a thousand are known from Guyana. Those in Suriname number fewer than 200; less than two score are reported from Guyane française. Certain elements common in the west are unknown in the

Figure 3.41. Elements of the Enumerative Petroglyph/Pictograph Series.

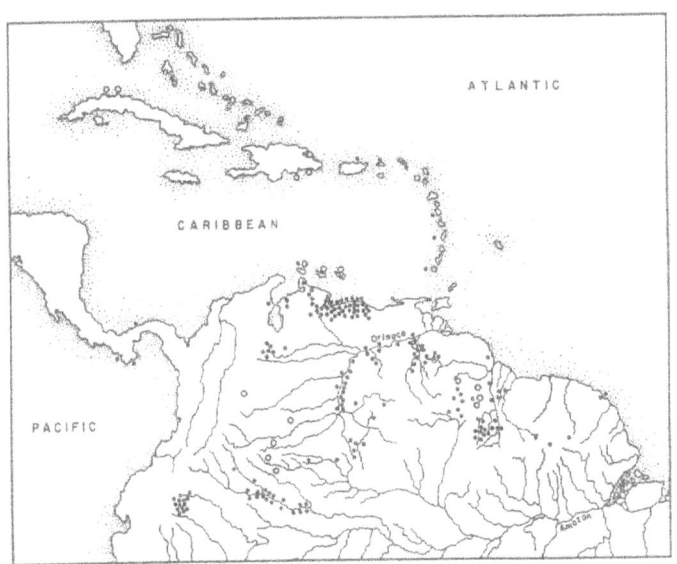

Figure 3.42. Distribution of the Enumerative Petroglyph/Pictograph Series.

east. Complicated rectilinear frets, which occur numerously from Venezuela to Argentina, are absent in the Guianas. Paired anthropomorphs, recorded in Venezuela, are unknown to the east. A single Pit-and-Groove boulder in the South Rupununi Savannas of Guyana represents the most easterly occurrence of its type. It is common in Venezuela and the Andes. The implication is that, as was the case with the large projectile points of the paleo-Indigenous and Archaic Periods, the various types of which have their correlates in Andean inventories, diffusion of the trait of petroglyph/pictograph imposition was eastward across northern Amazonia.

(ii) Radiations of Amazonian petroglyph elements into the Antilles. Certain Amazonian petroglyph elements are recorded in Antillean inventories (Williams 1985). As noted earlier, pictographs on the islands of the South Caribbean Chain (Aruba, Curacao and Bonaire) exhibit virtually the entire Amazonian petroglyph inventory; just two petroglyphs are known in those islands (Hummelinck 1953,1957, 1961 - 1962, 1972). A few Amazonian elements, some doubtful, have been recorded in petroglyphs on Grenada and St. Vincent in the Lesser Antilles (Dubelaar 1995; Kirby 1969). Numerous pictograph elements on Cuba in the Greater Antilles are identical to petroglyph elements in Amazonian inventories (Delmonte y Rodriguez 1980; Ntifiez Jimenez 1964, 1970). Among zoomorphs, the "enumerated" monkey of Amazonian inventories has been recorded on Cuba, Figure 3.37a. Enumerative petroglyph elements in the Caribbean are concentrated most densely in the Netherlands Antilles and in Cuba (Williams 1985: Table 7.1).

Implied by these distributions is an ancestral relationship between the Enumerative Petroglyph Series of northern Amazonia and the petroglyph/ pictograph traditions of certain islands of the Antilles. This relationship is important in a situation in which little is known of the Antillean Archaic. The relative densities of the diagnostic elements suggest a stronger relationship between northern Amazonia and the Greater Antilles than between northern Amazonia and the Lesser Antilles, where the mainland iconography appears to have exercised a weak influence only on Grenada and St. Vincent. As noted above, occurrences of these Archaic Amazonian petroglyphs on Cuba may be related to the development of the dugout canoe on the Western Guiana Littoral and the initial peopling of the Antilles toward the ending of the fourth millennium B.C. If so, they would seem to provide a base for relative dating of certain elements in the Enumerative Petroglyph Series of northern Amazonia.

Associated with the Archaic industry is the typologically and technologically distinctive Cuneiform petroglyph. The frequent presence of the symmetric anthropomorph in this inventory, which mainly comprises linear elements and punctates, permits its identification as a subtype of the Enumerative Petroglyph Series, the symmetric anthropomorph being the sign for 20. Technologically, this subtype is distinguished by incision with a wedge-shaped stylus which produced a characteristic shallow (+/- 5 mm), v-shaped furrow with dwindling tails reminiscent of Sumerian cuneiform writing.

(iii) Influence of the arid episode of around 4000 years ago on petroglyph distributions in Amazonia. Apart from their potentials for cultural reconstruction, petroglyphs in northern Amazonia are important as diagnostics of past climates.

This is because specimens imposed during one or other of the arid episodes of +/- 4000 b.p. or +/- 2000 b.p. (Absy 1982, 1985) lie well below today's water levels. They represent a landscape characterized by a lowered water table and probably an altered vegetation. In the normal water levels of the present day, such petroglyphs, as well as other items of the material culture (such as grinding surfaces and bedrock mortars) may be submerged most of the year under as much as three meters of water. On this "submerged horizon," these incomprehensively neglected prehistoric artifacts are visible only during the annual dry seasons of the present and even then not always completely; a few, permanently submerged, remain accessible only to the touch. Because modification of these presently submerged rocks appertained to their individual elevation above prevailing water level (pwl) during one period or another of sustained reduced precipitation, elevations above pwl of the grinding grooves imposed upon them from time to time differed and therefore may be diagnostic of fluctuating water levels in the remote past.

Implied is the potential for accurate mapping of the locations of these parietal artifacts on the submerged horizon of the Archaic using sonar equipment and a Global Positioning System receiver. In this way, the elevations of particular items of modified rock above the riverbed may be recorded as a basis for intersite comparisons directed at attributing relative values to prehistoric water level fluctuations regionwide.

Narrowing the area of petroglyph research to include only northern Amazonia and its neighbors simplifies restructuring prehistory by permitting discrimination between certain elements that are specific to northern Amazonia and other elements that occur only elsewhere. Thus, while according to Dubelaar (MS), Nandu prints occur in East Brazil and felines in North Venezuela, their combined occurrence together with cameloids is specifically Andean. All of these kinds of petroglyph elements are unknown in the Guianas. On the other hand, the range of elements that are associated with the depiction of different types of fish trap have been recorded so far only in northern Amazonia.

The above peculiarities of the northern Amazonian petroglyph data apply also to the apparently much younger Fish Trap Series. Age-area comparisons, which relate the antiquity of a cultural trait to the size of its distribution area, suggest that the bearers of the Enumerative petroglyph type occupied northern Amazonia and parts of the Antilles for several millennia before the onset of the conditions that led to the development of the Fish Trap petroglyph type. While elements of the Enumerative petroglyph type are distributed from Alaska to Argentina and into the Antilles as far to the north as Cuba, Fish Trap petroglyphs have been recorded mainly in the Guianas (Williams 1979a,b, 1985). On the age-area principle the Fish Trap petroglyph type is therefore incomparably younger than the Enumerative petroglyph type. Nonetheless, its distribution is impressive.

Fish Trap petroglyphs are known on the Aramatau, a headwater stream of the Corentyne, at Wonotobo and Bigi Bere Falls on the Corentyne mainstream, on the Zuid and Tapanahoni Rivers, right tributaries of the Corentyne, and on the Marouini River in Guyane française (Dubelaar 1986: Figures 12, 91, 106, 113).

Figure 3.43. Upper Waini River. Fish Trap petroglyph.

Fish Trap petroglyphs are known also on the Essequibo as far downstream as Waraputa Falls (Im Thurn 1883: Pl. IX; Brown 1873) as well as on its tributaries the Kassikaityu, Rupununi and Burro Burro Rivers (Williams 1979a, 1994, 1996). To the west, Fish Trap petroglyphs are known on the Kowarwaunau, a tributary of the Takutu, which flows into the Rio Branco (Williams 1979). On the upper Rio Branco, a spring basket fish trap was recorded, unrecognized, by Mentz Ribeiro et al (1989: Figure 4a). Fish Trap petroglyphs have been recorded on the Rio Sipapo, upper Orinoco, as well as on the Casiquiare-Orinoco confluence (de Valencia et al 1987:327, 333, 339). A specimen recorded on the Amazon left bank, below the mouth of the Rio Negro (Morrissey pers. comm. 1993) is visible only very rarely, at the lowest level of the dry season discharge. Fish Trap petroglyphs are known also on the New and the Honawau Rivers in the southeastern Guianas (Dubelaar 1986: Figures 21, 22; Farabee 1916). To the north, Fish Trap petroglyphs have been recorded on the edge of the swamp basin, on the upper Waini, Figure 3.43. Beyond the Guianas, possible Fish Trap petroglyphs have been recorded on the Caquetá River, in eastern Colombia (Von Hildebrandt 1975: Figures 32,33). Fish Trap petroglyphs are unknown throughout the Antilles.

Artificial depressions. Other parietal artifacts located on the submerged horizon of the Archaic include grinding surfaces associated with the manufacture and maintenance of stone tools. These comprise three types: *(a)* circular to ovoidal depressions *(grinding surfaces;* Fr: cupules) resulting from reducing the chipped surfaces of preforms , (*b*) ellipsoids resulting from longitudinal grinding of preforms into specific tools and implements (Fr: *trait a section recti-curviligne), (c)* narrow, pointed (sometimes keeled) ellipsoids resulting from sharpening/resharpening the working edges of tools and implements *(sharpening grooves;* Fr: *goutiére* or *trait en fuseau;* Spanish/Portuguese *amoladores;* Dutch: *slijpgroeven).* Because water was a necessary component of the tool-grinding process, these artificial depressions tend to concentrate on suitable rock outcrops in the riverbed or on the riverbank. The dispersion of these clusters on a given river drainage suggests that they represent specialized workshops under the control of a particular local group.

Also of very specific distribution and located on the submerged horizon of the Archaic is a distinctive bedrock mortar comprising a ring of around 30 cm diameter worn into the rock surface by sustained circular action using a *mano*. Numerous specimens have been reported on the Orenoque River (Williams 1985). They occur also on the Ile de Cayenne (Rostain and Le Roux 1990) and on the upper Rio Branco (Mentz Ribeiro et al 1989). Figure 3.44.

Figure 3.44. Bedrock mortar, upper Rio Branco *(after Mentz Ribeiro et al 1989)*.

The mobiliary artifacts

Tools lost or discarded during manufacture or maintenance may be recovered at the site of the associated sharpening grooves. Since the measurements of sharpening grooves are diagnostic of the sizes, and even types, of stone tools that had been manufactured or maintained in them, the *in situ* recovery of a discarded tool is a valuable aid to interpretation.

In situ tool manufacture during the Archaic may be evidenced also in riverain workshops that were submerged by rising water levels following on an arid interval and consequently abandoned. Such a workshop, beside a quartz vein traversing the Burro Burro River, a tributary of the Siparuni, upper Essequibo, presently lies undisturbed under around three meters of water. It comprises a pile of quartz pebbles, chipping waste and various finished or near-finished tools, Figure 3.45. All items are covered with a thick, black deposit.

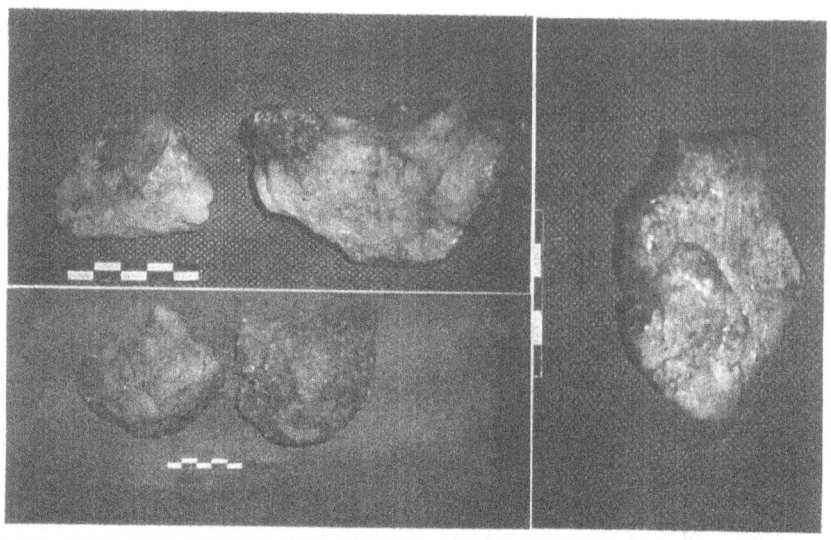

Figure 3.45. Upper Burro Burro River. Percussion flaked and pecked tools on quartz.

Modified rock in Archaic culture history

The potentials of petroglyphs for restructuring aspects of settlement pattern, subsistence systems, group migrations, religious behaviors and even the climates of the late Archaic have been noted. To some degree, and limited by the peculiarities of the data outlined above (p. 156), these potentials of petroglyphs are held by every other kind of modified rock as well. They are reviewed below.

Petroglyphs. In contrast to the restricted dispersion of the few available paleo-indigenous tools and implements, petroglyph/pictograph distributions show Archaic groups in occupation of virtually the entire Guiana land mass and parts of the Antilles as well. These differing spatial parameters constitute evidence for recognizing qualitative differences between the respective cultural levels. Paleo-indigenes pioneering the exploration of the Guianas during the millennia before the sea had attained its present level appear to have been tethered to specific rock exposures in the highlands while fishing the ponds of dried out riverbeds in the lowlands. Following on the sea level peak, exploitation of the now brimful rivers necessitated modifying the sizes of their characteristically large projectile points, some of which, e.g. the Paijan point, nonetheless retained their salient morphological characteristics.

Most probably, it was the descendants of these paleo-indigenes who initiated the shellfishing lifeway around 7000 years ago. Simultaneously other Archaic peoples were expanding across the dry transverse zone of the southern Guianas. Just as the subsistence systems of the coastal pioneers are evidenced in their various refuse heaps, the subsistence systems of their hinterland brethren are evidenced in numerous petroglyphs and other forms of modified rock, Figures 3.8, 3.42. And whereas the sizes and shapes of the distinctive, large points of paleo-indigenes in the Western Guiana Hinterland show them to have been specialist fishers and collectors, the small sizes of the stemmed and unstemmed points of their Archaic descendants show them, in turn, to have been generalized small-game hunters and fishers (e.g. see Barse 1997).

Interaction between coastal and hinterland communities is evidenced from paleo-Indigenous times by the occurrence of the above-mentioned Clovis-derived projectile point, albeit undated, on the Western Guiana Littoral. Clovis antecedents may be indicated also in northeastern Brazil, where the cultural sequence at Pedra Pintada runs from paleo-Indigenous to late prehistoric times. In both areas, early horticulture dates at around 3,500 years ago (see Roosevelt et al 1996) a fact which in itself probably attests to the preceding millennia of interaction between *terra firme* and coastal areas.

Thus, the refuse of Archaic shellfishers on the Western Guiana Littoral and the modified rocks of hunter-gatherers, fishers and collectors in the hinterland constitute complementary data sets in the restructuring of Guianese prehistory, Table B.

The dispersion of their petroglyphic boulders indicates that savanna hunter-gatherers typically were located near waterfalls along the major rivers, or in the neighborhood of small streams. They exploited nearby gallery forest or the rain-forest/savanna boundary seasonally. Their subsistence round was adapted to the annual flooding of the savannas as the Rio Branco and its tributary, the Takutu, backed up, converting much of the savannas into a vast lake across which each year it becomes possible to canoe continuously down to the Mouth of the Rio Negro. Following the rains, various game animals concentrated around the residual savanna pools, now well stocked with fish. In this annual cycle of scarcity and abundance, the settlement pattern of the savanna hunters was transhumant, though the link with the supernatural world that is evidenced in sustained petroglyph imposition at particular sites suggests that each local group was tethered to a fixed set of natural resources

Figure 3.46. The Enumerative Petroglyph Type.

and may have exercised proprietary rights over those resources. This is suggested by the stratified imposition of certain petroglyph/pictograph elements (Williams 1985:348) implying sedentary occupation of favored sites and at the same time signifying the responsibility of the local group to maintain a balance between the reproductive potentials of their marginal environment and their own reproductive potentials. The Enumerative petroglyph type represents a stratagem directed to this end.

Its comprehensive distribution in the Americas permits assigning the greatest antiquity to this Enumerative Series, elements of which have been recorded from Alaska to Argentina. Among the most diagnostic of these elements, the Pit-and-Groove boulder, Figure 3.46, has been estimated in Eastern California and Nevada archaeology to date at between 5000 and 3000 B.C. (Heizer and Baumhoff 1962:234). This estimate accords well with the available radiocarbon dates for the arrival of the founding propagules at Piraka and Barabina on the Western Guiana Littoral. Similar boulders have been reported or recorded in parts of Central America (Kennnedy 1973, Murray 1979, 1985,1987), South America Ortiz-Troncoso 1977; Cruxent 1971:41) and the Caribbean (Dubelaar 1995: Figures 104 - 106; Kirby 1976; Oliver 1973). Enumerative punctates are associated with directional elements on a Pit-and-Groove boulder in the South Rupununi Savannas.

In the vigesimal system of northern Amazonia, multiples of five are denoted by the hands and toes. Five is denoted by one hand, ten by all the fingers, and twenty by all twenty digits of a man. Hence 20 = one man, one Warao (Edwards 1980:160; Wilbert 1972:69). Similarly, among the Arawaks, 20 = one man, one Lokono (W.C.Bennett 1949:601; van Berkel 1948:19). The Chibcha sign for 20, *gueta*, is a symmetric anthropomorph (Brotherston 1979: Figure 8d). The outstanding element in the Enumerative Petroglyph Series is the symmetric anthropomorph, interpreted in petroglyph iconography as signifying a count of 20 (Williams 1985). Integers in the system are represented by punctates and straight furrows. These are combined with biomorphic elements to create *graphemes* (Proskouriakoff 1968), Figure 3.47.

Probably associated with its economic functions the enumerative petroglyph type may have been employed also in lunar counting (Murray 1979, 1982, 1982a, 1985, 1986, 1987), Figure 3.48. Their burial orientations, deriving from observations on more than 100 interments, imply that, among coastal shellfishers, a religious significance attached to the solstitial arc of the western sky. The associated beliefs appear to explain certain rare specimens of the Enumerative petroglyph type which combine directional (straight furrow) and enumerative (punctate) elements, Figure 3.49a,b.

In the Venezuelan specimen, three concentric-ring elements of the Enumerative Tradition are associated with small rings, some enclosing punctates. On the central element, four small, punctated rings are linked with four straight furrows forming

Figure 3.47. The petroglyphic grapheme. **a-h**, Guyana (after Williams 1985); **i-j, q-r, v,** Venezuela (Cruxent 1946-1947; de Abate 1973; Sujo Volksy 1975); **k,n,p,s,u,w,** Colombia (von Hildebrand 1975); **l**, Guyane française (Hurault et al 1963); **m**, Cuba (Delmonte y Rodriguez 1980); **o,t**, Netherlands Antilles (Hummelinck 1957, 1972); **x-e**; U.S.A (Cain 1950; Cordill 1948; Epperson 1936; Heizer and Hester 1978).

Figure 3.48. New Mexico. Petroglyphic Tallies Interpreted as Representing Lunar Counts.

Figure 3.49a,b. **a**. Venezuela. Combined directional and notational elements (*after de Valencia et al* 1987: 290). **b**. Kurupukari Falls, Guyana. Combined directional and notational elements.

a restricted arc. The conjunction suggests the solstitial burial orientations reconstructed in Figure 3.6.

The Kurupukari Falls glyphs were imposed on the top, eastern face, and base of a boulder of pink granite on a small island in the Essequibo River. The base of the boulder comprised two planes at an obtuse angle. To an ellipsoid located atop the now dislodged boulder are attached four large punctates and two straight furrows, the latter directed, respectively, E and ENE. The ENE furrow bifurcates, one bifurcation ending in a punctate. A zigzag furrow links the glyph atop the boulder with other elements comprising its face. This latter comprises four vertical zigzags whose linear arrangement and serial patterning of the associated punctates suggest enumeration. The resulting series of punctates and furrows is calibrated at two, perhaps three, points by single or crossed furrows. The base of the boulder repeats the zigzag and ellipsoid elements on its top and face.

The opposition of these ellipsoids on the two small sides of the boulder with calibrated/enumerated zigzags occupying its main surface suggests that once the boulder lay longitudinally with the two ellipsoids facing, respectively, east and west.

This is the way it was recorded in the nineteenth century (Brown 1873: Pl. XVI; Im Thurn 1883: Figure 36). Other petroglyphic boulders recorded by nineteenth century writers, e.g. at Waraputa Falls downriver (Im Thurn 1883: Pl. IX) and at Marlisa Falls on the Berbice River (Winter 1881) now are dislodged and in some cases lost to the currents. Therefore, it is to be supposed that, similarly, the Kurupukari Falls specimen has been toppled since the initial record was made. The east-west orientation of the ellipsoids, both also calibrated, suggests solar symbolism. The sum of furrows comprising each pair of the four zigzag elements on its face ($\underline{14 + 13}$ + $\underline{17 + 11}$) suggests potentials for their interpretation as lunar counts, though the apparent dislocation of the boulder from its original position introduces an element of doubt.

The Enumerative petroglyph indicates the erstwhile presence of Archaic bands occupying favorable niches across the dry transverse zone stretching from the Venezuelan llanos in the northwest to as far in the southeast as certain left tributaries of the lower Amazon such as the Mapuera and Paru de Oeste. Certain petroglyphs occur on the Tuhtakariwai River, a tributary of the Paru de Oeste, which, while displaying highly distinctinve gravure characteristics, nonetheless exhibit sufficient iconographic similarities to the Enumerative Petroglyph type (e.g. the symmetric anthropomorph, serial straight furrows, punctation) to be considered a subtype in that series. In contrast to the technique of pecking and abrasion which produces the characteristic furrow of the Enumerative petroglyph type (up to 20 mm depth), the incisions of this subtype typically are shallow and cuneiform in character, the characteristic that explains its designation -- the Cuneiform Subtype, Figure 3.50.

Specimens of the Cuneiform Subtype have been recorded across northern South America at Lake Maracaibo in Venezuela (de Valencia et al 1987), on the upper Rio Branco, Brazil (Mentz Ribeiro et al 1987), on the Siparuni, Takutu and Essequibo Rivers in Guyana (Williams 1994, 1996), on the coast of Guyane française (Rostain et Le Roux 1990) and on the Paru de Oeste in northeastern Brazil (Frikel 1969; Dubelaar 1986). The Cuneiform petroglyph is not known in the Antilles.

The unique method of imposition that distinguishes this subtype evidently restricted its distribution to suitable rock surfaces and therefore may be less than representative of the disperson of the communities involved. Its immense distribution area suggests a respectable antiquity for the Cuneiform Subtype, which appears to have spread west to east in conditions associated with the arid interval of +/- 2000 B.C., Figure 3.50.

The second great petroglyph tradition of northern Amazonia is represented by the Fish Trap Series. Commencing around 2000 B.C., small bands of erstwhile hunter-gatherers, extruded from traditional niches on the savannas or savanna-forest ecotone, began to adapt to the cataracts and deep pools of productive rain forest streams where, in the attenuated river discharges and diminished rainfall of the day,

Figure 3.50. Takutu River, Guyana. The Cuneiform Petroglyph Subtype.

fishing was good most of the time.

Petroglyph typology suggests that a small group of hunter-gatherers, fleeing the dessicating savannas, pioneered the exploitation of the Kassikaityu River to the south. The Kassikaityu petroglyph assemblage comprises depictions of four kinds of fish trap -- the maswah, box trap, cylindrical fall trap and the spring-basket trap -- all of which continue in use to the present day (Williams 1979a) Figure 3.51a,b.

Figure 3.51a,b. a. Types of Fish Trap petroglyphs. b. Fish traps in present-day use.

These traps indicate selective harvesting of fish occupying the 'deep pools' that characterized the upper Kassikaityu drainage at this time. In place of the divinely sanctioned enumerating conventions of their old savanna habitats, the problem of conserving the annually renewed fish stocks of the Kassikaityu River in the interests of their long-term survival there demanded empirical solutions deriving specifically from the new environment. Rigorous controls were instituted over resource exploitation. It was observed that at each pool a given fish population was characterized by specific behaviors, and since not all fish species made the same journey each year to the same pool, fish populations at a given pool varied from year to year (Reichel-Dolmatoff 1967). As a stratagem to limit exploitation of this variable resource, selective extraction was guaranteed by the imposition, on a nearby rock exposure, of the range of fish traps known to be efficacious in taking particular species at a given pool. Extractive efficiencies and biological diversity were maintained by sign-posting a given drainage with respect to the potential harvests of its respective pools.

Riverain niches varied from one to another with respect to water quality, depth and the availability of aquatic vegetation for maintaining fish stocks. The most permanent of such niches, centered on waterfalls, constituted the supermarkets of the subsistence system, with fish feeding on the vegetation in the midst of the cataracts, wading birds on the fish, reptiles on the waders and man on the reptiles. In such productive niches, the water boa *(Eunectes murinus)* may be encountered at maximum sizes, Figure 3.52a, b.

Figure 3.52a,b. Food web Horseshoe Falls, Guyana. **a**. The aquatic weed, weya, attracts dense fish populations. **b**. The water boa digests a meal. **c**. Wahana Island. Hairi fish poison in the garden.

Within each of these niches, there may have been further differentiation. Pools with sandy bottoms support species that are absent from those with rocky bottoms. Clear and muddy streams accommodate different faunas. There may also be stratification of species within a given pool, or diurnal changeover of species (McConnell 1967).

Fish trap locations differed in accordance with these differing types of microhabitat. Certain fish traps were anchored directly on the bed of shallow streams. Others were supported on a platform in the current. Yet others appear to have been operated just below the surface of the water. Others were set in wickerwork barriers across waterfalls (Chernela 1994). Certain types were extremely complex, with one-way valves, bait chambers, floats, balances, etc., evidently adapted to specific functions. Roth (1924:200) describes various applications of the basketwork *maswah*, the distribution of which is claimed to be pan-Guianan. In accordance with the diurnal changeover of species, the bait of the cylindrical fall trap varies according to whether it is set by day or night (Roth 1924:196).

Fish trap locations and designs were specific also to particular water bodies depending on the local topography. Turtle Pond, Arwarma Pond and Haimara House are located in close proximity to one another on the upper Essequibo River, above Siparuni Mouth. Each is claimed locally to be characterized by a particular water quality and therefore to support a particular fish species. Fish Trap petroglyphs occur only at Turtle Pond and, predictably, only a single type is represented there, the box trap. A few kilometers upstream, the Kurupukari Falls petroglyph assemblage includes the spring-basket fish trap, but not the box trap, while, at nearby Sharples Island, the configuration of the riverscape at low water permits damming rivulets between rocks after which this artificially created pond, or fish pen, is treated with plant piscicides.

Fish traps and baiting procedures evidenced by the petroglyphic data imply a wide knowledge of the habits and haunts of various fish species and of their respective food preferences. Archaic culture now was equipped with an intellectual armoury whose adaptive efficiencies ranged from the relatively sophisticated constructs of the new fishing technology to manipulation of the chemical properties of certain plants as piscicides. Rotenone, the active principle in the fish poison, Haiari (*Lonchocarpus*) is employed worldwide as a biodegradable insecticide (Plotkin 1993:301). Thus, the respectable antiquity suggested for the use of plant piscicides in South America, where indeed they may have originated (Heizer 1949:281), seems confirmed by archaeology, Figure 3.52c.

The dispersion of Fish Trap petroglyphs over an area extending from the Casiquiare Canal in the west to the lower Amazon in the east, and from the Amazon left bank in the south to the Western Guiana Littoral in the north parallels the distribution area recorded by Roth (1924:200) for various types of actual basketwork fish traps and indicates the level of socio-cultural integration that, by 2000 B.C., had come to characterize the Archaic in the Guianas, Figure 3.53a,b.

The outstanding trait of Archaic culture in the Guianas was the intimate relationship between petroglyph/pictograph imposition and the associated subsistence system. But whereas fish traps were represented only in petroglyphs, the

Figure 3.53. Fish Trap petroglyphs.

systematic enumeration of fauna and flora that necessarily were expropriated from the biota in the interests of long-term human survival involved imposition of both petroglyphs and pictographs, depending on the local topography. Pictographs particularly require a light-colored fine-grained rock surface. Such rocks mainly occur in the Roraima cover sediments of the Western Guiana Hinterland, Figure 3.54.

On the Western Guiana Littoral, excavation of shellfish refuse at the foot of a petroglyphic outcrop at Wahana Island on the upper Waini River permitted dating a tool employed in the imposition of a series of Fish Trap petroglyphs. The tool, an abrading stone, derived from a layer of refuse dating at 4570 +/- 80 B.P. Cal B.C. 3370 to 3290. The calibrated date would relate the series to the high water levels of the freshwater climax at around 3300 B. C. rather than to the low water levels of the Amazonian arid interval of around 2000 B. C. As the water level data firmly

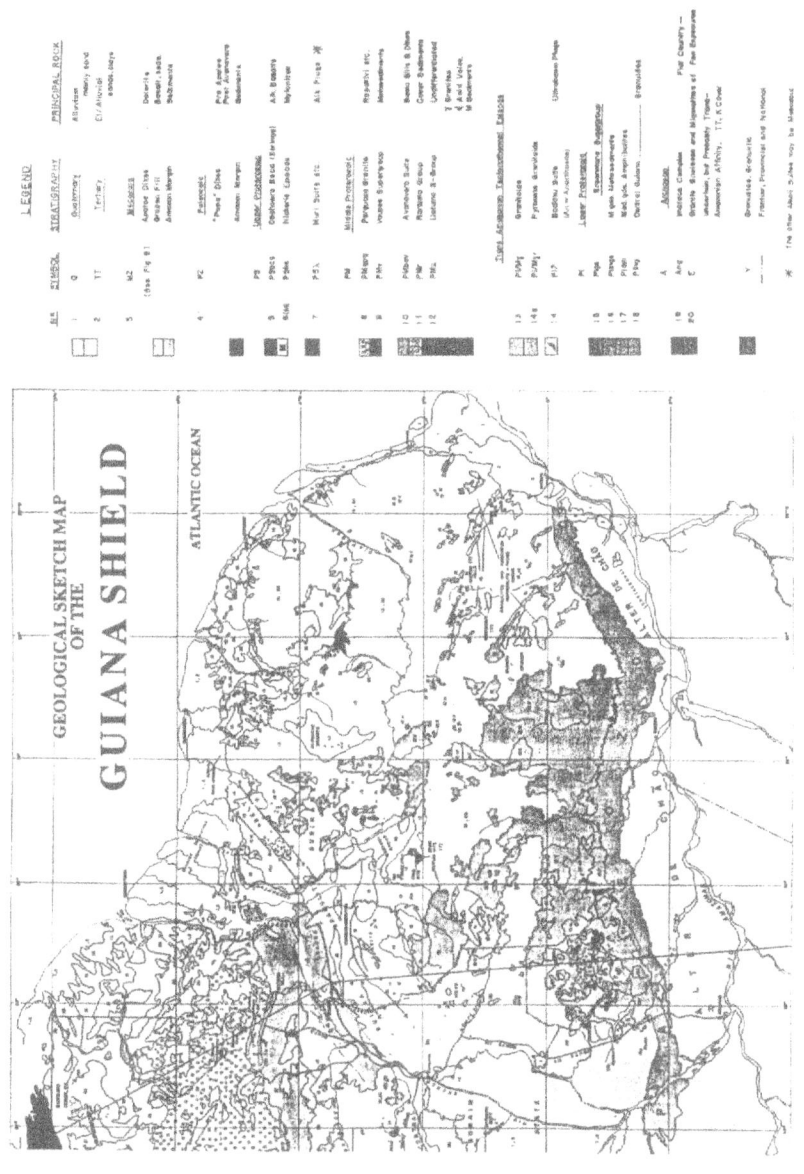

Figure 3.54. Geological Sketch Map of the Guiana Shield (*after Gibbs and Barron 1992 with permission*).

associate the makers of Fish Trap petroglyphs in the southern Guianas with the attenuated streams of the arid interval, the calibrated date of the Waini River Fish Trap petroglyph tool remains anomalous. The conventional C^{14} date (2620 B.C.) approximates more closely to the dating of the Amazonian arid interval (Absy 1982, 1985).

Once classified, petroglyphs display important potentials for reconstructing aspects of the associated subsistence system, and since such subsistence systems may correlate with environments different from those of the present day, the subsistence data may refer to conditions that have vanished forever. The data from Wahana Island are of this kind. The box traps and spring-basket fish traps of this petroglyph assemblage refer to the now vanished landscape of attenuated river discharges of the Amazonian arid interval. Appropriately, the excavated refuse comprised overwhelmingly the myriads of crab carapaces of a mudflat environment and the large skinfish of an estuarine environment, both still marked in cultural memory by the Warao name *Wahana Island*. Surviving Fish Trap petroglyphs on the granite outcrop that dominates the island attest to the economic resources of a stream that was much shallower than at present.

The stratification of food refuse at the Pedra Pintada rock shelter on the Parima River, a left tributary of the Uraricoera, shows occupation there to have lasted between 2000 - 1000 B.C., i.e., commencing around the time of the onset of and conditions regionwide. The refuse indicates heavy reliance on fish, freshwater snails and various small reptiles and mammals. In keeping with hunter-gatherer subsistence practices in the marginal environments of the savannas, numerous Enumerative petroglyphs and pictographs, including the Cuneiform Subtype, were imposed on the surrounding cave walls. Paint-stained exfoliation flakes occurring in the food refuse not only present a rare opportunity for dating these pictographs but also permit associating a specific range of pictograph elements with a particular assemblage of Archaic food refuse.

The potentials of the Enumerative petroglyph type for reconstructing its associated subsistence system are second only to those of direct excavation. These potentials are of especial value in the Guianas where Archaic sites, which occur mainly in eroded gravelly or sandy savanna environments, or in the impenetrable rain forest, are extremely difficult to locate. The Sipaliwini complex of southern Suriname is an example of the former, and the chipping station on the upper Burro Burro River, Figure 3.45, an example of the latter. The at times explicit petroglyph record of numbers and types of game animals taken in a given hunting episode remains so far an unacknowledged boon to archaeological inference. This seems all the more unfortunate when it is remembered that the authors of the record were, uniquely, the folk themselves.

At certain sites, petroglyph/pictograph imposition was episodic, the elements having been imposed from bottom to top over time. Discrete registers resulted, where successively longer ladders were employed as lower areas became saturated. A good example occurs at Aishalton, in the South Rupununi Savannas (Williams 1979: Figure 21). In the Merume Mountains, the Tramen pictograph besides exhibiting similar registers also displays horizontally defined clusters of elements that resulted from the limited lateral reach of the artificer perched on a ladder. Therefore each element cluster represents a single impositional event, while the game animals enumerated in each cluster represent a specific hunting episode. The range of species represented, and the numbers of each species taken suggest a communal hunt. Leadership of some sort and reciprocal distribution of game seem implied.

The size of the community involved is implied by the weight of meat available to it for distribution after a particular hunting episode. One of the element clusters selected for analysis, Figure 3.55, records game animals of the following estimated weights: a two-toed sloth *(Choloepus didactylus)* 12 kg; 15 monkeys *(Saimiri sciureus)* including a female with young, 0.7 kg each; an unidentified small mammal (*? Dasyprocta aguti*), 1.5 kg; and 11 powis (*Crax nigra*), 4 kg each. Though not known as a game animal at present, *Saimiri* was chosen among eight species of monkeys listed in the primate survey of Guyana (Muckenhirn et al 1975; Muckenhirn and Eisenberg 1978; Phillips-Conroy and Sussman 1995) and Suriname (Mittermeier and van Roosmalen 1981) because, in a situation in which the white sands of the Guiana Shield are known to be relatively depauperate in species density, the uniquely large group sizes of *Saimiri* (30 - 50 individuals) seemed best to correlate with the large numbers recorded in a single hunting event.

Animals represented in this element cluster approximate 68 kg live weight. At a minimum 65% of live weight (Hill and Hawkes 1983: 158), this cluster provided 44.2 kg edible meat. Assuming the typically small band sizes of the coastal shellfishers, the volume of these returns suggests that consumption was not immediate and that therefore the estimate should account also for weight loss by smoking or sundrying. Reducing the moisture level to 13% or lower prevents the growth of harmful micro-organisms and lessens chances of infestation (Pimentel and Pimentel 1979:117). For this, tropical sunlight is cheap, efficient and less labor intensive than smoking. Estimates of the moisture content of wild meat and fowl are based on values for dried meat and chicken, respectively (Watt et al 1959:246).

Dried to 13% of its original water content, the edible meat of mammals represented in this element cluster (initially 24 kg) finally weighed 14 kg (= 4750 g protein), while the edible meat of fowl in the same element cluster (initially 44 kg), finally weighed 16.82 kg (= 5920 g protein). Assuming an RDA of 65 g protein/day per adult male and 55 g protein/day per adult female, the complement of 10,670 g protein deriving from the recorded hunting episode would

Figure 3.55. Upper Mazaruni River. The Tramen Pictograph.

have been adequate for an Archaic reference group of around 16 adults over a period of six days.

A petroglyph recorded on the upper Marouini River (Hurault et al 1963: Figure 11) comprised 29 unidentified ground dwelling birds estimated to have weighed 29 kg; 35 monkeys (*Saimiri*) estimated to have weighed 24.5 kg; and seven unidentified wading birds estimated at 14 kg. The total, 67.5 kg live weight, compares well with the returns indicated for a single hunting episode in the Tramen pictograph. If these very rough estimates are acceptable, they indicate that Archaic band sizes on *terra firme* were comparable to those on the Western Guiana Littoral suggested by food refuse and housepost distributions.

Despite the contrasting floral and faunal environments represented by species depicted in the Tramen pictograph in the Pakaraima Highlands on the one hand and species depicted in the upper Marouini petroglyph on the other, the most common game animals consumed in both cases were ground dwelling birds, and monkeys. This is because, in all environments, monkeys generally are more visible and numerous than other kinds of game animals and therefore are more likely than others to be taken on short order, assuming use of the bow and arrow. Like the trees, animal communities in the rain forest are stratified. The emergent layer, 45 - 50 m high, is inhabited mostly by birds and insects which live their whole lives in that habitat. Below them, the greatest variety of animals inhabit the canopy layer, 25 - 35 m high, which forms an almost continuous cover and which absorbs some 70 - 80% of the incident light. Here dwell the monkeys, sloths, anteaters and small carnivores, who rarely descend to the ground but feature nonetheless in the menu pictured in Archaic petroglyphs. Ground dwellers are less diverse than arboreal types. They include deer, rodents and peccaries, all of which are represented in the petroglyph record, Figure 3.39. In Guyana, 31 out of 50 species are arboreal, five amphibious and the rest mainly ground dwellers (Simmons 1979:95).

Taking into account the low proportion of ground dwellers, their prominence in the menu of the savanna hunters probably reflects their closer proximity to man and consequent exposure to trapping, stalking, imitative calls and deadly casual encounters. The trait of petroglyph/pictograph monitoring of game animals necessarily extracted from the biota, Figures 3.39, 3.47, suggests a certain level of residential stability on the part of the group responsible for the record. This record inextricably linked human subsistence with the supernatural world (Reichel - Dolmatoff 1967, 1971, 1978). In this way a particular local group guaranteed the reproductive viability of its economic catchment area. The occurrence of petroglyph elements of savanna hunter-gatherers on a bark beater from a shell mound of the Western Guiana Litoral, made on local stone, Figure 3.13, indicates the socio-economic scope of Archaic groups in the Guianas. It also emphasizes the semantic power of the petroglyphic sign.

As noted by Reichel-Dolmatoff among the Tukano of the Colombian North West Amazon:

> Tukano graphic symbols, that is, their "decorative art," is a system of communication. It reminds the receptor to practice moderation in hunting and fishing, in eating, in needlessly destroying the environment, in fighting, in population increase, in sexual license, in interpersonal strife. Its origin is not in ritual but lies in the logical cause-and-effect reasoning of shamans and other intellectual leaders.

The petroglyph evidences suggest that this was typical of the political economy of *terra firme* as a whole, which differed from that of coastal areas in the stratagem by means of which a balance was maintained between the reproductive potentials of the biota and man's own reproductive potentials. In the absence of the abundant coastal, riverain and swamp resources of the shellfishers, exploitation of the biota on *terra firme* was possible only by means of a system of rigid controls. These were legitimated and maintained down the generations by divine sanction. A particular community achieved and maintained access to the domain of the supernaturals through the agency of hallucinogens. Control was exercised over the extractive behaviors of its members by the imposition of Enumerative petroglyphs and pictographs. The involvement of the headman or shaman is implied. Communities subject to such controls are identifiable since, across the Guianas and into the Antilles, petroglyph/pictograph iconographies reflect well defined socio-economic contrasts on both the Archaic and horticulturist time levels.

The Enumerative petroglyph of certain *terra firme* peoples is identifiable by virtue of the peculiar division of its diagnostic elements into geometric and biomorphic classes. As noted above, the geometric inventory is of extreme interest in light of the universal occurrence of its main elements across the region -- rings, concentric rings, rayed rings, rings circumscribing radiating straight furrows, concentric semicircles, concentric rectangles, curvilinear to rectilinear spirals, straight parallel furrows, serpentines, punctates, chevrons, diamonds, grids, crosses, meandering furrows, etc., Figure 3.46. In its opposition to the class of figurative elements that characterizes many inventories and in the sameness of its elements, the geometric class early attracted notice because of its distributional consistency. Reichel-Dolmatoff (1972:104, 1978:15) found not only that these elements were repeated frequently in Tukano decorative art, but also that each was of semantic significance to the indigenes. This resulted from repeated appearances of the same elements to different groups and on different occasions during altered states of consciousness induced by hallucinogens. More, the author was struck by how frequently these elements occurred in the petroglyphs and pictographs of the region, in explanation of which they were compared with those entoptic images, or phosphenes, that in certain conditions briefly illumine the field of vision independently of retinal observation.

Stimulated by the use of various hallucinogens, phosphenes can be experienced with closed eyes and are especially well perceived if the eyes are already dark-adapted, but they can be seen also with open eyes and, in that case, may appear as superimposed upon normal vision. Some of these photic sensations are hardly more than sudden flashes, stripes of light, or scintillating shapeless flickers that pass over the field of vision like lightning, but others may appear as well defined, abstract, geometrical patterns, sometimes of a remarkable complexity. To most people, these images are familiar in the sensation of "seeing stars," or, to Guyanese, "ning-ning." Under certain circumstances, phosphenes can appear quite spontaneously, though, more frequently, they are produced by external stimulants such as pressure on the eyeballs, a sudden fright or a sharp blow. On account of their origin within the eye and the brain, these phosphenes are common to all men and therefore are of special interest to neuro-psychologists, by whom they have been produced under laboratory conditions (e.g. Bradley 1989; Lewis-Williams and Dowson 1988, 1993; Seigel 1977).

Scientifically produced entoptic patterns have been employed in the study of non-figurative art, including Bushman, neolithic and megalithic art (Lewis-Williams and Dowson 1993), the art of the American Southwest (Hedges 1981, 1985, 1987), Tukano decorative art of the Colombian North West Amazon (Reichel-Dolmatoff 1967, 1972, 1978) and Mayan graffiti (Haviland and Haviland 1995). Based on the work of the German neurologist, Max Knoll, Reichel-Dolmatoff was able to compare eight types of motif occurring in modern Tukano art with a similar number of phosphene patterns produced by electrical stimulation of the temporal, frontal and occipital areas of the human brain. The similarities seem conclusive of the neural origin of imagery in certain forms of non-figurative art in Amazonia, Figure 3.56.

Application of Reichel-Dolmatoff's codification of phosphene patterns in Tukano art to the geometric class of elements deriving from Archaic pictographs and petroglyphs in the Guianas produces results that appear to support the findings of Knoll and others that a certain category of neural light pattern was widely present in prehistoric art, Figure 3.57. On the Amazon, the concentric ring motif has been dated to paleo-Indigenous time (Roosevelt et al 1996).

Universal though these phosphene patterns undoubtedly are, cultural predelictions governed their selection and use and thereby determined their semantic significance in any given case. Thus the conventions of petroglyph enumeration took many forms across the hemisphere, Figure 3.58.

Implied in the distributions of the Enumerative petroglyph type, Figure 3.42, is the local group adapted to a specific niche and exercising due control over exploitation of its natural resources in the interests of the group's indefinite survival there. Implied also is the function of the agency through whose mediation discourse

Figure 3.56. Comparison of Tukano and Knoll phosphene patterns (*after Reichel-Dolmatoff 1978*).

Figure 3.57. Comparative phosphene vocabularies. **a**. Modern Tukano, North West Amazon. **b**. Guiana Archaic, deriving from pictographs and petroglyphs.

Figure 3.58a-i. Contrasting forms of petroglyph enumeration in the Americas. **a.** Colombia (*von Hildebrandt 1975*), **b.** Cuba (*Delmonte y Rodriguez 1980*), **c.** Guyana (*Williams 1985*), **d.** Guyane française (*Hurault et al 1963*), **e.** United States (*after Heizer and Hester 1978*), M. Venezuela (*de Valencia et al 1987*).

was made possible with the supernatural world, apparently on a periodic basis. And implied by the manipulation of phosphene patterns in the generation of the socially recognized *grapheme* is the involvement of other specialists in petroglyph imposition. Data providing support for these three inferences are given below.

Controlled resource exploitation. On his ascent of Roraima, Schomburgk (1848:201) encountered a sandstone boulder on which had been imposed "several curved lines about 1/8 in deep that looked exactly as if some one had drawn both his hands in a curve over the stone, and left the impression behind" -- a good description of a common phosphene pattern, Figure 3.57 last line (middle). Various writers have reported petroglyphs; located at puzzling heights up cliff sides (von Humboldt 1852 - 1853,ii:513; Reichel-Dolmatoff 1967, 1971:82) or in remote mountain fastnesses (e.g. Peberdy 1945, 1948). An elaborate petroglyph imposed on the face of a large outcrop on a headwater stream of the Burro Burro River can be seen only at the cost of a rigorous climb up cloud-capped Iwokrama Mountain (Williams 1996). This remoteness from human habitation would appear to suggest the abode of the sacred, territory which remained unclaimed in the geography of cultural memory and hence constituted the terrain of the supernatural (Reichel-Dolmatoff 1971:131). The pictograph on Tramen Cliff out of whose dark, cavernous recesses the headwaters of the Mazaruni River issue with a continuous deep, hollow rumble, exemplifies such a sacred space, uninhabited and unmodified by the hand of man. In the Tramen pictograph may be encountered most of the phosphenes shown in Figure 3.57b. Thus, petroglyph/pictograph imposition would appear to have been, so to speak, stratified in the Archaic mind, apparently reflecting the cosmological structure of superimposed 'levels' or 'worlds' reported by various writers. Schematized by Roe (1982:129, Figure 3) and compared by that author to a 'cosmic layer cake' comprising upper, middle and lower worlds, this model varied from group to group mainly in the number of tiers constituting the celestial sphere, each tier being identified with a particular category of spirit. Such tiers may vary from four among the Yanomamo to ten among the Secoya of northeastern Ecuador. The model is symbolized in the domestic architecture of Amazonian and Antillean groups (reviewed in Roe 1982; Seigel 1992; see also Versteeg and Schinkel 1992; Hugh-Jones 1993) and also may have determined the functional stratification of petroglyphs -- sacred in the hills, hunter-gatherer on the savannas and Fish Trap in the rivers.

Notwithstanding its possibly remote location in the highest level, or world, a petroglyph constituted nonetheless but one feature in a wider "archaeological configuration" (Greider 1975) which included also the mine that provided the specialized raw materials for tool manufacture, the workshop or chipping station where such tools were produced, and the place where they were discarded after use. With the exception of the last, these locations may not have stood in close proximity to the petroglyphic site; indeed, the required raw materials may have needed to be manuported significant distances between locations. At the petroglyphic boulder proper, imposition over an extended period implies tool maintenance and discard, with certain tools having been cached for variable periods as the work progressed.

These variables constitute the research parameters that dictate the scope of investigations at a given petroglyphic boulder.

On the crystalline rocks of the Guiana Shield, petroglyph imposition was by the technique of pecking and abrasion, Figure 3.59.

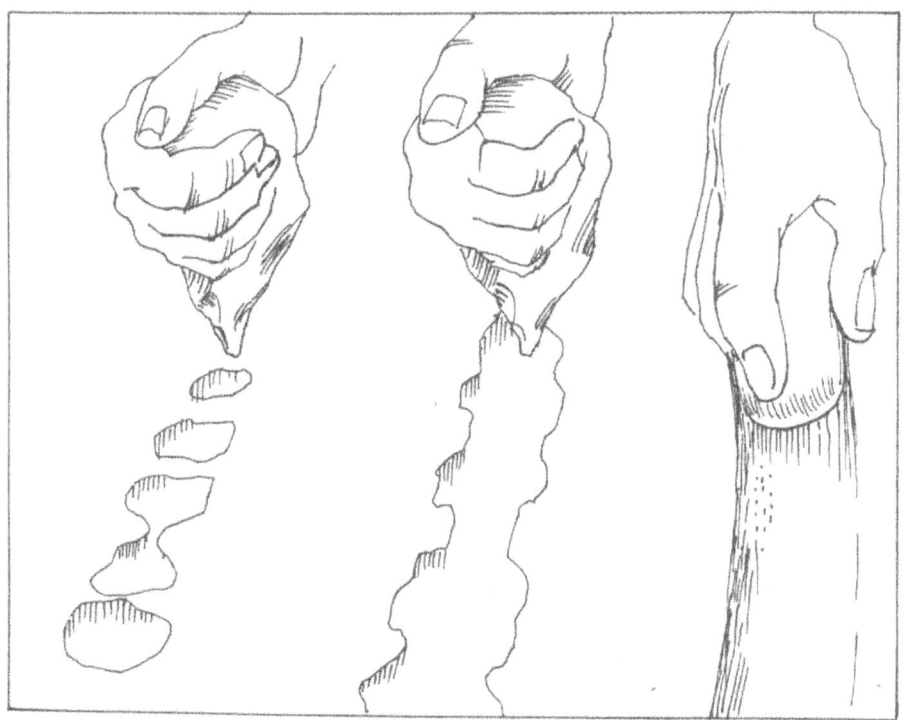

Figure 3.59. The technique of pecking and abrasion in petroglyph imposition.

Tools were made on quartz and granite, the latter exhibiting varying stages of kaolinization of the felspar. The majority were casually collected, unaltered pebbles or exfoliation flakes selected for characteristics of point, edge, roundness or relative hardness, Figure 3.60. Used as scrapers for preliminary sketching in of the desired phosphene pattern, the exfoliation flake produced a lean, chalk-like line by means of which the image could be modified indefinitely until the selected petroglyph element, e.g. concentric circles, grid, etc., was judged acceptably accurate. The exfoliation flakes utilized in this preliminary exercise consequently exhibit one or more telltale grinding facet. The unerring precision of geometric elements exhibited by the Enumerative petroglyph type clearly attests the preliminary function of these exfoliation flakes, Figure 3.41. Incision was then made into the cortex of the rock, 10 - 20 mm thick, by serial punctation with the quartz chopper. The irregular furrows created by running these punctates together were reduced by abrasion with

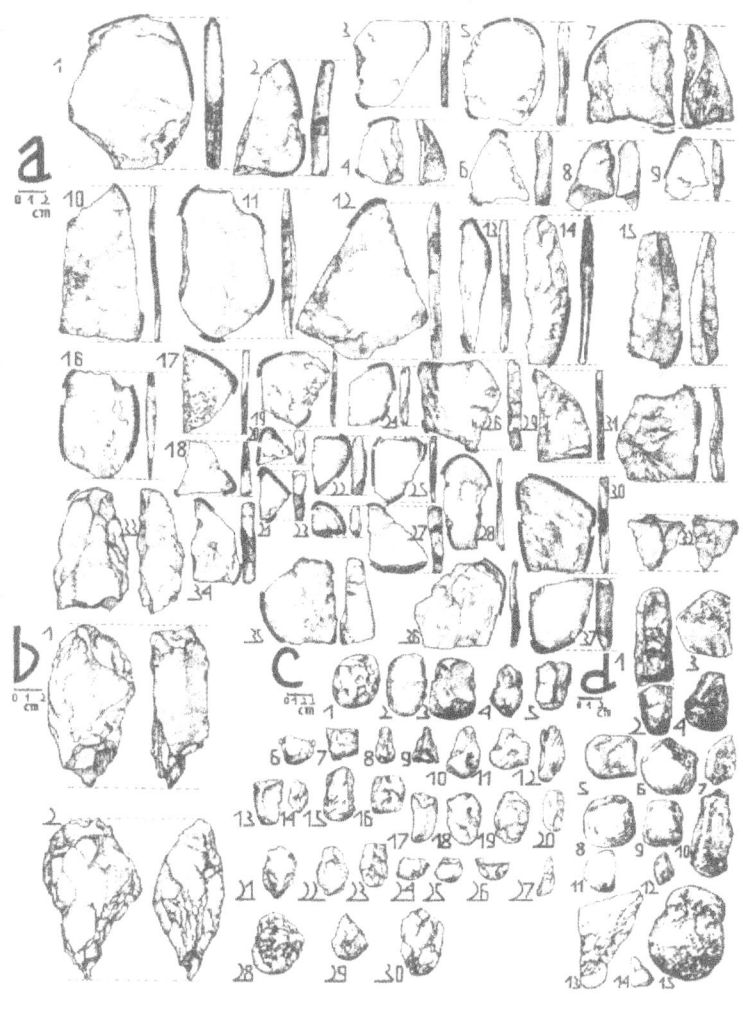

Figure 3.60. The petroglyph toolkit. a. Scraper, b. Chopper, c,d. abrader.

a quartz pebble. This was followed by polishing with two grades of granite abrader, each characterized by the degree of kaolinization of felspar in the granite. The finest grade of granite abrader was a pebble of almost pure kaolin.

The mediating agent. Granted incision on the crystalline rocks of the Guiana Shield, quantitative differences in this structurally two-stage operation suggest qualitative differences among the artificers. The implied altered state of consciousness of the purveyor of the phosphene pattern contrasts with the mechanical labors involved in incising the resulting petroglyphic element. A functional difference evidently existed between the artificer under trance and his fellows. Certain archaeological evidences may be cited in support of this scenario.

Excavation of three petroglyph sites near Makatau cave in the South Rupununi Savannas yielded the toolkit shown in Figure 3.60. Quartz pebbles and cobbles employed in the manufacture of these tools had been mined some distance away, where the savanna was littered with debris from a decomposed granite outcrop, and manuported to the foot of the petroglyph boulder for the characteristic crude, percussion flaking that is widely evidenced elsewhere in these savannas (see Evans and Meggers 1960:23; Meggers and Evans 1955; Williams 1978b) as well as further afield (Sanoja O. 1969).

The Aminge granite of the South Rupununi Savannas has weathered to a depth of around 12 mm. This represents the limit of penetration of the rock surface by the Archaic toolkit. Resulting from chemical action in cave interiors, the thickness of the weathered crust increases in direct proportion to distance from the cave mouth and exhibits progressive kaolinization of the felspar, so that in the innermost galleries the granite is completely kaolinized to a depth of around 35 mm. On these softer rocks, pecking and abrasion was abandoned and petroglyphs were imposed simply by scoring into the chalky material.

Thus, rock materials employed in the petroglyph toolkit had been quarried at the site of a decomposing boulder in the open savanna as well as in the depths of Makatau Cave, representing distances of 2 - 3 km in each direction from the petroglyphic boulder. These boulders were located within 2 - 3 km of one another around Makatau Mountain, some covered with a myriad of thimble-sized punctations, Figure 3.61. Similar punctations covering the entire western flank of Makatau Mountain represent the enumerating concerns of savanna hunter gatherers over the millennia.

Excavation at the foot of one of these boulders revealed a pattern of deposition of waste chips resulting from *in situ* manufacture of the quartz tools employed. These chips had fallen in a wide arc around a small, flat rock that evidently had been selected repeatedly among others to serve as the seat of the toolmaker. Whereas the coarser chips had fallen directly at the foot of the seated craftsman, the finer ones had radiated outward, their dimensions diminishing with distance from his position.

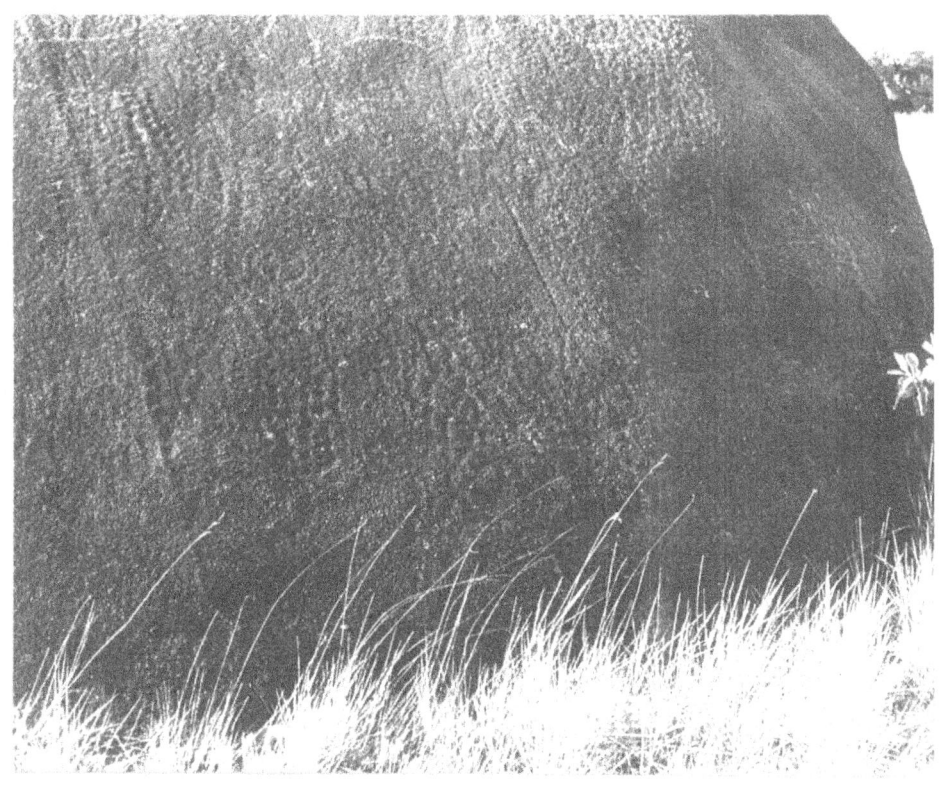

Figure 3.61. Makatau Mountain, South Rupununi Savannas. Massed punctation on western flank.

The ratio of fine to coarse chips, 10:1, Table H., indicates that *in situ* tool manufacture mainly had involved trimming quartz pebbles for use in abrading the petroglyphic furrow.

Table H. Size grades of waste chips in petroglyph tool manufacture.

Size	Number	Average wt (g)	Percentage
Coarse	52	3.69	7.60
Medium	85	12.42	12.42
Fine	547	0.29	79.97

The dispersion of waste chips about the toolmaker indicates that the same small outcrop had been utilized as a stool on each occasion of petroglyph imposition. No chips had fallen to his rear. During each impositional event the toolmaker had faced to the east among options which had permitted him to have faced either to the west or south had he so desired. A ritual posture associated with manufacture of petroglyph tools at the foot of the boulder seems suggested. After each impositional episode, the craftsman had cached his tools in a nearby crevice. Cached tools were recovered independently at two sites, suggesting that procurement of rock materials and manufacture of the tools in each case had been the work of a specialist.

Imposition of the petroglyphic grapheme. Apart from the technical competence evidenced by the *in situ* accumulation of chipping debris, this specialist was evidently also the purveyor of the phosphene pattern responsible for the petroglyph element that remained to be incised on the rock. However, as has been seen, elements of the geometric class, some apparently of neural origin, often occur in association with elements of a contrasting, biomorphic, class the origin of which seems associated with specific kinds of game animals extracted from the biota. It is by means of such combinations that, in any given case, a specific enumerative value was communicated. Thus, combinations of biomorphic and geometric elements indicate numbers of deer, fish, bird, monkeys, etc., taken in given hunting episodes, Figure 3.58a,b,d-i. This is the petroglyphic/pictographic *grapheme* by means of which the exploitation of the biota was controlled. The trait is hemispheric, suggesting the universality of the associated subsistence practices. Since the *compte rendu* of the petroglyphic *grapheme* was made on behalf of the entire community, its imposition, involving periods of sustained and apparently ecstatic labor, should be attributable to the shaman. The (neural) inverted anthropomorph of the Mont Alegre pictograph (Roosevelt et al 1996: Figure 3) may be a metaphor for the shaman's altered state of consciousness during an impositional episode.

Besides their potentials for contributing to the reconstruction of Archaic subsistence, petroglyphs are useful indicators of past climates, Figure 3.62a-c, 3.63. The dispersion of the Cuneiform Petroglyph Subtype implies a centripetal (coast to hinterland) pattern in the human migrations of the arid interval. Concurrently, the

Figure 3.62a-b. **a.** Turtle Pond, Essequibo River; **b.** Petroglyphs.

migrations of certain hunter-gatherers from the dessicating savannas of the Western Guiana Hinterland were following a centrifugal (hinterland to coast) pattern which now began to people the streams of the rain forest, some part of these two migrating movements appear to have met along the upper reaches of the Essequibo corridor where Cuneiform (coast to hinterland) and Fish Trap (hinterland to coast) petroglyphs co-occur on a horizon which, even during critical low water of the dry season, remains partly submerged, Figure 3.63.

Sharpening grooves. Also occurring on this submerged horizon are sharpening grooves *(amoladores, goutières, slijpgroeven),* long, narrow (sometimes keeled) ellipsoids resulting from sharpening working edges of ground stone tools (p. 163). Since they cluster near the prevailing waterline, their zonations suggest the

Since they cluster near the prevailing waterline, their zonations suggest the fluctuating water levels of past climates.

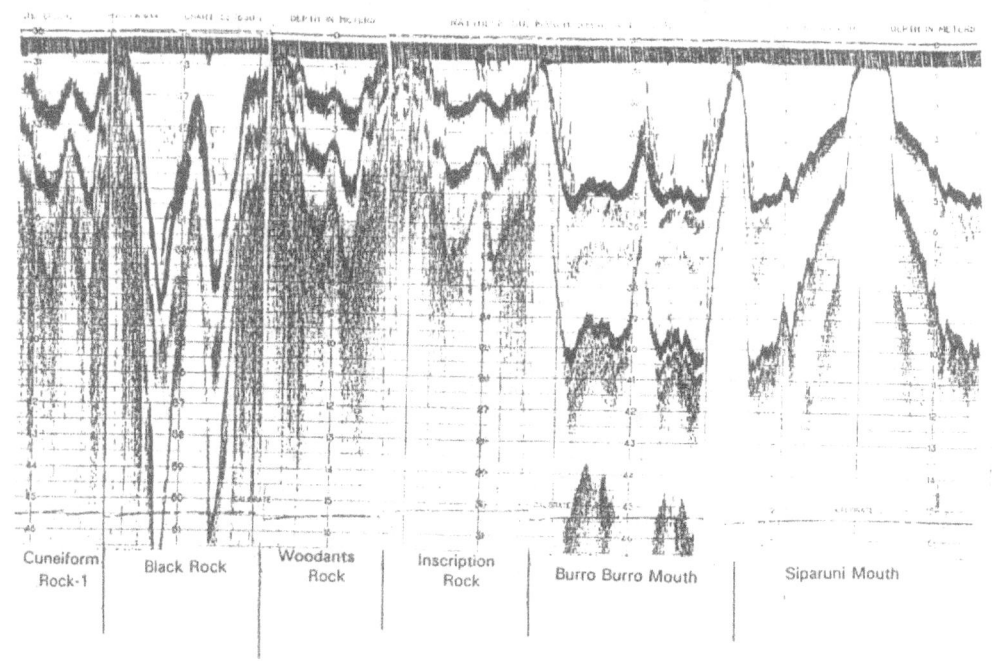

Figure 3.63. Sonar sections on Essequibo and Burro Burro riverbeds showing petroglyph locations ( ) above/below present water level 27 March 1994. (*Data on Raytheon DE719C Fathometer*).

By virtue of their close relationship to the tools prepared in them, sharpening grooves are a valuable diagnostic in reconstructing paleoclimates in a given river basin. If a direct relationship is assumed between the dimensions of a given sharpening groove on the one hand and, on the other, dimensions of working edges of the tools that had been manufactured or maintained in it, then granted a sample of the size obtained on the Siparuni River, upper Essequibo, analysis of these dimensions should prove rewarding, Table Ia,b.

Table Ia. Siparuni River, Guyana. Relationships of length to depth in sharpening grooves, n = 118.

Length (cm) 41 - 50		3	3	3	
31 - 40	7	18	8	3	1
21 - 30	24	21	11	5	
11 - 20	4	5			
0 - 10	2				
	0 - 10 Depth (mm)	11 - 20	21 - 30	31 - 40	41 - 50

Table Ib. Siparuni River, Guyana. Size-grades of tools derived from Table Ia.

Length (cm)	Depth (mm)	Size grade
11 - 20	0 - 2	Small (9) 7.6%
21 - 30	1 - 4	Medium (61) 51.6%
31 - 40	1 - 5	Large (37) 31.3%
		Other (11) 9.3%

Frequencies of hypothesized tool sizes deriving from Table Ia, are shown in Table Ib. Of the five size grades of tools represented in the sample, the two groups at either extreme in Figure 3.64 (between them totaling 11 specimens) are considered atypical (extra small or extra large). The remaining frequencies suggest that sharpening grooves at Big "S" Falls were associated with the consistent manufacture and maintenance of tools which clustered around three well defined size grades, tools of medium size having been overwhelmingly the most popular.

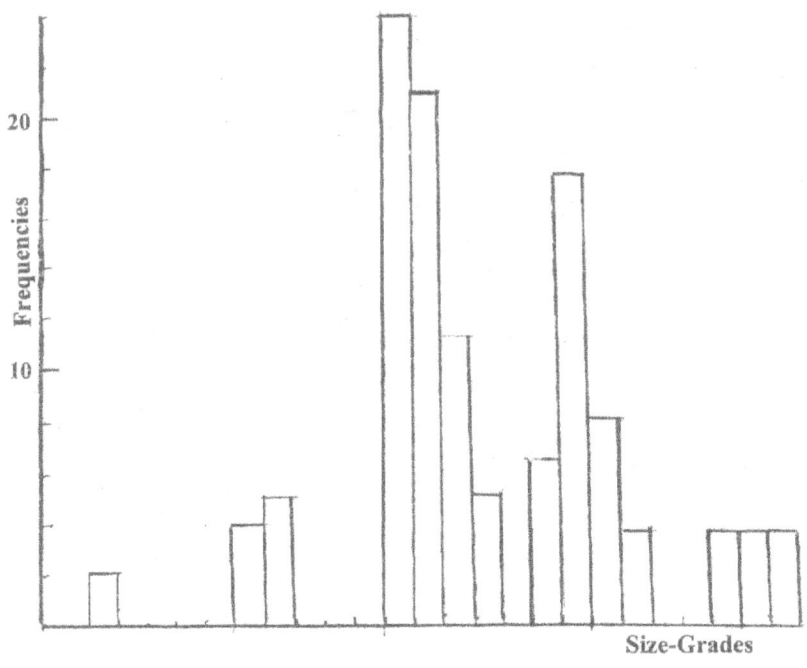

Figure 3.64. Size grades of tools probably manufactured/maintained in sharpening grooves.

Artificial depressions at Big "S" Falls on the Siparuni River are about equally distributed on the left and right banks, 414 and 439, respectively. On the left bank, sharpening grooves number 51 (12.3%), while on the right bank sharpening grooves number 76 (17.3%). In the total sample, sharpening grooves account for 14.9%. Thus, the right bank would appear to have been marginally more favored for tool manufacture. There, 14 sharpening grooves represent 23% of a total 60 depressions, or half again the average for the total sample. The preference may have resulted from the configuration of the right bank rocks. This is characterized by a larger area of rock exposures immediately below the waterfall. The most favored spot was a small, flat platform clear of turbulence and shelving gently into the stream.

On the left bank, sharpening grooves occupy a zone between -17 cm to 145 cm with respect to prevailing water level (pwl), i.e., water level represented by a fixed datum in the main channel at Kurupukari Falls *on the precise day of the survey*. (The timing was meant to recognize the variable discharge regimes of rivers in the Essequibo drainage). On the right bank, sharpening grooves occupy a zone between -8 cm to 145 cm with respect to pwl, with the overwhelming majority concentrated between 60 - 145 cm. Thus, whereas sharpening grooves on the left bank concentrate mainly in an 85 cm deep zone located around 60 cm above pwl, sharpening grooves on the right bank concentrate mainly in an 80 cm deep zone located at the same height above pwl. This collocation of sharpening grooves on a common presently submerged horizon on the two riverbanks suggests that, as elsewhere in the Essequibo Basin, they were imposed in phase with sustained low water levels at the time of manufacture or maintenance of the related tools. A functional relationship is implied between the zonation of sharpening grooves at Big "S" Falls and water levels prevailing at the time individual specimens of sharpening groove were imposed on the rock. This seems to suggest that the specialized sharpening or maintenance of working edges on stone tools required the close proximity of water (Abonnenc 1952; Deman et Lefebvre 1974; Toutouri 1983). These kinds of artificial depressions occur mainly in or on the banks of streams, and then on selected fine-grained igneous rocks.

The lowest artifical depression in the Big " S " Falls assemblage was located on -41 cm with respect to pwl. On the same day, the lowest artificial depression at the site of a Cuneiform petroglyph on the Essequibo mainstream stood on -11 cm with respect to pwl. Simultaneously other artificial depressions lower down the Siparuni stood on -21 cm at Tapir Rock (VIII - 2:37) and on -32 cm at Electric Eel Rock (VIII - 2:36) (Site numbers and co-ordinates in Williams 1994). Thus, artificial depressions on the Siparuni River were imposed on the same submerged horizon of the Archaic as is occupied by certain Enumerative, Fish Trap and Cuneiform petroglyphs in the Essequibo mainstream.

Excavation of a sand-filled crevice below one of the left-bank artificial depressions yielded a small, trapezoidal adze. Bit measurements on this specimen (15 mm depth) place it in the smallest of the three major size-grades shown above, Table Ib. Trapezoidal adzes of this size excavated in an Archaic coastal shell mound represented one of three size-grades employed in the manufacture of the earliest dugout canoes known so far in the archaeology of the Guianas. Grouped according to size, excavated specimens of these Archaic adzes weighed, respectively, 0.1-0.3 kg, 0.6 kg, and 1.8 kg (Williams 1992:240). The specimen from Big "S" Falls weighed 0.84 kg.

Nowadays, adzes of this size-grade are employed in smoothing charred chip marks on the burnt interior of the dugout canoe during the final stages of its

Table J. Comparative means of SHARPENING GROOVES Siparuni and Essequibo Rivers.

(i) Length

	Siparuni			Essequibo
	Group 1a (N = 3)	Group 1b (N = 48)	Group 2 (N = 76)	N = 9
Mean	28.0	28.92	27.89	24.3
Standard Deviation (n-1 parameter)	3.61	6.12	7.38	11.7

(ii) Breadth

	Siparuni			Essequibo
	Group 1a (N = 3)	Group 1b (N = 48)	Group 2 (N = 76)	N = 9
Mean	5.67	7.69	1.69	6.9
Standard Deviation (n-1 parameter)	0.58	3.97	0.99	2.76

(iii) Depth

	Siparuni			Essequibo
	Group 1a (N = 3)	Group 1b (N = 48)	Group 2 (N = 76)	N = 9
Mean	1.67	1.69	1.84	0.56
Standard Deviation (n-1 parameter)	0.76	0.99	1.15	0.47

manufacture. Use wear on the dorsal surface of the Big "S" Falls specimen suggests this function. Such a function would suggest a rate of discard for this minuscule implement that was appreciably lower than those of the larger size-grades, the working edges of which were employed in modifying fresh wood and which therefore would have been subject to higher rates of attrition and/or fracture. Fracture rates

Table K. Comparative means SHARPENING GROOVES Siparuni and Essequibo Rivers

(i) Length

	Siparuni			Essequibo
	Group 1a (N = 95)	Group 1b (N = 268)	Group 2 (N = 363)	N = 115
Mean	23.72	24.69	25.02	22.56
Standard Deviation (n-1 parameter)	7.78	7.38	8.66	4.71

(ii) Breadth

	Siparuni			Essequibo
	Group 1a (N = 95)	Group 1b (N = 268)	Group 2 (N = 363)	N = 115
Mean	14.11	11.82	11.59	12.71
Standard Deviation (n-1 parameter)	5.97	5.14	6.40	2.99

(iii) Depth

	Siparuni			Essequibo
	Group 1a (N = 95)	Group 1b (N = 268)	Group 2 (N = 363)	N = 115
Mean	1.14	1.09	0.94	0.09
Standard Deviation (n-1 parameter)	1.32	1.27	1.39	0.16

of specimens excavated in shell mounds on the Western Guiana Littoral were high, with fracture types varying according to the design of the tool, Figure 3.32.

Differentials in the discard rates of adzes according to individual size/shape factors imply differentials in attrition rates of the associated sharpening grooves. Therefore, as shown in Table J, the relative frequencies of medium and large sizes of sharpening grooves at particular sites should be diagnostic of frequencies of the associated tools, and hence of the potentials of such sites for the manufacture of dugout canoes. For example, assuming that the wide range of size differentials in the above sample indicates a good representation of adzes (axes do not exhibit such a wide size range) a canoe manufacturing industry at Big "S" Falls can be inferred with fair certainty.

A range of measurements in each size grade is indicated there also by the high standard deviations of sharpening grooves. These values remain consistent on both banks of the river, Table J., Groups 1,2.

Also, the cultural homogeneity of the site is reflected in the values of artificial depressions as a whole, which on both riverbanks (Groups 1,2) exhibit notable similarities in variation about the mean, Tables J, K.

Lengths and depths of sharpening grooves at one site on the Essequibo mainstream (Cuneiform Rock VIII - 2:45) exhibit marked contrasts with the situation at Big " S " Falls, Table J, though the smallness of the former sample precludes the possibility of drawing conclusions concerning the type of activity represented there -- systematic tool manufacture or opportunistic tool maintenance.

Of thirty-seven artificial depressions encountered on the Burro Burro River, twenty-four (68%) were encountered at Monkey Falls (VIII - 2:49) where riverbed outcrops are visible during the dry season at around 50 cm depth from bank to bank. With a further slight drop in the water level, this stretch of the river becomes a rapid, a factor probably explaining the numbers of artificial depressions there. The next largest inventory, recorded at an unnamed left bank site a bit further upstream, numbered eight specimens. The relative paucity of sharpening grooves at these sites when contrasted with those on the Siparuni, and their characteristic shallowness (< 1 mm), suggest seasonal fishing camps rather than habitations.

The elevations of artificial depressions at the Monkey Falls site ranged from just below pwl to 100 cm above pwl. Assuming a relationship between the zonation of these sharpening grooves on the Burro Burro River and water levels prevailing there at the time of their imposition, they seem to relate to a period of high water, apparently coincident with water levels indicated by the lower half of the zone of sharpening grooves at Big "S" Falls on the Siparuni. However, this comparison leaves out of account the contrasting catchments of these two streams, the Burro Burro rising in the Iwokrama Mountains and the Siparuni in the Pakaraimas.

The relative scarcity of sharpening grooves on the Burro Burro River suggests that subsistence activities there were considerably less than on the Siparuni and Essequibo Rivers and that the exploiting communities probably were small.

The relationship suggested here between the zonation of sharpening grooves and water levels probably prevailing at the time of manufacture and/or maintenance of the related tools derives from studies in the upper Essequibo Basin. It is provisional and experimental and needs to be supported by further accurate observations at sites elsewhere in the sample area where assemblages of artificial depressions of sufficient size occur. The potential exists for mapping the locations of individual sharpening grooves at such sites with respect to pwl as a basis for intersite comparisons directed at attributing relative values to regional water level fluctuations during the Archaic.

The literature does not want for descriptions of riverain sharpening grooves that are evident only at low water (e.g. Abonnenc 1952; Toutouri 1983 in Guyane française; Bubberman 1972, Versteeg 1980 in Suriname; Mentz Ribeiro et al 1987 in Brazil; and de Valencia et al 1987 in Venezuela), and therefore imply imposition during an arid interval. Unfortunately, sizes of the assemblage and dimensions of individual specimens invariably are lacking, nor are measurements ever presented with respect to elevation above or depth below the prevailing water level. Such data potentially are of regional significance when tied to sonar reading of the respective riverbeds. By relating the lowest sharpening groove at a given site (= water level prevailing at time of its imposition) to the maximum depth of the riverbed there, a picture is derived of the depth of the Archaic stream as well as of specific local features of the now submerged cultural horizon, Figure 3.63.

Data on differential water levels during periods of sustained reduced precipitation in the past would seem to hold potentials for inferring differences in prehistoric vegetation cover in the various river drainages, for example as evidenced in superimposed layers of orange and black patination on certain modified rocks of the upper Siparuni River. These contrasting layers appear to relate to past differences in vegetational cover locally. The orange patina is absent on rocks protected by the shade of the present day riverbank vegetation.

The restructuring of prehistory in the rain forest seems set to present interdisciplinary problems that are new in the archaeology of the Americas. Granted the overwhelming importance of riverbanks in the settlement of the Tropical Forest the cooperation of the geographers, geochemists and hydrologists may be required to explain observed contemporaneous water level differences in the streams of a particular drainage. For example, the 80 cm deep oscillation zone (O-Zone) on the Siparuni River is represented on the neighboring Burro Burro River by an O-Zone 40 cm deep which seems to correlate with only the lower half of the zone of sharpening grooves on the Siparuni into which it flows. On the Essequibo mainstream, into which the Siparuni flows, the O-Zone at Cuneiform Rock (VIII - 2:45) is comparable in depth (40 cm) to the O-Zone on the Burro Burro River, but occupies a lower position with respect to pwl.

The implications of these correlations are unclear in light of the observed (Hawkes and Wall 1993:18) ample conveyance capacity of the Siparuni drainage, network, the dynamic channel storage of which is thought too small to sustain prolonged flood recessions. An hypothesis therefore remaining to be tested is that the concentration of sharpening grooves in the 80 cm deep O-Zone on the Siparuni

River is an expression of *repeated flooding episodes* occurring toward the ending of the arid interval, earlier stages of which arid interval may be represented by the lower (-6 to 60 cm) and more dispersed sharpening grooves occurring there. In other words, these scattered lower specimens may represent an initial gradual but continuous rise in the water level which gave way in due course to a regime characterized by oscillating water levels (the O-Zone) and representing the terminal stages of the arid interval.

Water level oscillations in hinterland rivers provide a firm basis for correlating hinterland and coastal paleoclimates. It has been seen that, on the Western Guiana Littoral, the palynological and archaeological data indicate two discrete marine incursions commencing around 2000 B.C. each accompanied by marked vegetation change. Thus, the break-up of this arid interval would appear to have been expressed in more than one episode of pluviation there. This apparently phased break-up of the arid interval on the Western Guiana Littoral invites comparison with oscillating water levels on the Mazaruni River in the Western Guiana Hinterland. There, as will be seen, a regime of sustained low water levels, apparently representing the culmination of a later dry interval (or the final stages of the prevailing one) ended around the time of Christ in successive short-term episodes of torrential rainfall, each having been associated with massive transport of sediments deriving from the Pakaraima Highlands. Sediments transported in phase with rainfall episodes on the Mazaruni following on dessication in the Pakaraimas towards the end of an arid interval were deposited on certain riverbed outcrops and eventually formed wooded islands in the stream. So far, similar islands have not been observed on the Siparuni, which rises in the same highlands and is provided with numerous outcrops suitable for initiating such a fluvial island-building process. By contrast, transport of coarse sediments can be expected not to have occurred on the Burro Burro River and the Essequibo mainstream, each of which rises in dense rain forest devoid of sand. Although representing contrasting time levels, this pattern of an apparent phased break-up of prevailing arid conditions on the coast, as well as in the hinterland, by intermittent but torrential rainfall episodes provides a framework for interpreting the concentration of O-Zone specimens among the sharpening grooves of the upper Siparuni River.

Bedrock mortars. Also outstanding among artifacts of the submerged horizon of Archaic material culture are the channeled mortars on bedrock briefly noted above, Figure 3.44. As has been seen, this mortar has been reported along the entire Orenoque River from its junction with the Muri River to its confluence with the New River, and into the New River (Williams 1985: Figure 23), on the upper Rio Branco (Mentz Ribeiro et al. 1989, Figure 8a) and in Cayenne (Rostain et Le Roux 1990y, Rostain 1994), Figure 3.66.

The shape of this mortar appears to have resulted from sustained circular action with a mano during food preparation. As with other artifacts imposed on bedrock in the rivers of the Guianas during a period of sustained reduced precipitation, these channeled mortars are located on or below critical low water in the dry season. The most concentrated occurrences presently known were recorded on the Orenoque River and its tributaries the East Muri River and the West Muri River, which rise in the Akarai Chain. Unfortunately, the extremely decayed condition of surviving specimens offers no clues regarding the kinds of substances that once were ground in them. Evidently, however, their dispersion along some 225 km of the Orenoque

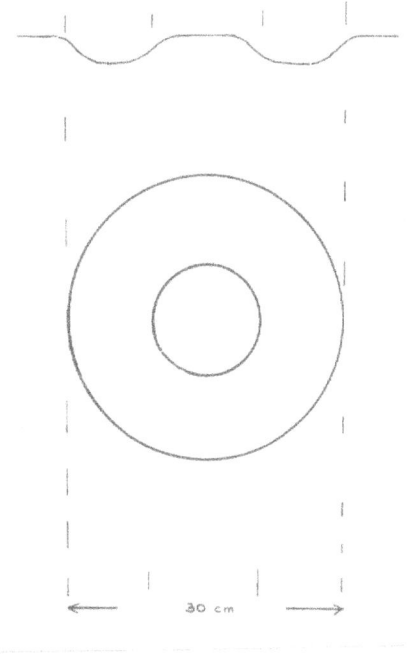

Figure 3.65. Bedrock mortar Orenoque River.

and New Rivers indicates heavy reliance on vegetal foods, probably the brazilnut. The Brazilnut tree (*Bertholletia excelsa*) is of extreme seasonal importance to surviving groups in the area. As the flowers of this plant depend for pollination on a particular bee *(Meliponidae)* (OAS 1987) which, in turn, is to be found only in areas occupied by the particular orchid from which that bee obtains the chemical needed to attract its mate (OTA 1984:52), this channeled mortar can be considered a specialized artifact of bio-diversity in a rain forest environment.

The Brazilnut is an evergreen, predominant, unbuttressed tree with large, spreading crown, occasionally attaining a diameter of 20 m and a height of around 45 m. It sheds its pods around the beginning of the year. The pods are the size of a coconut with a thick, hard shell, each shell containing the tightly packed, delicious, wedge-shaped kernels that are known in supermarkets around the world. The kernels contain 60 - 70% oil composed of elacine (74%) and stearine (26%) which can be used as a substitute for olive oil. The tree is widely distributed in northern South America, occurring locally in small reefs in seasonal forest below 500 m in the Rupununi and upper Essequibo areas. At the present time, its most northerly sighting is on Powawau (Pobawau) Creek in 3° 20' N, 59° 25' W, just north of the Kanuku Mountains (Barron pers. comm. 1988), though its most abundant occurrences in Guyana are on the right bank of the Essequibo as well as on the Kassikaityu and Kamoa Rivers (Fanshawe 1950). Its southerly distribution, high nutritional value and excellent storage properties constitute it a valued food item of the present day Waiwai, by whom it is collected in large quantities annually.

The New River Triangle is under rain forest which covers a typically polygonally dissected terrain of low, rounded, lateritic hills rising from seasonal swamps. This terrain stretches continuously across the Eastern Guiana Hinterland to the Oyapoc River, effectively restricting human occupancy to the riverbanks. Although the Orenoque River supports an extraordinarily rich fish fauna, petroglyphs of any description are lacking there. This suggests that interaction of its Archaic occupants with contemporary specialist fishers of the upper Essequibo River in the northwest and the Trombetas Basin to the south was weak or non-existent. The myriads of channeled mortars there are associated with numerous sharpening grooves indicating the manufacture and maintenance of ground stone tools. Interestingly, the channeled mortars do not co-occur with other kinds of artificial depression, which would seem to suggest a sexual division of labor among the widely scattered bands associated with their imposition.

Chipping station. The final feature of the submerged horizon of Archaic material culture of the Guianas is the chipping station centered on a rare, exposed quartz vein already noted on the upper Burro Burro River, Figure 3.45. The site is located at Dunari Falls in 4° 32' 53.7" N, 58° 50' 35.1" W, comprising a pile of waterworn quartz pebbles and cobbles, waste chips, finished tools and discards, all presently submerged below the critical low water of the dry season. Tools recovered at that time by wading in around 35 cm of water comprised percussion-made choppers, scrapers and knives, all bifacially thinned by pecking, a common technique of the Archaic. In certain specimens, thinning was carried to the extent of producing a translucent working edge of extreme fragility. Unquestionably, the inventory included other items though, on a second dry-season visit to augment the sample, the site lay under 135 cm of water, necessitating impromptu diving that produced few new specimens.

At the time of the earlier investigation, at a lower water level, maximum depth of the Burro Burro River at this point was 2.30 m. The lowest glyph inscribed on a nearby boulder on the riverbed was located 30 cm below pwl. During its imposition, the craftsman had perched in a stooping or kneeling posture on a ledge of rock 110 cm below pwl. Assuming him to have remained clear of the water during that operation, maximum depth of the Burro Burro at this point was 120 cm, at which time the chipping station remained permanently dry on a riverbank which then was around one meter below the lowest dry season water level of the present day, Figure 3.63. The submerged debris is estimated to be around 65 cm thick.

Regional demographic dispersals

The site specific nature of certain strategic resources provided the basis of reciprocal exchange among widely dispersed Archaic groups in the stressed environments of the Amazonian arid interval. Convergences of diagnostic traits in their respective kinds of modified rocks are symptomatic of the demographic upheavals of the period. These convergences indicate interactions of identifiably distinct subsistence systems over immense distances. For example, two separate petroglyph traditions -- those of, respectively, savanna hunter-gatherers and specialist fishers -- converge on the upper Essequibo River. A similar convergence of contrasting petroglyph traditions is in evidence at Kowarwaunau, on the Rupununi headwaters. Enumerative type petroglyphs converge with Fish Trap petroglyphs on the upper Kassikaityu River. Again, two discrete Archaic petroglyph traditions converge at sites around 500 m apart on the upper Rio Branco. There, the channeled mortars at Bem Querer, Figure 3.44, are associated with a spring-basket petroglyph element of specialist fishers which, incongruously, is enumerated. An enumerated caiman occurs at the same site (Mentz Ribeiro et al 1989).

Just as the identity of the pioneer occupants of the Kassikaityu River is suggested by inclusions of the symmetric anthropomorph of their erstwhile savanna environment in the newly developed inventory of Fish Trap petroglyph elements (Williams 1979a), so also the identity of the community at Bem Querer on the upper Rio Branco is suggested on the Kassikaityu River by the imposition of their characteristic caiman element on its headwaters. In contrast to the technique of simple abrasion that is employed for petroglyph imposition along the entire Kassikaityu River, this caiman element, which is located near to the track leading to the upper Rio Branco, was imposed by pecking *(picoteamento)*, the technique which, on the Rio Branco, was employed without distinction on both Fish Trap and Enumerative petroglyphs (Mentz Ribeiro et al 1989: 23, 25), and which evidently was associated with a local group there. These convergences of disparate subsistence systems are interpreted as indicating some measure of economic interdependence between the respective local groups notwithstanding the immense distances separating them.

The stratification of food refuse in the large rock shelter at Pedra Pintada on the Parima River, a left tributary of the lower Uraricoera, shows occupation there to have lasted between 2000 - 1000 B.C., i.e., commencing with the onset of and conditions in Amazonia. The refuse indicates consumption of fish, freshwater snails and various small reptiles and mammals. In keeping with hunter-gatherer practice on the savannas, numerous Enumerative pictographs were imposed on the surrounding cave walls, though the *grapheme* of savanna petroglyph iconography is rare or absent. Paint-stained exfoliation flakes deriving from these pictographs and recovered in the food refuse not only present a rare opportunity for their direct dating but also permit associating a specific range of pictograph elements with a particular assemblage of late Archaic food remains.

The Enumerative elements employed comprised only serially imposed tallies, free standing or set in a cartouche. Thus it is difficult to be certain as to the exact food items being enumerated. However, the refuse indicates in a general way that the tallies related to consumption of fish, deer, iguana, caiman, small carnivores and freshwater gastropods. It has been seen that exactly similar tallies occur at numerous petroglyph/pictograph sites elsewhere in the Rupunun-Rio Branco Savannas as well as further afield, e.g. Tramen, Figure 3.55.

The local environments indicated by the Pedra Pintada food refuse were river, gallery forest and open savannas, not rain forest. The present vegetation is described as mixed tropical forest and savanna (Mentz Ribeiro et al 1989:6, Figure 7a). Therefore, no source appears to have existed in the economic catchment area of the local group for use of the brazilnut as their starchy staple, as seems indicated by occurrences of around 50 channeled mortars locally. These suggest either a different prehistoric environment or an alternative resource area. In the latter case, these savanna hunter-gatherers would have enjoyed economic relations with the rain forest peoples to the southeast.

A clue to the implied economic relations with the rain forest is provided at Pedra Pintada on the Uraricoera. In the food refuse there, frequencies/level of caiman bones increase with decreasing depth from the surface of the ground. Whereas, together, the earliest five excavated levels yielded remains of just one caiman, the uppermost four levels each yielded the remains of at least one (Mentz Ribeiro et al 1987:29). The implied extension of the economic catchment area to the distant Kassikaityu River suggests intensification in the dessicating savanna environment. The "country road" from the Rio Branco used by Evelyn Waugh in 1933 is on a direct route 160 km long to the upper Rupununi and upper Kassikaityu Rivers where Fish Trap and Enumerative petroglyphs co-occur, Figure 3.67. The sole specimen of the intrusive *picteamento* petroglyph technique occurs on a large caiman on the Kassikaityu headwaters (Williams 1979: Figure 13).

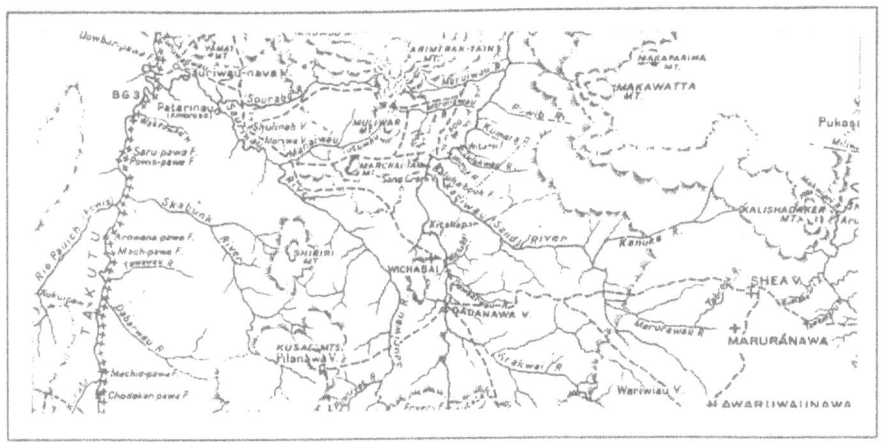

Figure 3.66. The Rio Branco - Rupununi trail

The convergence of the respective subsistence systems suggests that the route may have connected hunter-gatherers on the savannas of the upper Rio Branco and groups of Tropical Forest Collectors on the Kassikaityu in the younger half of the Pedra Pintada sequence, or around 1500 - 1000 B.C. In each area, certain strategic resources are sufficiently site specific to suggest a basis for reciprocal exchange. Rich stands of Brazilnut trees on the lower Kassikaityu right bank complement dense concentrations of sharpening grooves *(sulcos alongados, estreitos e canaletas em "V")* on granite exposures of the upper Rio Branco, Figure 3.67 (Mentz Ribeiro et al 1989:22).

A similar scenario is presented by complementary distributions of strategic resources in coastal and hinterland areas of Eastern Guiana where assemblages of channeled mortars and sharpening grooves on the Ile de Cayenne may represent the material remains of reciprocal exchanges in which ground stone tools from the coast were traded against brazilnuts from the Orenoque and New Rivers. Significantly, areas of dense concentrations of brazilnuts on hinterland rivers such as the Orenoque and the Kassikaityu, while exhibiting dense concentrations of artificial

Figure 3.67. Sharpening grooves.

depressions that characteristically result from tool maintenance, are lacking in the concentrations of sharpening grooves which invariably are associated with local manufacture of ground stone tools. The enormous distances represented by the dispersion of these channeled mortars suggest prolonged time periods and possibly the involvement of intermediaries. But it must be borne in mind that the demographic upheavals of the Amazonian arid interval were characterized, also, by the migrations of bearers of the Cuneiform Petroglyph Subtype southeastward from the Lake Maracaibo area of western Venezuela into the Rupununi-Rio Branco Savannas, the rain forests of the Siparuni Basin and into Guyane française and northeastern Brazil. These very long-range migrations of the arid interval, by initiating the first permanent settlement of the rain forest, facilitated interaction between *terra firme* and the Coast. But, they need to be set within an interaction sphere of the late Archaic that saw the Fish Trap petroglyph of the southern Guianas already in use on the Western Guiana Littoral by around 3300 B.C., at around which time seafarers from the mainland were pioneering the colonization of parts of the Antilles.

4. THE FIRST FARMERS

Introduction

The complex technoeconomic subsystems of late Archaic hunter-gatherers, specialized fishers and Tropical Forest collectors, each occupying a specific niche, their archaeologically attested wide dispersion across the Guianas, the ancient subsistence lore that is evidenced in the system of petroglyph/pictograph enumeration and, most importantly, the long-range interactions made possible by everyday use of the dugout canoe, all of these provided, cumulatively, a base for the shift to food production. This momentous cultural advance was triggered by conditions imposed regionwide during the Amazonian arid interval of +/- 2000 B.C. On presently available evidences, the step was taken initially by peoples occupying the two great deltas of northern Amazonia - the swamp edge near the Mouth of the Orinoco River (Williams 1992) and elevated terrain bordering *varzea* near the Mouth of the Amazon River (cf. Roosevelt et al 1991; Roosevelt et al 1996).

Occurring roughly around 1600 B.C., these seminal events appear to have shared a common origin in the demographic dispersals of the immediately preceding arid interval. At that time, apparently in response to a universal quest for potable water in saline or brackish coastal locations, the centripetally and centrifugally patterned migrations of the late Archaic brought contrasting peoples, defined in the archaeological record by their respective petroglyph/pictograph inventories, into contact with one another across vast areas of northern South America.

Processes leading to the emergence of the two presently known occurrences of first farming in the Guianas are not equally clear. This notwithstanding, detailed examination of these processes, particularly of the relationships, if any, between the subsistence technologies of the late Archaic and those of the incipient horticulturists involved, are prerequisite to any attempt at addressing still outstanding questions concerning the origin and dissemination of Tropical Forest Culture in the Guianas -- our central inquiry. The available data permit attention to be drawn to events that were unfolding in the Northwestern Subzone of the Western Guiana Littoral during the centuries immediately preceding the emergence of food production there.

The environment of the swamp edge

Around 2000 B.C., two marine incursions are evidenced by deposits of shell sand on various creek heads in the Aruka Basin located directly on the swamp edge of the Western Guiana Littoral. These are Seba, Iurukaikuru, Wanakai and Chinee Creeks on the Aruka River, the last left hand tributary of the Barima before it empties into the *Boca Grande* of the Orinoco Delta, the source of these shell sand deposits.

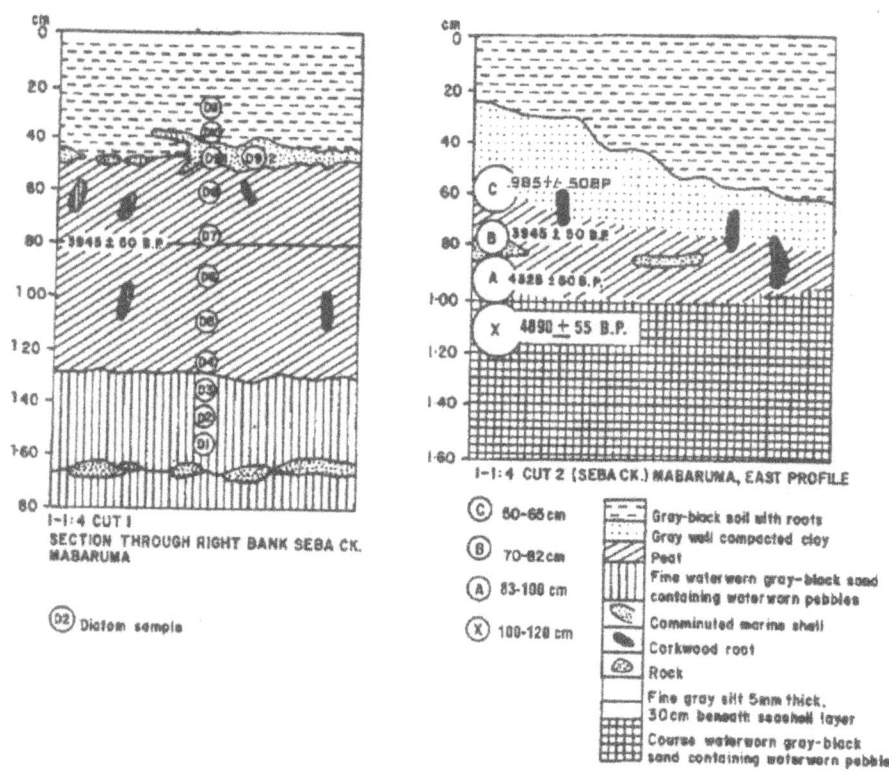

Figure 4.1. The Seba profile.

Excavations at Seba Creek (8° 13' N, 59° 46" W), a tributary of the Mabaruma River, which empties into the Aruka River, show these sediments to have been deposited in two discrete layers and at different times, Figure 4.1. On the right creek bank, a few meters from the creekhead on the footslopes of Mabaruma Hill, two layers of comminuted seashells varying between 2 - 14 cm in thickness are intercalated in a deposit of eustatic peat. The particles of this shell sand are well sorted, less than 5 mm maximum diameter, waterworn and mixed with fine quartz sand. The upper seashell deposit is located on 45 cm below the surface of the ground and the lower on 80 cm. Concurrent with the earlier of these two deposits, a thin (5mm) layer of fine, gray silt was deposited near the creek head, indicating zero water velocity there. The lower shell deposit returned a date at 3945 +/- 50 b.p., 1995 B.C. (SI 5449). The sediments indicate two separate marine incursions associated with a falling water table and apparently sustained reduced run-off. As shown in the pollen diagram from Laguna Agua Sucia in eastern Colombia, Figure 4.2, events at Seba were coterminous with the Amazonian arid interval of around 2000 B.C.

Excavation of the Barabina shell mound shows that on to the time of its abandonment, shortly after 4115 +/- 50 b.p., 2165 B.C., (SI 4332), Barabina Hill had been covered with rain forest and the swamps of the lower Aruka Basin continued brackish, Table F. On the interfleuves, meanwhile, freshwater swamps had been maintained by springs from the Aruka Hills. Seba Creek, not far from Barabina Hill, had begun to drain the Mabaruma foothills by around 3000 B.C. following on the "freshwater rebound" on the basement edge +/-3700 B.C. Already by 2300 B.C., inception of peat growth on Seba Creek signals an invasion of mangrove vegetation there and hence a continuing brackish envir-

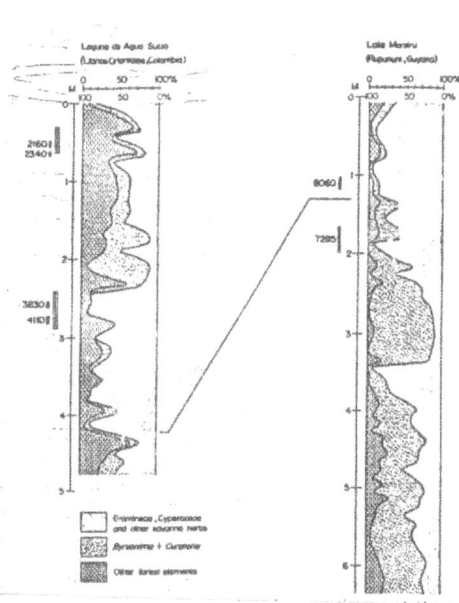

Figure 4.2. Pollen diagram. Colombia, Guyana

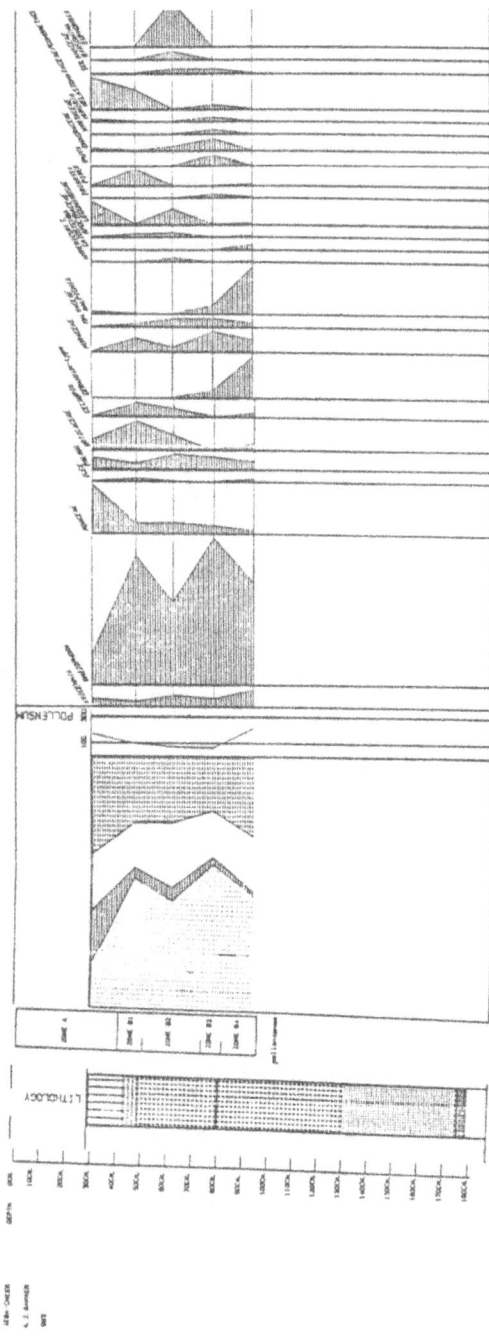

Figure 4.2. Seba Creek. The pollen diagram.

onment on these foothills (Williams 1981:91). With the advent of arid conditions around 2000 B.C., the freshwater swamps dried out and mangrove vegetation encoached to the limits of brackish water. The situation is exemplified on the Hosororo foothills where mangrove growth was initiated around 2000 B.C.

In the ameliorating climate of the following centuries the situation was gradually reversed. Salinity levels dropped locally and stands of riverain mangroves, still evidenced archaeologically as accumulating peat deposits, retreated, Figure 4.2a. This is the slowly freshening environment of increasing rainfall, re-emergent freshwater swamps and a new rain forest/swamp forest ecotone that was exploited by the first farmers, whose economic catchment area therefore differed profoundly from that of their Archaic predecessors.

A reportedly intact remnant of this ecotone was sampled on Barabina hillfoot by a 60 m x 8 m transect, Figure 4.3. The forest remnant measures 800 m x 80 m E-W (1988). It comprises a closed canopy, an emergent layer and a ground cover dominated by a swamp lily with occasional ferns. The canopy comprises rain forest species with juveniles in intervening spaces. Vines and lianas are abundant. Where gaps occur, Mukru *(Ichnosophon)*, used in basketry, grows 2 - 3 m high. Other economic species include Kakaralli *(Eschweilera sp.)* used for bark cloth, Kauta *(Licania laxiflora)* for ceramic temper, Crabwood *(Carapa guianensis)* for bodypaint, Yarula *(Aspidospenna sp.)* and Parakusan *(Swartiza sp.)* for paddles, Haiawa *(Protium heptaphylum)* (Incense Tree) for starting fires and in ritual, Trysil *(Pentaclethra macroloba)* for honey and beeswax, and Duka *(Tapirira marchandii)* for a variety of building purposes.

The pollen diagram for Seba Creek, also on this rain forest/swamp forest ecotone, Figure 4.2a, exhibits species that characterize the widely contrasting microhabitats of the ameliorating environment: herbaceous swamp *(Malvaceae, Saggitaria)*, freshwater swamp *(Iriartea, Pterocarpus officinalis)*, ponds *(Nymphea)*, soft mud *(Polypodium, Acrosticum)*, firm, wet soil *(Cyperaceae)*, marsh forest *(Cecropia)*, rain forest *(Euphorbiaceae)*, dry forest *(Didymopanax)*, and xerophytic uplands *(Curatella crassifolia)*.

Thus, humans inhabiting the swamp edge enjoyed an immense adaptive advantage over those located on *terra firme*. Ever since the pioneering of sedentary occupancy on the Western Guiana Littoral a good thousand years before the culmination of the eustatic sea level rise, human groups on the lower Aruka River had survived episodes of environmental change without recourse to relocation. As run-off diminished during the arid interval, salinization of the rivers and creeks resulting from the two marine incursions is evidenced in the Seba profile by advances of *Rhizophora mangle* at the expense of *Avicennia nitida* on 80 cm depth and again on 50 cm depth. After the first incursion, increases of *Byrsonima* and *Cecropia* followed in due course by *Curatella*, suggest a more or less simultaneous contraction of the rain forest. The pollen diagram indicates widespread replacing of the rain forest by secondary vegetation rather than by savanna.

With the second marine incursion, a simultaneous decline in the frequencies of *Palmae* and *Cyperaceae* suggests drying out of the freshwater swamps as run-off from the hills declined. The curves for *Curatella* and *Cecropia*, both second-growth species, peak during this second incursion. This is followed by a gradual expansion of *Pterocarpus,* only recently established. A concommitant rising water table and slow freshening of the environment locally witnessed the emergence of the present day vegetation.

Drying out of the freshwater swamps towards the ending of the Archaic is evidenced by the decline in frequencies of *Palmae*, the species diversity of which provided year-round resources of carbohydrates, fats, some vitamins and a range of industrial products -- oils, string, palm bast, etc. Principal economic palms were Dhalebana (*Geonoma spp*), Manicole (*Euterpe oleracea*), Kokoriti *(Maximilliana regia)*, Moriche (*Mauritia flexuosa*), Truli (*Manicaria saccifera*), Turu *(Jessenia bataua)*, Awara (*Astrocaryum tucuma*) and Akhoyoro (*Astrocaryum tucumoides*) representing a wide range of contrasting niches. Whereas Moriche and Truli palms exhibit a patchy distribution in the swamps, Manicole and Turu are more evenly distributed, the latter growing densely right up to the hillfoot. Dhalebana grows on elevated land under high bush, while Kokoriti is found all along the moisture gradient from freshwater swamp to the hill top. Therefore, the productivity of the palms was compromised differentially as arid conditions supervened and the swamps dried out. In drought conditions, the peat dries out sufficiently to generate spontaneous forest fires which burn to the mineral soil beneath. As the water table falls below around one meter, the roots of the Moriche palm, the traditional starch producer, themselves dry out and its productivity drops to zero. (Experimental planting of *Mauritia* on a Barabina hill top resulted in a plant which never flowered in 40 years). In such an environment, even on poor soils, the Kokoriti, Akhoyoro and Awara palms continue to flourish.

This level of resource variability permitted those micro-shifts in subsistence technology by means of which human occupancy of the swamp edge remained sustainable during the course of the arid interval, a time characterized by profound demographic upheavals across the Guianas. In these relatively benign exnvironmental conditions, the hillfoot of Hosororo Hill, near Barabina was occupied for the first time. The settlers derived from beyond the swamp basin. Apart from an inexhaustible resource of potable water, the Hosororo Hill environment presented the added bonus of proximity to an abundant new protein resource, the Mangrove Oyster (*Crassostrea rhizophorae*), unknown in such numbers on the lower Aruka River since the hypersaline environments of the sea level peak some 2000 years earlier. The folk now exploiting these products of the marine incursion were pottery

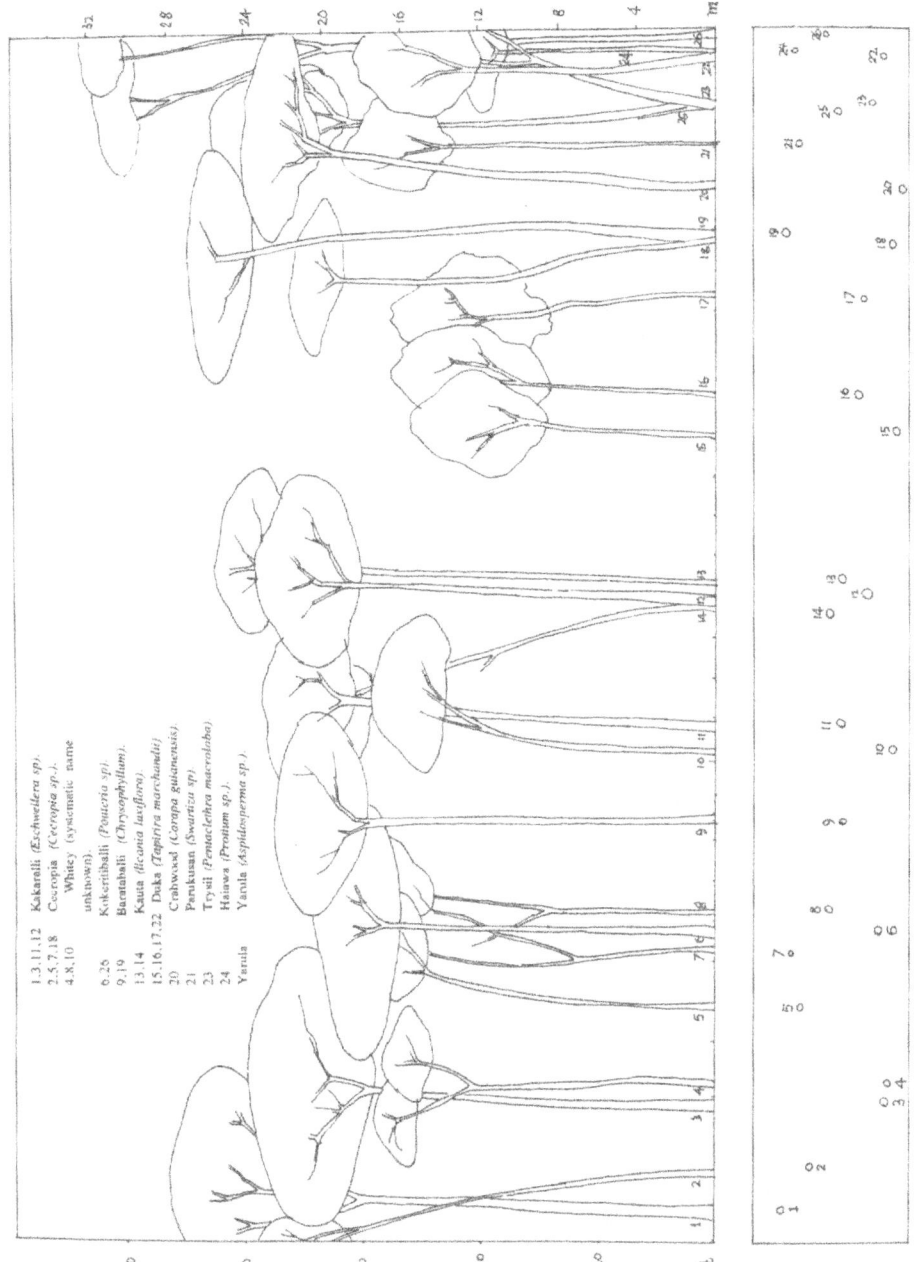

Figure 4.3. Transect through Barabina foothills.

makers. Their diagnostic pottery was a simple, shell-tempered ware which duplicated, exactly, the pottery of the Mina Tradition from the Mouth of the Amazon.

The immigrants set up camp on the left creek bank near the pioneering stands of mangroves. Henceforth this bivalve provided the overwhelming bulk of their protein. Their oyster refuse accumulated in the rotting mangrove vegetation nearby. The uniqueness of this refuse suggests that by this time the Warao already had abandoned the lower Aruka River, thus explaining the unopposed exploitation of its economic resources by immigrants of such remote origin.

Of the five creek heads exhibiting marine deposits, stratigraphic excavations conducted at the two nearest to the present day seashore indicate marked contrasts in their depositional histories as expressed in the effects of tectonic subsidence locally. Although both sites are located on the exact swamp edge, around 4 km apart, they exhibit differing depths of peat representing decayed mangrove vegetation once growing in phase with the relative rise in the sea level. Whereas at Hosororo Creek the peat deposit rests directly on the seashell deposit of the arid interval, at Seba Creek the peat deposit rests on a layer of fine, gray-black sand 30 cm thick overlying decomposing basement rock. Examination of the Seba Creek sand showed:

Quartz grains (angular with rare subangular grains)	38%
Amphibole grains (containing individual crystals)	39%
"Clay" (ex-felspar) grains, well rounded, polished	15%
Compound quartz-amphibole grains, crystalline	7%
Total	99%

The composition of this sand, proportions of its constituent grains and the presence of compound crystalline grains are consistent with its derivation from the underlying amphibole schist by *in situ* leaching of humic and carbonic acids from the peat forming above it. The layer of residual sand was not detected in an adjacent pit, where a relatively shallow peat deposit (10 - 30 cm) was underlain by coarse, waterworn black sand sediments containing waterworn pebbles of amphibole schist and quartz. These materials were identical to those forming the creek bed. Therefore this part of Seba Creek had shifted slightly.

A sample of vegetal matter deriving from the surface of the old creek bed returned a C^{14} date at 4890 +/- 50 b.p. (SI 5451). The bottom of the peat dates at 4325 +/- 50 b.p. (SI 5448). The lower deposit of shell sand dates at 3945 +/- 50 b.p. (SI 5449). The bottom of the clay which eventually formed over the peat dates at 985 +/- 50 b.p. (SI 5450). A root of *Pterocarpus* preserved in anaerobic conditions below the upper shell deposit but which represents growth occurring above it, returned a date at 915 +/- 55 b.p. (SI 5184).

Thus, around 3000 B. C., Seba Creek had just developed in the swamps. This was in response to the rising water table which, as freshwater backed up in the southeast of the Subzone, had been responsible for the freshwater climax which had submerged the intertidal mudflats there. The Seba Creek profile suggests that, in this part of the North West, the water table had remained stable for the ensuing 500 years and more (no peat deposition), after which peat growth had commenced in phase with a *relative* rise in the sea level.

At the time of the first marine incursion, 80 cm of peat had accumulated at the head of Seba Creek. At that time, the Hosororo Creek mudflats remained bare. Peat deposition commenced there only around 3975 +/- 45 b.p., 2025 B.C. (SI 6638). In phase with a still rising water table, it continued on to around 3550 +/- 50 b.p., 1600 B.C. (Beta 20007). The first of the two marine incursions on the Aruka River occurred at around 2000 B.C. and the second some time before 1600 B.C. This latter date saw the abrupt disappearance of mangrove vegetation in a rapidly freshening environment. This freshening brought the shellfishing lifeway in the Northwestern Subzone to an end. It also signaled the ending of tectonic subsidence locally, the ending of the relative rise in the sea level and cessation of the overwhelming influence of run-off. The hitherto rising water table (= peat deposition) now was stabilized on 40 cm below the surface of the ground. There it remains to the present day (p.59.vi).

The preagricultural ceramists of Hosororo Creek

Hosororo Creek (Warao: *Ho Sororo = Falling Water*) cascades down a rock staircase from a perennial spring on the southern flank of Hosororo Hill in 8° 11' N, 59° 49' W. At the base of the hill it traverses a narrow stretch of swamp and joins the Aruka River ca. 35 km from the sea coast. Water level fluctuates twice daily between 10 - 85 cm. The discharging stream encounters the incoming tide on a sharp right bend below the hillfoot. There, the water velocity drops to zero. During the arid interval, shell sand borne in on the tide was deposited in a 15 cm-thick layer at this point on the left creek bank. The volume of this sand is +/- 0.4 m. It lies beneath 85 cm of food remains, peat and dirt.

The mound stands around 150 m below the waterfall, and ca 100 m from Hosororo Creek Mouth. Destruction of the mound has been comprehensive (Verrill 1918a; Evans and Meggers 1960). In 1907, a drainage ditch had been cut through it *(Daily Chronicle, August 11, 1907, p.5)*. Later, it was excavated to ca. 1.0 m for laying a waterpipe to the Aruka River *(Daily Argosy, June 3, 1933, p.9)*. This had involved placing a hydro-ram at its center, the concrete foundation of which measured 2.7 x 5 m. The hydro-ram pumped fresh water to the Aruka River for the benefit of villagers living within the tidal range, Figure 4.30. To north of the drainage ditch, a laterite outcrop shelving into the swamp is covered with around 30 cm of peat containing cultural materials.

A test pit placed beside the hydro-ram encountered disturbed conditions. It yielded the following coins:

George V	One Penny	1940
Elizabeth II	One Penny	1965
Government of Guyana	Ten Cents	1975

Shells of the Mangrove Oyster accounted for between 63 - 70% of the refuse per level. Their relatively small sizes may be indicative of prevailing salinities, Table L. The upward trend suggests that maximum salinity locally was reached shortly before the end of shellfish deposition. The ensuing decline caused the disappearance of oysters in the economic catchment area, salinity having dropped below 3 ppm, at which point certain species of oyster cease to feed and die of tissue starvation (cf. Loosanoff 1950). The Zebra Nerite, a brackish-water species, likewise did not survive the indicated salinity decline.

Table L. Hosororo Creek. C. *Rhizophorae*/level

Level (cm)	Number	Mean (mm)	Range (mm)
70 - 80	36	35.5	15 - 82
80 - 90	70	41.4	16 - 82
90 - 100	140	37.3	17 - 87
100 - 110	141	36.0	11 - 82
110 - 120	66	29.7	10 - 65

Other food refuse included rare crab carapaces, bones of estuarine fish, e.g. gilbacker (*Silurus sciadeichthys*) and cuirass *(Arius spixi)*, scutes of the Yellow-foot Tortoise *(Geochelone denticulata)*, maxillae of two tapirs *(Tapirus terrestris)*, the humerus of a Giant Armadillo *(Priodontes giganteus)*, two humeri of large, unidentified birds, one specimen of which had been "sawn" through while the other exhibited butchering marks. The micro-habitats indicated by these food remains supports the picture of resource variability suggested by the vegetation: saline river mouths, mudflats and rain forest.

Thus, the long-range human dispersals which, elsewhere in Amazonia, accompanied the onset of arid conditions around 2000 B.C. appear to have had little effect on the lower Aruka River. When contrasted with the food refuse of contemporary occupants of Pedra Pintada on the upper Rio Branco -- fish, turtles, small mammals, reptiles, and freshwater snails -- the range of options on the swamp edge was relatively rich. Nonetheless, in the prevailing conditions of subsistence-lack stress on the Western Guiana Littoral, socio-cultural strain remained unambiguously evidenced in the ceramic history of the immigrants.

Immediately, the newcomers set about the revolutionary activity of pottery-making. They employed raw materials readily to hand in the swamps -- marine clay beneath the nearby mangroves tempered with crushed nerite shells from their accumulating food refuse. A distinctive though generally poor fabric resulted. Its major characteristic, shell temper, combined with its simple, unadorned vessel shapes, was employed to define the *Wanaina Plain* pottery type of the original excavators of the site (Evans and Meggers 1960).

Familiarity of the migrants with the ancient trade network of the swamps is implied by the fact that, beyond their home base, their diagnostic *Wanaina Plain* pottery is known only on Wahana Island, some 170 km to the southeast on the upper Waini River. Evidently, Wahana Island lay on their route of entry to Hosororo Creek at a time when the Essequibo delta margin extended as far as Charity on the Pomeroon River. While the dispersion of prehistoric Warao beyond the swamp basin remains unknown, the interaction sphere indicated by certain place-names, e.g. *Wara*-puta on the Essequibo, *Ore*-alla (Ohi-alla) on the Corentyne, and the *Ore*-noque (Ohi-noko) River on the Acarai watershed, suggest distant coastal-hinterland relationships during the Archaic.

This stratigraphically earliest pottery produced by the migrants is indicative of such long-distance inter-relationships. In every detail, their shell-tempered *Wanaina Plain* pottery was identical to the contemporary pottery of the Mina phase at the Mouth of the Amazon (Meggers and Evans 1978; Simões 1981). However, over the generations, the Hosororo Creek industry was characterized by increasing experimentation as growing familiarity with the new environment is evidenced in an increasingly wider knowledge of the sources, properties and behaviors of alternative ceramic raw materials, both clays and additives.

The original area of the shell mound was roughly 15 x 12 m, the northernmost portion presently lying under swamp forest beyond the drainage ditch originally reported by Verrill (1918a). Occurrences of what were described as seashells and shell sand in the Hosororo foothills convinced Verrill that the islands of the lower Aruka River once had been washed by the sea, in support of which notion Verrill reported "waveworn ledges" of rock locally. Repeated search of the area lends no support to Verrill's statement. Nonetheless, since the debate stimulated by Verrill's observations on these landlocked seashells and shell sand remained inconclusive (e.g. Osgood 1946) the area clearly merited further inquiry.

Investigation of the shell sand deposits of the Aruka Basin were undertaken during the excavation of the Barabina shell mound 1979 - 1984. Resulting from a report by a local resident (Ivan Santiago, pers. comm. 1981) of a shell sand deposit at the foot of Mabaruma Hill, Figure 4.4, the initial inquiry was made at Seba Creek there, with the results already noted. These results stimulated the re-excavation of the Hosororo Creek shell mound with the object of relocating and examining the shell sand deposits reported there by Verrill.

The deposit showed subangular to rounded grains of shell and quartz 1 - 3 mm maximum diameter, and larger, uneroded flakes of sea shells up to 12 mm maximum diameter and exhibiting razor-sharp edges. Occasional eroded flakes of nerite shell from the erstwhile mangroves suggested derivation of this fraction of the sample from an older shell mound in the neighborhood, i.e., erosion of the earlier shell mounds, suggesting their abandonment, already was in progress before the arrival of the Amazonian migrants on the lower Aruka River. Also included in the shell sand deposit were rare, rounded needles of amphibole schist, the prevailing rock material of hills in the lower Aruka Valley, microscopic charcoal particles (evidently deriving from the eroding shell mounds) and various minute seed parts from the freshwater swamps. The shell sand directly overlies the marine clay of the creek bank. It represents one or other, or both, of the marine incursions that characterized

Figure 4.4. Seba Creek. Mabaruma River.

the Amazonian arid interval on the Western Guiana Littoral. Implied by these incursions are lowering of the water table, diminishing run-off from the hills and drying out (or salinization) of the freshwater swamps. In the prevailing hypersaline environment, the advancing riverain mangroves carried rich harvests of *C. rhizophorae* to the doorstep of the migrants who, like the present inhabitants, were blessed with continual freshwater from the still discharging (*Ho Sororo*) spring uphill.

There was the added bonus of the flat, laterite outcrop shelving gently into the swamps upon which no vegetation could gain permanent foothold and which therefore afforded the migrants a place in the sun for at least the midday hours. Its restricted area indicates the small size of the propagule group.

The extent of post-depositional disturbance of the mound over the preceding 80 years, Figure 4.5, was realized only gradually over three field seasons. Our

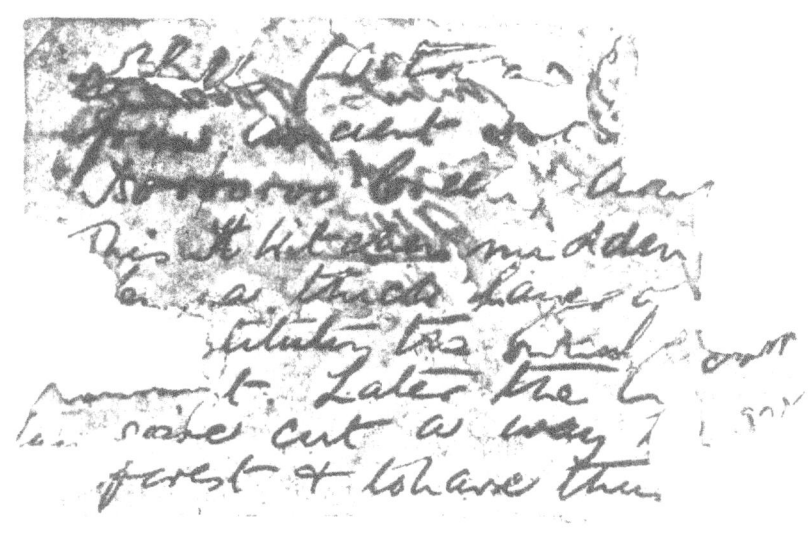

Figure 4.5. Hosororo Creek shell mound. Note by the unidentified traveller AWB 1905 (Im Thurn Collection, Walter Roth Museum).

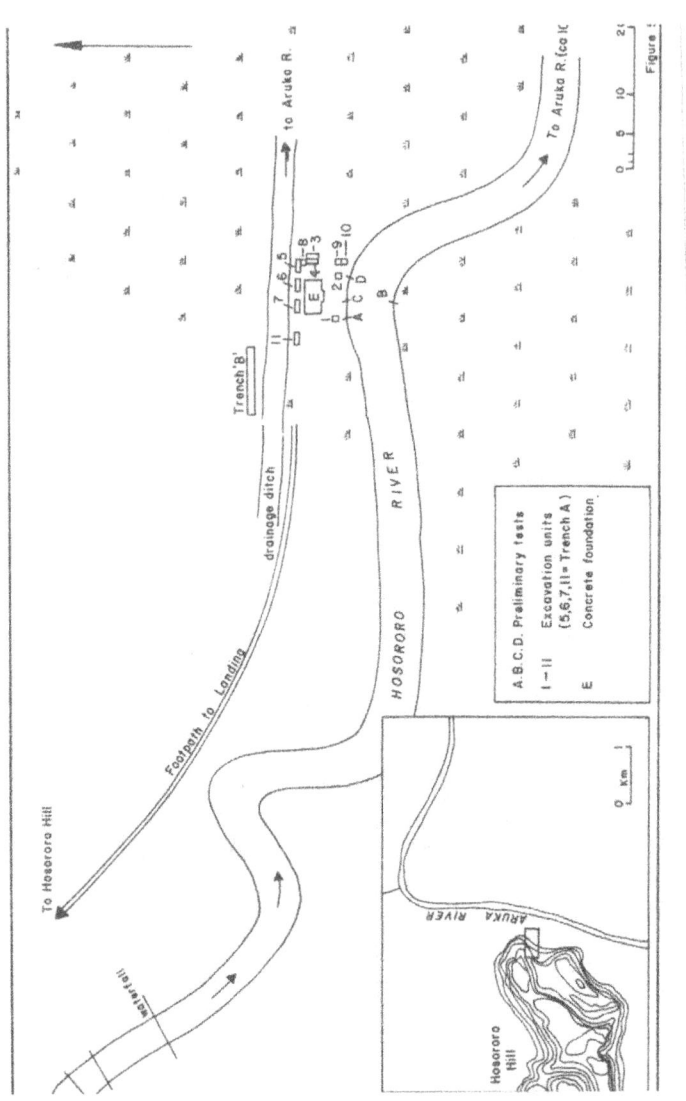

Figure 4.6. The Hosororo Creek Excavations.

excavation methodology was a cumulative response to the gradually unfolding configuration of the surviving refuse. Because, on the creek bank, the undercut concrete foundation of the water pump showed the surface of the mound buried at a depth of 40 cm, with the refuse of the shellfishers lying at a depth of 70 cm, the first of the preliminary tests was placed directly in the creek bank on either side at low water, Figure 4.6, A, B. This was done in order to (a) determine the elevation of the base of the mound in relation to the stream bed, and (b) to check for shell sand on the right creek bank. These queries were needed in order to establish whether the creek had cut through the shell deposit, as may have been suggested by the dense cultural debris littering the creek bed. In the event, these tests showed that, due to aggradation and deposition of humus from the overhanging vegetation, the creek bed lay a few centimeters higher than the bottom of the shell sand which floored the deposit. There was no shell sand on the right creek bank.

In order to check the stratification of the mound, two further tests, C, D, were cut directly into the riverbank on either side of the concrete foundation. These both showed compacted oyster shells overlying the shell sand. This oyster deposit, 35 cm thick, contained rare nerite shells, fish and animal bones and odd bits of carbonized wood. In turn, it underlay a layer of peat also containing cultural materials. Excavation units 1, 2 were placed adjacent to the tests C, D. Both of these units indicated disturbed conditions. Units 3,4, each measuring 2.0 x 0.8 m, were placed at the absolute limit of dry land, directly on the swamp edge. Preliminary study of the Unit 3 materials showed that its 20 cm levels did not reveal the already observed precise interface between shellfishing and later refuse. More, certain temper modes recognized in the ceramics of the shellfishers appeared to have survived unchanged in the later, horticulturist, industry, Table M.a.

Table M.a. Hosororo Creek. Unit 3 ceramic frequencies.

Level (cm)	Wan Pl.	S.Ck Pl.	Mab Pl.	Kob Pl.	Hot Pl.	Uncl Dec.	Total
20 - 40	-	-	19	-	1	-	20
40 - 60	-	-	14	-	-	-	14
60 - 80	7	1	18	-	-	2	28
80 - 100	123	13	-	-	-	1	137
100 - 120	61	1	-	-	-	-	
	191	15	51	-	1	3	261

KEY: **Wan Pl** (Wanaina Plain), **S.Ck Pl** (Sand Creek Plain), **Mab Pl** (Mabaruma Plain), **Kob Pl** (Koberimo Plain), **Hot Pl** (Hotokwai Pl), **Uncl Dec** (Unclssified decorated).

In order to ensure unequivocal separation of the shellfishing component of the deposit from later refuse, a subsequent excavation was undertaken at Unit 4. This was placed contiguous to Unit 3. Controlled in 10 cm levels, Unit 4 confirmed the uninterrupted survival of certain temper modes of the shellfishers in later (Mabaruma phase) pottery manufacture. Further, because of the anomalous position of the late Archaic *Wanaina Plain* ware in the conventional sequence for the Mabaruma phase (Evans and Meggers 1960:121), it was now necessary to establish beyond any doubt the relationship, if any, between occurrences of shellfish refuse and incidence of this pottery type. Therefore, a control block was retained at center of Unit 4. This also was excavated in 10 cm levels. It established that the cut-off points of shellfish refuse and shell-tempered ware were coterminous. Since they both marked the end of the shellfishing lifeway, a *terminus post quem* was established for the refuse of the horticulturist Mabaruma phase, Table M.b.

Table M.b. Hosororo Creek. Unit 4 ceramic frequencies.

Level (cm)	Wan Pl.	S.Ck Pl.	Mab Pl.	Kob Pl.	Hos Pl.	Hot Pl.	Uncl Dec.	Total
20 - 30	-	-	10	-	-	-	-	10
30 - 40	-	-	42	7	-	-	3	52
40 - 50	-	-	52	-	-	1	-	53
50 - 60	-	-	80	1	-	1	-	82
60 - 70	-	-	102	2	-	-	-	104
70 - 80	15	-	76	4	-	-	-	95
80 - 90	56	10	12	-	2	-	-	80
90 - 100	100	10	3	-	-	-	-	113
100 - 110	5	-	1	-	-	-	-	6
110 - 120	1	-	-	-	-	-	-	1
	177	20	378	14	2	2	3	596

KEY: **Wan Pl** (Wanaina Plain), **S.Ck Pl** (Sand Creek Plain), **Mab Pl** (Mabaruma Plain), **Kob Pl** (Koberimo Plain), **Hos Pl** (Hosororo Pl), **Hot Pl** (Hotokwai Pl), **Uncl Dec** (Unclssified decorated).

Apart from Units 3,4, cultural materials were recovered also from (a) Trench A, (b) Trench B, as well as from (c) the creek bed. These sources are described below.

(a) Trench A. In order to test the limits of this hidden shell mound, five contiguous 2 x 1 m units were dug in line along its main axis. Each unit encountered disturbed conditions, evidenced by the presence of laterite boulders, gravel, lenses of quartz sand, even an abandoned rubber boot. It was in this trench that the three coins described above were recovered. A water pipe (P), diameter 5 cm, located 35 cm below the surface of the ground, lay athwart this trench. Once, it had emptied

into the adjacent drainage ditch. A rubber hose attached to this outlet had directed freshwater into a concrete reservoir downhill, whence it was fed by gravity to power a sawmill on the Aruka left bank, Figure 4.7. These installations survive to the present. Trench A proved relatively rich in cultural materials. A number of boiling stones in the refuse suggests it represents at least part of the late Archaic component of the mound.

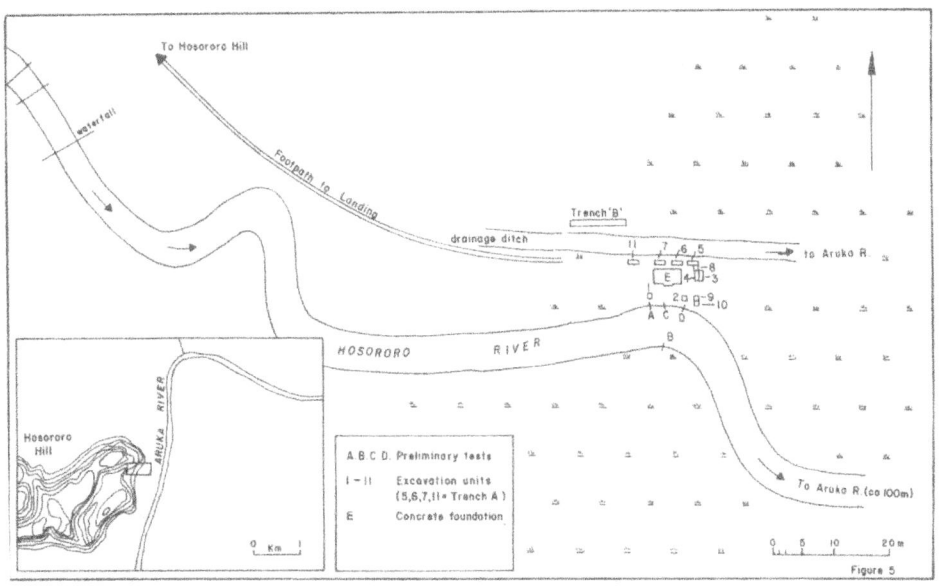

Figure 4.7a,b. **a.** Hosororo Creek. Composite north-south section showing relationship between Unit 4 and Trench B. (P = pipe).

(b) Trench B. Trench B was cut into the shallow deposit overlying the laterite outcrop on the northern edge of the site, beyond the drainage ditch. As the area is under swamp forest, it had formed no part of the original research design. It was investigated only after the final field season had been brought to an abrupt ending by a heavy downpour initiating the rainy season. The next few minutes of shelter uphill, unexpectedly in the company of some laborers from the nearby citrus plantation, produced the spontaneous information that cultural refuse was to be found also under the swamp vegetation beyond the ditch. There, certain cultural materials were relocated undisturbed. Most importantly, these materials appertained only to the horticultural component of the Hosororo Creek sequence, providing added support to the previously observed precise distinction between shellfishing and horticulturist refuse. Only with these terminal investigations were the full dimensions of the site, its stratification and the lateral spread of the Early Formative refuse realized. The deposit was trenched in five contiguous $2m^2$ units with the following results, Table N.a,b

c. The creek bed. As well as materials excavated in Units 3.4 and Trenches A, B, the sample included 229 sherds from the creek bed.

Table N.a. Hosororo Creek. Trench B: The Ceramic Inventory

Unit	Mab Pl Mode A	Mab Pl Mode B	Hot Pl	Kait Inc/Punc	Akw Inc/Mod	Wa Pl	S Ck Pl	Unc Dec	
1: 0-20	69	49	-	2	-	-	1	-	121
2: 0-20	45	34	-	-	-	13	4	-	96
3: 0-10	18	14	1	-	-	-	-	-	33
3: 10-20	22	22	-	-	-	-	-	-	44
4: 0-10	19	8	1	-	-	-	-	-	28
4: 10-20	37	27	2	2	-	-	-	-	68
4: 20-25	9	2	-	-	-	-	-	-	11
5: 0-10	13	4	-	-	-	1	-	-	18
5: 10-20	15	8	1	-	-	-	-	-	24
5: 20-30	42	30	4	-	2	-	-	4	82
	289	198	9	4	2	14	5		525

KEY: Knit Inc Punc Kaituma Incised and Punctate, **Akw Inc/Mod** Akawabi Incised and Modeled.

Table N.b. Hosororo Creek. The stone artifact inventory Trench B.

Level (cm)	Ax	Hammerstone	Chisel	Chopper	Spokeshave
0 - 10	-	-	-	1	1
10 - 20	5	1	1	2	-
20 - 30	1	-	-	-	-

First farmers on the Western Guiana Littoral

Since the Amazonian immigrants had arrived at Hosororo Creek with an already adequate knowledge of pottery making, their experimentations in the new environment were concerned mainly with learning the whereabouts and properties of strategic raw materials for developing their pioneering industry -- e.g., the range of clays and tempering materials suitable for producing the different ceramic pastes that are evidenced in their refuse, as well as clays for use as slips on some of their earliest vessels. Their concerns included *ad hoc* observations on water quality as, twice daily, this changed from fresh to brackish in the creek with contrasting effects on the hardness of certain fired clays. Since the sources of raw materials were located not in the swamps but at varying distances inland, on *terra firme*, the pioneering experiments were spread over the years, perhaps decades, it took to attain a working knowledge of the environment. Among their best known clay mines, Sebai, which yields *Mabaruma Plain*, is located some 90 km to the southeast on the Kaituma River and is reached only during the rains, when the Aruka-Kaituma watershed floods. The clay deposit at Hotaquai about 30 km up the Aruka, which gives *Hosororo Plain*, is of no great thickness. Exploitation of this rare resource over the millennia has cut back the riverbank far into the Hotaquai foothills. Therefore, *Hosororo Plain* was never popular.

Experimentation with contrasting clays yielded a variety of pastes, some better than others. The variable responses of these pastes to firing indicate the experimental nature of the early industry. These pastes were adopted at differing times. The earliest pottery at Hosororo Creek comprised the two plainwares *(Wanaina Plain, Sand Creek Plain)* used to define the Archaic Alaka phase (Evans and Meggers 1960:56). As shown in Table M.b, pastes of three of the four plainwares employed to define the horticultural Mabaruma phase that followed *(Mabaruma Plain, Koberimo Plain, Hosororo Plain)* had been developed in the Archaic. All of these pastes exhibit variable quantities of microscopic waterworn particles of amphibole schist, the prevailing rock material of the lower Aruka, Figure 4.8a.

Although shell tempering was of respectable antiquity at the Mouth of the

Amazon at the time of these initial experiments (Roosevelt et al 1996; Simões 1981; see Willey 1985) the *Wanaina Plain* pottery of the pioneers on the Aruka River was of very poor quality indeed, the sherds being soft and porous with a tendency to melt upon being washed and to fissure longitudinally through their thickness upon drying, Figure 4.8b. These difficulties are inherent in the use of shell temper in pottery. The destruction of pottery by hydration of CaO has been described frequently (Budak 1991; Goodyear 1971:176; Rye 1981:27; Shepard 1976:30). This can be countered by adding sodium chloride and possibly other salts to the clay before forming, by using clays or temper that contain these naturally, or by adding sea water to the clay. This last contingency is suggested by the variable hardnesses of *Wanaina Plain* sherds.

Figure 4.8a-e. Hosororo Creek. Characteristics of Wanaina Plain pottery.

The superior hardness of certain of these sherds resulted also from the fine size grades of the temper particles utilized. Replication experiments suggested the nerite shells employed in manufacturing this paste were crushed and sifted (probably through palm bast) into two size grades: 0-2 mm maximum diameter and 0 - 8 mm maximum diameter. In the former, temper particles may be so fine as to be invisible to the naked eye in sherd cross sections while, in the latter, they may be abundantly evident as coarse, white flakes in the gray paste, permitting ready identification of the parent shell, Figure 4.8c. Fine temper particles were associated with exceptional hardness in the respective sherds resulting from the greater surface area of tempering material contained in a given volume of paste (Rye 1981).

The viability of a shell-tempered clay body rested also on the firing temperature achieved, around 850° C. At temperatures above 900° C, the shell decomposes and the fabric is destroyed by escaping gases (Goodyear 1971:114). As open firing may produce temperatures up to 1000° C depending on the calorific value of the fuel utilized, this constituted another area of uncertainty for the pioneer potters of Hosororo Creek.

Methods employed to counter the characteristic porosity of the softer wares included (i) scoring and (ii) slipping. Leather-hard vessels were scored interiorly and exteriorly, or *vice versa*. Scoring on a given sherd was applied vertically on the exterior and horizontally on the interior, or *vice versa*, Figure 4.8d. Scoring was followed by application of a slip, 2 - 4 mm thick, the slip clay having derived from a source other than the body clay, as may be evidenced by natural inclusions of mica particles that are absent in the body paste, Figure 4.8e. On large, liquid-storage jars, slipping was applied without prior sealing of the surface of the vessel, probably to enhance evaporation and hence cooling of the stored liquid. The practice continues to the present.

The "technological tightrope" walked by potters of *Wanaina Plain* in a swamp environment poor in mineral resources dictated the use of the simplest vessel shapes. Attempts at controlling the hazards inherent in the manufacture of shell-tempered pottery were supplemented by an empirical understanding of the structural properties of forms. The spheroid and its derivatives were adhered to throughout, elaboration of any kind having been eschewed in the interests of thermal equilibrium in the fabric during firing. Since the thermal expansion of calcite is similar to that of average fired clays (Rye 1981:33), stresses generated by differential thermal expansion of clay matrix and tempering material remained minimal in such forms. Incipient eversion of the rims of certain vessels was a finishing feature that resulted, apparently, from pinching the rim between thumb and forefinger while attaching a terminal, thin, lip coil, the vessel having been rotated the while. This altered slightly the angle of the rim to the axis of rotation of the vessel, producing a distinctive modulation of the rim contour. This detail is worth noting because of its recurrence in vessels made on contrasting pastes.

Similar simple, undecorated vessel shapes also characterized the shell-tempered pottery of the Mina phase at the Mouth of the Amazon. The recourse to differential temper grades and scoring of vessel walls by way of improving the viability of a poorly understood technique likewise characterized these Mina vessels (cf. Simões 1981: Est. 2a,b., Est. 3a,b,g).

The next tempering material experimented with, fine quartz sand, yielded the *Sand Creek Plain* paste of the Alaka phase, distinguished by natural inclusions of minute to coarse flecks of mica (Evans and Meggers 1960:55). Hardness ranged between 2.4 - 3.5 on Moh's scale, though soft, porous specimens which, like

Wanaina Plain, fissured and fractured upon drying, continued to attest the experimental nature of the industry. As with *Wanaina Plain*, porosity in such vessels was countered by the use of slips interiorly and exteriorly. Rarely, slipping overlay scoring of the vessel wall. To these technological similarities with *Wanaina Plain* must be added the trait of incipient lip eversion mentioned above (see Evans and Meggers 1960: Figure 20, last specimen).

Interestingly, *Wanaina Plain* and *Sand Creek Plain* pottery ware both occurred on the surface or in the upper levels in certain Archaic shell mounds on the upper Waini River. These occurrences not only suggest the route of entry of the Amazonian immigrants, i.e., *via* the Waini-Barima network of inland waterways, but also provide a clue to the source of sand employed by them later on as a ceramic tempering material on the Aruka River. Sand Creek (N-10 in the terminology of Evans and Meggers 1960:31) is located within hailing distance of Wahana Island (N-9 Evans and Meggers 1960:29) and appears to have served as an entrepôt in the ancient canoe manufacturing industry. The sand associated with its name evidently derived from weathering and erosion in the unique granite ridge around which all these upper Waini sites cluster. In the swamp environment, sand is a rare commodity confined to such isolated granite outcrops on the basement edge. Of the locations of such deposits, the immigrants could have had no prior knowledge.

The next experiment was with two new tempering materials one of which later would be regarded as definitive of the *Mabaruma Plain* pottery type of the succeeding Mabaruma phase. These were felspar and fine quartz sand. Since very different pastes resulted from these additives, they are recognized here as *Mabaruma Plain* modes A, B, respectively. However, it must be emphasized that, typologically, vessels made on these pastes were in no way distinguishable from *Wanaina Plain* and *Sand Creek Plain* while also displaying a few of the technological shortcomings of these earlier experiments.

Mabaruma Plain Mode A. An unclassified plainware of the conventional Mabaruma phase was reported at two sites on the lower Aruka River which, together, yielded seven sherds of the following characteristics. "The paste is gray to tan to dark gray and full of holes. Most of the surfaces have eroded away" (Evans and Meggers 1960:114). Numerous specimens in the Hosororo Creek sample display cavities in the fabric or the fill of such cavities in various stages of decomposition. Their similartity to the specimens described above suggests they represent a variant of *Mabaruma Plain* in which the non-plastic inclusions comprised mainly fine (microscopic to 2 mm) felspar particles, with quartz grains of similar size occasionally present. The cavities resulted from weathering out of the felspar. This paste is here designated *Mabaruma Plain Mode A*. It accounted for more than two-thirds of the Hosororo Creek sample of *Mabaruma Plain*. Five stages were observed in the loss of the non-plastic inclusions in these sherds, Figure 4.9a.

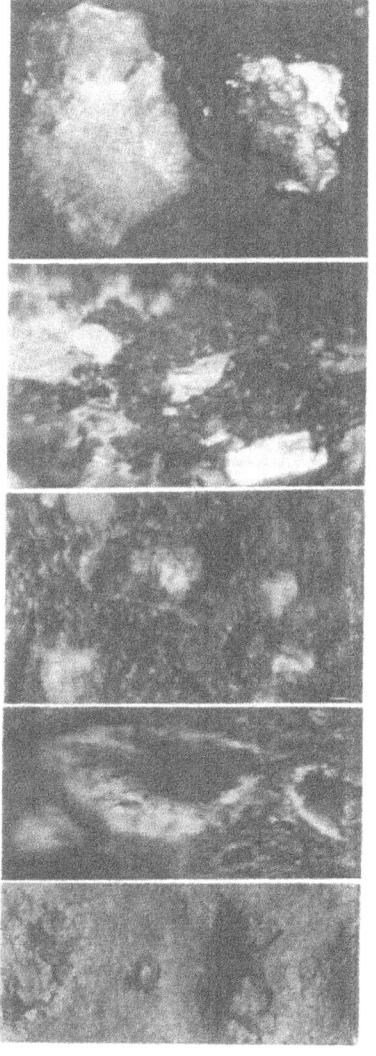

Figure 4.9a. Stages in the Loss of Felspar Temper.

1. Grains of unaltered felspar, indicating the original composition of the paste, survive in certain sherds.

2. Sherd sections display kaolinized felspar as creamy-white particles ranging from coarse to microscopic.

3. As weathering and erosion proceed, these kaolinized particles separate from the clay matrix, larger ones first, and drop out as rounded, waterworn grains, leaving cavities that may be conspicuously lined and rimmed with kaolin residues.

4. The kaolin residues were in turn leached out of the platy, rectangular-sectioned cavities.

5. The cavities erode, becoming progressively more rounded in contour. On badly eroded specimens, cavities may be worn to diameters many times that of the original grain.

Sherds of *Mabaruma Plain Mode A* display a hardness of 2.5 - 3.0 on Moh's scale, though, as with *Wanaina Plain* and *Sand Creek Plain,* some were soft, porous and soluble when washed, and similarly flaked and fissured through their thickness upon drying. Again, as with *Wanaina Plain* and *Sand Creek Plain,* this failing was countered by the use of slips interiorly and exteriorly. The slip having derived from an independent source exhibited mica inclusions that were absent in the body paste. Thus, a single clay source was mined for slip materials used on *Wanaina Plain, Sand Creek Plain* and *Mabaruma Plain Mode A* vessels. In addition, all three of the diagnostic vessel shapes of *Wanaina Plain* and *Sand Creek Plain* were recognized in the sample of *Mabaruma Plain Mode A.* The trait of incipient lip eversion was shared with *Wanaina Plain* and *Sand Creek Plain* vessels. A technological advantage of some sort may have ensured the survival of this finishing trait.

An alternative tempering experiment was represented in *Mabaruma Plain Mode B,* which accounted for 28.4% of the excavated sample of *Mabaruma Plain* sherds. Non-plastic inclusions comprised fine (microscopic to 1.0 mm maximum diameter) waterworn particles of quartz sand with occasional inclusions of waterworn felspar grains. Hardness was around 3.0 on Moh's scale. All of the diagnostic vessel shapes of *Wanaina Plain, Sand Creek Plain* and *Mabaruma Plain Mode A* were recognized in the sample for *Mabaruma Plain Mode B.*

The next experiment of these shellfishing potters was with *Hosororo Plain,* which co-occurred with *Mabaruma Plain Mode B* on the lower levels of their refuse. Though deriving from Hotaquai, a relatively nearby source, it was always poorly represented in the refuse of the shellfishers. This tempering material was much more popular in horticulturist times, but, even so, *Hosororo Plain* is known only from Hosororo Creek and nearby Akawabi Creek. Although the smallness of the excavated sample (0.6%) did not permit reconstruction of its vessel shapes, the position of *Hosororo Plain* early in the sequence is of the greatest importance, since, along with the natural inclusions of amphibole schist particles in most pastes, it indicates the *in situ* technological base of Formative pottery on the lower Aruka River.

First appearing in the uppermost level of the shellfishing refuse, mica-tempered *Koberimo Plain*, another of the pastes employed to define the Mabaruma phase of successor horticulturists, survived the demise of the shellfishing lifeway with a slight increase in popularity. *Koberimo Plain* exhibited the trait of incipient lip eversion of the other Archaic pastes.

Other tempering materials sporadically experimented with by these pre-agricultural potters were charcoal, caraipé and clay. As would be expected in the swamp environment, clay tempering was the most favored in these minor experiments. Certain of the vessels exhibit informal brushed decoration exteriorly, Figure 4.9b.

The various pastes of Early Formative pottery were produced down the generations by the same immigrant community which, in an environment under stress, occupied the swamp edge at Hosororo Creek equipped with a ceramic technology whose ultimate origins lay far to the southeast, at the Mouth of the Amazon. Over the years, the intractability of shell tempering triggered inquiry into a variety of alternative tempering materials, though with variable success. In most cases, the new pottery, while being more expensive to produce by virtue of the extended man-hours involved in acquiring the new raw materials, exhibited the major weaknesses of the old -- porosity, flaking and fissuring. Solutions to these technical problems differed. While the original *Wanaina Plain* potters had sought better control of the clay body by manipulating the particle size of their shell inclusions, a technique already tried in the ancestral Mina Tradition, the clay utilized for the *Mabaruma Plain Mode A* paste was changed completely. This clay, characterized by

Figure 4.9b. Clay tempered sherds

naturally occurring inclusions of felspar particles, permitted higher firing temperatures, some specimens being rock hard. This notwithstanding, failures remained significant throughout. *Mabaruma Plain Mode A* survived into the successor horticulturist period.

Next to be introduced was *Mabaruma Plain Mode B* characterized by natural inclusions of waterworn quartz sand. Although it provided a satisfactory alternative to *Wanaina Plain*, it was never a popular option among the shellfishers, though, like *Mabaruma Plain Mode A*, it survived as a dominant technological trait in the horticultural period.

Very soon after the *Wanaina Plain* experiment, *Sand Creek Plain* and *Hosororo Plain* pastes were being tested. As with the others, they both suffered from the effects of inadequate firing temperatures and were never popular, though in each case acceptable standards were achieved, albeit more or less fortuitously. Like *Wanaina Plain*, *Sand Creek Plain* was abandoned toward the ending of the shellfishing period.

Notwithstanding the unevenness of the results achieved, sustained experimentation with these pastes indicates the importance of fire-worthy vessels in late Archaic food technology. A range of vessels designed for direct contact with fire suggests an advance in food preparation when contrasted with the stone-boiling of the early Archaic. This advance facilitated acceptance of the manioc processing that later was introduced from the Orinoco. The response of the shellfishers to the introduction of the new food technology was predicated on a fund of local knowledge including the locations, properties and behaviors of different clays, sources of specialized organic and inorganic tempering materials, and perhaps observations regarding the variable effects on particular clay bodies of variable salinity in the local creek water. This knowledge was a function of the trade network that had moved men, materials and expertise across the swamps from the time of the pioneers. More than this, in the Northwestern Subzone, traditional experience of the complementarity between the resources of *terra firme* and those of the swamps had spread the ancient technologies of basketry, stone working and the extraction of toxins from vegetal substances across the entire swamp basin from time immemorial. Body paint, already evidenced in the Barabina shell mound around 5000 B.C., represents the earliest known use of a synthetic in the material culture of the Guianas. To the technologies of basketry, stone working and the extraction of vegetal toxins, all prerequisite to the elaborate manioc processing technology of middle and eastern parts of Amazonia (see Roosevelt 1980:135), the Hosororo Creek pioneers now added the final prerequisite of the process -- the fireworthy ceramic vessel. Thus, the local knowledge of these shellfishers, acquired by unaided trial and error over the preceding four hundred years, was combined with the ancient lore of the swamps to provide the economic base for the transition to horticulture on the

Western Guiana Littoral around 1600 B.C.
Antecedents of the pioneer horticulturists

Given the restricted area of the site, group sizes remained small throughout the four centuries of the shellfishing occupation. Assuming the potters to have been women, a matrilocal marriage rule is implied by extreme conservatism in vessel design as well as by the restriction of the distinctive shell-tempered *Wanaina Plain* pottery to the founding settlement on the Aruka River. Shell-tempered sherds recovered on the upper Waini represent the sustained interaction within the Warao trade network that had stimulated the bridging of the BarimaWaini watershed ever since the late fourth millennium B.C. Bridging of the watershed eventually permitted the pioneering occupation of Hosororo Creek by these migrants from the Mouth of the Amazon.

The distance of the trade link between the lower Aruka and upper Waini Rivers, around 170 km, once again attests Warao dominance of the swamp basin going back at least to the closing centuries of the sixth millennium B.C. Their kin-based trade network was already well over a thousand years old at the time of the initial occupation of Hosororo Creek, and Warao occupied the Western, as well as parts of the Eastern Guiana Littoral, as far as the Mouth of the Essequibo River. The intensive focus of modern Warao studies on the Orinoco Delta has obscured somewhat the extent of prehistoric Warao occupation of the Guianas, with the result that Warao settlements on the Berbice and Corentyne Rivers (e.g. van Berkel 1941 [1695]; Schomburgk 1886) are always assumed recent. They may not be. The Hosororo Creek pioneers enjoyed a long-term alliance with the Warao community on Wahana Island. Their oyster shell refuse is concentrated in a mound on the peripheries of the crabshell deposit there, Figures 3.27, 4.10. This oyster deposit is the only such concentration anywhere outside the Hosororo Creek home base (see Evans and Meggers 1960:3 1). Therefore the deposit should date between 2000 -1650 B. C., the period of the shellfishing occupation of the Hosororo Creek site. A sample from the center of the Wahana Island oyster deposit returned a C^{14} date at 4570 +/- 80 B.P. Cal. B.C. 3370 - 3290. Our reason for scepticism regarding this calibrated date has been advanced above (p. 178). Although on that and the present grounds the

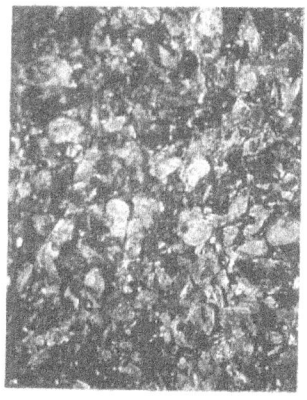

Figure 4.10. Oyster refuse, Wahana Is.

uncalibrated date is incomparably more acceptable, it still lies quite a bit outside the expected time period.

The presence of Hosororo Creek shellfishers on Wahana Island is attested, independently, by occurrences of their diagnostic pottery mixed with their oyster refuse. Represented are the principal pastes of their industry -- *Wanaina Plain, Sand Creek Plain, Mabaruma Plain Modes A, B* and an *Unclassified Clay-tempered Plain*. The first two of these pastes did not survive the transition to horticulture. In this refuse, an egg-shaped lump of unfired clay with fine sand inclusions may represent the raw material of *Mabaruma Plain Mode B*. Egg-shaped lumps of fired clay in upper levels of the main Wahana Island deposit (see Evans and Meggers 1960:31) may represent intrusive ceramic raw material.

Also mixed with the food refuse were unaltered pebbles and flakes of amphibole schist from the Aruka River, waste chips of andesite mined on the upper Barama River and odd tool discards on these rock materials. The stoneworking technique included chipping, chipping and abrasion and grinding, the latter two techniques restricted to the upper half of the deposit. Chipping and abrasion, and ground stone never were techniques of the shellfishers on the lower Aruka River. Their efficient percussion flaking of amphibole schist, the local rock material, survived into the latest levels of their refuse, Figure 4.11.

Figure 4.11. Hosororo Creek. Percussion made stone adze on amphibole schist.

Evidently, Hosororo Creek folk making the extended journey to the upper Waini traveled with supplies of Mangrove Oysters adequate for the period of their stay there. On Wahana Island, they were accommodated in a small cave away from the main campsite, Figure 4.12, where sherds of their diagnostic pottery were recovered in excavation. Their characteristic oyster refuse accumulated in an independent midden at the foot of the massive granite outcrop that dominates the island. Pebbles of amphibole schist in this refuse appear to represent trade items moved against local goods, probably including sand for use as tempering material in the swamps of the lower Aruka River.

Figure 4.12. Upper Waini River. Wahana Cave, Wahana Island.

Thus, the refuse of the visitors suggests their role as suppliers of strategic rock materials in the age-old canoe industry. This role would appear to have devolved upon them as a result of the abandonment of the Barabina shell mound in conditions of environmental stress associated with the arid interval of +/2000 B.C. (Williams 1982). As noted earlier, the uniqueness of their oyster refuse on the lower Aruka River suggests that during their entire occupancy they were the only inhabitants of the area. Hence their two earliest experimental ceramic pastes -- *Wanaina Plain* deriving from the marine clays of their immediate neighborhood and *Sand Creek*

Plain deriving from the neighborhood of the local group on the upper Waini River. (There is no sand on the lower Aruka River). The complete absence of any evidence of manufacture of the ground, or ground and polished stone tools that are diagnostic of the canoe industry points to their total dependence on the upper Waini River in this respect. There, their residential restriction to the cave on the camp peripheries, with their refuse accumulating in an independent deposit, indicates their, at least initially, non-kin status among the Warao of the upper Waini River.

The Formative
Adaptive responses to environmental freshening

It was a time of continuing climatic change and demographic upheaval. To these shellfishers on the lower Aruka River, adapted to the stringencies of the Amazonian arid interval, the stresses of the gradually ameliorating environment, evidenced by falling salinity levels locally, Table L, were entirely unfamiliar. The Mangrove Oyster and the Zebra Nerite, traditional protein resources of the preceding several millennia, now disappeared abruptly. Symptomatic of the correspondingly increased level of socio-cultural strain was a rapid diversification in ceramic technology. Two radically new temper modes were adopted, and these were accompanied by a wide new range of vessel shapes and decorative motifs. Outstanding in this enlarged ceramic inventory was the manioc griddle. Typologically, the new inventory suggests an affiliation with the lower Orinoco.

Use of the new tempering materials represented a technical innovation whose influence was to be permanent in the horticultural economy of the Western Guiana Littoral -- the apparent deliberate mining, crushing and sifting of rock as a non-plastic additive in ceramic manufacture. The resulting hardness and durability revolutionized the local food technology by permitting the manufacture of a wide range of fireworthy vessels, including that *sine qua non* of manioc processing -- the pottery griddle. This is because the bonding of rough fragments of rock with clay is superior to that achieved by the rounded grains of sand previously experimented with, and resulted in vessels of incomparably greater strength (Shepard 1976:27). The new tempering materials were crushed decayed granite and crushed decayed steatite, both implying exploitation of the preexisting trade network and the age-old alliances of the swamp basin. In the swamp environment, granite exfoliations (and sand) were obtainable only on the upper Waini River and on the nearby Koriabo River. Crushed and sifted, the exfoliations were now utilized in a new version of *Mabaruma Plain Mode B*.

The other new tempering material, steatite, derived from quarries on the upper Barama River that had been mined by shellfishers from the Barima River ever since the fourth millennium B.C. It was now employed in the manufacture of a distinctive new paste, *Hotaquai Plain*, which produced a fabric of great elasticity, later much favored for vessels that bear large, high-relief adornos. As had been the case with ground stone technology, knowledge of this resource was embedded in a system of alliances that already had been of hoary antiquity in the swamp basin when the need was felt to direct it to new ends. In due course, steatite temper came to provide the basis of local alliances from the lower Orinoco River to the Abary River on the Eastern Guiana Littoral.

These technological innovations at Hosororo Creek succeeded to the crushing and sifting of shell and charcoal that had characterized the quest for a viable paste in late Archaic pottery manufacture. So complete was the abandonment of the preagricultural inventory of vessel shapes with the advent of the new pottery that conquest and annihilation may have seemed implied but for the unbroken continuation of certain non-plastic additives in the new pastes, as well as continued use of clays from the traditional mines at Sebai and Hotaquai, both Warao villages (1978). Rather than conquest and subjugation, continuous technological development among these traditional ceramists seems implied. Local manufacture is indicated unambiguously by occurrences of minute particles of amphibole schist as natural inclusions in all of the new pastes. The evidently unbroken continuity of the technological tradition suggests an extension of alliances to the lower Orinoco as a function of diversification in the prevailing conditions of environmental stress.

The abrupt appearance of this new pottery suggests a marriage alliance that introduced the manioc root into the age-old swamp subsistence. Diminishing frequencies of stone tools/level were accompanied by a cumulative decline in potsherd frequencies. Simultaneously, fine, lateritic grit in the upper half of the peat deposit signaled forest clearing by these first farmers. Transportation of first the finer particles of this grit, followed by particles of successively coarser grain sizes, implies increasing precipitation, progressive expansion of the area of exposed soil and initiation of erosion on the hill slopes.

The Arawak dispersals

The climatic upheavals which, around 2000 B.C., were stimulating the movement of peoples and influences across the region appear to be evidenced in the linguistic record as well as the archaeological. At around this time, evidently spurred by the prevailing dry conditions, Proto-Maipuran Arawaks dispersing from a hearth somewhere along the upper Rio Negro are thought (Rouse 1985) to have commenced a "pincer movement" around the Island of Guiana. In Rouse's linguistically based reconstruction, an Orinocan, or Proto-Northern, group of these Maipuran Arawaks commenced moving down the Orinoco River, while, simultaneously, an Amazonian, or Proto-Eastern, group proceeding down the Amazon to its mouth, traveled along the Atlantic coast of northeastern South America and finally established contact with their kinsmen somewhere along the Guiana Coastal Plain. These migrations are thought to have commenced sometime during the second millennium B.C., and to have been completed by around the time of Christ.

The Proto-Northern migration down the Orinoco River is thought to have culminated in the colonization of the Antilles. In the process, certain migrants, reaching the Delta, "turned to the right onto the Guiana Coastal Plain and moved south to, or close to, Proto-Eastern speakers coming up from the south" (ibid). However, this Coastal Plain is separated from the Orinoco Delta by the 3500 km^2 of swamp forest, intertidal mudflats and seasonally inundated grass savannas which, combined, constitute the Western Guiana Littoral, Warao homelands for at least three millennia preceding the commencement of the Arawak radiation.

The postulated Proto-Northern route down the Orinoco is supported by the dispersion of the distinctive *Timehri* petroglyph which accompanied the Arawak migrations into the Antilles (Dubelaar 1995). Specimens have been recorded from the Casiquiare Canal to near Barrancas, Figure 4.13.

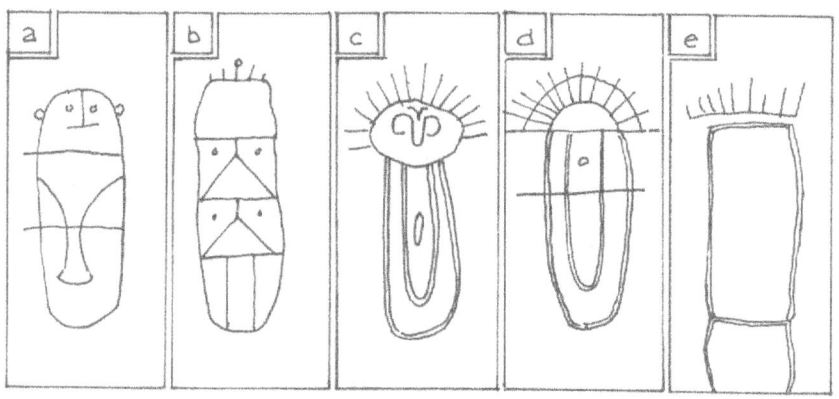

Figure 4.13. The *Timehri* petroglyph stereotype in the Orinoco Basin. **a.** Orinoco/Casiquiare, **b.** Amazonas Federal Territory, **c.** Caicara, Bolivar State, **d.** Rio Chiguao/Paragua, **e.** Rio Caroni.

The *Timehri* petroglyph is unique in the South American corpus as a representation of an identifiable deity, the Manioc Mother described in a fertility dance on the upper Vaupés (Koch-Grünberg 1917). The costume comprises three well defined features (1) rayed lunate crest, (2) bodice incorporating specific attributes, and (3) the raffia dance skirt, Figure 4.14 a,b.

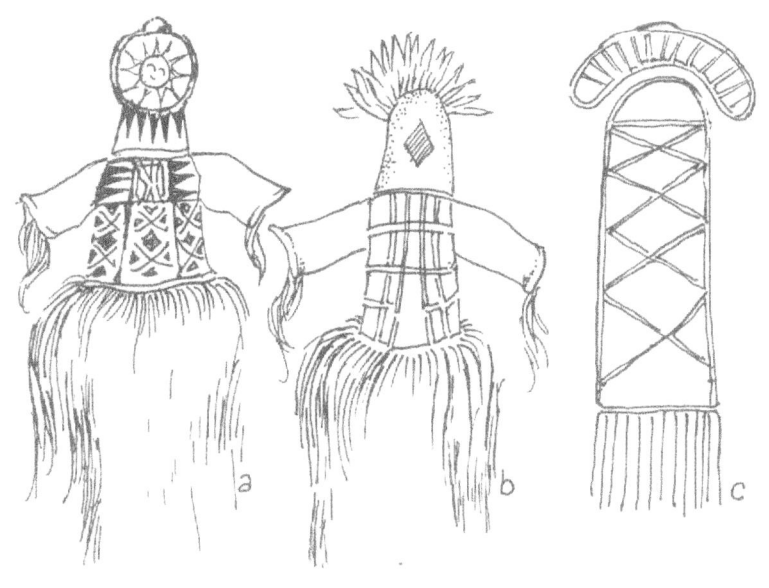

Figure 4.14a-c. Rio Vaupés, Colombia. **a,b.** Traditional costume in a fertility dance, Colombia, **c.** The petroglyphic stereotype, Colombia *(after von Hildebrand 1975)*.

The distribution of the *Timehri* petroglyph is as diagnostic of Maipuran Arawak dispersals across the Guianas as are their distinctive Saladoid/Barrancoid ceramics. Therefore, frequencies with which specific attributes of the associated dance costume of the Manioc Mother survive in this petroglyph type are considered diagnostic of relative distances of the respective migrants from a putative hearth on the upper Rio Negro (Williams 1985).

The Warao Manioc Mother (*Cassava Munia*) is the plant aruarani *(Phylanthus conani)*. Set in the midst of the cassava crop, it is believed to stimulate productivity (Edwards 1980). The tradition may represent a survival of the initial encounter between Arawak and Warao at Hosororo Creek around 1600 B.C. following the Proto-Northern Arawak migration down the Orinoco River. Harvest dances to the Manioc Mother of the Lokono on the Pomeroon River survive to the present day, but the distinctive raffia dance costume is forgotten.

Rouse's Proto-Eastern Maipuran Arawak migration down the Amazon also is evidenced by occurrences of this *Timehri* petroglyph stereotype. As well as on the lower Rio Negro, specimens occur along the Trombetas-Corentyne corridor, Figure 4.15. Thus, the route to the coast was across the Acarai watershed and not *via* the mouth of the Amazon, as Rouse supposed. The Eastern Guiana Littoral was colonized by these Arawaks during the early centuries of the Christian Era.

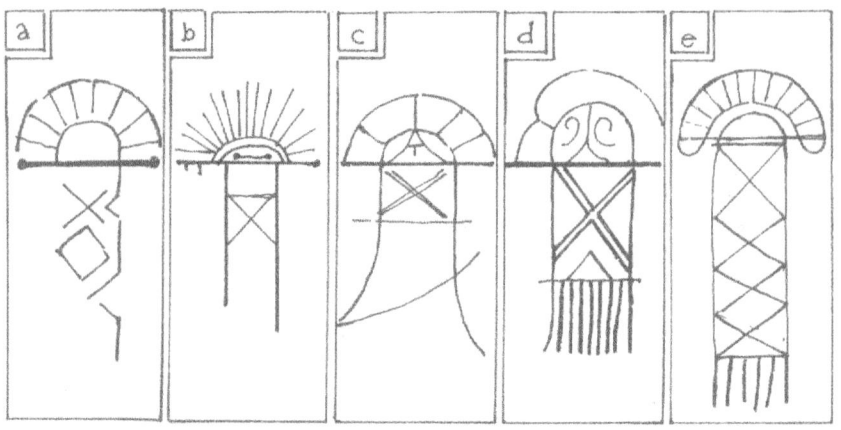

Figure 4.15a-e. The *Timehri* petroglyph stereotype on the lower Rio Negro and the Trombetas-Corentyne corridor. **a.** Lower Rio Negro *(after Mallery 1893/1972:691)*, **b.** Cumina/Trombetas *(after Coudreau 1901)*, **c.** Berbice River *(Williams 1978)*, **d.** Avanavero/Corentyne *(after Dubelaar 1986:Figure 95)*, **e.** Timehri/Corentyne, the type site *(after Im Thurn 1883:Figure 37)*.

Thus, Rouse's linguistic reconstruction is supported by the dispersion of the *Timehri* petroglyph stereotype, which, both on the mainland and in the Antilles, is associated with the distribution of Arawak Saladoid/Barrancoid ceramics.

The Carib dispersals. Linguistic evidences suggest that at this time Carib horticulturists also were spreading across vast areas of the Guianas. Since, unlike the Arawaks, they left no stone monuments by means of which the routes of their migrations may have been traced, their territorial advances and their inter-relations with the peoples they encountered can be established only on the basis of correlations between their diagnostic pottery styles and the available linguistic maps.

Linguistically based models of Carib dispersals (Durbin 1977; Migliazza 1982) postulate a divergence of Proto-Carib into northern and southern subgroups at around 2500 - 2000 B.C. According to Migliazza, the northern subgroup occupied virtually the entire Guiana land mass, which is believed to include Proto-Carib's original homeland and center of dispersal. Migliazza's reconstruction proposes that West Guiana Carib, and Coastal Carib, separated from Proto-Northern Carib around 1500 B.C. Out of the latter, an eastern subfamily, Coastal East, separated around 1000 B.C. Its major language, Galibi, differentiated shortly afterward. The Central crystalize around the time of Christ. Pemon and Makusi, widely spoken in Guyana, are the most recent of these, Figure 1.15. Durbin (1977) suggests a Carib migration across northern Venezuela and into Colombia. It penetrated southward up the Rip Magdalena as far as Tolima, and northward into into the Sierra de Perija, Figure 4.72. The internal relationships of the Carib languages are shown in Table O.

Table 0. Internal relationships of the Carib languages (*after Durbin 1977*)

I. *Northern Carib*
A. **Coastal Carib** (mostly outside Guiana)
 1. Venezuelan Coastal Carib
    a. Chayma
    b. Cumanagoto
    c. Yao
    d. Tamanaco (in Guiana land mass)
 2. Sierra de Perija (ColomNenez)
    a. Japreira
    b. Yukpa
    c. Yuko (Colombian Yukpa)
 3. Opone-Carare (Central Colombia)
B. **Western Guima Carib** (Western Venezuela)
 1. Mapoyo
 2. Yabarana
 3. Panare
 4. Quaca
 5. Pareca
C. **Galibi** (mostly Amazon-Orinoco Coast)
D. **East-West Guiana Carib** (the Guianas)
 1. Wayana-Apari
 2. Roucouyene (Guyane française)
 3. Aracaju
 4. Trio-Rangu
 5. wama(Akuriyu) (Suriname)
 6. Urukuyana
 7. Triometesen (Suriname)
 8. Kumayena (Suriname)
 9. Pianakoto
 10. Saluma
 11. Pauxi
 12. Cachuena
 13. Chikena
 14. Waiwai
 15. Paravilhana
 16. Wabui
 17. Sapara
 18. Yauapery
 19. Waimiri
 20. Crichana
 21. Pauxiana
 22. Bonari
 23. Makusi (Guyana)
 24. Purucoto (Venezuela)
 25. Pemon/Taulipang (Venezuela)
 26. Patamona (Guyana)
 27. Akawaio (Guyana)
 28. Arinagoto (Venezuela)
E. **Northern Brazilian Outliers**
 1. Palmella
 2. Pimenteira?
 3. Yaruma
 4. Txicao
 5. Pariri
 6. Apiaka
 7. Arara
 8. Yuma
II. *Southern Carib*
A. **Southeastern Colombia Carib**
 1. Hianacoto-Umaua
 2. Guaque
 3. Carijona
B. **Xingu Basin Carib** (Brazil)
 1. Bakairi
 2. Nashukwa
C. **Southern Guiana Carib** (Venez.,Brazil)
 Yecuana, Wayumara-Azumara, Parukoto, Hishkaryana, Warikyana.

These archaeologically attested reconstructions of Carib distributions indicate that Karinya occupancy, strictly so-called (Whitehead 1988:3 ff.), was broadly coastal, while their Carib-speaking descendants occupied hinterland areas.

The transition to horticulture on the Western Guiana Littoral
The Aruka Basin

Although the Northwestern Subzone of the Western Guiana Littoral has supported a traditional horticulture and sedentary occupation continuously for upward of the past three thousand years, it remained a No-Man's Land, claimed by both Venezuela and Great Britain, until the final decade of the nineteenth century. The British expeditions of Robert Schomburgk (1841) and Daniel Blair (1980/1857) both found thriving populations in the area, Kumaka Hill, on the Aruka River, being still occupied by its traditional "Apostaderan" (late Mabaruma) folk. In 1892, Everard Im Thurn, previously a magistrate on the Pomeroon River, pioneered British administration in the North West from a headquarters at Morawhanna, at the junction of the Barima River and the still then unopened Mora Passage, at the same time establishing outstations at the mouths of the Barima and Amacuro Rivers, both emptying into the *Boca Grande* of the Orinoco Delta. Thence, cargo boats ascended the river to service the colonial administration. The swamps around Morawhanna soon proving unsuitable for an administrative headquarters, a new site was chosen, 8 km upriver, on the basement edge once occupied by Archaic shellfishers.

Today, Mabaruma Headquarters is a sizeable settlement with all government services, river and air terminals and with direct access to the other inhabited hills of the Aruka Range. It is about 4 km from Kumaka Hill, and 8 km from Hosororo Hill. Government installations have destroyed a number of archaeological sites along the main road, notwithstanding which informative excavations have been conducted there in recent times (Osgood 1946; Evans and Meggers 1960; Meggers and Evans 1955). The designation "Mabaruma Headquarters" was employed by Osgood in recognition of the contiguity of these sites to the center of administration, and to avoid confusing them with the site on nearby Kumaka Hill.

In 1930, with "the sympathetic and generous help" of the Smithsonian Institution, Walter Roth pioneered a survey of ceramic sites in the Aruka Basin which took him as far as Naboni Creek, a right tributary of the Aruka, and up its left tributaries the Aruau and the Koriabo, the first as far as Barakwa and the second as far as Akawabi. Roth was astonished at the profusion of cultural remains he encountered. It seemed to him sufficient just to turn the sod anywhere to reveal potsherds. Whereas certain localized concentrations suggested an erstwhile campsite, in other areas the dispersion of such concentrations suggested the location of an entire village. Even taking into account the contribution of shifting cultivation to these dense accumulations of refuse, Roth found himself at a loss to explain the apparently sizeable populations on these small hills.

Roth could not but have been impressed, at first hand, by the immense volume of moving water constituting the environment of the now vanished pioneers of horticulture in the swamp basin. While the endless daily interaction with the sea on

Figure 4.16. Moriche palm (*Maurita flexuasa*) in swamp forest. (top left) Figure 4.17. Freshening diagram. (top right) Figure 4.18. Irrigation horticulture. Reclaimed swamp soil irrigated by the diurnal movement of the tidal counter currents. (bottom left) Figure 4.18a. Slash-and-burn horticulture on the hill slope. (bottom right)

about mean sea level is most evident in the fluctuating salinity gradients of the major rivers, the swamps themselves, though perennially fresh, are by no means beyond the influence of the tides. With the tidal countercurrents, the entire swamp system is a product of perpetual motion in the sheet of water that stretches continuously across 3500 km^2 between the basement edge and the sea.

Notwithstanding its relative harshness as a habitat for man, it needs to be borne in mind, as Roth could never have imagined, that the resources of these swamps have sustained sedentary human populations continuously over the past seven thousand years. A key subsistence resource was the elevational zoning of the vegetational environment from swamp forest, Figure 4.16, up the hill slopes to rain forest on *terra firme*, Figure 4.17. On the lowest elevations, open swamps alternated with seasonally inundated savannas bordered by groves of Moriche palms, and riverain mangroves extended well beyond the tidal limit. These distributions were reflected in the faunal variety in both space and time that characterizes the food refuse, and which determined patterns of human settlement and predation.

In this mosaic of environments, certain horticulturists occupying the borders of the swamps in the Northwestern Subzone nowadays exploit the peat soils there by the use of irrigation. As manioc will not tolerate excessive moisture, the soil is drained by a complex of ditches controlled by sluices and dikes, Figure 4.18. In this way, the diurnal movements of the tidal countercurrent are controlled, Figure 4.78a. This stratagem permits exploitation of a range of edaphic conditions from peat in the swamps to the mineral soils on the hill slopes and hilltops, Figure 4.78c. In the Northwest, the age of the stratagem is not known. On the Pomeroon River, it may date back to remote antiquity.

The horticulturist problem of segregating habitation sites and arable land from the surrounding swamps while at the same time enjoying a "home range" rich in energy reserves had been anticipated, by several millennia, in the sedentary adaptations of Archaic shellfishers on the basement edge. Indeed many of the horticulturist campsites identified by Roth, and before him by Verrill, also were shell mound sites. The revolution in the mode of production had been anticipated in the adaptive wisdom of generations of Warao shellfishers who had occupied these self-same hills over the millennia. A feature of this wisdom was sedentary occupancy. Sedentary occupancy of the swamp basin was a function of the trade network that had underpinned the settlement pattern since the development of the dugout canoe there during the Archaic. The nature and scope of this trade network were determined by variability in the niches comprising the Western Guiana Littoral, partly resulting from differences in local topographies, partly from differential rates of tectonic subsidence and partly from differences in the rates of environmental freshening resulting from the freshwater rebound which, commencing around 3700 B.C., had exercised a progressively ameliorating influence in the swamps. It will be recalled that differences existed in the rate and scope of this amelioration. In the South East, the effects of freshening had become definitive by around 3300 B.C. but, in the North West, due to the continuing relative rise in the sea level, the environment remained brackish on to around 1600 B.C. Subsequent environmental freshening in communities which had been adapted over the millennia to a brackish-to-marine coastal environment enforced a subsistence shift from exploiting the resources of the swamps (fishing/shellfishing combined with palm starch) to exploiting the resources of *terra firme* (fishing combined with manioc horticulture). In pursuance of this subsistence shift, the now acculturated migrants at Hosororo Creek turned not to their Warao "brethren" in the South East, but initiated an alliance with a so far unidentified Arawak group in the North West whose starchy staple was the manioc root. The long-term consequence was that, in contrast to the far-flung system of kin-based reciprocal exchange that had characterized swamp adaptation during the previous 3000 years, the cultural evolution of the now acculturated immigrants was restricted to the Aruka Basin. It, in its turn, spanned another 3000 years.

The Mabaruma chronologies

The Mabaruma phase is by far the most widely recognized archaeological culture of horticulturist Guyana, with a place in the literature that has proven as enduring as the infinitely more spectacular Aristé and Mazagão cultures of the Brazilian Territory of Amapá. Though extremely long-lived, its sustained recognition is by no means proportionate to its geographical extension and/or influence. Its unquestioned popularity is doubtless due to a perceived close affiliation with Barrancoid culture on the lower Orinoco. Entrenched in the literature, the nature and scope of this affiliation have never been examined.

Evidences now available for the supplanting of late Archaic by Formative culture on the lower Aruka River suggest the need for a revision of the generally held opinion that the inception of Formative culture on the Western Guiana Littoral is attributable to an "expansion" or "migration" of ceramic-using horticulturists from, according to some, Barrancas, according to others, Los Barrancos, on the lower Orinoco River. The origin of this notion has been traced to Carter's comment above, made on the basis of admittedly "limited work" at Seba, on the Demerara River, according to which the ceramic sites in the North West of Guyana represent a small southerly eddy in the mainstream current of Arawak culture that had passed down the Orinoco and flowed northward into the Antilles *via* the Island of Trinidad. Unfortunately, ripples of Carter's small eddy have continued to travel, unexamined, through the rising tide of the ensuing literature (Cruxent and Rouse 1961:39; Evans and Meggers 160:147; Hilbert 1982:80; Lathrap 1964:358, 1966:564, 1970:114; Meggers 1987:31; Meggers and Evans 1955:13; 1978:31; Osgood 1946; Rouse and Cruxent 1963:89; Sanoja O. 1979:286, 1983:40; Sanoja O. and Vargas 1983:240);

Willey 1971:373). Dates attributed to this entirely presumptive intrusion of Formative culture on the Aruka River range between 80 B.C. (Lathrap 1966:565) and A.D. 700 (Evans and Meggers 1960:147; Meggers and Evans 1978:571; Sanoja O. 1983:40; Sanoja O. and Vargas 1983:240).

The notion has provided the basis of three contrasting chronologies of the Mabaruma phase (Evans and Meggers 1960:147; Cruxent and Rouse 1959: Figure 5; Rouse 1983: Figure 3), besides which the Mabaruma phase has been slotted into certain widely differing area syntheses (e.g. Boomert 1986, 1993; Tarble 1985; Versteeg and Bubberman 1992). This continuing concern with Mabaruma chronology underscores Lathrap's (1964) observation concerning its extreme importance in the restructuring of the culture history of the Tropical Lowlands of South America. Lathrap's view was founded mainly on the longevity of the Mabaruma phase in a somewhat restricted area of northwestern Guyana. Other early ceramic cultures have come to light since on the upper Essequibo and the lower Amazon. The associated materials not only support Lathrap's intuitive retrodiction of the initiation of the Mabaruma sequence but also permit fine-grained examination of the issue of the origin and dissemination of Tropical Forest Culture raised by Steward. It is now clear that in the absence of a thorough understanding of Mabaruma chronology the issue can never be addressed satisfactorily, most particularly in light of its hitherto unsuspected technological inheritances from the preceding Mina Tradition of the lower Amazon (p. 224). Thus, the origins and affiliations of the Mabaruma phase have assumed an importance that could not have been suspected in Lathrap's day. For this reason, the already published chronologies of this phase merit special attention. Preliminary to presenting yet another, the three previous chronologies are reviewed below.

Following on Carter's (1943) identification of the ceramics of the North West with the passage of Arawaks down the Orinoco River, Osgood and Howard (1943: 105) drew attention to a number of decorative similarities with the ceramics of Los Barrancos which, in their view, constituted good evidence of a "close correlation" between the two complexes. The comparison did not extend to vessel shape.

Later Meggers and Evans (1955) observed that in the technique of modeling and incision employed in executing its characteristic designs, as well as in the design elements themselves, the decorated pottery of the Mabaruma phase exhibited closer resemblances to decorated materials deriving from the excavations of Osgood and Howard at Los Barrancos, "where incision prevails over modeled-incised decoration," rather than to materials deriving from Barrancas, where the reverse was found typical. As with Osgood and Howard, these comparisons did not extend to vessel shape.

Cross-dating of Mabaruma decorative elements with those of Los Barrancos permitted structuring of the earliest of the chronologies of the Mabaruma phase. The importance of Los Barrancos at the Mouth of the Orinoco River suggested to the authors an expanding culture of which the movement into northwestern Guyana indicated by the observed ceramic similarities was symptomatic. The only available date for Los Barrancos, around A.D. 500, was found acceptable as an approximate initial date for the Mabaruma phase. Postulating a terminal date at ca. A.D. 1600, the estimated time of European intrusion, permitted dividing the intervening 1100-year time span into early, middle and late periods, each characterized by particular characteristics in ceramic practice. Seriation of the levels of their five stratigraphic excavations permitted assigning peculiarities of vessel shape and/or decoration of the eight constituent pottery types of the phase (four plainwares, four decorated) to each of these time periods. Appearances and disappearances of particular traits provided a pattern that made it possible to divide the phase into approximately equal thirds. Assuming a smooth rate of change in pottery frequencies throughout the period, the sequence yielded to division into guess dates at A.D. 500 - 850 for the early period; A.D. 850 -1250 for the middle period; and A.D. 1250 - 1600 for the late period.

Interdigitation of the *Wanaina Plain* pottery type with the four Mabaruma phase plainwares at the bottom of the seriated sequence suggested to the authors the gradual replacement of Archaic Alaka phase pottery types by horticultural Mabaruma phase pottery types. It was emphasized, however, that co-occurrences of the two pottery types were not interpreted as representing the origin of the Mabaruma phase. Rather, they suggested trade or contact between it and the Alaka phase, which, therefore, was seen as approaching its demise around A.D. 500, probably after a lengthy period of co-existence in which agriculture was introduced gradually to an initially non-agricultural shellfishing economy. In this somewhat equivocal picture, the authors surmised that the adoption of pottery making on the Western Guiana Littoral, and probably also of agriculture, may have preceded the arrival of the Mabaruma phase from the Orinoco. Also, it may have stemmed from a different source.

Thus, two distinct and unrelated episodes of first farming were envisaged in northwestern Guyana. In the first place, the horticulturist Mabaruma phase may have intruded from Los Barrancos at around A.D. 500, and in the alternative, pottery making, and probably also agriculture, may have preceded this event at an unknown period during the Archaic. This latter possibility of local pottery making during the Archaic was never examined.

The views of Evans and Meggers on Mabaruma origins did not long remain unchallenged. Comparisons with other ceramic inventories on the lower Orinoco and on Trinidad did not appear to Cruxent and Rouse (1961:35) to support the contemporaneity claimed by the authors for the decorated pottery types they had presented as diagnostic of the Mabaruma phase. While regarding three of these decorated types as contemporaneous with the late prehistoric Apostaderan and

Guarguapan ceramic styles of the lower Orinoco, i.e., in each case dating after around A.D. 1150, Cruxent and Rouse referred the fourth decorated type, Mabaruma Incised, to the much earlier time level represented by the ceramic style at Palo Seco on Trinidad, dating at 180 B.C. to A.D. 470.

The above ambiguities prompted Boomert (1983:104) to suggest that the Mabaruma phase might actually have commenced earlier than its excavators had supposed. According to this view, the earliest part of the ceramic sequence for coastal Guyana is lacking, a conviction which led Boomert to detect what appeared to him to be characteristically Saladoid (lower Orinoco) features in pottery representing the Abary phase of the Eastern Guiana Littoral, interpreted by him as indicating an intrusion of Maritime Saladoid pottery (pottery of the Maipuran Arawak diaspora in the Antilles) from Trinidad.

This reiteration of the views of Cruxent and Rouse colored somewhat the structuring of Rouse's (1983) area synthesis for the Guiana Coast. Thus, Rouse continued to accept Evans and Meggers' date for inception of the Mabaruma phase, but "only in order to allow time for an earlier Saladoid style like those in Trinidad in the west and Suriname in the east," this latter being a reference to the apparently aberrant occurrence of Saladoid pottery at Wonotobo Falls on the Corentyne River. "On Boomert's advice" Rouse (loc. cit.) then divided the Mabaruma sequence into its three perceived components: (*i*) the Saladoid, (*ii*) the Barrancoid overlain by Arauquinoid and (*iii*) the Arauquinoid pottery styles. In this chronology, Rouse was obliged to posit an entirely hypothetical Saladoid transit of the Guiana Coast, presumably antedating the Wonotobo Falls deposit at A.D. 50.

As may be expected, the least speculative of the above chronologies has proven to be the one that was based on direct excavation. The conclusions of Evans and Meggers regarding two independent ceramic influences in the lower Aruka Basin most closely accords with the facts as they are presently known, though, resulting from the profile which they had obtained at Hosororo Creek, the chronological ordering of these two events remained unclear to the authors. As noted above, the viability of the second alternative in Evans and Meggers' interpretation of events antecedent to the arrival of the Mabaruma phase on the Western Guiana Littoral (an Archaic ceramic industry with possible horticulture) was never examined, notwithstanding the early challenge to their chronology posed by the observations of Cruxent and Rouse. As a result, the critical issue of the relationship between Mabaruma and the earlier Alaka phase remained unaddressed. The problem would stimulate heated debate (e.g. Lathrap 1966, 1970; cf. Willey 1971:365).

The Warao legacy

Renewed excavations at Hosororo Creek contributed to reconstructing the site layout, clearing up the ambiguous relationship between Mabaruma and its Archaic ancestors, to establishing the ethnic identity of these ancestors, and to explicating the relationship between Mabaruma and its supposed parent tradition at Barrancas. The date 1600 B.C. is one of four obtained for the inception of manioc horticulture there.

20 cm (peat)	3550 +/- 65 b.p.	Beta 20007
20 cm (peat)	3185 +/- 65 b.p.	SI-6635
35 cm (peat)	2660 +/- 45 b.p.	SI-6636
50 cm (shell)	3350 +/- 50 b.p.	SI-6637

The first date (Beta 20007) derived from sampling the horticulturist refuse on the far side of the deposit, beyond the drainage ditch, Figure 4.7. This overlay bedrock, eliminating any possibility of slumping of the deposit. The other sample (SI 6637), taken on 50 cm, was sealed, undisturbed, beneath 40 cm of roadmaking materials -- sand and gravel. Thus, these first and last dates derived from separate samples on peat and shell obtained from widely differing parts of the site. They were processed in separate laboratories.

Figure 4.19. **a.** Hosororo Creek, low tide -- freshwater (concrete foundation),
b. Hosororo Creek, high tide -- salt water.

A distinguishing feature of Hosororo Creek is its location in the intertidal zone, though with a nearby supply of perennial freshwater. Between tides, the creek receives freshwater from the waterfall, just upstream, Figure 4.19a. At high tide, salt water displaces the fresh and villagers travel many miles up the Aruka River to fill their buckets at the waterfall, Figure 4.19b. Villagers attracted to the site around

2000 B.C. were able to occupy a flat, laterite outcrop on the creek bank providing ready access not only to perennial freshwater nearby, but also to abundant new shellfish resources for the first time becoming available with the colonization of the immediate area by mangrove vegetation.

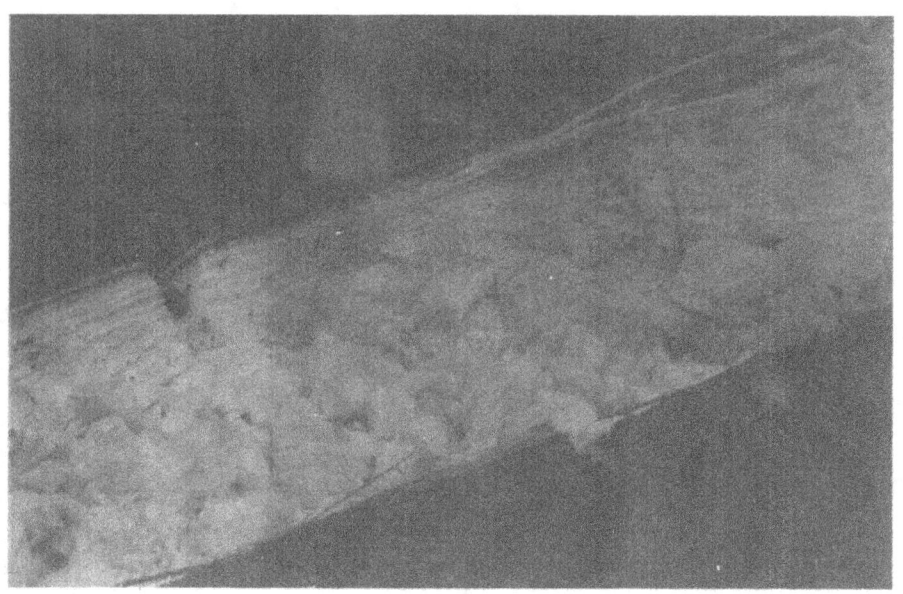

Figure 4.20. Extracting flour from the monicole palm.

Hosororo Creek is the most recent, by around a millennium, of three preagricultural coastal shell mounds in northern South America with a knowledge of pottery, Table P.

Table P. Initial dates of some Archaic coastal shell mounds

Late Archaic

Hosororo Creek (Beta 20007, SI 6638)	2025 B.C. (Williams 1981, 1992)
Puerto Hormiga (SI 173)	3090 B.C. (Reichel-Dolmatoff 1965)
Mina Complex (SI 1036)	3095 B.C. (Simões 1981)

Archaic

El Heneal	1450 B.C. (Rouse and Cruxent 1961)
Manicuare (T-295)	1730 B.C. (Rouse and Cruxent 1963)
Cubagua (Y-497)	2325 B.C. (Rouse and Cruxent 1963)
Las Varas	2600 B.C. (Sanoja O. 1989)
Guayana (Teledyne 751)	3650 B.C. (Sanoja O. 1989)
Banwari Trace (MC 888)	5230 B.C. (Harris 1976)
Piraka Alaka Series (Beta 27055)	5280 B.C. (Williams 1992, 1996)

The transition to horticulture at Hosororo Creek terminated over three millennia of sedentary occupation on the Western Guiana Littoral commencing at a time before the post-glacial sea had attained its present level. Since this sedentary occupancy of the Western Guiana Littoral represents the entire time period covered by the shellfishing adaptations of northern South America, and which it appears were initiated in the Alaka phase of northwestern Guyana, Table P, the socio-cultural revolution that eventually took place there must have related in some way to environmental specifics that were absent elsewhere. It might therefore be worthwhile to attempt to identify some of these specifics in so far as they are evidenced archaeologically.

The outstanding feature of the Western Guiana Littoral is the low gradient of its shelf. Because of its low elevation, marine influence alternating through time with the influence of run-off has resulted in a continually changing coastal zone (Clapperton 1994). A key feature of this coastal zone is variability in the magnitude of tectonic subsidence east to west toward the Orinoco Delta. This in turn resulted in extreme variability, through space and time, in the faunal resources of Eastern and Western Subzones. These conditions permitted a stability in the settlement pattern of northwestern areas of the Northwestern Subzone that was unknown to the southeast. The corresponding resource imbalances stimulated a system of reciprocal exchange in a material culture which the archaeological evidences show to have included canoe manufacture, bark cloth, body paint, basketware and possibly the hammock, all identifying traits of Tropical Forest Culture (Steward 1949:708). Dominating the system of reciprocal exchange was the movement of strategic rock materials from northwest to southeast, principal centers of extraction having been located on the upper Barama River and lower Aruka River. From these centers, a variety of specialized rocks materials were moved across the swamp basin and perhaps even further afield (cf. Harris 1976:37-40). Stimulated by the unique jasper exposures of the Pakaraima Highlands, similar long-range trade networks had been a feature of regional integration since paleo-Indigenous time. Thus, not only had the resources of the Western Guiana Littoral remained viable during the entire Amazonian arid interval of around 2000 B.C., but also the area represented the end of a migration route, down the Essequibo, which, during the period, had attracted shellfishers whose diagnostic shell tempered pottery indicates an ultimate affiliation with the lower Amazon.

Granted the biotic richness of the swamp edge (pp. 213) and the successful adaptation of the Warao there over the millennia, interpretation of the abrupt appearance of manioc horticulture on the lower Aruka River around 1600 B.C. must rest on a choice between alternative hypotheses: (*i*), The coming of horticulture was an *in situ* development reflecting continuity in the adaptation of Warao peoples to the swamps of the Western Guiana Littoral over the preceding three millennia, (*ii*), The coming of horticulture reflected the penetration of the lower Aruka River by Arawak migrants from the lower Orinoco Basin and their subsequent assimilation. Compelling arguments can be adduced in favor of either hypothesis (e.g. Williams 1996, 1996a), in respect of which the merits of each are outlined below.

(*i*). The continuing viability of the swamps during the Amazonian arid interval of +/- 2000 B.C. is sufficiently evidenced by the successful integration of certain migrants from the Mouth of the Amazon at around this time by Warao communities of the Western Guiana Littoral. This viability was a function of the varied starch resources of the swamps. Dominant among these resources was the Moriche palm (Mauritia flexuosa), the Tree of Life of the Warao, ambiguously represented (two badly corroded grains) in the pollen sample for the Archaic Barabina shell mound (Bakker 1981), at which elevation experiment shows that the Moriche palm will not fruit. The Moriche palm has been noted by many writers as the traditional starchy staple of the Warao (Barral 1980:29; Bennett 1866:247; Brett 1968:165; Gillin 1948:826, Gumilla 1791; Guppy MS; Heinen and Ruddle 1974; Heinen et al 1995; Kirchoff 1948:870; Osgood and Howard 1943:18; Ralegh 1848:95; Roth 1924:215; Schomburgk 1886:121; Wilbert 1972:93). A sample of its flour, extracted in replication experiment, Figure 4.20, yielded 80% carbohydrates, which is about equal to that of manioc, 81% (University of Guyana 1981). Its disadvantage as a starchy staple for small, sedentary groups on the swamp edge is its obligatory continual destruction by felling in order to harvest its manifold products. A 0.5 ha quadrat in the freshwater swamps to the north of Barabina Hill comprised 19 adults and five saplings concentrated in three-quarters of the area, Figure 4.20a. An adjacent quadrat contained no Moriche palms.

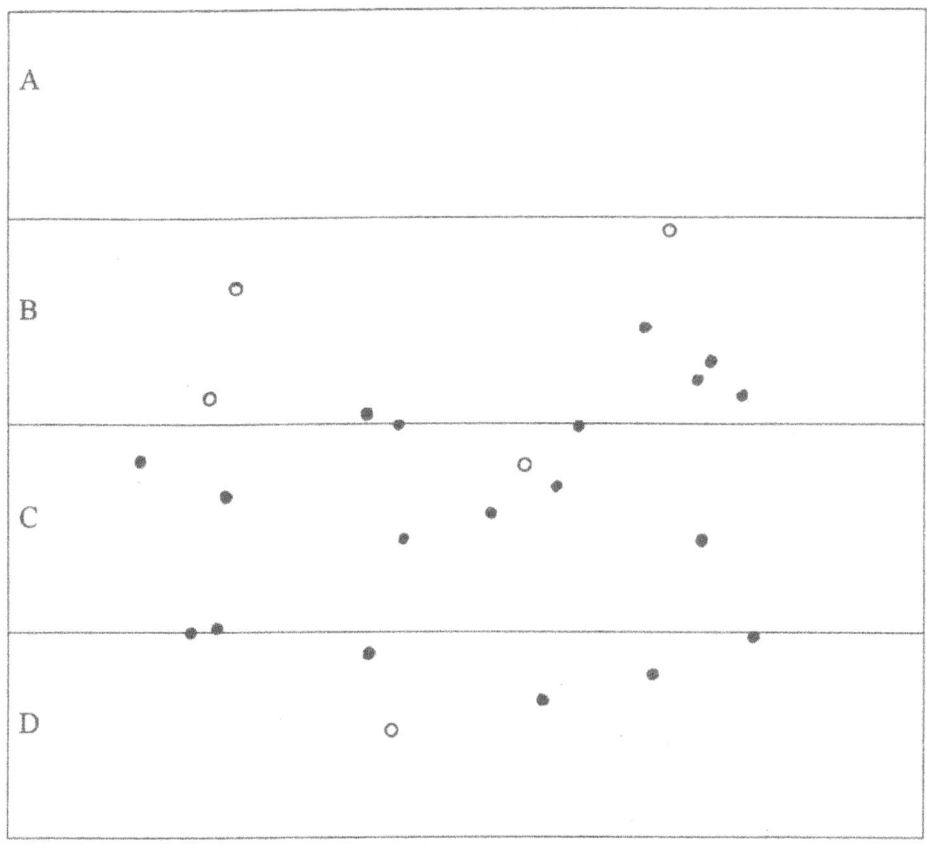

Figure 4.20a. Barabina foothills. Distribution of Moriche palms. Mature (●), sapling (○).

By way of assessing the viability of this palm as a starch resource in the economic catchment area of a small band on the swamp edge, an attempt was made to relate its characteristic disjunct distribution in the swamps to the harvesting needs of such a community, particularly during a period of sustained reduced precipitation.

Each moon, a leaf sheathe forms at the heart of the palm, Figure 4.21,1a. As this grows, a new leaf sheathe forms at the heart on the next moon, Figure 4.21,1b, and this is followed, on the next moon, by yet another, Figure 4.21,1c. Stems of this set of three new leaves, formed at the end of the first quarter, are joined on the trunk of the palm in a common ring. At the end of the second quarter, a new ring, comprising three leaf scars, forms on the trunk above the first. At the end of the third quarter, yet another ring of scars forms on the trunk above the second, and at the end of the final quarter (one year), the last ring is formed above the third by the newest set of opening leaves. In a mature palm, the annual cycle is marked by production of an inflorescence at this time, Figure 4.21A,B. The oldest triad of leaves, those forming the lowest ring of leaf scars, surviving from the previous

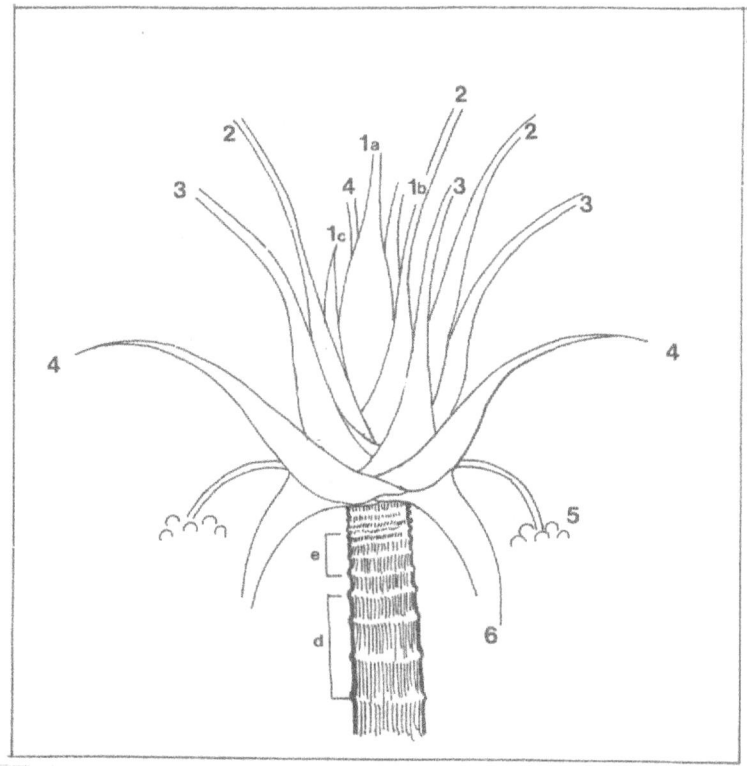

Figure 4.21. The Moriche palm. Age data.

annual cycle, now commence to decay and eventually will fall, Figure 4.21 Y,Z, Figure 4.16. This may take a year, or two, or more. Thus, four ring scars, representing four triads of leaves, mark an annual increment in the vertical growth of the trunk, Figure 4.21 I,II. In a given stand, therefore, the age of each palm can be estimated by dividing the total number of ring scars on each trunk by four. But since in each case the most recent rings remain unexpressed at the growing point of the trunk, the result will underestimate the true age by a count of these unexpressed rings plus those of the leaves representing the current year's growth.

254

Of the 19 mature specimens in the quadrat investigated, four had been felled recently and lay on the ground. The oldest standing specimen, 18 m high, was almost without leaf scars, which had "faded" with age. Number of rings among the 15 standing specimens ranged between 42 to 125, permitting age estimates of 10.5 to 31.3 years. The Moriche palm takes around 30 years to produce its first inflorescence. Only one of the specimens standing in the quadrat was fruiting. Using the rate of 19.17 years per human generation (Pianka 1974), palms in the quadrat represented two human generations, the first (0 - 20 yr) represented by 10 specimens including five saplings, and the second (20 - 40 yr) represented by 14 specimens including four already felled.

Shellfishers exploiting an identical sample from Barabina Hill would have encountered five mature palms. Their respective ages show that, during the ensuing decade, one or other individual of the remaining nine palms would have reached maturity at intervals ranging between six and 33 months.

Maximum starch production in the Moriche palm coincides with the months immediately preceding appearance of the inflorescence, i.e., in the dry season, February - April (Heinen and Ruddle 1974). The present investigations were conducted in October, when yields were minimal (1 - 2 kg/plant). Thus, during the ensuing decade, minimal yield of the above quadrat hardly would have exceeded 20 kg. Although ethnographic parallels show that maximum harvests permit storage (Heinen and Ruddle 1974), the accompanying destruction of the plant meant that year-round harvesting by a band of around 15 shellfishers would have involved continual extension of the search area in a given lifetime. Since the productivity of the Moriche palm is compromised when the ground water drops below its roots, the point of diminishing returns was reached at some stage in the arid interval of 2000 B.C. Intensification followed.

In the South East, freshening environment had resulted in the development of the dugout canoe with its critical demographic outcomes, around 3300 B.C. In the North West, the principal feature of environmental freshening was the replacing of palm starch by other starches, notably manoic, around 1600 B.C., Figure 4.17. As has been seen (p. 143), the development of canoe manufacture in the South East had seen recourse to exploitation of a technology of stone tool manufacture which, though always available in the socio-cultural system, had remained irrelevant in human subsistence until recruited there in the diversified economy symptomatic of socio-cultural strain. Similarly, though being aware of pottery making among their trade partners on Hosororo Creek, the industry was never adopted by the ancient Warao on Wahana Island, in whose traditional diet of land crabs and wild starch it was irrelevant.

In the stressed environment of the arid interval on the Western Guiana Littoral, diminishing returns/hectare of palm starch appears to have enforced recourse to already familiar alternatives, the most prominent of which, archaeologically, was the starch of the manioc root *Manihot esculenta*. Implied is an extension of alliances with some neighboring group capable of supplying the bundle of slips which is all that was needed by shellfishers already possessing the prerequisites for acceptance of manioc horticulture - an age-old ceramic technology, basketry, stoneworking, and a knowledge of manufacturing plant synthetics, Figure 4.23. From Hosororo Creek, contact with the Orinoco Basin was *via* the Aruau River upstream, a left tributary of the Aruka River. In such a scenario, it would be expected that the effect on local ceramic practice would have been a purely typological one reflecting the now enlarged functions of pottery vessels in manioc processing, and that the ceramic technology of the preceding centuries would have remained largely unaffected. As has been seen, this is precisely the situation that is revealed in the Hosororo Creek inventory, where three of the four traditional pastes of the shellfishers *(Mabaruma Plain, Hosororo Plain, Koberimo Plain)* survived the development of various new vessel forms, Table Mb. In this unremarkable adoption of first farming, the new manioc flour assumed the name of the traditional palm flour, *aru*; it was pressed in a Warao *aru*huba and the associated socio-cultural revolution was immortalized in the Warao name *Aru*akah - River of the Cassava Root. The critical alliance with the lower Orinoco was maintained along the *Aru*au River.

(*ii*). The other hypothesis that might explain the abrupt occurrence of first farming on the lower Aruka River requires, minimally, the intervention of an Arawak intruding agent. Acceptance of root crop horticulture at the hands of such an agent was predicated on a subsistence technology which, in the swamp environment, dated back continuously to the early Archaic and in the absence of which the arrival of innovative Arawak newcomers could have meant little to the Warao. Now, a ceramic technology characterized by centuries of *in situ* experimentation needed to be adapted to the particular requirements of manioc processing. Symptomatic of definitive solutions to this problem in the cultural refuse are occurrences, for the first time, of processed rock as new ceramic tempering materials -- crushed decayed granite and crushed decayed steatite, both of which, being highly exotic raw materials to swamp dwellers, required to be procured in distant strategic locations on *terra firme* (p. 114, Figure 3.17). In this particular, as well as in others (e.g. location of traditional clay mines) the ready cooperation of the Warao was obligatory.

Crushed-rock temper produced a wholly unaccustomed hardness and durability in the range of pottery vessels now utilized. Since their introduction, no non-ceramic substitute has existed, until the coming of metals, for the indispensable manioc griddle or for the large, open bowl, *kunki* (7.51) that is obligatory in the process of slow boiling and continual skimming of the gathering froth, *keheli kota* (Arawak *keheli* = cassava juice, *kota* = froth) associated with freeing the manioc root of its fatally toxic cyanogenic glucocides, Figures 4.22 (9,12). The process also constitutes the basis of the traditional fish pepperpot. Surprisingly, it is never mentioned in the literature (e.g. Lancaster et al 1981; cf. Dufour 1995), but should be noted because *keheli kota* is indispensable in the preservation of fish and therefore is critical in countering irregularities in the protein supply that are endemic in manioc subsistence. A capability to store protein indefinitely was obviously a critical concern in the traditional manioc diet, the protein content of which ranges between only 0.85 - 1.95% depending on the method of preparation employed. And just as the froth of the evaporation process provided an indispensable fish preservative, so also the toasted manioc juice, the thick, dark-brown residue that survives the evaporation process, provided *casareep*, the traditional meat preservative.

As will be shown, ceramic developments on the lower Aruka River favor the first of these alternatives.

The relations of production in manioc horticulture

The outstanding socio-cultural feature of manioc subsistence is its very high labor intensiveness. This set an inflexible limit on the potentials of Tropical Forest Culture to develop complexity on the interfleuves. From the obligatory underbushing of the rain forest, through felling the trees, burning and clearing the logs, allocating and planting the land; from the harvesting of the first tubers through all stages of their processing year round, the culture of manioc is communally organized within the kinship structure, with a functional reliance on part-time specializations in basketry, ceramics and stone working. The system could be maintained only on the basis of reciprocal exchange of labor and implies a level of political organization which, regardless of an infrastructural base that included the above part-time specializations, remained unknown among the shellfishers of Hosororo Creek.

Allied to the enhanced energy needs represented by the advent of manioc horticulture were the production and maintenance of stone axes. While it is obvious that the hardwoods of the Amazon rain forest could never have been felled by the use of stone axes (fire-felling of mora forest was observed on the upper Barima River as recently as 1988), that implement was indispensable in the endless production of the large quantities of firewood daily necessary in each household to process the manioc tuber. An assemblage of artificial depressions in the bed of Hosororo Creek attests to the expanded energy base of the new horticulturist lifeway.

A fragmentary ground and polished ax on andesite occurring early in the horticultural refuse at Hosororo Creek represents rock material imported from the upper Barama River and tooled locally in response to these expanding energy needs. Although ground stone technology and the specialized rock materials of the canoe manufacturing industry had constituted the base of the traditional trade network for well over the preceding millennium, ground tools occur nowhere in the refuse at Hosororo Creek before the coming of horticulture. Again evidencing local irrelevance of an available technology, chips and flakes of amphibole schist in the refuse of these first farmers attest to the survival of the traditional stone chipping of the late Archaic.

The small number of the Hosororo Creek artificial depressions (20) and particularly of the sharpening grooves (5) evidences the small size of the horticultural group involved and at the same time evidences their limited potentials for clearing the forest vegetation, maintaining productive farm plots and processing the harvested manioc tubers into its essential products. At such limited numbers (= the restricted band sizes of the late Archaic) it was impossible for any individual ever to have established political control over the manpower necessary to extract the enormous potential yields of the manioc plant, 4 - 10 tonnes/ha on the mineral-rich coastal alluvium (15-30 tonnes/ha tinder controlled conditions) and around half that yield on the leached soils of the Guiana Shield. Reciprocal exchange constituted the most efficient use of the labor force available in any given case to underbush, fell, burn and clear the projected farm plot during the obligatory last few weeks of the rainy season and the immediately succeeding first few weeks of the dry season prior to sowing. Given the time limits imposed by annually oscillating wet and dry seasons, and the resulting need for precise scheduling of the available labor, communal effort represented by far the most economical system in order to ensure viability in manioc horticulture. At the same time, the size of the available labor force set a rigid ceiling on the area of forest that could be cleared in a given season, using a traditional technology.

To this constraint was added the problem of satisfactory allocation of the available farm plots. Ethnographic analogy suggests that, in the interests of group cohesion, a one-to-one relationship could never have been permitted to exist between individual labor input and size of the plot allocated. Since group cohesion and unity implies the precedence of social order over individual considerations, the energy needs of the household were seen to prevail over those of the individual regardless of the magnitude of the individual contribution to land clearing measured in terms of man-hours (Mentore 1983-1984). The egalitarian social structure of the typically small, self-contained settlement was the most efficiently adaptive organizational stratagem in the rain forest of the Amazon Basin, linked as it was to the characteristically highly leached soils, the associated nutrient cycling regime and the cumulative stresses engendered by the imperatives of shifting cultivation on communities whose population growth may have failed to keep pace with their own energy demands. New fields needed to be cut every two or three years, irrespective of the size or age of the available manpower. Alternatively, as is suggested by declining ceramic frequencies in the Hosororo Creek profile (Williams 1996a), the productivity of the community declined.

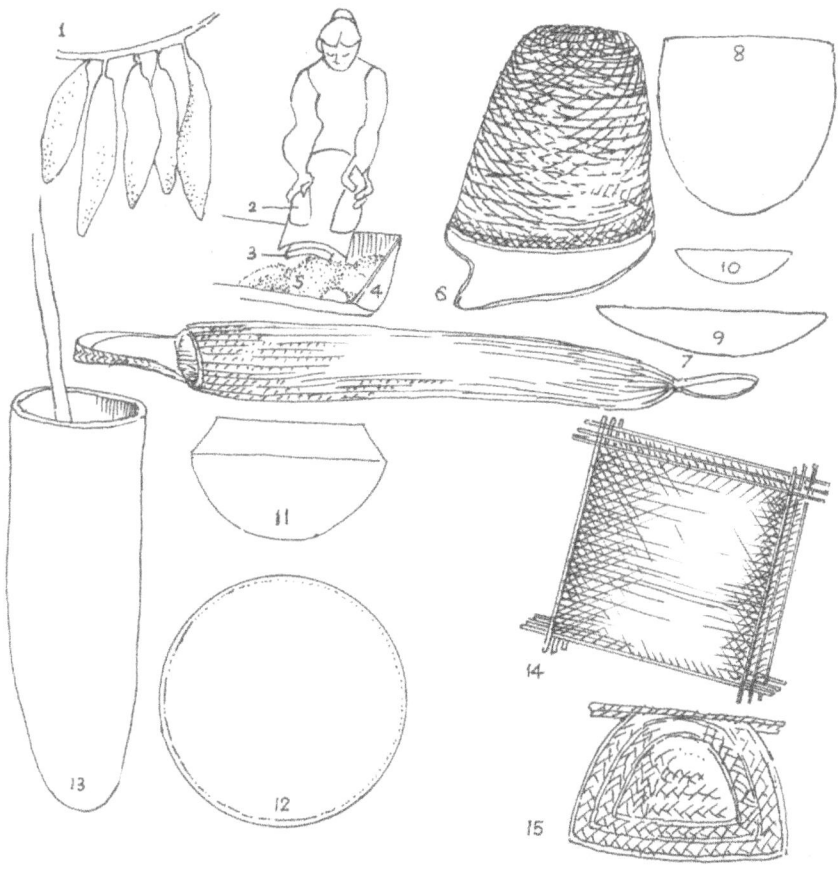

Figure 4.22. Arawak household utensils used in manioc processing. **1.** Manioc root, **2.** Tin grater (formerly stone chips) (*samari*), **3.** Wooden form (*samari daia*), **4.** Trough (*adisa*), **5.** Grated meal (*yoraha*), **6.** Carrying basket (*kuake*), **7.** Manioc press (*matapi*), **8.** Deep bowl for expressed juice (*dwada*) (7.51), **9.** Open bowl for boiling expressed juice (*kunki*) (7.5 1), **10.** Small open bowl (*kunki*) used to skim *keheli kota*, **11.** Pepperpot vessel *(tuma)*, **12.** Griddle (*bodali*), **13.** Wooden mortar *(hako)* and pestle (*hako-rech*), **14.** Basketry sifter (*manari*). **15.** Fire fan *(wari-wari)*.

Remains of items 8 - 12 are commonly recovered in archaeological contexts.

Essential utensils employed in contemporary Arawak manioc processing, Figure 4.22, combine the skills of males and females, males in basketware production and females in the manufacture of ceramic vessels. Because of its short life, +/- 3 months, demand for the basketwork *matapi* is almost continuous in a given household. Until recently, the stone-chip grater was the product of both sexes, women producing the micro-chips for setting into the wooden base by men (Roth 1924:278). Although the survival rate of utensils other than pottery is poor, the range of ceramic vessel shapes encountered in an archaeological context is usually diagnostic of the manioc processing technique involved and thus of the related female labor inputs. Since processing the raw materials of forest and farm lay squarely in the female domain, these labors, including reproduction, also constituted a critical element in the relations of production of the group. The processed *cassava* flour, *casareep* and *keheli kota* all demand female communal labor on a scale which may or may not be met in a given household. In the latter case, labor may be "borrowed" in the kinship network. Such labor needed to be "repaid."

The never-ending cycle of reciprocal exchange of female labor is best exemplified in the processing of the manioc root into its by-products. The constricting action of the *matapi* has been compared to the ingesting motions of the anaconda (Warao *aruhuba* = *cassava* snake). By means of this action, the volume of each load of grated manioc is reduced from around 7920 cm^3 to around 2500 cm^3, around 43% of it having been expressed as liquid. Liquid expressed from a *kwake* containing 45 kg of manioc tubers measures around 7 liters. Allowed to stand around 3 hours, the starch settles, following which the liquid is strained off and placed over a slow fire in order to drive off the toxins by evaporation. The process lasts around 7 hours, needing continual stirring and skimming, the froth being collected in a separate container to be boiled independently as *keheli kota*. Simultaneously, around 0.7 l of casareep has been produced.

Baked on a griddle, the processed manioc flour produces about 50 cassava cakes, each 50 cm in diameter and around 5 mm thick. Consumed at a rate of 2 to 3 cakes/person/day, a 45 kg load of tubers provides an adult with bread for just 17 - 25 days. Hence, as Butt (MS) observed among the Akawaio, a woman's trip to the farm to harvest tubers must be made twice or three times per week in order to meet the needs of an average nuclear family. Since the processing cycle for each 45 kg load of manioc tubers lasts 48 hours, production of bread, casareep and *keheli kota* never ceases year round. Combined with the obligations of reciprocal exchange of labor, this places an effective brake on surplus production.

The horticulturist radiation

The emergence of horticulture on the lower Aruka River around 1600 B.C. was just a single expression of the rise of Formative culture across the Guianas. Comparable dates have been obtained at the Mouth of the Amazon (See Roosevelt

1995, 1996 for discussion; Simões 1981). The hiatus separating this event from the occurrence of first farming elsewhere in the Guianas around 600 years later can be filled at present by little more than speculation. The period of climatic amelioration was extremely slow. This may have affected the productivity of the manioc plant regionwide. At this time of climatic amelioration, characterized by a freshening environment and continuing demographic upheaval, the diagnostic pottery of the new farmers, Figure 4.23, represents the campsites of small kin groups lacking as

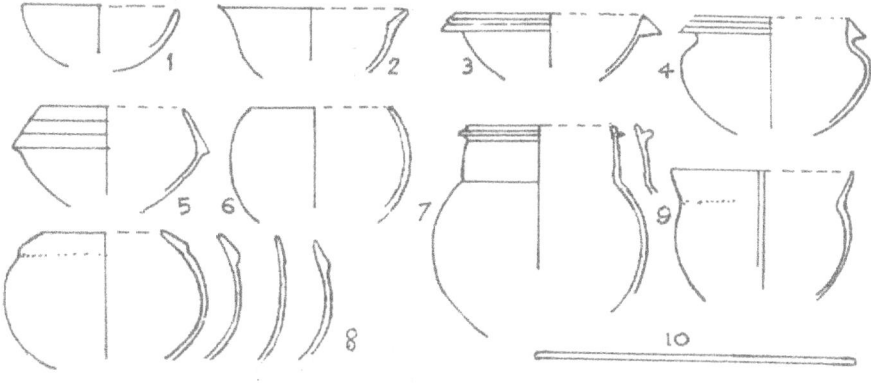

Figure 4.23. Hosororo Creek. Early Formative vessel shapes.

yet in the numerical size and political complexity that are necessary for the development of a full-blown manioc economy. Thus, although in due course the coming of horticulture was to prove of seminal importance in the cultural evolution of groups on the Western Guiana Littoral, initially it had prevailed there almost from the outset. Indeed, to the extent that this change in the mode of production was grounded in a pre-existing and rather complex socio-economic system, horticulture became in fact virtually a feature of that system, which thus remained unchanged in essentials, having been modified only by a shift (possibly opportunisic) in the choice of starch utilized in the traditional vegetal processing technology.

The effortless absorption of manioc horticulture into the Archaic socio-economic system of the swamps may itself explain the significance of Hosororo Creek in the light of a cultural advance which, at least initially, stopped short of representing a wholly comprehensive change in the mode of production. The Warao group there was unique as a host community rich in the range of pre-existent technoeconomic traits required for the effective transfer to root crop horticulture. They were in fact the only preagricultural community along the entire coast of northeastern South America at this time with a complex trade network in an environment sufficiently biotically rich and varied to have withstood the pressures of relocation induced by climate change. These resources underpinned alliances with groups on the lower Orinoco by means of which, apparently by intermarriage, manioc horticulture was transferred to the swamps of the Western Guiana Littoral.

Relationships engendered in these alliances were embedded in an interaction sphere that extended across the entire Guiana land mass. The pre-eminence achieved by the canoe manufacturing industry on the southeastern swamp edge had been based on strategic materials deriving from the geological resources of the northwestern swamp edge ever since the freshwater climax of the fourth millennium B. C. Perhaps the most outstanding example of this inter-relationship between the resources of the swamps and those of *terra firme* was the role now played by steatite as a non-plastic additive in the ceramic industries of Maipuran Arawaks intruding in the lower Orinoco Basin. This rock material was employed in the very earliest pottery at Barrancas, on which grounds Lathrap (1966) insisted on retrodicting the conventional date for these horticulturist pioneers on the lower Orinoco to around 700 or 800 B.C. The date has been established since at around 1000 B.C. (Sanoja O. 1979:186), though the alliance struck by Warao on Hosororo Creek with so far unidentified Arawaks on the lower Orinoco around 1600 B.C. suggests that the earliest Barrancoid sites in the area remain to be identified. Steatite continued to be employed as a ceramic tempering material into the latest levels of the Barrancoid Coporito subphase in the Orinoco Delta on to around A.D. 1345 (Sanoja O. 1979:214, 226). By this time it was also being traded far to the east, to Arawaks of the Abary phase on the Eastern Guiana Littoral (Evans and Meggers 1960:178).

Such a time span suggests a sustained monopoly of access to the steatite mines, which could be reached only *via* the ancient Warao entrepôt at Koriabo Point on the Barima River. As the last great tributary of the Barima River before it debouches into the Orinoco Delta, the Aruka River was strategically well placed to dominate relations with contemporary Arawak horticulturists at Barrancas *via* its tributary the Aruau. The expansion of steatite-tempered ceramics along the Guyana Coast suggests the eventual integration of the area in the economy of the lower Aruka River.

In this lengthy evolutionary period, a well defined hiatus in cultural development on the lower Orinoco River (Meggers (1987:30) needs to be borne in mind in light of its significance for understanding the course of events on the lower Aruka River. While six dates ranging between 1050 - 450 B.C. relate to the Pre-Classic Period at Barrancas, and 14 dates ranging between A.D. 450 and Contact times relate to Post-Classic Barrancas and its related phases, there remains a hiatus of around 800 years during which only a single date has been obtained for Classic Barrancas. This hiatus in the Barrancas date sequence relates to a similar gap occurring in radiocarbon sequences on the Western Llanos, the Middle Orinoco, the East Coast of Venezuela, and on Trinidad. The Barrancas hiatus has been seen as probably attributable to the submergence of riverain sites following on the return of the rains after an arid period dating between 2700 - 2000 b.p. At this time, a few radiocarbon dates on the Mazaruni River unequivocally indicate that, in hinterland areas, the low water levels of the late Archaic were giving way to increasing river discharges with the return of moister conditions. However, the evidence from Hosororo Creek suggests that the low water levels currently prevailing in coastal and estuarine areas may have been somewhat modified by the compensating influence of the tides.

While uncertainty persists regarding the duration of Holocene and conditions in Amazonia, generally accepted to have lasted either continuously or in disjunct stages between +/- 4000 and +/- 2000 b.p. (summarized in Meggers 1979), the degree to which the development and expansion of Formative culture on the lower Aruka River was affected is suggested by the apparent paucity of the associated refuse. Once the Hosororo Creek site had been abandoned, progressive occupation of other areas on the swamp edge as an immediate consequence is difficult to establish. Sites that may represent the lacuna on to the Arawak occupation of Barrancas six hundred years later are by no means easy to identify. Assuming the gradual expansion of farm plots up the hill slope, indicated by the graded grain sizes of transported grit in the peat layers of the Hosororo Creek profile, such sites probably yet remain to be identified on other foothills of the Aruka Range. Also, erosion attributable to continuous occupation of these lateritic hills over three millennia severely restricts opportunities for stratigraphic investigations, a situation made worse by the survival of various preagricultural pastes into the horticulturist period.

The picture becomes increasingly more unclear through time. The middle of the large (55 x 50 m) Akawabi Creek shell mound on the Koriabo River dates at around 2000 B.C. (4020 +/- 80 b.p. Beta 32187). Granted that it comprises mainly compacted crab shell, its accumulation, characterized by an unusual lateral spread, evidently represents the environment of exposed mudflats on the immediate swamp edge that preceded the marine incursion of +/-2000 B.C. at nearby Hosororo Creek. Appropriately, notwithstanding its contrast with the Hosororo Creek group in food procurement strategies, the recovery at Akawabi Hill of specimens of the diagnostic shell-tempered *Wanaina Plain* pottery of Hosororo Creek (Evans and Meggers 1960: Table A) indicates a degree of interaction between the two communities in the later stages. The felspar-tempered *Mabaruma Plain Mode A* paste of the shellfishers, though also well represented, continued into horticulturist times and therefore is of little value as a time marker. Also present were other late Archaic pastes that survived the transition to horticulture, e.g., *Mabaruma Plain Mode B* and *Koberimo Plain*. Sherds specific to the horticulturist occupation were steatite-tempered *Hotokwai Plain* and *Akawabi Incised and Modeled* motif 4 (Apostaderan). Unfortunately, two independent stratigraphic tests at different times failed to establish the local ceramic sequence at this site. Both tests yielded only a few potsherds in the overlying thin humus layer, associated with food refuse, boiling stones, etc. Although, as at Hosororo Creek, occupation evidently survived the end of the shellfishing lifeway, an unequivocal relationship could not be established between the late Archaic *Wanaina Plain* sherds reported at this site and the small horticultural sherd sample present in the overlying humus.

The apparent paucity of Early Mabaruma sites in the swamp basin needs to be considered in light of the continuation of the steatite trade during the two millennia following on its earliest known use as a ceramic temper at Barrancas (+/- 590 B.C.) and the demise of steatite-tempered pottery at Coporito (+/A.D. 1345). At Barrancas on the Orinoco, the prominent ceramic type of the Barrancas phase, *Barrancas Desgrasante de Esteatia*, occurred with variable frequencies on to around A.D. 800, attaining maximum popularity in the immediately preceding three centuries or so. After A.D. 800, it virtually disappeared in the Barrancas inventory (Sanoja O. 1979:193, 214).

In light of the above evidences, the shift in the mode of production that is represented by Warao adoption of manioc horticulture appears initially to have remained only skin deep. Already adapted by several millennia to the contrasting niches of the swamp basin, the return of benign climatic conditions and fresh, brimfull streams after around 1600 B.C. would have provided the powerfully attractive alternative of abundant harvests of Moriche flour as the starchy staple. Accordingly there is little presently available evidence of those changes in political organization that would have been expected following on the transition to horticulture and a concurrent shift to animal domestication. This latter eventually would have generated a viable standing stock of protein resources to replace the ever recurrent energy costs of hunting. It never occurred. As in the Archaic, fish continued to provide the essential protein complement to the starchy staple. Thus, the mere acceptance of the manioc plant did little to alter the domestic economy of these late Archaic peoples. The new starch resource merely represented an efficient alternative to the traditional palm starch of the swamps. Certain Warao, e.g., at Wahana Island on the upper Waini, steadfastly ignored the innovation notwithstanding centuries of contact with horticulture on the lower Aruka River. In any case, the surviving settlement pattern suggests that acceptance of the manioc plant initially failed to produce the outcomes expected of the transition to horticulture -- population growth, an attendant "demic diffusion," the emergence of settled village life and the beginnings of social complexity.

After decades of archaeological inquiry in the area, evidences of such developments remain singularly lacking. Acceptance of the new starchy staple did little, in itself, to alter the age-old socio-economic system of the swamp basin, where the settlement pattern continued to remain a function of the ancient trade networks linking the resources of the swamps with those of *terra firme*. Therefore, the small, single- or multi-household communities of the Archaic continued in occupation of isolated areas of elevated land around the swamp edge and with limited resources for clearing virgin rain forest and preparation of the land. This settlement pattern survives to the present day among manioc-based Warao kin-groups on the Moruka and upper Waini Rivers. They remained "tethered" to the resources of the swamp edge even after the advent of metal tools had mitigated their traditional dependence on the complementarity between swampland and upland resources.

Thus, the evidence suggests that the single- or multi-household communities of the Archaic (e.g. Akawabi on the Koriabo River) continued in occupation of isolated areas of elevated land around the swamp edge long after the incorporation of the manioc root in their traditional food processing technology. Their numbers remained always inadequate to achieving the complex relations of production that have been described above and which are concomitant on the development of a fully-fledged manioc-based economy with its inflexible demands on the reciprocal exchange of labor. Thus, instead of exhibiting the expected rapid rate of population growth following on the transition to horticulture there, the small group at Hosororo Creek displayed an immediate and irreversible *decline* in numbers.

The development of the Tropical Forest village of the lowlands, characteristically numbering around 60 - 80 persons with an upper limit of perhaps 200 - 250 (cf. Chagnon 1973:135; Meggers: 1995:27), was therefore a very tardy outcome of the transition to horticulture, which nowhere takes place overnight, but instead represents centuries of gradual change, as, for instance, in Europe, where agriculture began to spread decisively only after it had attained a substantial level of development (Cavalli-Sforza 1983:112). On the Western Guiana Littoral, resistance to social as against technological change may have militated for centuries against the transformation of these swamp communities into the fully-fledged, manioc-based economies of their *terra firme* mentors.

The earliest farming communities on the lower Orinoco River likewise appear to have remained numerically small and lacking in cultural development over several centuries during which their settlements hardly spread beyond a restricted area of the Saladero site. According to Sanoja O. (1979:269):

> A jugar por las caracteristicas de la alfareria coffespondiente a los niveles del periodo Preclássico, el espacio ocupada por los primeros habitantes del sitio debió haber side relativemente poco extenso

puesto que la alfarería correspondiente a este período se le ha encontrado limitada hasta el presente sólo a la parte occidental de la franja costera de Saladero. Asinfistno, representa un pottentage minimo del total de la alfareria recolectada en el sitio.

The tardiness that characterized the adoption of a fully-fledged manioc-based economy at these two early centers of first farming evidently were attributable, on the one hand, to the inherently slow rate of population growth that is implied by the respective settlement patterns and, on the other, to the absence of animal domestication that characterized the shift to food production in the lowlands as a whole. Slow population growth among these pioneer farmers delayed the attainment of the minimum group size which would have permitted deployment of the complex relations of production that are essential in a fully-fledged manioc-based economy. On the other hand, the lack of animal domestication, by perpetuating the reliance on aquatic protein, effectively denied the group the energy inputs of its able-bodied males in animal husbandry.

On the lower Orinoco, the population appears not to have attained viable numbers for the maintenance of a fully-fledged manioc economy until around the opening of the Christian era. On the lower Aruka River, that event appears to have occurred a few centuries later. As has been seen, one estimate (Evans and Meggers 1960:64) places the inception of the Mabaruma phase at around A.D. 500, with the important proviso that the diffusion and adoption of pottery making there, and probably also horticulture, may have preceded the "arrival" of the Mabaruma phase and perhaps even stemmed from a different source. Identification of that source of pottery making and horticulture at Hosororo Creek now establishes a time span for Early Mabaruma lasting from around 1600 B.C. to +/- A.D. 500. At around this latter date, the alliances on which the steatite trade had been based during the preceding centuries become more clearly visible in the archaeological record with sustained appearances in the Mabaruma inventory of selected pottery types of the Barrancas phase and its successor the Macapaima phase. Continuity in these ancient alliances is evidenced by rare occurrences of sherds of the Guarguapo phase on the lower Aruka River. The period represented by these alliances witnessed the slow expansion of farming groups across the Northwestern Subzone, notably up the Barima to Koriabo Point as well as throughout the Aruka Basin. Beyond the swamps, the diagnostic ceramics of this Classic Mabaruma period appeared in the ceramic inventories of Akawaio now in the process of spreading across the hinterland *via* the Mazaruni, Essequibo and Potaro Rivers. In this ceramic radiation, a coastwise expansion *via* Assakata in the Waini Basin and Recht-door-Zee at the Mouth of the Demerara River, reached eventually as far as the Abary River on the Eastern Guiana Littoral (Evans and Meggers 1960:154; see Figure 2.24), marking the ultimate eastward expansion of Rouse's Proto-Northern Maipuran Arawak influence.

Conversely, occurrences of decorative motifs from the lower Amazon in ceramic inventories on the Aruka River similarly illustrate the northward expansion of Rouse's Proto-Eastern Maipuran Arawak influence from the lower Amazon.

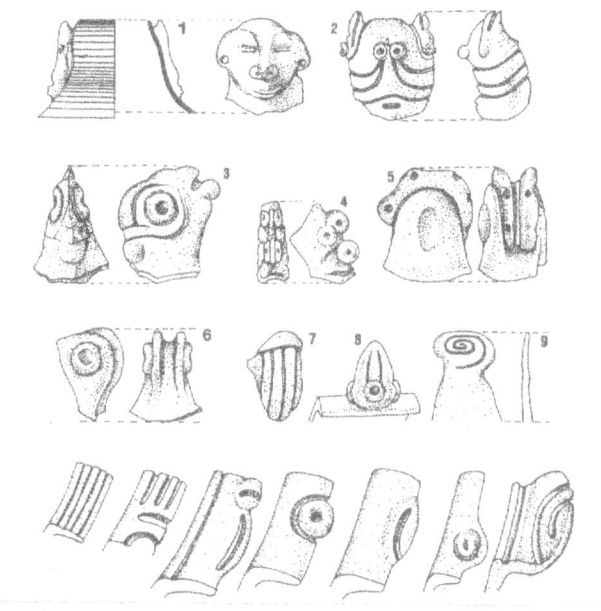

Figure 4.24. Barrancoid Traits of the Abary Phase, Recht-door-Zee, Eastern Guyana Littoral.

The Mabaruma phase: origin, characterization and chronology
The conventional Mabaruma phase

Decades after its initial identification and description and notwithstanding subsequent intense debate, the horticulturist Mabaruma phase remains to be adequately characterized and its relationship to the Archaic Alaka phase explicated. Since challenges to its conventional chronology have never been addressed, presentation of an alternative chronology involves an obligation to examine the still outstanding issues. These are (*i*) the perceived contemporaneity of certain Mabaruma phase ceramic types with late prehistoric types from the lower Orinoco (Cruxent and Rouse (1961:34) and (*ii*) the chronological implications of the occurrence of a steatite-tempered *Mabaruma Incised* (or *Barrancas Incised*) potsherd in early Barrancas refuse (Lathrap 1966). Excavation of the Hosororo Creek deposit now permits addressing these issues. It will be shown that, following on the demise of the alliance with the unidentified Barrancoid group that had stimulated first farming on the Aruka River around 1600 B.C., a continuing series of alliances with successive groups on the lower Orinoco resulted in the incorporation of *selected* decorative traits of the Guarguapan, Macapaiman and Apostaderan phases, and that these adventitious traits were incorporated into the definitions of three of the four decorated types in the conventional inventory of Mabaruma phase ceramics.

Our recharacterization of the Mabaruma phase confirms the identification of most of these extraneous decorative traits with late prehistoric groups (the Cruxent/Rouse issue), and identifies *Mabaruma Incised* ceramics with the horticulturist pioneers of the lower Aruka River (the Lathrap issue). At the same time, representing the local industry, certain unbroken continuities in vessel shape are recognized at various sites. The Mabaruma phase is presented as a function of diversification in conditions of subsistence-lack stress on the lower Aruka River during the second millennium B.C., and therefore as an *in situ* technological development from the late Archaic ceramic industry there.

Apostaderan decorative traits in the conventional Mabaruma phase.
Estimated to date after A.D. 1500 (Cruxent and Rouse 1959: Figure 170; 1961:275), the Apostadero style is the latest in the lower Orinoco ceramic sequence. It may represent the group encountered by the British explorer Daniel Blair on Kumaka Hill in 1857 (1980). Vessel shapes excavated there are shown in Figure 4.26. Decoration is by incision, punctation and three-dimensional modeling. Incisions are zoned, end in punctates, or radiate from ovoidal single or double nubbins. Biomorphic adornos are placed on neck and shoulders of a distinctive collared jar, Figure 4.26:6. Paired arcs of circles sometimes alternate with zoned gashes on interior surfaces of everted rims. With the associated vessel shapes, these decorative motifs permit ready identification of Apostaderan elements that have been incorporated in the definition of the conventional Mabaruma phase. [The ovoidal nubbin is a trait of the intrusive Koriabo phase, already established on nearby Koberimo Creek during the eighteenth and nineteenth centuries].

Vessel shapes

The Apostaderan globular jar with collared neck and flanged rim, Figure 4.26:6, characteristically decorated by incision and modeling, Figure 4.26:9, is classified in the conventional Mabaruma phase inventory as defining the *Akawibi Incised and Modeled* ceramic type, Form 4 (Evans and Meggers 1960: Figure 30 [4]). Two of the five stratigraphic cuts of the authors yielded specimens of this highly diagnostic vessel in their upper three levels (ibid Table 4). The vessel is seriated halfway through the authors' postulated middle period (ibid 120, Figure 49; see also Cruxent and Rouse 1961: Pl. 104, 5-11, 16, 17; Figure 196 [131]).

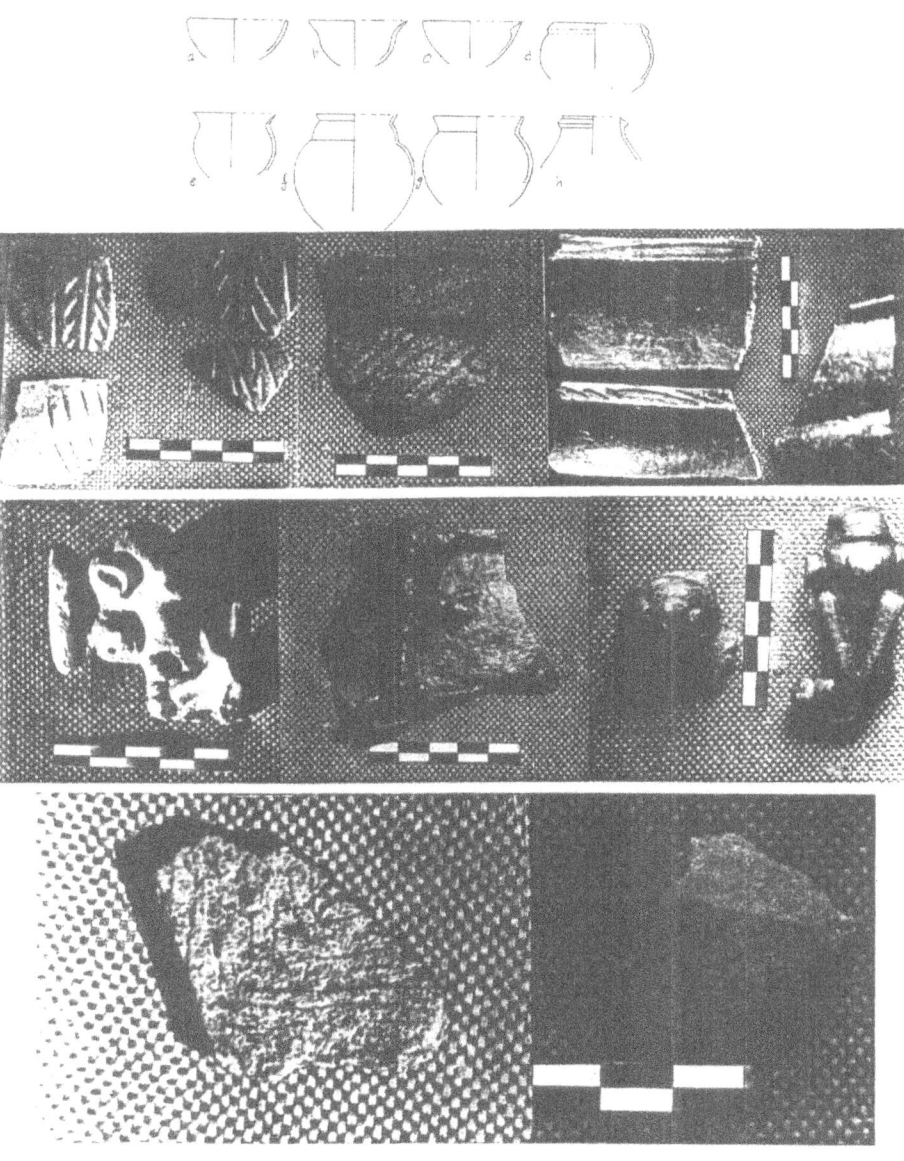

Figure 4.26. Kumaka Hill. Vessel shapes and decorative motifs of the Apostadero phase.

Decorative motifs

(a) Modeled. High relief or three dimensional modeling is employed in an array of distinctive Apostaderan biomorphic adornos that have contributed to the definition of the *Akawabi Incised and Modeled* ceramic type, Motif 4, of the conventional Mabaruma phase, Figure 4.26:9, 10. They represent middle to upper parts of the seriated sequence (Evans and Meggers 1960:94, Figures 32 - 37, Pls. 19, 20i, j, 26b; cf. Cruxent and Rouse 1961: Pl. 102).

(b) Incised. Unzoned curvilinear incisions, commonly in paired units, sometimes alternate with gashed incisions in interiors of everted rims, Figure 4.27a. These Apostaderan motifs were employed to define the *Aruka Incised* ceramic type of the conventional Mabarima phase, representing middle and upper parts of the seriated sequence (Evans and Meggers 1960: Pl. 21, l, n, Pl. 23. h, j; cf. Cruxent and Rouse 1961: Pl. 104: 7, 8, 11).

(c) Incised and Punctate. Apostaderan decorative motifs that have been employed to characterize the *Kaituma Incised and Punctate* ceramic type of the conventional Mabaruma phase include zoned incision ending in punctates (cf. Evans and Meggers 1060: Pl. 23a, b, d, g; Pl. 26a, d, f, h; Cruxent and Rouse 1961: Pl. 103:13), Figure 4.27d.

These vessel shapes and decorative motifs of unequivocal Apostaderan origin were employed to define three of the four decorated types of the conventional Mabaruma phase. Since all three of these decorated types were assigned by their excavators to middle to upper parts of their seriated sequence, the recency attributed to them at the outset (Cruxent and Rouse 1961:34) seems justified. Typologically, therefore, these defining types of the conventional Mabaruma phase, *Akawabi Incised and Modeled, Aruka Incised* and *Kaituma Incised and Punctate* must refer to the period after A.D. 1500.

Guarguapan decorative motifs in the conventional Mabaruma phase. Certain unzoned, incised curvilinear motifs of the Guarguapo style were employed in the definition of the *Aruka Incised* ceramic type of the conventional Mabaruma phase, Figure 4.27e (Evans and Meggers 1960:98, Pl. 22; Cruxent and Rouse 1961: Pl. 101 [1, 3]). Two cauxi-tempered Guarguapan decorated sherds recovered in surface collecting on Barabina Hill (Figure 4.27: f, g) suggest some degree of interaction with the lower Orinoco on the late prehistoric time level. Immediately antecedent to the Apostadero style on the lower Orinoco, Guarguapo has been estimated to date in the latter half of Period IV (A.D. 1150 - 1500) (Cruxent and Rouse 1961:266).

Macapaima decorative motifs in the conventional Mabaruma phase

The Macapaima phase was identified at Los Culises, El Pailon and Macapaima, located within short distances of one another on the left bank of the Orinoco River opposite the Caroni confluence and about 100 km above the horticulturist Barrancas site. Eight ceramic types comprise seven incised, punctated or modeled, and one

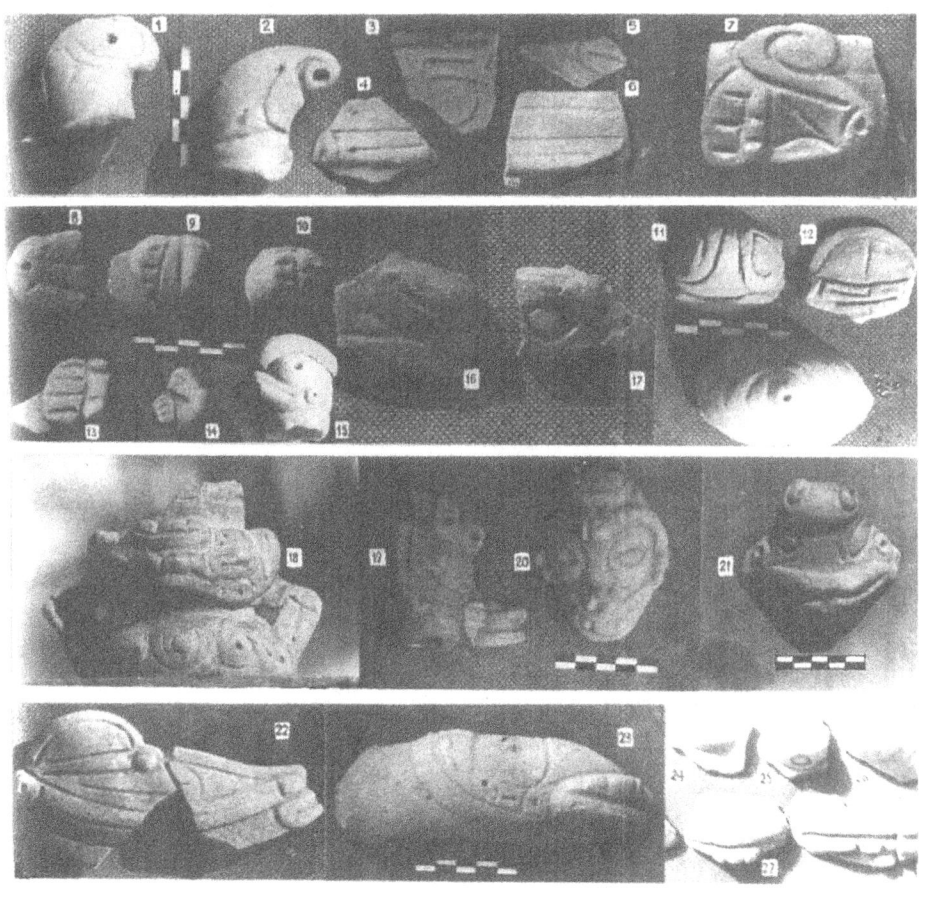

Figure 4.27. Apostaderan decorative motifs incorporated in the conventional Mabaruma phase.

painted. Two of these decorated types *Macapaima Zoned Punctated*, Figure 4.27 h-j, and *Macapaima Incision Corta*, Figure 4.27 j-l were employed in the definition of the ceramic type *Kaituma Incised and Punctate* of the conventional Mabaruma phase (Evans and Meggers 1960: Pl. 27i, j, h; cf. Sanoja O. 1979; Lamina 81, 8a; Roth MS Pls. 14 [11, 161, Pl. 27 110]). *Macapaima Zoned Punctated* is thought to date after A.D. 945 and *Macapaima Incision Corta* between A.D. 700 - 945/1000 (Sanoja O. 1979:193). Although a few of its sherds occurred in the early part of the Mabaruma sequence, *Kaituma Incised and Punctate* is thought characteristic of its middle to upper parts (Evans and Meggers 1960:108).

Thus, the three decorated types from the lower Orinoco that were employed in the definition of the conventional Mabaruma phase *(Kaituma Incised and Punctate, Akawabi Incised and Modeled and Aruka Incised)* relate to the middle to upper parts of the seriated sequence, with a few sherds of the first present in the early part.

The maximum time span represented by occurrences of Macapaima decorative motifs on the lower Aruka River is ca A.D. 700 - 1500 or later. Though occurring throughout, the remaining decorated type of the conventional Mabaruma phase, *Mabaruma Incised*, is most popular in the early part of the seriated sequence of the conventional chronology. However, as suspected by Cruxent and Rouse (1961:34), and as has been suggested by Lathrap (1966), *Mabaruma Incised* is typologically antecedent to other types of the conventional Mabaruma phase. Whereas *Mabaruma Incised* represents the horticulturist pioneers of around 1600 B.C., and their immediate descendants, decorative element, characterizing other ceramic types of the conventional Mabaruma phase, pertain to a period well in excess of two millennia later. This is borne out by the relative antiquity of soils containing Formative and Protohistoric Mabaruma pottery. The former, a humus-rich sandy loam, is extremely rare in the Aruka Basin, while the latter comprises the ubiquitous red hills described by Verrill.

Domestication of the land on the Aruka River

Hosororo Creek, 8° 11' N, 59° 49' W, conveniently divides the Aruka Basin into upper and lower sectors, the inhabited hills to the north (e.g. Barabina, Hosororo, Koberimo, Mabaruma, Wanaina) interacting *via* the Barima and Waini Rivers with the coast and the sea, Figure 4.28, and those to the south (e.g. Akawabi, Hotaquai, Hobediah) interacting, *via* its main tributary streams, with the Kaituma River in the east and the Amacuro River in the west, Figure 4.29. In the south, the hills of the Aruka-Amacuro watershed are underlain by gneisses (Pollard 1956) and, in the north, by amphibolites capped by laterite. Accordingly, the soils of the south typically are sandy loams whereas, the "red hills" of the north described by Verrill (1918) comprise shallow, lateritic clay and gravel overlying bedrock. All known sites of prehistoric horticulture in the Aruka Basin are located on these hills. The current practice of empoldering the swamps for farming is of unknown antiquity.

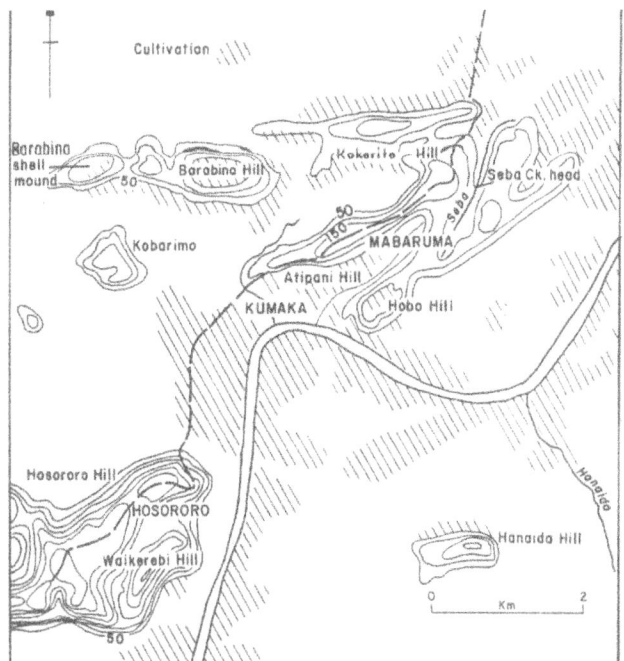

Figure 4.28. The lower Aruka River.

In its lower reaches, the Aruka River traverses uninterrupted freshwater swamp, but further up, around 7° 57' N, it drains land rising above 4 m on the swamp edge. Farming plots located on the drained, peaty soils of the immediate riverbank occur more or less continuously above Kumaka Creek but cease absolutely around Hotabuina Creek in 7° 55' N, which probably represents the limit of the peat. At any rate, this boundary lies quite near to the territorial boundary between Hotaquai and Hobediah, located on Bacquehana Creek in 7° 57' 56" N, 59° 49' 23" W. Further upstream the riverbank, continuously elevated at +/- 4.0 m, is cut by numerous small streams draining the swamps. On both riverbanks, settlements occur on the resulting "islands" of elevated ground (i.e., surrounded by swamp), though, around Hobediah, potsherds are said locally to occur only on the right riverbank. Streams draining these local swamps may become salty seasonally, at which time recourse must be had to shallow wells near the riverbank. This notwithstanding, Hobediah is the earliest Formative site so far known on the Aruka Basin. Erosion of the granite hills there is advanced, with potsherds weathering out of the hilltops and redeposited on the riverbank.

An immediate consequence of the shift to manioc cultivation by late Archaic communities occupying Hosororo Creek was the clearing of the hillfoot for farmland. Inevitably, this initiated a process of cumulative removal of the topsoil, evidenced in the stratigraphic profile by sustained deposition of grit in the accumulating peat. In due course, the topsoil was removed entirely, exposing lateritic gravel. Over time,

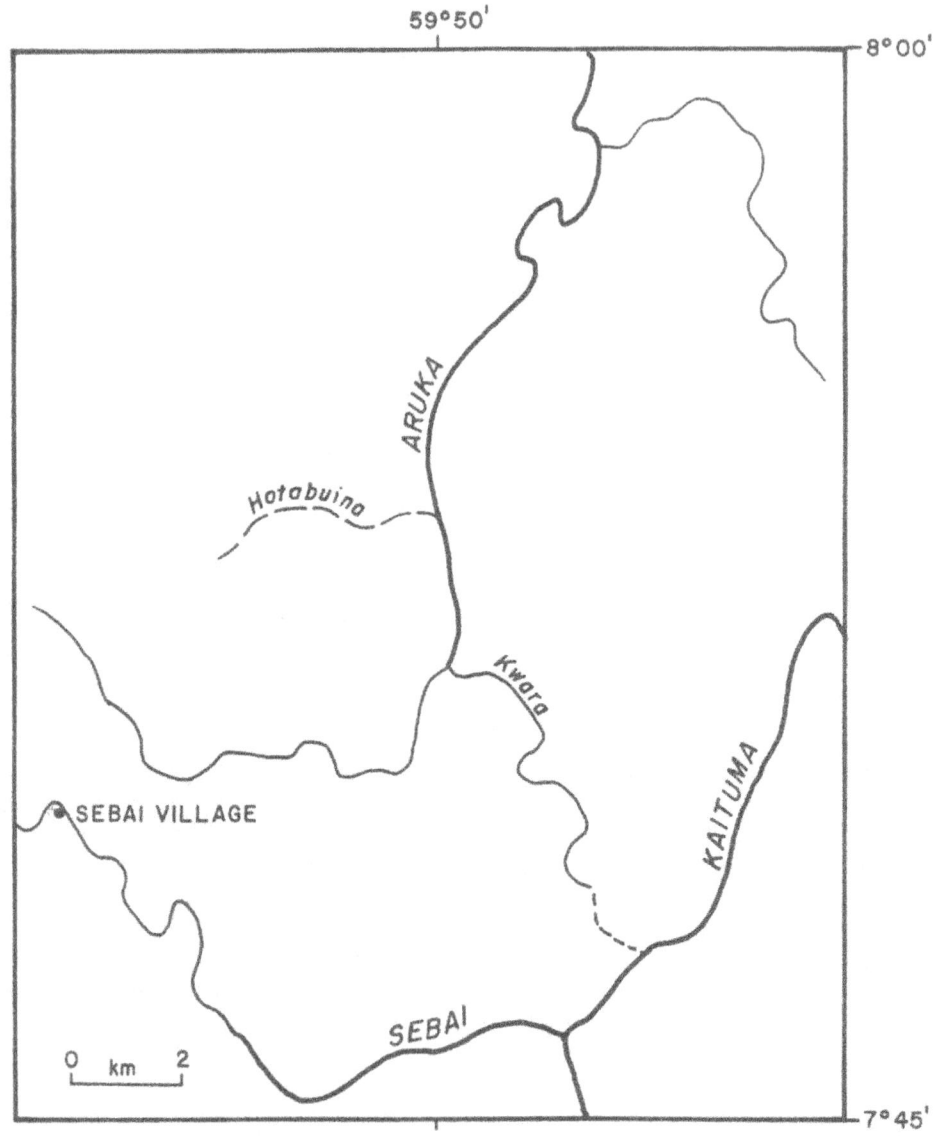

Figure 4.29. The upper Aruka-Kaituma watershed.

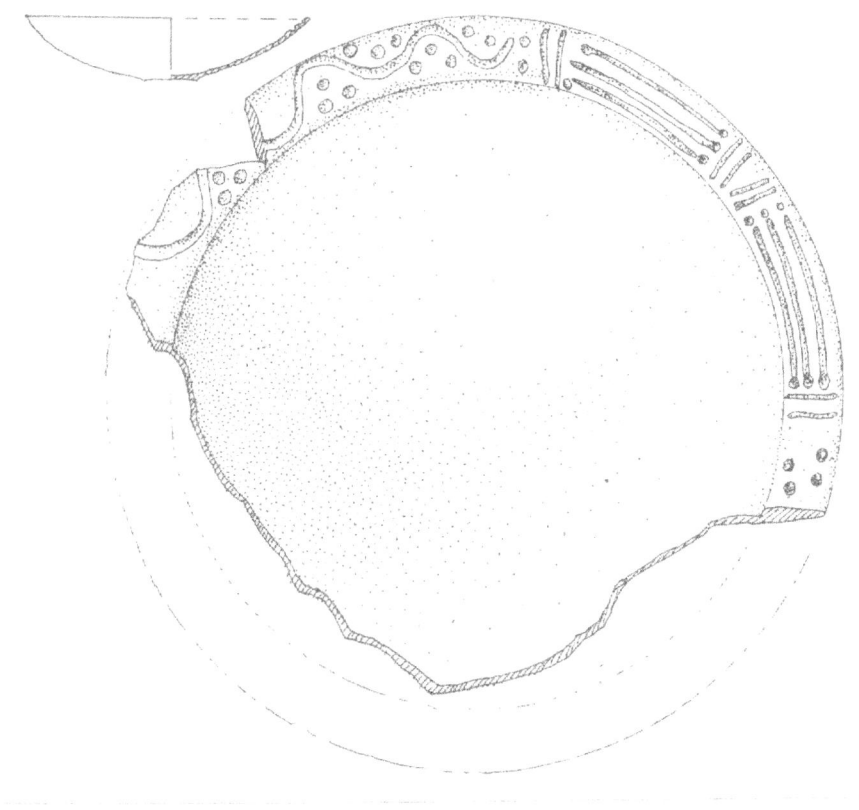

Figure 4.30. Formative vessel shapes: (a) Hobediah (b) Hotaquai

gravel migrating from this source commenced covering the shell mound on the low lying swamp edge. Concurrently, potsherd frequencies/level decline, probably in phase with progressive degradation of the agricultural soil. Thus, at 1600 B.C., the Hosororo Creek site presents the earliest record of comprehensive topsoil loss through horticulture anywhere in the Aruka Basin.

Dating appreciably later, a similar picture of cumulative topsoil loss is in evidence on Barabina Hill, which comprises two east-west-trending elevations rising above 60 m and connected by a narrow saddle, Figure 4.28. These elevations are Barabina Hill East and Barabina Hill West, the latter first occupied by shellfishers around 7000 years ago. Whereas the shell mound on Barabina Hill West is covered by a rich deposit of fine-textured humus 5 - 16 cm thick, reflecting the respect felt by later arrivals for the undisturbed human remains described in its Warao name *Muhu ina* (Bone Swamp), Barabina Hill East is now virtually bereft of topsoil. Excavation of a rare surviving patch of pristine soil overlying bedrock near its crown showed only Formative refuse. This refuse had accumulated to 32 cm depth in the topsoil. Thus, this small patch of pristine soil provides a reference for the edaphic status of other inhabited hills of the lower Aruka Basin. Ceramics in this soil date between 1030 +/- 90 b.p. (Beta 108107) and 740 +/- 710 b.p. (Beta 108108).

In the extreme west of this elevation, where it slopes down to the saddle that connects it with Barabina Hill West, horticulturist refuse survives in around 20 cm of badly leached gravelly loam presently supporting a manioc patch. Around 10 cm of topsoil can be assumed lost since initial clearing of the land.

Across the swamps to the south, Koberimo Hill is now a terminally eroded "red hill" (see Evans and Meggers 1960:78 sites N-21, N-22). A test placed on the hillfoot near the creek yielded cultural refuse to a depth of 30 cm in a rich, dark brown loam presently under second-growth bush. Interestingly, this evidently redeposited soil contained refuse of Akawaio (Koriabo phase) allies of the eighteenth century Dutch colonists on the Essequibo River.

Mabaruma Hill, similarly, is eroded over large areas. The pathway from Ivan Santiago's house spot down to the swamp edge on the headwaters of Seba Creek revealed odd sherds of feldspar-tempered *Maharuma Plain Mode A* weathering out of the residual clay. As *Mabaruma Plain Mode A* is a paste of the Archaic which enjoyed a long life among horticulturists, loss of the topsoil at this site may have commenced any time after 2000 B.C.

Until it was landscaped recently, as the setting of a new hotel (1988), *Kumaka Hill* was the typical "red hill" of the lower Aruka River. A test pit near its crown showed 35 cm of badly leached, gravelly soil overlying bedrock. On the hilltop proper, the topsoil had eroded completely. Whereas in the uppermost 15 cm of the excavated profile (Zone i), European items of metal and glass were associated with Apostaderan potsherds, the lower levels (Zone ii) were fully prehistoric. On the lowest level, Apostaderan sherds overlay a few Formative sherds. The severely leached soils of the two zones were separated by a dark, humus-rich layer apparently representing partial regeneration during a lengthy period of abandonment. Stages in the process of recovery of leached and degraded soil were observed in no other profile in the Aruka Basin.

On the sandy, or sandy loam hill tops of the upper Aruka River, excavated topsoil rarely reaches 20 cm depth. This follows a history of denudation by repeated clearing of the vegetation for habitation, maintenance of campsites by weeding and sweeping in the absence of slope management, followed by successive abandonments and reoccupations. The results are evidenced everywhere by differential levels of erosion and/or loss of soil structure. In five widely spaced test pits at Hobediah, relatively deep topsoil (20 cm) was encountered at only one site, on the upper slope of the riverbank under dense regrowth bush, and here it was by no means clear whether or not the soil had been redeposited from the now bald and dessicated hilltop. On an adjacent hilltop, downslope migration of potsherds had resulted in their inverted stratification at a point where slopewash had been intercepted by a 30 cm-deep channel formed under the drip line of a now vanished roof. Nearby, the crown of the hill, constituting the floor of the erstwhile dwelling, showed deep burning at several points from prehistoric fireplaces, but no trace of the topsoil.

Barring a minuscule patch of humus-rich loam under regrowth bush on the eastern-most extremity of the hill, loss of the topsoil at Hotaquai again has been comprehensive. Surviving depth of the topsoil in this patch was 20 cm.

Sampling these soils of the Aruka Basin provides a sketchy picture of consequences attendant on the domestication of the lower Aruka Basin by horticulturists. The picture needs to be fleshed out by the associated radiocarbon dates and the assessments of soil scientists. This notwithstanding, even in its present form the picture links varying levels of soil erosion and soil degradation over the millennia to farming activities represented by the evolving Mabaruma Subseries of the Barrancoid Tradition, or Series. Thus, a physical background is provided for addressing the issue raised by Cruxent and Rouse several decades ago concerning the typological priority of *Mabaruma Incised* ceramics in the chronology of the Mabaruma phase. At the same time, occurrences of steatite-tempered pottery in a pristine soil matrix dating to 1600 B.C. at Hosororo Creek permits addressing the issue of early relations with the lower Orinoco raised by Lathrap, also several decades ago.

Recharacterization of the Mabaruma phase

As has been seen (p. 224), Hosororo Creek is a bicultural deposit at the foot of Hosororo Hill. The early food refuse there is associated with mainly shell-tempered potsherds affiliated to the Archaic Mina phase at the Mouth of the Amazon. Since the Mina phase dates to at least 3000 B.C., the chronological gradient suggested by similarities between the early ceramics of Hosororo Creek and those of the Mina phase would have had a bearing on our central theme -- the origin and dissemination of Tropical Forest Culture in the lowlands -- had similar pottery been found at a few intermediate sites. In the persistent absence of such pottery, particularly along the Essequibo corridor, the recency and aberrancy of the earliest Hosororo Creek pottery and its demonstrable Mina affiliations suggest that the conventional assigning of the Hosororo Creek shell mound to the Alaka phase (Evans and Meggers 1960) must be called in question.

Notwithstanding the long, sedentary occupation of the Western Guiana Littoral, the earliest pottery there, shell tempered *Wanaina Plain* at Hosororo Creek, dates only to around 2000 B.C. "Pottery with this temper was not found in any other site in the whole of British Guiana" (Evans and Meggers 1960:59). When contrasted with the preceramic cultural level of all other shellfishing sites, the similarity of *Wanaina Plain* to the pottery of the Mina phase constitutes unassailably good grounds for eliminating Hosororo Creek from the Alaka phase.

The Hosororo Creek midden is aberrant also in its deposit of oyster refuse. Elsewhere, oyster refuse occurs only on Wahana Island about 170 km to the southeast, Figure 4.10 (Evans and Meggers 1960:31). Thus, definitively, the Hosororo Creek group was intrusive in Warao culture. Their importance lies in alliances these Amazonian migrants were able to form initially with groups on the upper Waini and, later, with groups on the lower Orinoco, Figure 4.31.

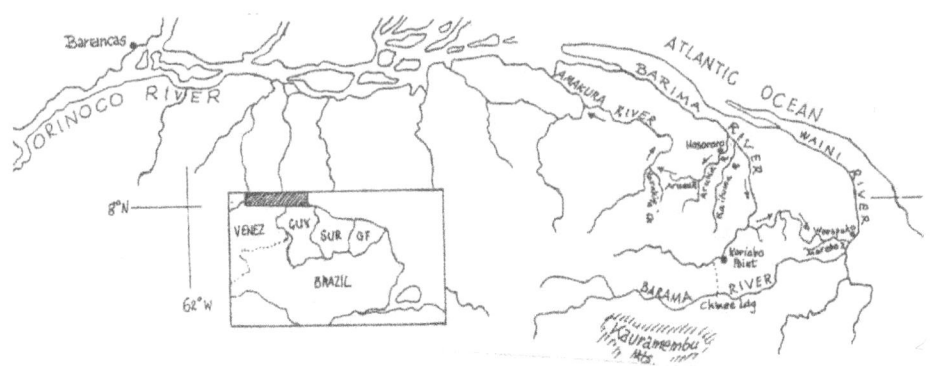

Figure 4.31. Routes of Hosororo-Barrancas and Hosororo-Waini interaction.

Alliances maintained with their Warao hosts down the generations facilitated their apparently effortless transition to horticulture when, abruptly around 1600 B.C., the exigencies of subsistence-lack stress enforced an alliance with certain as yet unidentified manioc horticulturists on the lower Orinoco River.

The successful introduction of Formative pottery at Hosororo Creek was predicated on the existence of the preagricultural pottery technology of these erstwhile Amazonian migrants. To this was added their ready access to certain strategic resources of the Archaic trade network, e.g. nodules of decayed steatite or micaceous sand from rare and remote outcrops on the swamp edge some 200 km to the southeast. The recovery at Alaka Creek on the upper Waini of an *Aruka Incised* potsherd of the horticulturist industry and of several sherds of *Mabaruma Plain Modes A,B* on Kabakaburi Hill, Pomeroon River indicates the wide scope of the alliances that underpinned horticulturist pioneering in the swamp basin. Clays utilized for the late Archaic *Koberimo Plain, Hosororo Plain* and *Mabaruma Plain Modes A B* pastes all survived the coming of horticulture around 1600 B.C. Some continue in use to the present day. As noted above, all of these pastes were employed (Evans and Meggers 1960) in the definition of diagnostic ceramic types of the horticulturist Mabaruma Phase.

On the level of typology, certain vessel shapes and decorative motifs of the Hosororo Creek assemblage have provided the basis for identification of diagnostic ceramic types in the conventional Mabaruma phase. Prominent among these vessels is the bowl with incised flanged rim, Figure 4.23.4, which has been recognized as Form I of the *Mabaruma Incised* ceramic type (Evans and Meggers 1960: Figure 45, 1).

Specimens of this vessel from Hosororo Creek were made on the steatite-tempered paste, *Holaquai Plain*. At the time of Lathrap's (1966) report of his find of a *Mabaruma Incised* (or *Barrancas Incised*) flanged rim in a Barrancas deposit at the Saladero site on the Orinoco, it was not known that steatite had been employed in ceramic clay bodies there at a date prior to 590 B.C. Lacking comparative materials, Lathrap had no recourse to an explanation of his observations. In fact, Lathrap's steatite-tempered rim sherd *(ibid* Figure 1, f) incorporates a design of twin circumscribed, centrally gashed nubbins (motif 2 in the nomenclature of Sanoja O: 1979:138) that seems already anticipated in the Early Formative inventory on Hosororo Creek, Figure 4.7b. At any rate, Lathrap's steatite-tempered *Barrancas Incised/Mabaruma Incised* sherd is vastly antecedent typologically to other decorated types in the conventional inventory of the Mabaruma phase. At the same time, it remained contemporaneous with the earliest use of other pastes that are definitive of that inventory.

Horticulturist alliances

By far the most comprehensive collection ever made of Formative ceramics on the Western Guiana Littoral derives from recent excavations on Barabina Hill. There, four contiguous test pits yielded in excess of 4000 sherds; on four 8 cm levels. Study of the collection permitted motif by motif comparisons with Roth's (MS) report on the Aruka River Basin survey of 1930, as well as with published inventories of the Barrancas Tradition on the lower Orinoco River (Cruxent and Rouse 1959, 1961; Sanoja O. 1976, 1979). These comparisons reveal that of 16 decorated types comprising the Barrancoid ceramic sequence on the Orinoco, only two, *Barrancas Incised* and *Barrancas Modeled Incised* were ever known on the Aruka River, Figure 4.32. The indicated picture of limited interaction between the two complexes must be set against the background of an almost complete lack of concordance between the respective vessel shapes.

Sites yielding *Barrancas Incised* and *Barrancas Modeled Incised* ceramics are distributed on the Aruka River between Mabaruma and Hobediah, the area surveyed.

They may exist elsewhere. The surviving refuse indicates that the respective groups occupied small contiguous hills either supplied with freshwater springs (Barabina Hill East, Hosororo, Mabaruma), or located near freshwater creeks (Akawabi, Hotaquai, Hobediah, Kumaka Hill). The territorially-based descent groups that are implied by potsherd densities on these hills (Roth MS; Verrill 1918) may have originated in the need for absolute control of this strategic resource. This settlement pattern survives to the present day on Barabina Hill East, individual families of this multi-household compound each being tethered to its particular spring or creek. As seems implied by the unchanging occurrences through time of exclusively *Barrancas Incised* and *Barrancas Modeled Incised* ceramic types in the Classic Mabaruma refuse, a particular descent group on the Aruka River constituted at any given time the basis of an alliance with a corresponding group at Barrancas on the lower Orinoco River. The basis of such alliances evidently were the nodules of decayed steatite that had been mined on the upper Barama River ever since Archaic times the corollary having been, apparently, acquisition of the marriage partners that seem implied by the accurate incorporation of specific Barrancas decorative motifs in Classic Mabaruma pottery, always characterized by the inevitable "Aruka fingerprint" indicating local manufacture.

Periodification of the recharacterized Mabaruma phase

The Mabaruma phase is characterized here as an *in situ* development out of the late Archaic on the lower Aruka River. Its inception was stimulated by Warao interaction with Arawak horticulturists migrating down the Orinoco River in conditions of environmental stress around 1600 B.C. It ended with the British expedition of Daniel Blair from Guyana to the Orinoco in 1857. The ceramic refuse permits identification of three well defined periods: Early Formative, Formative and Protohistoric.

Early Formative. The sample was derived partly from the upper levels of the late Archaic Hosororo Creek shell mound and partly from refuse on its northern peripheries. It included well over 2000 sherds of the Incised and Modeled Horizon Style, around a quarter that had remained sealed under swamp forest in 30 cm of pristine, peaty clay overlying bedrock. Decoration was comprised mainly of U-sectioned, broad-line incisions. Occasional rudimentary modeling was restricted to appliqué strips and plain or punctated nubbins.

Vessel shapes included open bowls, deep bowls, carinated bowls, large jars and griddles. Rims were interiorly or exteriorly thickened, flanged or concavo-convex in vertical cross section, Figure 4.23. The globular jar with constricted mouth and exteriorly thickened rim (4.23.8), and the globular jar with concavo-convex rim (4.23.9) were survivals from the late Archaic inventory. The Early Formative was characterized by the introduction of crushed decayed granite and crushed decayed steatite as non-plastic additives in ceramic manufacture. Two charcoal samples from the deposit returned dates at around 1600 B.C.

Formative. A deposit of Incised and Modeled materials, also recovered in pristine soil, on Barabina Hill East, represents a typologically richer ceramic inventory comprising four classes of vessel shapes: (*i*) inherited from the Early Formative, Figure 4.32.i, (*ii*), developed locally but unknown earlier, Figure 4.32.ii, (*iii*), probably adopted from the Barrancas inventory, Figure 4.32.iii, and iv, developed locally but of only rare occurrence (one specimen each), Figure 4.32.iv. Decoration includes the entire inventory of *Barrancas Incised* and *Barrancas Incised and Modeled* motifs. When the water quality permitted locally, the representative Formative peoples expanded into the upper Aruka River at least as far as Hobediah. Simultaneously, they began to interact, *via* the *itabo* opened by their Archaic ancestors across the Barima-Waini watershed, with horticulturists to the southwest,

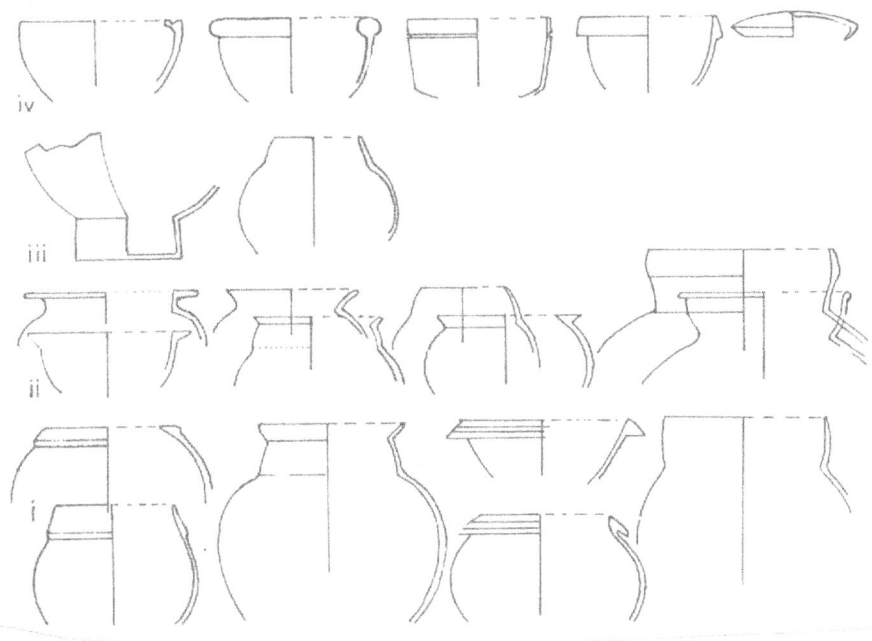

Figure 4.32. i-iv. Barabina East: Formative vessel shapes.

on the lower Amazon. To the southeast, their entrepôt at Recht-door-Zee, at the Mouth of the Demerara River, was the point of convergence of Orinocan (Aruka River) and Amazonian (Coremyne River) ceramic traits. From Recht-door-Zee, the precious rock materials of *terra firme* now were traded to the stoneless swamps inhabited by Arawaks of the Abary phase on the Eastern Guiana Littoral (cf. Evans and Meggers 1960:160, 198; Quelch 1894).

Protohistoric is represented on Kumaka Hill by occurrences of Incised and Punctate ceramics. This rich deposit of Apostaderan (Protohistoric) sherds represents the integration of certain Formative vessel shapes and Arauquinoid decorative motifs. In addition, the Protohistoric ceramic industry on Kumaka Hill continued to be characterized by vessel shapes and decoration specific to the Early Formative inventory on nearby Hosororo Creek, e.g., Figure 4.26 (cf. 4.26d, 4.23 i). Decoration of the Macapaima phase appears to be absent at the coastal sites, all of which had been brought into the interaction sphere of the lower Aruka River since Formative times, e.g., Recht-door-Zee and sites of the Abary phase. However, precisely these Protohistoric traits eventually were distributed, through Akawaio agency, along the great hinterland rivers reaching as far as the North Pakaraimas in the west and Suriname in the east. Through the Akawaio, also, Apostaderan decorative motifs were distributed both along the Guyana Coast and on northern tributaries of the lower Amazon (see Hilbert 1982: Figure M). These distributions appear to have resulted from Akawaio alliances with the Dutch on the Essequibo River during the eighteenth century. An Akawaio presence on the lower Aruka River is represented at this time by the refuse on Koberimo Creek.

Iconography

With respect to its strictly technological base, the pottery of the Mabaruma phase was a direct development out of the late Archaic ceramic industry, itself deriving, ultimately, from the Mouth of the Amazon. On the other hand, many of its typological traits resulted from alliances, over time, with one or other local group on the lower Orinoco River. These alliances date back to the middle of the second millennium B.C. It has been shown that the two decorative repertories that characterize the Incised and Modeled component of the Mabaruma phase derived from independent complexes and at different times. Whereas incised decoration represents elements that were introduced on the lower Aruka River by Early Formative potters in the alliance of + /- 1600 B. C., incised and modeled decoration typified, among other traits, by large, biomorphic adornos, relates to an alliance with a local group on the lower Orinoco commencing in the early centuries of the Christian Era. The definition of the conventional Mabaruma phase was based on an unfortunate conflation of these two entirely independent decorative repertories. Whereas the decoration of Early Formative ceramics at Hosororo Creek during the second millennium B.C. had comprised only incision and punctation with simple applique, Figure 4.7b, the *Barrancas Modeled Incised* forms that were assimilated in the ceramic inventory of the Mabaruma phase some two thousand years later were characterized by large, hollow biomorphic adornos of a distinctive technique and inconography, Figure 4.33a. Assuming women potters, this iconography indicates

Figure 4.33 a,b. Aruka River. **a.** The Barrancoid Distended-Mouth adorno. **b.** Metaphors for the Distended-Mouth adorno.

a social structure that now was a good deal more developed than that of the Early Formative, with women performing functions of enhanced economic and social importance.

The emergence of certain biomorphic motifs in *Barrancas Modeled Incised* ceramics implies the ritualizing of the manioc root at this time and the concurrent rise of females to critical importance in manioc production and processing. This was epitomized in certain magical practices by means of which women sought to control the potency of the intoxicating drink they brewed from the manioc root and by means of which they came to exercise a degree of control over the politically dominant male.

Barrancas Modeled Incised motif 4 comprises a distinctive human head with distended mouth which occasionally features a protruding tongue (Cruxent and Rouse 1963: Figure 33b, 34a; Sanoja O. 1979; Lamina 52, 54, 60e, 61c). This Distended-Mouth adorno is diagnostic of the ritualizing of the manioc root. In both a technological and a typological sense, the motif represents an advanced evolutionary stage as a semantic sign, characterized as it is by a combination of several socially recognized visual schemata, Figure 4.34a,b. A lengthy local development seems implied. Earliest known specimens date between the eighth and tenth centuries at Hobediah. A more competently executed specimen from Barabina Hill East dates to the tenth century.

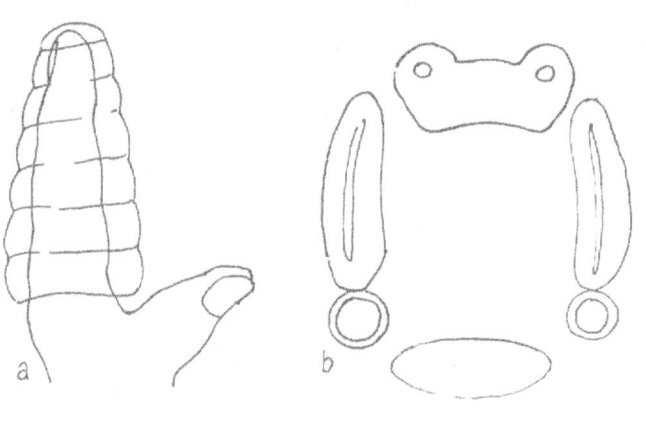

Figure 4.34 ab. The Classic Mabaruma biomorphic adorno. **a.** Armature. **b.** Schemata for human, animal and bird heads.

The typically large sizes of these adornos (3 - 5 cm maximum diameter, rarely as much as 9cm) derived from their relationship to the hand of the potter during manufacture. The majority were made on a cylindrical armature formed by winding a clay coil around the index finger, Figure 4.34a. Onto this armature were appended fillets of clay each representing a schematized facial feature, e.g. forehead, eyes, ears, mouth of man or animal. These features were rigidly conventionalized, Figure 4.34b, while permitting a range of variation at the hands of the individual potter. Heads of humans, animals or birds differed from one another not physiognomically but by their orientation -- human and bird vertical, animal horizontal (cf. Palmatary 1960:57), Figure 4.35a-c.

These schemata constituted highly specific categories in the visual perception of the local group such that they were employed with equal effect in a wide range of social contexts. While the Distended Mouth adorno at Figure 4.35a is associated with manioc processing, the bush-hog motif, Figure 4.35b is associated with the hunt. The King Vulture, Figure 4.35c, is a symbol of shamanic flight. The specimen shown in Figure 4.36a, recovered in an Enmore cemetery, embodies the widely distributed Hands-to-Face motif of Amazonian funerary art. In Figure 4.36b the Turtle Head, another funerary symbol, is similarly schematized. In all these cases, the same schemata were employed to produce contrasting types of socially recognized sign.

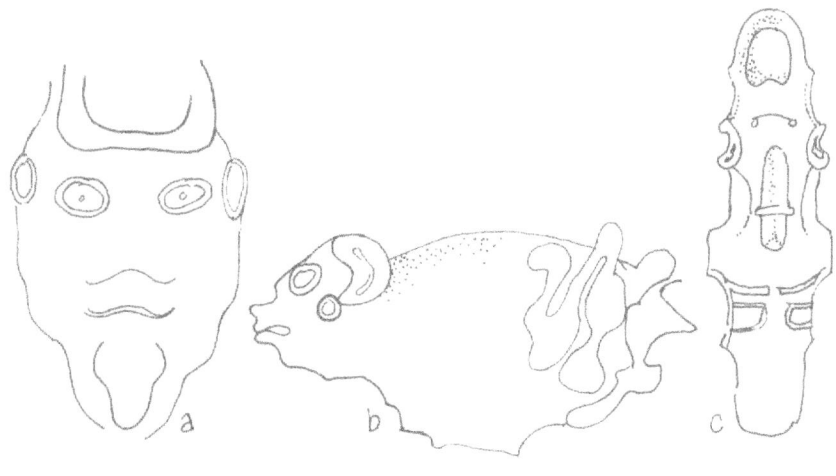

Figure 4.35 a-c. The Classic Mabaruma adorno. **a.** human, **b.** animal, **c.** bird.

In a variant of the method, appliqué fillets were placed on a hemispheric armature built up in the palm of the potter. On this armature, the image was developed additively by methods approaching true modeling, Figure 4.36c.

Figure 4.36a-e. **a.** Enmore cemetery, Demerara. Classic Mabaruma Hands-to-Face motif, **b.** Barabina. Turtle Head motif, **c.** Barabina. Bush Hog adorno, **d.** Vessel spout. Coporito, lower Orinoco, **e.** Barabina. Tattooed arm.

These techniques diverge significantly from practice on the lower Orinoco, where adornos were built up by coiling or were modeled in the solid (Sanoja O. 1979:127). The technique employed in the Barrancoid Coporito Subphase approximated conventional clay sculpture, as is indicated by the Incised and Modeled vessel spout shown in Figure 4.36d. Enough of the vessel wall survives to indicate that the cone-shaped nozzle was additionally built up with kneaded pellets

286

of clay on a circular base cut into the still plastic clay. These pellets remain clearly visible interiorly. Sutures produced by forcing more and more of them against one another on the ever decreasing nozzle diameter run transverse to the direction of the developing nozzle. As the nozzle diameter was progressively narrowed in the process, there was less and less possibility of eradicating these sutures which, accordingly, remain more clearly in evidence toward the tip of the spout, the shape and size of which exactly duplicate the proportions of the finger that was extracted from it upon completion. The animal face was built up by appliqué modeled and incised fillets deriving from contrasting schemata. The contrast with the spirally coiled armature employed on the lower Aruka River in the manufacture of an identical shape suggests a contrasting technology.

The various applications of *Barrancas Modeled Incised* ceramics on the lower Aruka River imply a relatively high level of social complexity when contrasted with the small, scattered communities of the Early Formative. Commencing at the latest sometime during the first millennium A.D., the female played a hitherto unknown role in rituals associated with key aspects of manioc subsistence, with hunting and with death.

The Distended Mouth adorno, the most widely distributed of these *Barrancas Modeled Incised* signs on the Aruka River, appears to have been associated with ritual chewing and tongue-tatooing in the preparation of the intoxicating beverage, *paiwari*, which is made from the manioc root. In the manufacturing process, the burnt cassava bread is chewed by women of the group by way of inducing fermentation. The quality of the resulting drink was believed to inhere in the chewing, the efficacy of which could be enhanced by the use of various charms that guaranteed sweetness, potency, sting, etc. in the drink. The mediating agency, a tattoo pattern applied to the lips, cheeks or tongue, conveyed these properties,

Figure 4.37. Akawaio Tattoo patterns (*after Batt 1957*). a. *Tedzang*, a bee pattern. b. *Aluai bipa*, (fish) skin pattern. c, j. *Arai*, spider patterns. d. *Tedzang*, a bee pattern (right forearm). e. *Tedzang*, a bee pattern (tattooed on knee). f-i, k. *Kanzuk*, scorpion's tail patterns.

themselves deriving from the natural world (honey bee, snake, scorpion, etc.) to the drink. The sting of the scorpion, bee or ant, the bite of the spider and of the camoudi snake were selected to represent the sweet, strong drink which the women desired to produce (Butt 1957; cf. Roth 1924:421). In the associated repertory of signs, particular tattoo patterns were applied to the lips, tongue or cheeks of women preparing the drink. Similarly, the arm used by the woman brewer in proffering the processed drink to the men was appropriately tattooed (cf. Gillin 1936:30), Figure 4.36e.

Occasionally, the significance of the Distended Mouth motif was emphasized by the incorporation of a salivating tongue, Figure 4.33a. Other drinking vessels were embellished with only this outsize mouth serving as a metaphor for the head, Figure 4.33b [23,27,28].

Figure 4.38. Karinya pottery vessels embellished with *kanzuk* motifs (Coll: *Walter Roth Museum*).

Another prominent *Barrancas Modeled Incised* motif, the King Vulture, Figure 4.34c, appears to have been associated with shamanic flight, and this may explain frequent representations of birds in funerary ceramics (e.g. Meggers and Evans 1957:Pls. 9c, 52c). At El Topacio in Colombia, Bray et al (1988:6) observed: "It is interesting to note the preponderance of birds and the total absence of anthropomorphic vessels in this cemetery." Bird bones are described among horticulturist grave offerings on the Suriname Coast (Boomert 1980:85). In Guyane française, the funerary regalia of the shaman included "wings" of macaw tail feathers attached to his arms, Figure 4.39a.

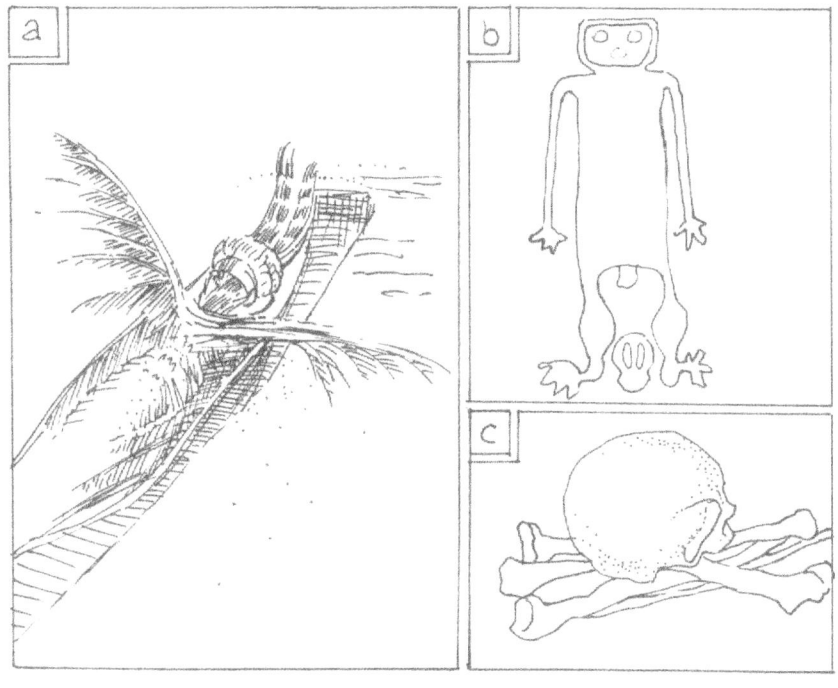

Figure 4.39a,c. a. Guyane française. Burial of a shaman *(after Rostain 1994:Figure 212)*, **b**. Head/foot symbol, Venezuela *(de Valencia et al 1987)*, c. Head-foot symbol, Guyana.

Concerning the so called Hands-to-Face motif, which occurs in *Barrancas Modeled Incised* decoration, Figure 4.36a, Reithel-Dolmatoff (1971:122) observed among the Desana of the North West Amazon: "To be seated in a crouching position, with the head between the hands, symbolizes death." The motif is very widespread in northern Amazonia (Palmatary 1960:98), where it appears to refer to an extremely ancient model of the universe. Schematized by Roe (1982:129) and compared by him to a cosmic layer cake comprising middle, upper and lower worlds connected by an *axis mundi*, this model varies from group to group in Amazonia mainly in the number of tiers constituting the celestial sphere, each tier being identified with a particular category of spirits and varying from four among the Yanomano to ten among the Secoya of northeastern Ecuador. The Hands-to-Face motif, elbows on knees, symbolically connects the head (up) and the legs (down) in a stereotype that has been widely interpreted in Amazonian art. The model is also widely symbolized in the domestic architecture of Amazonian and Antillean groups (reviewed in Roe 1982; Seigel 1992; see also Versteeg and Schinkel 1992).

This posture in horticulturist ceramics is already evidenced in Archaic mortuary practice on the Western Guiana Littoral. The entire skeletal series from the Piraka shell mound, comprising 17 adults, young adults and infants, had each been gilded on the head and legs before having been shrouded in a flexed or tightly flexed position and cremated. The mineral employed, an altered biotite indistinguishable from gold except in laboratory conditions (analysis by Golden Star Resources Limited, Guyana, 1995) adhered in particulate form to bones of the skull, lower legs and feet. The Barabina, excavations yielded a burial comprising a human skull atop a few postcranial bones, Figure 4.39c. Head/foot polarization is represented in an Archaic petroglyph from Carabobo State, Venezuela, by a human figure whose bulbous lower legs frame a skull, Figure 4.39b. This bulbous-legged stereotype survived in various ceramic cultures on the lower Amazon (Meggers and Evans 1957: Pl. 18), in Guyana (Williams 1993:Figure 8a), Suriname (Boomert 1980:Figure 19[4,5], Versteeg 1985:Figure 48d), in Colombia (Willey 1949: Pl. 39b,c), and Ecuador (Evans and Meggers 1968: Pis. 56, 57, 58a, 59, 60, 61b, 62b, 63). Head/foot symbolism occurs in a mortuary context among horticulturists on the Orinoco in the transition from the Corozal-111 and Camoruco-1 phases, ca. A.D. 400 (see Roosevelt 1980:Figures 85, 91), Figure 4.65h, as well as on Marajó Island at the Mouth of the Amazon (see Roosevelt 1991:1.22[5]), Figure 4.65i. An unusual specimen in stone from Guyane française represents a bird motif and a human foot in polar opposition, the concave back of the bird probably having served as an incense burner, with celestial conotations, Figure 1.11.

In the Antilles, an eighteenth century burial on Dominica incorporates the head-foot symbolism typical of Amazonian horticulturists:

> It [the grave] was fashioned like a well, about four feet in diameter, & six to seven feet deep. The corpse was here nearly in the same posture that I have described for those who were around the fire. His elbows rested on his knees, & the palms of his hands supported his cheeks ... He had sand only up to his knees.   (*Jean Baptiste Labat* cited in Whitehead 1992:159).

The Formative interaction sphere

Being themselves the potters, women of the Formative period were the sole manipulators of these sacred or magical signs, and thereby exercised a high level of social control. The sanctions of such power lay in the unique relationship held to exist between potter and clay. Among present-day Makusi, the Clay Mother (*Eshang*) is propitiated by food offerings at each mining episode. Warao and

Arawaks propitiate a similar deity (p. 398). The "living" properties of the clay were potentially exploitable through the agency of a specific repertory of schematized signs, each relating to a particular ritual system. The formal stability of these signs through time implies the rigidity of controls exercised by the Formative potters over key aspects of the associated ritual. These rituals related to the culture of the manioc root in all stages of its production and processing, Figure 4.35a, and thus ensured the very survival of the group. They related also to specific beliefs governing group practices in protein capture, Figure 4.35b, as well as to the thanatological activities of the shaman, Figure 4.35c, in which ceramic signs, deriving from an Archaic iconography, were used to speed the departing soul on its journey to the Land of the Dead in the western sky.

Such inter-related ritual systems imply a level of social complexity and population sizes that now were adequate to the functioning of a fully-fledged manioc-based economy. The "demic diffusion" that would be expected to have accompanied the rise of social complexity is now unequivocally evidenced in the archaeological record, notably in the wide dispersion of semantic signs diagnostic of Formative beliefs and practices relating to human subsistence and to death. In order to understand the routes followed in the diffusion of these beliefs and practices, attention needs to be paid to the importance of Kumaka Hill, representing, then as now, the last dry land connecting *terra firme* and the coastal swamps, Figure 4.40.

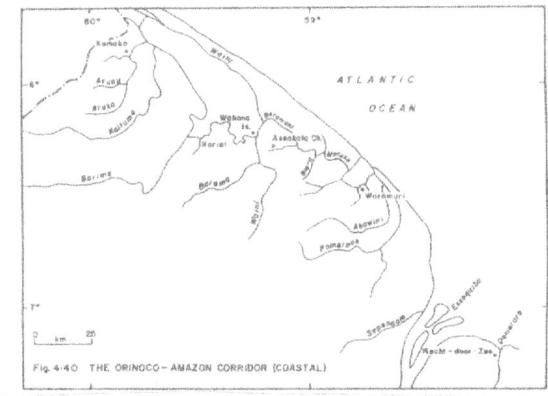

Figure 4.40. The Orinoco-Amazon corridor (Coastal).

Like their ancestors at Hosororo Creek, Arawak horticulturists occupying the hills of the lower Aruka River had been oriented, traditionally, to the lower Orinoco, *via* the Aruau-Amacuro watershed. Now, probably as a function of the indicated population growth, economic interest shifted from the hinterland to the coast as northwestern Guyana was drawn gradually into the interaction sphere of the lower

Amazon. This resulted from the re-establishment of contact with Proto-Eastern Maipurans whose long odyssey, begun on the Rio Negro some time during the second millennium B.C. or earlier, had taken them into the lower Amazon. There, they were bearers of the Incised and Modeled tradition, first recognized and defined at Barrancas on the lower Orinoco River. Like their Proto-Northern brethren, they made an early appearance in the Guianas, being already in evidence on the upper Essequibo by the closing centuries of the second millennium or the early centuries of the first millennium B.C. In due course, *via* the southeastern sector of the Amazon-Orinoco communications corridor, they re-established contact with their Orinocan brethren at Recht-door-Zee, the trade entrepôt at the Mouth of the Demerara River, Figure 4.41.

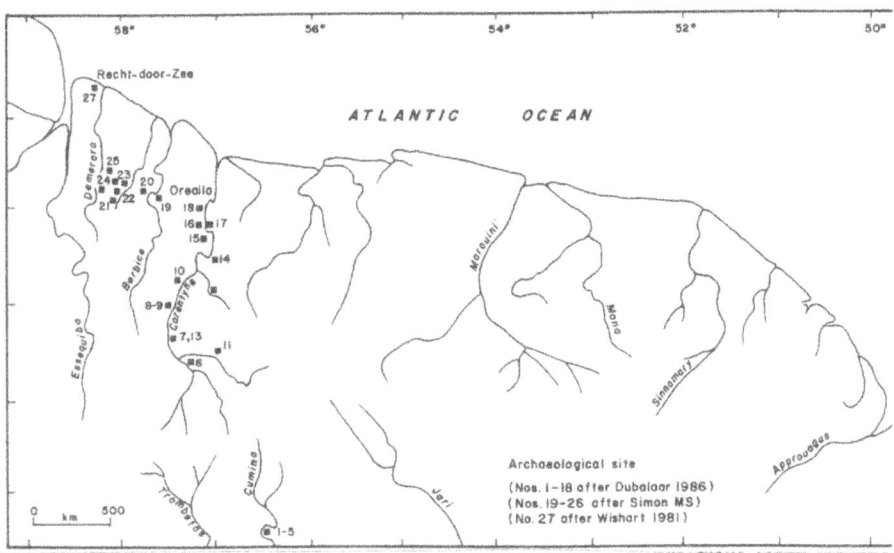

Figure 4.41. The southeastern sector of the Amazon-Orinoco communications corridor.

So named by seventeenth century Dutch colonists on the Berbice River, Recht-door-Zee was a waystation on their route across the Intermediate Savannas to Kykoveral on the Essequibo River. From Soesdyke, on the Demerara River, passage was had by canoe to the settlement at the river mouth, situated on one of the sand reefs that traverse the Guiana Coast east to west as far as the Essequibo River. Overland or by sea, the route then led to the mouth of the Essequibo River and thence *via* the streams of the northwestern sector of the Orinoco-Amazon communications corridor (Pomeroon-Koria-Barabara-Waini-Barima) to the Aruka River and the lower Orinoco, Figure 4.41a.

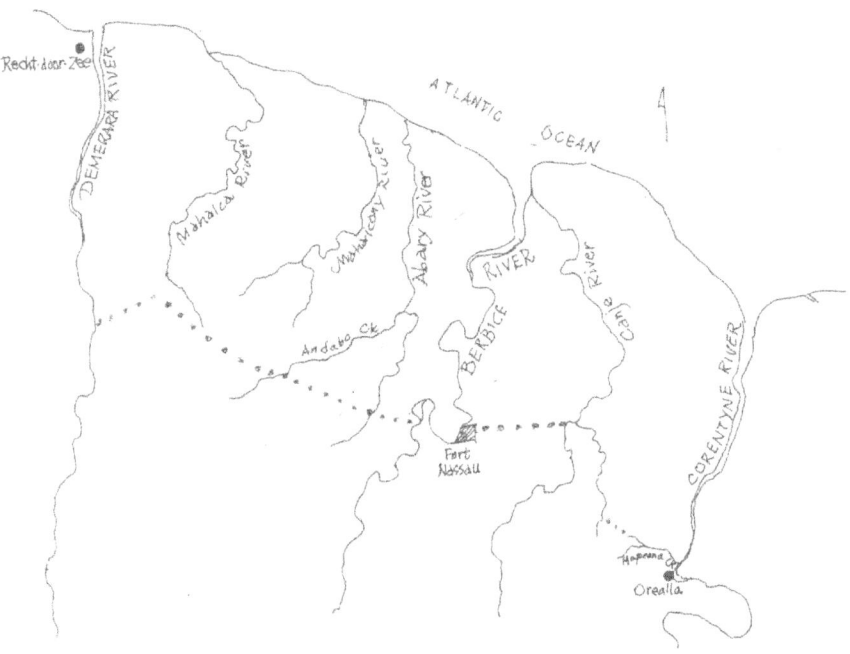

Figure 4.41a. The Amazon-Orinoco communications corridor (The Coastal Hinterland).

Where two contrasting though related linguistic groups meet over an extended period, their concourse, even if not inherently amicable, will be evidenced by an interchange of characteristic traits in the respective material cultures. The equivalent of a pidgin will emerge. The convergence of Arawaks representing the Incised and Modeled Classic Mabaruma ceramics of the lower Aruka River, and Arawaks representing the Incised and Punctate Arauquinoid ceramics of the trade entrepôt at Orealla on the Corentyne River was marked at Recht-door-Zee by a corresponding pidgin in ceramic typology, Figure 4.42.

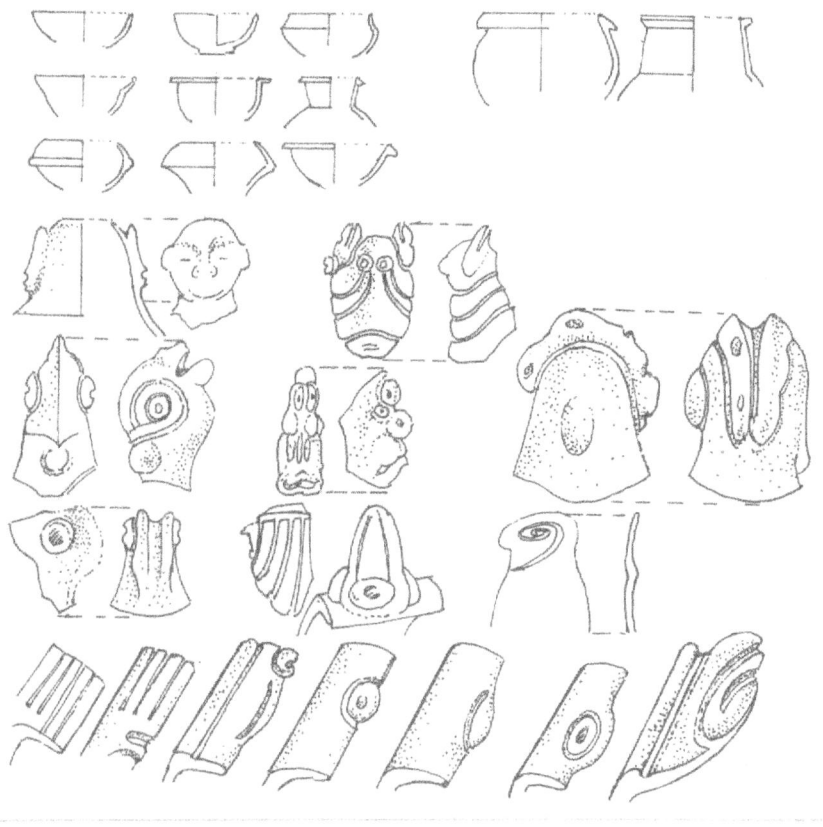

Figure 4.42. Classic Mabaruma, pottery encounters coastal Arauquinoid pottery at Recht-door-Zee, Demerara River.

Certain incised and modeled specimens of the Formative period at Recht-door-Zee were made on a kaolin-tempered paste typical of the Orealla complex on the Corentyne River, the raw material of which evidently had been manuported across the Intermediate Savannas from the Orealla Cliffs. Other specimens were on sand-tempered pastes that may or may not have been of the Mabaruma phase. A flanged bowl displaying a wide variety of incised and appliqué motifs of evident originality was the most popular shape at Recht-door-Zee. Significantly, it is precisely the two ceramic types of the Formative period on the Aruka River, *Barrancas Incised* and *Barrancas Modeled Incised*, long appropriated from the lower Orinoco inventory in the exigencies of the steatite trade, that now were incorporated in the [Arauquinoid] Orealla inventory at Recht-door-Zee. Equally significant in this polyglot assemblage, which included, also, the turtle (mortuary) element of the Karinya (Wishart 1982: Figure 5d), is the total absence of *Macapaima Punteado en Zonas* and *Macapaima Incision Corta* the incorporation of which had marked the demise of Formative on the Aruka River. Thus, the relationship between Recht-door-Zee and the lower Aruka River would appear to have been initiated in the Formative period, characterized by occurrences of only selected *Barrancas Incised* and *Barrancas Modeled Incised* decorative motifs.

At Recht-door-Zee, bowl flanges are characteristically massive, in some cases as much as 30 mm wide, and exhibit one to four deep, broad-line incisions concentric to the vessel rim and large, ovoidal or circular nubbins applied to the outer edges of rims, these nubbins being sometimes placed uniquely oblique to the direction of the flange. Typically, they are circumscribed by a broad-line incision. Incised and modeled decoration encompassed a new range of motifs or treated the traditional Mabaruma phase motifs, e.g., the Distended Mouth adorno (Wishart 1982:Figure 6k), in novel ways. Thus, by around A.D. 1000, the trading interests of Arawak groups at Orealla on the Corentyne River had come to exercise a profound influence on the original Formative pottery decoration of the lower Demerara River. This trade brought into being a string of settlements across the savannas, some of them linked, *via* the Abary, Mahaica and Mahaicony headwaters, with expanding settlements on the coastal sand reefs and sand ridges. The development of this coastal network, the Abary phase of the literature, hinged on the ready supply of strategic raw materials from *terra firme*. In due course, these coastal developments were felt as far inland as the complex of sites on the lower Aruka River, the source of amphibole schist.

Along this route, a small, badly eroded sherd sample recovered in the mantle of white sand covering Assakata Hill is all that has survived the loss of its topsoil and the disappearance of the village that once stood there. The founding of the present village by "Simon Lucas' father, who came from the Orinoco" to flee the Venezuelan War of Independence (1821), was evidently the immediate cause of this soil loss. The villagers who now farm the swamp edge report a shell mound in the neighborhood.

Assakata is located in the maze of inland waterways linking Arawak groups on the lower Aruka River with those at Recht-door-Zee on the Demerara River. The route traverses immense uninhabited expanses of freshwater swamp forest and the seasonally inundated grass savannas which once had been the open intertidal mudflats exploited by early Archaic Warao of the upper Waini shell mound complex. Just two speedboat hours from the Waini River, the as yet unexcavated Assakata shell mound probably served as a waystation on the route between the Waini and Moruka Rivers followed by craftsmen of the early Archaic canoe manufacturing industry (Arawak *sakada* v.t. = meet). Possibly it served a similar purpose in horticulturist times, for the ceramic refuse there affiliates both with the Aruka River and with Recht-door-Zee at the Mouth of the Demerara River. At the present time, Assakata is the only Mabaruma phase (Arawak) village so far known in the extensive swamps between the Moruka River and the upper Waini River. It is therefore of extreme value as the reciprocal of the waystation at Koriabo Point across the watershed on the Barima. River (N-4 in the terminology of Evans and Meggers 1960). There, the ceramic inventory is purely Mabaruman, i.e., with no sherds of Recht-door-Zee derivation, Figure 4.43. Downstream, at Drum Hill on the Barima right bank, recent recovery of a single sherd of *Mabaruma Plain* suggests another waystation on this ancient trade route.

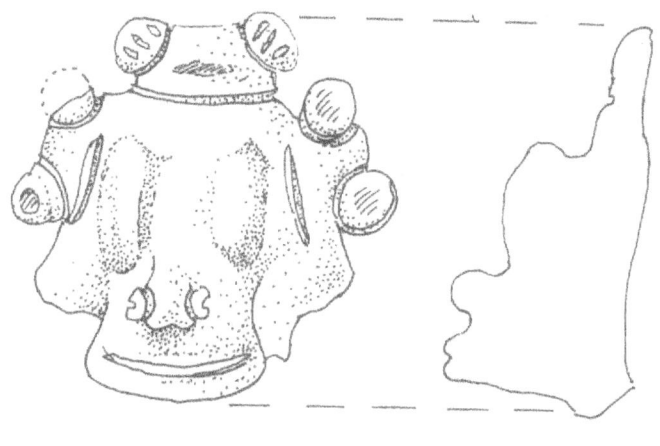

Figure 4.43. Koriabo Point, Barima River. A Classic Mabaruma trade entrepôt.

This settlement pattern seems to suggest that, as in Archaic times, the indicated trade network was maintained by a system of local relays. Occurrences of Hosororo Plain in the Assakata inventory, for which the clay was mined at Hotaquai on the upper Aruka River, may indicate that pottery clay, rather than finished vessels, traveled great distances as a trade item in Protohistoric times. Relays are even more unambiguously evidenced in the movement of steatite nodules through the system and along the Aruka River, *via* Kumaka Hill, into the lower Orinoco. With economic interchange went spiritual and religious communication. But while certain semantic signs evidently retained their value over great distances, with increasing distance from the Orinocan source there was an inevitable erosion of their formal integrity, e.g., Figures 4.42, 4.43. In due course, European artifacts began moving along the traditional routes.

The Protohistoric Mabaruma interaction sphere

In 1658, a Dutch colony planted in the previous year was already prospering some eleven miles up the Pomeroon River, with peaceful native villages stretching to around 40 miles upriver (Netto and Pereira 1962[1658]). Although this colony did not survive, Dutch interest in the area remained keen on account of Spanish activity further west. Accordingly, by 1746 a trading post was already functioning on the Moruka River

> ... under the direction of which are the rivers of Pomeroon and Waini... The road to the Spaniards leads past this Post, so that no one can go that road without the knowledge of the Postholder, who therefore, if he wishes, can generally get to know what is going on in Orinoco. (Harris and de Villiers 1911:80).

A French post had been sited at the Mouth of the Waini River in 1669. By 1684, unidentified Europeans were on the Barima River. Swedish prospectors were settled on the lower Waini in 1732, and various Dutch plantations were on the Barima, between 1768 - 1779. The last reported settler, possibly also Dutch, lived on the upper Barima around 1800 (Historical map, 1814). Thus, commencing in the mid-seventeenth century, European activity on the Western Guiana Littoral, initially intermittent, was to prove decisive in the destruction of the peoples of the Mabaruma phase over the next three hundred years.

Accordingly, the upper levels of the Apostaderan refuse on Kumaka Hill, which yielded also odd European items, corresponds with some part of the period between the first appearance of Europeans on the Pomeroon River in 1657 and Blair's expedition up the Waini River, *via* Kumaka Hill, in 1857. The lower levels of the deposit, i.e., below 15 cm depth, in which such items are absent, is wholly indigenous. Co-occurrences of Koriabo and Apostaderan potsherds in association with European artifacts in the uppermost levels of the Kumaka Hill deposit reflect the role of the Akawaio in Dutch surveillance of the Spanish on the lower Orinoco River. An Akawaio settlement on Koberimo Creek associated with datable Dutch wine jars and beer bottles seems to mark the Dutch frontier during the eighteenth century. By the mid-nineteenth century, the population at Kumaka Hill included, also, some Warao as well as Spanish Indians from the Moruka River who, earlier in the century, had fled the Bolivar Revolution (Blair 1980). The disintegration of the traditional economy was now irreversible. During the Postclassic period, elements of coastal culture were taken to the furthest limits of the hinterland by the Akawaio. Accordingly, Apostaderan refuse is mixed with Akawaio refuse at sites of the Koriabo phase along the Mazaruni River as far as the escarpment.

With the destruction of traditional infrastructures, radical changes in religious behaviors become evident, notably with regard to funerary ritual. An outstanding feature of these long-range interactions region-wide during the Postclassic period was the exchange of mortuary symbolism across ethnic frontiers. Thus, an unequivocal Classic Mabaruma Hands-to-Face motif of the Aruka River was recovered in a Postclassic cemetery of the Abary phase at Mon Repos on the Demerara Coast, Figure 4.36a., in direct association with a crescent-based figurine relating to funerary ritual on the Tapajós River and Marajó Island at the Mouth of the Amazon, Figure 4.44a. A distinctive feature of this figurine, comprising wavy locks placed on the occiput or the back of the neck as a directional device in mortuary ritual (i.e., to point the face of the deceased to the Land of the Dead in the western sky), was recovered in the Apostaderan assemblage on Kumaka Hill, Figure 4.44b. The device was likewise assimilated by Akawaio on the Mazaruni River, Figure 4.44c-e, who at the same time were purveyors of a mortuary symbolism of considerable antiquity on the upper Amazon, Figure 4.44f. The King Vulture motif symbolizing shamanic flight in the (Incised and Modeled) ceramics of the lower Aruka, Figure 4.24, appears in the (Incised and Punctate) Orealla inventory on the Corentyne River, Figure 4.25. Conversely, a version of this motif from Santarem, on the lower Amazon, depicting a King Vulture bearing on its beak a small bird (? a metaphor for the departing soul), is incorporated in the Classic Mabaruma inventory on the lower Aruka River, Figure 4.44g.

At the same time, resulting from their integration in the Postclassic coastal economies, certain decorative motifs, notably the Hands-to-Face adorno, the Distended-Mouth adorno, and the *Macapaima Incision Corta* and *Macapaima Punteado en Zonas* decorative elements were being carried by Akawaio potters up the Essequibo River to as far as Apoteri on the Rupununi confluence, as well as up the Potaro River and into the North Pakaraimas. This latter migration was still in progress during the later years of the nineteenth century, at which time Im Thurn

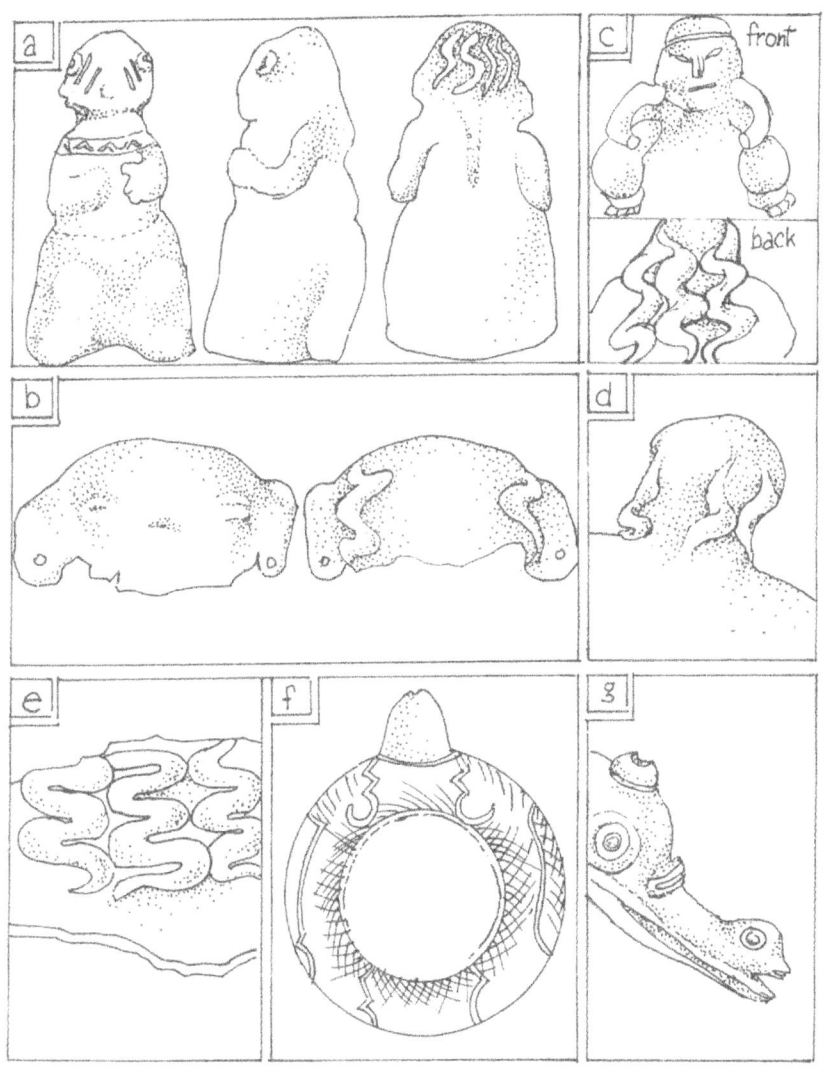

Figure 4.44 a-g. Dispersion of certain Postclassic traits. **a.** Mon Repos, **b-e.** Mazaruni River, **f.** Barabina, North West.

(1883:60) described a community of "at least two hundred men, women and children" attending a ceremonial gathering just below Amatuk Falls on the Potaro River. Postclassic Mabaruma phase decorative motifs, including *Macapaima Incision Corta*, have been recorded here, Figure 44h, and as far to the west as the Yawong Valley, in the Pakaraima foothills, Figure 44i, where they were absorbed by an incomparably older tradition. Protohistoric (Apostaderan) decorative motifs were taken as far to the east as the Rio Cajuaçú in the Trombetas Basin (Hilbert 1982: Figure 3J). As the great traders of the Guianas, the Akawaio were bearers of Protohistoric ceramic decoration *(Macapaima Inciso, Macapaima Punteado en Zonas)* across *terra firme* into Suriname, Figure 4.44j,k, and Guyane française, Figure 4.44l. The destruction of traditional polities following upon the various European incursions after the mid-seventeenth century is thus widely evidenced in the ceramic hybridizations that characterized the major horticulturist complexes of the Protohistoric period regionwide as, evidently, increasing secularization eroded reverence for the traditional icons.

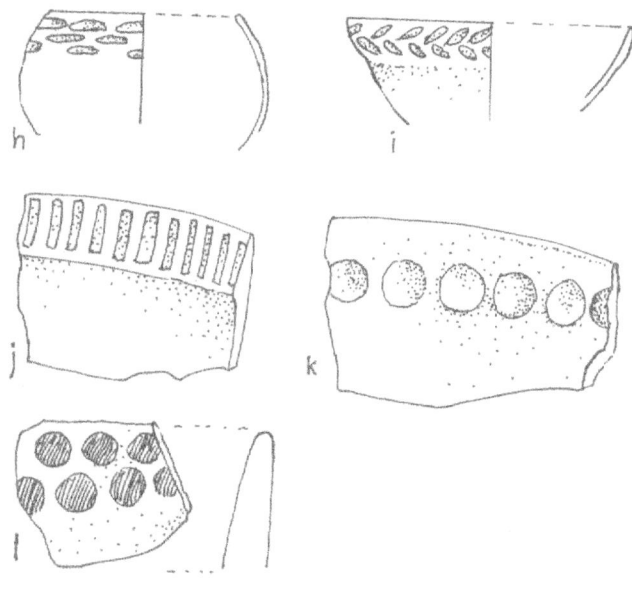

Figure 4.44h-l. **h**. Kuriebrong Mouth, Potaro River, **i**. Yawong Valley, Pakaraimas, **j, k**. Commetewane Creek, Commewijne, Suriname *(after Geijskes 1960-1961: 101)*. **l**. Rorota, Ile Ile de Cayenne *(after Roget et Roy 1975:6)*.

The Proto-Eastern Maipuran Arawak migrations
Introduction

Evidences of certain long-range inter-relationships now coming to light seem to lend support to the thesis (Lathrap, 1973) that Tropical Forest Culture was an artifact of Lowland adaptation dating possibly as far back as 4000 to 5000 B.C. Although Lathrap could adduce very little archaeological evidence in support of his views and despite the fact that the three known centers of agricultural origin in the Americas date no earlier than between about 5500 and 4000 years ago (Smith 1995), it is now becoming clear that certain of the traits considered definitive of Tropical Forest Culture, e.g., frame houses, the dugout canoe, pepperpot, bark cloth, basketry, and others (Steward 1949:708) in fact are of hoary antiquity in the Guianas, though, as suspected by Steward (1948:886) and as has been shown above, their times and places of origin differed. These differences contributed to early regional integration (Figure 3.1). While the earliest known pottery of the Guiana Coast derived from pre-agricultural shellfishing communities at the Mouth of the Amazon, its temporal survival was limited. On the other hand, the ceramic types and technologies that are diagnostic of the region-wide spread of a definitive horticultural adaptation also appear to have derived in an as yet unidentified area beyond the Guianas.

To Lathrap (1970:127), the dating and distribution of the Barrancoid ceramic styles of northern South America suggested that they had originated on the central Amazon or perhaps on the network of waterways connecting the Rio Negro and the Orinoco, their spread having accompanied the dispersal of the Maipuran Arawak languages during the first millennium B.C. As presently known, the representative Modeled Incised pottery enjoys a distribution from the Ucayali on the upper Amazon to Santarem on the lower Amazon and from the Casiquiare Canal on the upper Orinoco to Barrancas at its mouth. The postulated dispersal of Rouse's Proto-Northern Maipuran Arawaks is evidently coterminous with the distributions of Barrancoid Modeled Incised ceramics as well as with their diagnostic petroglyphs in the Orinoco Basin. Their earliest known site dates at Hosororo Creek, on the Aruka River, at around 1600 B.C. It should therefore be of interest to determine to what extent, if at all, presently available archaeological evidences may be found compatible with Rouse's hypothetical Proto-Eastern Maipuran Arawak dispersal down the middle and lower Amazon.

As on the Orinoco, distributions of the diagnostic *Timehri* petroglyphs constitute a clue to the route of this postulated Proto-Eastern migration. Occurrences of this highly distinctive petroglyph type are known on the Vaupés, the Negro, Cuminà, Corentyne and Berbice Rivers. Other than in the Orinoco Basin, *Timehri* petroglyphs are unknown elsewhere in the Guianas, Figure 4.15a-e.

On the Corentyne, important assemblages are known at the type site, Timehri Rock, as well as at Wonotobo Falls. An assemblage at Marlisa Falls on the Berbice

River suggests local penetration from the Corentyne. Thus, the route of Rouse's Proto-Eastern Maipuran Arawak migration incorporated an important hinterland component and indeed may never have reached the Mouth of the Amazon. Just as the Proto-Northern contribution to the spread of horticulture in the Guianas was made *via* the Western Guiana Littoral, so now the Proto-Eastern contribution was made *via* the Eastern Guiana Hinterland.

Representative specimens of this Timehri-type petroglyph on the Berbice and Corentyne Rivers are located on a presently submerged horizon indicating their imposition during a period of sustained reduced precipitation and therefore in an environment very different from that of the dense rain forest of the present day. During an "extreme drought" in 1975, a visitor (cited in Dubelaar 1986:76) described the low water level prevailing at the Wonotobo Falls site. The boulders constituting today's waterfalls there, Figure 4.45, stood high and dry in the sand of the riverbed.

> One could walk between them as between the walls of the houses in a street. The soil was a magnificent sandy plain where we found countless washed up potsherds and roughly chipped-off pieces of green and white quartz.

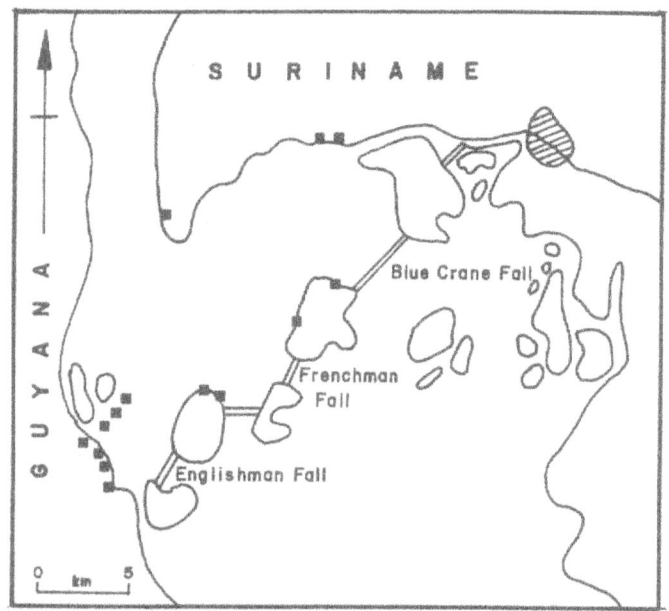

Figure 4.45. Wonotobo Falls. A site of the Proto-Eastern Maipuran Arawak migration. (*redrawn after Boomert 1983*).

Overlying a deposit of Saladoid pottery there, in an 85 cm deep profile, was a deposit of Barrancoid sherds, unfortunately undated. Barrancoid sherds at the Buckleburg-1 site on the Suriname Coast yielded a date sequence ranging between A.D. 115 - 635 (Versteeg 1985:Table 27). Unfortunately, since the archaeology of the Corentyne River remains unknown, the Barrancoid occupation of Wonotobo Falls can only be estimated to have dated some time before A.D. 700. To the present, Wonotobo Falls represents the only Saladoid-Barrancoid sequence so far known anywhere in the Eastern Guiana Hinterland. In the diagnostic test pit (Cut 1), the profile exhibited no clearly defined interface between its Saladoid and Barrancoid components. Its four lowest levels (50 to 85 cm) yielded exclusively Saladoid ceramics. In the overlying 30 cm (i.e., between 20 - 50 cm) Saladoid pottery still dominates, though, in the uppermost two levels (0 - 20 cm) its popularity declines in favor of the Barrancoid component (Boomert 1983:98). The overlap suggests a gradual transition from the one ceramic type to the other rather than an abrupt replacement of one by the other. (cf. Cruxent and Rouse 1961: Tables 9 - 12).

The correspondence between this Corentyne Saladoid-Barrancoid sequence and the known Saladoid-Barrancoid sequence on the lower Orinoco River lends support to Lathrap's notion (1970:112) of ultimately an upper Amazon origin of the Saladoid ceramics of Venezuela. In Lathrap's view, the ancestral complex on the upper Amazon should date a millennium or more earlier than the date of its earliest presently known representatives.

In such a scenario, the Corentyne sites would represent a late stage in the postulated Proto-Eastern Maipuran Arawak migration down the Amazon, earlier sites of which should be identifiable elsewhere, for example in the northern drainages of the lower Amazon. This Barrancoid migration should have been preceded by a Saladoid one. Lathrap's reconstruction of the Barrancoid migration rested on his identification of certain decorative traits and vessel shapes which spread out of the Central Amazon mainly during the first millennium B.C. and remained detectable as an early component in certain middle and lower Amazon complexes such as Jauari on the Rio Curuá, early Konduri at the Mouth of the Trombetas, early Santarem at the Mouth of the Tapajós and early Itacoatiara, just above Manaus, among others. Unfortunately, these sites all remain undated. Thus, Lathrap noted, "At present no securely dated styles of a sufficient age to be picked as the source of Barrancas are known." But although the author was able (1970:121) to suggest a Barrancoid-to-Polychrome transition on the Rio Japurá by around A.D. 700, no painted decoration antecedent to the Incised and Modeled tradition, and in which a Saladoid-to-Barrancoid transition may have been perceived, was detected by Lathrap at any site on the lower Amazon. Therefore, the Saladoid-to-Barrancoid sequence reported at Wonotobo Falls on the Corentyne raised expectations that painted pottery antecedent to the Incised and Modeled specimens identified by

Lathrap (1970: Figure 17) must exist elsewhere in the southern Guianas.

Proto-Eastern Maipuran Arawaks on the upper Essequibo

These expectations were heightened somewhat by the subsequent recovery of a single red-on-white painted, caraipé-tempered rim sherd on Seba Creek, a small tributary of the Corentyne River, during investigations at the extensive Hertenrits site at nearby Orealla. Unfortunately, persistent test pitting over a wide area of the badly eroded high ground of the right creek bank failed to increase the sample of decorated sherds. The associated surface collection of Hertenrits (Arauquinoid) sherds suggested that the solitary painted specimen had survived removal of the top soil and had become mixed with later materials. Thus, in the absence of other, more unequivocally diagnostic traits, a Saladoid presence on the Corentyne River other than at Wonotobo Falls could not be demonstrated at this site.

Subsequent excavations in *terra preta* at Kurupukari Falls on the upper Essequibo River provided a better demonstration of the sequence, Figure 4.46.

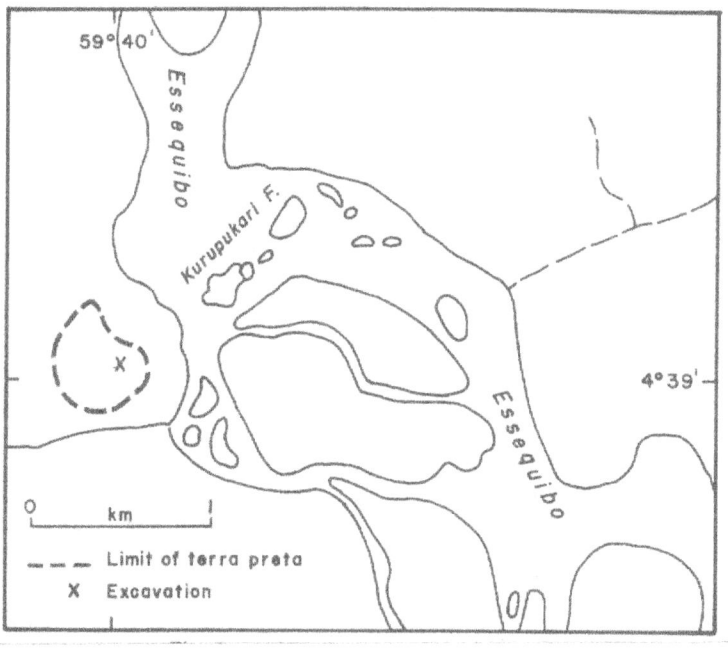

Figure 4.46. Kurupukari Falls, Essequibo River.

The Kurupukari Falls site is located on the left bank Essequibo River, some 320 km above its mouth. At this point, the riverbank stands around 3 m above the dry season water level and rises immediately inland perhaps another meter, where higher ground is presently occupied by a multi-household compound, garden plots and regrowth bush. The appeal of the spot to its original occupants was undoubtedly the feeding ground provided by the waterfall for an abundant supply of pacu fish *(Myleus pacu)*. The associated petroglyph complex shows the site to have been exploited by fish poisoning, spear fishing, and a variety of fish traps since at least Archaic time. The midden lies in 80 cm of *terra preta* measuring 700 x 600 m.

The earliest three levels of the profile displayed an array of vessel shapes which in various details exactly duplicated Saladoid specimens in the Wonotobo Falls inventory, Figure 4.47a-e, while others were specific to Kurupukari Falls, Figure 47f-j. Notable among the shared vessel shapes were the bowl with constricted neck and everted rim, Figure 4.47a, specimens with concavo-convex side walls and tapered, rounded or beveled lips, Figure 4.47c, and carinated bowls, Figure 4.47d, all three being also prominent in Venezuelan Saladoid inventories. The collared jar at Figure 4.47f, an Archaic shape not represented at Wonotobo Falls, was nonetheless a favored vessel in the Venezuelan Saladoid (e.g. Vargas 1979:Figure 41).

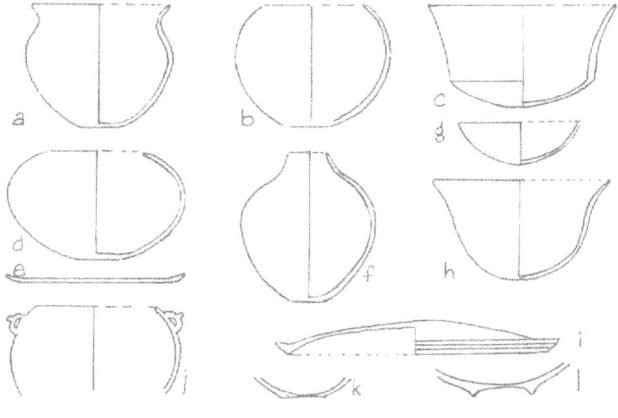

Figure 4.47 a-l. Kurupukari Falls. Saladoid vessel shapes.

Decoration was by painting, red wash and incision, with some rim lobing. Occasionally, a circular or ovoidal-sectioned peg was attached to the tops of vertical strap handles. Painting was white-on-red or red-on-white with both techniques occasionally employed on a single vessel. Many vessels were red painted or white-slipped interiorly. White slip was sometimes erased in parts in order to produce a negative red design of narrow, parallel bars. Although, mostly, sherds are too badly eroded to permit recognition of particular design elements, rectilinear vertical/horizontal bands, sometimes set at right angles, survive in a few cases on the upper walls of concavo-convex vessels, and on the interior rims of shallow, inverted dishes that in other contexts served as covers of burial urns, Figure 4.48.

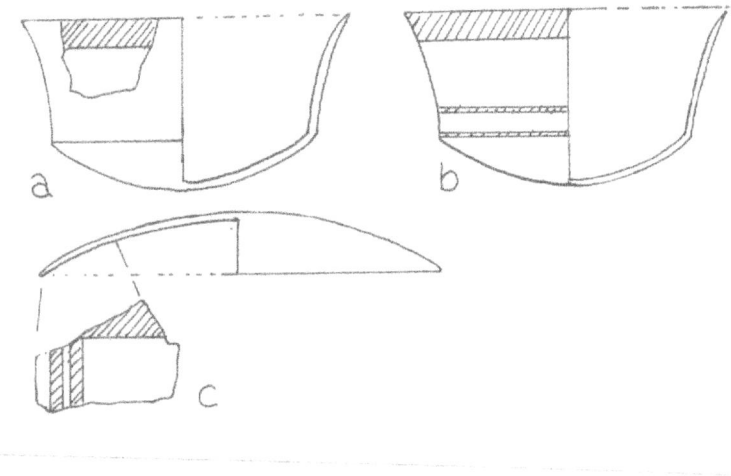

Figure 4.48. Kurupukari Falls. Saladoid white-on-red decoration.

Incision was dominantly fine-line, *(Apoteri Incised)*, Figure 4.49a-d. An alternative mode, *Apoteri Zoned Incised* (motif 1), opposed double, sometimes triple, vertical half-moon elements, somewhat like parentheses, in zones delimited by horizontal incisions, Figure 4.49e-g. Fine-line incision was employed, also, to delimit the boundaries of painted zones. Certain specimens display an alternative technique of ragged incision into a white slip on a leatherhard paste, *Apoteri Zoned Incised* (motif 2), Figure 4.49h-j.

Zoned Incised hachure, Figure 4.49 k, l, was applied on the interiors of what may be covers of burial urns.

Broad-line incision was early employed for the distinctive Scroll-and-step-fret element that constitutes the basis of *Apoteri Incised* decoration, Figure 4.49m. The scroll was extremely long-lived as a minor element in Saladoid incised or painted decoration.

Figure 4.49. Apoteri Incised motifs in Saladoid decoration.

Ceramic tempering materials were caraipé and sand, the latter either fine and waterworn or crushed decayed granite. Caraipé was mixed with either type in proportions varying from almost pure caraipé to almost pure sand. Classification of the sherd sample by temper was therefore approximate. Moreover, such classification revealed no correlation between temper mode and vessel shape. Therefore, for purposes of description and intersite comparison, ceramic categories could be recognized only on the basis of decoration.

Besides confirming the Saladoid identity of early Kurupukari Falls ceramics, such comparisons raise a few puzzling questions. The Scroll-and-step-fret element appears to suggest an affiliation with Early Tutishcainyo pottery on the central Ucayali (cf. Lathrap 1970: Figure 7f). The significance of this remains unclear. Early Tutishcainyo dates at around 2000 B.C. The early levels at Kurupukari date between 2910 +/- 80 B.P., Cal B.C. 1315-890 (Beta 76247) on 45-60 cm, and 2660 +/- 70 B.P., Cal B.C. 925-770 (Beta 96854) on 60-70 cm. Obviously, more early Saladoid sites remain to be investigated on the central and lower Amazon. In the meantime, the present occurrence seems to provide support for Lathrap's (1970:112) hypothesis of an upper Amazon origin for Saladoid ceramics a thousand or more years before the date of the earliest presently known Saladoid site. The popularity of the Scroll-and-step-fret design element increased through time at Kurupukari Falls. In due course, it was assimilated in broad-line Barrancoid decoration, representing an important difference with Orinocan design inventories. The Scroll-and-step-fret was widely employed in ceramic decoration on Marajó Island at the Mouth of the Amazon (e.g. Meggers and Evans 1957:Pl. 60).

The specimen of *Apoteri Zoned Incised* decoration shown in Figure 4.49j appears also to suggest affiliation with a distinctive meander pattern in Early Tutishcainyo pottery (cf. Lathrap 1970:Figure 7f), and the comparison may be thought to extend, also, to the vessel on which the design occurs -- the open bowl with concavo-convex upper wall that was characterized by Lathrap (1970:85) as the most common Early Tutishcainyo form. The carinated bowl occurring in early Saladoid levels at Kurupukari Falls is another common form in Early Tutishcainyo ceramics.

On this time level, Zoned Incised Hachure was being employed in ceramics of the Ananatuba phase on Marajó Island, at the Mouth of the Amazon (Meggers 1987: Figure 2). It is also well represented in the undated Jauari phase on the lower Amazon left bank (Hilbert and Hilbert 1957).

Certain early Saladoid vessels exhibit rims with exteriorly thickened lips or with narrow flanges displaying one or more broad-line incision on the interior surface. Appliqué nubbins atop vertical strap handles may be thought a form of incipient modeling which in due course provided a base for the *in situ* development of the more typically Barrancoid Incised and Modeled motifs that are characterized by *Kurupukari Incised and Modeled* decoration, Figure 4.50. Continuing occurrences of Saladoid painted decoration and vessel shapes representing *Kurupukari Painted*, Figures 4.47, 4.48, suggest a slow *in situ* development. However, on the basis of their relative frequencies, Saladoid decoration gave way to Barrancoid in the upper six levels of the Kurupukari profile. With the apparently still developing motifs of *Apoteri Incised* and *Apoteri Zoned Incised*, the Kurupukari Falls inventory now comprised a highly distinctive mix of decoration. However, tempering materials, and to a large extent vessel shapes, remained unchanged.

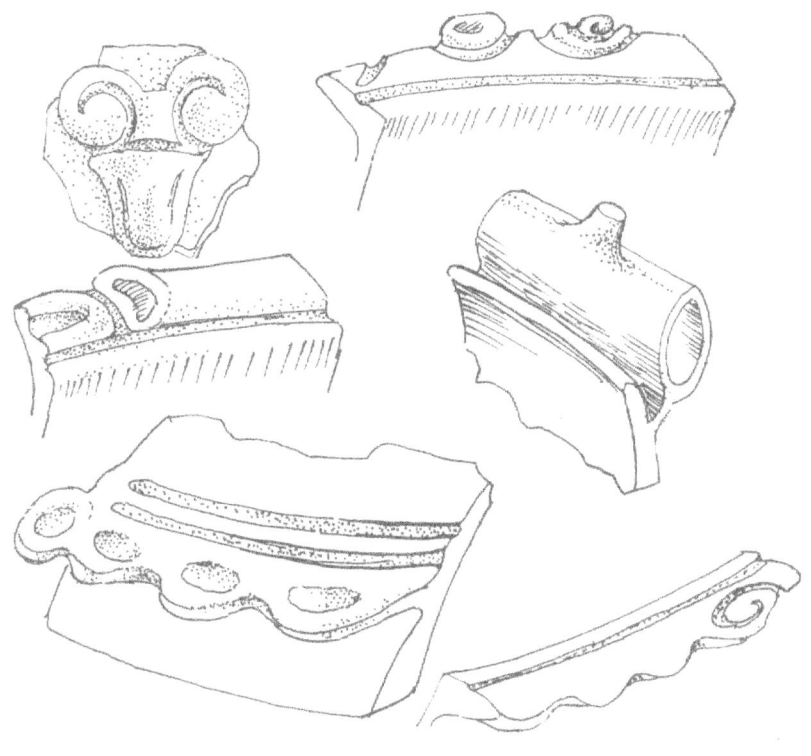

Figure 4.50. *Kurupukari Incised and Modeled* decoration.

On certain specimens of *Kurupukari Incised*, Figure 4.51a, and *Kurupukari Painted* vessels, from the earliest Saladoid levels, e.g. Figure 4.49c, the design element was applied on the interior of a shallow inverted bowl which, from its shape and the interiorly placed decoration, has been interpreted as the lid of a burial urn. This distinctive vessel is of extremely wide distribution in time and space. Rare specimens bear zoned incised hachuring, the elements of which appear to have served a directional function in mortuary ritual, Figure 4.49k, l, (Williams 1993). Urn lids, Figure 4.51a, are distinguished from bowls, Figure 4.51b, by an extremely shallow angle of body-wall to the horizontal at their rims, usually 25° - 40°, the majority being around 30°. At their rims, body-walls of bowls typically range between 55° - 80° from the horizontal.

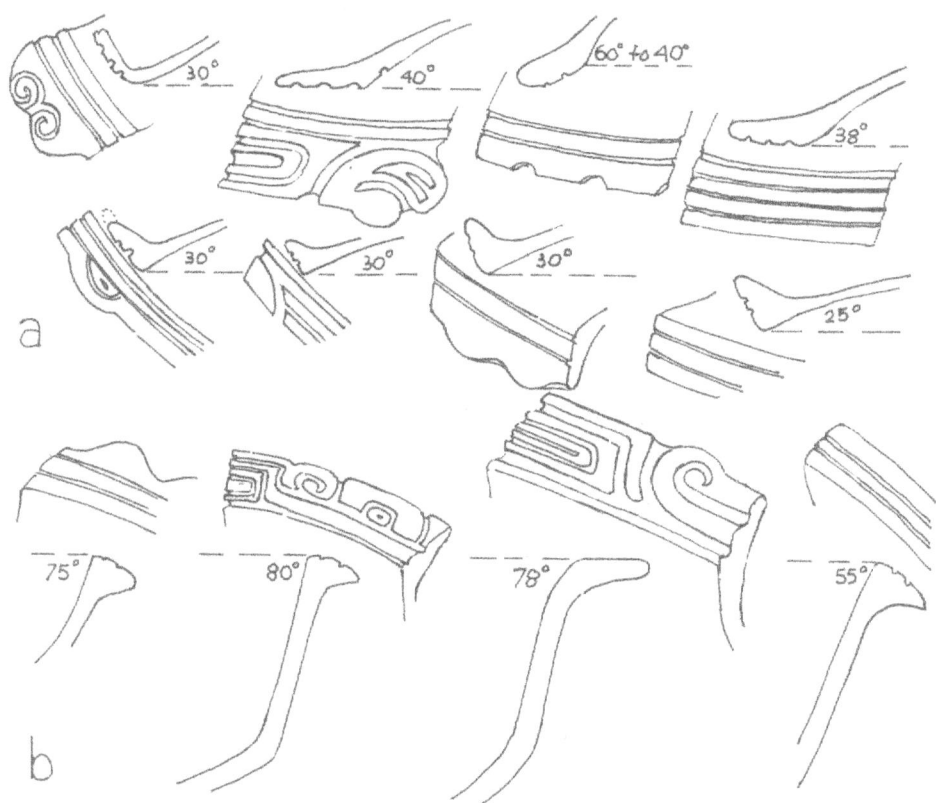

Figure 4.51. Kurupukari Falls. **a.** Incised urn lids, **b.** incised bowls.

Though rare, occasional reports of these vessels encountered *in situ* leave no doubt concerning their function. At Akawabi Hill in northwestern Guyana, Verrill (1918:15, Figures 10 - 12) excavated a seated burial above whose occiput had been placed an inverted ceramic dish, the illustrations of which exactly conform to the shallow, inverted vessel that is indicated in various complexes by the surviving sherds. Urn burials on the Abary River were found similarly covered upon excavation (Verrill 1918a:Figure 4). In an Abary phase cemetery, Quelch (1894:4) described

> a large and deep basin of strong make, the rim and inner portions are very considerably and elaborately ornamented by indented patterns...

A specimen was recovered intact at Kwatta, on the Suriname Coast (Goethals MS Pl. 7.4). Other excavated specimens have been reported by Boomert (1980:85) in Suriname and Rostain (1994:Figure 7.1) in Guyane française. Interiorly incised urn lids of the Mazagão phase at the Mouth of the Amazon were provided with a deep collar which, in an inverted position, suggests an annular base. According to their investigators (Meggers and Evans 1957:64):

> If the lid had not been found *in situ* on the jar mouth and neck, one might reconstruct quite differently the position and usage of this inverted basinlike lid. It appears as if these elaborately incised basins on a high pedestal might have been made for some other use than as lids because the applique and incising along the inner edge of the bowl were completely hidden by inversion over a burial.

Certain specimens in the Kurupukari Falls inventory were provided with holes in the rim presumably to secure immovably the attachment of lid to urn. The arrangement would appear to confirm their directional function. These urn lids occurred on the earliest, Saladoid, levels and continued throughout the sequence. The highest frequencies occurred in *Kurupukari Incised and Modeled* ceramics. Their probable function is reconstructed from sherds in Figure 4.52.

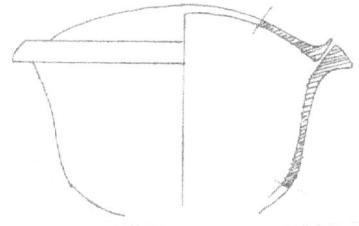

Figure 4.52. Kurupukari Falls. Hypothetical reconstruction of the function of urn lids.

Other vessels in the Kurupukari Falls inventory, e.g., Figure 4.53a, similarly invite comparison with ceramics recovered in burial contexts. An unprovenanced (Apostaderan ?) bowl recorded by Roth, Figure 4.53b, comprises an inward-facing adorno similar to an Apostaderan specimen dredged up in the Mazaruni River, Figure 4.53c. This latter incorporates the wavy locks that have been interpreted as a directional sign in the mortuary ritual (cf. Figure 4.44a-e).

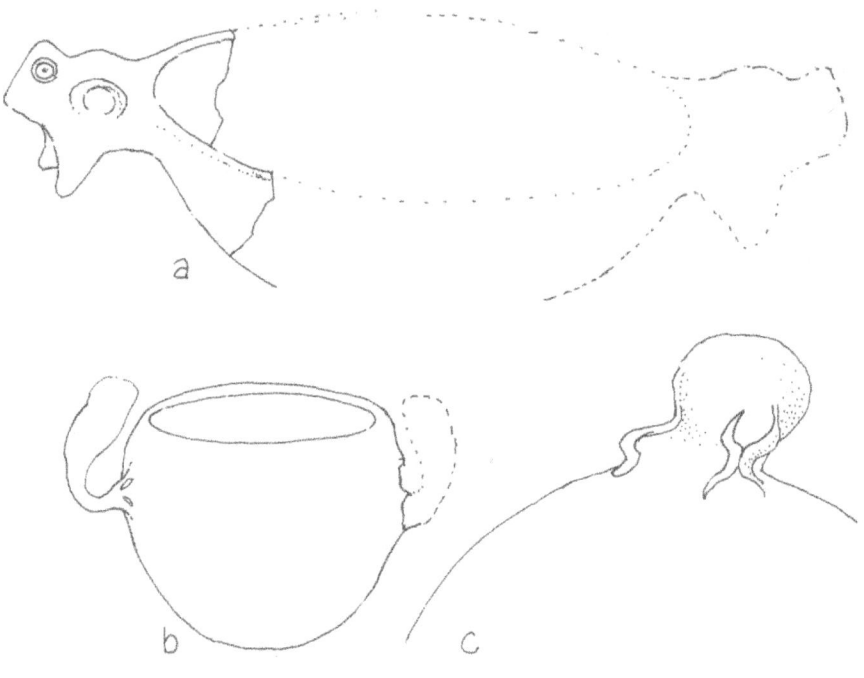

Figure 4.53. Probable funerary ceramic vessels. a. Kurupukari Falls, b. unprovenanced, after Roth 1924: Figure 32, c. Mazaruni River.

At Kurupukari Falls, a distinctive collared jar provided with a pair of strap handles on or above the shoulder apparently also served in mortuary ritual, Figure 4.54a. A specimen was recovered in a probable burial cache at Seba on the Demerara River, Figure 4.54b. A similar specimen was recovered in an Abary phase cemetery at Mon Repos, Figure 4.54c. The specimen at Figure 4.54d was recorded in a burial context at Palo Seco, Trinidad. A specimen representing the transition between the Corozal-III and Camoruco-I phases on the Orinoco River (ca. A.D. 400) was recovered near the knees of an intact human skeleton at Corozal (Roosevelt 1980:Figure 91).

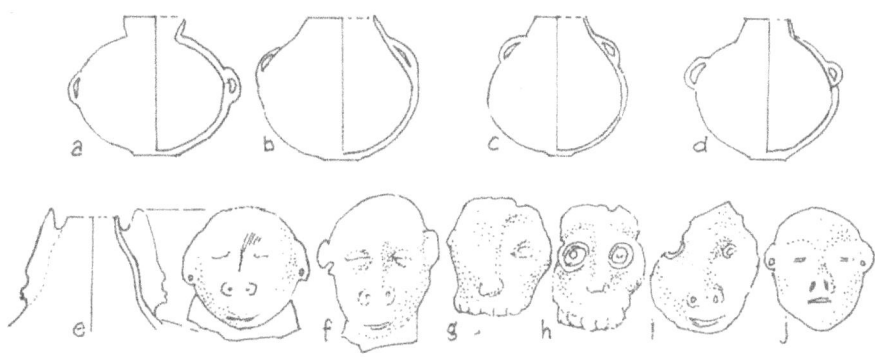

Figure 4.54. a-j. Ceramic funerary furniture. **a**. Kurupukari Falls, **b**. Seba, Demerara River *(after Carter 1943)*, **c**. Abary phase, Mon Repos *(Coll. Walter Roth Museum)*, **d**. Palo Seco, Trinidad, *(after Bullbrook 1953: Figure 9a)*, **e**. Recht-door-Zee, Demerara River, **f**. Funerary anthropomorph, Abary phase, *(after Wishart 1982)*, **g**. Mazaruni River, **h**. Commewijne District, Suriname, **i**. Rupununi Savannas *(after Evans ad Meggers 1969: Figure 123 a)*, **j**. Silver Sands, Barbados, *(after Drewett 1991: Pl. 18)*.

Modeled and/or incised specimens of this collared jar sometimes incorporated a distinctive funerary anthropomorph, Figures 4.54e-j.

An incised nozzle fragment at Kurupukari Falls may have derived from a small, spouted bowl. A spouted bowl bearing the fine-line Scroll-and-step-fret motif of the upper Amazon, thought to permit access to the supernatural world (Roosevelt 1991:79), occurs in Koriabo phase pottery on the Mazaruni River, Figure 4.44f.

The role of women in mortuary ritual is again suggested by the elaborate urn lids of the Kurupukari phase, though, unlike the situation obtaining in Classic Mabartima times on the lower Aruka River, the ceramics provide no evidence of the ritualizing of manioc.

Judged on the basis of sherd density/level, the Kurupukari Falls population peaked around 2080 +/- 70 B.P., Cal 215 B.C. to A.D. 75 (level 4) (Beta 76246). There was a corresponding enhanced elaboration in ceramic decoration, particularly in the incised types, *Kurupukari Incised and Modeled, Apoteri Incised* and *Apoteri Zoned Incised*. While vessel shapes and temper modes remained the same, heavy rim and waist flanges characterized by deep broadline incisions now began to appear. Rare three-dimensional adornos were added to the rims of certain vessels for the first time, one specimen comprising an inward-facing zoomorph with coffee-bean eyes on a small open bowl of asymmetrical plan, Figure 4.53a. The "parentheses" element in *Apoteri Zoned Incised* (motif 2) was combined with parallel incisions on the interiors of urn lids. The "Saladoid" design motifs of *Kurupukari Painted* unfortunately have not survived, though vestigial red or white paint on several specimens show that this decorative mode remained popular into level 2. Thus, having initiated the sequence, Saladoid decoration co-occurred with Barrancoid during the middle levels, and disappeared completely before abandonment of the site.

With the peaking of the Kurupukari Falls population in the closing centuries B.C., other design elements that now are associated with the Polychrome Tradition began to appear. These included grooving *(acanalado)*, fingernail ridging, scraping, brushing and serial fingertip impressions, Figure 4.55a-g.

These upper (Barrancoid) levels of the Kurupukari Falls site display a number of decorative motifs of *Apoteri Incised* that are virtually identical to those on certain sherds from Itacoatiara on the Lower Amazon left bank where they have been assigned to the Polychrome Guarita Subtradition.

Since this raises again the as yet unresolved issue of the origin of the Polychrome Tradition, it may be useful to invoke Lathrap (1970:157) once more.

> ... characteristics of the Guarita sub-tradition were present in the Central Amazon by AD 500 to 600 at the latest. The emergence of the Guarita tradition occurs as a gradual evolution out of the previous Barrancoid styles and there is no logical necessity for invoking a separate wave of migration.

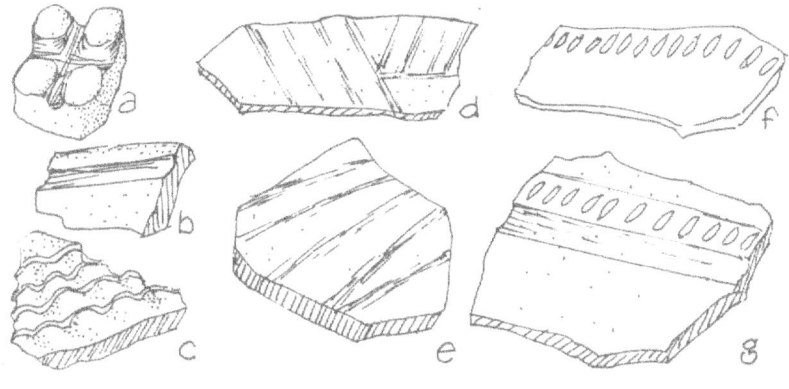

Figure 4.55 a-g. Polychrome techniques in the Kurupukari Falls inventory. **a,b**. Grooving, **c**. Fingernail ridged *(serrungulado)*. **d**. Scraping, **e**. Brushing, **f,g**. Serial fingertip impressions.

In light of the co-occurrence of their respective diagnostic design motifs in the Kurupukari Falls inventory during the apogée of the Barrancoid style there, this site on the upper Essequibo River would appear not to have been far removed from the heartland of both the Guarita and Saracá Subtraditions of the Polychrome Horizon Style, Figure 4.56a-h.

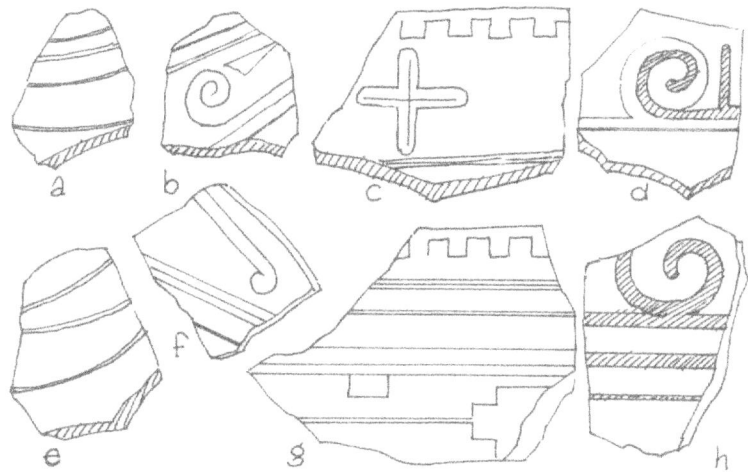

Figure 4.56 a-h. Comparative decorative traits in the Polychrome Guarita Subtradition. **a-d**. Itacoatiara *(after Evans and Meggers 1968:Pl. 81 h,j,k,n)*. **e-k**. Kurupukari Falls.

Dating as it does around the opening years of the Christian Era and the immediately preceding centuries, the ancestral position assigned to Itacoatiara with respect to Guarita in Lathrap's (1970) chronological chart would seem to have resulted from the extraordinary survival of *Apoteri Incised* techniques and motifs, Figure 4.57 a-c, occurring in earlier Saladoid decoration. Already nearly a thousand years old on the upper Essequibo River, *Apoteri Incised* appears to have been preceded there by Saladoid white-on-red/red-on-white painting, zoned incision, and the Scroll-and-step-fret motif. Along with zoned incision and the Scroll-and-step-fret motif, *Apoteri Incised* appears to have been absorbed locally in earlier Saladoid decoration. By around the time of Christ, an *Apoteri Incised* component still survived in a Saladoid deposit at Wonotobo Falls on the Corentyne River, Figure 4.57d. Indeed, *Apoteri Incised* continued to play an important role in Polychrome ceramics on the lower Amazon over the ensuing centuries, notably in the Caparu phase (Saracá Subtradition) immediately beyond the Acarai watershed, on the Rio Uatimã, Figure 4.57e-g. As has been seen, Figure 4.55c, the drag-and-jab technique which is definitive of the Saracá Subtradition, already occurs at Kurupukari Falls at +/- 0 A.D. Initiation of the Caparu phase has been placed at around A.D. 990 (Miller 1992).

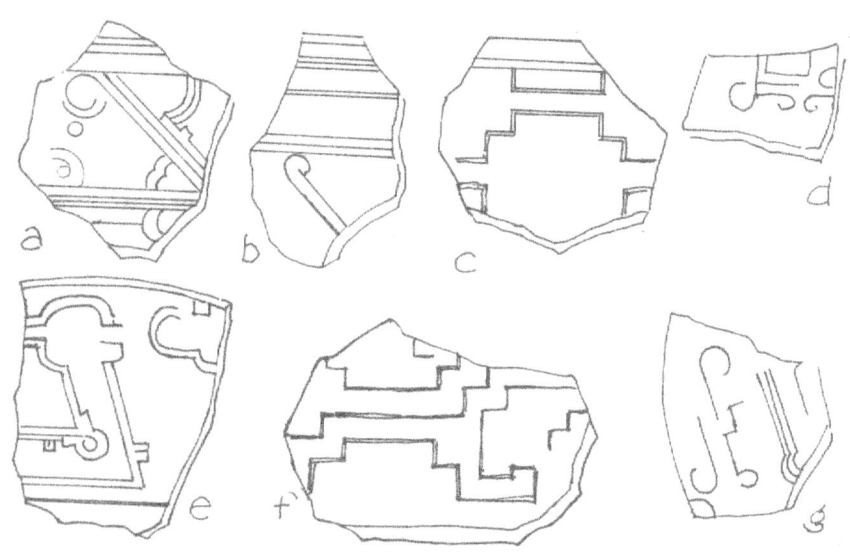

Figure 4.57. a-c. Kurupukari Falls, Essequibo River. Apoteri Incised motifs. d. Wonotobo Falls, Corentyne River (*after Boomert 1983*), e-g. Caparu Inciso, Rio Uatumã (*after Miller 1992*).

Thus, on the basis of both petroglyphic and ceramic distributions, the archaeological evidences lend ready support to Rouse's linguistic reconstruction of a Proto-Eastern Maipuran Arawak dispersal down the Orinoco and the Amazon Rivers. The latter route lay across the Acarai watershed and down the Corentyne River, and not *via* the Mouth of the Amazon as Rouse supposed. In the process, *via* the various decorative motifs characterizing the ceramics of the group at Kurupukari Falls during the centuries immediately preceding the opening of the Christian Era, the Proto-Easterners contributed to the rise of the Guarita and Saracá Subtraditions of the Polychrome Horizon Style.

At around this time, Barrancoid decoration there reached its apogée in the context of an expanded population. Granted the introduction of certain radically new motifs in ceramic decoration, Figure 4.55 a-g, this population expansion may not have been entirely natural. However, the new influences, the sources of which remain in doubt, did nothing to modify the traditional broad-line Incised and Modeled traits of the Barrancoid Tradition.

By this time, *Apoteri Incised* motifs, already present on the earlier levels at Kurupukari Falls and the source of which also remains unknown, had been integrated in Saladoid decoration well beyond Kurupukari Falls, on the Corentyne River, Figure 4.57d.

Therefore, Lathrap was correct in rejecting the need to explain the Guarita Subphase in the light of an independent migration. Occurrences of *Apoteri Incised* motifs in both the Guarita and Saracá Subtraditions suggest that they shared a common origin somewhere in the Acarai watershed area during the final centuries before Christ. By this time, the first Proto-Northern Maipuran Arawak migrants were already venturing into the Caribbean from the Eastern Venezuelan Coast, but with a ceramic repertory which lacked the fine-line motifs of *Apoteri Incised*. Likewise, as suggested by Rouse (1985), their Proto-Eastern brethren, also, may have been putting to sea at around this time from the Eastern Guiana Littoral with a by now wholly Barrancoid inventory.

Mound dwellers of the Eastern Guiana Littoral and their successors
Introduction

The earliest known arrivals on the Eastern Guiana Littoral, a landscape of mudflats, marshes, seasonally inundated grass savannas, estuaries and shallow coastal streams, would have been struck, as one still can be today, by its extremely high biological productivity. True, in its pristine state, this landscape may have been anything but attractive as a habitat for man, but this would have been offset by the prominence of its subsistence resources, particularly as regards the fauna. As on the Western Guiana Littoral, the annual migrations of land crabs to the sea provided a daily harvest of high-quality protein over a period of four months each year, while the converse but no less striking migrations of giant sea turtles to the sand or shell beaches between February and July offered a similarly accessible harvest of meat and eggs. As at the present time, dense populations of wading birds roosted in the mangroves and fed off the mudflats, most particularly in areas of Nickerie and West Coronie (Schultz 1976), though environmental changes possibly wrought by conditions associated with the archaeologically attested arid interval in Amazonia of around 2000 b.p. should be borne in mind.

The soils of these coastal wetlands are comparable to the Amazonian *varzea* soils, particularly when contrasted with the characteristically poor, highly leached soils of *terra firme*. However, being of marine rather than of riverain origin, their effective utilization by man presents fewer disadvantages relating to uneven deposition of sediments, alternating deficits and surpluses of water, changing river channels, etc. (e.g. see Meggers 1971:28).

From the time of the earliest utilization of these coastal soils by man, the principal adaptive strategy has centered on the problem of segregating habitable sites and arable lands from the surrounding seasonal swamps. On to the time of European colonization, and indeed to the present day, this problem has determined the settlement pattern of all coastal groups, that of the European no less than that of their immigrant labor.

As will be seen, recent investigations on the Mazaruni River in central Guyana yielded evidences of a more or less abrupt breakup of arid conditions, around 80 B.C., characterized by successive local episodes of torrential rainfall and rising water levels. Extrapolating these conditions to the Suriname Coast, the Arawak pioneers there would have occupied a landscape subject to escalating levels of inundation and gradual freshening during the early centuries of the Christian Era. Accordingly, when a group of pioneering Proto-Eastern Maipuran Arawaks eventually reached the Mouth of the Corentyne River and initiated settlement on the alluvial clays around Buckleburg-1, these clays displayed evidence of a recent change from a salty to a fresh environment (Versteeg 1985:714), Figure 4.58. The immigrants cultivated their crops, probably manioc, on the extensive seasonally inundated grass savannas, Figure 4.59a. Commencing around A.D. 250, they built the very first habitation mound on the Guiana Coast, at the same time elevating their farming plots which were drained by a network of narrow canals. In due course, evidently in response to the increasing discharge regime of the Corentyne River (as on the neighboring Berbice River) they found it expedient to raise the levels of their habitation and farming plots. Successive elevations of various other habitation mounds and farming plots in the complex over the ensuing centuries probably was a function of sustained rising water levels as wetter conditions supervened in the hinterland.

This first habitation mound, Buckleburg-1, eventually attained a height of two meters above the swamps. In this way was initiated the system by which large areas

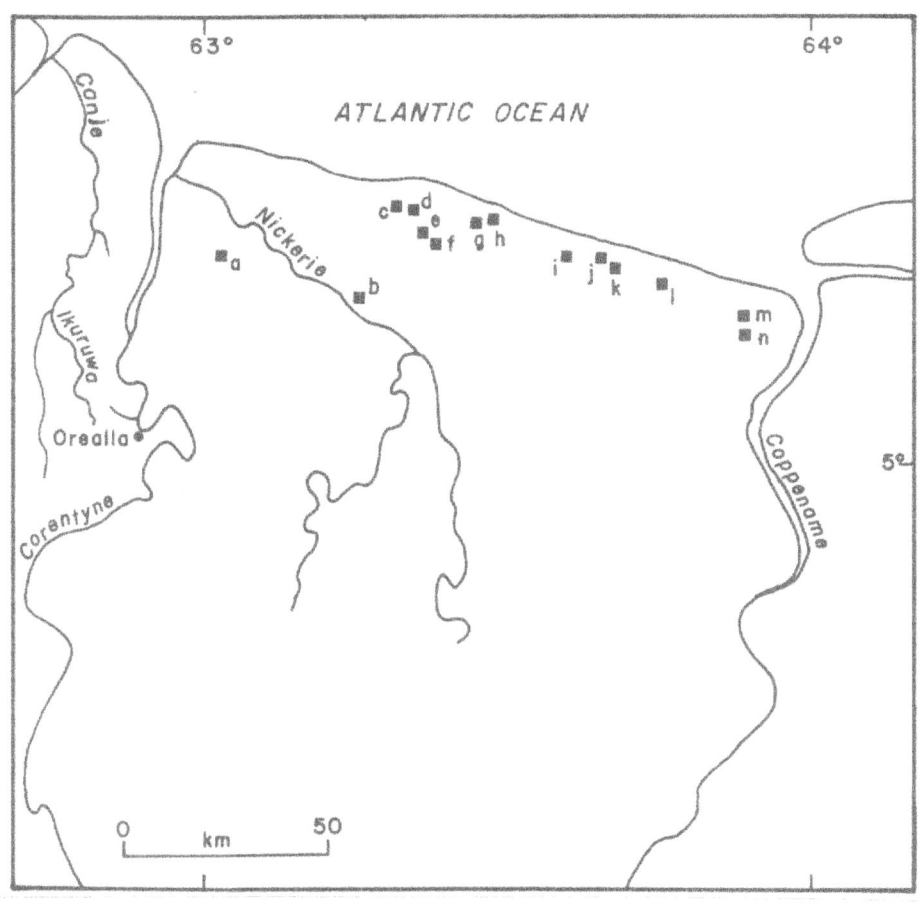

Figure 4.58. Pioneering settlements on the Eastern Guiana Littoral. **a.** Prins Bernhard Polder; **b.** Nickerie-2; **c.** Wageningen-3; **d.** Hertenrits; **e.** Wageningen-2; **f.** Wageningen-1; **g.** Buckleburg-1; **h.** Buckleburg-2; **i.** Burnside; **j.** Belladrum; **k.** Friendship; **l.** Ingiekondre; **m.** Peruvia-1; **n.** Peruvia-2 (*after Versteeg 1985*).

Figure 4.59 a,b. a. Seasonally inundated grass savannas. b. Hillock suitable for habitation and farming in seasonally inundated grass savannas.

of the Eastern Guiana Littoral were brought under perennial cultivation by an expanding complex of earthworks that permanently separated areas of utilizable land from the seasonal swamps. The system may be thought a form of irrigation horticulture which, in effect, brought land, rather than water, to the crops in conditions of progressive freshwater inundation of the ground surface in phase with ever-increasing run-off, a situation somewhat reminiscent of the rising water levels of the "freshwater crisis" of 3,300 B.C. in the swamp basin of the Western Guiana Littoral. The system never developed on the Western Guiana Littoral for the reason that, there, numerous forested hillocks on the swamp edge provided natural elevations for habitation, Figure 4.59b.

This system of drainage ditches and canals linking the artificial elevations of the Eastern Guiana Littoral was not a far cry from the irrigation horticulture of preceding centuries; or the canals, dykes and sluices of pioneering Dutch colonists in the eighteenth century; nor did it much differ in effect from the stilt-lift architecture of the swamplands introduced by British colonists during the nineteenth century or, indeed, the massive hydraulic operations of the post-colonial era in Guyana which dammed the headwaters of principal coastal streams such as the Mahaica, Mahaicony and Abary to provide irrigation for thousands of hectares of this rich, low-lying alluvium. Settlements based on one or another of these infrastructural stratagems occur along the entire Eastern Guiana Littoral, i.e., the narrow band of mudflats, estuaries, intertidal swamps and seasonally inundated grass savannas stretching between the mouths of the Essequibo and Amazon Rivers.

Over the centuries and millennia, the settlement pattern of these pioneering Arawaks on the Eastern Guiana Littoral underwent various important changes in response to developing technologies and expanding populations in an area which, notwithstanding its biological richness, was circumscribed by the White Sand Plateau to the south and the Atlantic Ocean to north and east.

Stated in biogeographical terms (Pianka 1976:89), initial occupation of such a niche is a density-independent event favoring r selection, which is characterized by rapid production of numerous offspring that are energetically inexpensive to produce but which, though small, are likely to strive because competition is negligible. But with continued occupation of the same niche, density effects come to operate on the population. Competition becomes keen, enforcing an opposing selective strategy, K selection, which requires fewer and larger offspring endowed with more substantial competitive attributes. Since such offspring are energetically more expensive, fewer are produced. At an increasingly slower reproductive rate, population growth gradually approaches carrying capacity, which is the density at which the net reproductive rate is zero.

Thus, over the centuries following on the arrival of these pioneers, population growth would have followed a predictable trajectory to carrying capacity, at which point a change in the selective strategy would have occurred. Their earliest habitation mound, Buckleburg-1, was characterized by occurrences of Barrancoid ceramics which, technologically and typologically, betrayed their Amazonian origin. As noted by its excavator (Versteeg 1985:684):

> Initially, the Buckleburg-1 potters used several kinds of temper. The exclusive use of crushed pottery temper in the later stages of occupation is probably an adaptation to the coastal habitat. This implies that they lived earlier in a habitat situated further inland where the other tempers were more readily available.

The stratigraphic sequence is illustrated in Table Q.

Table Q. The Buckleburg-1 site. Temper types/level

Depth (m)	Crushed pottery	Quartz sand	Charcoal/ caraipe	Shell	Micaceous sand
2.55	42	-	-	-	-
2.41	1805	-	-	-	-
2.26	593	-	-	-	-
2.17	1139	-	-	-	-
2.05	782	-	-	-	-
1.95	637	-	1	-	-
1.82	631	-	-	-	-
1.71	367	-	-	-	-
1.59	271	-	1	-	-
1.52	196	3	1	1	-
1.43	95	-	2	-	-
1.34	110	-	13	2	-
1.15	124	25	35	8	-
1.05	24	12	9	2	2
0.92	18	13	5	2	7
0.79	11	6	2	-	2
0.66	5	5	-	-	2
0.60	1	1	-	-	1
	6887	65	69	15	14

Source: Versteeg 1985:Table 2.

In the above table, "micaceous sand" has been substituted for the author's "mica" (Shepard 1977:162). The crushed granite of Barrancoid tradition, both Orinocan and Amazonian, may have been the source involved. Also "quartz" has been substituted by "quartz sand." As will be seen, "crushed pottery" may at least partly represent kaolin temper.

Initial reliance on the tempering materials of *terra firme* gave way in the early years of settlement (i.e., around 1.15 m depth) to an almost exclusive reliance on crushed potsherds, use of which evidently developed in phase with population growth. More than one kind of tempering material was utilized in some of the early vessels, a common trait in the pottery of the Corentyne River (Versteeg 1978). This confirms the hinterland origin of early Barrancoid pottery on the Eastern Guiana Littoral. But notwithstanding the indicated steadily increasing reliance on the alternative temper, the link with the hinterland was never completely broken. As continues the case to the present day, the viability of these coastal settlements rested to a large extent on the age-old complementarity between the resources of the swamps and those of *terra firme*.

Typologically, the Buckleburg-1 inventory betrays its Amazonian heritage in the survival of the Barrancoid scroll element, unknown in the Mabaruma complexes but a common trait on the upper Essequibo. Wide, Barrancoid-flanged rims and inward-facing zoomorphic adornos are recorded on a range of vessel shapes that include the carinated bowl of the earliest inventories (Versteeg 1985:Figures 14-18). As on the upper Essequibo, the distinctive Distended Mouth adorno of the middle (cf. Roosevelt 1980:Figure 53, bottom) and lower (Sanoja O. 1979:Lamina 54c) Orinoco is lacking.

The two Buckleburg mounds were occupied over a period of around 400 years. During that time, the volume of Buckleburg-1, ca. 38,250 m^3, as well as the sizes of its associated farm plots, + /- 53 ha, and those of the Barrancoid Buckleburg-2 mound located on the same creek nearby, attest sustained population growth with attendant continuous expansion of the adjacent raised fields. But, as population growth climaxed on these pioneering mounds, construction of new ones became necessary.

Around A.D. 645, i.e., toward the ending of occupancy of Buckleburg-1, work was commenced on Wageningen-1, *ca.* 10 km to the southwest. Soon after inception of this new mound, yet another was begun, this time at Hertenrits, around 4 km to the northwest. The population growth rate continued to increase. Whereas the much smaller Buckleburg-1 mound had grown over a period of around four centuries, the Hertenrits mound attained an estimated volume of + /- 100,000 m^3 in less than a century and a half. Girdled by a moat-like water body 20 - 100 m wide representing the progressively extended borrow pits that accompanied its accumulation in several vertical stages, Hertenrits soon became the political and administrative center of the complex, a virtual island village with a commanding view across the swamps. From this location, numerous pathways radiated to raised-field complexes annexed in a sprawling pattern over something on the order of 150 - 160 ha (Boomert 1980).

It was probably as a result of this rapid rate of population growth that the similarly moated, but smaller, mound at Joanna across the Corentyne estuary was constructed on Canje Creek. Joanna pottery shares a number of vessel shapes and their dominant tempering material with the Wageningen-1 and Hertenrits mounds but lacks Barrancoid pottery entirely.

Hertenrits pottery is predominantly tempered with kaolin or the crushed potsherds of late Buckleburg-1 practice. The kaolin derived from the Orealla Cliffs on the left bank Corentyne River, 90 km up. Certain kaolin-tempered specimens of Hertenrits pottery display a total loss of the kaolin particles through erosion, presenting in their place numerous irregularly shaped cavities that are inconsistent with use of sherd temper, as described by previous authors (e.g. Boomert 1980; Versteeg 1985). Kaolin-tempered pottery with a high percentage of sherds displaying loss of the temper particles is likewise characteristic of Joanna ceramics.

The location of the solitary Joanna mound on the Guyana side of the Corentyne River is probably best interpreted as the site of a waystation on the route to Orealla, upriver, *via* the Canje River and its headwater tributary, the Ikuruwa. From this latter stream, a short portage leads to Mapenna Creek, just below Orealla Cliffs, where, as mentioned above, Hertenrits pottery was recovered at Seba, on the right creek bank, Figure 4.58. The predominant use of kaolin from these cliffs in Joanna pottery as well as in Hertenrits pottery suggests that this route was judged preferable to the direct ascent of the Corentyne River, since it avoided the formidable tidal action in the sector between the cliffs and the sea. This interpretation was aided by direct experience of a tidal bore on the Corentyne River above Mapenna Creek during the excavation of Orealla Cliffs.

The route was already well established by A.D. 870 (1080 +/- 60 B.P., Beta 20008). The date derives from a charcoal sample near the bottom of the Orealla profile, which yielded a rich deposit of Hertenrits (Arauquinoid) pottery. By this date, Arawaks on the Eastern Guiana Littoral had expanded eastward as far as the Peruvia-2 site near the Coppename River, occupying there -- a new experiment -- a naturally elevated *chenier* ridge instead of a mound. Peruvia-2 potters, likewise representing the Arauquinoid Incised and Punctate Horizon style, which had begun expanding out of a hearth on the upper Orinoco sometime around A.D. 500, employed mixed tempering agents in a given vessel, a trait common to ceramic practice at Buckleburg-1, Wageningen-1 and Orealla. The presence of this trait in early Buckleburg-1 pottery suggests that a trade entrepôt already existed on the Corentyne during the early years of the Christian Era. As seems suggested by the location of sites of the Orealla Complex on both banks of the river as well as up Mapenna and Epira Creeks, the subsequent route of Arauquinoid influence on the pottery of the Eastern Guiana Littoral may have been along the Corentyne corridor. Settlements of Proto-Eastern Maipuran Arawaks now extended from the Coppename River, 60 km to the east, to Joanna on the Canje Creek some 80 km to the west and to the south at least as far as Orealla Cliffs, around 90 km up the Corentyne River.

Thus, at some point, the initial rapid growth rate of the propagule group that is represented by Barrancoid Incised and Modeled pottery on the coast gave way to the slower, more density-dependent growth rate of sites of the later Incised and Punctate Tradition. Following on the raising of the pioneering mounds at Buckleburg-1 and 2, early Wageningen-1 and early Hertenrits, the raising of new mounds at Wageningen-2 and 3, Prins Bernhard Polder, and occupation of the reef site at Peruvia-2 became imperative within a relatively short time of one another. Evidently, sustained population growth, now implying a K selection adaptive strategy, was militating against the continued efficacy of the settlement pattern of the pioneers. During its short life, population pressure at Hertenrits thrice enforced the expansion of the mound area by increments which, while successively increasing its elevation, at the same time enlarged the surrounding moat. Whereas the mantle representing the first increment doubled the areal extension of the original mound, the second doubled the area of the first. With the mound now standing 1.4 m above the level of the surrounding swamps and with a growing moat in the way, the third mantle then elevated the mound area by a further one meter. As well as meeting the needs of the indicated population growth, these extensions also made good the inevitable loss of surface area in a tropical environment through erosion (cf. Rostain et Frenay 1991:Figure 12). At the same time, they were possibly a cumulative response to increasing water levels in the swamps during the centuries following on the end of the arid interval of +/- 2000 b. p. However, the solution had its limits.

Population growth at Hertenrits is unequivocally evidenced by consistent increases in potsherd frequencies per level, and by the introduction of new vessel forms accompanied by an enhanced vocabulary of decorative motifs (Boomert 1980:Table 3 a,b). Ceremonial gewgaws, such as Amazon stones, as well as beads, lip plugs, pendants, etc, manufactured on shell and bone, combined with an evidently selective mortuary ceremonial, suggest a degree of social differentiation unusual in the Tropical Forest lowlands. However, although differential burial modes suggest the vesting of title to valued land in particular descent groups related to a common apical ancestor, there is no evidence of the chiefdom. As in Archaic cultures on the Western Guiana Littoral, generalized reciprocity appears to have provided the base of the economic system. In due course, however, population growth and the concurrent expansion of the associated raised-field complexes indicate the approach of carrying capacity. Intensification seems already indicated with the final increment on the Hertenrits mound surface (see Boomert 1980:Tables 4, 5 a,b). This was followed by the ultimate adaptive stratagem -- desertion of the now optimally extended raised-field complex.

The habitation-mound *cum* raised-field settlement pattern of the pioneers no longer could survive in its traditional form in face of the population expansion which it had itself made possible in the biotically rich swamp environment. Population growth had meant, simultaneouly, both mound expansion and expansion of the raised-field network. Of these two kinds of capital inputs, returns evidently had been realized more rapidly on investment in more fields (new ones or extensions to the old) especially since, in the swamp environment and bearing in mind that manioc thrives best in dry conditions, yields probably had been chronically uneconomic. Be that as it may, the effect of unrestrained expansion of the farm plots to feed the steadily growing population that is implied by ever-increasing potsherd densities on successive levels of the Hertenrits mound was to limit the energy inputs available for the obligatory reciprocal expansion of the mound platform. Granted the limitations of the available earth-moving technology of wooden spades and, presumably, baskets, Figure 4.60, the viability of Hertenrits as the political and economic hub of the system was increasingly compromised through time. An alternative accommodation between agricultural productivity and residential site structure became imperative.

Occupation of the sand or shell reefs that traverse these seasonally inundated swamplands at depths varying between 8 - 16 km from the seashore presented an economically viable alternative to the settlement pattern of the pioneers. With the ready made segregation of residential and farm lands, the energy costs of occupying the swamps were reduced to primary clearing of dry forest on the reefs. Farm plots were raised directly against the reef edge in an economical linear pattern adjacent to the associated house plot. This was the settlement pattern at Peruvia-2. The energy subsidy that accrued was accompanied by enhancement of the dietary pattern. In addition to the swamp and forest-based food items of the mound culture at Wageningen-1 (manatee, tapir, anteater, capybara, otter, racoon, caiman and other reptiles), consumption of reef foods (reef fish, invertebrates, etc.) more than doubled (Versteeg 1991:Table 8.4).

Thus, the first stage of settling the swamps of the Eastern Guiana Littoral by Proto-Eastern Maipuran Arawaks from the lower Amazon, characterized by the mound-platform/raised-field settlement pattern of Buckleburg-1 and 2, Hertenrits, Wageningen-1 and Joanna, lasted between A.D. 250 and approximately A.D. 650. This stage was brought to an end with the initiation of reef settlement at Peruvia-2, which represented the alternative and incomparably more extensive settlement pattern of the future.

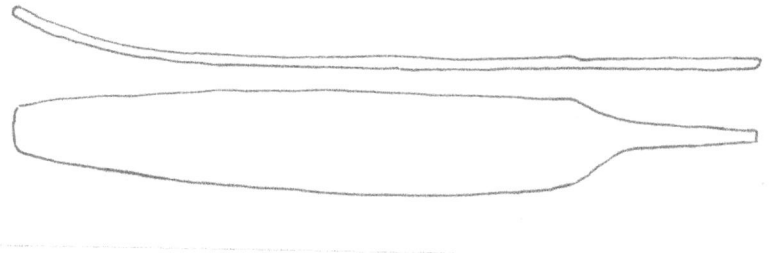

Figure 4.60. Prins Bernhard Polder. Wooden (?) shovel (*after Versteeg 1985:Figure 51*).

Hertenrits and its aftermath
The reef dwellers

The abandonment of the habitation mounds of the pioneers and their occupation of the sand and shell reefs was a function of population expansion in this uniquely productive environment. With Peruvia-2 the nucleated mound villages of the pioneers began to give way during the eighth century to a pattern of dispersed homesteads which, by virtue of their location on the *chenier* ridges that traverse the length of the Young Coastal Plain, allowed for virtually indefinite southeastward and northwestward expansion and with minimal energy costs in the exploitation of arable land. Typifying the new system were complexes at Kwatta on the central Suriname coast, Barbakoeba between the Commewijne and Mani Rivers, and Themire stretching between the Sinnamary River and the Ile de Cayenne in Guyane française. Raised fields are not known to have been associated with the Kwatta Complex, which, however, like Barbakoeba, appears to have derived ultimately from the Arauquinoid Hertenrits Complex.

A C^{14} sequence from the reef site at Kwatta Tingiholo ranged between A.D. 810 - 890. The only available date for the Barbakoeba Complex is A.D. 975. Dates for the Themire Complex range between A.D. 1140 - 1690, though it is thought that earlier sites there may date as early as A.D. 950 (Rostain 1994a:Table 85). These homesteads were located on the absolute reef edge, Figure 4.61.

Figure 4.61. Eastern Guiana Littoral. The Barbakoeba reef site (*after Boomert 1978*).

Some of the horticultural plots measure as much as a hectare, with individul plots as much as 30 m long, 1.3 m wide and varying in height between 0.3 m -0.8 m (Rostain 1991, 1994; Rostain et Frenay 1991).

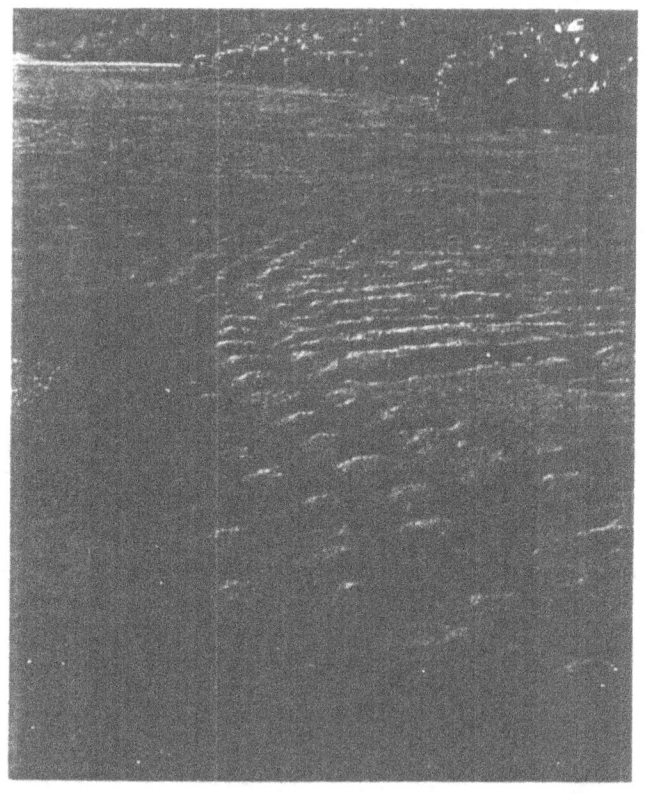

Figure 4.62 a,b. The Eastern Guiana Littoral. Guyane française. a. Karouabo, b. Diamant.
Courtesy Stéphen Rostain.

Long, straight access routes between the farm plots made more efficient use of space than did the torturous lanes of the traditional Hertenrits raised-field complexes. The new efficiencies released further energies for food production, the success of the new settlement pattern being attested in its eventual wide distribution. Eventually, concentrations of raised fields stretched across the watershed of the Canje and Berbice Rivers, as well as westward toward the Abary River. Although presently located on dry land deep in the hinterland, these plots apparently were raised at a time when the low-lying watersheds were inundated year-round, permitting recourse to extensive water table horticulture, Figure 4.63a,b. (cf. West 1979). An uncontexted charcoal sample from the base of one of these mounds returned a date at around 1000 A.D. (Whitehead pers. comm.) which is not incompatible with continuing back-up of flood waters following on the end of the arid interval around the time of Christ.

Figure 4.63 a,b. The low-lying watersheds of the Eastern Guiana Littoral. a. Abary River and floodplain. b. Raised horticultural plots on the Berbice-Canje watershed.

The immense labor inputs required for the maintenance and development of the raised-field system down the generations more likely denote reciprocal exchange of labor rather than conscription within a putative hierarchical social structure. It has been seen that the outstanding socio-economic feature of manioc subsistence is its very high labor intensiveness, and that this in turn sets an inflexible limit to the potentials of Tropical Forest cultures to develop complexity, at any rate on *terra firme*. The egalitarian social structure of the typically small, self-contained settlement was evidently the most efficiently adaptive organizational stratagem there, linked as it was to shifting cultivation on highly leached soils whose nutrient cycling regime, combined with alternating wet and dry seasons, engendered strict socio-political controls for their efficient exploitation. As these controls related directly to the size of the available labor force (which below a certain strength could not keep pace with the continual or escalating needs of forest clearing), stresses were generated in communities whose population failed to keep pace with the imperatives of efficient land management. Symptomatic of these stresses was the disadvantaging of the old and the infirm. At the same time, in the female domain (including juveniles) the reciprocal exchange of labor was imperative for processing the raw materials of forest and farm. The resulting brake on surplus production effectively ensured against the emergence of social complexity in the interests of the long-term survival of the group.

As had been the case from Archaic times, the economies of coastal cultures were linked by complementarity to those of *terra firme*. Thus, the supply of strategic rock materials to the Arawaks was mediated by Akawaio (Kapon) traders located in the hinterland. Accordingly, the Koriabo phase potsherds of the Akawaio occur in certain coastal inventories, e.g. at sites of the Suriname Barbakoeba Complex and of the Abary phase on the Guyana coast. Certain Arawak potters on the Suriname Coast copied elements of Akawaio ceramics, while, conversely, decorative elements of coastal Arawak ceramics were copied by Akawaio potters inland (Boomert 1993).

Underpinning this inter-ethnic coastal-hinterland interaction in the east was a trade in stone tools made mainly on metabasalt, metadolerite and dolerite deriving from the Nassau and Lely Mountains of central and east Suriname. This trade was centered in the Brownsberg Complex, comprising the Brownsberg, Afobaka and Kaaimankreek ceramic sites located under rain forest on *terra firme*. Technologically and typologically, Brownsberg pottery remains unaffiliated to any of the other ceramic complexes so far known from the Guianas. Tempered with quartz sand or caraipé, its affiliation would appear to have been with the rain forest rather than with any of the coastal cultures. Appropriately, interaction with the Koriabo phase is indicated in the Brownsberg refuse as well (Boomert and Kroonenberg 1977).

Thus, stone artifacts of the Akawaio moved down the Suriname, Saramacca and possibly also the Marouini Rivers to the coast and along the *cheniers* to the otherwise stoneless Arawak complexes at Kwatta and Barbakoeba. Based on the indicated interaction with these Akawaio, the Brownsberg trade has been estimated to date at between A.D. 1200 - 1500. The earlier date is thought to have marked the initial appearance of their Koriabo phase ceramics in Suriname (Boomert and Kroonenberg 1977; Versteeg and Bubberman 1992:45). However, stone tools of even earlier date on Brownsberg materials occurring at certain coastal sites indicate exploitation of Brownsberg resources well before A.D. 1200. As will be seen, the Akawaio may have been in Suriname much earlier than has been supposed.

While the community that is represented by the distinctive Brownsberg pottery remains to be identified, its centralized control of tool manufacture in eastern Suriname is implied by local concentrations of debitage in their refuse (Boomert and Kroonenburg 1977). Evidences from the canoe industry of the Western Guiana Littoral suggest they may have controlled access to the local rock outcrops that were indispensible in manufacturing stone tools. Refuse from stool manufacture is uniformly absent at the sites of their coastal trade partners. Just as the rock materials and stoneworking technology of the hinterland was subsumed in Late Archaic canoe manufacture, so also the viability of horticultural adaptations on the Eastern Guiana Littoral was underpinned by sustained interaction with specialized hinterland stone tool industries at Brownsberg and elsewhere (Boomert and Kroonenburg 1977: Figure 2).

By the mid-seventeenth century, the low-density settlement pattern of these reef dwellers had reached its ultimate eastward extension in the Thenure complex of coastal Guyane française. From this time onward, the presence of Europeans along this stretch of coast introduced a new factor in the competition for reef space. The Arawak migrations of the preceding thousand and more years now approached its ending. Following the founding of the Dutch West India Company in 1621, the first European colonists arrived on the Oyapoc River in 1623 under Jesse de Forest, and on the Berbice River in 1625 under Abraham van Pere. Thus, de Forest's map of 1625, Figure 4.64, is an especially valuable source for reconstructing the settlement pattern on this sector of the Eastern Guiana Littoral before it was destroyed forever. The map shows present-day Portal Island in the Marouini, the border river between Suriname and Guyane française. Arawaks occupied reef sites on both banks at the mouth of the river. Carib-speaking Yaos were located in the St. Laurent area a bit further upstream, again occupying both banks of the river, while, farthest inland, in the area of present-day Bigiston, was a settlement of "Caribs" on the left bank. As this latter site has since yielded pottery of the (Kapon) Koriabo phase, the designation "Carib," as employed by early European writers in the Guianas must be considered suspect until supported by archaeological evidence.

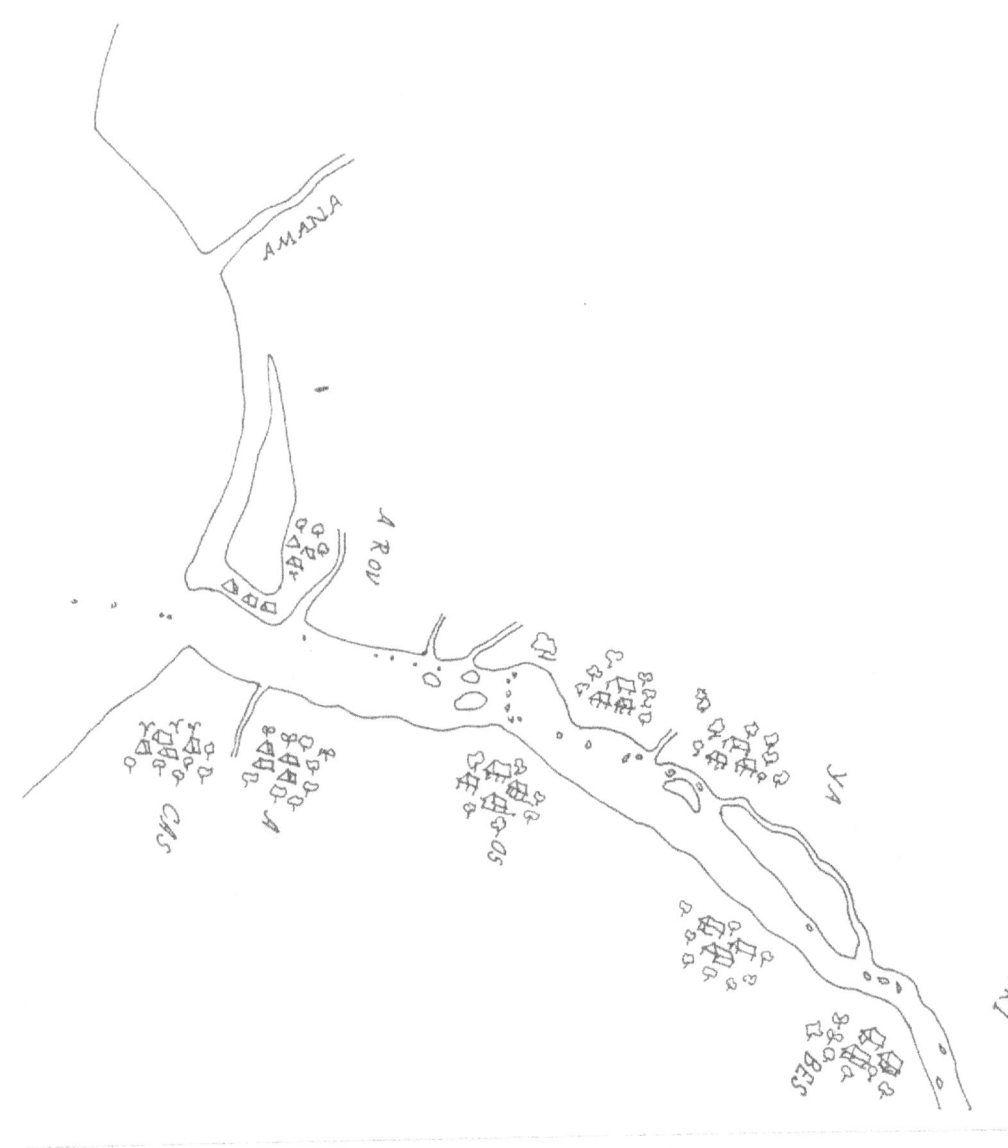

Figure 4.64. The Proto-Eastern Maipuran Arawak expansion on the Eastern Guiana Littoral. Arawaks occupy the reefs on both banks of the Marowijne, "Caribes" (Kapon) are located upriver. (*After map of J. de Forest, 1625*).

Although raised-field complexes associated with these Arawak settlements were extensive, the habitation sites themselves typically were small, comprising multi-household compounds of around three to four dwellings each. The relatively large area now occupied by the raised field complexes evidently were the result of fissioning over more than a thousand years. If the settlement pattern pictured on this early seventeenth century map truly represents the precontact situation, the absence of large villages, taken with the above evidences of sedentary occupancy of the reefs, suggests that these dispersed homesteads in fact represented various small kin-groups each tethered to a specific plot of ancestral land. This is the settlement pattern that seems indicated by both the archaeological (Boomert 1993; Rostain 1994a; Versteeg 1985) and ethnographic (Im Thurn 1884; Quelch 1894) evidences. They suggest an egalitarian social structure based on reciprocal exchange and comprising matrilineal descent groups which, while enjoying title to ancestral land and thus a certain degree of prestige, exercised no coercive power.

Meanwhile, another arm of the Proto-Eastern Maipuran Arawak migration had crossed the Corentyne River and initiated occupation on the western reefs. As has been seen, Joanna had been planted on the Canje Creek some time during the late first millennium apparently to serve as a waystation on the route to Orealla Cliffs, upriver. Measuring around 90 m maximum diameter and 2.5 m high, the Joanna mound is surrounded by the typical moat-like water body of late Hertenrits construction. Evidently, over the years it had grown into a settlement of some consequence. Thence, late Hertenrits culture commenced a slow westward movement along the Eastern Guiana Littoral. Most of the sites unfortunately were put to the plough during the development of the sugar industry in the nineteenth century, but the scanty literature and the unfortunately limited excavations carried out to date reveal that, with the crossing of the Corentyne River, the settlement pattern of the reef dwellers, with their raised horticultural beds extending directly from the reef edges, gave way to yet another, which dispensed altogether with cultivating the swamps. The immense concentrations of raised agricultural beds located on the Canje-Berbice-Abary watersheds, Figure 4.65a, must therefore belong to the earlier period.

As the free-draining reef soils were found equally satisfactory for either habitation or cultivation, population expansion was limited now only by the availability of areas of satisfactory elevation. Suitable elevations, mostly forested, rose irregularly from the swamps between the Corentyne Coast and the Canje Valley (Poonai 1962) and continued along the coast to the Abary River where Verrill (1918a) claimed to have excavated 30,000 densely packed burial urns, though the accuracy of the estimate has been questioned (Evans and Meggers 1960:182). Im Thurn (1884) recorded forested "islands" at Enmore and Bachelor's Adventure, concluding that such raised islands probably occurred at irregular intervals along the entire course of the reefs (see also Vincent Roth 1944), Figure 4.59b.

The density of urn burials associated with these reef sites (Im Thurn 1884; Poonai 1962; Verrill 1918a) suggests that their necessarily limited numbers constituted these forested islands ancestral property in any given case, in precisely the sense of the mound builders farther to the east, or indeed, the reef dwellers of de Forest's map. Selective mortuary rituals imply descent groups claiming title to land in perpetuity by virtue of their affiliation to an apical ancestor (Saxe 1971). From the earliest times, such claims were legitimated by religious sanction. On the Western Guiana Littoral, title similarly was claimed by late Archaic groups with respect to particular productive niches, hence the universal custom among shellfishers of *in situ* burial in the dwelling places of the living. This custom unifies horticulturist groups on the Guiana Coast from the Mouth of the Amazon to the Orinoco. The bounded cemetery was a feature of the settlement pattern on the Amazon deltaic islands (Meggers and Evans 1957; Roosevelt 1992) as well as on the Orinoco foodplain (Roosevelt 1990: Figures 69,85,91). The antiquity of the trait among horticulturists is suggested in the Formiga phase on Marajó, the largest of the Amazon deltaic islands. With inception dating at around the time of Christ, the Formiga phase is known from various artificially constructed habitation mounds on the north and central portions of the island. Villages comprised one to six independent mounds, some artificially raised while others were simple piles of rubbish. Lumps of clay with twig impressions suggest the wattle and daub house type that later would characterize the architecture of the entire Eastern Guiana Littoral. Burial appears to have been by cremation and interment in the floor of the dwelling (Meggers and Evans 1957:241).

The bounded cemetery is exemplified *par excellence* in the successor Marajoara phase (A.D. 500 - 1400). There, artificial mounds were employed as both habitation sites and urn cemeteries. In the Arua phase, which succeeded to the Marajoara phase in late prehistoric times, there is also a well defined relationship between habitation and cemetery sites. All the way to the Oyapoc, the coastal swamps restricted habitation and cemetery sites to low elevations that remained above flood level, or to higher ground up rivers and creeks where caves and rock shelters were favored repositories for burial urns. In both cases, cemeteries typically were incorporated in the lifespace of the community.

Associated burial and habitation sites again characterized the Aristé phase in the north of the Territory of Amapá. Here, urn burial took two well defined forms (*i*) secondary burial of bones following upon decomposition of the flesh, and (*ii*) cremation followed by interment of the carbonized bones. It is thought (Grenand and Grenand 1987) that the first type was characteristic of the Arua and Mazagão phases and the second of the Maracá and Aristé phases. Both types were employed on the Guiana Coast beyond the Territory of Amapá (Boomert 1980; Verrill 1918, 1918a; Versteeg 1985).

Manipulation of the dead in the interests of particular descent groups is evidenced in Archaic burials that represent polarization between the head and feet of the deceased in terms of a cosmological structure that appears to be of hoary antiquity in the Americas, Figure 4.39c. Gilding of the head and legs in the Piraka shell mound burials on the Pomeroon River is the earliest dated example of the custom so far known in the Guianas -- 7230 +/- 90 B.P. (Beta 27055). Apparently resulting from the cohabitation of the swamp edge by Warao and early Arawaks, aspects of the associated mortuary ritual were assimilated by these early horticulturists and, over the centuries, disseminated across the Guianas and beyond, Figure 4.65a-i.

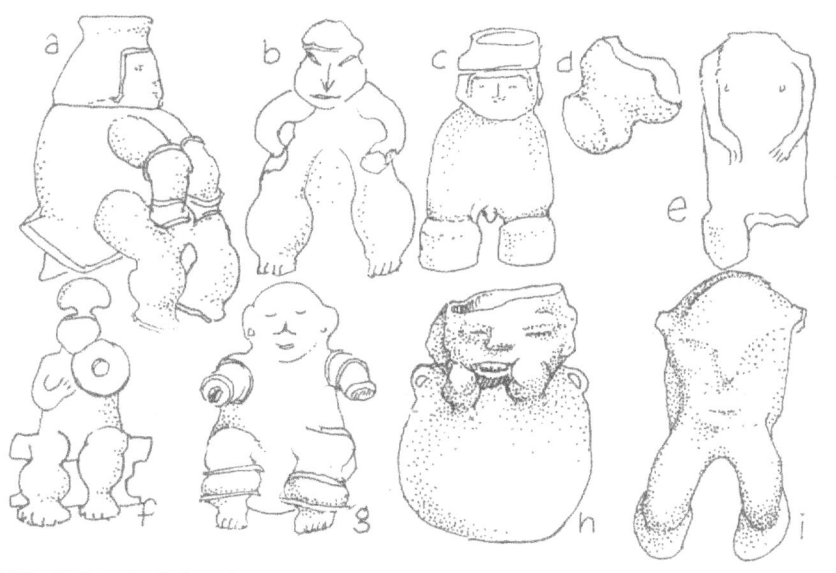

Figure 4.65 a-i. Head/foot symbols among horticulturists. a. Territory of Amapá, Brazil, (*after Meggers and Evans 1957:Pl. 18*), b. Mazaruni River, Guyana (*Coll. James Krakowski*), c. Mon Repos, Guyana (*Coll. Walter Roth Museum*), d. Suriname (*after Boomert 1980:Figure 19 [4,5]*), e. Suriname (*after Versteeg 1985:Figure 48d*), f. Colombia (*after Willey 1949:Pl.39 b,c*), g. Ecuador (*after Meggers and Evans 1968:Pl. 57*), h. Orinoco River (*after Roosevelt 1980:Figure 9*), i. Marajó Island, (*after Roosevelt 1991:Figure 1. 22[5]*).

Cemeteries of these new denizens of the reefs similarly were located within the life space of the community (Im Thurn 1884; Quelch 1894). Verrill (1918a) described urns packed side-by-side over an area of around 600 x 150 feet, which, even granted Verrill's penchant for impressive estimates, indicates the bounded cemetery of an appreciable population circumscribed by the fixed dimensions of a particular "forested island." Im Thurn (1884:127) described similarly dense concentrations of burial urns at Enmore, all now broken but each still occupying a small heap at the center of which a pile of human bones survived. On another reef at Mon Repos, Quelch (1894) described an actual head/foot burial in refuse that included fish bones, stone artifacts and potsherds:

> ... the bodies had been buried in a sitting posture in the hole, with the knees drawn up towards the chin. It was also distinctly noticeable that a somewhat shallow and open pot had been placed, like a hat pressed down, over the head of each ...

Small, delicately formed pots, "some hardly big enough to fit the top of one's thumb" (Im Thurn 1884), together with basins and jars or goblets and hollow funerary figurines in the Santarem style, Figure 4.65c, were recovered at the Enmore cemetery site in a collection which included a Classic Mabaruma Hands-to-Face figurine, Figure 4.36a. Similar small ceramic vessels placed inside burial urns in the Mazagão phase contained teeth and small bones (Meggers and Evans 1957:53).

Life spans of these reef sites, estimated at between 50.1 - 213.5 years, suggest a total duration for the culture, archaeologically identified as the Abary phase, at between 298 - 417 years. Granted these durations, the depth of refuse at three sites, 48 - 56 cm, yielding 1002 - 2463 sherds per 1 x 1 m pit, suggest reasonable population densities throughout (Evans and Meggers 1960:181).

Sedentary occupation is suggested also by relatively high labor inputs into domestic structures. Wattle and daub was the preferred building technique. Framework and rafters were lashed together using several kinds of plaiting fibers. For walls, the wattle was partly covered with palm leaves before application of the daub. The species of palm utilized is sometimes identifiable, Figure 1.4d,e. At the same time, modern Arawaks using the bark of the Baromalli (*Catostemma sp.*) for walls and/or floors may be utilizing an ancient technology of poor survival potential, Figure 4.66 (cf. the seventeenth century map, Figure 4.64).

As the culture migrated westward, certain technological and typological traits of the Hertenrits Complex were lost and others, deriving from the Western Guiana

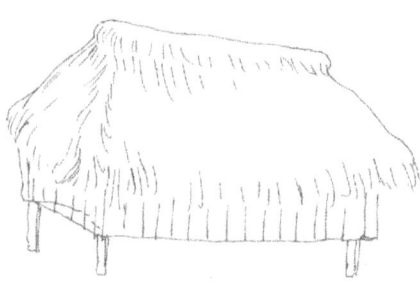

Figure 4.66. Arawak stilt house, Oreaila.

Littoral, were adopted. Thus, by the time the Abary River was reached and crossed, most of the Hertenrits vessel shapes and decoration had given way to ceramic types of the Mabaruma and even the Koriabo phases. Surviving Hertenrits traits were the sherd temper of the *Taurakuli Plain* ceramic type of the Abary phase and certain appliqué motifs from the Hertenrits inventory. On the other hand, various Incised or Modeled-Incised motifs of the Mabaruma phase were incorporated. The Abary River thus appears to mark a late point of contact between the migrating Proto-Eastern and Proto-Northern Maipuran Arawaks of the Rouse hypothesis, evidently *via* the entrepôt at Recht-door-Zee at the Mouth of the Demerara River where continuity with Hertenrits culture remained in evidence in the survival of the traditional wattle-and-daub dwelling (Wishart 1982) as well as in ceramics with the kaolin temper of the Orealla Cliffs. As has been shown, the trait of kaolin temper was transmitted, *via* Recht-door-Zee, as far into the North West as the entrepôt at Assakata on the upper Waini, evidently an ethnic frontier since Archaic times.

A bead-making industry at Karapa Creek on the Mahaica River utilized quartz crystals, amethyst and jasper (Roth 1944), all rock materials of *terra firme*. The quartz crystals probably derived from known occurrences in the Roraima Highlands, suggesting a trade link with the upper Mazaruni River. Amethyst and jasper suggest the long-distance trade route by means of which the earliest Clovis-type projectile points reached the coast, i.e., from the unique local exposures in the Pakaraimas *via* the Wenamu and the Barama, the latter a tributary of the Waini. Polished quartz beads perforated through the center were recovered at Enmore. Similar beads and blanks on agate, amethyst and jasper from Recht-door-Zee suggest a local bead-making industry (Wishart 1982a). Alternatively, the beads may reflect the role of Recht-door-Zee as a trade entrepôt on the Orinoco-Amazon route. Bead-making is weakly attested on the Abary River, where the sole surviving specimen is on felspar (Evans and Meggers 1960:161). The blanks, unfinished or discarded specimens and unutilized chips indicate an *in situ* industry under specialist craftsmen. Besides having been polished to perfection, individual beads were biconically drilled, transversely or longitudinally, by a technique unknown elsewhere on the coast. While bead-making was a traditional feature of the Hertenrits Complex, materials utilized there were ceramics, shell or bone (Boomert 1980). Ceramic bead-making traveled as far to the west as the Abary River (Evans and Meggers 1960: Figure 67 d), but if the drilling of each stone bead there did not, as Roth (1944:45) supposed, consume the spare time of three generations of craftsmen, then modification of these semi-precious stones suggests a relationship with some more advanced technology, probably European, on *terra firme*. Already toward the ending of the sixteenth century, Dutch ships trading in salt along the Venezuelan Coast were bartering axes, knives, beads, trinkets and gaudy ornaments to Arawaks at Nibi (Idaballi), on Captain Creek, upper Mahaica River, against cotton, hammocks, hemp, annatto, letterwood, balsam and tobacco (Leechman 1913). Unfortunately, Leechman did not provide the source of his information, but upgrading the local industry by supplying simple drills may well have contributed to creating the economic dependency which, as on the West African coast, was essential in furthering early Dutch trade interests in these parts.

The indicated movement of semi-precious stones from the hinterland to the coast was embedded in a larger and older trade network involving more utilitarian stone products such as the axes, adzes, whetstones and manioc graters upon which rested the viability of these full-blown manioc economies. In the Enmore inventory, Verrill recorded:

> ... granite polishers or rubbers, granite plates, and granite baking slab or pounding pot, besides rough and partially polished fragments of hornblende schist from which *the greater number* of stone implements found in the mound seem to have been made - rock materials which are distinctly derived from the interior parts of the colony. (italics added).

Verrill's assumption regarding the hinterland source of the hornblende schist was correct. Other than in the North West, a greenstone belt occurs only in the New River Triangle, in the far southeast of Guyana. Amphibole schist was the principal export of groups on the lower Aruka River since the canoe manufacturing industry of Archaic times. The trade from the North West also carried the andesite, quartzite, granite and quartz that has been recovered in habitation refuse in the Abary phase, as well as the steatite employed in its ceramic industry. All these materials derived from the upper Barama River. They all passed through Recht-door-Zee *via* the system of inland waterways linking the mouths of the Essequibo and Orinoco Rivers, Figures 4.31.,4.40.

Inception of the Abary phase has been estimated at between A.D. 1200-1300 (Evans and Meggers 1960:189), i.e., partly contemporaneous with other Hertenrits successor complexes such as Kwatta, Barbakoeba and Themire. In its westward migration, Abary phase pottery came to represent a congeries of influences deriving from Mabaruma and Koriabo ceramics superimposed on a surviving Hertenrits base. The most characteristic survival among Hertenrits vessel shapes in the Abary phase is the ubiquitous Form 5 bowl (see Boomert 1980). Certain small, collared jars in the Recht-door-Zee inventory, apparently of mortuary function, also represent survival of a Hertenrits type. Decoration in the Abary phase was by fine-line and broad-line incision, punctation and modeling, with motifs ranging from arbitrary incisions on vessel exteriors to more ordered design elements deriving from other complexes. These influences are diagnostic of the age-old imperatives of complementarity between coastal and hinterland economies in the Guianas.

Nearest to the Mouth of the Demerara River, Chateau Margôt, just outside

Georgetown, is dominantly characterized by Apostaderan ceramics (Osgood 1946). The laying of railway tracks on sand reefs traversing the city a century and a half ago may explain the fact that not a single potsherd has ever been reported on the site of present-day Georgetown. The area appears never to have enjoyed an Amerindian name, which is perhaps significant where, though it has functioned as a Dutch highway since the early seventeenth century, traditional names survive across the entire Coastal Hinterland. Yet, immediately across the Demerara River, at Recht-door-Zee, the influence of the Mabaruma phase is overwhelming. However, the Incised, and Incised and Modeled types in the ceramic inventory there refer to a much earlier period, Figure 4.42. Here, evidently, Rouse's Proto-Northern, or Orinocan, Maipuran Arawaks had made contact with their Proto-Eastern, or Amazonian brethren long before the advance of the Abary phase petered out just outside Georgetown. Evidently, the main communication route had been along the east-west trending Intermediate Savannas, some distance inland, between the Corentyne and the Demerara Rivers. This is part of the narrow belt of savannas stretching between the hinterland forests and the sea and stretching north and northwestward from the Mouth of the Amazon. Along this route, finally, the great Arawak migrations had converged at Recht-door-Zee well before sites of the coastal Abary phase had reached the Demerara River.

The Proto-Northern/Proto-Eastern Maipuran Arawo convergence

Long before the settlement pattern of the mound building pioneers of the Eastern Guiana Littoral had given way to the dispersed homesteads of reef dwellers occupying the swamp edges, settlements of the Orealla Complex, located above the brackish mangrove wetlands, on the great bulge of the Corentyne River, had grown to importance as the gateway to the west.

Although the prehistoric archaeology of the Guiana Coastal Plain has attracted sustained interest for well over the past hundred years (Boomert 1980, 1993; Evans and Meggers 1960; Goodland n.d., Goodland 1964; Im Thurn 1884; Osgood 1946; Poonai 1978; Quelch 1894; Verrill 1918a; Versteeg 1983, 1985; Versteeg and Bubberman 1993; Wishart 1982), investigations in the adjacent Coastal Hinterland have been sporadic and in any case a good deal more recent (Carter 1943; Geijskes 1960-1961; Simon MS; Versteeg 1978). As noted above, the Corentyne River remains virtually a terra incognita.

Orealla is located above the tidal reach of the Corentyne at the apex of an immense fan-shaped deposit of estuarine and riverain clays some 90 km from the sea coast. From its flood plain, its spectacular chalk cliffs rise sheer to the Tertiary White Sand Plateau of the Coastal Hinterland, Figure 4.67a.

The White Sand Plateau is a landscape of wet savannas interspersed by bush islands, clumps of moriche palms and gallery forest. The soil comprises coarse sands with intercalated clays, gray clays and lignitic beds extending to a maximum 300 km

Figure 4.67 a,b. Orealla, Corentyne River. **a**. The chalk cliffs, **b**. Excavation of Marjorie Landing overlooking the river.

inland behind the Coastal Plain. Marjorie Landing, situated on a bluff overlooking the river, is one of several sites of the Orealla Complex stretching from Epira in the south to Seba in the north, a distance of around 40 km along the Corentyne left bank, and from Kaurikreek to Apwaka on the right bank, Figure 4.67 b. As noted above, Seba, on Mapenna Creek, is conveniently located to have functioned as a waystation on the route to Joanna on the coastal reefs. The sole date so far obtained for a site of the Orealla Complex, 1080 +/- 60 B.P., A.D. 880, (Beta 20008) may therefore date Joanna as well.

Orealla pottery is affiliated to the Arauquinoid late Hertenrits style, though distinguished by an unusual array of tempering materials. Most characteristic are ignimbrite, kaolin, quartz sand, laterite, charcoal and caraipé. Ignimbrite is an intermediate to acid rock of the Precambrian Iwokrama Formation which runs across Guyana from the upper Essequibo to Governor Falls on the left bank Corentyne (Barron pers. comm. 1980). Kaolin derived from the Orealla Cliffs. Typically, a single sherd combined two or more of these aplastics. While major vessel shapes derive from the Hertenrits inventory, decorative elements of the Santarem, Koriabo and Mabaruma phases are also present, Figure 4.68.

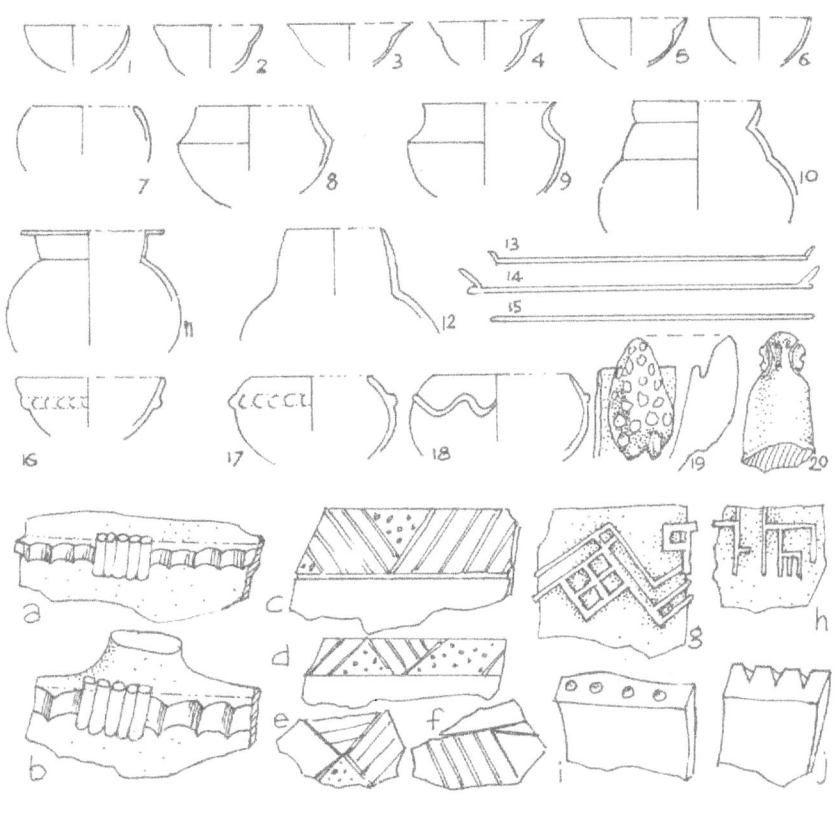

Figure 4.68. The Orealla Complex. Vessel shapes and decoration.

By far the largest number of Hertenrits vessel shapes occur at Marjorie Landing. By comparison, the site at Orealla Creekmouth on the floodplain yielded few vessel shapes and these, as also at Apwaka in Suriname, were associated with artifacts of the eighteenth century Lutheran Mission. No Dutch relics were reported from the Kaurikreek site further upstream, where, again, the recorded inventory of vessel shapes is relatively poor. However, Kaurikreek yielded numerous specimens of circular-sectioned strap handles, sometimes pegged, as well as a variety of lugs and adornos that suggest a wider range of vessel shapes than were actually reported

(Versteeg 1978). Incised designs are geometric, mainly comprising parallel diagonals opposed at right angles, sometimes combined with zoned punctates -- typical of Arauquinoid rims. More unusually, appliqué strips were employed as frets, serpentines or continuously nicked bands on shoulders or rims of vessels. Short, contiguously arranged cylindrical elements were combined with a nicked appliqué motif on the shoulders of certain vessels. Large, biomorphic adornos were attached to direct rims. Among these, a turtle element, a symbol of head/foot polarization in Guianese funerary art, Figure 4.68,19, derived from the Akawaio who in turn had inherited it from their Karinya Carib ancestors. A distinctive appliqué fret in the Hertenrits inventory, Figure 4.68 g,h, is well represented at Kaurikreek, while a vulture motif in the Santarem style on the lower Amazon, Figure 4.68,20, evidently also a mortuary symbol, occurs in the Orealla Complex as well as in the Mabaruma phase, Figure 4.35c. Trade with the lower Amazon is evidenced in the movement of stone tools along the Trombetas/Corentyne corridor. Thus, the diversity of styles and artifacts comprising the Orealla Complex emphasizes its role as the main trade entrepôt on the route between the lower Amazon and the lower Orinoco in Classic Mabaruma times.

Reciprocally, Recht-door-Zee on the Demerara River displays evidence of technological interaction with Orealla on the Corentyne River. The kaolin of the Orealla Cliffs occurs in local ceramics there. This technological link with the Corentyne River survived the crossing of the Essequibo Delta (35 km wide) and, *via* the Moruka River, penetrated the swamp basin of the Western Guiana Littoral to as far as Assakata, on the upper Waini. At the same time, a potsherd sample from Assakata exhibited the micaceous temper of the *Koberimo Plain* ceramics of the Western Guiana Littoral. The trait of kaolin temper appears not to have crossed the Waini-Barima watershed into northwestern Guyana. It is absent at Koriabo Point (N-4 in the terminology of Evans and Meggers 1960:67). Koriabo Point is the port of arrival of goods dispatched across the Barima-Waini watershed from the upper Waini. Therefore, as its name implies, Assakata appears to have been the "meeting point" of the two great interaction spheres linking the lower Amazon and lower Orinoco Rivers.

These distributions doubtless reflect the traditional custom by which, for convenience and expediency, factors in a given alliance traveled great distances with prepared pottery clays rather than with made-up vessels that were subject to breakage or loss *en route*. Contemporary Patamona traveling from the North Pakaraimas to the upper Essequibo River equip themselves with unfired clay for the journey. They manufacture their pottery, as needed, at the site of their hosts. This custom is already evidenced in the refuse of preagricultural potters from the lower Aruka assigned by their shellfishing hosts on Wahana Island to occupancy of the nearby cave during protracted trade visits. It would seem to explain occurrences of fired or unfired lumps of clay often encountered in the refuse of these shellfishers (e.g. Evans and Meggers 1960:31). Specimens of a peg-topped, tubular adorno recovered in Saladoid refuse at Kurupukari Falls on the upper Essequibo River, Figure 4.50d., and therefore dating early in the first millennium B.C., occur also in the pottery of recent Patamona in the North Pakaraimas (Williams 1994:Figure 2) as well as on the Tapajós (Palmatary 1960:99). Thus, as seems indicated by the refuse on Wahana Island, at Kurupukari Falls and at Recht-door-Zee, typologically or technologically abberant potsherds in a given assemblage would appear to represent the exigencies of local travel within sometimes quite vast trade networks.

As evidenced in the canoe manufacturing industry of the Archaic, strategic raw materials moving either way across the Waini-Barima watershed had been directed through Koriabo Point. The as yet unexcavated shell mounds at Honobo, Drum Hill and Mount Everard on the Barima River evidently were the reciprocals, *via* Koriabo Point, of the shell mound complex on the upper Waini. Similarly, in horticulturist times, it was to Koriabo Point that goods from the lower Aruka River were directed across the watershed apparently *via* Drum Hill on the Barima, Figure 4.43. More work needs to be directed to determine the extent to which resource complimentarities on both the Archaic and horticulturist time levels may have patterned the associated migrations and therefore contributed to regional integration. In any case, after their lengthy odyssey, which had commenced in remote antiquity somewhere on the upper Rio Negro, the convergence of Proto-Northern and Proto-Eastern Maipuran Arawaks appears to have eventuated on the basis of various local transactions within interlocking trade networks. In stages, these local trade networks finally linked horticulturists on the lower Amazon and the lower Orinoco Rivers.

The demise of the Orinoco-Amazon interaction corridor

The disruption of traditional economies on the Coastal Hinterland is indicated toward the end of the sixteenth century by the advent at Nibi on the upper Mabaica River of Dutch salt traders from the Venezuelan Coast. The demand of these traders for a variety of products of forest and farm appears to have brought into being a number of settlements clustering around the Mahaica headwaters -- Abe, Barabara-Shanle, Marwa, Yamora -- whose ceramic refuse, while exhibiting clear affiliations with the Orealla Complex, lacks the variety and richness of its major decorative elements. At the same time, a few traits of Mabaruma ceramics are weakly represented at these sites, suggesting their emergence after the Recht-door-Zee entrepôt had gone into decline.

More definitively disruptive and more permanent was the arrival of Dutch settlers at Wironie Creek on the Berbice River in 1627. Just as de Forest's map (1625) affords a final view of traditional settlements on the Eastern Guiana Littoral before Contact, so also does van Stapels' map (1629) afford a glimpse of contemporary settlement on the Berbice and Canje Rivers, Figure 4.69 a. By the mid-eighteenth century, their influence on traditional polities had been profound, Figure 4.69b. To the Dutch presence is probably to be attributed the emergence of uncharacteristically large villages at Hitia, upstream, as well as on the Abary River a few hours' walk across the watershed (van Berkel 1948/1695). Refuse at the more recent administrative center at Fort Nassau yielded potsherds of the Abary phase, Figure 4.70. These vessels include the globular jar with collarlike neck which, at other Arawak sites, e.g. Seba on the Demerara River, Figure 4.69c, or Mon Repos on the Demerara coast, is included in funerary ritual.

While admitting the possibility that the Seba artifacts represented a burial, Carter (1943) was puzzled at the absence of human skeletal remains, concluding that the body had been buried elsewhere. Repeated investigations at dated Dutch tombs have shown that in the acid soils of Guyana human skeletal remains do not survive longer than 250 years. Indeed, Carter's own data suggest *in situ* burial.

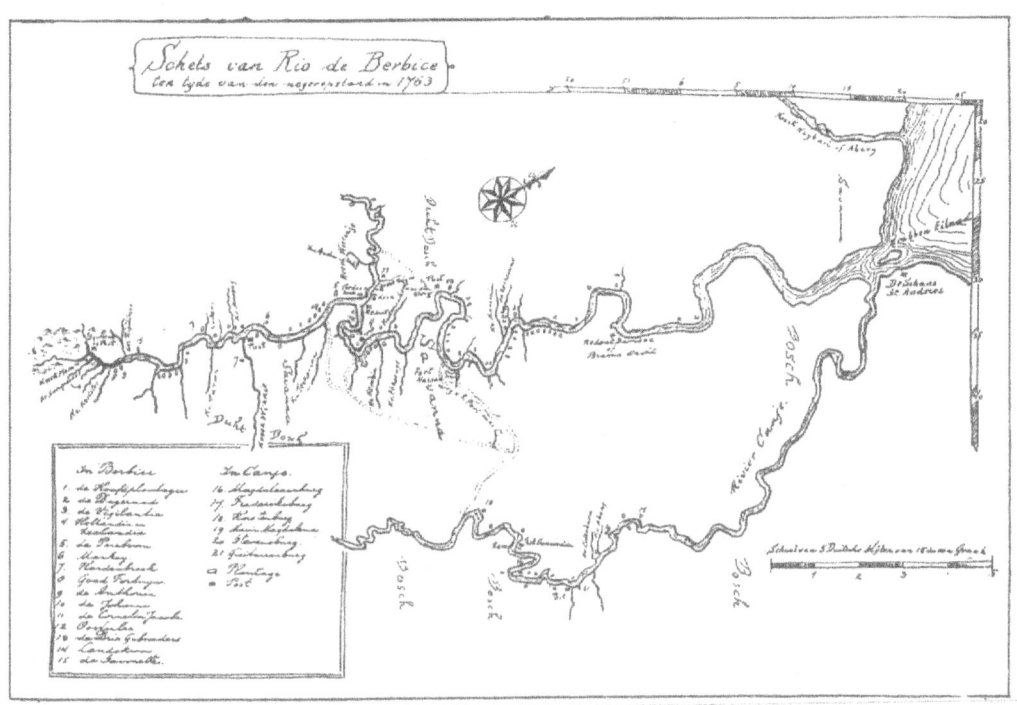

Figure 4.69a. Dutch colonists on the Berbice and Canje Rivers 1629 (*after van Wallenburg 1995*).

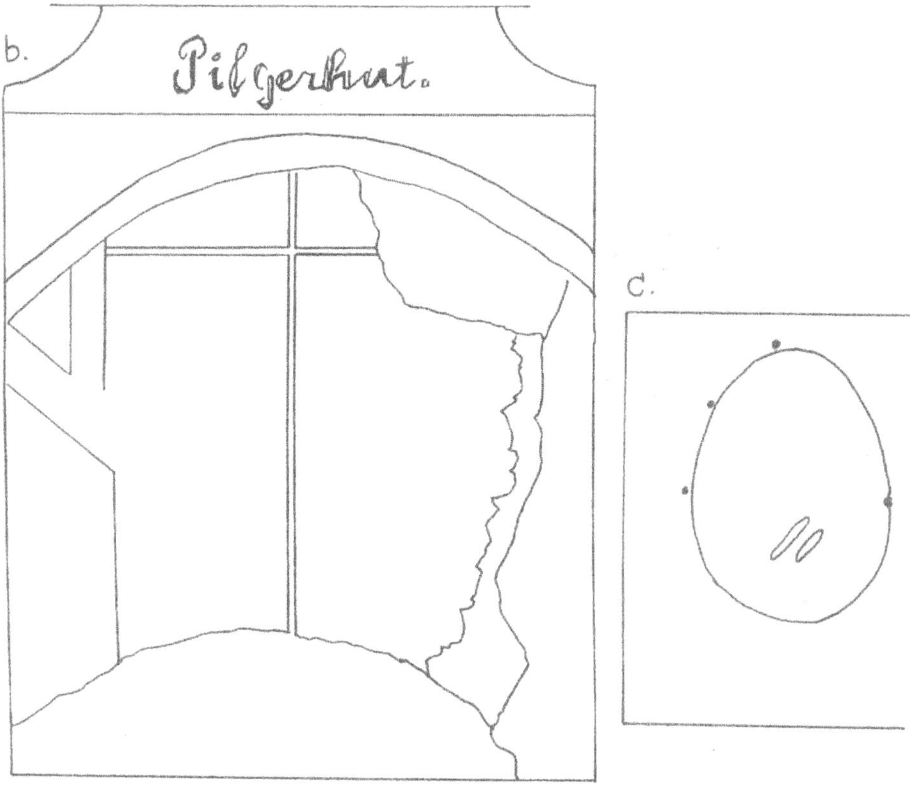

Figure 4.69. **b.** Pilgerhut Mission, Berbice River ca. 1750. **c.** Burial, Seba Creek, Demerara River.

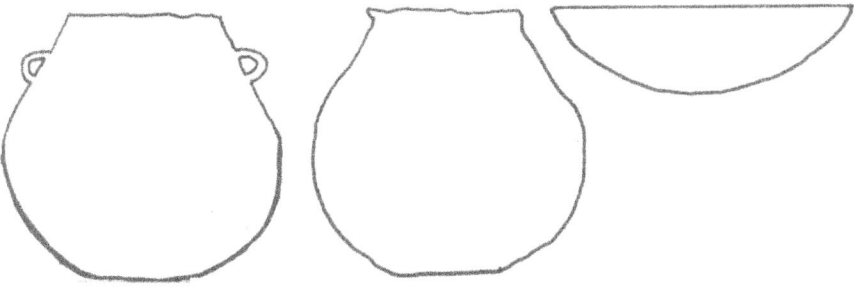

Figure 4.70. Fort Nassau, Berbice River. Dredged up Arawak vessels.

The pottery vessels had been carefully laid out in an asymmetrical oval oriented on an east-west axis.

> ... the two principal stone artifacts [two large boat-building adzes] lay side by side resting against each other with their points in the same direction. They appeared to have been laid very carefully in position on the undisturbed subsoil. On top of them was the mass of pottery ... On the perimeter of the pile lay the four hammerstones.

These materials are held in the collections of the Walter Roth Museum. In the above description "points" should read "butts," while "hammerstones" should read "whetstones." With these substitutions made, the picture is of a westward oriented burial with the adzes carefully deposited on the undisturbed subsoil, butt ends directed to the northwest, before the pottery vessels and whetstones were laid out around the perimeter of the pit. The configuration of these artifacts around the peripheries of the pit leaves room for the inference that its now vacant center had once been occupied by the individual, evidently a builder of canoes, whose identity had been symbolized by the tools of his erstwhile craft. The careful excavation and mapping of this burial is a unique contribution to Arawak studies in so far as it probably constitutes the final record of Arawak traditional funerary practice on the Coastal Hinterland before this sector of the ancient Orinoco-Amazon trade route was transformed into a Dutch highway during the seventeenth century.

The Carib migrations
Introduction

By the time of our earliest record of a Carib presence in the Guianas, around 200 B.C., Arawak occupation of the circum-Guiana lowlands was already well advanced. By this time, as has been seen, Proto-Northern Maipuran Arawak horticulturists had been in occupation on the lower Aruka River for more than a thousand years, while, not much later in the lower Amazon area, commencing around 1000 B.C., their Proto-Eastern brethren had been in occupation on the upper Essequibo River. By around the time of Christ, these Proto-Easterners were located on the Eastern Guiana Littoral, at the Mouth of the Corentyne River. However, there are indications that continuing inquiries on the Western Guiana Littoral might yet locate an even earlier Carib presence there, possibly also dating into the second millennium B.C.

At the present time, there are two main dialects of Katinya, an eastern and a western. The eastern dialect is spoken by 250-500 persons in Brazil and by 1200 in Guyane française and in the Marowijne River area of northeastern Suriname. The western dialect is spoken in the center and west of Suriname (2400 speakers of both dialects), in Guyana, by 450 people, and in Venezuela by 1500. This western dialect

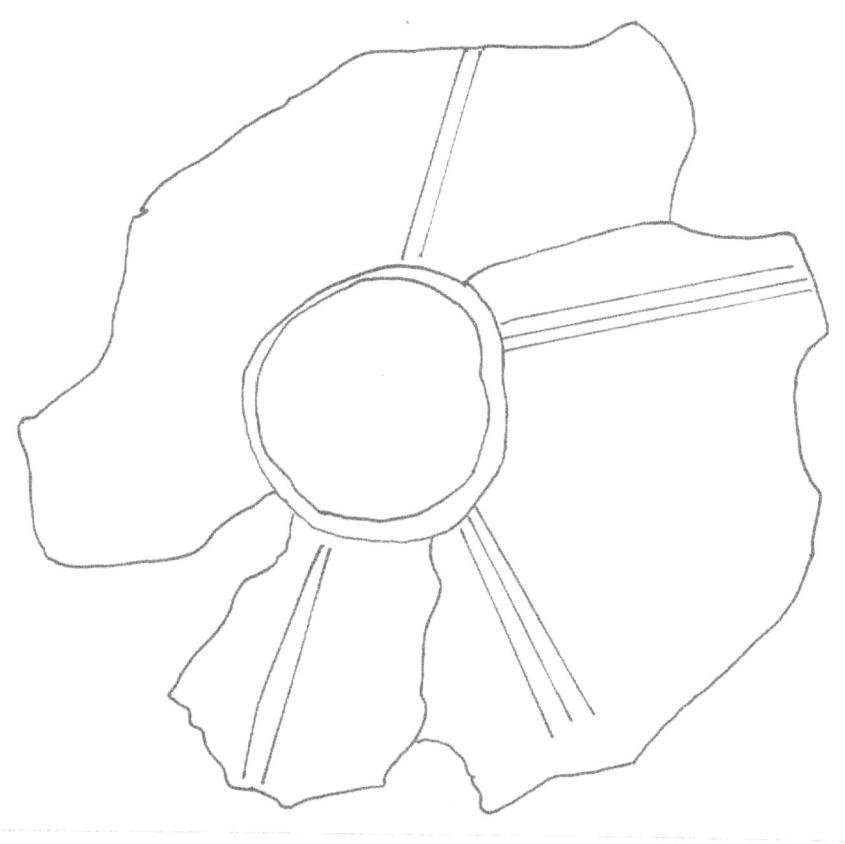

Figure 4.71. Waiwaru Creek, Pomeroon River. Zones Incised Crosshatch on interior of Karinya (?) burial urn *(Photo: Walter Roth Museum)*.

itself comprises two subdialects, one in central and western Suriname, and another in Guyana and Venezuela (Peasgood 1972). As has been seen, the Corentyne River, which represents the division between the eastern and western subdialects of Karinya, was the route of entry of the Proto-Eastern Maipuran Arawaks who had initiated settlement on the Eastern Guiana Littoral during the first centuries of the Christian Era.

After Contact, "Caribs" were located by various European authors upstream on the major rivers, behind the Arawaks (see Benjamin 1982). This situation resulted from our demonstrated Proto-Eastern Maipuran Arawak expansion along the Eastern Guiana Littoral during the first millennium A.D. The refuse of these Arawaks has been recognized at Buckleberg-1, Hertenrits and its successor cultures, with an aftermath that was felt across the Coastal Hinterland *via* Recht-door-Zee and into the Waini drainage at Assakata. However, it is worth repeating here, in advance of later evidences, that the "Caribs" of the European record invariably prove on archaeological evidence to have been confused with their linguistic descendants, the Kapon (Akawaio), denizens of the rain forest, where already they were pioneering exploration during the closing centuries before Christ.

By contrast, as the distribution of their language group shows, the Karinya were, and remain to the present, strictly coast-adapted in the Guianas. They were first recognized by a distinctive, archaeological complex in the swamps between the mouths of the Essequibo and the Orinoco Rivers. Later, this group expanded southeastward along the Eastern Guiana Littoral almost as far as to the Mouth of the Amazon. This expansion to the southeast was modified by the prior presence of Proto-Easterners on parts of the Eastern Guiana Littoral. To the west, their affiliations appear to have been with the Coastal Caribs of Venezuela, and they may have extended even farther to the west, into the upper Cauca Valley of Colombia, Figure 4.72. In view of certain surviving traits in Karinya ceramics to which attention will be drawn in due course, Durbin (1977:30) ought to be included in this linguistic review:

> ... we believe that we can posit a close unity among the Venezuelan coastal groups, the groups in Sierra de Perija, and the Opone-Carare. This would seem to represent a western migration across the plains into the Lake Maracaibo area, then north into the Siera de Perija, and also south through the foothills of the Sierra and down the Magdalena.

While prior Arawak occupation of large areas of the Eastern Guiana Littoral effectively limited the southeastward expansion of the Karinya to hitherto unoccupied stretches of the Eastern Guiana Littoral, the reverse situation was obtained in the hinterland. Here, in turn, Arawak expansion was limited by the prior occupancy of the rain forest by the Carib-speaking Kapon (Akawaio). This is the

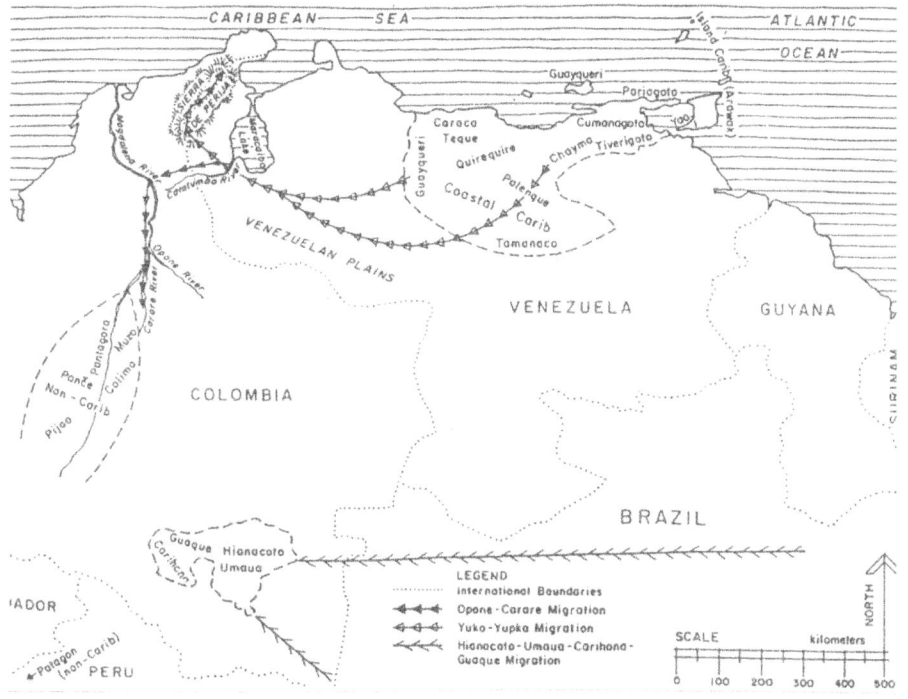

Figure 4.72. Some Carib tribes of Colombia and northern Venezuela and their possible migration routes. (*after Durbin 1977*).

situation that has been described by most European writers, Arawaks on the lower courses of the rivers, "Carib" (= Akawaio) on the upper.

In fact, behind the coastal dispersion of the Karinya lay the vast hinterland expanse of speakers of the Central Guiana and Western Guiana subfamilies of the Carib language group (Migliazza 1982), the East-West Guiana Caribs of Durbin (1977). Dominating these hinterland Carib-speakers in time as well as in space were the Akawaio. Their diagnostic Koriabo phase ceramics indicate that the Akawaio dispersal from coastal Karinya stock at around the time of Christ followed two routes into the hinterland. The first was *via* the great streams of the Essequibo Basin, eventually to encounter the cultures of the North Pakaraimas and the Rupununi-Rio Branco Savannas. In the second route, Akawaio traders traversed the rain forest west to east, descending the north-flowing and south-flowing streams of the Acarai and Tumac Humac watersheds and reached the Eastern Guiana Littoral. There they encountered, on the one hand, *via* the great coastal streams of the Eastern Guiana Hinterland, the Oyapoc, Approuague, Marouini, Suriname and Saramacca, the Proto-Eastern Maipuran Arawaks of coastal Suriname and Guyane française and, on the other, apparently *via* the Rio Jari, groups of their Western Karinya ancestors around the Mouth of the Amazon. As we attempted to do with the ancient Arawak migrations around the Guiana land mass, the remainder of our inquiry will cite the available archaeological evidences in support of linguistic reconstructions that identify more recent Carib-speaking peoples expanding across it.

The Western Karinya. The Pomeroon empties into the Atlantic about 30 km to the west of the Essequibo Delta. Waiwaru Creek (*Waiwaru* is a Karinya proper noun), a small left tributary, drains the basement edge just above the Arapiako River, a main tributary of the Pomeroon about 65 km up, Figure 4.73.

Figure 4.73. Waiwaru Creek. Depth of the canoe landing suggests centuries of cutting into its floodplain.

A peat sample taken on 70 cm below the surface of the ground at Jacobus Farm on the Pomeroon floodplain just above the Arapiako returned a C^{14} date at $3120 +/- 70$ B.P., or 1170 B.C. (Beta 44743). This implies that brackish conditions survived on the upper Pomeroon River well beyond the freshwater climax which, on the nearby Moruka River, had commenced around 3300 B.C. It will be recalled (p. 145) that, at around this latter date, environmental stress generated by freshening, and accompanied by an imperceptibly rising water level in the swamps, had produced symptoms of socio-cultural strain among the Waramuri shellfishers. Among these symptoms was the development of the dugout canoe on Haimarakabra Creek and an enforced residential shift to Kabakaburi on the neighboring Pomeroon River. The continuing brackish environment of the Pomeroon River at this time, evidenced by its complex of shell mounds comprising entirely refuse of the brackish-water *Zebra Nerite*, was a function of a once much wider Essequibo Delta. The recovery of a shell of *Strombus pugilis* in horticulturist refuse on Waiwaru Creek, dating at 2150 +/- 70 b.p., 200 B.C. (Beta 27649), attests to the late survival of brackish conditions on parts of the Pomeroon swamp edge. The levees of the Essequibo deltaic islands and the estuarine levees to east and west of its present mouth exhibit a common stratigraphic connection with marine clays of the Commowine sedimentation phase on the Guiana Coastal Plain which dates later than A.D. 1000 (Brinkman and Pons 1968:27). As shown in the profile at Jacobus Farm, Figure 4.74, mangrove vegetation established along the western delta margin of the Essequibo during the preceding thousand and more years had been overtaken by progradation of the coastline and consequent contraction of the delta.

Therefore, two potsherds recovered on the basement edge in sterile clay underlying the peat layer on Jacobus' Farm suggest alternative possibilities for interpretation: (*i*) they represent human exploitation of the Essequibo delta margin well in advance of the initial encroachment of mangrove vegetation there; (*ii*) when recovered, these potsherds no longer were in true association; their deposition may have postdated the emergence of the peat layer.

The peat deposit varies between 20-50 cm thick, and underlies 30-60 cm of brownish-clay soil, probably clays of the Commowijne phase, supporting the present vegetation.

Figure 4.74. Jacobus Farm.

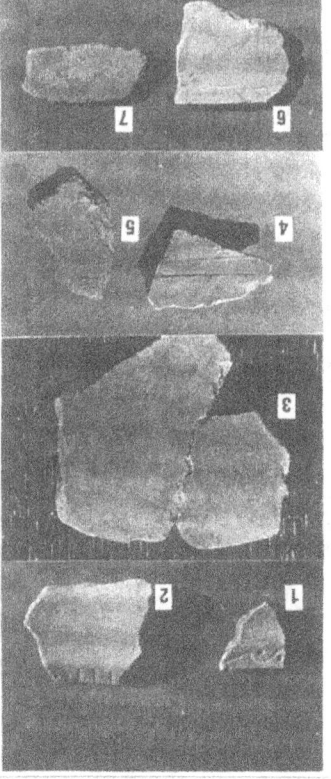

Figure 4.75. Karinya pottery.

The sherds derived from a deep bowl with incurving sidewalls, direct rim and beveled lip (a Waiwaru trait) on a paste including fine, water-worn sand. Search over a wide area for a more substantial sherd sample proved futile.

Recovery of evidently stray sherds of the Waiwaru phase below peat on the swamp edge favors the second of the above interpretations: they derived from irrigation horticulture on the swamp edge some time after the peat deposit there had been submerged and the present soil cover had commenced to develop.

A habitation site of the ancient Karinya lay on white sand some two kilometers inland, on the Pomeroon-Akawini watershed, at an elevation of around 15 meters. At the present time (1987), the site is used as a weekly marketplace. Post-holes sunk in the white sand of the hill top during the erection of market stalls encountered a midden on 50-55 cm below the surface of the ground and extending some 100-120 meters over the hill top. The excavated sample comprised potsherds, a broken ground and polished trapezoidal adze of the type employed in Archaic canoe manufacture at the Kabakaburi mound and the just mentioned shell of *Strombus pugilis* fractured for extracting the meat, Figure 4.75.

The overwhelming bulk of the pottery (66.6%) was tempered with caraipé. Clay employed for the remaining 33.3% was characterized by natural inclusions of fine, waterworn quartz sand, particle sizes of which ranged from microscopic to 1.0 mm maximum diameter. Clay mined by today's Karinya at the traditional quarry at Paiwari Creek, on the Issororo River upstream, exhibits similar natural inclusions of fine quartz sand. Sherds with these characteristics from the contemporary industry are indistinguishable from the prehistoric specimens.

Decoration of the pottery of Waiwaru Market is by appliqué, incision, scraping, white slipping and red-on-white painting. Appliqué typically includes biomorphic nubbins, single or double ovoidal nubbins, and lugs with strap handles. Incised decoration is broad-line varying between 1-2 mm wide, 5 mm deep. Fine-line is generally deep and irregular. Shallow, scraped bands up to 8 mm wide, with no depth, are also characteristic. On interior surfaces of rims are placed deep, triangular incisions, serpentines alternating with punctates, single or double incisions following the rim contour, and circumscribed punctates. Fine-line zoned hachure motifs, either cross-hatched or comprising parallel-line incisions, occur on the inner surfaces of urn lids. Red-on-white painting was applied on upper exteriors of collared jars, though the apparently geometric bands comprising the designs are now almost totally eroded.

Diagnostic vessel shapes of the Waiwaru phase are shown in Figure 4.76.

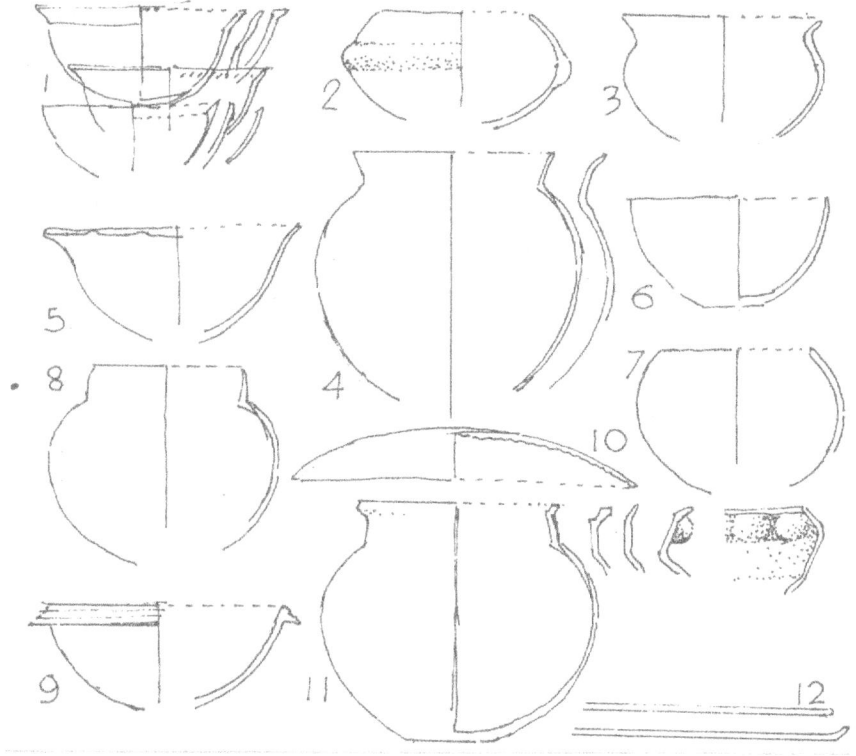

Figure 4.76. Waiwaru Market. Diagnostic vessel shapes.

Up and downriver from Waiwaru Creek, undated assemblages at St. Monica, Maupendu, Piraka Landing, Kabakaburi and Wakapao-Kokorichi exhibit the main characteristics of the Waiwaru inventory. Among popular vessel shapes are the *tomaien*, Form 3, universally favored to the present for the preparation of the pepperpot *(tuma)*, the Form 5 open bowl with wide, flaring, frequently lobed rim and the Form 11 collared jar, probably of mortuary associations. Along with others, these three vessels are well represented at Maupendu and Piraka Landing. Long obscured under second-growth forest, these two sites were relocated by Karinya guides whose ancestors had occupied them during the nineteenth century.

The Karinya of Waiwaru Market represent a model of adaptation to the swamp edge of the Western Guiana Littoral which, over the ensuing millennia, has proven extremely resistant to change. The available evidences suggest that irrigation horticulture has provided the basis of the Karinya settlement pattern from at least the closing centuries of the first millennium B.C., when the landscape differed profoundly from the present. To that time, the Pomeroon landscape had remained a landscape of the Archaic.

This is because the freshening which had caused the demise of the shellfishing lifeway around 3300 B.C. in the neighboring Moruka drainage had had little or no effect on the Pomeroon over the ensuing millennia. Progradation around the margins of the old Essequibo Delta had partitioned the Moruka and Pomeroon Basins. Sealed from freshening on the Moruka, the Pomeroon River had remained brackish, discharging into the old Essequibo delta margin at Charity. Its brackish-water flora and fauna survived into relatively late times. Eventually, its mouth shifted westward with the longshore drift, thereby initiating the progradation on its right bank which sequestered its old mouth at Charity and which continues to the present day, Figure 4.77.

4.77. Pomeroon River.

Irrigation farmers on the Western Guiana Littoral exploit the rich peat soils of the swamp edge by relatively high capital investments in land clearing, empoldering and control of the diurnal movement of the tidal counter-currents in the freshwater swamps or on the flood-plains of creeks draining the swamp edge (p.247). The projected farm plot is empoldered and drained by a system of ditches. Seepage from the rising current is countered by laying a "blind trench" around the plot. Digging this trench permits replacing decaying vegetal matter with pure clay which renders it impervious. The empoldering dam is constructed atop this now "blind" trench. The main drainage channel is controlled by a sluice, the door of which is activated by the force of floodwaters entering the creek twice daily, Figure 4.78a. As water level in the swamps rises above the surface of the farm plot, the crops remain dry, Figure 4.78b. Thus, an edaphic gradient is created from peat or peaty clay on the floodplain, through sandy loam overlying residual clay on the hillslope, to the leached, coarse white sand of the hill top, Figure 4.78c. This gradient supports the wide range of crops that provide the basis of the subsistence round. Since man cannot live by bread alone, the subsistence round on the swamp edge includes the herbaries and orchards needed to supplement the starchy staple of the manioc patch.

Figure 4.78 a-c. a. Irrigation farm plot, b. Slash-and-burn plot on hilltop. c. Soil gradient.

Rewards of these capital investments are sustained-yield cropping and a high level of sedentary occupation. The perennial resource represented by the peat soils constitutes a mitigating factor in the cumulative degradation of mineral soils on the hills by slash-and-burn practices. Already adapted by the time of Christ to a niche on the direct swamp edge that permitted exploiting the edaphic gradient from floodplain to hilltop, the Karinya showed little subsequent interest in occupying any other niche on the Western Guiana Littoral.

The Waiwaru Complex exhibits no evidences whatsoever of the fumbling experimentation that characterized the advent of pottery making on the lower Aruka River during the early centuries of the second millennium B.C. The clay utilized, with its natural inclusions of fine, water-worn quartz sand, suggests that the quarries of the present day Karinya on the Issororo River and on Basher Creek, on the upper Pomeroon, were features of the economic catchment area of their ancestors. Its technical and typological competencies suggest that this pottery was affiliated to a tradition already of respectable antiquity at the time of initial occupation of the Waiwaru Market site. Typologically, the inventory suggests interaction with more western complexes of greater age. The erstwhile distribution of Coastal Carib in northern Venezuela, Figure 4.72, might explain the survival of certain traits of Quimbaya and Calima ceramics of Colombia on this part of the Western Guiana Littoral. Outstanding are certain zoned incised hachure decorative elements that duplicate exactly specimens in the the Ilama phase on the Rio Calima, Figure 4.71, 4.79a-d.

Figure 4.79. a-c. Barabina shell mound (surface). d. Ilama phase, Rio Calima, Colombia (d. after Bray et al 1988).

These occurrences must be placed within the wider context of interaction between the Guiana Coast and Andean ceramic cultures from apparently remote antiquity. The specimens from Barabina Hill recall an ancient Peruvian vessel shape. The incisions occur on wall fragments of a large flat-based pan recovered in humus overlying the shellfish deposit. Large, pan-shaped pottery vessels with flat bases, walls that are relatively low in proportion to the vessel diameter and rise from the base at a sharp angle slanting slightly outward occur early in Mesoamerican chronologies but appear to be missing from early Colombian and Ecuadorian sequences. The type is said to occur in both highland and coastal sequences in Peru, being present at Kotosh from around 1200 B.C. It appeared on the coast around 1500 B.C. (Ford 1969:98, chart 13; see also Tolstoy 1974: Figure 2.1c).

The Waiwaru Market specimen is of interest in its association with funerary ritual. It constitutes a design motif which appears of directional significance in relation to the solstitial arc of the western sky -- the Land of the Dead in ancient Warao cosmology, Figure 3.6. Dissemination of the associated religious beliefs is indicated by the widespread adoption of the motif by various other horticulturist groups across the Guianas from the Venezuelan Coast to the Mouth of the Amazon, Figure 4.80a-f. A rare specimen from a Colombian burial, being plain, suggested the shape of a plate (Bray et al 1988).

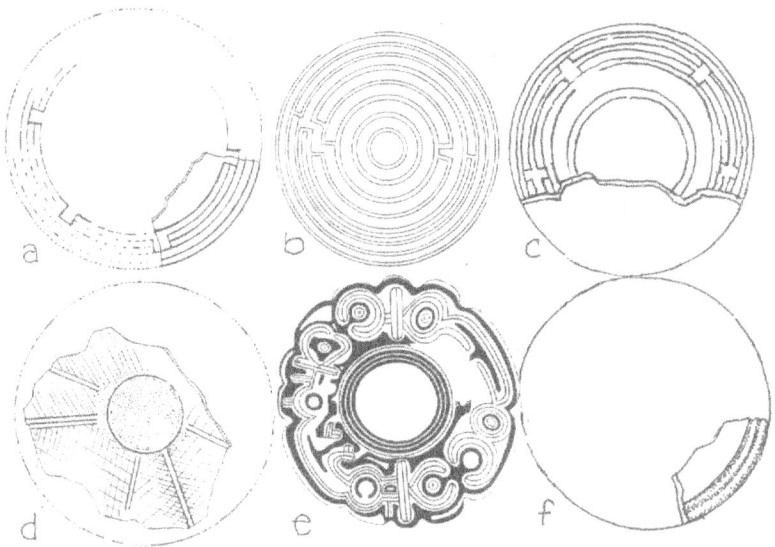

Figure 4.80. Mortuary symbolism among early horticulturists. **a,b**. Waiwaru Market, Pomeroon River, **c**. Eastern Venezuela (*after Vargas 1979:Figure 11*), **d**. Territory of Amapá, Brazil (*after Meggers and Evans 1957:Pl. 15*), **e,f**. Mazaruni River, Guyana.

The hachure motifs indicating the function of these vessels as urn lids among the Western Karinya and elsewhere suggest that all of these peoples shared the ancient Warao, trait of solar orientation of the dead, which, in turn, is of remote antiquity in American cosmology (Hudson and Underhay 1978; Metraux 1949; Roe 1982:272; Yarrow 1881). In various shaft graves of the Colombian Pavas-La Cumbre region on the upper Rio Dagua the trait is indicated by the westward orientation of the burial chambers (Gähwiler-Walder 1988:54).

Besides the Pomeroon, Western Karinya inhabited also the Moruka River, where their red-on-white painted and modeled ceramics attained a remarkable level of excellence, Figure 4.81 a-g. Practitioners of this 2000 year-old craft describe their ceramic coloring techniques: red is obtained from the bark of a tree called *Itara*. After firing, the design is painted on and dried. An extract from the bark of another tree, called *Maporokon*, yields white pigment, which is painted on and left to dry. If the pot is fired, the *Maporokon* gives a black color. *Maporokon* grows on the brown sandy loam of the hill slopes.

Figure 4.81 a-b. Moruka River. Karinya ceramics and ceramists. a. Moruka River *(Walter Roth Museum Collection)*, b. Pomeroon River, made by Rachel Smith.

The Eastern Karinya. A large globular jar with a cover in the shape of a truncated cone, discovered intact on the archaeologically unknown stretch of coast between the Marouini River and the Ile de Cayenne, contained the skeletal remains of an adult. Four vertical segmented appliqué strips placed equidistantly on the shoulder circumference appear to have served the directional end of similar devices on certain *Chaton fantastique* jars of the Aristé phase in Guyane française, Figure 4.82a-c. In its turn, *Chaton fantastique* pottery incorporates major vessel shapes of the Karinya Waiwaru phase on the Pomeroon River, Figure 4.82d-g. An anonymous nineteenth century illustrator of Karinya ceramics in Guyane française depicted a specimen of the double-bellied pottery trumpet of the Galibi, Figure 4.82h., which also characterised the Karinya inventory on the Moruka River, Figure 4.82i. Thus, the typology of the Karinya Waiwaru phase is well represented along the Guiana Coast from the Moruka to the Oyapoc as well as on the Approuague.

Also diagnostic of the Eastern Karinya are the sand-tempered *Ouanary Encoche*, caraipé-and-sand-tempered *Caripo Kwep* and sherd-tempered *Enfer Polychrome* ceramic types of the Aristé phase. Five C^{14} dates representing this sequence commence around A.D. 350 and survive the arrival of Europeans. An earlier initial date at $2070 +/- 45$ B.P., or 164-39 B.C. (calibrated) was rejected by its excavator as unacceptably out of phase with this C^{14} sequence (Rostain 1994a:421). But granted the temporal priority of *Ouanary Encoche* at these earliest of Eastern Karinya sites this rejected C^{14} date is of potential interest. This is because of the above-mentioned typological affiliations between this ceramic type of the pioneering Eastern Karinya and specimens from the Western Karinya on the Pomeroon River dating at +/- 200 B.C.

Among these affiliations is the diagnostic trait of the *Ouanary Encoche* ceramic type -- excision with a stylus to produce a deep, triangular-shaped or quadrangular element. Serially imposed, this element constitutes the *rangée d'encoches* motif of this ceramic type (Rostain 1994a:209). The motif has been recorded in the Waiwaru phase in coastal Guyana, Figure 4.76i, as well as at Paramaribo in coastal Suriname (Goethals MS: PIA). Among various similarly incised specimens from Guyane française, an open bowl with an interiorly thickened everted rim, Figure 4.82j, duplicates the above mentioned specimen from the Waiwaru phase, Figure 4.76i. Two other vessel shapes of the Waiwaru phase occur in *Ouanary Encoche* ceramics, Figure 4.82k,l. In Paramaribo, the *rangée d'encoches* motif occurs in a burial context on the shoulders of a globular jar with collared neck. This vessel shape occurs also both in Guyane française and on Waiwaru Creek on the Pomeroon. White and red paint were associated with sherds exhibiting this *rangée d'encoches* motif. In Guyane française, a specimen of *Ouanary Encoche* was combined with the incised crosshatching of the Pomeroon River Waiwaru phase. Incised crosshatch was employed, also, in the later ceramic type *Caripo Kwep*. Fine-line incision combined with red painting on an urn lid in the *Ouanary Encoche* ceramic type of Guyane française duplicates a highly distinctive motif in the mortuary ceramics of the Waiwaru Complex on the Pomeroon, Figure 4.82l.

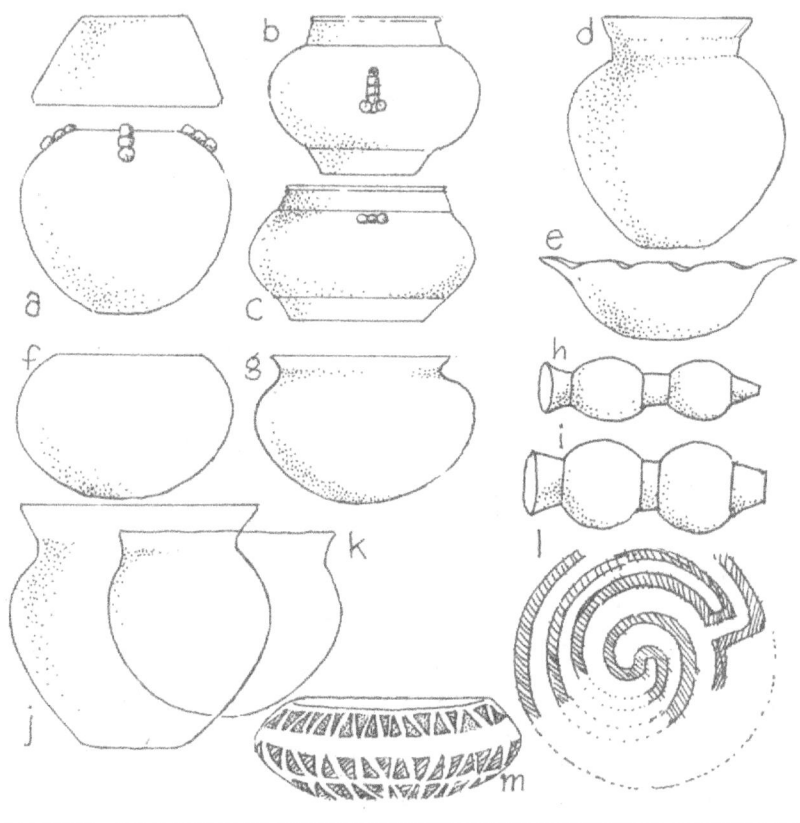

Figure 4.82. a-m. Comparative traits in Eastern and Western Karinya ceramics. **a.** Burial urn (*after Rostain 1994, ii:50*); **b-g.** The Chaton fantastique ceramic type (cf. Koriabo phase of Guyana and Suriname (*after Rostain 1994, ii [nos. 107.2, 107.3, 104.3, 104.7, 104.12, 108.1]*); **h.** Galibi clay trumpet, Guyane française (*after Rostain 1994, ii:136*); **i.** Karinya clay trumpet, Moruka River Guyana (*Coll. Walter Roth Museum*); **j,k.** Vessel shapes of the *Ouanary Encoche* ceramic type; **l.** Red-painted and incised "plate", Guyane française (*after Rostain 1994,ii:86, cf. Waiwaru phase, Figure 4.80 a*); **m.** Champleve decoration, upper Rio Cauca, Colombia.

Granted the affiliation with the ceramics of the upper Cauca Valley in Colombia that is suggested by the trait of zoned incised crosshatch, it seems reasonable to seek comparisons between the *rangée d'encoches* motif of the *Ouanary Encoche* ceramic type in Guyane française and the champlevé element in the Quimbaya ceramics of the Cauca Valley. The comparison seems compelling, Figure 4.82m.

Indications of a relationship of some kind between the Colombian Highlands and the Guiana Coast seem further supported by occurrences of Colombian shaft tombs in the Brazilian Territory of Amapá, Figure 4.83a,b.

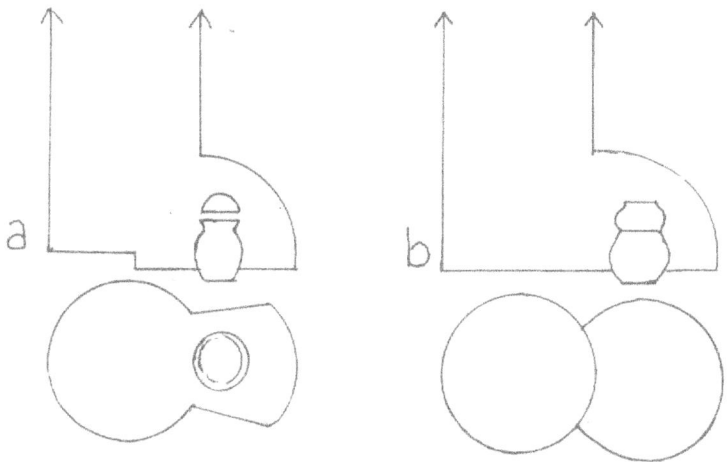

Figure 4.83 a,b. Shaft tombs. **a.** La Cumbre, Colombia *(after Gähwiler-Walder 1988)*, **b.** Amapá, Brazil *(after Meggers and Evans 1957)*.

An explanation of these remarkable relationships over so vast a stretch of territory seems to be given in Hakluyt's account (*Voyages* No. 3, cited in Quelch 1887) of a traditional trade in canoes on the Corentyne River against gold ornaments evidently deriving from the Tairona and Sinu Complexes on the Caribbean Coast of Colombia:

> This river, as also most of the rest, is not navigable above six days' journey by reason of rocks. It is ten days' journey to the head, where the Guianans do dwell. Honey, yarn or cotton, silk, balsamum, and brasil-beds, are here to be had in plenty, and so all the coast along eastward. Some images of gold, spleenstones, and others, may be gotten on this coast, but they do somewhat extraordinarily esteem of them, because everwhere they are current money. They get their moons, and other pieces of gold, by exchange, taking for each one of their greater canoes, *one piece or image of gold, with three heads*; and after that rate for their lesser canoes, they received pieces of gold of less value. One hatchet is the ordinary price of a canoe (*italics added*).

One of these "images of gold," Figure 4.84a, claimed by its vendor to have been dredged up from the bed of the Mazaruni River, in Guyana, suggests that the trade in these objects was an overland rather than a seaborne one, probably mediated by Cariban groups thought by Durbin (1977:30) to have been numerously distributed in the past across northwestern Venezuela and northeastern Colombia. Traditional interaction with northwestern Venezuela seems strongly suggested by the recovery in the Muribang River, a headwater tributary of the Potaro in the North Pakaraimas, of the pottery figurine shown in Figure 4.84b,c. (e.g. see Cruxent 1971:Figures 180/181,188). The mediating agency may have been the Akawaio, in sole occupation of the Mazaruni River, the major communications corridor with the lower Orinoco, ever since the time of Christ. Appropriately, their diagnostic Koriabo phase pottery characterizes the Charlesburg site near Paramaribo not far from the reef that yielded typical refuse of the Eastern Karinya (Goethals MS. Pl. 4:10-18).

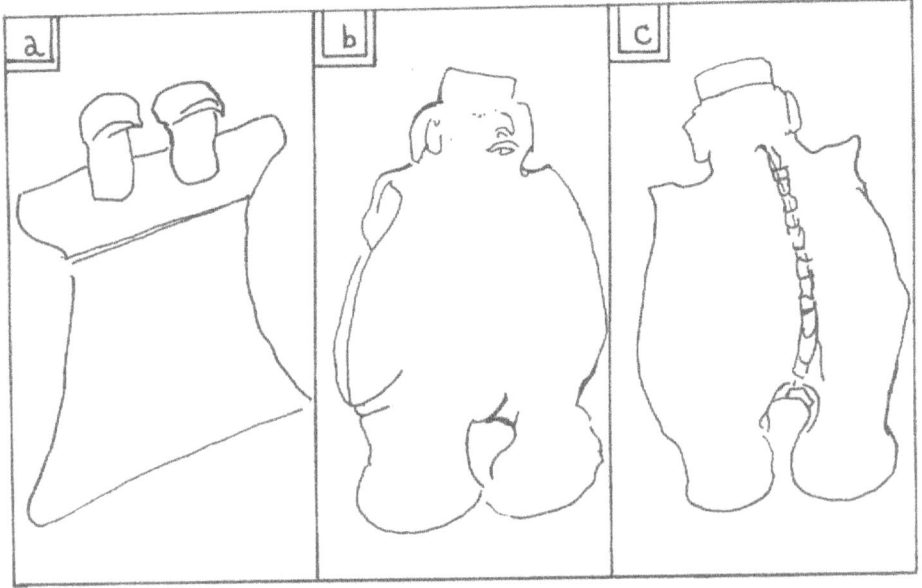

Figure 4.84 a-c. **a.** Gold pectoral. Presented for sale to the Walter Roth Museum by a miner claiming to have dredged it up in the Mazaruni River. **b-c.** Ceramic figurine, probably western Venezuela. Claimed by a miner to have been dredged up in the Muribang River, upper Potaro, Guyana, "under a nine-foot thick layer of gravel, on top of a layer of multicolored clay."

More locally, traits of Aristé phase pottery of the Brazilian Territory of Amapá have been recognized in coastal Suriname inventories (Meggers and Evans 1957:165) though, hitherto, this ceramic style has not been credited to the Karinya. Notable among these traits are the open bowl with wide, flaring rim lobes and the carinated bowl of the Aristé phase inventory. (These vessels represent Form 5 and Form 3, respectively, in the Waiwaru Market inventory). In addition, numerous design elements in the Suriname inventory have their counterparts in Aristé phase decoration, notably the application of red paint to lips and rim edges, common on vessel forms 3 and 4 of *Aristé Painted* and Form 1 of *Serra Painted*. Further similarities were scraped and incised design elements identical to specimens of the Uaçá *Incised, Davi Incised* and *Flexal Scraped* ceramic types of the Aristé phase. Struck by these numerous similarities, Meggers and Evans (1957:165) concluded that the Suriname coastal materials must represent a late intrusion from the south, and conjectured that the more elaborate painted ceramics of the Aristé phase, believed to date to post-Contact times, probably would not be found to occur in these northern areas, at any rate no further north than the northern portion of the Territory of Amapá. There, the indigenous culture was thought to have escaped for longer than in the south the disrupting effects suffered in adjacent parts of the Guianas.

These conclusions derived from a scenario in which Aristé phase ceramics had been considered to represent a northward migration of peoples sharing a common origin, in a so far undetermined time and place, with others representing the Mazagão phase of the southern portion of the Territory of Amapá. Through time, it was thought, these "first cousins" came to be located, mutually exclusively, to north and south of their common frontier, the Rio Araguari.

In the event, and as a result of the later investigations of Rostain (1994, 1994a) and to a lesser extent Goethals (MS) in, respectively Guyane française and Suriname, the prominent presence of *Ouanary Encoche* along this portion of the Eastern Guiana Littoral definitively located these ceramic complexes in the early part of the Aristé phase sequence, with the chronologically later sherd-tempered *Enfer Polychrome* (= sherd-tempered *Serra Plain* of the Aristé phase) already present in Guyane française. With the now firmly established affiliation of the earliest of these ceramic types, *Ouanary Encoche*, to the Waiwaru phase ceramics of the Western Karinya, their occupation of the Guiana Coast appears to have commenced in a Karinya heartland located somewhere to the west, with a lengthy subsequent migration southeastward which eventually led them into the Brazilian Territory of Amapá. Thus, as with the earlier Proto-Maipuran Arawak dispersal, the archaeological and linguistic evidences defining the Karinya Carib dispersal appear to concur (cf. Migliazza 1982:504).

The Karinya group pioneering the settlement of the Eastern Guiana Littoral were early horticulturists who, like their near ancestors on the Western Guiana

Littoral, remained opportunistic shellfishers in an environment that continued brackish into at least the middle of the first millennium A.D. As on the Pomeroon, this is evidenced by shells of Mangrove Oyster, conch and other brackish to marine shellfish among the cultural remains of the Abri Marcel, one of the two earliest rock shelters so far known on the coast of Guyane française. Abri Marcel has been assigned C^{14} dates in the time range A.D. 550-850, while a date range between A.D. 345-427 (calibrated) has been accepted for nearby Carbet Milan (Rostain 1994:81,173). The indicated relationship with the ancestral Waiwaru Complex (+/- 200 B.C.) implies at least a degree of plausibility for the earliest date returned on Carbet Milan (A.D. 120), rejection of which (Rostain 1994:173) creates an unwarranted lacuna in the southeastward movement of these early Karinya.

At present, Mangrove Oysters on the coast of Guyane française occur only on the Rivière de Montsinery to the far west of Cayenne. Thus, significant freshening can be assumed since Karinya groups first occupied the coast ranges, encountering there a landscape of seasonally inundated savannas to seaward of the mountains with vast peat deposits inland, Figure 4.85.

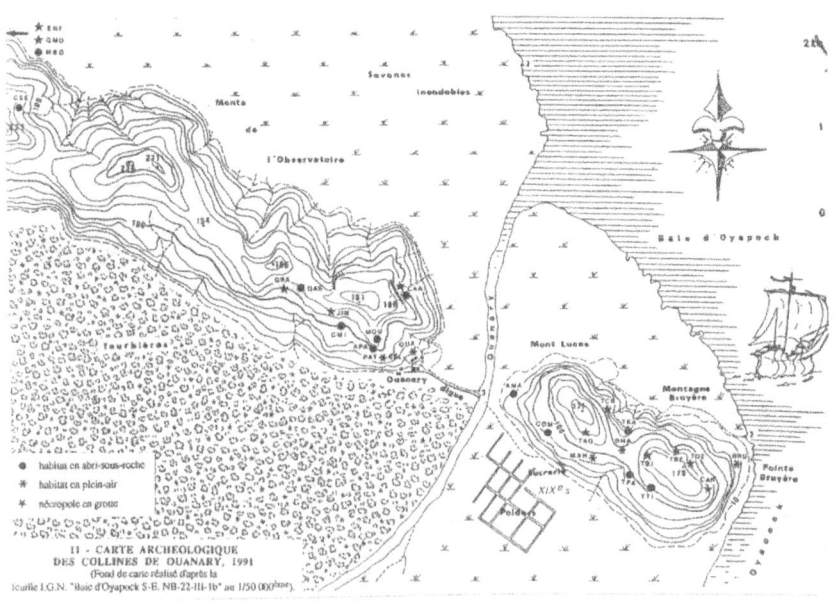

Figure 4.85. Guyane française. Settlement pattern of the early Eastern Karinya (*after Rostain 1994*).

Such a landscape permitted settlement beyond the tidal reach of streams draining northern and southern flanks of the mountains probably with empoldered horticultural plots located on the swamp edge -- a farming stratagem long familiar to their Western Karinya ancestors. Although such polders have not been reported archaeologically, sedentary occupation at these habitation sites combined with the tradition of the bound cemetery are more readily associated with the practice of irrigation horticulture than with the practice of slash-and-burn. The many small rock shelters occupied domestically suggest that the early population comprised small kin groups concentrated on high ground on both banks of the Oyapoc in close proximity to their cemetery sites, which, as elsewhere on the circum-Guiana alluvium, may have established title to ancestral land among particular descent groups. As the population expanded, open air sites were taken up as habitations.

Over the centuries, the ceramics of Eastern Karinya centered on Oyapoc Bay developed certain traits that remained unknown in the west, notably the increasing decorative elaboration of their *Caripo Kwep* pottery. *Caripo Kwep* marks the gradual change from incised and punctate decoration to the painted decoration of *Enfer Polychrome*, a transition that has been estimated to date at between A.D. 750 (the terminal date of *Ouanary Encoche*) and A.D. 1450 (the estimated inception date of *Enfer Polychrome*). In this transition, the incised, punctated and scraped techniques of the Eastern Karinya potter came into direct or indirect contact with certain elements of the Polychrome Horizon Style apparently filtering northward from the lower Amazon. On this frontier, a few of the old decorative elements survived as defining traits in the ceramics of the Aristé phase, e.g., in the *Aristé Plain, Davi Incised, Uaça Incised* and *Flexal Scraped* ceramic types of the Territory of Amapá. At the same time, one of the earliest decorative motifs of coastal Guyane française, the *rangée d'encoches*, which had survived into the latest periods in *Enfer Polychrome*, failed to appear in the repertoire of the Aristé phase of Amapá.

Thus, by the mid-fifteenth century, the defining traits of Aristé phase ceramics had been developed by Eastern Karinya potters around the Bay of Oyapoc. Nonetheless, these Eastern Karinya retained certain ceramic traits bespeaking their ultimate western origins. In due course, their habitations spread along the lower Oyapoc into the Territory of Amapá, where they encountered a familiar landscape of swamps and lakes drained by numerous coastal streams flowing into the Atlantic, undulating uplands, low mountain ranges, savanna and rain forest. By far the largest of these coastal streams, the Rio Araguari, which with its tributary the Amapari rises in the Tumuc Humac Mountains, represents the common frontier with the related Mazagão horticulturists to the south. Beyond the Araguari, the streams all empty into the lower Amazon. Largest of these, the Rio Jari marks the frontier with the State of Pará to the west, Figure 4.86.

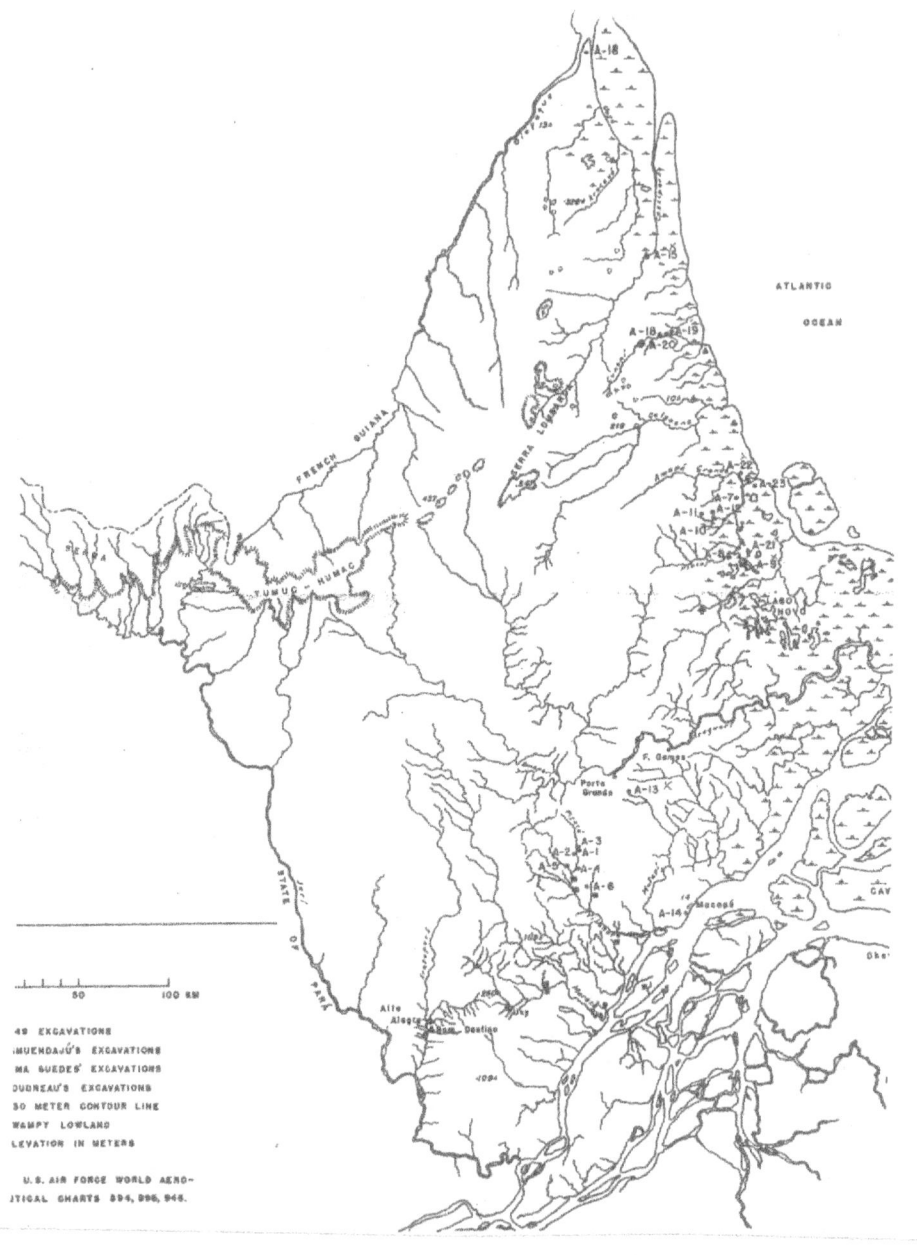

Figure 4.86. The Territory of Amapá, Brazil.

The strictly coastal route of the Karinya migration across the Guianas was determined by their initial adaptation to the swampland-upland ecotone of the Western Guiana Littoral. A critical constraint in their southeasterly expansion was the concurrent occupation of the forests of the Eastern Guiana Hinterland by their Akawaio kinfolk. The expansion of the Akawaio out of a hearth somewhere in northwestern Guyana had peopled the lower Mazaruni River, at least as far as Issano, by around 80 B.C This arm of the Akawaio radiation is evidenced in the dispersion of their diagnostic Koriabo phase ceramics, notably on Quartz Island.

It was a time of profound demographic upheaval, occasioned by the effects of the Amazonian arid interval of around 2100 B.P. (Absy 1982, 1985). One result of this upheaval was the interception of the southeastward expansion of the Karinya by Rouse's Proto-Eastern Maipuran Arawak pioneers, who had occupied the Mouth of the Corentyne River during the opening centuries of the present era. As seems implied by the disjunct distribution of the Karinya language group on the Guiana Coastal Plain, Figure 1.16, (p. 348), this event cut or at least curtailed severely communication with the ancestral Karinya culture on the Western Guiana Littoral. A consequence of the Proto-Eastern Maipuran Arawak wedge driven into the distribution area of the still expanding Eastern Karinya was that the ceramics of the Aristé phase came to florescence in the Territory of Amapá in complete isolation from the ceramics of its ancestral beginnings in the west. Problems of interpretation originally posed by this apparent stylistic isolation of the Aristé phase in northern Amapá (e.g. Meggers and Evans 1957:596) seem less formidable as the archaeological and linguistic evidences become available (e.g. Durbin 1977; Migliazza 1982; Rostain 1994, 1994a). At the same time, identification of the Karinya with the ceramics of the Aristé phase goes a long way toward clarifying the apparent isolation of the Aristé phase to the north of the Rio Araguari notwithstanding indisputable ceramic evidences of a common origin with peoples to the south represented by the Mazagão phase (Meggers and Evans 1957:158). Our attempt to explicate the relationships involved must take inquiry back to the linguistically reconstructed Kapon divergence from the Karinya somewhere in the west.

The Akawaio dispersal

By around the time of Christ, the languages of the Central Guiana subfamily (Trio, Pemon, Kapon, Pauxiana, Wayana, etc.) had crystalized. If, as the archaeological evidence now seems to suggest, the ceramics of the Waiwaru Complex represent the situation on the Western Guiana Littoral before this crystalization occurred, then the emergence of Kapon ought to be identifiable archaeologically and to date no earlier than around this time. On the basis of their hinterland location and surviving ceramic practice, the Akawaio, today mainly distributed on the lower and upper Mazaruni River but once the dominant group in the Guiana hinterland, are unequivocally identifiable with the ceramics of the Koriabo phase, defined on the Western Guiana Littoral by Evans and Meggers (1960:124). Koriabo phase ceramics are produced on the upper Mazaruni to the present day (1977). Akawaio, Ingarico and Patamona are names for three small groups, geographically distinct but speaking the same language, designated by their autodenomination *Kapon*. *Ingarico* is a collective Makusi name for the Akawaio and Patamona (Migliazza 1980).

The original characterization of the Koriabo phase was based on stratigraphic excavations at four habitation sites in northwestern Guyana, three on the basement edge on the Barima River and one on Warapoko Creek, a left tributary of the Waini River (Evans and Meggers 1960:124). In that characterization, Koriabo phase ceramics comprise two major and a minor plain ware *(Koriabo Plain, Warapoko Plain, Barima Plain)* and two decorated *(Koriabo Incised, Koriabo Scraped)*. The two decorated types are highly distinctive. *Koriabo Incised* is characterized by sharp, carefully executed, V-shaped incisions, sometimes combined with low appliqué ridges, nubbins and schematized faces. *Koriabo Scraped* consists of wide, shallow, incised lines usually made with a flat-edged, sometimes slightly serrated stylus. Such scraped incisions are frequently combined with low, appliqué nubbins, eyes, and faces comprising only eyes, nose and mouth. These may be placed on the edges of wide rims with the incisions spaced in between (Evans and Meggers 1960: Pls. 33-37).

A vastly expanded sample of Koriabo phase ceramics is available from more recent investigations which, together, now extend the research area considerably (Boomert 1986; Boomert and Kroonenberg 1977; Cruxent and Rouse 1961; Geijskes 1960-1961; Groene 1976; Hilbert 1982; Rostain 1994,1994a; Rostain et le Roux 1990; Williams 1978a, 1988, 1990, 1990a). Just as the distribution area of the Karinya ceramic sample has been found closely congruent with the dispersion of surviving speakers of the Karinya language group (Galibi, Coastal East and even with the Opone-Carare in Colombia), so the now expanded sample of Koriabo phase ceramics has been found to exhibit a close correlation with the dispersion of the major Carib language groups in Central and Western Guiana (Kapon, Pemon and Wayana especially, as well as with speakers of the Tapajós-Xingu languages). This expanded sample, Figure 4.87, permits a fuller characterization of the origin and affiliations of the Koriabo phase, its chronology and dispersion, than was possible at the time it was identified and described.

Koriabo phase pottery now emerges as *par excellence* the pottery of the rain forest, where its distribution on major arteries such as the Cuyuni and Mazaruni Rivers, which rise in the Pakaraima Highlands, emphasizes the role played by the Kapon, and especially the Akawaio Kapon, in the bridging of the Orinoco-Amazon

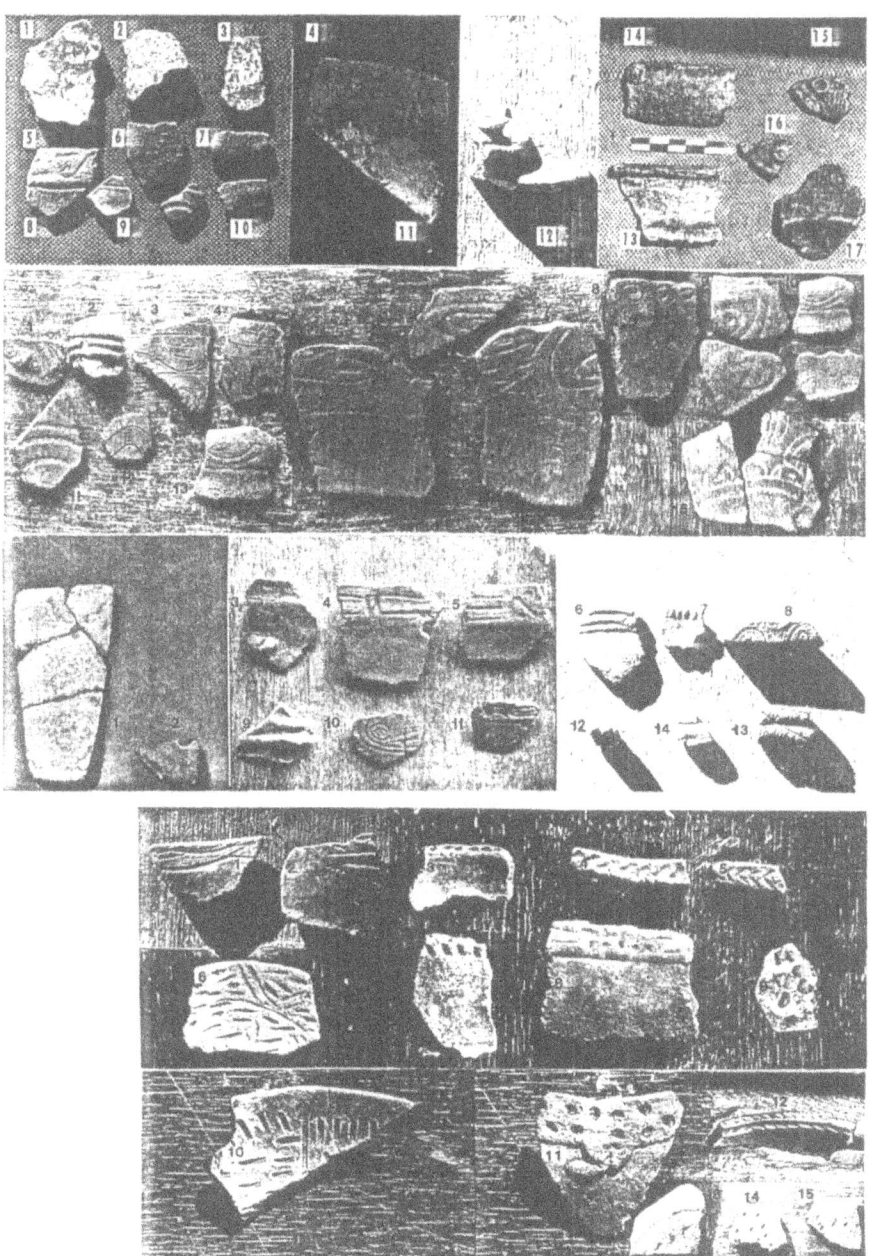

Figure 4.87 a,b. **a**. Ceramics of the Koriabo phase. **b**. Macapaima decorative motifs in Koriabo phase ceramics. **1,2,6,10.** *Macapaima Zoned Incised*; **3,11,14,15.** *Macapaima Punctated*; **4,5,7,12.** *Macapaima Incision Corta*; **8,13.** *Macapaima Zoned Punctated*.

watershed ever since the time of Christ.

At the time of the initial identification and description of the Koriabo phase, the archaeology of the Pomeroon River remained unknown. A ceramic complex exclusively definitive of the Karinya there has remained unsuspected to the present time. Hitherto, in the absence of direct excavations in its heartland area, knowledge of Karinya ceramics has derived from historic and ethnographic sources, and therefore relates only to its protohistoric manifestations. The resulting incompleteness of the record, especially with regard to the inventory, dispersion and history of Karinya ceramics was therefore inevitable (e.g. see Boomert 1986). The archaeology of the Pomeroon Basin now fills these *lacunae* and provides the added bonus of permitting comparisons between the traditional and modern ceramic industries of the Karinya, representing 2000 years of continuous technological and typological transmission through their women potters, Figure 4.81.

Derivation of Koriabo phase pottery from the Karinya ceramic tradition should locate Koriabo origins somewhere on the Western Guiana Littoral more or less concurrently with the crystallization of Kapon among the languages of the Central Guiana subfamily, i.e., during the terminal centuries of the last millennium B.C. These expectations are fulfilled in the location and antiquity of the Waiwaru Market site on the upper Pomeroon River.

Already at around 200 B.C., the Waiwaru Market inventory exhibits certain traits in ceramic design which, not much later, would be definitive of the Koriabo phase as its earliest known sites enter the archaeological record. While the Karinya remained settled in productive niches on the immediate swamp edge, apparently anchored there by a traditional practice of irrigation horticulture, their descendants, the Kapon, pioneered the exploration and settlement of the hinterland forests by slash-and-burn horticulturists. Their earliest known site, now permanently submerged on the bed of the Mazaruni River, was occupied toward the ending of the Amazonian arid interval of +/- 2100 b. p., i.e., during the demographic upheavals that, simultaneously, were witnessing the Proto-Eastern Maipuran Arawak migration down the Corentyne River and onto the Eastern Guiana Littoral as well as the southeastward expansion of the Karinya themselves out of their ancestral territory on the Western Guiana Littoral.

The Mazaruni rises in the Roraima Highlands and flows into the Essequibo River, draining an estimated 3.1 of the 16 million hectares that comprise the total area of rain forest in Guyana (Carter MS; Ben Ter Welle, Tropenbos Prqject, pers. comm. 1990). It is therefore a dominant distributary for cultural influences moving eastward from the Roraima Highlands, and ultimately the lower Orinoco, as well as for influences moving southward *via* its parent stream, the Essequibo, to the lower Amazon.

The route by which the early Kapon reached the Mazaruni remains unknown.

Their oral tradition of having traveled *via* the Cuyuni River has not been authenticated so far for the reason that, barring the occasional accidental dredging up of odd pottery vessels from the riverbed, archaeological investigations have never been conducted in this legendarily challenging river.

An old museum photograph showing a well forested Quartz Island inhabited by an Akawaio nuclear family during a flood stage of the Mazaruni River ca. 1960, Figure 4.88, is of interest as a record of an annual event that has contributed greatly to the recovery of that island's prehistory. During the seasonal flooding of the river, a further rise of just a few centimeters would inundate Quartz Island completely. This is because Quartz Island is the cumulative result of several such inundations in the remote past, the earliest having covered the refuse of its pioneer occupants on the then dried out riverbed, now lying some two meters below the surface of the ground. The rectangular house on wooden stilts is a contemporary architectural convention of the coastal swamps introduced in the hinterland by an enthusiastic government official during the previous decade. Beside it, now relegated to serving as a kitchen and daytime workplace, is the traditional wall-less camp house with its circular thatched roof.

Figure 4.88. Quartz Island, 1960.

The site was abandoned in the early sixties. Therefore the record represents the ethnographic present in our attempt to reconstruct the various prehistoric occupations of which, unfortunately, this has proven the last. Soon afterwards, the soil cover began being progressively eroded in the annual floods, revealing the cultural stratigraphy of the island. The 1960 site proved the fifth in a series of residential units, each located in roughly the same position on its crown. The accumulated refuse represented a time span of two millennia.

The remarkable longevity of the settlement pattern represented in the, Quartz Island sequence is to be explained, at least partly, by its principal feature, the braided channel of the Mazaruni River at this point, Figure 4.89a,b.

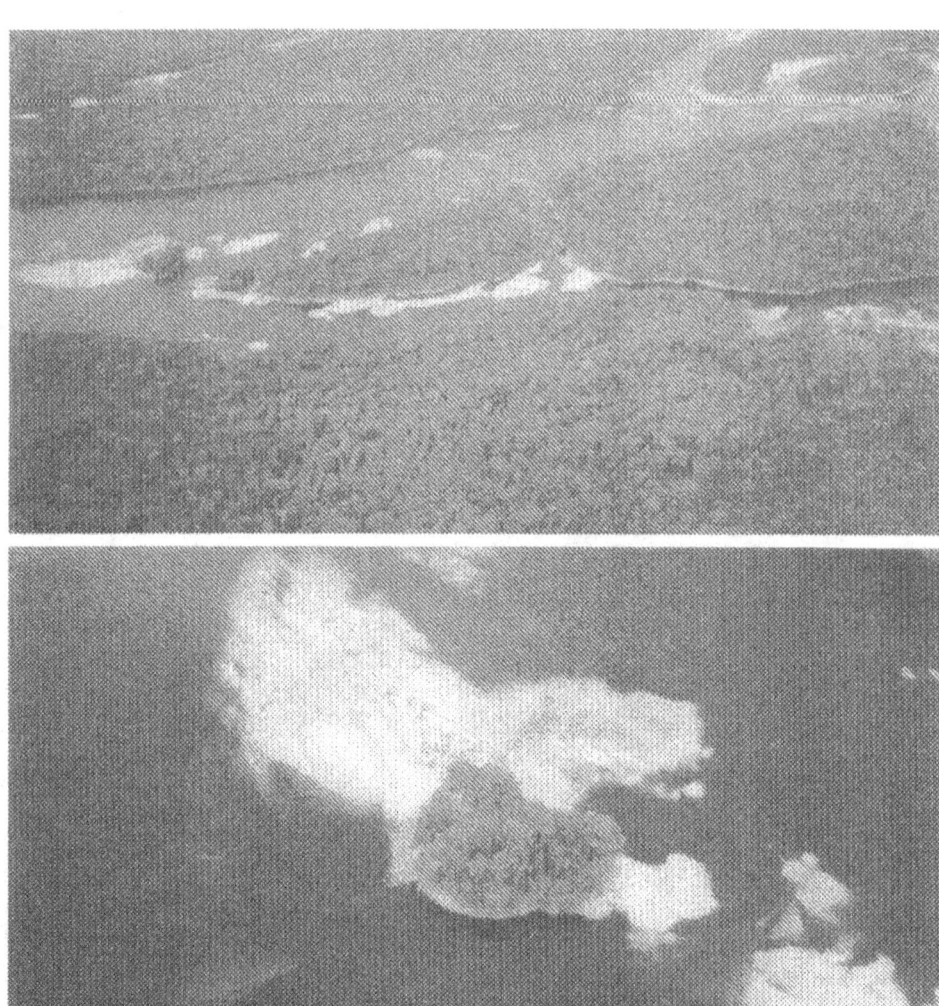

Figure 4.89 a,b. **a.** Part of the braided channel of the Mazaruni River in the vicinity of Quartz Island, located to far left, **b.** Quartz Island in an advanced state of decay, showing the quartz barrier which comprises its core.

It is thought that the braided pattern in the rivers of the Guiana Shield represent a change from and to humid climatic conditions. An arid climate causes the disappearance of the original deep river channel through erosion of the surrounding areas and deposition of huge amounts of coarse materials on the stream bed. With the return of more humid conditions, the braided pattern of such rivers results from the redistribution of run-off across these coarse sediments (Krook 1970; Whitmore 1990:92). Stone artifacts recovered on the surface of gravels deposited on the braided bed of the Lawa River, in Suriname, underlay recent sandy clays and have been estimated to date no earlier than 1500 years ago (Krook 1970). Refuse of the Taruma phase is associated with the braided channel of the New River, a tributary of the Corentyne. On Quartz Island, the earliest cultural refuse likewise directly overlies river gravels in a braided channel. In such major rivers, the various islands and sandbanks of braided channels appear to have provided attractive conditions for settlement by virtue of the abundant fish life in the rapids which occur there at low water. Thus, braided channels are of interest in rain forest archaeology by virtue of their potentials for explicating the environments of early horticulturists in the hinterland, and to some extent, also, for explicating the history of the forests. The present bankfull state of the rivers and the associated lush vegetation most certainly do not represent conditions prevailing at the time the Akawaio were pioneering manioc horticulture on the Mazaruni River.

The low water levels in the river encountered by these pioneers carried important implications for their settlement pattern. This is because sustained low water in the mainstream results in drying out of the creeks and enforces the relocation of camp sites. At such times, permanent water is available only in the drastically attenuated discharge of the mainstream. Large expanses of the riverbed are exposed, revealing its sandbanks, outcrops, rock barriers and forested islands. By virtue of the proximity of permanent water, these islands are attractive as alternative camp sites.

The Quartz Island profile is of the utmost value in explicating the importance of the braided channel in the settlement pattern. Unusually deep sequences there and on neighboring Lanciana Island display a stratification that permits reconstructing the changing environments of the Mazaruni Basin from the closing years of the last millennium B.C.

The sequence commences with water level lying > 2.0 meters lower than at present. The island then was a terminally decomposed outcrop comprising a pile of uneroded cobbles and pebbles located around a massive, one-meter-high quartz barrier, Figure 4.90(B). Chipping waste and potsherds in this pile of rocks, Figure 4.90 inset (I), indicate that initial occupation was on the crown of the island immediately downstream from the quartz barrier.

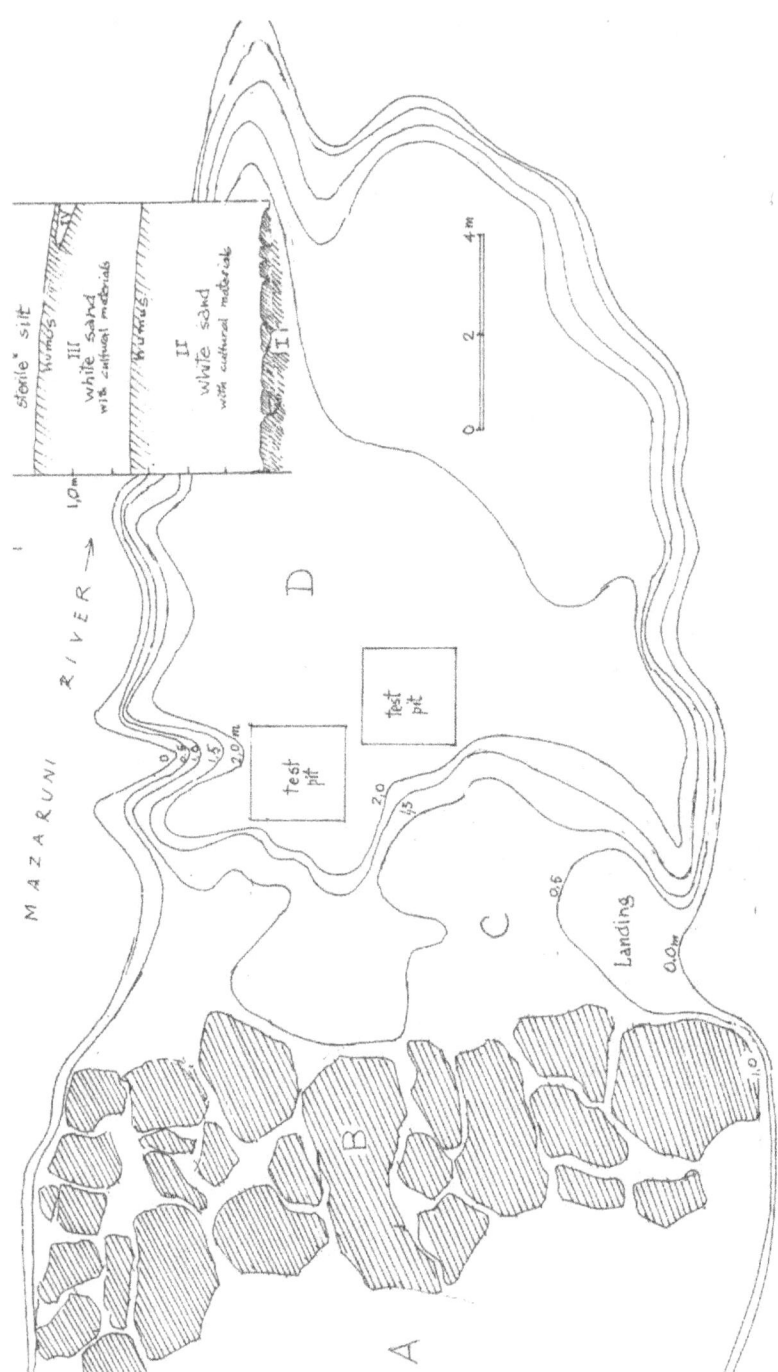

Figure 4.90. Quartz Island. Sketch plan showing eroded section (A), rock barrier (B), sediment basin (C), remnant forest (D). Profile (insert)

As the climate became wetter during the ensuing years, increments of coarse, white sand, 70 cm thick, were deposited on top of this refuse, Figure 4.90 inset (II). The angular particles of this sand imply rapid transport of erosion products from the Pakaraima Highlands following on recession of the forest cover there. While increasing its elevation, these increments of sand, co-occurring with seasonally deposited cultural refuse, simultaneously increased the girth of the island. Light vegetation cover (= a hiatus in flooding episodes) is implied by a thin layer of humus on this enlarged island. Cultural refuse mixed in this humus implies an extended occupation. This occupation was brought to an end by a resumption of torrential rainfall, evidenced by rapid deposition of fresh increments of coarse white sand, 50 cm thick, Figure 4.90 inset (III). These increments again added to the girth of the island. Another extended occupation left cultural refuse in a fresh deposit of humus. In the course of this occupation, resumption of torrential rainfall deposited a further increment of coarse, white sand, this time only around the peripheries of the island while adding nothing to its height, Figure 4.90 inset (IV). The elevation of the island resulting from these increments of coarse sand (1.20 m) was achieved relatively rapidly. The successive flooding episodes that had accompanied the break-up of the arid interval evidently had crested. Deposition of transported sand ceased. Re-establishment of dry forest around the Mazaruni headwaters after an evidently phased break-up of the arid interval is implied. The quartz barrier which forms the core of the island now was submerged. The humus cover at Figure 4.90 inset III, IV indicates that sediments comprising the now enlarged island eventually were stabilized under rain forest. The occupation associated with deposition of the peripheral layer of coarse sand (= end of the arid interval) Figure 4.90 inset (IV) dates at 2030 +/- 70 b.p., or 80 B.C. (Beta 41946). The rapid growth of the island up to this point suggests that initiation of its formation and the arrival of the earliest known Akawaio on the Mazaruni River had not long preceded this date. Evidently their migrations into the hinterland had been facilitated by the prevailing severely attenuated river discharges and probably extensive recession of the rain forest.

Deposition of a crowning 80 cm of silt in the Quartz Island profile now occurred in an altered regime of the river. This new sedimentation phase was extremely slow, since the sediments no longer derived from rapid transport of coarse sand, but accrued instead in extremely small increments in forested conditions that differed little, if at all, from those prevailing at the present time. As a typical blackwater stream in Amazonia, the Mazaruni and its tributaries are poor in nutrients, with limited primary productivity and a characteristically low concentration of suspended sediments. Nine samples from its tributary, the Kamarang River, showed total solids to range between 30 - 130 ppm, with only one sample greater than 65 ppm (median 48 ppm). The pH ranges between 4.9 - 6.7 (median 5.2). Resultingly, the water is extraordinarily pure and translucent, depositing virtually nothing during its annual flood stages. Located as it is in the northern part of the country, where the wet-marine climate is characterized by rainfall normally in excess of 2000 mm/yr., the maximum flood stage of the Mazaruni at Quartz Island may exceed 1.0 m between May - July (Persaud 1983; Hawkes and Wall 1993).

Sediments now accruing on Quartz Island are represented in the profile by a hard, dry, compact deposit of silt 80 cm thick. The initial 20 cm of this silt remained sterile, Figure 4.90 inset (V), representing an appreciable period of non-occupancy of the island. Cultural remains occurred in the uppermost 60 cm, Figure 4.90 inset (Va). The +20 fraction of a sample from the bottom of the upper silt layer showed rootlets, wood, charcoal particles and grains of pottery, with particles of quartz and rounded quartz grains held loosely together in occasional, friable, microscopic balls. Individual charcoal particles were also coated with this tight, creamy, clayey material. In the -20 fraction, rounded quartz grains dominated, with particles of charcoal and various minerals present (Guyana Geology and Mines Commission 1977). At the present time, the amount of suspended sediment in the Mazaruni River is negligible: 5 - 25 ppm (Hydrometeorological Department Georgetown). Lanciana Island upstream was already occupied at around 1780 +/- 100 b.p., A.D. 170 (Beta 57594) and continued to be occupied long after 1470 + /- 90 b.p., A.D. 480 (Beta 57593).

At some stage after the river had developed its present regime, Quartz Island began to erode from its upstream end. In due course, this process reduced its upstream two-thirds to the lowest level of the present day dry season discharge, Figure 4.90 (A). Downstream from the now re-exposed quartz barrier Figure 4.90 (B), the remaining one-third of the island commenced being eroded by the centrifugal, scouring action of the current. Annually, the process removes a portion of soil and sand in suspension while depositing heavier materials, such as ceramic and stone artifacts, on the floor of a slowly widening sediment basin, Figure 4.90 (C). At the time of our excavations (1972-1977), this basin was bordered downstream by remnant forest capping the most recent layer of soil, Figure 4.90 (D).

Surface collecting in the sediment basin recovered sherds representing various pottery styles of the past 2000 years, Figure 4.91. In addition, two $2m^2$ test pits were sunk in undisturbed soil below the remnant forest. These provided the stratification of the refuse and a C^{14} date, Figure 4.92. Recovery from these two sources of diagnostic sherds or decorative motifs representing the Waiwaru phase of the Pomeroon River, the Barrancoid, Macapaiman and Apostaderan phases of the lower Orinoco, and some distinctive Rupununi phase adornos from the North Pakaraimas indicates the very long-range nature of the alliances that had supported this classic rain forest adaptation continuously during the past two thousand years. The Waiwaru Market inventory was represented on Quartz Island by the serial incisions on vessel

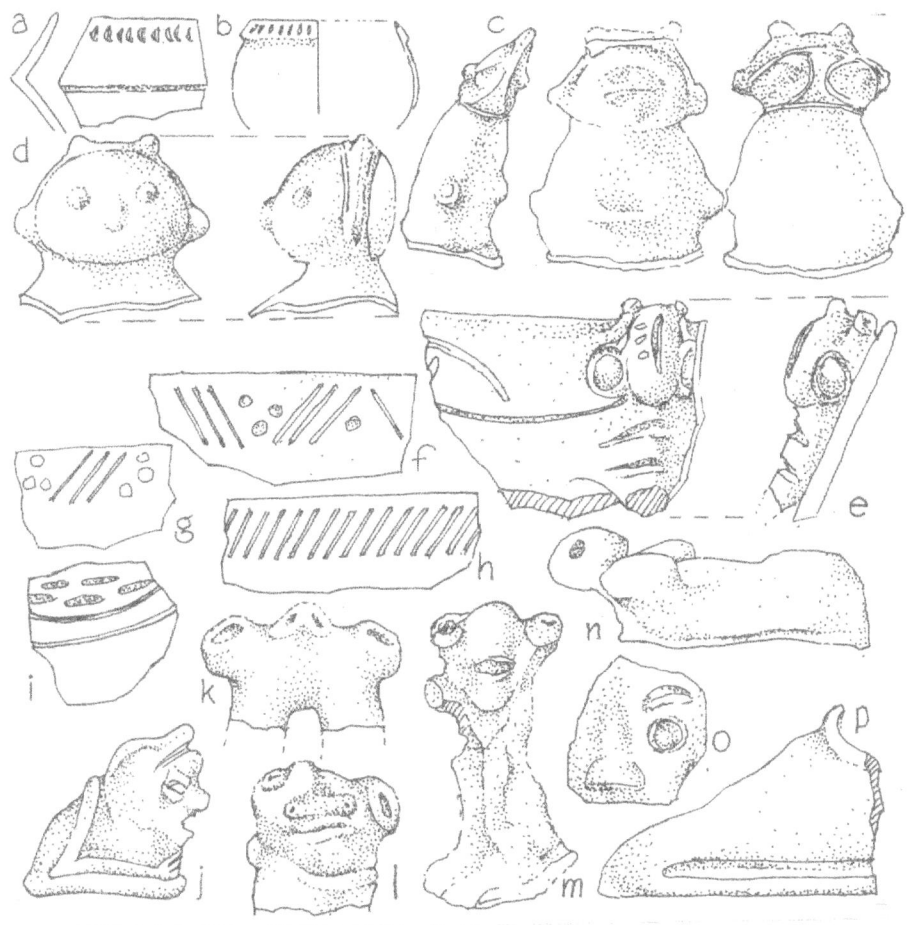

Figure 4.91. Intrusive decorative traits in the Quartz Island ceramic inventory. **a,b.** Waiwaru phase, **c-e.** Barrancoid adornos, **f,g.** Macapaima Zoned Punctated, **h.** Macapaima Incised, **i.** Macapaima Incision Corta, **j-n.** Apostaderan adornos, **o,p.** Rupununi phase adornos.

rims which, in Eastern Karinya ceramics, represents the *rangée d'encoches* motif of the *Ouanary Encoche* ceramic type, Figure 4.91a, (cf. Figure 4.76,1), as well as by the large jar with flaring rims (cf. Figure 4.76,4) the urn lid (cf Figure 4.76,10) and the *tomaien* of the Western Karinya (cf. Figure 4.76,3). The single or double nubbin motif at the point of carination in the Waiwaru Market specimens is replaced by a continuous modeled appliqué strip in the Quartz Island inventory. This motif of Karinya potters on the Pomeroon River also survived on other vessels in the inventory of early Akawaio potters on the Mazaruni River.

Incised flanged rims and Classic Barrancas adornos in the Quartz Island inventory reflect interaction with the lower Orinoco, probably *via* Classic Mabaruma groups on the lower Aruka River. However, a specimen of that Classic Barrancas marker, the double-spout-and-bridge bottle (Willey 1971:429 fn. 49), dredged up at Tumereng on the upper Mazaruni (Williams 1978a: Figure 3) more probably represents an alliance with Barrancas *via* the Caroni River on the other side of the Guiana Highlands., cf. Figure 4.91c-e. The alliance represented by occurrences of *Barrancas, Incised* and *Barrancas Modeled Incised* decoration in Classic Mabaruma inventories on the lower Aruka River may have come to an end by around A.D. 800. Therefore, occurrences of precisely these two ceramic types on the Mazaruni suggest the antiquity of relations between *terra firme* (Koriabo) and coastal (Mabaruma) horticulturists.

As noted above (p. 270), alliances between communities on the lower Aruka River and communities on the lower Orinoco did not end with the demise of *Barrancas Incised* and *Barrancas Modeled Incised* ceramics. After around A.D. 700, certain decorative motifs in the pottery of the Macapaima subphase of the Barrancoid tradition, now being absorbed in the Barrancas inventory, came to be represented in the Mabaruma phase inventory on the lower Aruka River. The only two ceramic types of the Macapaima subphase that made an appearance on the lower Aruka River, *Macapaima Punteado en Zonas* and *Macapaima Incision Corta* were precisely the two that are represented in the Quartz Island inventory on the Mazaruni. As has been seen, these two ceramic types were never represented at Recht-door-Zee, in the trade between Arawaks on the lower Aruka and Arawaks on the Eastern Guiana Littoral. The presence of these two ceramic types in the Koriabo phase inventory on the Mazaruni attests coastal interaction with the Akawaio *via* a hinterland route, probably the old highway from the North Pakaraimas down the Wenamu River and across the Cuyuni-Waini watershed into the Barama, thence *via* the Barama-Barima watershed at Chinee Landing to Koriabo Point and into the Barima Basin, cf, Figure 4.31. The lower levels of the profile on Kumaka Hill yielded specimens of *Macapaima Incision Corta*.

Specimens of Macapaima phase ceramics in the early Koriabo phase inventory on the Mazaruni River include decorative motifs of *Macapaima Inciso*, an early ceramic type on the lower Orinoco River (i.e., commencing +/A.D. 500) which remained unknown to groups on the lower Aruka River. Since Macapaima is located on the Orinoco left bank opposite the Mouth of the Caroni River, direct interaction between the Akawio of the Mazarum River and Arawaks on the lower Orinoco *via* the Caroni River seems implied.

Apostaderan adornos are well represented in pre-Contact levels of the Kumaka Hill profile. The Quartz Island surface collection included excellent specimens of these distinctive adornos. Figure 4.91j-m.

A memory of the Akawaio coastal heritage survived in their adornos depicting the giant sea turtle, Figure 4.91n, a head-foot symbol of their Karinya ancestors. Seasonally familiar to coast dwellers, the sea turtle is unknown to denizens of the forest. The turtle symbol survived in Eastern Karinya communities in the *Cayenne Peint* and *Enfer Polychrome* ceramic types (cf. Rostain 1994: Figures 102.1,2,5; 114.3,5). It has been recorded in the Maracá phase in the Territory of Amapá (cf. Meggers and Evans 1957:Pl. 17) and survives in Western Karinya symbolism to the present day, Figure 4.91A. The independent turtle head motif serves as a metaphor for the head-foot symbol in Formative pottery, Figure 36b, and occurs also in the Eastern Karinya (Rostain 1994:Figure 102.1,14), Recht-door-Zee (Wishart 1982:Figure 6c) and Orealla inventories. For turtle ritual on St. Eustatius see Versteeg (1986); Versteeg and Schinkel (1992:195).

The independent foot, another metaphor for the head-foot symbol, has been recorded in a Mazagão phase cemetery (Meggers and Evans 1957:Figure 6). An independent foot specimen was recovered in the Quartz Island inventory, Figure 4.91. p.

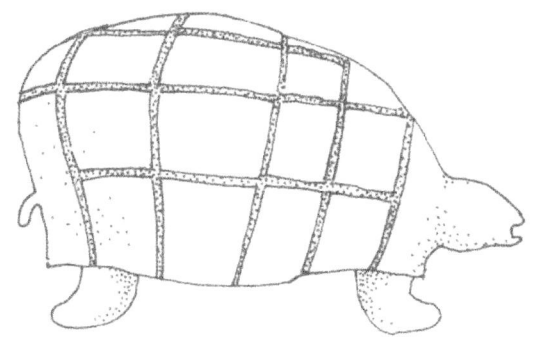

As well as the independent-foot motif, the mortuary symbolism of the Akawaio on Quartz Island included also the independent-head motif (cf. Evans and Meggers 1960:Figure 123 a,c,d,e), Figure 4.91 o. The independent-head was of extremely wide distribution, occurring also in the Antilles, Figure 4.54 e-j. (see Drewett 1991: Figures 31,20, 53,187, Pls. 16,18).

Figure 4.91A. Waiwaru Market, Pomeroon River. Red-on-white painted turtle (contemporary).

Vessel shapes deriving from the stratified sample reveal something of the chronology of the Akawaio Koriabo phase ceramics, Figure 4.92. The ceramic typology reflects the two contrasting regimes of the Mazaruni River described above. Period I was characterized by rapid deposition of 120 cm of coarse sand associated with apparently intermittent occupation toward the ending of the Amazonian arid interval in the closing years of the last millennium B.C.

Period II materials were deposited in only the upper portion of an 80 cm-deep layer of silt representing sedimentation in an increasingly wetter climate. Period II ended with the river attaining present discharge levels in a climate comparable to that of the present day. The remains of the badly eroded island now are under rain forest, Figure 4.89b.

Period I

The sequence commenced with an inventory that included the open bowl with wide, flaring, frequently lobed rim already recognized in the Waiwaru Market inventory, Figure 4.92 (200.3) and a rare ovoidal bowl with constricted neck, Figure 4.92 (180.2). The vessel with lobed rim was the most popular in both Periods I and II. It achieved wide distribution at sites of the Koriabo phase throughout the Guianas (Boomert 1986:Figure 12.5; Evans and Meggers 1960: Figure 53.1; Geijskes 1960-1961: Figure 49a; Meggers and Evans 1957:Figure 39.5; Rostain 1994: Figure 108. 1). In late Period I, certain specimens of this open bowl exhibit Barrancoid-like broad-line incisions on interior rim lobes (100.6, 120.4, 140.3). Motifs are curvilinear or spiral, the latter already present in earlier levels. Certain rim lobes were provided with stepped contours.

Also deriving from the Waiwaru Market inventory, the *tomaien* appeared toward the end of Period I. This late place in the sequence evidently results from sampling error. This is the best known of all "Carib" vessels (Allaire 1980; Boomert 1986:50; Geijskes 1960-1961:Afb.2-4; Im Thurn 1883:Figure 19a; Roth 1924: Pl. 86b, 88B). It continues in use to the present day as the *tuma* pot of the Mazaruni and Pomeroon Rivers (see also Roth 1924:306). In the middle of Period I, a bowl with steeply outsloping sidewall and almost vertical upper wall exhibits incised curvilinear motifs filled with white slip, a technique that is more reminiscent of Amazonian than of Orinocan inventories. Along with the Barrancoid decoration and a plain, tanga-like object, the specimen seems already to suggest the interaction of the Akawaio with the lower Amazon which will become more evident at a later date in the ceramics of the Mazagão phase.

To Period I probably is to be attributed the high point in painted decoration in Koriabo phase ceramics that is represented by, for example, the red-on-white specimen shown in Figure 4.80e. Not many specimens of Koriabo phase painted decoration have survived. The trait is not considered in the original definition of the Koriabo phase.

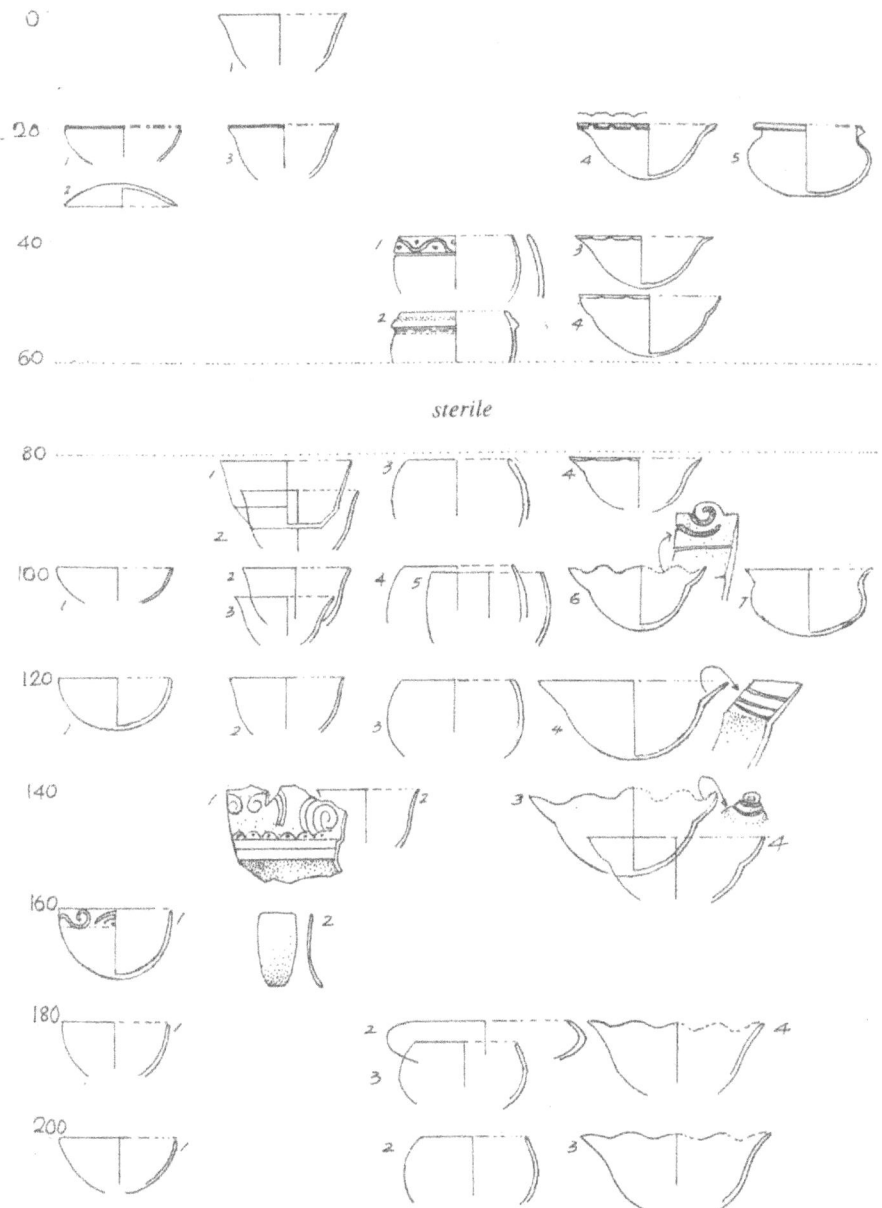

Figure 4.92. Quartz Island. The stratified sample.

Typologically, the carved wooden staff shown in Figure 4.93 may derive from this period. The end of the period is marked by the introducton of vessels with stark, angular contours, Figure 4.92 (80.1), a trait which survived into later periods, Figure 4.94 (2.1, 4.4).

Figure 4.93. Mazaruni River. Carved wooden staff of the (?) Akawaio Kapon. Koriabo phase.

Period II

The open bowl with wide, flaring, sometimes lobed rim continued to dominate the Period II inventory, but by now decoration had been abandoned. A site in regrowth forest on Woi Creek, a tributary of the Mahdia River, yielded plain specimens of this vessel dating at 1090 +/- 50 b.p., or A.D. 860 (Beta 40998).

Akawaio expansion into the Potaro Basin by this date suggests an ameliorating climate and still rising water levels in the rivers. On Lanciana Island, upstream, deposition of the silt layer overlying the coarse sand transported from the Pakaraimas was still in progress at around 1470 +/- 90 b.p., or A.D. 480 (Beta 57593). A similar date (1470 +/- 40 b.p., or A.D. 480) was returned on refuse at Abri Marcel on the Eastern Guiana Littoral (Rostain 1994:173) where continuing brackish conditions imply that the discharge of the Oyapoc yet remained well below its present volume. Thus, the slowly rising water levels that are evidenced in the silt deposit of the Mazaruni River during Period II, having commenced around the time of Christ, still remained well below optimum half a millennium later.

The location of the Woi Creek site suggests that one direction of Akawaio expansion during Period II was *via* the Essequibo River. This seems indicated also in ceramic typology, Figure 4.94. Sites at Bartica and Saxacalli, near the Mazaruni confluence, exhibit no extraneous decorative influences, but at Head Falls and Kuruabu, upstream, a few vessels incorporate motifs of *Macapaima Incision Corta* as well as adornos of the late prehistoric Apostadero phase. As pottery of the Macapaima phase remained unrepresented in coastal Arawak inventories throughout, occurrences of its decorative motifs in Akawaio pottery on the Essequibo River tend to confirm the oral traditions of the latter of their migration inland *via* the Essequibo tributaries, the Cuyuni and Mazaruni.

Apostaderan decoration was incorporated also in Akawaio pottery at Head Falls, Yukuribo, and Apoteri on the confluence of the Essequibo and Rupununi Rivers. Thus, the upriver Akawaio migration spanned the transition from late Macapaima to Apostaderan times (+/- A.D. 1700). By this time, the upper Essequibo River had been deserted by those Arawaks whose habitation sites had clustered around Kurupukari Falls at least on to the time of Christ. An account of an Arawak expedition up the Essequibo River and across the watershed to the Amazon in 1553 suggests that the Akawaio were not dominant in the Essequibo Basin in the middle of the sixteenth century:

> [Yayua] cacique Arawak, the year 1553, ascended the Esquibo River to its upper region with four piraguas, and carried these on shoulder across the mountain ridge, and came upon another river on the other side, and traveled through it to come upon the great river of the Amazonas, and found so many people [that he returned]. *(Mapa de los rios Amazonas, Esequivo o Dulce* cited in Benjamin 1982).

383

10. *Apoteri*

9. *Yukuribo*

8. *Waraputa Falls*

7. *Crab Falls*

6. *Omai*

5. *Rockstone*

4. *Kuruabu*

3. *Head Falls*

2. *Bartica*

1. *Saxacalli*

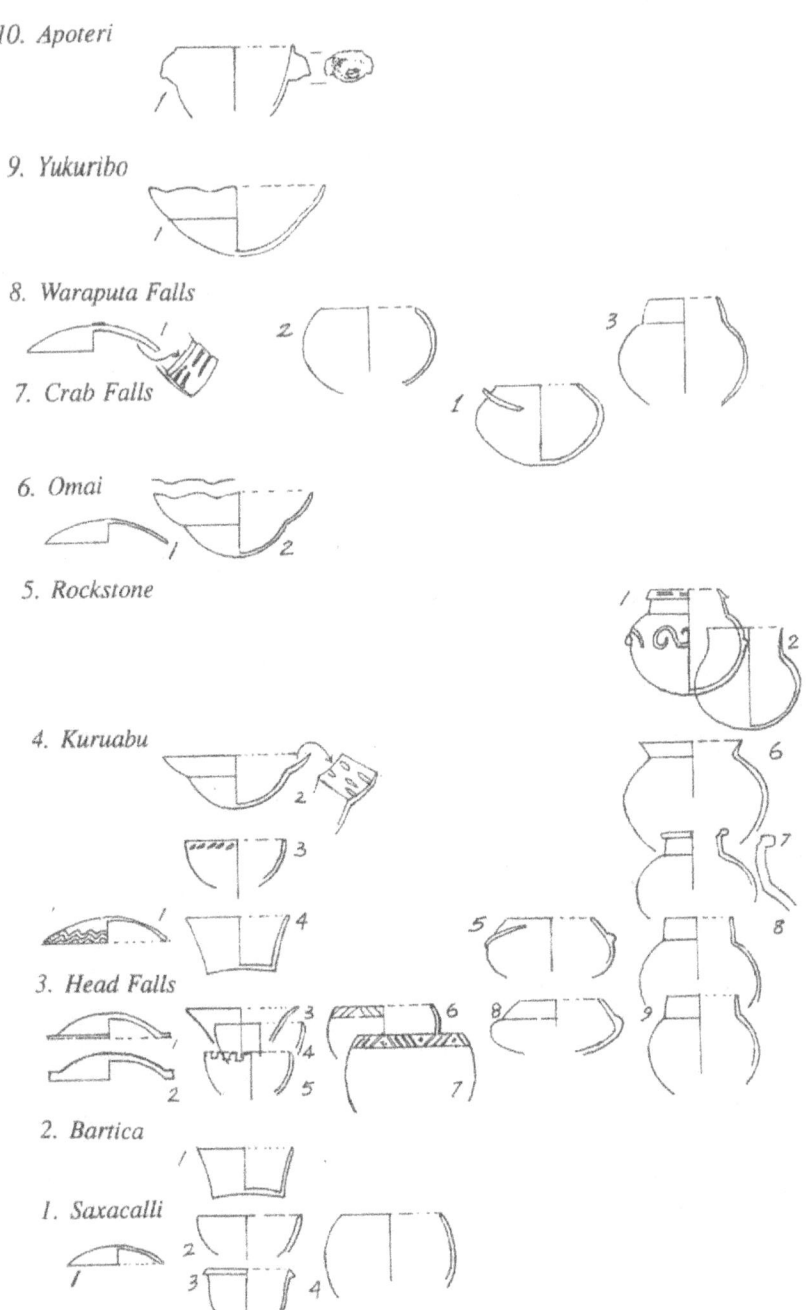

Figure 4.94. Essequibo River. Late prehistoric Akawaio migration upstream.

Indeed, their expansion up the Essequibo may have resulted only from the alliance a local group on the Mazaruni/Cuyuni/Essequibo confluence was able to strike with the newly arrived early seventeenth century Dutch. Likewise, the large village [of the Parahans] at the Mouth of the Siparuni at which the German explorer, Horstman, spent the 1739 dry season, probably had come into being in response to the establishment of the Dutch Post Arinda there in 1734. Therefore, Horstman's guides up the Siparuni probably were Akawaio. The founding of Essequibo Village on the Rupununi confluence after 1750 (Harris and de Villiers 1911:254) probably also was a result of the transfer of Post Arinda to Apoteri. The eighteenth century trade route from Fort Nassau led to Cannister Falls on the Demerara River, thence across the Demerara-Essequibo watershed to Post Arinda, overland to Dutchman Point on the Siparuni, thence up the Siparuni to the North Pakaraimas. Ceramic inventories at Kurupukari Falls, Essequibo Village and Paramakatoi all exhibit Koriabo phase traits. Big "S" Falls on the upper Siparuni River yielded stratified mixed sherds of the Koriabo and Taruma phases, suggesting that, over time, it had functioned as a waystation to the west.

The urn lid of the Koriabo phase which appears at this time in the ceramic inventory at Paramakatoi comprises a rim made up of two or three unerased coils. This distinctive rim is a feature of the Macapaima phase inventory on the Orinoco, which apparently had derived from Banador at the Mouth of the Caroni. It is thought to have been adopted at Barrancas some time during the closing centuries of the first millennium A.D. (Sanoja O. 1979:174., Lam. 74). Across the Roraima Highlands, it accompanied the migration of Macapaima phase decoration downstream along the Mazaruni River and into the Essequibo mainstream, whence, in due course, it entered the ceramic inventory of the Makusi and Patamona *via*, respectively, the Siparuni and Potaro Rivers. Its distribution constitutes further evidence of the role of the Akawaio in the economic integration of the region. Equally importantly, it points to a shared mortuary ritual between lower Orinoco Arawaks on the one hand and the Carib-speaking Akawaio on the other, commencing at least during the closing years of the first millennium A.D. It has been seen that, among the Karinya ancestors of the Akawaio, similar urn lids were in customary use since at least the closing centuries of the first millennium B.C., by which time the associated religious observances were already of hoary antiquity on the Western Guiana Littoral.

Notwithstanding the antiquity of the Woi Creek site on the Mahdia River, a relatively late date is suggested for Akawaio expansion up the Potaro mainstream. This is evidenced by high frequencies of Macapaima phase decorative motifs in Koriabo phase inventories there. Motifs of *Macapaima Incision Corta* and *Macapaima Punteado en Zonas* dominate these Koriabo phase inventories. However, Apostaderan traits occur at only one of seven sites surveyed between the Mouth of the Potaro and its tributary the Kuriebrong River, Figure 4.95. In its terminal stages, witnessed by Im Thurn (1883:60) toward the end of the nineteenth century, Akawaio expansion up the Potaro introduced *Macapaima Incision Corta* into the vocabulary of Carib-speaking Patamona potters in the North Pakaraimas, Figure 4.95. There, a traditional Rupununi phase pottery affiliates with sites on the Rio Branco Savannas dating back to at least 1070 +/- 50 b.p., or A.D. 880 (Mentz Ribeiro, et al 1989).

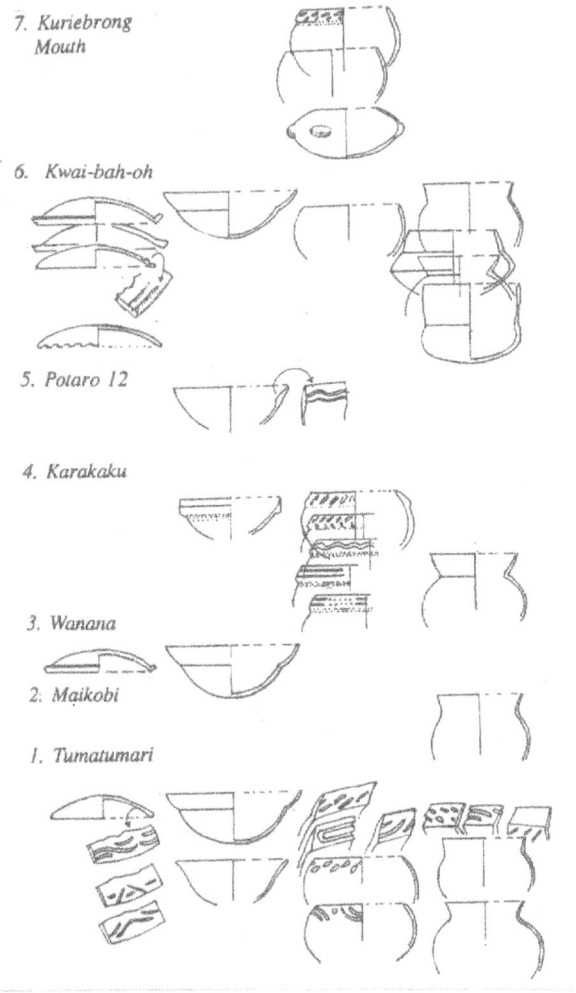

Figure 4.95. Potaro River. Late Prehistoric migrations of the Akawaio Kapon.

As it applies to Akawaio expansion up the major rivers, the concept "migration" implies a conscious goal for which, obviously, there can never be archaeological evidence. Akawaio expansion across *terra firme* was more demonstrably a function of their settlement pattern. Ethnographic parallels show this to have comprised a number of satellite garden places centering, at a convenient distance, on a village which may have been as much as a hundred years in the same place. But, by virtue of the practice of shifting cultivation on the leached soils of *terra firme*, the life of garden places is inherently short, seldom longer than five or six years. Because, as a rule, garden places attract eventual habitation, each one in due course may come to support a family group of variable size. On the other hand, social and ceremonial activities tend to be centered in a village, and this, over time, would develop into a community of up to perhaps 50-60 persons. The village and its satellite garden places eventually constituted the unit of expansion up or down a productive stream.

In order to remain viable, such a village needed to command the labor of the minimum number of able-bodied individuals required to support a fully fledged manioc-based economy in any given case. Larger group sizes were maladaptive for the reason that the leached soils of *terra firme* impose a strict limit on the cropping period that is feasible for manioc horticulture, usually 2-3 years. Controlled experiments in a farm plot on the upper Rio Negro showed that total net primary productivity of manioc vegetation dropped from 5.3 to 3.1 t/ha/yr, and the dry weight of the edible tubers dropped from 1.46 to 0.70 t/ha/yr between the first and third years (Jordan 1987). The penalty for exceeding this limit is invasion of the abandoned farm plot by pioneering plant species, weeds and pests which may be difficult to eliminate during the ensuing fallow. Farmers therefore know when the manioc plot should be abandoned to allow for successful regrowth with the option of returning for another cycle of cultivation after the appropriate lapse of time, perhaps a generation, sometimes less. Soil nutrients accumulated during such a period, as indicated by the appropriate vegetation, would be deemed about sufficient to support a renewed cycle of manioc cropping. Since it is easier to fell and burn secondary forest rather than virgin forest, repeated rotation through a given area is the adaptively optimal strategy of land management generated by manioc horticulture in the Tropical Forest environment. This system, in which land rather than crops is rotated, is a sustainable low-input form of cultivation which can continue indefinitely on these infertile soils provided the carrying capacity of the land is not exceeded. Its obvious limitation is that it can usually support only 10-20 persons/km^2 because at any time only around 10 percent of the available land is under cultivation. The system breaks down if either the bush fallow period is excessively shortened or if the period of cultivation is extended too long, either of which is likely to occur if population increases in the settled territory and a land shortage develops (Whitmore 1990:134). Communities therefore remained small, though, as is implied by the inherent labor intensiveness of fully-fledged manioc horticulture, the term shifting cultivation in fact conceals a high level of relatively sedentary habitation by families scattered over a wide area. Consequently, horticulturist habitation sites in the Guianas either exhibit significant depth of refuse in *terra preta*, at times indicating occupancies of up to a thousand years, or show evidences of cultural discontinuities resulting from repeated abandonments and reoccupations of the sections of a given stream that constituted the home range of a particular group, i.e., the area where the extraction of resources shows a positive energy balance, or a series of these areas that grade the energy balance (Foley 1977:181). Combined with a matrilocal marriage rule, this system of land use ensures a high level of residential stability and therefore stability in ceramic practice.

The transect shown in Table R traverses 10 kilometers of satellite farmland between the Kamarang left bank and a currently (1977) cultivated plot at Agupu. The Akawaio village of Waramabia lay a further 3 km inland, in the mountains.

Table R. Regrowth farmland at Waramabia Village, Kamarang, over the past 100 years

	60-100 yrs	40-60 yrs rare stumps	20-40 yrs stumps burned trunks	10-20 yrs trees trunks	
Laterite	*Sand*	*Sand*	*Sand*	*Sand* (farm)	**Agupu**
					> 10km
Tropical Evergreen Forest	**Sukabi**				
	regrowth forest	Savanna 3	Savanna 2	Savanna 1	Forest
	12-15cm dbh regrowing to Evergreen Forest (edaphic sub-climax)	6.0m orchard. Cashew *(Anacardium occidentale)*	2.5m grass *(Pteridium aquilinum)*	0.9-1.5m bracken	cassava. etc.

Source: Dale Jenkins PAHO, pers. comm. 1977; see also Scott 1987.

Contrasting seral stages of the vegetation permitted estimates of relative time since abandonment of the respective farm plots, the earliest of which, Sukabi, had been last abandoned around 1965.

With the seasonal drying out of water level in the rivers and the associated drying out of particular creeks, families occupying such creeks are obliged to move temporarily to the mainstream to await the coming of the rains. An area of riverbank or a particular island in the river might thus be seasonally occupied over several years by a single family group. Interpreted as but a single site in a settlement pattern comprising several dispersed homesteads tethered to a complex of strategic resources, the existence of related sites might be hypothesized with a high level of certainty on neighboring islands, if any, as well as in nearby creeks. As shown above, if the settlement is younger than a century or two, such sites usually are identifiable by the associated second-growth vegetation. But as shown in Table 8, sites of greater age are unlikely to be detected by the untrained eye.

Table 8. Diversity at several stages of succession in an Amazonian floodplain

	Number of species			
	Pioneer stage 3 to 5 years	Early succession 30 - 50 years	Late succession 100 - 150 years	Mature forest > 300 years
Birds	21	49	127	236
Primates	0	2-6	6-8	8-12
Trees*	19	33	50	112

* Number of species with a diameter of at least 10cm at breast height contained in 0.5 ha samp plots. *Source*: Terborgh 1992.

The excavation of Quartz Island showed its occupation to have been seasonal. However, rather than having been annual, in phase with the onset of the main dry season, the occupation cycle reflects an irregular alternation between dry and wet episodes, each variably prolonged, toward the ending of a regional arid interval spanning the closing centuries of the last millennium B.C. and the opening centuries of the present era. Besides Quartz Island, neighboring Lanciana Island, 2-3 km upstream, was similarly seasonally occupied on to at least the middle of the first millennium A.D. Cultural refuse was recovered in surface collecting on nearby Morabisi Creek on the Mazaruni left bank, just above Quartz Island; on Bombomparu Creek, right bank Mazaruni up the Issano River; and at Issano Rest House right bank Mazaruni, downstream. The village of which these satellite sites constituted a sample was located while clearing an old terrace of the Mazaruni River a kilometer or two below Quartz Island. Potsherds of the Koriabo phase were recovered in soil clinging to the roots of a bulldozed forest giant (Iron Mary, *Licania grisea*). The site covered an area of some 40,000 m^2 with discrete lenses of refuse at around 20 cm depth yielding the same array of ceramic styles as subsequently were represented in the Quartz Island surface collection -- the Mabaruma, early Koriabo, Apostadero and Rupununi phases. The cleared land had been thought virgin rain forest. Thus, although no radiocarbon dates are available for the occupation of Quartz Island after Period I had come to an end with deposition of the final increment of coarse, white sand from the Pakaraimas, settlements evidently continued to expand locally as slowly rising water levels in the mainstream permitted renewed access to hitherto abandoned creeks.

The available evidences suggest that a few centuries remained before a still ameliorating environment and rising water levels permitted Akawaio expansion from the Mazaruni and Cuyuni into the Essequibo mainstream and thence into the upriver (? still dry) streams of the Essequibo Basin. The expansion of the Akawaio that marked the latter half of Period II had reached Woi Creek on the Mahdia River, a tributary of the Potaro, by around A.D. 1000. Beyond the Essequibo, there is an ambivalent but in the light of Woi Creek entirely credible C^{14} date at A.D. 1165 +/- 50 b.p. (GrN 2174) for Akawaio (Koriabo phase) refuse on Coeroni Island on the upper Corentyne River (Boomert 1979:83).

The regrowth sequence at Waramabia, taken with the Periods I, II Quartz Island sequences, show that the repeated reoccupations associated with slash-and-burn horticulture constituted a significant brake on the rate of riverain migration.

Beyond the Essequibo Basin, occurrences of certain Koriabo phase ceramic traits in inventories at the Mouth of the Amazon suggest that Akawaio expansion *via* the dried-out watercourses of the day might have commenced as far back as as early Period I, proceeding by routes which led, ultimately, into the Tumuc Humac range of southeastern Guiana and down the Rio Jari, which empties into the Mouth of the Amazon.

The evidence so far available comprises a small sherd collection made on the lower Rio Jari (cited in Meggers and Evans 1957:68). In this collection, traits of the as yet undefined Koriabo phase are many and striking, Figure 4.96B. Even more striking in this collection are the presence of key ceramic traits of the Waiwaru Complex, representing the Karinya ancestors of the Akawaio, Figure 4.96A. The collection was identified with the Mazagão phase of southern Amapá, Figure 4.96C. The indicated affiliations between these three widely separated archaeological complexes -- Waiwaru, Koriabo and Mazagão -- suggest contact at a time when the Karinya were themselves still expanding out of a hearth somewhere to the far northwest.

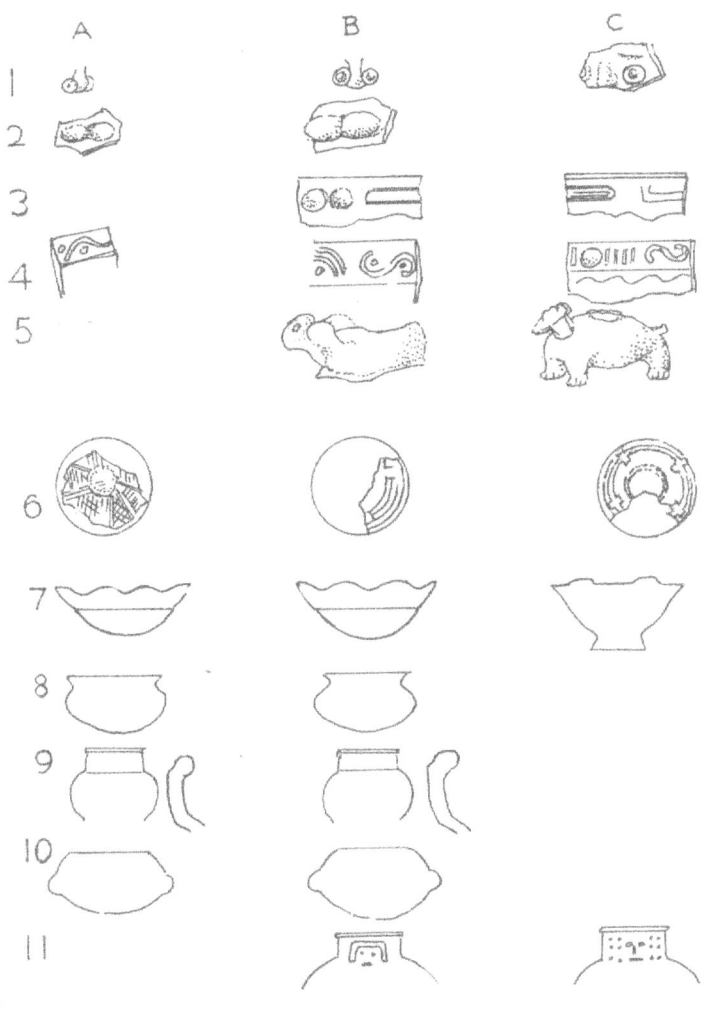

Figure 4.96. Comparative ceramic traits Waiwaru (**A**), Koriabo (**B**) and Mazagão (**C**) Complexes. 1. Small, punctated nubbins, 2. Large, ovoidal nubbins, 3. Fine- or broad-line subangular incisions on rims, 4. Double-spiral alternating with or enclosing punctates, etc., 5. Turtle motif, a mortuary symbol, 6. Urn lid, with (?) directional markings, 7. Large, open bowl with lobed rim, a mortuary vessel in the Mazagão phase (Meggers and Evans 1957:64), 8. The *tomaien*, 9. Globular jar with upright collared neck, shallow channel scraped into inner surface of exteriorly thickened rim, 10. Carinated bowl, 11. Effigy jar, probably a directional sign in funerary ceramics.

It must be borne in mind that this was a time of continuing low water levels in the hinterland rivers. Therefore, as is indicated in the refuse of cave dwellers at the Abri Marcel site on Oyapoc Bay in Guyane française, a compensating brackish environment survived on the coast there on to at least the seventh century A.D. Surviving shellfish refuse suggests that similar conditions may be hypothesized on Waiwaru Creek at around this date. In these conditions of continuing environmental stress, Proto-Eastern Miapuran Arawaks were expanding westward along the coastal reefs bearing with them the ceramics of the Incised and Punctate Horizon Style. At the same time, Karinya Caribs adapted to the swamp edge were expanding southeastward along the Guiana Coast, eventually creating in the Territory of Amapá the cultural florescence that is now recognized in the elaborately painted ceramics of the Aristé phase.

In this period of low water levels in the rivers, the Kapon descendants of the Karinya had pioneered the settlement of the Mazaruni Basin by horticulturists before 80 B.C. Although their subsequent fortunes can be traced during Period II in the ceramic distributions of the Essequibo Basin, the circumstances of their occupation of the Eastern Guiana Hinterland are less clear. This is mainly a function of the pioneering state of the study of prehistory in the Guianas. As has been seen, this study was put on a systematic basis only within the past half century, just before the advent of the radiocarbon era. Consequently, C^{14} sequences now available for the major ceramic complexes of the Guianas retrodict appreciably the age estimates that originally were assigned to them. Most radically affected are the Mabaruma and Koriabo phases. Inception of the latter has been retrodicted by upwards of a millennium, and of the former by upwards of two. Derivation of the initial date for the Koriabo phase from "guess dates" (Evans and Meggers 1960:150) of a putative Mabaruma middle period commencing around A.D. 1200 assigned to the Koriabo phase an estimated life span of a mere 400 years ending at Contact.

Unfortunately, this very modest estimate of the life-span of the Koriabo phase has been incorporated, unquestioned, into various prominently published chronological charts (Boomert 1986, 1993; Cruxent and Rouse 1959; Rouse 1983). Thus, entrenched in the literature, this attenuated perception of the Koriabo life-span has proven a formidable obstacle to restructuring the chronology of the Guiana Coast. But, as has been seen, potsherds exhibiting the diagnostic scraped, modeled and painted decoration of the (Akawaio) Koriabo phase have been recovered at the Paramarica Creek and Boekoe Creek sites of the Arauquinoid (Arawak) Barbakoeba Complex in coastal Suriname estimated to date at between A.D. 650 and 1250. On the other hand, sherds decorated with biomorphic adornos typical of the Barbakoeba Complex have been recovered at the Koriabo phase settlement of Peprepasi. Barbakoeba potters appear to have been in the habit of copying decorative elements of Koriabo phase ceramics. The sole available date for the Barbakoeba Complex,

975 +/- 50 b.p. (Boomert 1993) derives from the upper part of the Boekoe site, suggesting a much earlier Akawaio presence on the eastern Suriname Coast than has been acknowledged so far.

This notwithstanding, the notion has persisted in Suriname archaeology that the earlier sites of the Koriabo phase were hinterland sites, dating after around A.D. 1250, and the later ones coastal (Versteeg and Bubberman 1992). Resultingly, one investigator (Versteeg 1979; 1980a) has felt obliged to reject as too early a series of C^{14} dates deriving from his own excavations at four sites on the central and eastern Suriname Coasts which yielded ceramics of the Koriabo phase, Table T.

Table T. Early sites of the Koriabo phase in Coastal Suriname

Site	Locality	Sample no:	Date b.p.
Onverdcht	Central Coast	GrN 846	2290 +/- 50
Commetewane	Eastern Coast	GrN 1899	1310 +/- 45
Hanover	Central Coast	GrN 4414	1130 +/- 40
Moengo-Doesmanhil	Eastern Coast	GrN 439	970 +/- 70

Source: Versteeg 1979,1980a

The decision to reject the evidence of his own C^{14} dated investigations in favor of the admitted "guess dates" of the original Koriabo phase report was made at a time of uncertainty regarding the origin of the Koriabo phase. The retrodicted inception date for the Koriabo phase and its subsequent dated expansion throughout the Essequibo Basin now makes it easily possible to accommodate the notion of an Akawaio presence on the Suriname Coast at these relatively early dates, even the earliest of which conveys a measure of plausibility in light of the 200 B.C. date of the parent culture on the Pomeroon River. But the dating of Waiwaru ceramics still leaves open the question of the place and time of inception of Karinya ceramics. Obviously, a good deal more work needs to be done on the Barama River and possibly even further west.

Likewise, rejection of the earliest C^{14} date on a sample from Carbet Mitan in Guyane française (p. 367) might have seemed less necessary had the antiquity of Karinya ceramics at Waiwaru Market on the Western Guiana Littoral been known to its excavator.

Ceramics of the Koriabo phase are unknown along the Atlantic Coast of the Territory of Amapá. Therefore, the early Koriabo dates from the Suriname Coast now suggest a progressive occupation of the major rivers of the hinterland by Akawaio who followed the north-flowing rivers to the sea and whose eventual crossing of the Tumuc Humac watershed left a permanent mark on the ceramics of the Rio Jari Basin. The antiquity of the encounter at the Mouth of the Amazon is suggested by the temporal priority enjoyed by the *Uxy Incised, Jari Scraped* and *Mazagão Plain* ceramic types in the ceramic sequence for the Mazagão phase (Meggers and Evans 1957:Figure 23).

So long as the origin of the Koriabo phase had remained an equivocal issue (e.g. Boomert 1978a; Evans and Meggers 1960:150; Hilbert 1982; Rostain 1994a:460; Versteeg and Bubberman 1992; Williams 1985) every attempt at restructuring the history of the Guiana Coastal Plain was destined to remain inconclusive. Because Koriabo phase ceramic typology bears such an ineradicable imprint of its ancestral beginnings in the Waiwaru Complex, our erstwhile ignorance of the existence of Waiwaru phase ceramics inevitably resulted in an inability to distinguish between traits shared by the two complexes. Obviously, more work is needed on this issue at sites in the Eastern Guiana Hinterland, where the Akawaio were responsible for diffusing major cultural traits from the west. For example, the rim lobing, scraped decoration, incised scrolls and biomorphic nubbins of the Mazagão phase all unquestionably now seem to have derived, *via* the Akawaio, from their Karinya ancestors in the Waiwaru phase of the Western Guiana Littoral.

To these diagnostics of a relationship between Karinya and Akawaio must be added the rim-lobing, rim-nicking, scraped decoration, red-on-white painting and certain vessel shapes of the Aristé phase to the north of the Rio Araguari. These technological and typological similarities suggested to the pioneer excavators of the Territory of Amapá an affiliation between the early Mazagão and early Aristé phases. A common ancestor in an unidentified earlier ceramic style was implied. No direct dates are available for the Mazagão phase. A date sequence between A.D. 350 (or earlier) and Contact times has been accepted for the Aristé phase. Our identification of the Karinya of the Western Guiana Littoral as the common ancestor of peoples represented by the Aristé and Mazagão phases sheds new light on this long outstanding issue. As the Waiwaru phase of the Pomeroon River is to the Aristé phase of northern Amapá, so is the Koriabo phase of the Mazaruni River to the Mazagão phase of southern Amapá.

Belief, magic, death and the forms of art

Key forms in the indigenous art of the Guianas reflect the close inter-relationship that was held to exist between the opposed concepts of being and death. At the center of human being is subsistence, the total product of man's labor and which determined the social organization of his group. But man's access to the fruits of the natural world, on which this subsistence was based, was qualified by limits inhering in his available technologies. Therefore, Archaic man's inability to increase in any way the productivity of the biota subjected his subsistence activities to divine authority. In order to ensure his indefinite survival in various marginal environments of the New World, Archaic man was obliged to provide food for the gods in the form of souls of the human departed. The cosmological structure that expressed this relationship of indefinite clientship to the gods was reflected in the forms of a metaphoric architecture comprising the earth disc with its celestial dome and underworld connected by an *axis mundi*. As has been seen, this ethnographically evidenced structure (Wilbert 1975) is evidenced also in the archaeology of the Warao on the Western Guiana Littoral. In his economically centered discourse with the supernaturals, which articulated man's eternal clientship to the spirit world, the shaman generated various semantic signs, some of extreme antiquity.

Of these, three appertain to the Archaic. These are the Enumerative petroglyph sign which accounted for man's extractive behaviors in the biota, the polarization of head and foot in mortuary ritual that established the location of the group along the *axis mundi*, and the solsticial orientation of the dead which directed the departing soul toward the Land of the Dead in the western sky. Significantly, despite the economic revolution that is often thought to have been signaled by the transition to horticulture, the latter two classes of sign survived among various horticulturist groups well into the protohistoric period, e.g., the famous effigy urns of the Maracá phase in the Brazilian Territory of Amapá (Meggers and Evans 1957: Pl. 18).

A ground stone object from Guyane française which sets the figures of a bird and a human foot in vertical opposition, Figure 1.11, may or may not appertain to the Archaic time level. At any rate it suggests a metaphor for the head/foot (spirit/flesh, mind/body) dichotomy in which the concavity in the back of the bird may have served as an incense-burner. A similar symbolism may attach to a bird finial capping the *axis mundi* of a house in Guyane française (see Rostain 1994a, ii:Pl.27). Bird adornos were associated with mortuary vessels in the Mazagão phase (Meggers and Evans 1957:Pl./9c), while in the Orealla, Mabaruma and Santarem ceramic inventories an adorno, representing the King Vulture Figure 4.35c may have been associated with shamanic flight. In Guyane française, the shaman was buried in symbolic wings of macaw feathers, Figure 4.39a. Bird bones in a ceramic vessel placed next to the head in Hertenrits burial (Boomert 1980) may symbolize the flight of the soul to the spirit world.

Anthropomorphs signifying the head/foot dichotomy may comprise a pair of lower limbs attached directly to the human head (Roosevelt 1980:Figure 91; 1992: Figure 1.22,5), lower limbs connected to the head by means of the upper limbs resting on the knees (the so-called Hands-to-Face motif) (Palmatary 1960:Pl.72fh) or outsized lower limbs (the so-called "swollen calves" motif), this latter having derived from Archaic iconography, Figure 4.39b. With only head and legs protruding from its carapace, the turtle provided an excellent ready-made image in head/foot symbolism, Figure 4.97, B5, C5. Species utilized were the giant sea turtles, the Hawksbill *(Eretinochelys imbricata)*, Leatherback *(Dermochelys coriacea)*, Pacific Ridley *(Lepidochelys ofivacea)* and Green Turtle *(Chelonia mydas)*.

Concepts of a solticial map in horticulturist iconography derived from the early adoption of Warao, mortuary ritual among the Karinya. On both the Western and Eastern Guiana Littorals the late survival of shellfishing in Karinya subsistence suggests that adoption of these mortuary rituals, and the associated star lore, may have predated the advent of horticulture. As has been observed by Butt-Colson and Armellada (1989:182):

> It is noteworthy that all the figures which Kapon and Pemon constellations represent refer to the three activities of hunting, fishing and collecting. Their constellations are visual representations of stellar heroes which embody and control birds, crabs, turtles and their eggs, fish and game animals and also the creatures associated with these. Although cultivation has long been a basic economic activity, now often the primary one with manioc the staple starch food, it is conspicuous by its absence from Kapon and Pemon astronomy.

The star lore of the Karinya involves the same stellar heroes and constellations as that of the Kapon and Pemon, their linguistic descendants, and this star lore in turn displays close similarities to that of the Warao (Heinen and Lavandero 1973). The assimilation of Arawak horticulturist beliefs within the cosmological structure of the Archaic Warao seems evidenced in the place name of a small creek on the upper Pomeroon River -- *Aruquiaha*. In Arawak lore, *-koyaha* signifies the permanent home in a given star of the vitalizing spirit of a particular animal or plant species. Attainment by such a star of a given position in the heavens signals the season of its substrate animal or plant in a particular locality. Being the same each year, this locality acquires an appropriate place name. Several such place names are given in Roth (1924:716).

> The breeding places on earth where the *kuyuhas* specially assemble, ready to breathe the breath of life over animal or plant, receive names identical with those of their spirit-derived star. Thus, we have just spoken of the *kamma-kuyuha* star, which is the home of the body spirit of the tapir. Now, there is a creek on the left bank of the Demerara River called the Kammakwear* (a corruption of *Kamma-Kuyuha*), which points to the fact that at some previous period, or possibly even now, at a certain season of the year when its namesake star reached a definite point in the heavens, the female tapir and its young were very plentiful in the area, i.e., it was a recognized breeding ground of that creature. Thus, there are the *Kassa* (porpoise) *-Kwai*, the *Oma* (perai fish) *-Kwai*, the Barema (Giant anteater) *-Kwai*, the Tibikuri freshwater fish) *-Kwai*, etc.
>
> * Kamakuru: left bank Demerara 88km up.

In the example from the Pomeroon River, *Aru* the Warao word for flour is combined with *-koyaha,* Arawak for the guiding principle (Bennett 1994). In the absence of animal domestication, and in the prevailing stressed environments, the advent of food production did not signal the more or less rapid socio-cultural revolution that is sometimes attributed to that event. The provision of bread continued to be apprehended among horticulturists as a function of the will of the gods. Accordingly, the religion of the Archaic, with its repertory of sacred signs, survived more or less unaltered among the Karinya, and prominently so in the hands of their traditional women potters.

The woman potter in sacred and secular art

In the comparative ceramic traits shown in Figure 4.97, vessels numbered 4,5,6 and 11 comprise, specifically, funerary furniture. Assuming women potters, production of this repertory of sacred vessels implies a range of thanatological skills combined with competence in the manipulation of such signs in two- and three-dimensional design. The symbolism involved in the depositional pattern of secondary bones inside their respective urns, appropriately oriented by means of their associated signs towards the western sky, suggests a specialized role in the final manipulation of the mortal remains of the departed. Women thus appear to have functioned down the generations not only as arbiters of the vocabulary of semantic signs which constituted imagery in the funerary arts but also on some level to have served as accomplices of the shaman in the conduct of the final rites. In the characteristically matrilocal cultures of the Guianas, this body of sacred knowledge constituted a strictly gender-based specialization which, by virtue of its relationship to death, ensured its survival and dissemination through time. Mortuary imagery was therefore highly group specific. Moreover, its forms having been inherently resistant to change through time, yield readily to classification. Certain signs generated in two- and three-dimensional elements or vessel shapes are readily recognizable in the funerary ceramics of the Marajoara, Mazagão, Maracá and Aristé phases (Meggers and Evans 1957:103,154,375). Specialization in the forms of funerary furniture similarly characterized the ceramics of the Kurupukari phase, upper Essequibo.

This group specificity in funerary art permits recognition of iconographic relationships on various time levels. For example, the distinctive mortuary symbolism of the Maracá phase at the Mouth of the Amazon, Figure 4.65a, and of the Karinya in Guyane française, Figure 4.82 l, both occur in the refuse of Akawaio on the lower Mazaruni River, 4.65b, 4.80e. In light of their evident ceramic affliations, this should not seem surprising. Less expected in the ceramic inventories of the Akawaio are occurrences of the Scroll-and-stepfret (? funerary) sign, Figure 5.6b, and various anthropomorphic signs of possibly directional import deriving from Amazonian (? mortuary) iconography, Figure 4.53c.

Granted their semantic value in the ceramics of a given group, these distributions indicate at least the voluntary or involuntary movement of especially valued women across ethnic lines, emphasizing their social role as the bearers of life, providers of the essential manioc food technologies and, finally, as monitors of the flight of the departing soul to the world of the supernaturals. In this latter role, individual women may have functioned as the ultimate repositories of social power in their respective communities, and this may explain the numerous occurrences of *tangas* in certain burials of the Marajoara phase. Rare *tanga*-like objects recovered in the Koriabo phase inventory on the Essequibo River, Figure 4.97, likewise might signify the specialized role of individual potters among the Akawaio.

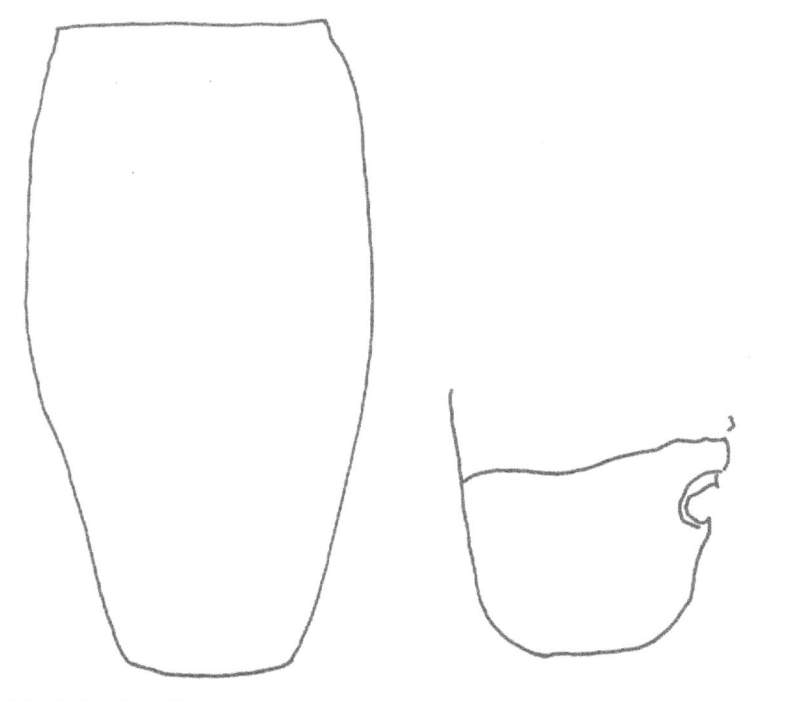

Figure 4.97. Koriabo phase. Possible ceramic *tangas*.

The sanctions of such power lay in the relationship of potter to clay. In this relationship, the Clay Mother (Warao *Konani;* Arawak *Konali;* Makusi *Eshang)* is propitiated by songs and offerings of food. As its "Owner," the Clay Mother resides in the subsurface deposit and controls its availability by means of bubbles breaking the surface. The spirit inhering in the clay was exploitable through the appropriate repertory of semantic signs. The elements of such signs were schematized and remained unchanged down the generations irrespective of the kinds of referent involved, human, animal or bird. This is exemplified in certain magical forms of the Arawaks and the Akawaio. Among the latter, the Scorpion's Tail motif tattooed around a woman's mouth assists in imparting the required "sting" to the intoxicating beverage under preparation. So, also, the appropriate metaphor for her brewing skills, modeled by the potter onto the drinking vessel, will transfer the attributes of the beverage (sting, sweetness) to the males who consume it (Butt 1957; Roth 1924:419). The Distended-Mouth adorno of Arawak ceramics, incorporating standard schemata for the cassava-chewing process and the salivating tongue that assists in fermentation in that process, constitutes such a metaphor. Stereotype elements employed equally in representations of animals in secular art or birds in sacred art imply identical sanctions in the Clay Mother, Figures 4.33, 4.35a-c.

These large Arawak adornos of the Aruka River reflect the final emergence of an artistic vocabulary of rigidly observed schemata completely lacking among their pre-horticultural ceramist hosts who had migrated from the Mouth of the Amazon. Their characteristic figurative repertory took many centuries to develop. The Distended-Mouth adorno remained unknown among Proto-Eastern Arawaks on the Amazon throughout. The unique achievement of these Orinoco Arawaks was the emergence of the professional figurative potter after around 590 B.C. (see Sanoja O. 1979:190). In response to evidently increasing institutionalization of the perceived interrelatedness between being and death, the corresponding ceramic motifs now attained explicit and permanent semantic value. In due course, they were adopted in the Koriabo phase, Figure 4.98.

Figure 4.98. Adoption of the Arawak Distended-Mouth adorno in Akawaio ceramics. **a-c.** Cuyuni, Mazaruni, Potato Rivers, respectively *(Coll. Walter Roth Museum).*

Inter-ethnic frontiers

Already during the Archaic, resource complementarities had opened certain trade routes between coastal groups and groups in occupation of *terra firme*. Probably, these groups already shared their parasitic, infectious and respiratory diseases. From the evidence of a later mortuary symbolism, they certainly shared their experiences of death. Along these trade routes, points of convergence are identifiable in the bi- or tri-component nature of the associated ceramic inventories. These points of convergence served as foci at which occurred a degree of cross-fertilization of local religious beliefs and practices, in this way contributing to the spiritual integration of the region. Cultural frontiers have been recognized in the southern part of the Brazilian Territory of Amapá, on the Guyana Coast, in the North Rupununi Savannas and in the North Pakaraimas. They date at different times and thus, to a degree, reveal process in cultural evolution. They are reviewed below in order of decreasing antiquity.

Southern Amapá 164 - 39 B.C. Koriabo phase ceramics on the Jari drainage suggest the early bridging of the Tumuc Humac watershed, probably from certain as yet undated sites on the Approuague and Oyapoc Rivers (Rostain 1994a). Samples from the Rio Jari and the Uxy site on the upper Rio Maracá produced the earliest ceramic types in the Mazagão sequence. Significantly, they represent Akawaio and Karinya refuse in close association. Between 164-39 B.C., the typologically and technologically equivalent ceramic types of the Aristé phase -- *Uaçá Incised* and *Flexal Scraped* -- were penetrating northern Amapá from the coast of Guyane française (Rostain 1994, 1994a:172). The compelling similarities between these ceramic types of northern and southern Amapá (Meggers and Evans 1957:596) suggest a degree of contemporaneity in the respective incursions. The early time level represented by these incursions is further emphasized by the near identity of the *Uxy Incised* urn lid from the Rio Maracá and the Karinya specimen from Waiwaru Creek, Figure 4.97, A6, C6. Appropriately, the indicated early Karinya migration into Amapá is closely congruent with the known migration of their Akawaio kinsmen into the Mazaruni Basin some time before 80 B.C., where, again, the urn lid occurs in painted and modeled forms, Figure 4.51f. And just as Karinya potsherds, Figure 4.91a,b co-occur with Akawaio potsherds on the Mazaruni, so also Karinya potsherds co-occur with Akawaio potsherds in southern Amapá. The restriction of *Uaçá Incised* ceramics to the northern portion of the Territory suggests that the indicated convergence of Karinya and Akawaio kinsmen in the south was along a hinterland route. Significantly, key items in their refuse derived from cemeteries.

The Guyana Coast +/- A.D. 870. The remarkable convergence of ceramic traits at the now destroyed reef site at Recht-door-Zee, at the Mouth of the Demerara River, reflects its role as the nexus of trade routes linking the Mabaruma, Abary and

Orealla Complexes. Orealla, an entrepôt on the Corentyne-Trombetas corridor dating to the ninth century A.D., was the point of departure of a route which led, across the Coastal Hinterland to Soesdyke on the Demerara River, thence to Recht-door-Zee at the Mouth of the Demerara River. Here, also, certain Amazonian traits of the coastal Suriname Hertenrits Complex, transmitted *via* the east-west trending *chenier* ridges, encountered a frontier that was characterized by a ceramic inventory predominantly comprising decorative elements of the Mabaruma Subseries of the Barrancoid Tradition on the lower Orinoco. Ultimately, *via* the tortuous inland waterways of the Western Guiana Littoral, the Recht-door-Zee interaction sphere established limits on the lower Aruka River, which had been peopled by Proto-Northern Maipuran Arawak horticulturists since around 1600 B.C., Figure 4.41.

Under the control of these Arawaks, whose entrepôt at Assakata on the Waini Basin was the reciprocal, across the Waini-Barima watershed, of their entrepôt at Koriabo Point on the Barima, rock materials from the *terra firme* quarries of the Western Guiana Littoral, prominent among them steatite from the upper Barama River, were moved into the stoneless reef sites of the Eastern Guiana Littoral to at least as far as the Abary River an the Demerara Coast. Complementarily, kaolin from the chalk cliffs at Orealla, on the Corentyne River, was moved as tempering material across the Coastal Hinterland *via* Recht-door-Zee and the Moruka River to as far into the North West as Assakata on the Biara River, Figure 4.40.

Thus, on this cultural frontier, descendants of Proto-Northern Maipuran Arawaks of the (Orinocan) Mabaruma phase were interacting, at least from Early Formative times, with their Proto-Eastern Maipuran Arawak brethren of the (Amazonian) Orealla and Hertenrits Complexes. These Proto-Eastern Maipuran Arawaks had penetrated the upper Essequibo River as early as 1000 B.C. and the upper Corentyne as early as A.D. 50, so that, by the time of their "reunion" with their Proto-Northern kinsfolk at Recht-door-Zee, their respective dialects had diverged somewhat, a situation that persists to the present day.

There was a corresponding divergence in material culture. For example, the large, heavy Saladoid/Barracoid adornos of Arawaks on the middle and lower Orinoco, and of the Mabaruma phase on the lower Aruka River (associated here with the ritualizing of manioc), while being present in the Recht-door-Zee inventory, was absent throughout in the ceramic inventories of the Amazonian Arawaks.

On the other hand, the dominant feature of the convergence of traits at Recht-door-Zee was the survival of the mortuary symbolism of particular factors in the indicated trade relationships. The local ceramic inventory therefore displays the head/foot turtle motif of the Karinya, the mortuary anthropomorph of the Akawaio and the 'directional' anthropomorphic head on burial urns of the (? Karinya/Akawaio) Mazagão phase, Figure 4.99a-e.

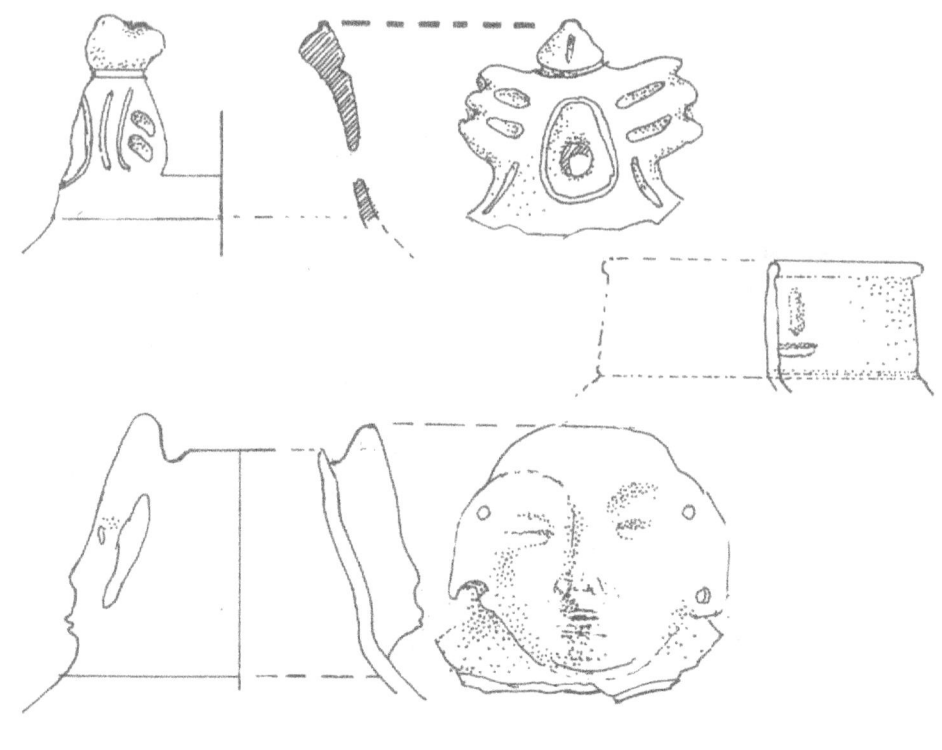

Figure 4.99. Convergence of disparate mortuary symbols at Recht-door-Zee, near the Mouth of the Demerara River, commencing +/- ninth century A-D. **a.** Incised and Modeled Tradition. **b,c.** Incised and Punctate Tradition.

The North Rupununi Savannas +/-A.D. 880.

Not recorded in the official *Gazetteer of Guyana,* Arua Creek is described (C.R. Jones, cited in Evans and Meggers 1960:298) as located around 30 km to the north of Yupukari, on the right bank Rupununi River. A surface collection made there on a small lateritic hill comprised potsherds of the Koriabo, Taruma and Rupununi phases. Associated were anthropomorphic figurines representing the head/foot mortuary symbol, known elsewhere at various late prehistoric sites, including Silver Sands on the Barbados south coast, dated between the tenth and fourteenth centuries (Drewett 1991). White slipping and caraipé temper support the indicated Akawaio presence. The Taruma were represented by their distinctive *Onoro Stamped* and *Kanashen Incised* ceramic types.

Essequibo Village is located on the left bank Essequibo about 2 km above the Essequibo-Rupununi confluence. A short pathway leads to Apoteri Village on the right bank of the Rupununi River. Surface collecting at both villages again included sherds of the Koriabo, Taruma and Rupununi phases, with, in addition, a few diagnostic sherds of the Kurupukari phase, further downstream.

Two nearly complete vessels of *Onoro Stamped* of the Taruma phase were represented. The Kurupukari phase was represented by two *Apoteri Incised* flanged rims from an interiorly red-painted bowl. This vessel is unknown in Koriabo, Taruma and Rupununi phase inventories. Evidently it represents a now destroyed camp site of the old Kurupukari Arawak settlers on the upper Essequibo River. The Akawaio, Taruma and Makusi refuse is evidently much more recent, probably dating no earlier than the planting of the Dutch outpost at Apoteri some time during the latter half of the eighteenth century. Such a contingency would explain this convergence of Carib speakers "on the direct route of the tribes who come from the Orinoco and Corentyne and pass through the country to trade or make war higher up" (Gravesande cited in Harris and de Villiers 1911:254). Higher up were the Taruma and the Waiwai, apparently late prehistoric peoples.

The North Pakaraimas. Nineteenth century. Suggestive of this trade is a ceramic sample from Paramakatoi that included a few specimens of *Macapaima Incision Corta* decorative motifs. This Orinocan influence evidently had been mediated by Akawaio traders who had derived it in relays with Arawaks on the Caroni, on the other side of the watershed on the upper Mazaruni River (i.e., *via* the Essequibo and Potaro Rivers and overland from Chinowieng Village). More apposite to this discussion is the acceptance by the Makusi and Patamona from the Akawaio of the concept of *kenaima* (witch doctor). As a method of social control among peoples who deny the possibility of death from natural causes, the operation of the *kenaima*, through whose agency a particular death is avenged on an unsuspecting individual, is evidenced in Makusi inventories by a globular ceramic jar whose constricted neck is girdled by a snake motif. Containing the fragmentary and sometimes charred human bones that are employed to sever the *External sphincter ani* of his victim, this vessel represents the most important possession of the *kenaima*. Being thus an unerring clue to his identity, which must never be known, its concealment from the remainder of the community was imperative. Recently, such a vessel was recovered in the dark recesses of a cave around Paramakatoi Village, Figure 4.100. Judiciously, it was left intact by the horrified community. A similar pot derives from Makusi territory in the North Rupununi Savannas. The snake motif occurred also in the ceramic sample from Apoteri.

Notwithstanding the presence of horticulturists on the peripheries of the Guiana land mass during at least the second millennium B.C. (Roosevelt et al 1995; Weber 1990), our earliest evidences of inter-ethnic convergence date toward the

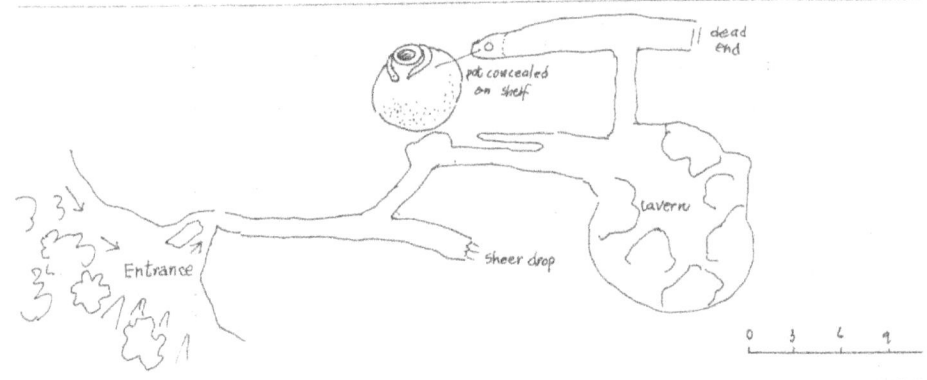

Figure 4.100. The impedimenta of the *kenaima* concealed in a cave in the North Pakaraimas. *(Courtesy Col. John Blashford-Snell).*

ending of the first millennium with the meeting of Akawaio and Karinya groups in southern Amapá. The evidence of the cave dwellers on the coast of Guyane française suggests that these were small kin groups not yet enjoying the economic base of a fully-fledged manioc horticulture with its inflexible demands on organized labor, but who already had developed the trait of the bounded cemetery, Figure 4.85, and appropriate mortuary ceramics, certain forms of which, e.g., the zoned incised hachure decorated urn lid were already of a respectable antiquity in the Intermediate Area. Its apparent association with title to ancestral land would seem to account for the formal rigidity of funerary art and the wide dispersion of its two- and three-dimensional elements across the circum-Guiana alluvium. Specificity of mortuary ritual to a given group would seem to explain the tenacity with which its forms were preserved in any given case, even where death occurred, or was caused, in alien territory. Hence, evidently, the similarities in funerary ritual that are implied by the convergence of specific ceramic traits of the Karinya and Akawaio in southern Amapá.

Almost another thousand years elapsed before the convergence of Orinocan and Amazonian Arawak speakers is evidenced at the Mouth of the Demerara River. By this time, the ninth century A.D., the volume of refuse accumulating around the entrepôts at Orealla and at Recht-door-Zee suggests that the groups involved were incomparably larger, with subsistence based on a fully-fledged manioc economy. By this time, also, Akawaio on the Mazaruni River had been interacting with Arawaks on the Orinoco *via* the Pakaraima Highlands during the previous several centuries. The movement of mortuary symbolism, evidenced in the respective ceramic inventories (e.g. the urn lid, perhaps the double-spout-and-bridge bottle) suggests that, along with thanatological lore may have occurred the transmission of communicable diseases and experiences of other peoples' mortuary behaviors.

By the nineteenth century, ceramic evidences of the operations of *kenaima* among the Patamona and their Makusi neighbors co-occur with the dispersion of the basin urn lid in their funerary furniture. Again, the dispersal of this distinctive ceramic utensil points to an ancient trade route which ultimately linked the North Pakaraimas and the Intermediate Area.

Thus, key mortuary symbols in their respective ceramic inventories indicate that, by means of a complex of ancient trade networks, the contrasting late prehistoric groups of northeastern South America, and even of part of the Eastern Caribbean, were unified in a rich lore of healing, of disease and of death that evidently had been accumulating among groups of contrasting language and dialect and in specific environments during at least the six thousand years since the initial colonization of the Antilles following on the development of the dugout canoe. That this cumulative heritage of adaptation to specific ecological zones in the mosaic of the Tropical Forest environment did not long survive the incursion of Europeans is eloquently evidenced in the congeries of ceramic styles and traditions concentrating on the Essequibo-Rupununi confluence in the wake of the Dutch trading outpost there in the late eighteenth century and in the subsequent universal demise of the age-old mortuary arts.

5. THE ORIGIN AND DISSEMINATION OF TROPICAL FOREST CULTURE IN THE GUIANAS

Introduction

At the time of Steward's ethnographically based classification of South American cultures, the archaeology of the Guianas remained virtually unknown, comprising mainly the results of chance finds reported by travelers, missionaries, soldiers and colonial administrators. Although, in Guyana, the best known research area of the region, the history of excavation went back to Brett's pioneering Classificatory-Descriptive investigations commencing 1865, the associated trends (past environments, relative levels of cultural development) had stimulated little interest outside the country over the ensuing many decades. Because of the coastal and riverain base of the early investigators, notably the missionaries, administrators and military men, knowledge of indigenous cultures remained confined to the geographical margins of the area. Unfortunately, this restricted picture was all that existed at the time by way of providing a background to Steward's characterization of Tropical Forest Culture, a situation to which Gillin's (1948:819) cautionary observation gave considerable point:

> In the absence of a comprehensive picture (if the actual archaeological resources of the interior, statements regarding prehistoric distributions of culture and population for the Guianas as a whole must remain highly tentative.

In Steward's characterization, Tropical Forest peoples were thought to have been mainly riparian and maritime, water resources having been no less important to them than crops. Fish, a major food resource, were taken with drags, baskets, nets, weirs, multi-prong and harpoon arrows, and, frequently, hooks. They used the spear and spear-thrower, bow-and-arrow, and blow gun. Other traits were the dugout canoe, thatched-covered frame houses, hammocks, basketry, weaving, ceramics, body-painting, mosquito shelters, pepper-pot, rubber, bark-cloth, the climbing ring, hollow-log drum, the babracot and poisoned arrows (Steward 1949:708).

Inevitably, the question arose concerning the relative ages of these traits and the mechanisms of their spread across the region. Because the Guianas were found to have the greatest number regarded as characteristic of the Tropical Forests, and in light of their supposedly rich archaeological remains, they were postulated (Steward 1948:886) as a center of dispersal, though not necessarily of all items. But as shown by Gillin (1948:799), the Guianas were not culturally homogeneous; differences between the physiographic zones identified there (coastal, mountain-savanna and Amazonian areas) needed further definition. In particular, systematic comparisons were required between its Arawakan and Cariban cultures, especially with respect to their differential dispersion in coastal and hinterland areas. As, it was claimed, these cultures disappeared before they were recorded, the challenge of reconstructing them was thrown squarely to archaeology.

During the past several decades, enough has been learned of the archaeology of the Guianas to permit taking up the challenge thrown out by Steward. Indeed, the task had been initiated by Osgood in northwestern Guyana even before the appearance of the first volume of Steward's *Handbook of South American Indians*. Osgood's undertaking was refined and developed by Clifford Evans and Betty J. Meggers commencing in the early fifties, and the study has gained momentum in work undertaken since by specialists in the various territories. But it is to the pioneering endeavors of Evans and Meggers that we owe the earliest identification of the archaeological cultures of the territory, the coastal cultures of Guyana and the Territory of Amapá and, particularly, the hinterland cultures represented by the Koriabo phase of the Akawaio, as well as by the Rupununi and the Waiwai phases. All these were manioc horticulturists adapted to the lowlands and exhibiting in varying degree the defining traits of Tropical Forest Culture. Since, with the exception of the Rupununi and Waiwai phases, methodological rigor precluded any attempt by the authors at identifying these archaeological cultures with particular ethnic groups, the systematic comparisons of Arawakan and Cariban cultures and the explication of their respective dispersions, required in Steward's characterization, unfortunately never materialized. Accordingly, this has been the central concern of the present inquiry.

In part, also, systematic comparison of Arawak and Cariban cultures has been a concern because representatives of these cultures are still very much with us. As a number of more recent works have shown, it is by no means the case that their demise eliminated the possibility of structuring the ethnographic record. The continuing, though obviously reduced, presence of representatives of these peoples in strictly the areas inhabited by their forefathers over the millennia constitutes a most welcome bonus in archaeological interpretation.

The most ancient archaeologically attested adaptation on the Guiana Coast is of the Warao on the edge of the intertidal swamps which, during the eighth millennium, developed in extreme northwestern Guyana as the sea approached its present level, separating Trinidad from the northeastern coast of South America. Warao refuse on this time level indicates a prevailing set of cosmological beliefs which appear already to have been of respectable antiquity elsewhere in the Americas. An analog of the model of the universe that is implied by their archaeologically reconstructed burial practices has been illustrated in the domestic architecture of various Amazonian peoples, notably the Yecuana of the upper Orinoco (Barandiaran 1979), and the model survives among the ethnographic Warao to the present day (Wilbert 1986).

Likewise, the Proto-Eastern Maipuran Arawaks of the Corentyne River continue to occupy precisely the site of the medieval entrepôt of their ancestors on the edge of the Intermediate Savannas and with a cultural memory that goes back to at least the time of the Dutch trade routes of the seventeenth century. Their Proto-Northern brethren at Assakata recall the route of their flight from the Venezuelan War of Independence (1821).

Finally, pottery techniques of contemporary Karinya on the upper Pomeroon River explain archaeological refuse suggesting a link between certain peoples on the Cauca Valley in Colombia and peoples along the Guiana Coast as far as the Brazilian Territory of Amapá. Recognition of the possible heartland of Karinya culture some place in or near the Western Guiana Littoral provided the key to restructuring subsequent horticultural evolution on the Coast and contributed to an understanding of Kapon penetration of the hinterland and their eventual encounter, in the North Pakaraimas, with horticulturists coming up from the Amazon *via* the Rupununi/Rio Branco Savannas.

These regionwide dispersals of horticulturists across the Guianas converged at certain key points both on the Coast and in the Hinterland. These points of convergence correlate with ethnic, linguistic and physiographic boundaries and therefore are potentially useful in the reconstruction of ancient demographies, particularly in suggesting possible patterns of disease transmission, the effects of epidemics on migration and the settlement pattern, etc.

It will have been observed that Gillin's tripartite division of the physiographic areas of the Guianas, which recognizes a specific culture type in the Amazonian Area, has been dropped in favor of a two-part (littoral/hinterland) division which recognizes contrasts between the subsistence potentials of the circum-Guiana alluvium (coastal swamps, rivers, estuaries) and *terra firme* (tropical forest, savannas, mountains). This has permitted interpreting the archaeological data from early Archaic times in terms of coastal-hinterland resource complementarities which, tending over time to accentuate rather than obliterate the adaptive effects of these physiographic contrasts, have contributed to sharpening rather than blurring the defining limits of the ethnicities (Carib, Arawak) recognized by Steward within the abiding framework of Tropical Forest Culture. Identifying contrasting coastal/hinterland resource complementaries yielded, also, an immediate bonus in the recognition of the adaptive value of niche variation through time, both on the Coast and in the Hinterland.

The principal migrations
The Coast and Coastal Hinterland

Exclusion of the Pomeroon River in the research design of the pioneering excavators precluded recognition of the culture of the Karinya on the coast. The resulting lacuna had a bearing on evidences for or against Steward's (1949:697) notion of the origin of Tropical Forest Culture in a movement which supposedly had carried Circum-Caribbean traits down the Atlantic Coast and up the Orinoco and/or the Amazon. The Steward hypothesis was put to the test at the Mouth of the Amazon and rejected (Meggers and Evans 1957:604). But had that test included the Pomeroon River, this rejection might have been somewhat less absolute. The technological and typological characteristics of Waiwaru phase ceramics on the Pomeroon at around 200 B.C. might have suggested the source of the cultural unity already recognized in certain shared characteristics of the Mazagão, Aristé and Maracá phases in the Territory of Amapá (Meggers and Evans 1957:158).

Granted the dispersion of the Carib languages cited above, Figures 1.15, 1.16, 4.72, the coastal distribution of Karinya ceramics suggests their migration from an as yet unidentified heartland more to the west during the centuries preceding the birth of Christ. It has been seen that occurrences of aberrant funerary furniture, in particular ceramic inventories, imply the intrusion of alien mortuary practices. Intrusive at the Waiwaru Market site on the Pomeroon are basin urn lids of the Zoned Incised Hachure Horizon Style characteristic of burials on the upper Rio Cauca, in Colombia, dating at the 5th and early 6th centuries B.C. Figure 4.79d. There, the Ilama phase inventory at the El Topacio cemetery included "a single example of a rather crude plate, a shape not hitherto recognized for the Ilama period" (Bray et al 1988). This "plate" is the basin urn lid of various ceramic inventories in the Guianas.

Aberrant occurrences of Colombian shaft tombs in the Territory of Amapá similarly point to intrusion of an alien mortuary practice among Eastern Karinya, Figure 4.83a,b this time on a much later time level. The shaft tomb, shown in Figure 4.83a, contained an urn burial dated at A.D. 920 +/- 80, though earlier and later dates were obtained from the same cemetery (Gähwiler-Walder 1988). Ceramic types in the shaft tombs of the Territory of Amapá, *Serra Plain* and *Serra Painted*, represent the late part of the Aristé phase sequence there (Meggers and Evans 1957:153). In neighboring Guyane française, the equivalent ceramic type, *Enfer Polychrome*, dates at between A.D. 1450-1750 (Rostain 1994a: 197). Thus, the ceramic evidences indicate interaction between Karinya on the Guiana Coast and communities on the upper Cauca in Colombia between 200 B.C. and A.D. 1750. To this time span probably is to be attributed the trade in canoes against Colombian gold ornaments that is reported by the early explorers, Figure 4.84a. What part of this period is represented by the associated migrations, the precise route involved in these migrations (consider Figure 4.84b,c) and the part possibly played by the canoe trade in the associated interactions remain unclear.

During roughly this same period, the Eastern and Western Guiana Littorals were being peopled in the terminal stages of the Proto-Maipuran Arawak migrations that had been initiated somewhere on the upper Rio Negro. Arrived at the Mouth of the Corentyne during the opening centuries of the Christian Era, these earliest Arawaks on the Eastern Guiana Littoral moved southeastward along the reefs toward the Coast of Guyane française, where the emergent rocks of the Guiana Shield Complex meet the sea. In due course, the crossing of the Corentyne estuary opened the way for their westward expansion along the reefs and across the Intermediate Savannas of the Coastal Hinterland. Along this latter route, contact was established with their brethren from the lower Orinoco who, commencing around 1600 B.C., had peopled the swamps apparently *via* the route across the Aruka-Amacuro watershed. Thus, the Arawak migrations across the Guiana Coast and Coastal Hinterland covered the period 1600 B.C. to around A.D. 1000. On the Coast, these Arawak migrations were partly concurrent with the southeastward expansion of the Karinya, who, however, appear to have avoided the already occupied *chenier* ridges.

The Hinterland. The early migrations of the Akawaio had reached the middle Mazaruni River by 80 B.C. and the Territory of Amapá, Brazil, not long afterward. The route remains to be identified. By 1000 A.D., the Akawaio had reached the lower Potaro River on the Essequibo. Their penetration of the remainder of the Essequibo Basin occupied most of the ensuing millennium.

The circum-Guiana migrations. Commencing probably around 2000 B.C., Arawaks were migrating simultaneously down the Orinoco and Amazon Rivers. At sites on both rivers, these migrations are represented by potsherds of Saladoid ceramics overlain by potsherds of Barrancoid ceramics. Associated with both Orinocan and Amazonian migrations was the distinctive *Timehri* petroglyph type, representing the continuing role of the supernatural in horticulturist economy. On the Orinoco, distributions of this petroglyph indicate that certain early Arawaks moved up the Caroni River, Figure 4.13d,e. Early Arawak settlements there would appear to explain occurrences of Barrancoid ceramics in the early part of the Quartz Island sequence on the Mazaruni River, across the Guiana Highlands. Saladoid ceramics were absent on Quartz Island.

By around the time of Christ, Arawak horticulturists had encircled the portion of the Island of Guiana lying to the west of the Corentyne River, in the process crossing the Acarai watershed into the Essequibo Basin. By around the time of Christ, also, Karinya Caribs migrating southeastward from a hearth somewhere on or near the Western Guiana Littoral, had initiated settlement in north Amapá, thereby completing the occupation of the Guianas by horticulturists. These migrations are mapped in Figure 5.1.

The above archaeologically attested migrations accord quite well with the peripheral distributions of Arawaks around the Guiana land mass. An isolated area at its center apparently represents penetration of the upper Essequibo River by Proto-Eastern Maipurans of the Kurupukari Complex around 1000 B.C. The

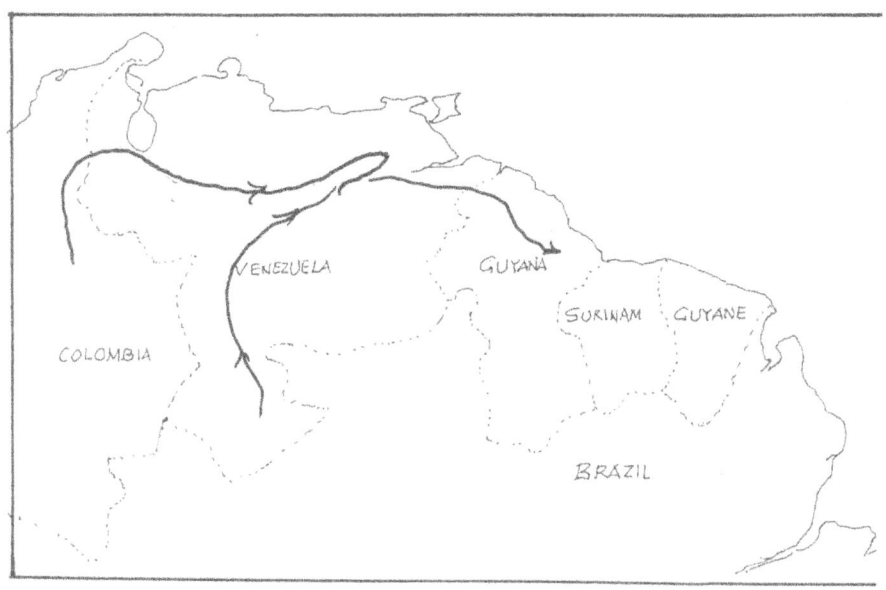

Figure 5.1. Principal migrations in the peopling of the Guianas by horticulturists.

contiguity of Galibi (Karinya) with Coastal Carib suggests a direction for future inquiry into prehistoric interactions between central Colombia and the Atlantic Coast of the Guianas. In the meantime, archaeological evidences of an ancestral relationship between ceramics of the Waiwaru Complex and the ceramics of the Koriabo phase lend support to the linguistic reconstruction of a similarly ancestral relationship between Galibi (Karinya) and the languages of the East-West Guiana Carib (including Kapon, Pemon, Makusi, Waiwai and others). The archaeologically attested early peopling of the Territory of Amapá by Karinya (Aristé phase) in the north and a Kapon or Kapon-related group (Koriabo phase) in the south is unequivocally evidenced in the linguistic partitioning of the region by the Rio Araguari.

Contrasting horticulturist adaptations

Available evidences from both the littoral and *terra firme* suggest that populations remained small and relatively immobile long after the manioc option had become available. Notwithstanding the early date for this event on the lower Aruka River, the attainment of the minimum population size required for establishing this highly labor intensive crop on a viable economic basis appears to have taken these coastal (Proto-Northern Maipuran) Arawaks well over a thousand years. The situation appears to have been not a lot better among their hinterland (Proto-Eastern Maipuran) brethren whose *terra preta* campsite on the upper Essequibo River covered only around 40 ha at its greatest extent after almost a thousand years of sedentary occupation. Their situation is comparable to that of Arawaks pioneering a horticultural economy at Barrancas on the lower Orinoco River at around the same date (p. 269).

While appearing much later in the archaeological record, and having received their farming from a different source, the Karinya exhibited a similar tardiness in achieving a fully sustainable manioc horticulture. This event probably did not long precede the introduction of *Uaça Incised* pottery in northern Amapá around the mid-fourteenth century (Rostain 1994a:197), before which, as has been seen (Figure 4.85) the rock shelters and small caves inhabited by Eastern Karinya on the Coast of Guyane française do not suggest the large concentrations of labor required for fully-fledged manioc farming.

The profiles at Quartz Island and Lanciana Island indicate an only slowly ameliorating environment at this time. These conditions, characterized by a very slow rate of rise in water level in the Mazaruni River and deposition of fine silt particles during its annual flood stages, were reflected in a continuing marine influence on the coasts and estuaries, possibly including the estuary of the Orinoco River.

This process of island building remains in evidence well into the latter half of the first millennium A. D. Thus, although population expansion is implied in the coastal migrations of both Arawaks and Caribs at this time, population growth among Karinya on the swamp edge of the Eastern Guiana Littoral appears to have been less rapid than among Arawaks on the *chenier* ridges there. It will be recalled that at this time these Arawaks were expanding not only eastward and westward along the reefs, but also had already crossed the Intermediate Savannas from Orealla and established an emporium at the Mouth of the Demerara River. It may be speculated that differentials in the respective rates of expansion may have been due to relative differences in productivity in the contrasting farming strategies of Caribs and Arawaks: irrigation horticulture and high residential stability on the swamp edge among the Karinya, contrasted with slash-and-burn horticulture and high residential mobility among Arawaks on the reefs. A good deal more work is needed on this topic. The adaptive potentials of niche variability on the rich coastal alluvium remain to be examined. On presently available evidences, the Karinya settlement pattern on high ground bordering small streams on the direct swamp edge, where the tidal counter-currents permitted their version of irrigation horticulture, Figure 4.85, appears to contrast with the Arawak strategy of exploiting the swamps from, first, artificially raised habitation mounds combined with raised fields; next, by raised fields directly annexed to habitation plots on the reef edge; and, finally, by combined cultivation and habitation on the reefs proper. The last stratagem appears to have been associated with the highest growth rates and most rapid westward expansion, as represented in the Abary phase east of the Demerara River (p. 339). If so, the reason remains to be sought.

In the Hinterland, Akawaio expansion also had been relatively slow when compared with that of the coastal Arawaks. Although the Akawaio had reached the lower Potaro River already by A.D. 1000, (by which time Arawak entrepôts were flourishing at Orealla on the Corentyne and Recht-door-Zee on the Demerara), Akawaio slash-and-burn exploitation of the remainder of the Essequibo Basin remained still incomplete at Contact (ca. A.D. 1619). Even by this time, the rainfall regime and bankfull streams of the present day probably had not yet been achieved. In fact, it remains an open question whether or not, in the ameliorating environment that followed on the ending of the Amazonian arid interval at around 80 B.C., the Essequibo River has yet reached its maximum discharge capacity.

In 1739, in advance of the construction of Fort Zeelandia on Flag Island near the Mouth of the Essequibo River, Commander Gravesande

> had the ground examined to a depth of eight feet, and found that it consisted of hard firm clay and well able to carry the heaviest masonry (Harris and de Villiers 1911:198).

At its completion, in 1744, Gravesande reported:

> The said fort consists of a redoubt fifty feet square, the wall of which will stand against the heaviest ordnance. There are two stories, the lower serving for provisions and holding also a safe powder magazine (Harris and de Villiers 1911:208).

Today, on Flag Island, the water table stands 2" higher than the surface of the ground (Cox pers. comm. 1977) and the floor where gunpowder was kept dry two and a half centuries ago, like the remainder of the island, now lies under a mantle of permanently wet mud. The hard, firm clay of the mid-eighteenth century no longer supports Gravesande's gun emplacements, which have collapsed into the river.

A water table located around eight foot lower than at present suggests a still severely attenuated discharge of the Essequibo River during the mid-eighteenth century. This implies more pronounced drying out of the creeks and increased mobility of the Akawaio during the dry season. It was in these still testing environmental conditions that the traditional polities of the Akawaio encountered the bounty of the first Dutch settlers on the Essequibo. Within a generation the Akawaio were bearing Dutch arms against Africans in the Berbice War [their Koriabo phase potsherds can still be recovered around the fort]. The decline in their fortunes that followed on the political demise of the Dutch toward the end of the nineteenth century is evidenced in their subsequent slow rate of expansion in the Essequibo Basin (p. 391).

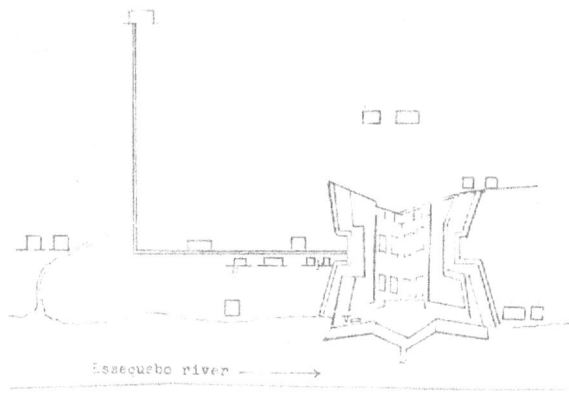

Figure 5.2. Following the ending of the Amazonian arid interval around 80 B.C., water level was still rising in the Essequibo River when Fort Zeelandia was completed 1744.

The Intermediate Area and the Guianas

The near congruence of initial dates for the earliest shell mounds on Trinidad and on the Western Guiana Littoral may explain the recovery, on that island, of a large, chipped-stone, stemmed, trianguloid projectile point on local chert similar to the large points from western Guyana. On Trinidad, this point is thought roughly contemporaneous with the Guyana points, dating around 9000 - 8000 B.C., at which time Trinidad remained part of the mainland and the lowlands already were interacting with the Andes. Indeed, the initial peopling of Western Guiana may have been stimulated by its unique jasper exposures.

Around 5000 B. C., certain defining traits of Tropical Forest Culture, notably the synthetic bodypaint, begin to enter the archaeological record. The dugout canoe was developed later. This was an artifact of rebounding water levels in the sediment basin around 3300 B.C. following on the peaking of the sea level rise around 4000 B.C. A long-term consequence of this development was the emergence, around 3200 B.C. (p. 148), of an Archaic interaction sphere defined by Cuba in the north, the South Caribbean Island Chain in the west and the Mouth of the Amazon in the south. Around 2000 B.C., pottery-making was introduced on the Western Guiana Littoral from the Mouth of the Amazon. This development was adventitious and without influence on the traditional shellfishing economies there. The affiliation of the Alaka phase remained with shell mounds extending westward along the old littoral line of northern South America, with diminishing antiquity, to as far as El Heneal in Venezuela.

Thus, Tropical Forest Culture is much older in the Guianas than Steward could have suspected granted the archaeological data available in the forties. It emerged in conditions of continuous adaptation to the continually changing environments of the late Pleistocene. While specialist fishers and collectors were exploiting the rare jasper outcrops of the Pakaraima Highlands to produce the large projectile points needed to exploit the deep pools of the dried-out stream beds of the day, small-game hunters and collectors representing a contrasting adaptation on the eastern tropical lowlands of South America appeared around the Mouth of the Amazon.

The various niches that developed on the Western Guiana Littoral in response to changing relationships between the sea and a low-lying coastal zone generated the resource complementarities between these areas and the Western Guiana Hinterland which, after the "freshwater climax" of +/- 3300 B.C., were exploited in a complex kin-based system of reciprocal exchange that moved strategic rock materials from one end to the other of the swamp basin in the development of the canoe manufacturing industry. The economic catchment area was vast. Occurrences of the Amazonian (Mina phase) trapezoidal stone adze of this industry at Las Varas on the eastern Venezuelan coast (Sanoja O. 1989) suggest that, with the expansion of the industry on the lower Moruka River, the kin-based trade network of the swamp basin had been integrated into the more complex system of relationships that is suggested by the coastwise dispersion of Warao-like languages noted by Granberry (1993:31):

> We know ... from toponymic data that Warao-like languages, such as the Guayqueri of Margarita Island, were at one time spoken from an indeterminate position on the Caribbean coast of Colombia-Venezuela between Lake Maracaibo and the Magdalena east through the Orinoco Delta. Speakers of these languages occupied the northern segment of South America as far south as the Amazonian rain forest and the confluence of the Rio Vaupés and the Rio Negro. From ethnographic evidence it is also clear that the origin of the present-day Warao lay far to the west of the Orinoco Delta, quite likely as far west as the Maracaibo region itself or even lower Central America to judge from modern Warao myths and cosmology.

While the distribution of Archaic shell mounds along the old littoral line of South America lends support to the dispersion of ancient Warao-like languages there, the chronology of these mounds seems to indicate a westward expansion of Warao peoples rather than the eastward movement postulated above. It was into this complex of relationships along the north coast of South America that horticulture was introduced on the Western Guiana Littoral during the second millennium B.C.

In the northwestern sector of the swamp basin, Late Archaic peoples had continued to enjoy a diversity of economic resources unknown in the southeast since the subsistence crisis that had been induced by the inundation of the intertidal mudflats there during the freshwater climax of +/- 3300 B.C. Accordingly, the subsistence technologies of the North West survived with little or no change the introduction of a root carbohydrate (manioc) in a domestic economy that traditionally had been based on the processing of a stem carbohydrate (moriche flour). Proto-Northern Maipuran Arawaks entering at this time into an alliance with a Warao local group on the lower Aruka River inherited an Archaic system of reciprocal exchange that permitted access to the entire swamp basin and beyond. At the same time, their introduction of the manioc root was predicated not only on the prior existence among the Warao of the technologies of basketry, ceramics and stoneworking, but also on the knowledge, now critical in detoxifying this root, of synthesizing vegetal substances. This seminal alliance with Arawak horticulturists survives in Warao cultural memory to the present day and, to some extent, in the Warao language of Guyana, which, significantly, includes more words for manioc plant parts and manioc processing than either Arawak or Carib. Even more significantly, the event is immortalized in the name *Aru-akah* (Aruka): River of the Cassava Root. The above clears the way for a return to the Steward hypothesis (1949:762). This postulated that

> Tropical Forest Culture derived its essential technology from the Circum-Caribbean culture and that it also acquired certain rain forest traits, but it failed to borrow the Circum-Caribbean sociopolitical and religious patterns. In becoming adapted to fluvial, littoral, and rain forest areas, the technological complex spread *via* the main waterways. Specifically, it seems to have spread from Venezuela down the Atlantic Coast and up the Amazon and its tributaries (perhaps secondarily it spread up the Orinoco and down the Rio Negro), suffering successive losses as it reached the headwaters ...

The available evidences now indicate that the "essential technology" of Tropical Forest Culture, including the slow development of the sociopolitical system that is required for the emergence of a full-blown manioc-based economy; development of the irrigation, water-table or slash-and-burn strategies of land use that ensure sustainability in manioc horticulture; development of the various processes of detoxifying the manioc root; of the use of plant piscicides; of a range of ingenious fish traps and fish weirs; of the manufacture of synthetics such as the bodypaint that permits sustained human occupancy of the rain forests and the swamps; of the extensive pharmacopoeia that to the present day supports the survival of healthy human forest communities (cf. Waterlow 1945); of the complex of trade networks that linked littoral, fluvial, rain forest and Andean groups and by means of which were transmitted the lore and learning of antiquity (e.g. Langdon 1981) -- all these represent a heritage of adaptation to one of the most complex environments ever peopled by man and certainly not a devolution from or adaptation of Circum-Caribbean culture.

While data now available from the Guiana Coast firmly support Meggers and Evans' rejection of the Steward hypothesis, interaction with the Intermediate Area is nonetheless of very remote antiquity, involving, first, the shellfishing Warao and later, in the centuries before the opening of the Christian Era, the horticulturist Karinya. Among the Karinya, the basin urn lid of Waiwaru Market and the shaft tomb of the Territory of Amapá both have their correlates in Central Colombia. The shaft burial of Amapá may have been a function of the long-distance trade that seems implied by the recovery on the Mazaruni River of the gold pectoral of the Tairona or Sinu peoples of the Caribbean Coast of Colombia, Figure 4.84a. These "eagles" were quite common trade items on the lower Orinoco toward the ending of the sixteenth century (Whitehead 1990). Thus, the Mazaruni specimen may have been carried up the Caroni River and across the watershed *en route* further east. The ceramic figurine from the North Pakaraimas, Figure 4.84b,c, also suggests that the route from western Venezuela led across country *via* the territories of Carib-speakers on the lower Orinoco and the Caroni, into the Guiana Highlands and further east. This route accords with Durbin's disjunct distribution of Galibi across the Guianas when contrasted with the strictly coastal distribution of Arawak.

Occurrences of typologically aberrant items of funerary furniture in local ceramic inventories regionwide was the logical corollary of such long-distance trade. As evidenced in the distribution of the Colombian shaft tomb, Figure 4.83a,b, or the basin urn lid of the Pomeroon River, death in alien territory permitted the intrusion of the mortuary rituals of the guest into the ancestral territory of the host. One of the earliest instances of the mobility of mortuary symbolism in the Guianas is represented by the two basin urn lids from the Saladoid levels at the Kurupukari Falls site. On separate C^{14} assays, these basin urn lids date at between Cal. B.C. 1315-770 (p. 311). These specimens display Zoned Incised Hachure motifs interiorly, Figure 4.49k,l. Although at this time zoned incision represented an already old tradition in the Andes (see Evans and Meggers 1968:89; Meggers and Evans 1961), the technique appears to have been relatively new at the Mouth of the Amazon where occurrences in the Ananatuba phase, the earliest in the cultural sequence, date at around 980 B.C. Zoned Incised Hachure occurs also in the undated

Jauari shell mound at the Mouth of the Trombetas.

Zoned Incised Hachure elements identical to the Kurupukari Falls specimens occur in the El Topacio burials on the upper Rio Cauca, in Colombia, where such incision is thought to date at between the sixth and fifth centuries B.C. Identical elements occurring at the Waiwaru Market site around 200 B.C., Figure 4.76:10, imply the Archaic mortuary ritual of solar orientation of the dead. On Trinidad, specimens of zoned incision in the Saladoid levels of the Cedros site date at around 190 B.C. (Olsen 1973), but evidence for attributing a mortuary significance to these designs is lacking. Zoned Incised Hachure is recorded next on the interiors of two Saladoid rim sherds from the Wonotobo Falls site on the Corentyne River (Boomert 1983:Figure 7:8,9). There, the specimens appear to have derived from basin urn lids. Urn lids implying solar orientation of the dead have been recovered at El Mayal, on the Venezuelan coast, Figure 4.80e, thought a successor of Cedros on Trinidad (Olsen 1973). El Mayal dates at A.D. 155 (Bullen and Bullen 1976).

Specimens of Zoned Incised Hachure from the Saladoid levels of the Kurupukari Falls site represent the earliest dated occurrences of the trait known so far in the ceramics of the Guianas. The designs are of mortuary significance there and are typologically intrusive in the associated Saladoid ceramic inventory. Occurrences of this distinctive design on the upper Essequibo River, on the upper Rio Cauca and on the upper Pomeroon suggest the sustained interaction between the Amazonian and Intermediate Areas of the Steward hypothesis.

With respect to this hypothesis, use of the associated funerary motif among Arawaks on the upper Essequibo River around 1000 B.C. antedated by several centuries its earliest known occurrence in Colombia and its subsequent diffusion on the Western Guiana Littoral. This evidently ancient zoned incised mortuary symbol was only one of various cultural traits that apparently were converging or being developed on the Central Amazon at around this date. Others were the scroll-and-step-fret motif of the Upper Amazon and the motifs of *Apoteri Incised* and *Apoteri Zoned Incised* in the Kurupukari Falls inventory. Certain *Apoteri Incised* and *Apoteri Zoned Incised* motifs were still present in Saladoid inventories on the Corentyne River almost a thousand years later, Figure 4.57d. More importantly, lead motifs based on these highly distinctive design elements have been recognized as defining traits in the Guarita Subtradition of the Polychrome Horizon Style, Figure 4.56a-h.

Taken with occurences at Kurupukari Falls of diagnostic traits of the Saracá Subtradition, the presence of Guarita motifs in the early inventory there seems to reverse the Andes-to-Amazon expectations of the original investigators with respect to Polychrome origins and subsequent expansion. These expectations were based on comparisons between the greater antiquity of pottery-making and the higher level of general cultural development characteristic of the Andean area when contrasted with the situation on the Lower Amazon (Evans and Meggers 1968:108; Meggers and Evans 1961). Accordingly, in rejecting the Steward hypothesis, the authors postulated a diffusion of cultural traits from the Andes eastward. In this view, the superlative Polychrome pottery of the Marajoara phase at the Mouth of the Amazon, with its perceived implications of occupational division of labor, was out of adjustment with the resources of the tropical forest environment, where the yield per unit of land was considered insufficient to support the large population concentrations inferred at Marajoara. Therefore, Marajoara culture was interpreted as a degeneration from one of the more advanced Andean cultures, probably deriving from a source somewhere in the area of highland Colombia. As Meggers (1971:148) has observed, when the Marajoara culture appeared on Marajó Island, it seems to have possessed a more highly stratified society than that of more recent varzea groups, but during its history on Marajó it underwent a decline in complexity that is reflected archaeologically in the disappearance of elaborate kinds of pottery decoration and special ritual practices. Accordingly, Meggers and Evans (1973:45) concluded:

1) a society with advanced social stratification and occupational division of labor cannot evolve in a tropical forest environment where agriculture is by slash-and-burn, and ...
2) should such a culture penetrate into the tropical lowlands, it will not be able to develop further or even to maintain the level it has already achieved, but will decline until it reaches the simplicity characteristic of tropical forest tribes.

The early dates now available for diagnostic Polychrome traits at Kurupukari Falls provide a basis for evaluating the above statements. They suggest that notwithstanding the apparently early interaction between the Amazonian and Intermediate Areas, Marajoara origins may be sought locally. Dating at around A.D. 400, Marajoara is thought to represent an early Subtradition of the Polychrome Horizon Style on the Central and Lower Amazon. This opinion is based on the absence there of the diagnostic grooving of the Guarita Subtradition and the drag-and-jab of the Saracá Subtradition, both of which traits are considered late in the Polychrome inventory (Meggers pers. comm. 1995; but see Roosevelt 1991: Figure 6.3C). However, the diagnostic grooving of the Guarita Subtradition at Kurupukari Falls was contemporaneous with the apogée of Barrancoid ceramic decoration there (Cal B.C. 215 to A.D. 75 (Beta 76246). At around the time of Christ, Guarita refuse characterized by the "distinctive kind of fine-line incision" (Lathrap 1970:121) that now is known to characterize the *Apoteri Incised* ceramic type, Figure 4.56, was accumulating on top of Barrancoid refuse at Itacoatiara, on the Central Amazon. The Saracá Subtradition also is represented at the Barrancoid apogée at Kurupukari Falls by a few salient traits, including fingernail nicking and fingertip impressing.

The relative stratigraphic positions of Barrancoid and Guarita refuse at

Kurupukari Falls and Itacoatiara differed appreciably due to the years, or perhaps centuries, separating them. At Kurupukari Falls, divergence had not yet occurred between what later would be regarded as the diagnostic traits of the Guarita and Saracá Subtraditions, nor had these traits yet separated from traits characterizing the Barrancoid Tradition there. They all co-occurred, mutually exclusively, on the same levels in the upper two-thirds of the stratigraphic sequence. But by the time of the initial occupation of Itacoatiara, the divergence between these traits was clear, permitting recognition of a Barrancoid-to-Polychrome replacement there at around the opening of the Christian Era. Since, evidently, on to this time the various traits that later would characterize Guarita and Saracá ceramics had not yet diverged into separate subtraditions, the Kurupukari Falls deposit must be located very close to the source of the Guarita Subtradition. In view of its extreme longevity, which permitted the development of a unique vocabulary of motifs based on the scroll-and-step-fret element of the upper Amazon, Kurupukari Falls may even be thought the actual source of the Guarita Subtradition. There, the scroll-and-step-fret, Figure 5.3a, co-occurred on the earliest level with Saladoid white/red bell-shaped bowls and basin

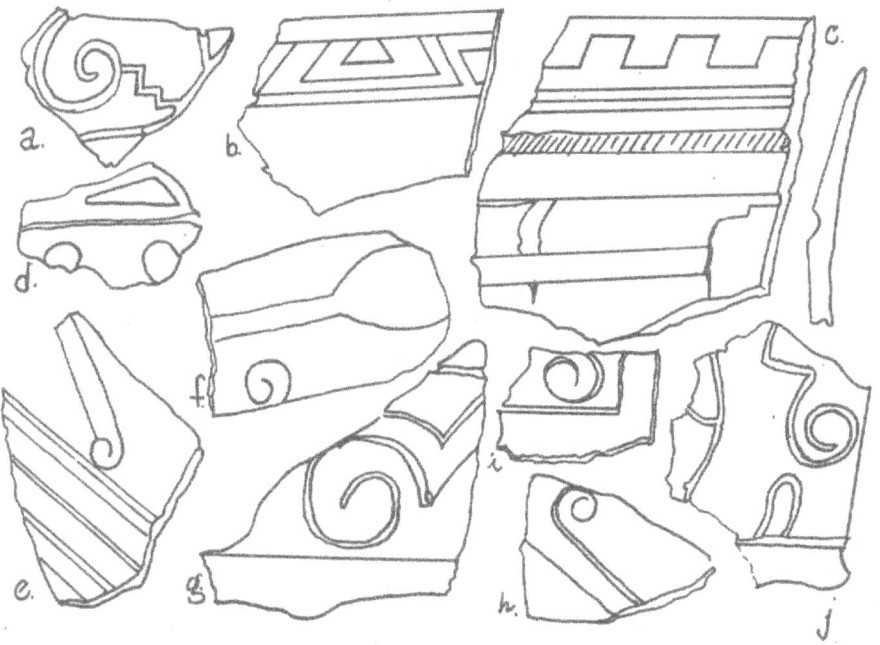

Figure 5.3 a-j. Kurupukari Falls. Early motifs of the Guarita Subtradition.

Figure 5.4 a-l. Pocó phase, lower Nhamunda and Trombetas Rivers. Ceramics of the Barrancoid and Polychrome Traditions co-occurring at the opening of the Christian Era (after Hilbert 1980).

urn lids, as well as with basin urn lids of the Zoned Hachure horizon style. Coming in a bit later, other typically fine-line *Apoteri Incised* motifs co-occurred with early specimens of Barrancoid broad-line incision (with modeling absent) Figure 5.3b-d. Yet other typically *Apoteri Incised* motifs came in on successively later levels, Figure 5.3e-j. *Apoteri Zoned Incised* appears to have followed *Apoteri Incised* in the sequence. Whether or not an evolutionary trend is represented over this period of several centuries it is too early to say.

On the other side of the Acarai watershed, at the Mouths of the Nhamunda and Trombetas Rivers, the Pocó phase, dating at between 65 B.C. and A.D. 205 (Hilbert and Hilbert 1980), appropriately yielded Saladoid red-on-white sherds, Barrancoid broad-line Incised and Modeled sherds, and overwhelmingly, sherds displaying Polychrome motifs such as fingernail nicking, fingertip impressing, cord-impressing, massed punctation and red wash. Figure 5.4a-l. Evidently, these latter traits had not yet converged there as a subtradition of the Polychrome Horizon Style. Thus, in the area, the Barrancoid-to-Polychrome transition had not yet come about. The sample was overlain by refuse of the Konduri phase of the later Incised and Punctate Horizon Style, dating at +/- 1200-1300 A.D. (Willey 1971:414).

Further upstream on the Amazon, at Manacapuru, the Barrancoid-to-Polychrome transition is thought to date after A.D. 425, while further yet, on the Rio Japurá, ceramics representing this transition have been dated at A.D. 635 (Lathrap 1970:121).

The possibility of an upriver expansion of the Polychrome Horizon Style into the upper Amazon (Evans and Meggers 1968:104-106; Lathrap 1970:121; Willey 1971:420), now seems supported by the data from Kurupukari Falls. If so, it represents yet another episode of cross-fertilization in the continuing interaction between the Lowlands and the Intermediate Area. By around 1000 B.C., the scroll-and-step-fret was a key element in the emerging *Apoteri Incised* vocabulary at Kurupukari Falls. Thereafter, apparently as a semantic sign in mortuary ceramics, it developed in parallel with the still developing Barrancoid style. This may explain the mutually exclusive ocurrences of these two ceramic styles on the same levels.

If the exact time of emergence of a recognizable subtradition of the Polychrome Horizon Style is beyond detection at the moment, *Apoteri Incised* undoubtedly played a role in the early evolution of the Polychrome Horizon Style on the Central and Lower Amazon. Its characteristic single-, double- or triple-line incision, with small, annexed linear, square or step elements, survived among other traits in the design vocabulary of the Caparu phase on the nearby Rio Uatumá across the Acarai watershed between A.D. 890 and 1520, Figure 4.57e-g. *Apoteri Incised* design elements likewise contributed to the design vocabulary of the Marajoara phase, Figure 5.5a-g.

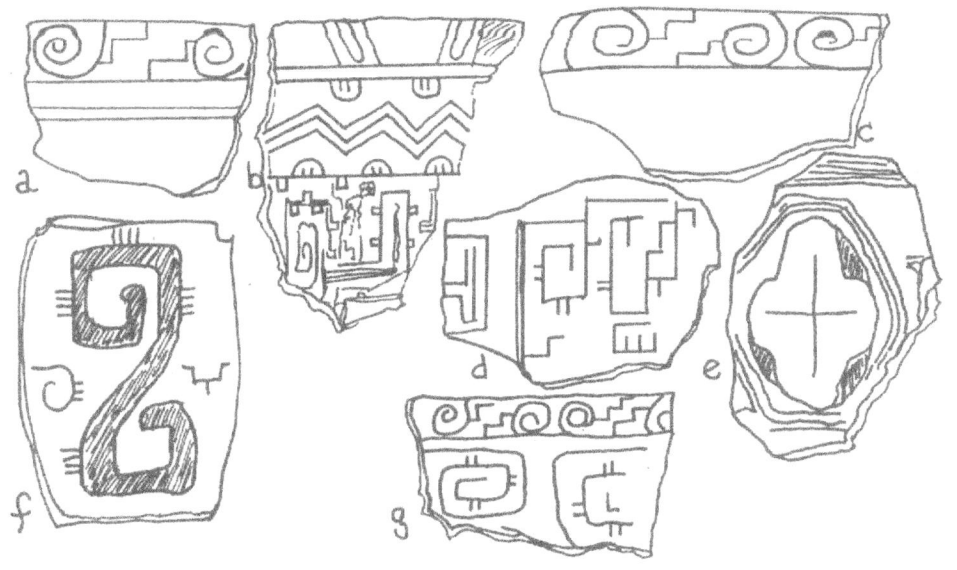

Figure 5.5 a-g. *Apoteri Incised* elements in the Marajoara phase. **a-b.** *(after Roosevelt 1991:Figure 63 B,G);* **c-e.** *(after Evans and Meggers 1968:Pl.85 b,d,f);* **f,g.** *(after Meggers and Evans 1957:Pls. 62b, 77f).* cf. Figures 4.56b-d, f, 4.57a.

Thus, at least in the iconography of death, the ceramics of the Marajoara phase seem securely linked to the very beginnings of ceramic design on the upper Essequibo River commencing during the last millennium before Christ.

On the question of the viability of stratified societies in the Tropical Forest environment, the law-like statements cited above might have benefitted from recourse to a causal postulate of some kind capable of standing up to investigation in other Tropical Forest societies, for, at least partly contemporaneously with Marajoara, the great city states of the Yoruba and Benin Kingdoms across the Atlantic were creating some of the finest art known to mankind and these cities flourished in hardwood tropical forests that are identical to the forests of the Amazon Basin.

A *propos* the viability of the Guinea Coast environment for maintaining an intruding stratified society, or indeed for developing complex culture on its own, recent opinion (Penny et al 1995:56) notes:

> Generally speaking, tropical forests are less hospitable to cultural life than the savannah region to the north ... Nonetheless, Congo-Kordofan speakers pushed into the forested coastal belt three to four thousand years ago *and brought the institutions of Western Sudanic civilization with them.* The cultivation of ... the east Asian yam, banana, and taro resulted in tremendous population

growth for this culturally marginal region. *By the fourteenth century, the Guinea Coast supported impressive kingdoms of its own.* (Italics added).

Since there appears to be nothing inherently limiting on cultural development in the Tropical Forest environment, differences between the respective cultural levels attained there and on the Guinea Coast may be explainable in terms of contrasting world views. The highly elaborate designs on Marajoara funerary urns derived from a concept of human existence as the reciprocal of divine order, Figure 4.65i. Once manufactured, these vessels with their contents of human remains appropriately directed toward the setting sun, were destined for the burial mound, never again to be seen by human eyes. By way of contrast, the secular bronzes of the courts of Ife and Benin were palace furnishings meant to enhance the prestige of a divine king here on earth, at the same time maintaining contact with the ancestral spirits. At Marajoara, as elsewhere in the marginal environments of the Tropical Forest Lowlands, the obligation was eternally to provide nourishment for the gods in the form of the souls of the human departed, Figure 4.65a-h. Human mortality was thus at once the testament and guarantee of divine immortality. Accordingly, human discourse with the supernaturals found its highest expression in the forms of a sacred art. The authors of this art, unlike the court artists of Guinea, and as is evidenced by the innumerable ornate *tangus* recovered in the Marajoara cemeteries, were women potters. The semantic value of design motifs manipulated by these women potters is evidenced in their formal rigidity and incredible longevity. Hence the unaltered survival of the scroll-and-step-fret motif of Early Tutishcainyo ceramics in the funerary ceramics of Arawaks on the upper Essequibo a thousand and more years later and, beyond that, in the Marajoara fluorescence half a millennium after that.

Developments and divergences in the evolution of these mortuary signs was evidently a function of the spread of the associated thanatological beliefs, initially at the hands of Arawak women on the Central and Lower Amazon, and, later, across ethnic frontiers on *terra firme*. Thus, quite early, the scroll-and-step-fret occurs on a basin urn lid in the Cariban Mazagão culture in southern Amapá, Figure 5.6a. Centuries later, it was absorbed in Kapon (Cariban) funerary art on the lower Mazaruni River, Figure 5.6b.

The cosmological structure from which derived this image of man was of hoary antiquity in the Americas. In the Guianas, it generated a metaphoric space which located the group along the axis of vertical opposition between the celestial and nether regions. This was imaged by the Archaic symbol of human head/foot polarization, Figure 4.39b. The corollary opposition between the rising and the setting sun -- the Land of the Dead -- was imaged by various symbols of solar orientation, Figure 3.6. From this location at the center of cosmic space, the flight of the departing human soul toward the spirit world was controlled by the appropriate repertory of directional signs inherited and transmitted by the woman potter. The remarkable inflexibility of these signs is best appreciated within the evolutionary trajectory that is first evidenced in the archaeological record 7000 years ago by ritual gilding of the head and legs of the departed. This inflexibility was the treasured contribution of women to the commonwealth as the bearers of life, as the agents of its succour and, finally, as custodians of the semantic signs that facilitated the flight of the departing soul to the world of the supernaturals. As the modern Waiwai sagely pronounce: "Men rule the universe; women contain men."

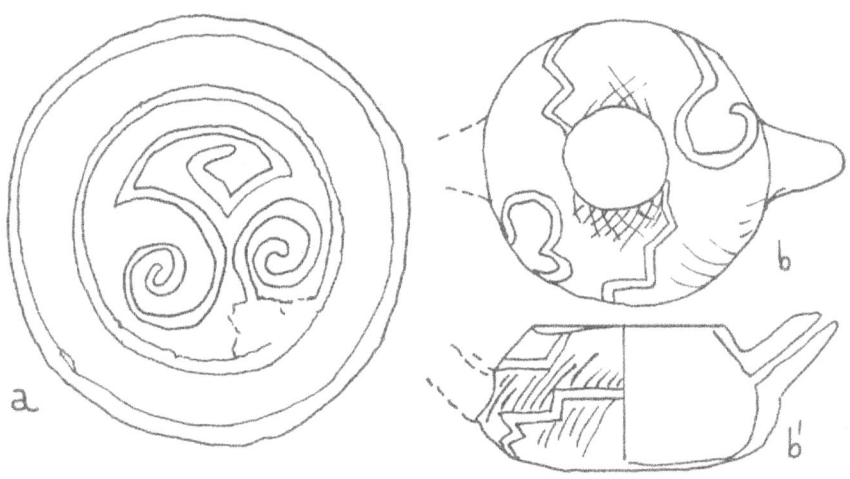

Figure 5.6 a,b. The scroll-and-step-fret funerary symbol. a. Southern Amapá. b. Lower Mazaruni.

APPENDIX A. Western Guiana Littoral. Shell mounds and shell deposits

Northwestern Subzone

Site no./name	Coordinates	References
i-1:1 Barabina N23	8° 13'N, 59° 49'W	Bakker 1981, Bleackley 1956, Evans/Meggers 1960, Jansma 1981, Osgood 1946, Verrill 1918a, Williams 1981, 1982, 1985a, Wishart 1982.
i-1:5 Hosororo Ck N-11	8° 11'N, 59° 49'W	AWB [1907], Cooksey 1919, Evans/ Meggers 1960, Roth MS, Williams 1985b.
i-1:8 Akawabi N16	8° 8'N, 59° 53'W	Cooksey 1919, Evans/Meggers 1960, Osgood 1946, Poonai 1978, Roth MS, Verrill 1918a, Williams 1981.
i-1:20 Hobo Hill	8° 13'N, 59° 46'W	Osgood 1946, Verrill 1918a, Williams 1981.
i-1:23 Hotahana	7° 55'N, 59° 42'W	Osgood 1946, Roth MS, Verrill 1918a, Williams 1981.
i-1:32 Koriabo Pt.	7° 37'N, 59° 38'W	Evans/Meggers 1960, Verrill 1918a, Williams 1981.
i-1:35 Anabisi	7° 42'N, 59° 38'W	Osgood 1946, Verrill 1918a, Williams MS.
i-1:39 Mt. Everard		Verrill 1918a, Williams MS.
i-1:40 Honobo Hill		Williams MS.
i-1:41 Drum Hill		Williams MS.
i-1:42 Kokerital	8° 13'N, 59° 49'W	Williams MS.
i-1:19 Hosororo Ck (*shell sand*)	8° 11'N, 59° 49'W	Williams 1985a, MS.
i-1:4 Seba Ck (*shell sand*)	8° 13'N, 59° 46'W	Osgood 1946, Pollard 1956; Roth MS, Will-iams 1981, 1982, 1985b.
i-1:26 Wanakai Ck (*shell sand*)	8° 00'N, 59° 52'W	Williams 1982.
i-1:27 Iurukaikuru (*shell sand*)	8° 01'N, 59° 54'W	Williams 1982.
i-1:28 Chinee Ck (*shell sand*)	8° 00'N, 59° 54'W	Williams 1982.
i-2:2 Alaka Ck N8	7° 47'N, 59° 16'W	Brett 1868, Evans/Meggers 1960, Osgood 1946, Roth MS, Williams 1981
i-2:3 Alaka Is. N9	7° 48'N, 59° 16'W	Evans/Meggers 1960, Williams 1981.
i-2:5 Lt. Kaniaballi N6	7° 43'N, 59° 14'W	Brett 1868, Evans/Meggers 1960, Osgood 1946, Roth MS.
i-2:6 Pawaieykeymoo	7° 36'N, 59° 07'W	Evans/Meggers 1960, Im Thurn 1883, Osgood 1946.
i-2:7 Kwaiarau (Quiaro)	7° 36'N, 59° 07'W	Evans/Meggers 1960, Im Thurn 1883, Osgood 1946.
i-2:8 Sand Ck N10	7° 48'N, 59° 16'W	Evans/Meggers 1960, Map *Lands/ Surveys Dept.* nd.
i-2:12 Waramuri	7° 55'N, 58° 66'W	Anon [J.L. Smith] 1866, Bennett 1866, Brett 1868, Evans/Meggers 1960, Osgood 1946, Poonai 1978, Williams 1981.
i-2: Haimaracabra	7° 55'N, 58° 56'W	Evans/Meggers 1960, Williams MS.
i-2:13 Manawarin	7° 30'N, 58° 56'W	Williams 1981.

Southeastern Subzone

ii-1:2 Kabakaburi	7° 15'N, 59° 14'W	Brett 1868; Evans/Meggers 1960, Im Thurn 1879, 1883, Osgood 1946, Poonai 1978, Williams 1981.
ii-1:3 Warapana	7° 10'N, 58° 40'W	Brett 1868, Im Thurn 1879, 1883.
ii-1:4 Piraka	7° 25'N, 58° 40'W	Evans/Meggers 1960, Im Thurn 1879, 1883, Osgood 1946, Williams 1981.
ii-1:5 Siriki	7° 10'N, 58° 56'W	Anon [J.L. Smith] 1866, Bennet 1866, Brett 1868, Evans/Meggers 1960, Poonai 1978.

With the exception of Cooksey (1919), the above references are given in the **Literature Cited**. The Cooksey reference is as follows:

Cooksey, Rev. C., S.J
1919   Letters to the Editor, *Timehri* 23.

Appendix B. Manufacture of the dugout canoe
(Recorded at Orealla, Corentyne River, 1986)

A suitable log (usu. Silverballi [*Ocotea glomerata*]) is left to "cure" several months (around six). It is squared on three sides with a broadax, and cut off head and tail to the length of the desired vessel. The fourth side is left natural. Upper surface and sides of the log are grooved transversely at 15 cm intervals to prevent the ax from following the grain of the wood.

The vessel is drawn in plan on the upper surface of the log, the stern being marginally wider than the bow. Around 4 cm on the inside of the gunwales represents the limit for initial rough-hewing of the cavity, Figure a,a'. On the outside, a further 3 cm is reserved for the thickness of the hull, Figure I b,b'.

In the cavity area, a zigzag incision from bow to stern, Figure 1 A, determines the maximum size of the chips removed with each blow of the adze. As the cavity develops, Figure I a, a', sculpturing of the exterior surface of the hull is guided by the interior contour, Figure I b, b'. This yields the desired symmetry. The thickness of the hull is monitored by drilling a horizontal row of holes below each gunwale. A third row is placed along the bottom, bow to stern. These holes are 1 cm each in diameter and are spaced about 1.0 m apart, Figure 2. They permit the hull to be cut to 2 cm thickness along its sides and 3 cm along the bottom. The holes are sealed with wooden pegs.

The hull is expanded by simultneous internal and external firing. Palm leaves tied into bundles provide fuel. Leaves of the Moriche palm are preferred for their reportedly slow-burning properties and high calorific value. Burning exploits the fact that water expands with heating; it is not part of the hollowing-out process. It chars the hull only slightly inside and out. Water and wet clay are kept at the ready to control the flames. A pole terminating in a wet pad is employed for the purpose. An optimum level of burning chars only the chip marks of the adze. Upon cooling, these are scraped off with a blade, yielding a smooth, sometimes silky, surface. At bow and stern, expansion is restricted by sturdy wooden clamps, Figure 3.

The hull is kept expanded by *(a)* a series of sticks of increasing length placed horizontally between the gunwales about 30 cm apart, Figure 4a, and (*b*) a corresponding series of crossed sticks placed below the initial row of horizontal sticks, Figure 4b.

The degree of expansion achieved is a matter of local preference. Corentyne Arawaks prefer almost vertical side walls, whereas Arawaks of the Coastal Hinterland prefer a flatter hull, resistant to rolling. There are also local differences in sculpture of the bow, e.g., Figure 5a (Corentyne), Figure 5b (Coastal Hinterland).

LITERATURE CITED

Abonnenc, Emile
    1952   Inventaire et distribution des sites archeologique en Guyane française. *Journal de la Societe des Americanistes* 41:44-62.

Absy, Maria Lucia
    1982   Quaternary palynological studies in the Amazon Basin. *Biological diversification in the Tropics.* Edited by Ghillean T.Prance. New York: New York University Press, pp. 67-73.
    1985   Palynology of Amazonia: the history of the forests as revealed by the palynological record. *Amazonia.* Edited by Ghillean T. Prance and Thomas Lovejoy.

Ahlbrinck, C.R.W
    1929   *Vijf Maanden in Het Oerwoud.* Rotterdam.

Allaire, Louis
    1980   On the historicity of Carib migrations in the Anilles. *American Antiquity* 45(2): 238-245.

Allersma, E
    1968   Mud on the Ocean Shelf off Guiana. Curacao: *Cigar Symposium.* 11 pp.

Anon [J.L.Smith]
    1866   The Governor's visit to the shell mound at Waramuri. *The Royal Gazette.* Georgetown: Steam Press.

Augustinus, P.G.E.F
    1978   *The changing shoreline of Surinam (South America).* Utrecht: Uitgaven "Natuurwetenschappelijke Studiekring voor Suriname en de Nederlandse Antillen".

A.W.B
    1905   MS. National Anthropological Archives Walter Roth Museum of Anthropology.

Bacon, Peter
    1970   Studies on the biology and cultivation of the Mangrove Oyster in Trinidad with notes on other shellfish resources. *Tropical Science* 12(4):265-278.

Bakker, Arno J
    1981   Palynological investigations of the Barabina shell mound. *Archaeology and Anthropology* 4(1,2):35-36.

Baldwin, Richard
    1946   *The Rupununi Record.* Georgetown: Bureau of Publicity and Information.

Barbosa, Altair Sales
    1992   A tradacao Itaparica: uma compreensao ecologica e cultural do povoamento inicial do planalto central brasileiro. *Prehistoria Sudamericana: Nuevas Perspectivas*. Washington: Taraxacum. pp. 145-160.

Barandarian, Daniel de
    1979   *Introduccion a la cosmovision de los indios Ye'kuana-Makiritare*. Caracas: Universidad Catolica Andres Bello.

Barral, P Basilio Maria de
    1980   La musica teurigico-magica de los Indios Guaranos. *Montalban 10*. Caracas: Universidad Catolica Andres Bello. pp.7-201.

Barse, William P.
    1989   *A preliminary archaeological sequence in the Upper Orinoco Valley, Territorio Federal Amazonas, Venezuela*. Ph D thesis. The Catholic University of America.
    1990   Preceramic occupation in the Orinoco River Valley. *Science*. Volume 250. pp. 1388-1390.
    1997   Dating a Paleoindian site in the Amazon in comparison with Clovis culture. *Science* 275:1949-1950.
    MS   *A preliminary archaeological sequence for the upper Orinoco River in the vicinity of Puerto Ayacucho, Territorio Federal Amazonas, Venezuela*. Unpublished.

Bell, Robert E
    1960   Evidence of a fluted point tradition in Ecuador. *American Antiquity* 26(1):102-106.

Benjamin Joel P
    1982   The naming of the Essequibo River. *Archaeology and Anthropology* 5(1):29-66.

Bennett, George
    1866   *An illustrated history of British Guiana*. Georgetown: Richardson and Co.

Bennett, W.C
    1949   Numbers, measures, weights and calendars. *Handbook of South American Indians*. Edited by Julian H. Steward. Volume 5. Washington D.C: United States Government Printing Office. pp.601-610.

Bennett, John Peter
    1994   *An Arawak-English Dictionary. With an English Word List*. Georgetown: Walter Roth Museum of Anthropology.

Bird, Junius B
1969 A comparison of South Chilean and Ecuadorian "Fishtail" projectile points. *Kroeber Anthropological Society Papers* 40:52-71.
1988 *Travels and Archaeology in South Chile.* Iowa City: University of Iowa Press.
1993 *Viajes y Arquelogia en Chile Austral.* Magallanes: Ediciones de la Universidad de Magallanes.

Blair, Daniel
1980 Notes of an expedition from Georgetown to the gold diggings on the borders of Venezuela. *Archaeology and Anthropology* 3:3-64. MS notebook 1857 University of Guyana.

Bleackley, D
1956 *Report on the Geological Survey Department for the Year 1955.* Georgetown: The Daily Chronicle.

Boomert, Aad
1977 Prehistorie. *Encyclopedie van Suriname.* Edited by C.F.A Bruijning, J. Voorhoeve and W. Gordijn. Amsterdam/Brussel. pp.506-517.
1978 Prehistoric habitation mounds in the Canje River area? *Archaeology and Anthropology* 2(1):78-86.
1979 An analysis of the ceramic finds from Itabru, Berbice River. *Archaeology and Anthropology* 2(1):78-86.
1979a The prehistoric stone axes from Suriname: a typological classification. *Archaeology and Anthropology* 2(2):99-124.
1980 Hertenrits: an Arauquinoid complex in northwest Suriname, Part 1. *Archaeology & Anthropology* 3(2):68-104.
1981 The Taruma phase of southern Suriname. *Archaeology and Anthropology* 4(1,2):104-159.
1983 The Saladoid occupation of Wonotobo Falls, western Suriname. *Proceedings of the Ninth International Congress for the study of the Precolumbian Cultures of the Lesser Antilles.* Montreal: Universite de Montreal.
1986 The Cayo complex of St. Vincent: ethnohistorical and archaeological aspects of the Islan Carib problem. *Antropologica* 66:3-68.
1987 Gifts of the Amazons: "green stone" pendants and beads as items of ceremonial exchange in Amazonia and the Caribbean. *Antropologica* 67:33-54.
1993 The Barbakoeba archaeological complex of northeast Suriname.

OSO: *Tijdschrift voor Surinaamse taalkunde, letterkunde, cultuur en geschiedenis* 12(2). Manuscript copy presented by the author.

Boomert, Aad., and S.B. Kroonenberg
1977 Manufacture and trade of stone artifacts in prehistoric Suriname. *Ex Horreo*. Universiteit van Amsterdam. Cingula 1V:2-46.

Borgstrom, G
1962 Shellfish protein: nutritive aspects. *Fish as food*. Vol. 2: Nutrition, sanitation and utilization. New York: Academic Press, pp. 115-147.

Boye, M
1974 Contribution a Fetude des roches marquees de Mahury (Ile de Cayenne, Guyane française). Connaissance de la Guyane 1:3-12.

Bradley, Richard
1989 Deaths and entrances: a contextual analysis of Megalithic art. *Current Anthropology* 30(1):68-75.

Bray, Warwick, Leonor Fleffera and Marianne Cardale Schrimpff
1988 Report on the 1988 field season. Pro *Calima* 5:2-42.

Brett, W. H
1868 *The Indian tribes of Guiana: their condition and habits*. London: Bell and Daldy.

Brinkman, R., and L.J. Pons
1968 A *pedo-geomorphological classification and map of the Holocene sediments in the Coastal Plain of the three Guianas*. Wageningen: Netherlands Soil Survey Institute.

Brotherston, Gordon
1979 What's written in Timehri. *Archaeology and Anthropology* 2:5-9.

Brothwell, D.R
1981 *Digging up bones*. Third edition. New York: Cornell University Press.

Brown, H.H
1943 *The fisheries of British Guiana*. Appendix to Vincent Roth. *Notes and observations on fish life in British Guiana*. Georgetown: The Daily Chronicle.

Brown, C. Barrington
1873 Indian picture writings in British Guiana. *Journal of the Royal Anthropological Institute of Gt Britain and Ireland*, 2:254-257.
1876 *Canoe and camp life in British Guiana*. London: Edward Stanford.

Brown, K.S
1977 Centros de evolucao, refugios Quatemarios, e conservacao de

patrimonios geneticos no regiao neotropical: padroes de diferenciacao em Ithomiinae *(Lepidoptera: Nymphalidae)*. *Acta Amazonica 7(1):75-137.*

Brown, K.S., and A.N. Ab'Saber
1979   Ice-age refuges and evolution in the Neotropics: correlation of paleoclimatological, geornorphological and pedological data with modern biological endemism. *Paleoclimas 5.*

Bubberman, F. C
1972   Stenen schrijven geschiedenis. *Mededelingen Surinaamse Musea* 9:3-18.
1973   Rotstekeningen in de Sipaliwini Savanna. En bijdrage tot de archeologie van Zuid-Suriname. *Nieuwe West-Indische Gids* 3:129-142.
1974   Archaeologie, de basis onzer kennis. *Suralco Magazine* 1: 1-9.
1977   Rotstekeningen. *Encyclopedie van Suriname.* Edited by C. F. A Bruijning, J. Voorhoeve and W. Gordijn. Amsterdam/Brussel. pp. 538-540.

Budak, M
1991   The function of shell temper in pottery. *The Minnesota Archaeologist* 50(2):53-59

Bullbrook, J. A.
1953   On the excavation of a shell mound at Palo Seco, Trinidad, B.W.I. *Yale University Publications in Anthropology* 2:83-90.

Butlen, Ripley P
1974   Certain petroglyphs of the Antilles. *Proceedings of the Fifth International Congress for the study of the Precolumbian Cultures of the Lesser Antilles.* Antigua 1973. pp. 94-109.

Bullen, Ripley P., and A. Bullen
1976   Culture areas and climaxes in Antillean prehistory. *Proceedings of the Sixth International Congress for the study of the Precolumbian Cultures of the Lesser Antilles.* Guadeloupe. pp. 1-10.

Burnham, L.F.S
1978   Archaeology and Anthropology 1(1). Inaugural foreword.

Butt, Audrey
1957   The Mazaruni scorpion. *Timehri* 36:40-54.
MS   *Systems of belief in relation to social structure and organisation with reference to the Carib-speaking tribes of the Guianas.* Unpublished Ph.D thesis. Oxford 1954.

Butt-Colson, Audrey, and C. de Armellada
    1989   The Pleiades, Hyades and Orion *(Tamokan)* in the conceptual and ritual system of Kapon and Pemon groups in the Guiana Highlands. *Scripta Ethnologica. Supplementa* 9. pp. 153-200.

Cain, H. Thomas
    1950   *Petroglyphs of Central Washington.* Seattle: University of Washington Press.

Cardich, Augusta
    1987   Arquelogia de Los Toldos y El Ceiba (Provincia de Santa Crux, Argentina). *Estudios Atacamenos* 8:98-117. San Pedro de Atacama: Universidad del Norte.

Carter, J.E.L
    1943   An account of some recent excavations at Seba, British Guiana. *American Antiquity* 9:3-18.

Carter, J.W
    MS   Preliminary report on the Kukui Valley: Chinowieng -Ayangana expedition. *Department of Soil Surveys* [1960].

Cavalli-Sforza, L.L
    1983   The transition to agriculture and some of its consequences. *How humans adapt: a bio-cultural odyssey.* D. J. Ortner ed. Washington: Smithsonian Institution Press. pp. 103-120.

Chagnon, Napoleon A
    1973   The culture-ecology of shifting cultivation among the Yanomamo Indians. *Peoples and cultures of native South America.* Daniel Gross ed. New York: Doubleday, pp. 126-142.

Chernela, Janel M
    1994   Tukanoan know-how: the importance of the forested river margin to Neotropical fishing populations. *Research and Exploration* 10(4):440-457.

Clapperton, C
    1993   *Quaternary geology and geomorphology of South America.* Amsterdam: Elsevier.

Coe, Michael
    1960   A fluted point from highland Guatemala. *American Antiquity* 25(3):412-413.

Cordill, Robert H
    1948   *Photographic prints showing petroglyphs from San Bernadino, California.* National Anthropological Archives, Smithsonian Institution, MS 4330.

Coudreau, Henri Anatole
    1887   *Voyage a travers les Guyanes et lAmazonie*. Paris.
Coudreau, Octavie
    1901   *Voyage a Cumina*. Paris.
Crevaux, Jules Nicolas
    1883   *Voyage dans l'Amerique du Sud*. Paris.
Cruxent, Jose M
    1946-1947   Pinturas rupestres en El Carmen, en el Rio Parguaza, Estado Bolivar, Venezuela. *Acta Venezolana* 2:83-90.
    1971   Apuntes sobre arquelogia Venezolana. *Arte prehispanico de Venezuela*. Caracas: Fundacion Eugenio Mendoza.
    1972   El paleoindia en Venezuela. *Revista Venezuela suya* 1:4-13.
    1972a   Tupuquen: un yacimiento con litica de tipo paleo-indio. *Acta Cientifica Venezolana*.
Cruxent, Jose M., and Irving Rouse
    1959   *An archaeological chronology of Venezuela*. Washington: Pan American Union. Two volumes. Volume 2.
    1961   *An archaeological chronology of Venezuela*. Washington: Pan American Union.
D'Abate, John
    1973   A key to the interpretation of the petroglyphs of the Orinoco. *Proceedings Fourth International Congress study Precolumbian Cultures Lesser Antilles*. Castries, St. Lucia. pp.57-64.
Dangour, Alan D., and Suraiya Ismail
    1995   Growth and nutritional status of Guyanese Patamona Indians. *Archaeology and Anthropology* 10:43-47.
D'Audretsch, F.C
    1957   *Geologische kaart*. Geologisch mijnbouwkundige dienst Suriname, Paramaribo.
De Goeje, C. H
    1906   Brijdrage tot de Ethnographie der Surinaamsche Indianen. *International Archiv fur Ethnographie 17*. Supplement.
De Granville, J.J
    1982   Rain forest and xeric flora refuges in French Guiana. *Biological diversification in the Tropics*. Edited by Ghillean T. Prance. New York: Columbia University Press. pp. 159-181.
Delmonte, J.M.Guarch, y Caridad Rodriguez Cullel
    1980   Consideraciones acera e la morfologia y el desarrollo de los pictogramas Cubenos. *Cuba arquelogica*.

Deman, R., et G. Lefebvre
    1974   L'Archaeologie dans l'Ile de Cayenne. *Connaissance de la Guyane.* 1:13-19. Cayenne.

De Milde, R., and D. de Groot
    1970   *Reconnaissance survey of the more accessible forest areas, Zone 2.* Georgetown: United Nations Development Programme.

De Valencia, Ruby, Jeannine Sujo Volsky, R. Lairet and P. Alminana
    1987   *Design in Venezuelan petroglyphs.* Caracas: Fundacion Pampero.

Dillehay, Tom D
    1984   A Late Ice-Age settlement in Southern Chile. *Scientific American* 25(4):106-117.

Di Peso C.C
    1955   Two Cerro Guamas Clovis points from Sonoro, Mexico. *Kiva* 121:13-15.

Drewett, Peter L., E. Wing, M.H. Harris, C. Cartwright, R.G. Scaife, S. Rogers and D. Rudling.
    1991   *Prehistoric Barbados.* London: University College London and Barbados Museum and Historical Society.

Dubelaar, C. N
    1974-1976   Review: El *estudio del arte rupestre en Venezuela* by Jeannine Sujo-Volsky. *Journal de la Societe des Americanistes.* Paris.
    1976   Some remarks on petroglyphs in Suriname and on petroglyph investigation in general. *International Congress of Americanists* 42., volume 9B:381-386.
    1977   De rotstekeningen van Suriname. *Iros* 2(t):20-28.
    1979   Petroglyphs in the Guianas. *Proceedings of the Valcamonica symposium.* Brescia: Centro Camuni di studi prehistorici, pp. 349-353.
    1981   The distribution of Im Thurn's elaborate type petroglyphs in South America. *International Congress for the study of the Precolumbian Cultures of the Lesser Antilles* 9:375-397.
    1981a   Petroglyphs in Suriname: a survey. *Archaeology and Anthropology* 4(1,2):64-80.
    1982   Interpretation of South American petroglyphs. *Proceedings of the International Congress of Americanists* 44:13 1.
    1983   A comparison between petroglyphs of the Antilles and of North-East South America. *International Congress for the study of the Precolumbian Cultures of the Lesser Antilles* 10:421-435.
    1986   *The petroglyphs in the Guianas and adjacent areas of Brazil and Venezuela: an inventory. With a comprehensive bibliography of*

	South American and Antillean petroglyphs. University of California. Monumenta Archaeologica 12.
1995	*The petroglyphs of the Lesser Antilles, the Virgin Islands and Trinidad.* Amsterdam: Publications Foundation for Scientific Research in the Caribbean Region 135.
MS	*A study on South American and Antillean petroglyphs.* Unpublished Ph D thesis. University of Leiden.

Dubelaar, C.N., and Jevan P. Berrange
    1979   Some recent petroglyph finds in Southern Guyana. *Archaeology and Anthropology* 2(1):60-77.

Dufour, Darna L
    1982   Nutrition in the Northwest Amazon: Household and dietary intake and time-energy expenditure. *Adaptive responses of Native Amazonians.* New York: Academic Press, pp. 329-355.

Durbin, Marshall
    1977   A survey of the Carib language family. *Carib-speaking Indians: culture, society and language.* Ellen Basso ed. Tucson: Arizona University Press. pp.23-38.

Edwards, Walter F (ed)
    1980   *A short dictionary of the Warau language of Guyana.* Turkeyen: University of Guyana.

Eisenberg, John F., M.A. O'Connell and Peter V. August
    1979   Density, productivity, and distribution of mammals in two Venezuelan habitats. *Vertebrate ecology in the northern neotropics.* J. F. Eisenberg ed. Washington: The National Zoological Park. pp. 187-207.

Epperson, S
    1936   *Photographs of petroglyphs from Wyoming.* National Anthropological Archives, Smithsonian Institution, MS 4455.

Evans, Clifford
    1971[1955]   New archaeological interpretations in northeastern South America. *New interpretations of aboriginal American culture history.* Washington: Anthropological Society of Washington. pp. 82-94.

Evans, Clifford, and Betty J. Meggers
    MS   Letters: Vincent Roth to Clifford Evans and Betty Meggers, 1953-1965. Georgetown: National Anthropological Archives Walter Roth Museum.
    1960   *Archaeological investigations in British Guiana.* Washington: United States Government Printing Office.
    1964   British Guiana archaeology: a return to the original

interpretations. *American Antiquity* 30(1):83-84.
1968 *Archaeological investigations on the Rio Napo, Eastern Ecuador.* Washington: Smithsonian Institution Press.

Evans, Clifford, Betty J. Meggers and Jose M. Cruxent
1960 Preliminary results of archaeological investigations along the Orinoco and Ventuari Rivers. *Actas del XXXIII Congreso Internacional de Americanistas.* Costa Rica. pp.359-369.

Fairbridge, Rhodes W
1976 Shellfish-eating preceramic Indians in coastal Brazil. *Science.* 191(4225): 353-359.

Fanshawe, Dennis B
1950 *Minor forest products.* Pt.2. Georgetown: Forest Department.

Farabee, William Curtis.
1916 Some South American petroglyphs. *Holmes anniversary volume: Anthropological essays presented to William Henry Holmes in honor of his seventieth birthday, December 1, 1916.* Washington: James William Bryan Press. pp. 88-95.

Feriz, H
1956 *Report on the 32nd International Congress of Americanistes at Copenhagen.* Amsterdam: Royal Tropical Institute.

Flenniken, J. Jeffrey
1985 Stone tool reduction techniques as cultural markers. *Stone tool analysis.* Edited by Mark G. Plew, James C. Woods, Max C. Pavesic. Albuquerque: University New Mexico Press. pp. 265-276.

Foley, Robert
1977 A method for analyzing habitat value and utilization in relation to archaeological sites. *Spatial archaeology.* New York: Academic Press. pp. 163-187.

Ford, James A
1969 *A comparison of Formative cultures in the Americas: Diffusion or the psychic unity of man.* Washington: Smithsonian Institution Press.

Frikel, Potasio
1969 Tradition und archeologie im Tumuk=Humuk/Nordbrasillien. *Zeitschrift fur Ethnologie* 94:103-130.

Gahwiler-Walder, Theres
1988 Archaeological investigations in the Pavas-La Curnbre Region. *Pro Calima* 5:50-60.

Geay, Francois
1903 Gravures rupestre de la table du Mahury. *Journal de la Societe*

                des Americanistes IV:244-246.
Geijskes, Dirk Cornelis
    1960-1961   History of archaeological investigations in Surinam. *Mededelingen van de Stichting Surinaams Museum.*
Gibbon, Guy
    1984   *Anthropological archaeology.* New York: Columbia University Press.
Gibbs, Alan K., and Christopher Barron
    1994   *The geology of the Guiana Shield.* New York: Oxford University Press.
Gillin, John
    1948   Tribes of the Guianas and left Amazon tributaries. *Handbook of South American Indians.* Julian H. Steward ed. Volume 3:799-860. Washington: United States Government Printing Office.
Goethals, Peter R
    MS   *An archaeological reconnaissance of coastal Suriname.* MS Department of Anthropology, Yale University.
Goldstein, Lynne ed
    1987   Current Research. *American Antiquity* 52:175.
Gonggryp, Justus Wilhelm
    1920   Sporen van voorhistorische bewoners van Suriname. *WestIndische Gids* 2:1-16.
Goodland, Arthur Edward
    1964   The mound. *Journal of the British Guiana Museum and Zoo.* 39:9-17.
    1979   Schomburgh's ships. *Nieuwe West-Indische Gids* 53(3,4):141-146.
    n.d.   *The Goodland papers.* National Anthropological Archives Walter Roth Museum. MS 1976. 1.
Goodyear, F. H
    1971   *Archaeological site science.* London: Heineman.
Granberry, Julian
    1971   Final collation of texts, vocabulary lists, grammar of Timucua. *Yearbook of the American Philosophical Society 1970.* Philadelphia, pp. 606-607.
    1990   A grammatical sketch of Timucua. *International Journal of American Linguistics* 56(1):60-101.
    1993   Mysteriously missing for no reason at all. Since it has to be in the study somewhere, a space can confidently be left here.

Grayson, Donald K
1988 Americans before Columbus: Perspectives on the archaeology of the first Americans. *Americans Before Columbus: Ice-age origins.* University of Pittsburgh Ethnology Monographs 12:107-123.

Greenberg, Joseph H
1960 The general classification of Central and South American languages. *Proceedings of the Fifth International Congress of Anthropological and Ethnological Sciences.* A.F.C. Wallace ed. Philadelphia: University of Philadelphia Press.

Greenberg, J.H., Christy G. Turner and Stephen L. Zegura
1986 The settlement of the Americas: A comparison of the linguistic, dental and genetic evidence. *Current Anthropology* 27(5):472-497.

Greider, Terence
1975 The interpretation of ancient symbols. *American Anthropologist* 77(4):849-856.

Grenand, Francoise, et Pierre Grenand
1987 La cote d'Amapá, de la bouche de l'Amazone a la Baie d'Oyapock, a travers la tradition orale Palikur. *Boletim do Museu Paraense Emilio Goeldi.* Serie antropologia 3(1):1-77.

Groene, Denis
1976 Note sur le site Kormontibo, Guyane française. *Proceedings of the Sixth International Congress for the study of the Precolumbian cultures of the Lesser Antilles.* Guadeloupe.

Gumilla, Joseph
1791 *Historia natural, civil y geografica de las naciones situadas en la riveras del Rio Orinoco.* 2 vols. Barcelona.

Guppy, Nicholas
MS *Plant exploration in the Sierra Acarai.* Georgetown: Forest Department.

Hilbert, Peter Paul and Klaus Hilbert
1980 Resultados preliminaries da pesquisa arquelogica nos Rio Nhamunda e Trombetas, Baixo Amazonas. *Boletim do Museu Paraense Emilio Goeldi.* Nova serie 75:2-17.

Huber, Otto
1982 Significance of savanna vegetation in the Amazon Territory of Venezuela. Biological diversification in *the Tropics.* Ghillean T. Prance ed. New York: Columbia University Press.

Hudson Travis, and Ernest Underhay
1978 *Crystals in the sky: An intellectual odyssey involving Chumash*

astronomy, cosmology and rock art. Ballena Press Anthropological Papers No. 10.

Hugh-Jones, Stephen
 1993 Clear descent or ambiguous houses? A re-examination of Tukanoan social organization. L'Homme XXXIII (2-4):95-120.

Humboldt, Alexander von
 1852-1853 *Personal narrative of travels to the equinoctial regions of America, 1799-1804*. London: Bell and Daldy.

Hummelinck, P. Wagenaar
 1953 Rotstekeningen van Curacao, Aruba en Bonaire. Deel I. *Nieuwe West-Indische Gids* 34:173-209.
 1957 Rotstekeningen van Curacao, Aruba en Bonaire. Deel II. *Nieuwe West-Indische Gids* 37:93-126.
 1961-1962 Rotstekeningen van Curacao, Aruba en Bonaire. Deel III. *Nieuwe West-Indische Gids* 41:83-126.
 1972 *Rotstekeningen van Curacao, Aruba en Bonaire*. Deel IV. Curacao: Uitgaven van de Natuurwetenschappelijke Werkgroep Nederlandse Antillen.

Hurault, Jean-Marcel
 1972 *Français et Indiens en Guyane 1604-1972*. Paris: Union Generale d'Editions.
 1989 *Français et Indiens en Guyane 1604-1972*. Cayenne: Guyane Press Diffusion.

Hurault, J., P. Frenay et Y. Raoux
 1963 Petroglyphes et assemblages dans le sud-est de la Guyane française. *Journal de la Societe des Americanistes* 52:157-166.

Hurtado de Mendoza, Luis
 1987 Cazadores de las Punas de Junin y Cerro de Pasco, Peru. *Estudios Atacamenos: Investigaciones paleoindias al sur de la linea equatorial*. Lautaro Nunez and Betty J. Meggers eds. San Pedro de Atacama: Universidad del Norte, pp. 198-243.

IJzerman, R
 1931 *Outline of the geology and petrology of Surinam (Dutch Guiana)*. The Hague.

Im Thurn, Everard
 1879 Notes on the Indians of Guiana: No. 2. Indian Antiquities. *Demerara papers, Being papers on different subjects concerning British Guiana, contributed to the Royal Gazette of that colony*. Georgetown: Royal Gazette.
 1883 *Among the Indians of Guiana*. London: Kegan Paul, Trench and

	Company. Reprint edition, New York: Dover, 1967.
1884	Notes on West Indian stone implements and other Indian relics, Parts 3,4. *Timehri* 111:123-137.
Jansma, M. J	
1981	Diatom analysis of a section in the Barabina shell midden. *Archaeology and Anthropology* 4(1,2).
Janssen, J.J	
1976	The genesis of the Coastal Plain. *Suralco Magazine.* September 1-7.
Jordan, C.F	
1987	Slash and burn agriculture near San Carlos de Rio Negro, Venezuela. *Amazonian rainforests. Ecosystem disturbance and recovery.* New York: Springer-Verlag, pp. 9-23.
Joyce, T. A	
1916	*Central American and West Indian archaeology. Being an introduction to the archaeology of the states of Nicaragua, Costa Rica, Panama and the West Indies.* London.
Kayser, C. C	
1912	Verslag der Corantijn-expeditie. *Tijdschrift van het Koninklijk Nederlandsch Aardrijkskundig Genootschap te Amsterdam.* Amsterdam.
Kelly, Thomas C	
1993	Preceramic projectile-point typology in Belize. *Ancient Mesoamerica* 4:205-227. Cambridge University Press.
Kennedy, William Jarrold	
1970	A comparison of certain Costa Rica petroglyph designs with those of adjacent areas. *Proceedings of the Fourth International Congress for the study of the Precolumbian cultures of the Lesser Antilles.*
Khudabux, M.R	
1989	Physical anthropological investigations of precolumbian skeletal remains from the "Tingi Holo Ridge" in Suriname. *Paper presented at the Thirtieth Congress of the International Association of Caribbean Archaeology.* Curacao.
1991	*Effects of life conditions on the health of a Negro slave community in Suriname. With reference to similar aspects in local precolumbian Amerindians.* 's-Gravenhage: Pasmans Offsetdrukkerij BV.
Kirby, I.A. Earle	
1969	*Precolumbian Monuments in Stone.* St. Vincent: St. Vincent

	Archaeological and Historical Society.
1976	A newly found petroglyphic rock on St. Vincent. *Proceedings of the Sixth International Congress for the Study of the Precolumbian cultures of the Lesser Antilles.*

Kirchoff, Paul
1948 The Warrau. *Handbook of South American Indians.* Ed. Julian H. Steward. Vol. 3. Washington: US Government Printing Office.

Koch-Grünberg, T
1907 *Sudamerikanische Felszeichnungen.* Berlin: Ernst Wasmuth.
1917 From Roraima to the Orinoco: results of a journey in north Brazil and Venezuela in the years 1911-1913. Translated by Walter E. Roth. Ms. Caribbean Research Library, University of Guyana.

Krook, L
1970 Climate and Sedimentation in the Guianas. *Proceedings of the Eighth Geological Conference.* Georgetown: Geology and Mines Commission.

Kroonenberg, S.B., and P.J. Mellitz
1983 Summit levels, bedrock control and the etchplain concept in the basement of Suriname. *Geologie en Mijnbouw* 62:389-399.

Lancaster, P.A., J.S. Ingram, M.Y. Lim and D.G. Coursey
1981 Traditional cassava-based foods: survey of processing techniques. *Economic Botany* 36(1):12-45.

Langdon, Jean
1981 Cultural bases for trading of visions and spiritual knowledge. *Networks of the Past: Regional Interaction in Archaeology.* Archaeological Association University of Calgary. Proceedings of the Twelfth Annual Conference.

Lathrap, Donald
1964 An alternative seriation of the Mabaruma phase, northwestern British Guiana. *American Antiquity* 29(3).
1966 The Mabaruma phase: a return to the more probable interpretation. *American Antiquity* 31(4).
1970 *The Upper Amazon.* London: Thames and Hudson.
1973 The "Hunting" Economies of the Tropical Forest Zone of South America: An attempt at historical perspective. In: *Peoples and Cultures of Native South America.* Ed. Daniel Gross. New York: Natural History Press.
1975 *Ancient Ecuador; Culture, Clay and Creativity 3000-300 B.C.* Chicago: Field Museum of Natural History.

Laurie, C.K. and D.L. Matheson
 1973 The Petroglyphs of St. Kitts, West Indies. *Proceedings of the Fourth International Congress for the Study of the Precolumbian Cultures of the Lesser Antilles.*

Leechman, Alleyne
 1913 Notes on the ancient sites and historical monuments now existing in the colony of British Guiana. Georgetown: *The Official Gazette* 12 July.

Leemans, C
 1878 Description de quelques antiquites americaines conservees dans le Musee Royal Neerlandais d'Antiquites, a Leide. *Compte rendu du Congres International des Americanistes* 11: 283-302. Luxembourg/Paris.
 1879 Antiquites americaines recemment acquises pour le Musee Royal Neerlandais d'Antiquites a Leide. *Compte rendu du Congres International des Americanistes.* Bruxelles 1: 657-675.
 1884 Verslag omtrent het Rijks Museum van Oudheden te Leiden 1882-1883. Leiden.

Lefebvre, G
 1975 Le gisement de l'Anse Remire-Montjoly (Il de Cayenne). *Connaissance de la Guyane 2:33-39.*

Lewis-Williams, J.D., and T.A. Dowson
 1988 The signs of all times. Entoptic phenomena in Upper Paleolithic art. *Current Anthropology* 29(2):201-245.
 1993 On vision and power in the Neolithic: Evidence from the decorated monuments. *Current Anthropology* 34:55-65.

Loosanoff, V. L
 1950 On the behavior of oysters transferred from low to high salinities. *The Anatomical Record* 108(3):579.

Lorenzo, Jose L
 1953 A fluted point from Durango, Mexico. *American Antiquity* 18(4):394-395.
 1964 Das puntas acanaladas en la region de Chapala, Mexico. Instituto Nacional de Antropologia e Historia, Mexico D.F. *Boletim* 18:1-6.

Lothhrop, S.K
 1961 Early migrations to Central and South America: An anthropological problem in the light of other sciences. *Jour. Royal Anthropological Institute of Gt Britain and Ireland* 91:97-123.

Loven, Sven
 1935 *Origins of the Tainan culture, West Indies.* Goteborg: Elanders

Botryckeri Aktiebolag.

Lumbreras, Luis G
1974 *The peoples and cultures of ancient Peru.* Trans. Betty J. Meggers. Washington: Smithsonian Institution Press.

Lynch, Thomas F
1978 The South American Paleo-Indians. *Ancient Native Americans.* Jesse D. Jennings ed. San Francisco: W. H. Freeman and Company, pp. 455-489.
1990 Glacial-age man in South America? A critical review. *American Antiquity* 55(1):12-36.

Mallery, Garrick
1893 Picture writing of the American Indians. *Tenth Annual Report of the Bureau of American Ethnology, 1888-1889.* Washington: Smithsonian Institution.

Marett, R, R
1934 *Thoughts, talks and tramps. A collection of papers by Sir Everard Im Thurn.* R.R. Marett ed. Oxford University Press.

Martin, Robert Montgomery
1967 *History of the colonies of the British Empire.* London: Dawsons.

Mason, J. Alden
1950 The languages of South American Indians. *Handbook of South American Indians.* Julian H. Steward ed. Volume 6. Washington: United States Government Printing Office.

Mayer-Oakes, William J
1963 Early man in the Andes. *New World Archaeology.* Introductions by Ezra B. Zubrow, M. C. Fritz and John M. Fritz. San Francisco: W.H. Freeman and Company, pp. 51-59.

Maziere, Marlene
1995 Montagne couronnee Fortunat Kapiri. *Bilan scientifique 1994.* Cayenne: Ministere de la Culture.

McConnell, Rosemary
1967 The fish fauna of the Rupununi District, Guyana. *Timehri* 43:58-69.

McGimpsey, Charles R
1956 Cerro Mangote: A preceramic site in Panama. *American Antiquity* XX 11(2):151-167.
1958 Fuller data and a date from Cerro Mangote, Panama. *American Antiquity* XX 111(4):434-435.

McNeish, Richard S
1971 Early Man in the Andes. In *Pre-Columbian archaeology.* San

Francisco: W.H. Freeman and Company.
McTurk, Michael
  1911   Journey from Kalacoon to the Orinoco. *Timehri* 1:88-97.
Meggers, Betty J
  1947   *The Beal-Steere collection of pottery from Marajó Island, Brazil.* Papers of the Michigan Academy of Science, Arts and Letters XXXI (1945):193-213.
  1954   Environmental limitation on the development of culture. *American Anthropologist* 56:801-824.
  1971   *Amazonia: Man and culture in a counterfeit paradise.* Chicago: Aldine Publishing Company.
  1975   Application of the biological model of diversification to cultural distributions in tropical lowland South America. *Biotropica* 7:141-161.
  1977   Vegetational fluctuation and prehistoric cultural adaptation in Amazonia. *World Archaeology* 8(3):287-303.
  1979   Climatic oscillation as a factor in the prehistory of Amazonia. *American Antiquity* 44(2):252-266.
  1982   Archaeological and ethnographic evidence compatible with the model of forest fragmentation. *Biological diversification in the Tropics.* Ghillean T. Prance ed. New York: Columbia University Press, pp. 483-496.
  1984   The indigenous peoples of Amazonia, their cultures, land use patterns and effects on the landscape and biota. *The Amazon: Limnology and landscape ecology of a mighty tropical river and its basin.* H. Sioli ed. Dordrecht, Boston: Dr W. Junk Publishers, pp. 627-648.
  1987   Oscilacion climatica y cronologia cultural en el Caribe. *Actas del tercer simposia de la Fundacion de Arquelogia del Caribe.* Mario Sanoja O. ed. Washington.
  1994   Biogeographical approaches to reconstructing the prehistory of Amazonia. *Biogeographica* 70(3):97-10.
  1995   Archaeological perspectives on the potential of Amazonia for intensive exploitation. *The fragile tropics of Latin America: Sustainable management of changing environments.* United Nations University Press, pp. 68-93.
Meggers, Betty J., and Clifford Evans
  1955   Preliminary results of archaeological investigations in British Guiana. *Timehri* 34:5-25.
  1957   *Archaeological investigations at the Mouth of the Amazon.*

	Washington: United States Government Printing Office.
1961	An experimental formulation of horizon styles in the tropical forest area of South America. *Essays in Pre-Columbian art and archaeology.* Samuel K. Lothrop ed. Cambridge: Harvard University Press, pp. 372-388.
1973	An interpretation of the cultures of Marajó Island. *Peoples and cultures, of native South America.* Daniel R. Gross ed. Doubleday: The Natural History Press, pp. 39-47.
1978	Lowland South America and the Antilles. *Ancient Native Americans.* Jesse D. Jennings ed. San Francisco: W.H. Freeman and Company.
1979	An experimental reconstruction of Taruma village succession and some implications. *Brazil: Anthropological Perspectives.* M.L. Margoulis and W.E. Carter eds. New York: Columbia University Press, pp. 39-60.

Meggers, Betty J., Ondemar Dias, Eurico Th. Miller and Celso Perota
 1988 *Implications of archaeological distributions in Amazonia.* W.R. Heyer and P.E.Vanzolini eds. Academia Brasileira de Ciencias Rio de Janeiro, pp. 275-294.

Meltzer, David J., James M. Adovasio and Tom D. Dillehay
 1994 On a Pleistocene human occupation at Pedra Furada, Brazil. *Antiquity* 68:695-714.

Mentore, George
 1983-1984 Waiwai labour relations in the production of cassava. *Antropologica* 59-62:199-221.

Mentz-Ribeiro, P.A., C.T. Ribeiro, Vera L. Calandrini Guapindaia, F.C. Bezerra Pinto and Luis Aranjo Felix
 1986 Projeto arquelogico de salvamento na regiao de Boa Vista, Terrritorio Federal de Roraima, Brazil. *Revista do Cepa* 13(16):33-91.

Mentz-Ribeiro, P.A., Ana Lucia Machado and Vera L. Calandrini Guapindaia
 1987 Projeto arquelogico de salvamento na regiao de Boa Vista, Ter. Fed. de Roraima, Brasil. *Revista do Cepa* 14(17):3-82.

Mentz-Ribeiro, P.A., C.T. Ribeiro and Francisca C. Bezerra Pinto
 1989 Levantmentos arquelogicos no Territorio Federal de Roraima, Brasil. *Revista do Cepa* 16(19):5-46.

Metraux, Alfred
 1949 Religion and shamanism. *Handbook of South American Indians.* Julian H. Steward ed. Washington: United States Government Printing Office, pp. 559-599.

Migliazza, Ernesto
 1980 Languages of the Orinoco-Amazon basin: Current status. *Antropologica* 53:95-162.
 1982 Linguistic prehistory and the refuge model in Amazonia. *Biological diversification in the Tropics.* Ghillean T. Prance ed. New York: Columbia University Press, pp. 497-519.

Miller, Eurico T.
 1992 *Arquelogia: Ambiente desenvolvintento.* Programa das Nacaos Unidas para o Desenvolvimento (PNUD)/Smithsonian Institution.

Mittermeier, Russel A., and M.G.M. van Roosmalen
 1981 Preliminary observations on habitat utilization and diet in eight Surinam monkeys. *Folia Primatologica* 36:1-39.

Morlan, Richard E
 1988 Pre-Clovis people: Early discoveries in America. *Americans before Columbus.* Ronald C. Carlisle ed. University of Pittsburgh Ethnology monograph 12:31-43.

Muckenhim, Nancy A., and J.F. Eisenberg
 1978 *The status of primates in Guyana and ecological correlations for Neotropical primates,* Washington: National Zoological Park, pp. 27-30.

Muckenhirn, Nancy A., B.K. Mortensen, S.Vessey, C.E.O. Fraser, Balram Singh
 1975 *Report on a primate survey of Guyana.* Washington: Pan American Sanitary Bureau, PAHO.

Murray, William Breen
 1979 Interpretive perspectives on the rock art traditions of northeastern and north central Mexico with special reference to Nuevo Leon. *STJRH* 3(1):27-51.
 1982 A closer look at petroglyphic counting in northeastern Mexico. *Pantoc* 3:39-45.
 1982a Rock art and site environment at Boca de Potrerillos, Nuevo Leon. Mexico. *American Indian Rock Art* VII-VIII:57-65.
 1985 Petroglyphic counts at Icamole, Neuvo Leon (Mexico). *Current Anthropology* 26(2):276-279.
 1986 Numerical representations in North American rock art. *Native American Mathematics.* Michael P. Closs ed. Austin: University of Texas Press.
 1987 *Arte rapestre en Nuevo Leon: Numeracion prehistorica.* Monterry: Cuadernos del Archivo No. 13.

Netto, Jeosua Nunez, and Joseph Pereira
 1658[1962] Copy *of a commentary dated 15 September 1658, written by*

Jeosua Nunes Netto and Joseph Pereira, on the beach of Pauroma (Pomeroon) on the Wild Coast, in which they describe their journey and the conditions they could observe that day of the country. J. Melier ed. *Timehri* 33:47-51.

Noble, G. Kingsley
- 1965 *Proto-Arawakan and its descendants.* Bloomington: Indiana University Publication in Anthropology and Linguistics, 18.

Nunez-Jimenez, A
- 1964 *Cuevas y pictografias.* La Habana: Edicion Revolucionaria.
- 1970 *Caguanes pictografico.* Serie Espeleologica, y carsologica 16. La Habana.

Organization of American States (OAS).
- 1987 *Minimum conflict: Guidelines for planning the use of American humid tropic environments.* Washington: Secretariat for Economic and Social Affairs, p. 30.

Odum, William E
- 1984 The relationship between protected coastal areas and marine fisheries genetic resources. *National parks, conservation and development: The role of protected areas in sustaining society.* Jeffrey A. McNeely and K.R. Miller eds. Washington: Smithsonian Institution Press.

Ogden, John C
- 1987-1988 Caribbean coastal ecology at Caribbean marine laboratories. Oceanus 30(4):9-14.

Oliver, J.R
- 1973 Petroglyphs en La Mina. *Boletin Inforinativo.* Fundacion Arquelogia, Antropologia e Historia de Puerto Rico 1(6):1-2.

Olsen, Fred
- 1973 On the trail of the Arawaks: When did they arrive in Trinidad? *Proceedings of the Fourth International Congress for the study of the Precolumbian cultures of the Lesser Antilles.* Castries: St. Lucia, pp. 181-191.

Ortiz-Troncoso, O.R
- 1977 Documents pour la pre- et proto-histoire de la zone Central-Sud du Chili. *Ex Horreo* IV: 165-184.

Osgood, Cornelius
- 1946 *British Guiana archaeology to 1945.* New Haven: Yale University Press.

Osgood, Cornelius, and George D. Howard
- 1943 *An anthropological survey of Venezuela.* New Haven: Yale

University Press.
Office of Technology Assessment
1984 *Technologies to sustain tropical forest resources OTA-F-214*. See "Environment" Ch. 2, p. 52. Congress of the United States. Washington D.C: United States Government Printing Office.

Palmatary, Helen C
1960 *The archaeology of the lower Tapajos Valley, Brazil*. Philadelphia: The American Philosophical Society.

Palmer, Jay, and J.R. Williams
1977 The formation of goethite and calcareous lenses in shell mounds in Florida. *Florida Anthropologist* 30:24-27.

Peasgood, Edward T
1972 Carib phonology. *Languages of the Guianas*. Joseph E. Grimes ed. Summer Institute of Linguistics University of Oklahoma.

Peberdy, J. Storer
1945 Progress report by the Amerindian Welfare Officer covering the period 13 February to 23 April, 1945. Amerindian Welfare Scheme, British Guiana. No. 1/17/2/4. Unpublished. National Anthropological Archives Walter Roth Museum.
1948 Amerindian rock paintings in British Guiana. *Timehri* 28:54-58.

Pelegrin, Jacques, and Claude Chauchat
1993 Tecnologia y funcion on de las puntas de Paijan: El aporte de la experimentacion. *Latin American Antiquity* 4(4):367-382.

Penard, A.P., and T.E. Penard
1917 Popular notions pertaining to primitive stone artifacts in Surinam. *Journal of American Folklore* XXX(CXV 1): 251-261. New York.

Penna, Domingos Soares Ferreira
1877 Apontamentos sobre os ceramios do Para. *Archivos do Museu nacional do Rio Janeiro* 2:47-67.

Penney, David W., M.N. Roberts, and H.M. Shannon
1995 African masterworks in the Detroit Institute of Arts. Washington: Smithsonian Institution Press.

Perlman, Stephen M
1980 An optimum diet model, coastal variability, and hunter gatherer behavior. *Advances in archaeological method and theory*. Volume 3:257-310. New York: Academic Press.

Persaud, Chander
1983 Regional variations of the rainfall climate of Guyana and its application in planning. *A paper presented at the seminar on Spatial Aspects, of Development and Planning*. Turkeyen:

University of Guyana.
Phillips-Conroy, Jane, and Robert Sussman
　1994　　　A study of the primates of Guyana: Survey and 20-year comparison. *Archaeology and Anthropology* 10: 3-18.
Pianka
　1974　　　*Evolutionary ecology*. New York: Harper and Row, Publishers.
Pimentel, David, and Marcia Pimentel
　1979　　　*Food, energy and society*. London: Edward Arnold.
Plotkin, Mark
　1993　　　*Tales of a shaman's apprentice*. New York: Viking.
Pollak-Eltz, Angelina
　1976　　　Venezuelan petroglyphs. *Proceedings of the Fourth International Congress for the study of the Precolumbian cultures of the Lesser Antilles*. Guadeloupe, pp. 221-231.
Pollard, R
　1956　　　*Geological survey of British Guiana Annual Report for 1954*. Appendix 11, pp. 39-45. Georgetown: Geology and Mines Commission.
Poonai
　1962　　　Archaeological sites on the Corentyne Coast. *Journal of the British Guiana Museum and Zoo* 33:52-53.
　1970　　　*Stone-age Guyana*. Georgetown: National History and Arts Council.
　1978　　　Stone-age Guyana. *Archaeology and Anthropology* 1(1):5-23.
Porras G., P.I
　1961　　　Contribucion al estudio de la arquelogia e historia de los valles Qukjos y Misagualli (Alto Napo) en ta Region Oriental del Ecuador. Quito: Editora Fenix.
Prance, Ghillean T
　1973　　　Phytogeographic support for the theory of Pleistocene forest refuges in the Amazon Basin, based on evidence from distribution patterns in *Caryocaraceae, Chrysobalanaceae, Dichapetelaceae and Lecythidaceae*. *Acta Amazonica* 3(3):103-137.
　1982　　　Forest refuges: Evidence from woody angiosperms. *Biological diversification in the Tropics*. Edited by Ghillean T. Prance. New York: Columbia University Press, pp. 137-158.
Price, Barbara
　1982　　　Cultural materialism: A theoretical review. *American Antiquity* 47(4):709-741.

Proskouriakoff, Tatiana
- 1968 The jog and the jaguar sign in Maya writing. *American Antiquity* 33(2):247-251.

Quelch, J.J
- 1887 Value of gold to the Indians in the past. *Timehri* 6:350.
- 1894 *Carib remains on Pln. Mon Repos.* Georgetown: The Argosy Office.

Ralegh, Walter
- 1848 *The discovery of the large, rich and beautiful empire of Guiana [...] performed in the year 1595.* R. H. Schomburgk ed. London: The Hakluyt Society.

Ray, G. Carleton, B.P. Hayden, R.Dolan
- 1984 Development of a biophysical coastal and marine classification system. *National parks, conservation, and development: The role of protected areas in sustaining society.* Edited by J.A. McNeely, K.R.Miller. Washington: Smithsonian Institution Press.

Reichel-Dolmatoff, Gerardo
- 1965 *Excavaciones arquelogicas en Puerto Hormiga (Department de Bolivar).* Bogota: Ediciones Universidad de los Andes Publicaciones Antropologia 2.
- 1967 Rock paintings of the Vaupés: An essay of interpretation. *Folklore Americas XXV* 11(2):107-113.
- 1971 *Amazonian cosmos.* Chicago: University of Chicago Press.
- 1972 The cultural context of an aboriginal hallucinogen. *Flesh of the gods: The ritual use of hallucinogens.* P.T. Furst, ed. London: Allen and Unwin.
- 1978 *Under the Milky Way.* Los Angeles: UCLA Latin American Center.

Reichlen, H., and P. Reichlen
- 1943-1945 Contribution a l'archeologie de la Guyane française. *Journal de la Societe des Americanistes* 35:1-24.

Roe, Peter G
- 1982 *The cosmic zygote. Cosmology in the Amazon Basin.* New Jersey: Rutgers University Press.

Roe, Peter G., and Peter Seigel
- 1982 The life history of a Shipibo compound: Ethnoarchaeology in the Peruvian montana. *Archaeology and Anthropology* 5(2):95-118.

Roeleveld, W
- 1969 Pollen analysis of two sections in the Young Coastal Plain of Suriname. *Geologie en Mijnbouw* 48(2):215-224.

Roget, Hughes Petitjean, and Dornique Roy
    1975   *Contributions a la connaissance prehistorique de la Guyane.* Cayenne.

Roosevelt, Anna Curtenius
    1980   *Parmana. Prehistoric maize and manioc subsistence along the Amazon and Orinoco.* New York: Academic Press.
    1991   *Moundbuilders of the Amazon. Geophysical archaeology on Marajó Island, Brazil.* New York: Academic Press.
    1995   Early pottery in the Amazon. Twenty years of scholarly obscurity. *The emergence of pottery: Technology and innovation in ancient societies.* W. K. Barnett and J.W. Hoopes eds. Washington: Smithsonian Institution Press.

Roosevelt, A. C., R.A. Housley, M. Imazio da Silveira, S. Maranca, R. Johnson.
    1991   Eighth millennium pottery from a prehistoric shell midden in the Brazilian Amazon. *Science* 254:1621-1624.

Roosevelt, A. C., M. Lima da Costa, C. Lopes Machado, M. Michab, N. Mercier, H. Valladas, J. Feathers, W. Barnett, M. Imazio da Silveira, A. Henderson, J. Sliva, B. Chernoff, D.S. Reese, J.A. Holman, N. Toth, K. Schick.
    1996   Paleoindian cave dwellers in the Amazon: The peopling of the Americas. *Science* 272:373-384.

Rostain, Stephen
    1991   *Projet savanes. Champs sureleves Amerindiens de la Guyane.* Cayenne: ORSTOM/IGN.
    1994   L'Occupation Amerindienne ancienne du littoral de Guyane. PhD thesis Universite de Paris, Sorbonne.
    1994a   Archeologie du littoral de Guyane, un region charniere entre les influences culturelles de l'Orenoque et de l'Amazone. *Journal de la Societe des Americanistes* 80:9-46.
    1995   L'occupation Amerindienne ancienne de littoral de Guyane. Ministere de la Culture, pp. 67-70.

Rostain, Stephen, et Pierre Frenay
    1991   Projet savanes, champs sureleves amerindiens du littoral de la Guyane. *Rapport de recherche.* ORSTOM/I.G.N. Cayenne.

Rostain, Stephen and Yannick Le Roux
    1990   *Archeologie. La documentation guyanaise.* Cayenne: Saga.

Roth, Vincent
    1944   A stone-age bead factory on the Mahaica River. *Timehri* 26:42-48.
    MS   Letters: Roth/Evans and Meggers. Walter Roth Museum.

Roth, Walter Edmund
    1924   *An introductory study of the arts, crafts and customs of the Guiana Indians.* Bureau of American Ethnology thirty-eighth annual report. Washington: U.S. Government Printing Office.
    1925   Animal names, place names, linguistics, vocabularies and miscellany relating to the aboriginal Indians of Dutch and British Guiana. Univ. Guyana Caribbean Research Library.
    1902-1931   Letters received. Walter Roth Museum.
    MS   A preliminary survey of certain prehistoric pottery ware from the North-Western District of British Guiana. Washington: National Anthropological Archives.
    1902-1931   Letters received. University of Guyana Caribbean Research Library. [Copy Walter Roth Museum of Anthropology].

Rouse, Irving B
    1953   Indian sites in Trinidad. In J.A. Bullbrook *On the excavation of a shell mound at Palo Seco, Trinidad, BWI.* Yale University Publications in Anthropology 50:94-111.
    1983   Diffusion and interaction in the Orinoco Valley and on the coast. *Proceedings of the Ninth International Congress for the study of the Precolumbian cultures of the Lesser Antilles.* Montreal: Universite de Montreal, pp. 3-13.
    1985   Arawakan phylogeny, Caribbean chronology, and their implications for the study of popular movement. *Antropologica* 63/64:9-21.

Rouse, I, B., and L. Allaire
    1978   Caribbean. *Chronologies in New World archaeology.* C. Meighan and T. Taylor eds. New York: Seminar Press.

Rouse, I, B., and Jose M. Cruxent
    1963   Venezuelan archaeology. New Haven: Yale University Press.

Roy, Dominique
    1978   Decouverte du site de Jaffe Indien (Guyane). *Proceedings of the Seventh International Congress for the study of the Precolumbian cultures of the Lesser Antilles.* Montreal: Universite de Montreal, pp. 137-147.

Rull, Valenti
    1991   Contribucion a la paleoecologia de Pantepui y la Gran Sabana (Guayana Venezolana): clima, biogeografia y ecologia. *Scientia Guaianae* 2.

Rutzler, Klaus, and Candy Feller
    1987/1988   Mangrove swamp communities. *Oceanus* 30(4):16-23. Woods

Hole Oceanographic Institution.
Rye, Owen S
 1981 *Pottery technology: Principles and reconstruction.* Washington: Taraxacum.
Sanoja, O
 1969 La arquelogia de Guayana. *Las relaciones culturas.* Caracas: Corporacion Venezolana de Guayana, pp. 54-86.
 1979 *Las culturas formativas del oriente de Venezuela. La Tradicion Barrancas del bajo Orinoco.* Caracas: Biblioteca de la Academia Nacional de la Historia.
 1983 El origen de la sociedad Taina y el Formativo Suramericano. *La cultura Taino.* Madrid: Biblioteca del V Centenario.
 1989 Origins of cultivation around the Gulf of Paria, northeastern Venezuela. *National Geographic Research* 5:445-458.
Sanoja O. M., and I. Vargas A.
 1983 New light on the prehistory of eastern Venezuela: *Advances in World archaeology* 2. F. Wendorf and A. Close, eds. New York: Academic Press.
Sarmiento, Guillermo
 1984 *The ecology of neotropical savannas.* Cambridge, Massachusetts: Harvard University Press.
Sauer, Carl O
 1952 *Agricultural origins and dispersals.* New York: The American Geographical Society.
Saxe, Arthur
 1971 Social dimensions of mortuary practices in a Mesolithic population from Wadi Haifa, Sudan. *Approaches to the social dimensions of mortuary practices.* James A. Brown ed. *American Antiquity* 36(3), Part 2:39-57.
Schmeltz, J. D
 1904 Uber sammlungen aus Neiderlands West-indien und Surinam, *Mitteilungen aus dem Niederlands Reichsmuseum fur volkerkunde* 2,9:1-7.
Schmitz, Pedro Ignacio
 1987 Prehistoric hunters and gathers of Brazil. *Journal of World Prehistory* 1(1):53-126.
Schomburgk, Richard
 1848 *Richard Schomburgk's travels in British Guiana 1840-1844.* Trans. ed. Walter Roth. Two volumes 1922, 1923. Georgetown: The Daily Chronicle.

Schomburgk
1841   *Robert Hermann Schomburgk's travels in British Guiana during the years 1835-1839*. E. O. Schomburgk ed. Georgetown: The Argosy Company Ltd [Reprint ed. 1931].
1886   Sir Robert Schomburgk on the *Aeta* palm. *Timehri* 5:121-122.

Schubert, Carlos
1986   Paleoenvironmental studies in the Guayana region southeastern Venezuela. *Current Research in the Pleistocene* 3:88-89.
1995   Origin of the Gran Sabana in southeastern Venezuela: no longer a "lost world." *Scientia Guaianae* 5:147-174.

Schultz, J
1976   The genesis of the Coastal Plain. *Suralco Magazine* Sept: 1-7.

Scott, Geoffrey A
1987   Shifting cultivation where land is limited. Campa Indian agriculture in the Gran Pajonal of Peru. *Amazonian rain forests. Ecosystem disturbance and recovery.* New York: Springer-Verlag, pp. 34-45.

Seigel, Peter
1987   Small village demographic and architectural organization: an example from the tropical lowlands. Paper presented in the symposium *Site structure and spatial organization of sedentary communities*. 52nd annual meeting of the Society for American Archaeology, Toronto.
1992   Lowland cosmology as an interpretive framework for prehistoric community organization. 57th annual meeting of the Society for American Archaeology, Pittsburgh.

Seigel, Ronald K
1977   Hallucinations. *Scientific American* 237(4):132-140.

Shaw, Paul
1979   Preliminary report on the geomorphology of Makatau Mt., South Rupununi. *Archaeology and Anthropology* 2(1):54-57.

Shepard, Anna O
1976   *Ceramics for the archaeologist*. Washington: Carnegie Institution.

Silva Celis, E
1961   Pinturas rupestres precolumbians de Sachira, Valle de Heiva. *Revista Colombiana de Antropologia* 10:33-35.

Simmons, I. G
1979   *Biogeography: natural and cultural*. London: Edward Arnold.

Simões, Mario
1981   Coletadores-pescadores ceramistas do tittoral do Salgado (Para).

Nota preliminar. Belem: *Boletim do Museu Paraense Emilio Goeldi* 78:1-32.

Simões, Mario, and F. Araujo-Costa
   1978   *Areas da Amazonia legal Brasileira para pesquisa e cadastro de sitios arquelogicos*. Belem: Museu Paraense Emilio Goeldi.

Simon, George
   MS   Report: Field trip upper Mahaica River January 1986. MS National Anthropological Archives Walter Roth Museum.

Smith, Nigel J. H
   1981   Man, fishes, and the Amazon. New York: Columbia University Press.

Snarkis, Michael
   1979   Turrialba: a paleo-Indian quarry and workshop site in eastern Costa Rica. *American Antiquity* 44(1):125-138.

Spitzly, J. H
   1890   Notes on three stone adzes from Surinam (Dutch Guiana) and on eight stone implements from the islands of St. Vincent and St. Lucie. *Internationales Archiv fur Ethnographie* 3:231-233.

Stahel, Gerold
   1927   De expeditie naar het Wilhelminagebergte (Suriname) in 1926. *Tijdschrift van het Koninklijk Nederlandsch Aardrijkskundig Genootschap te Amsterdam* 44:383-392.

Steere, J.B.
   1927   *The archaeology of the Amazon*. University of Michigan Official Publication 29(9): Part II:20-26.

Stephens, William M
   1963   Mangroves: trees that make land. *Smithsonian Report for 1962*. Washington: Smithsonian Institution, pp. 491-496.

Steward, Julian H
   1948   Culture areas of the Tropical Forest. *Handbook of South American Indians*. Julian H. Steward ed. Volume 3:883-899. Washington: U.S. Government Printing Office.
   1949   South American cultures: an interpretive summary. *Handbook of South American Indians*. Julian H. Steward, ed. Volume 5:669-772. Washington: U.S. Government Printing Office.

Steyermark, Julian A
   1982   Relationships of some Venezuelan forest refuges with lowland tropical floras. *Biological diversification in the Tropics*. Ghillean T. Prance ed. New York: Columbia University Press, pp. 182-220.

Stothert, Karen
    1985   The preceramic Las Vegas culture of coastal Ecuador. *American Antiquity* 50(3):613-637.

Strahler, Arthur N
    1975   *Physical geography.* New York: John Willey and Sons.

Sujo-Volsky, Jeannine
    1975   *El estudio del arte rupestre en Venezuela.* Caracas: Universidad Catolica Andres Bello.

Swauger, James L., and W.J. Mayer-Oakes
    1952   A fluted point from Costa Rica. *American Antiquity* (3):264-265.

Tacoma, J
    1963   *American Indians from Suriname. A physical anthropological study.* PhD thesis University of Utrecht.

Tankersley, Kenneth B
    1994   The effects of stone and technology on fluted-point morphometry. *American Antiquity* 59(3):498-510.

Tarble, Kay
    1985   Un nuevo modelo de expansion caribe para la epoca prehispanica. *Antropologica* 63-64:45-81.

Tarble, Kay, y Alberta Zucchi
    1984   Nuevas datos sobre la arquelogia tardia del Orinoco: La serie Valloide. *Acta Scientifica Venezolana* 35:434-445.

Ten Kate, H.F.C
    1889   Notes on some West Indian stone implements, and other Indian relics. Bijdragen tot de taal, land- en volkenkunde van Nederlandsch Indie 38.-153-160.
    1914-1917   "Oudheden I. Suriname." *Encyclopaedie van Nederlandsch West Indie.* Edited by H.D. Benjamins and J.F. Snellman, pp. 541-543.

Terborgh, John
    1995   *Diversity and the tropical rain forest.* New York: Scientific American Library.

Thompson, J. Eric S
    1963   *Mayan archaeologist.* London: Robert Hale Limited.

Toutouri, Christian
    1983   La roche gravee de l'Inipi, Guyane française. *Proceedings of the Ninth International Congress for the study of the Precolumbian cultures of the Lesser Antilles.* Montreal: Universite de Montreal, pp. 363-374.

Tolstoy, Paul
    1974   Mesoamerica. *Prehispanic America.* S. Gorenstein, ed. New York:

St Martin's Press, pp. 29-64.

Ubelaker, Douglas H
 1989 *Human skeletal remains.* Washington: Taraxacum.

Van Andel, Tj, H
 1967 The Orinoco delta. *Journal of Sedimentary Petrology* 37(2):297-310.

Van Berkel, Adriaan
 1948[1695] *Adriaan van Berkel's travels in South America between the Berbice and Essequibo rivers, and in Surinam.* Walter E. Roth, ed. Georgetown: The Daily Chronicle.

Van der Harnmen, T
 1963 A palynological study of the Quaternary of British Guiana. *Leidse Geologische Mededelingen* 29:125-180.
 1974 The Pleistocene changes of vegetation and climate in tropical South America. *Journal of Biogeography* 1:3-36.

Van der Hammen, T., and M.L. Absy
 1994 Amazonia during the Last Glacial. *Palaeogeography, palaeoclimatology, palaeoecology* 109:247-261.

Vanzolini, P. E
 1970 *Zoologia sistematica, geografia e a origem das species.* Sao Paulo: Universidad de Sao Paulo, Instituto Geografia. Teses e monografias 3.

Van Wallenberg, Martin
 1995 Sites of fortifications and administrative headquarters of early Dutch colonists on the Berbice River. *Archaeology and Anthropology* 10:48-57.

Vargas, Iraida
 1979 *La Tradicion Saladoide del oriente de Venezuela: La phase Quartel.* Caracas: Biblioteca de la Academia Nacional de la Historia.

Vargas, Iraida, and Mario Sanoja O
 1970 The Orinoco project: preliminary report 1968-1969. *Proceedings of the Third International Congress for the study of the Precolumbian cultures of the Lesser Antilles* pp. 107-113.

Veloz-Maggiolo, Marcio, Elpido Ortega, Joaquin Nadar, Fernando Luna Calderon, and Renato O. Rimoli
 1977 *Arquelogia de Cueva de Berna.* Republica Dominicano: San Pedro de Macoris.

Verrill, A. Hyatt
 1918 Prehistoric mounds and relics of the North West District of British

      Guiana. *Timehri* 5:11-20.
 1918a   A remarkable mound discovered in British Guiana. *Timehri* 5:20-25.

Versteeg, Aad H
 1978   A distinctive kind of pottery in western Suriname. *Mededelingen Surinaams Museum* 23/24:15-26.
 1979   The first C^{14} datings of archaeological material from Suriname. *Mededelingen Surinaams Museum* No. 29:39-48.
 1980   Archaeological investigations at Kwamalasamotoe, south Suriname. *Stichting Surinaams Museum* 30:23-46.
 1980a C^{14} datings from archaeological sites in Suriname. *Mededelingen Surinaams Museum* No. 32:38-56.
 1981   A fortified pre-Columbian village in east Suriname? *Mededelingen der Surinaamse Musea* 33:38-48.
 1983   Recent archaeological investigations in Suriname. *Suralco Magazine* 15(1):1-8.
 1985   The prehistory of the Young Coastal Plain of west Suriname. *Berichten van de Rijksdeinst voor het Oudheidkundig Bodemonderzoek* 35:653-750.
 1991   Application of isotopic analysis of total bone collagen to studies of ancient human populations in the Caribbean region. In C.J. Van Klinken: *Dating and dietary reconstruction by isotopic analysis of amino acids, in fossil bone collagen, with special reference to the Caribbean.* Amsterdam: Publications Foundation for Scientific Research in the Caribbean Region, pp. 79-102.

Versteeg, A. H., and F.C. Bubberman
 1992   *Suriname before Columbus.* Paramaribo: Stichting Surinaams Museum.

Versteeg, A. H., and Kees Schinkel
 1992   *The archaeology of St Eustatius. The Golden Rock site.* Amsterdam: St. Eustatius Historical Foundation 2.

Von Hildebrand, Elizabeth
 1975   Levantan-tiento de los petroglifos del Rio Caqueta entre La Pedrera y Araracuara. *Revista Colombiana de Antropologia* 19:303-370.

Von Humboldt, Alexander
 1852-1853   *Personal narrative of travels to the equinoctial regions of America.* London: Bell and Daldy.

Wallace, Alfred Russell
 1889   A narrative of travels on the Amazon and Rio Negro, with an

account of the native tribes, and observations on climate, geology and natural history of the Amazon valley. London: Ward Lock.

Waselkov, Gregory A
   1987   Shellfish gathering and shell midden archaeology. *Advances in archaeological method and theory.* New York: Academic Press, pp. 93-209.

Waterlow, J
   1945   Nutritional survey of the Akowio Indians in the villages and settlements around Imbaimadai, Upper Mazaruni River (British Guiana). Unpubl. MS. Walter Roth Museum National Anthropological Archives.

Watt, B.K., A.L. Merrill, M.L. Orr
   1959   A table of food values. *Food. The yearbook of agriculture 1959.* Washington: United States Department of Agriculture.

Watters, David R
   1976   Caribbean prehistory: a century of researchers, models and trends. MA thesis, University of Nevada.

Weber, Ronald
   1990   Current Research. *American Antiquity* 55(1):169-172.

Weihrauch, F., S. Narain, J.C. Inasi
   1977   Quartz crystal occurrences in Guyana. Georgetown: Geological Surveys and Mines Department.

Wells, John T., and J.M. Coleman
   1981   Periodic mudflat progradation, northeastern coast of South America: a hypothesis. *Journal of Sedimentary Petrology* 51(4):1069-1075.

West, Michael
   1979   Early watertable farming on the north coast of Peru. *American Antiquity* 44(1):138-144.

Whitehead, Neil L
   1988   Lords of the tiger spirit. A history of the Caribs in Colonial Venezuela and Guyana. Dordrecht: Foris Publications.
   1990   The Mazaruni pectoral: a golden artefact discovered in Guyana and the historical sources concerning native metallurgy in the Caribbean, Orinoco and northern Amazonia. *Archaeology and Anthropology* 7:19-38.
   1992   *Wild majesty. Encounters with Caribs from Columbia to the present day.* Oxford: The Clarendon Press.
   1996   *The Patamona of Paramakatoi and the Yawong Valley: An oral history.* Georgetown: The Hamburg Register.

Whitmore, T.C.
1990 *An introduction to the tropical rainforest.* New York: Oxford University Press.

Wijmstra, T.A., and T. van der Hammen
1966 Palynological data on the history of tropical savannas in northern South America. *Leidse Geologische Mededelingen* 38:71-83.

Wilbert, Johannes
1972 *Survivors of El Dorado.* New York: Praeger.
1975 Eschatology in a participatory universe: destinies of the soul among the Warao Indians of Venezuela. *Death and the afterlife in pre-Columbian America.* Edited by Elizabeth P. Benson. Washington: Dumbarton Oaks, pp. 163-189.
1979 Geography and telluric lore of the Orinoco Delta. *Journal of Latin American Lore* 5(1):129-150.
1985 The house of the swallow-tailed kite: Warao myth and the art of thinking in images. *Animal myths and metaphors in South America.* Gary Norton ed. Salt Lake City: University of Utah Press, pp. 145-181.
1986 Warao cosmology and Yekuana roundhouse symbolism. Myth and the imaginary in the New World. Edmundo Magana and Peter Mason eds. *Latin American Studies* 34:427-458. Dordrecht: Foris Publications.

Willey, Gordon R
1949 Ceramics. *Handbook of South American Indians.* Edited by Julian H. Steward. Vol. 5: 139-204.
1971 *An introduction to American archaeology.* Volume 2: South America. Englewood Cliffs: Prentice-Hall.
1985 Some continuing problems in New World culture history. *American Antiquity* 50(2):351-363.

Willey, Gordon R., and Jeremy A. Sabloff
1974 *A history of American archaeology.* London: Thames and Hudson.

Williams, Denis
1978 Petroglyphs at Marlisa, Berbice River. *Archaeology and Anthropology* 1(1):24-31.
1978a An unusual ceramic vessel. *Archaeology and Anthropology* 1(1):56.
1978b Prehistoric rock art in Guyana and the Antilles. Paper presented at the Tenth Conference of Caribbean Historians, St. Thomas, U.S. Virgin Islands 27 March - 1 April, 1978.
1979 A report on preceramic lithic artifacts in the South Rupununi

	Savannas. *Archaeology and Anthropology* 2(1):10-53.
1979a	Preceramic fish traps on the upper Essequibo: Report on a survey of unusual petroglyphs on the Upper Essequibo and Kassikaityu rivers 12-28 March 1979. *Archaeology and Anthropology* 2(2):125-140.
1979b	Controlled resource exploitation in contrasting neotropical environments evidenced by meso-Indian petroglyphs in Southern Guyana. *Archaeology and Anthropology* 2(2):141-148.
1981	Excavation of the Barabina shell mound North West District: An interim report. *Archaeology and Anthropology* 1(2):16-34.
1982	Some subsistence implications of Holocene climate change in northwestern Guyana. *Archaeology and Anthropology* 5(2):82-94.
1985	Petroglyphs in the prehistory of northern Amazonia and the Antilles. Advances in *world archaeology*. Fred Wendorf and A. Close eds. New York: Academic Press. Volume 4:335-387.
1985a	*Ancient Guyana*. Georgetown: Department of Culture.
1988	Archaeological reconnaissance in the Omai River area, Essequibo River. Environmental impact survey *RESCAN*, Ontario.
1990	Mahdia Gold Project. Environmental Impact Survey *RESCAN*, Ontario.
1990a	Archaeological reconnaissance on the lower Potaro River. Environmental Impact Survey *RESCAN*, Ontario.
1992	El Arcaico en el noroeste de Guyana y los cornienzos de la horticultura. *Prehistoria Sudamericana: Nuevas perspectivas*, pp. 233-251.
1993	The forms of the shamanic sign in the prehistoric Guianas. *Archaeology and Anthropology* 9:3-21.
1994	*Iwokrama: The Commonwealth and Government of Guyana Rain Forest Programme*. Georgetown: Guyana Natural Resources Agency.
1996	*Prehistoric cultures of the Iwokrama rainforest*. Georgetown: Guyana Natural Resources Agency.
1996a	Archaeology in the Guianas. *Society for American Archaeology Bulletin* 14:10-12.
1997	Early pottery on the Amazon: a correction. *American Antiquity* 62(2):342-352.
Unpubl MS	Excavation of the Kokerital Mound, Northwest District. National Anthropological Archives, Walter Roth Museum.

Williams, E., R.T. Cannon, R.B. McConnell
    1967   *The folded Precambrian of northern Guyana related to the geology of the Guiana Shield.* Georgetown: Geological Survey of Guyana. Volume 5.

Wing, Elizabeth S., and A.B. Brown
    1979   *Paleonutrition. Method and theory in prehistoric foodways.* New York: Academic Press.

Winter, Alexander
    1881   *Indian pictured rocks in British Guiana.* London: Judd.

Wishart, Jennifer E
    1982   A note on Abary phase house construction. *Archaeology and Anthropology* 5(1):68-69.
    1982a   Recht-door-Zee: a site of the Abary phase on the West Bank Demerara River. *Archaeology and Anthropology* 5(2):119-124.

Yarrow, H.C
    1881   A further contribution to the study of the mortuary customs of the North American Indians. *Annual Report of the Bureau of American Ethnology* 1879-1880, pp. 87-203.

Zucchi, Alberta
    1985   Evidencias arquelogicas sobre grupos de possible lengua Caribe. *Antropologica* 63-64:23-44.
    1991   Las migraciones Maipures: diversas, lineas de evidencias para la interpretacion arqueologica. *America Negra* 1: 113-138.

Zucchi, Alberta, and Kay Tarble
    1984   Los Cedenoides: Un neuvo grupo prehispanico del Orinoco medio. *Acta Scientifica Venezolana* 35:293-309.

Zucchi, A., Kay Tarble, J.Eduardo Vaz
    1984   The ceramic sequence and new TL and C^{14} dates for the Aguerito site of the middle Orinoco, Venezuela. *Journal of Field Archaeology,* vol. 11: 155-180.

INDEX

Abary phase, 11, 248, 262, 267, 282, 295, 298, 311, 313, 330, 336-339, 344, 413

Aishalton Petroglyph Complex, 156, 177

Aiyekowa Creek, 9, 133

Akawabi, 9, 100, 224, 231, 242, 263-265, 270, 272, 280, 311, 426

Akawaio, ii, 241, 260, 266, 276, 282, 287, 298, 300, 330, 331, 342, 348-350, 362, 367, 368, 371, 373, 375, 378-380, 382-388, 390, 392-394, 397-405, 407, 410, 413, 414

Alaka Creek, 9, 133, 278

Alaka phase, 27-32, 117, 225, 227, 247, 248, 251, 267, 277, 415

Amapa, 365

Anabisi Creek, 107, 113, 132, 426

Apoteri Incised, 306, 307, 309, 314, 316, 317, 403, 418, 419, 422

Apoteri Zoned Incised, 306, 308, 309, 314, 418, 422

Apwaka, 340, 341

Arauquinoid pottery, 248, 294

Arawak, ii, xix, 26, 27, 49-51, 83, 104, 165, 237-240, 245, 246, 248, 252, 256, 260, 262, 263, 266, 267, 280, 282, 291, 294-296, 301-304, 317, 318, 321, 324, 326, 330-333, 335-337, 339, 343, 344, 346, 348-350, 363, 367, 370, 378, 379, 383, 385, 392, 396, 397, 399, 401, 403, 405, 407-410, 412, 413, 416-418, 424

Archaic, 7, 10-12, 15, 31, 47, 71, 73, 74, 76, 78, 83, 92-95, 99, 100, 147-149, 154, 158-163, 173, 179, 180, 195, 200, 202, 203, 207, 261, 297, 305, 325, 330, 334, 337, 343, 354, 395, 400, 408, 415

Ariste phase, xix, 45, 245, 334, 359, 363, 365, 367, 392, 394, 397, 400, 409, 412

Aritificial depressions, 14, 39, 40, 334, 413

Artificial depressions, 6-8, 10, 154, 160, 194, 195, 198, 202, 205, 257, 258

Arua phase, 45, 334

Aruka Basin, 54, 132, 207, 209, 217, 242, 245, 248, 266, 272, 273, 275-277

Aruka River, ii, 9, 22, 24, 26, 31, 34, 50, 88, 100, 104, 111, 113, 128, 129, 135, 137, 141, 143, 144, 207, 209, 211, 212, 214-218, 223, 225, 226, 228, 231, 233-236, 242, 245, 246, 249, 251, 252, 256, 257, 260, 262-264, 266-268, 272, 273, 276, 279-282, 287, 291, 293-298, 301, 314, 338, 342, 343, 346, 356, 378, 379, 399, 401, 412, 416

465

Assakata, 9, 133, 266, 295-297, 337, 342, 348, 401, 408
Barabina shell mounds, 27, 73, 82-85, 90, 108-111, 113, 124, 130, 146, 209, 217, 232, 235, 252, 356
Barbakoeba Complex, 327, 330, 392
Barima Basin, 111, 113, 132, 378
Barima River, 2, 9, 26, 57, 88, 100, 101, 103, 104, 106-108, 129, 132, 133, 135, 141, 143, 144, 207, 228, 233, 236, 242, 257, 262, 272, 281, 296, 297, 342, 343, 368, 378, 401
Bark-beater, 143
Barrancoid pottery, 322, 323
Beeswax, 73, 211
Brownsberg Complex, 330
Buckleburg-1, 40, 303, 318, 319, 321, 323, 324, 326
Caicara, 238
Canaima Savannas, 39, 48, 71
Canoe manufacturing industry, 95, 124-126, 128-133, 135, 136, 138, 140-145, 147, 149, 158, 195, 198, 228, 235, 236, 244, 251, 255, 257, 262, 296, 331, 338, 343, 351, 352, 405, 409, 415, 428
Ceramic sequence, 248, 264, 268, 279
Chateau Margot, 338
Chipping station, 7, 93, 95, 113, 176, 185, 202, 203
Corentyne River, 5, 33, 37, 39, 160, 217, 233, 248, 294, 295, 298, 301-304, 316-318, 322-324, 333, 339, 340, 342, 346, 348, 361, 367, 370, 373, 390, 401, 408, 410, 418
Cosmology, 14, 357, 358, 415
Cueva del Elefante, 96
Cuneiform Subtype, 92, 156, 169, 176
Cuyuni River, 5, 64, 68, 368, 371, 378, 383, 385, 390
Demerara River, 16, 22, 26, 56, 245, 266, 282, 292, 293, 295, 296, 313, 337-339, 342, 344, 385, 400, 401, 405, 412, 413
Domestic economy, 264, 416
Drum Hill, 113, 132, 296, 343, 426
Dutch, 276, 282, 408
Eastern Guiana Littoral, 2, 4, 11, 25, 39, 52, 53, 57, 77, 82, 83, 99, 100, 237, 239, 248, 262, 266, 282, 317, 320-322, 324, 326, 331, 333, 334, 339, 343, 346, 348, 350, 363, 370, 378, 383, 396, 401, 410, 412
Economy, 62, 69, 99, 100, 106, 108, 130, 133, 180, 236, 247, 255, 261, 262, 264-266, 291, 298, 387, 405, 410, 412, 416
El Carmen, 97
Enumerative Type, 154, 156-159, 164, 165, 169, 176, 180, 181, 187, 190, 195, 203, 204, 395
Essequibo River, 1, 2, 29, 66, 78, 86, 88, 93, 105, 111, 114, 133, 145, 147, 168, 169, 173, 198, 202, 203, 233, 276, 282, 293, 298, 304, 315,

316, 342, 343, 346, 370, 383, 398, 401, 403, 410, 412-414, 418, 423
Essequibo Village, 385, 403
Euterpe oleracea, 212
Evans, Clifford, xviii, xx, 5, 8, 9, 11-13, 16, 22, 27-32, 34, 35, 37, 43-46, 48, 49, 53, 54, 62, 66, 67, 73, 107, 113, 117, 132, 153, 154, 188, 215, 217, 222, 225, 227, 228, 233, 234, 242, 262, 266, 268, 270, 277, 279, 282, 290, 296, 308, 333, 336, 342, 363, 379, 380, 390, 395, 397, 400, 407, 417, 419
Farabee, William Curtis, 16, 24, 73, 153, 160
Fish Trap Type, 92, 94, 100, 154, 156, 159, 160, 169, 171, 173, 174, 176, 185, 191, 195, 203, 204, 206
Freshwater climax, 80, 106, 107, 125, 129-132, 135, 136, 143, 148, 174, 215, 262, 350, 415, 416
Haimarakabra, 120, 124, 135, 136, 138, 142, 143, 351
Head-foot symbol, 289, 290, 379
Hertenrits, 38, 39, 304, 323-328, 333, 336-338, 340-342, 348, 395, 401
Honobo, 113, 132, 343, 426
Horticulture, 6, 29, 40, 47, 48, 163, 232, 234, 242, 245, 248, 249, 251, 252, 256-258, 260-262, 264-266, 272, 275, 278, 279, 302, 320, 321, 329, 352, 354, 365,

370, 373, 387, 388, 390, 395, 396, 404, 412, 413, 416
Horticulturist, 10, 11, 24, 26, 27, 31-33, 47, 50, 56, 77, 81, 83, 92, 180, 207, 221, 222, 224, 231-233, 240, 244, 245, 247, 249, 257, 260, 262-264, 267, 268, 270, 272, 276-280, 290, 296, 300, 334, 343, 346, 357, 363, 370, 388, 392, 397, 403, 408, 410, 412
Hosororo Creek, 9, 47, 133, 214, 215, 217, 218, 224, 225, 227, 228, 231-234, 237, 239, 245, 248-251, 255-258, 262-267, 272, 273, 275, 277-280, 282, 291, 301
Issano, 367, 389
Itacoatiara, 44, 73, 303, 314-316, 419, 420
Iwokrama Formation, 185, 198, 340
Jacobus Farm, 114, 115, 350, 351
Jari scraped pottery, 394
Kabakaburi, 20, 76, 80, 101, 117, 121, 131, 135, 136, 138, 144, 278, 351, 352, 354
Kaituma River, 9, 88, 129, 143, 225, 272
Kaniaballi, 133
Karinya, 104, 241, 288, 295, 342, 348-350, 352, 354, 356, 358-360, 362-365, 367, 368, 370, 378, 379, 385, 390, 392-394, 396, 397, 400, 401, 404, 408-413, 417
Kassikaityu River, 94, 160, 170, 171,

202-205
Koriabo phase, xix, 27, 37, 43, 268, 276, 298, 314, 330, 331, 337, 340, 349, 362, 367, 368, 370, 378, 385, 390, 392-394, 398-400, 407, 411
Koriabo Point, 57, 101, 106-108, 111, 113, 117, 129, 132, 137, 141-143, 262, 266, 296, 342, 343, 378, 401
Kurupukari Complex, 410
Kurupukari Falls, 93, 168, 169, 173, 195, 304, 305, 308, 309, 311-317, 343, 383, 385, 417-420, 422
Kurupukari phase, 314, 397, 403
Kwatta Tingiholo, 327
Lanciana Island, 373, 376, 383, 389, 412
Luri Creek, 102
Mabaruma Headquarters, 242
Mabaruma phase, 22, 30, 32, 222, 225, 228, 231, 245-248, 266-268, 270, 272, 277, 279, 280, 282, 283, 295-297, 300, 337, 339, 340, 342, 378, 401
Magic, 284, 290, 394, 399
Mahaica River, 13, 33, 295, 321, 337, 343
Makusi, ii, 24, 240, 241, 290, 368, 385, 399, 403, 405, 411
Manacapuru, 422
Mangroves, 3, 24, 55-57, 78, 80, 82, 86, 88, 89, 100, 103, 104, 106, 107, 113, 114, 119-121, 123, 125, 126, 136, 144, 209, 211, 214, 215, 217-219, 244, 250,

318, 339, 351
Manioc Mother, 238, 239
Mapenna Creek, 324, 340
Maraca phase, 44, 45, 334, 379, 395, 397, 400, 409
Marajo Island, xix, 37, 44-46, 290, 298, 308, 334, 335, 419
Marine incursions, 10, 55, 200, 207, 209, 211, 212, 215, 218, 263
Marjorie Landing, 340, 341
Mazagao phase, 45, 245, 311, 334, 336, 363, 365, 367, 379, 380, 390, 394, 395, 397, 400, 401, 409
Meggers, Betty J., xviii, xx, 5, 8, 9, 11, 12, 15, 22, 27, 29-31, 35, 37, 44, 45, 53, 54, 67, 107, 117, 215, 222, 233, 242, 246-248, 270, 279, 342, 363, 368, 392, 402, 407, 417, 419
Migrations, 6, 19, 20, 25, 27, 29, 45, 48, 49, 63, 68, 69, 104, 105, 129, 144, 147-149, 162, 190, 191, 206, 207, 237-241, 245, 252, 276, 298, 301-303, 317, 318, 331, 333, 338, 339, 343, 346, 350, 363, 367, 370, 375, 383-385, 387, 390, 400, 408-412
Mina phase, 30, 100, 217, 227, 277, 415
Morabisi Creek, 389
Mortuary practices, xix, 14, 25, 83, 290, 295, 298, 310, 312-314, 325, 334, 335, 338, 342, 354, 357, 360, 379, 385, 395-397,

400-402, 404, 405, 409, 417, 418, 422, 424
Mt Everard, 104, 113, 132, 343
Mudflats, 4, 55, 78-80, 86, 88, 100, 103, 104, 107, 110, 111, 115, 118-121, 123, 125, 126, 128-132, 135, 136, 176, 215, 216, 238, 263, 296, 317, 318, 321, 416
Muribang River, 362
Naboni Creek, 242
Orealla, 294, 295, 298, 304, 323, 324, 333, 336, 337, 339-343, 379, 395, 401, 405, 412, 413
Osgood, Cornelius, 5, 8, 9, 16, 25-27, 31, 32, 34, 54, 107, 113, 217, 242, 245, 252, 339, 407
Ouanary Enoche pottery, 359-361, 363, 365, 378
Pakaraimas, ii, 5, 33, 64-66, 75, 97, 147, 198, 200, 282, 298, 337, 342, 343, 350, 362, 376, 378, 383, 385, 386, 390, 400, 403-405, 408, 417
Paneo-Indigenous period, 7, 15, 47, 48, 55, 57, 65, 68, 69, 71, 74, 75, 90, 93, 104, 126, 130, 158, 162, 163, 181, 252
Paramakatoi, 385, 403
Patamona, 75, 241, 342, 343, 368, 385, 386, 403, 405
Pedra Pintada, 47, 69, 92, 95, 96, 151, 163, 176, 204, 205, 216
Petroglyphs, xix, 6, 10, 20, 33, 36, 42, 44, 72, 90, 92, 95, 97, 98, 147, 148, 150, 154, 162, 165, 169, 180, 185, 290, 301, 305, 317
Pictographs, 6, 7, 10, 11, 92, 95, 96, 98, 99, 147, 149, 152-154, 156, 158, 174, 176, 180, 181, 204
Piraka, 20, 57, 76, 77, 79, 83, 86, 100, 101, 104, 105, 111, 113, 115, 119, 131, 135, 149, 165, 290, 335, 354
Poco phase, 421
Potaro River, 5, 68, 266, 298, 300, 362, 385, 386, 390, 403, 410, 413
Preagricultural ceramists, 215
Prins Bernhard Polder, 319, 324, 326
Puruni River, 64-66
Quartz Island, 367, 371-373, 375-379, 381, 389, 390, 410, 412
Quiaro, 8, 133
Raised-field complexes, 11, 323, 325, 326, 328, 330, 332
Recht-door-Zee, 266, 282, 292-296, 337-339, 342, 343, 348, 378, 379, 400, 401, 405, 413
Religious practices, ii, 14, 21, 149, 162, 165, 297, 298, 334, 357, 385, 400, 416
Rio Caroni, 5, 238, 270, 378, 379, 385, 403, 410, 417
Rio Casiquiare, 1, 50, 51, 160, 173, 238, 301
Rio Paragua, 238
Rio Parguaza, 97
Rio Sipapo, 160
Rio Uatuma, 316, 422
Rock alignments, 6, 12, 15

Roth, Walter Edmund, iii, 16, 22, 23, 152, 173, 242, 260, 279, 380, 399
Rupununi phase, 376, 377, 386, 390, 402, 403, 407
Rupununi River, 7, 93, 383, 402, 403
Rupununi Savannas, 5, 14, 33, 58, 66, 68, 88, 90, 93, 97, 153, 157, 165, 177, 188, 400, 402, 403
Sand Creek, 9, 133, 143, 221, 222, 225, 227, 228, 230, 232
Sand Creek Plain pottery, 228, 230, 232, 234, 235
Santarem pottery, 298, 301, 303, 336, 340, 342, 395
Seba Creek, 209, 211, 214, 215, 217, 276, 304
Settlement pattern, 34, 67, 86, 339, 364, 373, 389
Shaft tombs, 361, 409, 417
Shell mounds, 7-9, 14, 16, 18, 20, 26, 28, 30, 53, 54, 83, 89, 90, 104, 111, 113, 117-119, 128, 132, 133, 144, 197, 218, 228, 250, 343, 351, 414-416, 426
Sipaliwini Savannas, 38, 39, 71, 147, 176
Siriki, 80, 144, 146
Soil erosion, 277
Suriname, iii, 1, 4, 6, 11, 14, 35-40, 44, 48, 53, 57-59, 82, 147, 152, 156, 176, 177, 199, 241, 248, 282, 288, 290, 300, 303, 311, 318, 330, 331, 341, 346, 348, 350, 359, 363, 373, 392, 393, 401
Taruma, 34, 373, 385, 402, 403

Timehri, 92, 156, 238-240, 301, 302, 410
Timehri petroglyphs, 238-240, 301, 410
Trade practices, xvii, 12, 37, 48, 111, 113, 132, 133, 135, 141-144, 147, 205, 217, 232, 233, 235, 236, 244, 247, 252, 255, 257, 262, 264, 265, 278, 292, 294-297, 324, 330, 331, 337, 338, 342, 343, 346, 350, 361, 362, 378, 385, 400, 401, 403, 405, 408, 409, 415, 417
Tramen pictograph, 97, 177-179, 185
Tropical Forest Culture, 11, 12, 15, 26, 28-31, 34, 44, 45, 53, 54, 83, 98, 111, 149, 199, 205, 207, 246, 251, 257, 265, 277, 301, 325, 330, 387, 405-409, 414-416, 423, 424
Tupuken, 68
Upper Waini Complex, 9, 97, 100, 129-132, 135, 143, 144, 160, 174, 217, 228, 233, 234, 236, 264, 265, 278, 296, 337, 342, 343
Uraricoera, 176, 204
Urn burial, 311, 333, 334, 409
Wageningen, 319, 323, 324, 326
Wahana Island, 97, 118, 126, 131-133, 135, 136, 141, 143, 144, 174, 176, 217, 228, 233-235, 255, 264, 278, 342, 343
Waiwai, ii, 32, 202, 241, 403, 407, 411, 425
Waiwaru, 347, 350-352, 354,

358-360, 364, 367, 376, 377, 390-394, 400, 409, 411
Waiwaru Market, 114, 353, 354, 356, 357, 363, 370, 376, 378-380, 393, 409, 417, 418
Walter Roth Museum, iii, 8, 32, 136, 346
Waramabia, 388, 390
Waramuri, 8, 16-18, 20, 115, 116, 118-121, 123, 125, 126, 128, 130, 131, 133, 135, 136, 351
Warapana, 8, 80, 133, 144, 146, 427
Waraputa, 93, 133, 160, 169
Waropoko, 8, 9, 133, 135
Wenamu River, 5, 64, 68, 105, 337, 378

Western Guiana Littoral, 2, 3, 8, 9, 11, 16, 18, 20, 21, 24-26, 28-32, 47, 53, 54, 56, 57, 63, 64, 68, 69, 73, 76, 77, 83, 86-89, 99-101, 103, 104, 107-111, 117, 119, 124-126, 130, 131, 133, 136, 144-147, 149, 150, 158, 163, 173, 197, 206, 219, 225, 236, 242, 252, 265, 297, 317, 320, 331, 342, 346, 354, 356, 367, 385, 393, 401, 408, 410, 414, 415, 418
White Sand Plateau, 321, 339
witchcraft, 397
Witchcraft practices, 403
Wonotobo Falls, 160, 248, 301-305, 316, 418
Yamora, 343
Zoned Hachure Horizon Style, 422

www.ingramcontent.com/pod-product-compliance
Lightning Source LLC
Chambersburg PA
CBHW060512230426
43665CB00013B/1489